GENERA GRAMINUM

KEW BULLETIN ADDITIONAL SERIES XIII

GENERA GRAMINUM

Grasses of the World

W.D. Clayton
&
S.A. Renvoize

LONDON

HER MAJESTY'S STATIONERY OFFICE

First published 1986
Second impression 1989

General editor of series M.J.E. Coode.
Special editor of this number T.A. Cope.
Cover design by L. Giuffrida and J. Ruddy.
Set by Mrs P. Arnold, Mrs E. Attwood, Mrs B.
Carey & Mrs A. Magee. Illustrations prepared
by Eleanor Catherine.

ISBN 0 11 250006 4

PREFACE

Identification is the keystone of biology. Unless organisms are correctly named knowledge about them cannot be communicated universally; the science of taxonomy is thus of fundamental importance. It is a difficult and undervalued skill, whose comparative neglect frequently hinders the progress of biological enquiry and the economic development of natural resources. Research at Kew has always taken a special interest in the resolution of this problem and some 10% of the world's flowering plants have been revised in a series of major Floras published here since the Second World War.

The position is particularly serious with regard to the large cosmopolitan families, for few institutions have sufficiently comprehensive collections or adequately experienced staff to tackle them. The present authors have devoted a total of 50 years to the study of grasses, and present here the first complete reworking of the Gramineae at generic level since 1883. It comes at a particularly opportune moment in the history of grass taxonomy when classical morphology is being wedded to modern ideas on the evolutionary role of metabolism. These ideas have given fresh impetus to a traditional discipline, though our understanding of them and their bearing on classification is far from complete. Consequently, as the authors themselves have said, "There is something here to annoy everyone; so do not bother to chastise — think rather to improve".

Professor E.A. Bell
Director
Royal Botanic Gardens, Kew

CONTENTS

PART 1.   THE GRASS PLANT

PART 2.   ENUMERATION OF GENERA

FIGURES

TABLES

PART 1. THE GRASS PLANT

INTRODUCTION

Taxonomy, in the first instance, is essentially a practical science whose aim is to distinguish, to name, and then to arrange plants in some logical manner that eases the task of identifying and remembering them. However, the orderly classification of form discloses patterns of similarity that indicate the possibility of a wider synthesis. This has been achieved, firstly, by developing a system of sufficient generality to map the distribution of many different properties,thereby supporting the introduction of versatile polyclave identification techniques, and at the same time generating a useful predictive capability; and secondly, in alliance with evolutionary theory, by incorporating in the classification some explanation as to how these patterns might have arisen. Thus taxonomy, while still fulfilling its original role as the methodology of identification, has expanded into a means of biological enquiry in its own right, capable of assembling a disorganized mass of observations into a coherent working hypothesis that reveals something of the factors responsible for diversity. It is in this spirit that we have approached the classification of grasses.

The grass family is not the largest in terms of species and genera, coming after Compositae, Leguminosae, Orchidaceae and Rubiaceae, but its importance is beyond doubt for it provides the grasslands which occupy a third of the land's surface (Schantz 1954), and the cereal crops upon which much of the world's population depends for its food. By any reckoning the grasses are a successful family, in which three themes constantly recur: their adaptability to changeable environments; their ability to coexist with grazing herbivores and with man; and their possession of a distinctive lifeform, in which fidelity to a single architectural scheme is counterbalanced by the endless ingenuity of its variations. The following discussion is mainly concerned with herbaceous grasses, the peculiarities of woody bamboos being deferred to the tribal entry.

MORPHOLOGY

Root, culm & leaf

The life cycle of most grasses is strongly seasonal. Perennials become dormant when the season is adverse to growth, allowing some or all of their foliage to wither after recovering any useful nutrients contained in it; truly deciduous leaves are very rare. Annuals overwinter as seed, a strategy generally regarded as more advanced because of the high standard of reproductive efficiency required. Perennials may be recognized by the presence of dormant buds or innovation shoots at their base, but these are not always obvious in the weedy

1

short lived perennials produced by some tropical genera, nor in rambling species that are difficult to trace back to their rootstock.

The root system is fibrous and relatively shallow, seldom penetrating more than 2 m and often less than 1 m (Troughton 1957). Commonly about half of it dies and is replaced each year. The main branch system and the perennating buds occur just above (tussock grasses), at (stoloniferous and sward-forming grasses) or just below (rhizomatous grasses) the soil surface. It is relatively inaccessible to grazing, and readily produces new shoots ('tillers') from its axils to make good any loss of the aerial parts. Adventitious roots develop freely, so that typically each tiller is sustained by its own independent root system. The tillers eventually develop into upright inflorescence-bearing culms. The culms are usually unbranched, though there are some notable exceptions especially in Andropogoneae; they are mostly hollow, but may be solid particularly in Chloridoideae and Panicoideae (Brown et al 1959a). In a few species the base of the culm develops into a food-storing bulb or corm (Burns 1946).

The usual Monocotyledonous division of the leaf into sheath and blade is highly developed in grasses, and gives rise to their characteristic life-form. The most obvious manifestation is the manner in which the stem and sheath combine to form a structural unit. As a result the apical primordium is protected within a nest of concentric sheaths, and the internode can elongate at a soft basal intercalary meristem which extrudes it from the supporting sheath. Intercalary meristems also feature in the node (or sheath base, Brown et al 1959b), which retains the ability to turn the culm upright after lodging by rain or trampling; and in the blade, which grows from a basal meristem (the 'collar') and can thus recover from loss of its distal parts by cropping. The blade is typically linear with the ability to roll or fold under desiccation, but a wide range of other shapes occasionally occurs. It is the primary photosynthetic organ, but the sheath (Throne 1959) and even the awns (Grandbacher 1963) can make an important contribution. At the junction of sheath and blade stands the ligule, represented by a membrane or by a line of hairs. Its function is obscure but may plausibly be to deter insects from entering the sheath; it is a novel structure, not homologous with any other organ (Philipson 1935). Very rarely there is a ligule-like structure on the abaxial side of the sheath (Tran 1971), or auricles at base of blade or summit of sheath (Tran 1972). Other variations are an abscission zone at the collar, or a basal narrowing of the blade so extreme that it imitates a petiole.

Note that the first leaf of an axillary branch is adaxial, highly modified and termed a prophyll. It is membranous and 2-keeled, scale-like on basal branches but linear on aerial branches. It is often difficult to find and seems to be of slight practical importance, but it is of interest in establishing homologies.

The ligule is often a useful aid to tribal recognition, though prone to erratic exceptions. Otherwise vegetative characters are seldom of much taxonomic significance above generic level.

Inflorescence

The inflorescence is a special branch system whose subtending leaves have been suppressed. It may be a panicle, open or contracted; a spiciform panicle, where contraction has proceeded to the point of fusing most of the branches to the central axis; a single raceme with spikelets on one side of the rhachis, on opposite sides, or all around like a bottle-brush; or multiple racemes arranged digitately or scattered along an axis.

Terminology is sometimes rather strained, as when a panicle is so sparse that its branches resemble racemes, when a raceme bears little spikelet clusters instead of single spikelets, or when its spikelets have no pedicel. The latter is sometimes distinguished as a spike, but the difference is often so slight, or downright contradictory in Andropogoneae, that this refinement is more confusing than helpful. The terminology in any case is technically incorrect as it is derived by treating its basic unit, the spikelet, as analogous to the normal petaloid flower. However, there seems little point in replacing a well established convention with a plethora of new terms.

The inflorescence is often quite characteristic of a tribe, and is so obvious that it can scarcely be ignored. However, it should be treated with caution, as it is also the character most likely to mislead.

Spikelet

The spikelet is composed of bracts borne distichously on a rhachilla (fig. 1). The two lowest bracts ('glumes') are empty scales which protect the immature spikelet; the rest ('lemmas') are each opposed by a palea. Lemma and palea together enclose a set of floral organs, the whole forming a structural unit known, by functional analogy rather than morphological homology, as a floret. The base of the spikelet or floret is sometmes enlarged into a little knob or stalk called a callus. An enormous range of spikelet variation has been achieved by reducing the number of scales, elaborating their shape, or extending them into bristles called awns; yet the overall structural pattern is remarkably consistent, and there is seldom any difficulty in relating its variants to the standard form. Note that the suppression of a scale, which happens in a few genera, can be inferred from its interruption of the distichous sequence.

The floral organs typically consist of 2 tiny lodicules, 3 stamens and 2 plumose stigmas. Morphologically they are rather uniform, but there is some variation in their number (Clifford 1961). This is often associated with varying degrees of sexual segregation, in which the most significant comparison is female or bisexual against male or barren. It is a convenient, though inexact, abbreviation to unite the two ovary-bearing forms under the term 'fertile'.

It has been shown that glumes and lemmas are mainly derived from leaf-sheaths, though their upper part may involve more complex homologies with ligule, auricles and blade (Tran 1973). The palea is commonly a hyaline 2-keeled structure, best regarded as the prophyll of a diminished axillary branch. The lodicules are usually interpreted as a vestigial perianth, which swells to open the floret for anther emergence, and then allows it to spring shut until the stigmas are ready for extrusion (Pissarek 1971). They are commonly lacking in cleistogamous and protogynous florets. It may be postulated that the spikelet is derived by condensation from a spike with axillary petaloid flowers; aggregation of the spikelets coupled with suppression of the intervening leaves then formed the grass panicle. Nor is that the end of it, for second order reduction-aggregation cycles may be observed in Bambuseae and Andropogoneae (fig. 2).

The multiplication of floral envelopes is a notable feature of the grass life-form. Thus the function of the lemma is often duplicated by an enlarged glume, and sometimes by sterile outer florets; in the most complex examples it may be further reinforced by an involucre of sterile spikelets or sterile branchlets, or by a modification of the uppermost leaf-sheath. This trend is evidently of importance to the plant, but its purpose is largely a matter for speculation. The most obvious effect is to increase the protection of flower and fruit. Also, since

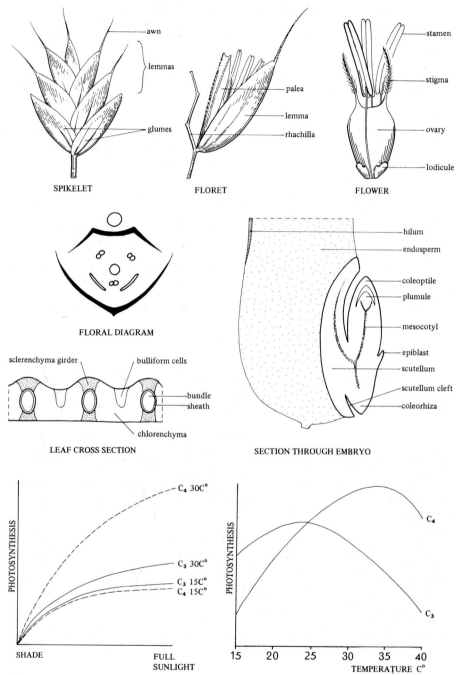

Fig. 1   Parts of the grass plant and the terminology employed. Graphs comparing C_3 and C_4 photosynthesis under a range of illumination and temperature conditions.

the 'sterile' florets are in fact often male, it increases the ratio of stamens to ovaries. Furthermore it has been shown that a large proportion of the seed's food store is photosynthesized in the flag leaf and inflorescence itself (Redman & Reekie in Estes et al 1982), so that the additional envelopes may be a means of enhancing this process without obstructing the exposure of the inflorescence to anemophilous pollination.

Characters drawn from the spikelet are fundamental to the taxonomy of grasses, and identification is invariably hazardous without careful dissection to observe their structure.

Cleistogamy

Cleistogamous spikelets in which self-fertilization occurs within the closed floret, are quite common, being reported for over 300 species. These spikelets, which are additional to the normal form, show varying degrees of modification (Campbell et al 1983).

1. Spikelet fertilization. Inflorescence exposed, but florets fail to open. Rare, or at least difficult to detect since spikelet modification is minimal.
2. Sheath fertilization. Infloresence or spikelets remain within upper sheaths during fertilization, but may be exserted later; spikelets usually smaller than normal. The commonest form.
3. Cleistogenes. Modified spikelets within lowermost sheaths, sometimes associated with specialized tumbleweed dispersal involving parts of the culm and subtending leaves.
4. Rhizanthogenes. Highly modified spikelets on specialized underground rhizomes.

Fruit

The grass fruit normally has a thin pericarp firmly adherent to the seed, and is thus a caryopsis. However it is by no means rare to find the pericarp free, the fruit then being a utricle if the pericarp is soft, or an achene if it is hard. The attachment of the ovule to the pericarp wall leaves a visible scar ('hilum') on the adaxial side, which is of some taxonomic value.

The bulk of the seed is made up of endosperm, that curious triploid tissue common to Angiosperms which is formed by fusion of two polar nuclei from the ovule with a secondary nucleus from the pollen. It contains starch and protein which provide the initial food supply for the seedling. Investigation of its sugar and amino acid chemistry has shown broad taxonomic correlations, but provides little of diagnostic significance. Characters of local interest, including starch grains (Bromeae), serology (Bromeae) and lipids (Aveneae), are mentioned under the relevant tribe.

The embryo has a flat haustorial cotyledon ('scutellum'), and a special outer sheath ('coleoptile') protecting the plumule during soil penetration (Negbi 1984). These and other embryo structures are shown in figs. 1 & 2. Numerous attempts have been made to establish precise homologies with foliage leaves (Brown 1960, Guignard & Mestre 1970), but it seems just as likely that these are novel organs evolved to meet the special needs of germination. For taxonomic purposes the embryo structure may be expressed in a simple formula; its terms, and the principal combinations, are set out below. Other combinations also occur, the epiblast being particularly prone to erratic variation, but the

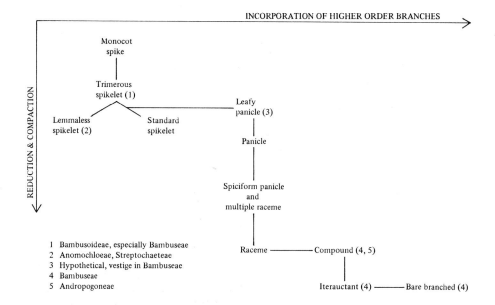

Fig. 2   Diagram showing hypothetical evolution of spikelet and inflorescence.

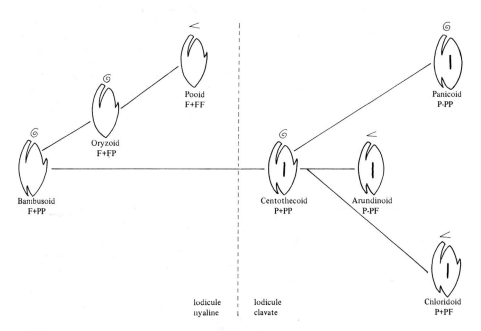

Fig. 3   Postulated evolutionary sequence of embryo types. Vernation of first
          leaf and presence of a mesocotyl are indicated diagrammatically.

microscope preparations are not always easy to interpret and this may account for some of the apparent anomalies. The most important sources are Reeder 1960 & 1962, Kinges 1961, Decker 1962 and Mlada 1977.

1 Mesocotyl present (P), absent (F)
2 Epiblast present (+), absent (-)
3 Scutellum cleft present (P), absent (F)
4 First leaf rolled (P), folded (F)

Principal combinations:	Bambusoid	F+PP	Arundinoid	P-PF
	Oryzoid	F+FP	Chloridoid	P+PF
	Pooid	F+FF	Panicoid	P-PP
	Centothecoid	P+PP		

The dispersal unit is rarely a seed, sometimes a caryopsis, more often a false fruit incorporating various parts of the spikelet or inflorescence. The false fruits are exceedingly diverse, and are often equipped with elaborate appendages. Awns that propel the fruit along the ground by hygroscopic flexing or coiling are particularly common, backward movement being prevented by a beard on the callus. The awn is often complex with a straight limb set geniculately upon a twisted column; and sometimes the moving awn is designed to catch on a fixed awn until the mounting tension springs it free, making the fruit hop. Such devices are loosely referred to as dispersal mechanisms, but in fact many of them seem more concerned with establishment of the germinating seed. It is very difficult to secure experimental evidence relating form to function, but Peart (1984) has demonstrated the role of such devices in moving the fruit to a favourable microsite, orienting it to facilitate initial water uptake, and anchoring it securely against the thrust of the radicle. When the fruit incorporates a hard lemma there is usually a neatly dehiscing germination flap at its base through which the radicle emerges (Johnston & Watson 1983). The fruits of many species survive burial in the ground for up 10 years; few exceed 30 years (Toole & Brown 1946).

REPRODUCTION

Pollination

Grasses are wind pollinated. Bees and other insects have been observed feeding on pollen, but their contribution to pollination would appear to be slight (Bogdan 1962), except for *Pariana* and a few other forest floor genera, where the entomophilous mode is evidently a secondary adaptation. The pollen itself is unique to the family, but too uniform to be helpful taxonomically (Page 1978). It is the shortest lived of all Angiosperm pollen being viable for only a few hours in the open air; nor does it usually travel far in a viable condition, effective pollination distances being measurable in tens of metres (Jones & Newall 1946, 1948). The structure of the androecium hardly varies, and seems insulated from the selection pressures that have created such diversity of form in the fruit. Nevertheless there is a strong evolutionary trend towards suppression of the gynoecium in a proportion of the florets or spikelets, thereby shifting the balance in favour of pollen production. It is probably consequential to another characteristic of the grasses, their brief anthesis, the florets usually opening for only 2—3 hours. This is perhaps to reduce the chance of trapping destructive fungal spores, but whatever the reasons they are sufficiently pressing to have induced a small marvel of seasonal and diurnal synchronization.

Recognition of a suitable reproductive partner is mediated by a complex spectrum of antigens produced in the pollen. It is unfortunate that these also have allergenic properties, wind-borne aerosols of pollen causing hay-fever in susceptible individuals. The patient's sensitivity to different grasses has a taxonomic component, but this is difficult to disentangle as many antigens are concerned, some of which have wide taxonomic spans (Watson & Knox 1976).

Breeding behaviour

Grasses have developed a wide range of breeding behaviour (Connor 1980, 1981), broadly divisible into two opposing strategies. Some have countered the incestuous promiscuity of anemophily by developing a complex incompatibility system that ensures outbreeding (Heslop-Harrison 1982); or, less often, by adopting dioecy. Others, particularly annuals, have reduced the uncertainty of anemophily by self-fertility or cleistogamy. The more extreme forms of inbreeding are invariably facultative and often mediated by environmental conditions, thus mitigating their restrictive effect on genetic diversity.

Cytogenetic systems are likewise extremely varied, with extensive development of polyploidy (Carnahan & Hill 1961, Stebbins in Younger & McKell 1972), hybridization (Knobloch 1968) and facultative apomixis (Nygren 1954, Brown 1958, Brown & Emery 1958); polyhaploidy, the reversion of polyploids to the diploid condition, has been reported in *Bromus, Dactylis* and *Sorghum* (Kimber & Riley 1963). Taken together these processes have produced systems of great flexibility, capable of responding conservatively or adaptively according to the exigencies of selection pressure. Their ability to proliferate segregate populations, which yet retain some capacity for gene exchange, has often created polymorphic complexes of fearsome taxonomic difficulty, but their versatility has been a potent factor in the success of the grasses.

The chromosomes themselves are of limited taxonomic interest, as the karyotype is relatively constant and the chromosome count, though variable, shows only broad statistical correlation with the classification. Their evolutionary history is largely speculative, but it seems likely that 12 was the primitive basic number, with 10 and 9 derived from it. The most significant deviation occurs in the Pooideae, where large chromosomes with a basic number of 7 are associated with the more advanced tribes.

Vivipary and proliferation

True vivipary, the precocious germination of the seed while still attached to the parent, is unusual. However, the term is commonly applied to a few species, mainly Arctic-alpine Pooideae, that regularly propagate by means of plantlets formed by vegetative proliferation of the spikelets (Langer & Ryle 1958, Beetle 1980). A teratological version of proliferation is not uncommon, particularly in the autumn when it seems to be induced by the effect of cold and short days on genetically predisposed races. Hormone weedkillers and pathological invasions can have a similar effect.

Vegetative reproduction.

Seed set in perennials is often surprisingly low, and vegetative reproduction is evidently of considerable importance as an alternative strategy, its effectiveness being greatly enhanced by the evolution of stolons and rhizomes as a means of dispersal. The size and age of single clones is difficult to investigate but Harberd (1961, 1962), using self-incompatibility as an indicator of clonal membership, has estimated 200 metres and 400 years for *Festuca rubra*, 8 meters and 1000 years for *F. ovina*.

ANATOMY AND METABOLISM

Anatomy

The structure of the grass leaf is determined by the longitudinal vascular bundles, its tissues being arranged as a module around each bundle (fig. 1). In addition to chlorenchyma these tissues usually include sclerenchymatous girders to give mechanical strength, and a number of colourless thin-walled cells — termed bulliform cells in the epidermal layer, motor cells in the mesophyll. The function of these is obscure, but it may be to enhance penetration of light to the innermost chlorenchyma cells. It is not, as is sometimes supposed, concerned with rolling the leaf (Shields 1951).

The photosynthetic apparatus comprises the chlorenchyma cells of the mesophyll, and two sheaths surrounding the vascular bundle. The inner (mestome) sheath is of small thick-walled cells corresponding to an endodermis and derived from the vascular tissue; the outer (parenchyma) sheath is of large thin-walled cells originating in the mesophyll (Dengler et al 1985).

The following basic patterns occur, using the terminology of Brown (1975, 1977).

1. Non-kranz. Chlorenchyma irregular, with more than 4 cells between adjacent sheaths. Both bundle sheaths present. Starch formed principally in mesophyll.
2. Kranz (German for wreath, referring to the prominent sheath cells). Chlorenchyma with only 2—4 cells between adjacent sheaths. Starch formed principally in sheath.
   a. PS (parenchyma sheath) type. Chlorenchyma strongly radiate surrounding bundles of approximately equal size. Both sheaths present, only the parenchyma sheath forming starch.
      i. Chloroplasts centripetal in sheath cells.
      ii. Chloroplasts centrifugal in sheath cells.
   b. MS (mestome sheath) type. Chlorenchyma irregular or weakly radiate, surrounding bundles of often widely differing size. One sheath present, this forming starch and apparently derived from the mestome sheath.

The epidermis is composed primarily of elongate 'long-cells', which may or may not be interspersed with equidimensional 'short-cells'. Two zones are usually perceptible, the intercostal zone and the costal zone. The costal zones are narrow tracts overlying the vascular bundles and their associated sclerenchyma. They are characterized by the presence of opaline silica-bodies which, regardless of the shape of the cell containing them, assume characteristic shapes according to the different tribes; unfortunately there is so much intergradation that their diagnostic value is limited. The intercostal zones are usually much broader than the costal zones and may contain, in addition to the long and short cells, stomata, microhairs and silica-containing cells. Intercostal silica-bodies are not of any characteristic shape. The stomata are of an unusual kind in which the two guard cells are each supported by a subsidiary cell. Microhairs are fragile microscopic 2-celled hairs of unknown function (not to be confused with macrohairs of visibly hairy leaves). For a detailed account of grass leaf anatomy see Metcalfe (1960).

Metabolism

Normal, or C_3, photosynthesis commences with the diffusion of CO_2 into the mesophyll, where it is taken up by a ribulose diphosphate (5-carbon) acceptor molecule. This then splits into 2 molecules of phosphoglycerate, a 3-carbon compound (whence the term 'C_3 pathway'). There follows a complex sequence of molecular rearrangements that has the capacity to return more acceptor than it receives — an important requirement in allowing for the growth of the plant, and also manufacture an end-product. The latter tends to accumulate during daylight, and is temporarily stored as starch pending translocation at night; it is easily detected by staining with iodine. The whole process takes place in the mesophyll.

Some plants, including many grasses, have added an extra loop to this system. CO_2 is initially taken up in the mesophyll by pyruvate to form a 4-carbon compound (hence 'C_4 pathway'). This migrates to the bundle sheath where its CO_2 is removed by a decarboxylating enzyme and fed into the C_3 cycle. There are several versions of the C_4 pathway, which have been found to match the variations in kranz structure.

1. Non-kranz C_3 pathway
2. Kranz C_4 pathway

	Principal 4-carbon compound	Decarboxylating enzyme
a. PS		
i. Centripetal	Aspartate	NAD-ME
ii. Centrifugal	Aspartate	PEP-CK
b. MS	Malate	NADP-ME

Chemical elucidation of the pathway is a complex affair, and in practice it is usually inferred from the anatomy. However it is worth noting that the C_4 pathway takes up the isotopes ^{12}C and ^{13}C in nearly atmospheric proportions, whereas the C_3 pathway discriminates against ^{13}C. Determination of the carbon isotope ratio therefore affords a rapid means of obtaining chemical confirmation. An expansion of this simplified account of photosynthesis can be found in Edwards & Walker (1983).

Physiological significance

In C_3 plants CO_2 uptake and transport is by diffusion, a process which may become the limiting factor in rate of assimilation. When this is so the extra loop of the C_4 cycle, acting in effect as a CO_2 pump, can considerably enhance performance; but at the same time it introduces its own set of limitations.

1. Higher temperatures increase the rate of photosynthesis, but in C_3 plants the effect is overtaken by a decrease in CO_2 solubility. The C_4 mechanism overcomes the disability, and can run at a higher optimum temperature with

consequently higher overall assimilation rates. By contrast it is handicapped by low temperatures, probably due to an adverse effect on the enzyme system (fig. 1).

2. Higher illumination raises the rate of photosynthesis, but in C_3 plants this outruns the rate of CO_2 transport, reaching saturation well short of full sunlight; saturation point is almost independent of temperature. There is no such limitation on C_4 plants, which can maintain an almost linear response to increasing illumination; but their ability to respond falls sharply at less than optimum temperatures (fig. 1).

3. Photorespiration is a curious side reaction of the C_3 pathway, releasing CO_2 in daylight at a rate higher than the usual dark reaction. Its purpose is unknown, but some competition between CO_2 and O_2 for receptor sites may be an inevitable feature in the enzyme system employed. As a result the C_3 pathway habitually runs at less than theoretical efficiency; in fact when internal CO_2 is reduced to 15% of atmospheric level (the 'compensation point') photorespiration balances photosynthesis and assimilation effectively ceases. The C_4 pathway counters this effect by its ability to scavenge CO_2 down to zero level and return it to the assimilation cycle.

4. Water stress is relieved by reducing stomatal aperture and thus slowing the outward diffusion of water vapour, but this also reduces CO_2 intake so that internal levels may reach the compensation point of C_3 plants when photosynthesis ceases. C_4 plants can maintain photosynthesis at very low rates of CO_2 intake through partially closed stomata, and consequently display markedly higher water use efficiency.

In summary, C_4 is at an advantage in hot climates with some additional advantage if the climate is also dry, but is ineffective or disadvantageous in cool climates and shady habitats. However both metabolic groups are capable of considerable climatic adaptation, especially if they are occupying specialized habitats in which competition is limited. Consequently there is no sharp transition in their geographical distribution; in fact there is often an almost linear correlation between temperature gradient and percentage of C_4 species in the grass flora (Ellis et al 1980, Hattersley 1983).

The kranz variants

A remarkable feature of C_4 photosynthesis is its division of labour between mesophyll and sheath. This is associated with a structural modification, kranz anatomy, which places chlorenchyma and sheath cells in direct contact or at least never more than one cell apart. The PS type achieves this by radial elongation of chlorenchyma cells around secondary bundles (the enzyme variants show no clear taxonomic correlation and are not further considered). The MS type pursues a different strategy by interpolating minor bundles in the mesophyll located under the bulliform cells, their vascular core sometimes reduced to a few cells scarcely differentiated into phloem and xylem. The concomitant change to a single sheath is not fully explained, but it increases the proportion of photosynthetic tissue present, particularly in the smaller bundles.

The selection for PS or MS types is sometimes ascribed to environmental factors but this assertion is dubious, for although Chloridoideae (all PS) are associated with stressful habitats, Panicoideae, in which PS and MS types occur together, show no such correlation. It seems certain that kranz anatomy is polyphyletic, and likely that the two forms have evolved independently and more

11

or less at random at least 5 times — Chloridoideae (PS), *Centropodia* (PS), Aristideae (PS), Arundinelleae-Andropogoneae (MS) and Paniceae (PS & MS). For further discussion of unusual or intermediate forms see under Aristideae, Arundinelleae, Triodiinae and Paniceae.

Many C_4 species have adapted to cool, wet or shady habitats, but there are no proven examples of reversion to C_3 metabolism and it is conjectured that this never happens (but see *Eragrostis walteri*).

Leaf architecture

A horizontal leaf is inefficient in bright light for it intercepts most of the incident light, only 5—10% being transmitted, but the C_3 photosynthetic process becomes saturated at about 25% of full sunlight and can make no use of the surplus. By contrast a narrow vertical leaf permits light to penetrate deeply into the canopy, thereby admitting useful levels of illumination to a greater leaf area (Newton & Blackman 1970). A corollary is that grass-like leaves are able to pack a greater biomass into a given volume of space (Lonsdale & Watkinson 1983). Taken together these facts do much to explain the success of the grass life-form, and its association with a large herbivorous fauna.

Most grass leaves have their stomata mainly in the upper epidermis, this lying inside when the leaf rolls up to reduce water stress. However, the broad horizontal bambusoid type of leaf has its stomata mainly in the lower epidermis, as do most other broad-leaved plants; Phareae and Phaenospermateae achieve the same effect by twisting their false petiole to invert the leaf.

Phytochemistry

The metabolic pathway is of crucial importance in grass taxonomy. Other phytochemical investigations have yielded little of significance, presumably because the anemophilous life style makes no call for the elaboration of scents or pigments, and the advantageous association with herbivores negates the development of chemical defences.

The foliage of *Sorghum* and a few other genera occasionally develops a dangerously high content of hydrocyanic acid through the breakdown of glucosides; the process is often associated with the wilting of lush growth, but is difficult to predict with any certainty. Otherwise poisonous properties attributed to grass are mostly due to fungal infection; the most notorious is *Claviceps* (Ergot) whose fruiting bodies may be eaten by cattle or harvested with the grain of cereal crops.

CLASSIFICATION

History

Grass taxonomy has traditionally been based upon spikelet structure, and there gradually developed an 'arithmetic' system derived from counting the florets, lemma nerves, awns and so on. It is a method well suited to its primary purpose of cataloguing the grasses, and is still the most effective approach for the construction of artificial keys. However, it was apparent at least 100 years ago that parallel evolution of spikelet structure could lead to artificial groupings, but even when these were recognized and disentangled — as in the separation of Eragrostideae from Poeae — there was no criterion by which true kinship could be established.

The next stage came in the 1930's with the discovery that numerous cryptic characters derived from anatomy, cytology and physiology were correlated with spikelet structure, and that their incorporation in the system could resolve many of the problems posed by parallel evolution. The characters have been summarized by Auquier (1963), Gould (1983), Jacques-Félix (1962), Prat (1960) and Stebbins (1956). With their help the tribes were purged of discordant elements and assembled into broad natural groups. However, many of the new characters proved too indefinite to be of much practical diagnostic value; others were contradictory, and evidently themselves subject to parallel evolution albeit to a lesser degree than the spikelets. Consequently, although the outlines of an improved classification were amply demonstrated, its details were often blurred and its biological implications uncertain.

Finally, during the last 20 years, it has been established that many of the characters defining major groups are associated with differences in photosynthetic metabolism. An awakening understanding of the significance of this phenomenon has provided criteria for reassessing the relevance of phenetic characters, and for relating at least some of them to fundamental developments in the biology of the living plant. The insight thus gained has opened the way for a fresh approach to the classification of grasses in which physiology stands alongside classical morphology.

Method

The present study is essentially pragmatic, being based on the description and diagnosis of genera, for which all species represented at Kew were examined, thence proceeding upwards through the hierarchy of classification. The method employed for the higher levels was eclectic, pursuing no particular preconceived theory. Its steps are briefly outlined below.

1. Assemble the genera into clusters according to overall morphological similarity.
2. Construct a parallel anatomical classification.
3. Verify doubtful links and eliminate false homologies by reciprocal comparison between the two classifications, gradually building the clusters up to about tribal size. Other classifications, such as cytological or phytochemical, could be used to refine the process, but the data currently available are inadequate for a comprehensive overview.
4. Use this first approximation to discard variable characters, selecting those that are constant within clusters and discriminatory between them.
5. Consolidate boundaries, arrange the clusters in sequence and allocate outliers by applying cladistic reasoning to the selected characters. At its simplest this approach seeks to establish the phylogenetic polarity of each character and then to plot relationships as the progressive accumulation of advanced character states. No formal cladistic treatment has been attempted in the present, primarily descriptive, account.

The suite of primary characters that emerges from this process is listed below.

First approximation

1. Only Bambusoideae have fusoid cells; they also have primitive spikelet characters.
2. C_4 metabolism occurs in only about 20 Angiosperm families, and is evidently an advanced character.

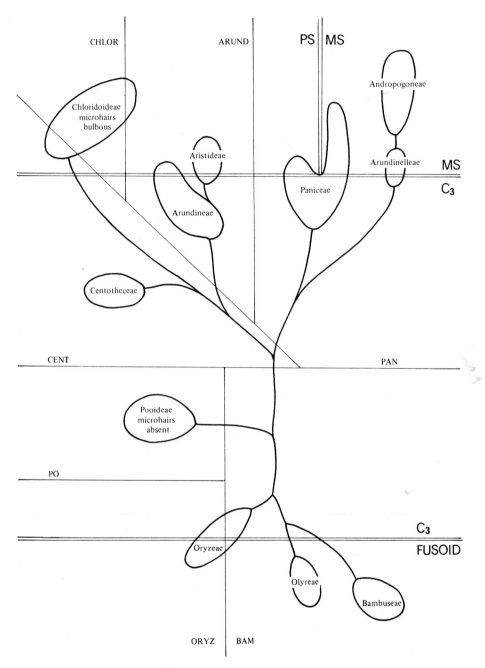

Fig. 4   First approximation to a classification of grasses, with superimposed grids for major differences in anatomy (double lines) and embryo structure (thin lines).

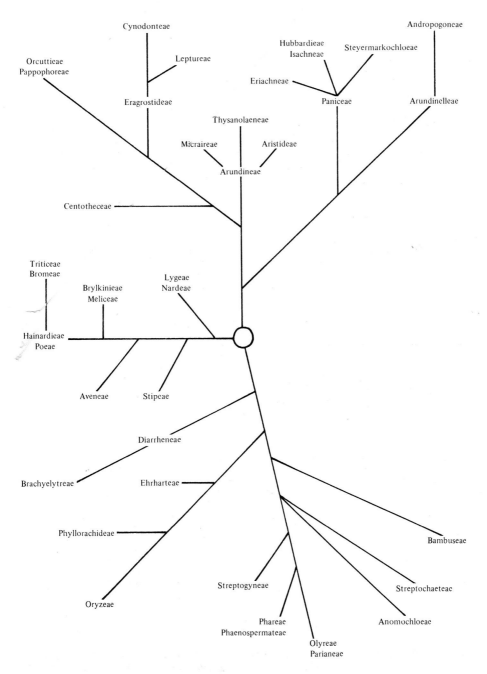

Fig. 5   Second approximation showing relationships between the tribes.

3. A plausible evolutionary sequence of embryo structure is shown in fig. 3.
4. The major distinction between membranous and pointed or bilobed lodicules against fleshy and truncate correlates with a change in embryo structure. See Jirasek & Josifova (1968) for range of variation.
5. Microhairs are usually slender; swollen hairs (Chloridoideae) or lack of hairs (Pooideae) are good markers for two subfamilies. See Tateoka et al (1959) for full range of variation.
6. Large chromosomes with a basic number of 7 are unique; they mark advancement in the Pooid line.
7. Both on theoretical considerations of the foliar origin of spikelet scales and by comparison with the primitive bamboo spikelet, many-flowered spikelets and many-nerved lemmas are more primitive than 1-flowered and 3-nerved. However, the reduction has occurred rather frequently, which limits its taxonomic usefulness. The strictly 2-flowered spikelet is of more limited occurrence, and its special form with a sterile lower floret is a good marker for Panicoideae.

The application of these criteria leads to the phylogenetic tree shown in fig.4. It is based on a primary anatomical sequence: fusoid — non-kranz — kranz. Its secondary branches are mainly dictated by differences in embryo structure.

Second approximation.

The validity of the above principles can best be judged by reference to the subfamily and tribal entries where the evidence, and the exceptions, are set out in some detail. The most serious discrepancy concerns the Bambuseae. Certainly their spikelets are relatively primitive, but their woody culms, complex branch and inflorescence structure and specialized fusoid cells are highly advanced. The evidence cannot support an unqualified assumption of primitiveness, and a direct progression from bambusoid to panicoid grasses is evidently an oversimplification. Hence the revised phylogeny of fig. 5, which shows three lines radiating from an unknown ancestor.

GRASSLANDS

The productivity of grasses is critically determined by light and water, and the great grasslands of the world are to be found in the zone between desert and forest, where a marked seasonality in the rainfall provides adequate moisture during a limited growing season, but is insufficient for the development of a closed forest canopy casting dense shade. However, their growth cycle is not well adapted to a cold weather rainy season, and sclerophyll becomes the dominant vegetation formation in a Mediterranean climatic regime (though they have responded to this challenge by producing an extraordinary number of early spring annuals). Their productivity is also sensitive to nitrogen, and they tend to be replaced by heathland on oligotrophic soils; but they are physiologically adaptable to saline, alkaline and seasonally waterlogged soils, forming edaphic grasslands in these environments.

These generalizations require two qualifications. The first is the extraordinary versatility of the family, so that individual species have adapted to special niches in most other vegetation types, and grasses will be found almost everywhere that Angiosperms will grow. The second is the enormous significance of biotic factors in moderating the competitiveness of grasses, and relaxing the influence of climate as a controlling factor. Indeed the classical climax concept is difficult to apply to the grasslands, for more often than not the evidence points to some form of disclimax, leaving the nature of the true climatic climax in doubt.

The first of the moderating factors is fire. Withered grass burns readily in the dry season and fires, started naturally by lightning or latterly by man, are a normal feature of the grassland environment of sufficient regularity and antiquity for the savanna trees to have co-evolved a significant degree of fire tolerance. The grasses themselves are dormant at the time and actually benefit, by clearance of dead litter and recycling of nutrients in ash, from a fire regime that is lethal to many other plants. In particular burning severely restricts the competitiveness of trees, and enables the grasslands to extend their domain into what would otherwise be closed woodland. Grassland is thus an ecosystem that supplies the fuel to ensure its own survival (Vogl in Kozlowski & Ahlgren 1974).

The second factor is grazing. Grassland represents a considerable food resource, but the abrasive silica-bodies in its leaves limited its exploitation by herbivores until the evolution of the hypsodont tooth by animals such as the horses, antelopes and bovines. The grass life-form, with its ground level branching and recuperative intercalary meristems, was pre-adapted to withstand the subsequent proliferation of grazing mammals. The grasses did not elaborate their defences, except in subtle competition to shift the burden of grazing from one species to another, but instead engaged in a quasi-symbiotic partnership of co-evolution with herbivores, developing an ecosystem that attracts and sustains a level of predation sufficient to cripple many of its competitors.

Lastly there came man, to exploit the unique nutritional and keeping qualities of the grass endosperm. 'Ramassage', the opportunistic harvesting of pure stands of wild grass, was the first stage in this process, and even today some of the minor crops of subsistence farming lie on this borderline of agriculture. Deliberate cultivation began some 10,000 years ago with the appropriation of weedy annual species that could be reliably established from seed in a wide range of habitats. The cycle of sowing and harvesting then automatically exerted selection pressure for such traits as loss of dormancy, simultaneous flowering and retention of fruit, leading to a domesticated plant dependent on man for its survival (de Wet 1981)

Agriculture, by removing the forest cover, opened up new territory for occupation by the grasses as fallow land weeds. These new grasslands were themselves exploited, with consequent changes in their composition (Scholz 1975), to provide forage and hay for increasing herds of domestic cattle. From about the 17th century they have also been subjected to some degree of domestication with the introduction of sown pastures. In short the cereal and pasture grasses, by their usefulness to man, have created another self-sustaining ecosystem favourable to their own kind.

The story of the grasslands suggests that the success of the grasses lies primarily in the evolution of a versatile life-style adapted to unstable or fluctuating environments, particularly those associated with strongly seasonal rainfall regimes or the early stages of succession following disturbance. This life-form then proved readily adaptable to a partnership with fire and herbivores, creating the highly competitive grassland ecosystem. Finally their propensity for exploiting instability has made them partner to the revolutionary changes in landscape induced by man.

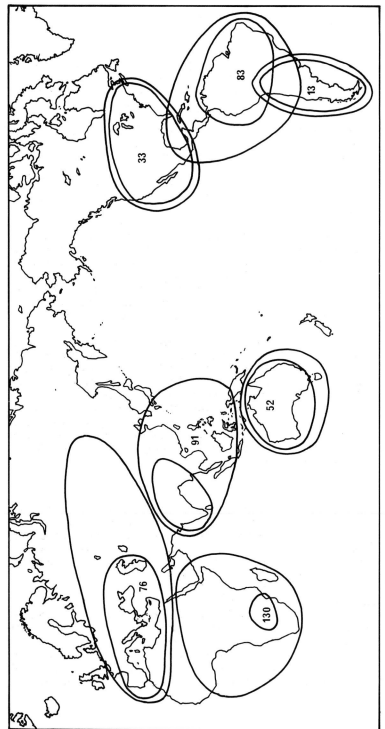

Fig. 6   The seven major continental distributions showing number of genera restricted to each. At least 50% of these genera are present within the inner line; at least 25% within the outer line.

EVOLUTION

Origin

The origin of the grasses is obscure, for whatever link existed with the rest of the Monocotyledons is now extinct. Their nearest living relatives are found in the group of little families that includes Joinvilleaceae, Flagellariaceae and Restionaceae, whose broadly tropical distribution hints at a tropical origin for the grasses (Dahlgren & Rasmussen 1983, Anton & Cocucci 1984, Linder & Ferguson 1985). The similarity between Gramineae and Cyperaceae is a matter of convergence rather than kinship.

On taxonomic evidence the grasses can be divided into three evolutionary lines:

Bambusoideae; tropical, specializing in forest and aquatic habitats.

Arundinoideae - Chloridoideae - Panicoideae; mainly tropical, but Arundinoideae biased towards the southern hemisphere.

Pooideae; temperate.

The base of each line is now extinct, leaving little to indicate the nature of their common ancestor. The most likely indications come from Bambusoideae whose diversity and fragmentation bespeak of age, whose spikelets (at least in Bambuseae) retain traces of a primitive trimerous symmetry, and whose origins seem to lie in the relatively benign forest margin environment. However, in proposing Bambusoideae as the most primitive of the subfamilies it is necessary to add the caveat that subsequent adaptation to specialized habitats has carried it a long way from the original prototype.

The implication of a forest origin for the grasses is contradicted by their anemophilous pollination, and by their possession of a life-form so eminently well adapted to open environments. It is therefore more likely that the bambusoids are savanna grasses that have moved into the forest rather than vice versa. In practice the antithesis is less than it seems, for the forest boundary is a broad ecotone in which, with decreasing rainfall, the forest first thins out on the well drained interfluves, then open woodland and bushland gradually extend down the valley flanks, until eventually the closed canopy is confined to narrow riverine tracts. The mosaic of open mesic habitats within the ecotone belt may well represent the birthplace of the grasses.

Fossils

It is desirable to fit a time scale to the evolution of grasses, but direct evidence from fossils is scanty. The earliest reports of grass-type pollen are dubious, and probably refer to Restionaceae which has similar grains. Authentic grass pollen first occurred in the Palaeocene, becoming abundant by the Oligocene (Muller 1981). The earliest macrofossils may likewise be dismissed as misidentifications (Thomasson 1980), but caryopses and cuticles occur in the Eocene (Daghlian 1981), and fruits of the genus *Stipa* in the Oligocene (see generic entry). Mammals acquired hypsodont teeth in the Oligocene, implying that grassland had emerged as an ecological formation by this time (Stebbins 1981). Silica-bodies are recoverable from the soil as 'phytoliths', but their palaeontological value seems limited to the Quarternary (Twiss 1969).

These snippets of evidence clearly indicate that grasses were in existence in the early Tertiary, at a time when the continents were in their final stages of separation. The details of this separation are controversial, but there is reasonable evidence for a temperate climate connection between South America, Antarctica and Australia until the Eocene, and for feasible indirect routes for seed dispersal between Eurasia, Africa and the Americas during most of the first half of the Tertiary (Clayton 1981a).

Geographical distribution

The subfamiles and major tribes of grasses are distributed across the world in broad latitudinal belts (Hartley 1950, Cross 1980). This accords with the evidence that their evolution has been strongly influenced by physiological adaptation to divergent climatic factors. The belts are particularly clear in the Old World, where latitudinal barriers of mountain, sea and desert have restricted intermingling, less so in the New World where longitudinal mountain chains have afforded no obstacle to the incursion of, for example, Paniceae and Cynodonteae to temperate regions of North America.

The pattern is quite different for genera, which tend to be restricted to a single land mass (Clayton 1975). Fig. 6 shows the seven major continental distributions which account for 73% of the genera. Of the remainder, 19% are relatively widespread and 8% are distributed disjunctly between various pairs of adjacent continents. The disjunct distributions are fascinating, but their members are too few to form a statistically sound base for overmuch theorizing. Table 1 shows the subfamily spectrum in each distribution type, revealing some irregularities which will be discussed under the subfamily concerned.

Table 1. Numbers of genera restricted to each distribution pattern, subdivided by subfamily or tribal group ('Pan' includes Isachneae, Eriachneae, Hubbardieae, Steyermarkochloeae; 'Andro' includes Arundinelleae). 'Africa' includes Madagascar and the Saharo-Sindian region. Tropical Asia includes 14 genera that extend to Australia. Subtotals group the wide, continental and disjunct distributions.

	Bamb	Po	Cent	Arund	Chlor	Pan	Andro	Sub-total
Pan-temperate	—	28	—	3	1	—	—	
Pan-tropical	4	—	—	1	13	17	17	
Old World trop	3	1	1	1	7	7	18	122
Eurasia	—	70	—	3	3	—	—	
N America	—	6	1	—	24	2	—	
S America	—	12	—	—	1	—	—	
Trop Asia	26	9	1	5	7	9	34	
Africa	14	1	3	19	51	26	16	
Trop America	37	—	3	3	12	25	3	
Australia	1	8	—	10	12	19	2	478
N Am/S Am	—	4	—	—	8	—	—	
N Asia/N Am	4	3	—	—	—	—	—	
Eur/N Am	—	11	—	—	—	—	—	
Africa/Am	1	—	1	—	4	5	7	
Trop Am/Asia	1	—	—	—	2	—	—	51

Evidently the genera are not good travellers, yet paradoxically the tribes have become widely dispersed with little heed to ocean barriers. It has been shown that grasses emerged in the early Tertiary. The evidence from geographical distributions now implies that the basic stock of the major tribes was established in an initial bout of adaptive radiation, spreading through the world in the first half of the Tertiary when the continents were closer together. Subsequently the widening oceans reduced the probability of intercontinental dispersal to the point at which the continuing evolution of genera was effectively isolated on separate continents.

At species level distributions are usually confined to a single land mass. The exceptions can mainly be attributed to introduction, which has been proceeding at an accelerating pace ever since man's trading activities provided a convenient vector, though many introductions are so ancient that their history is difficult to trace (Parsons 1970). In general, distributions coincide with the major ecological formations, though some apparent anomalies may be the consequence of vegetation disturbance induced by Pleistocene climatic changes (Clayton & Cope 1980 a & b). The anomalous tropical pooid flora of African mountain peaks seems to have been evolving in situ for a considerable time (Clayton 1976), affording evidence for long-standing stepping-stone routes between northern and southern temperate zones.

Endemic species are fairly common. They are prolific on the southern tips of continents, where partial isolation is evidently an important factor. They are also characteristic of mountain ranges, whose rich variety of ecological niches encourages micro-speciation, and where shifts in altitudinal zonation can compensate for the effects of climatic change (Clayton & Cope 1980a). Mountain endemism is not divisible into discrete centres and, though doubtless important as a refugium, its role in evolution has probably been exaggerated. Speciation by competitive replacement on the plains is likely to have been the more significant process.

Historical summary

The evidence may now be brought together in a working hypothesis.

1. Bambusoideae are the most primitive extant grasses, whose ancestors evolved in what is now the tropical forest-savanna ecotone. They have retained their hold upon the moister end of the environment by specializing in forest, forest floor and aquatic habitats. They are also represented by a number of small, often bizarre, relict tribes of forest and woodland which hint at their former diversity. However, their exploitation of open environments was curtailed by the emergence of new groups better adapted to dry conditions, though Ehrharteae survived this decline by retreating to the southern hemisphere.
2. Arundineae and Stipeae were the new groups of the open savanna, initiating the partnership with burning and grazing which expanded the grasslands into a major ecosystem.
3. They in turn were ousted from the tropics by the emergence of the more efficient C_4 tribes. Panicoideae took the mesic and climax environments; Chloridoideae specialized in pioneer and stressful habitats.
4. Arundineae survived extinction by retreating to the southern hemisphere where they successfully adapted to temperate conditions, leaving a sprinkling of isolated genera in specialized habitats elsewhere.

5. Stipeae also moved outwards, eventually giving rise to the Pooid tribes which became paramount in the extensive temperate latitudes of the northern hemisphere. By stepping across the tropical mountains they have also colonized the smaller temperate zones of the southern hemisphere.

Size of genera

The grouping of species into genera marks a particular level of evolutionary divergence, though it is exceedingly difficult to match this level with any objective criterion (Clayton 1983). However, some of its properties may be glimpsed by examining the size of genera.

The frequency distribution of genera containing 1, 2, 3 etc species approximates to a logarithmic curve, though the first term is always much higher than predicted (Fig. 7). This curve is typical of Angiosperm families, and has been stable in the Gramineae at least since Steudel's Syn. Pl. Glum. of 1854, suggesting that it is a natural consequence of the evolutionary process, though doubtless with some modification imposed by our own psychology. The fact that evolution

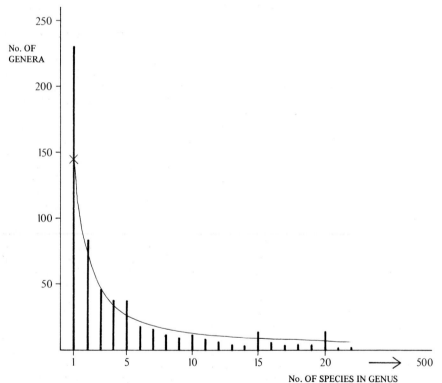

Fig. 7   Frequency distribution of generic size, with fitted logarithmic curve whose end point is marked X.

works in this way means that any concept of average generic size is almost meaningless, and that taxonomic systems will normally be strongly polarized, having some 80% of the genera smaller than average, but 80% of the species concentrated in genera larger than average (Clayton 1972, 1974). The asymmetric pattern is counter-intuitive, and a source of some perplexity to taxonomists for it does not lend itself to the construction of neat hierarchies.

Size, age and area tend to be correlated. Widespread genera are presumably old enough to have spread across the world when the continents were closer. They are certainly larger than continental genera. Moreover they remain larger when calculated as species per continent. It suggests a certain dichotomy in evolutionary strategies between large genera quietly speciating in the niches of a stable environment from which they are not easily dislodged, and small genera in labile environments subject to a continuing process of disruption and replacement (Clayton 1975).

DESCRIPTIVE TREATMENT

A three-level classification has been adopted, with the following approximate meanings:

Subfamily; basic anatomical differences.

Tribe; major differences in spikelet structure (see Clayton 1981b for note on nomenclature).

Subtribe; facies differences, of no great taxonomic significance, but forming recognizable groups.

For subfamilies an informal summary of morphology replaces the formal description, as the latter is so wide as to be almost meaningless. Otherwise the suprageneric descriptions should be treated as augmenting the generic diagnoses; in this connection words such as 'usually' mean applicable unless contradicted. The anatomical descriptions are based on the examination of at least one species in every genus. The chromosome tables, compiled from Fedorov 1969 and Moore 1973, are not a critical summation, but intended to serve as a guide to relative frequency of occurrence; counts of very low frequency, amounting to 20 or 30 different numbers in a large tribe, have been omitted. The diagrams are intended to give a visual impression of phenetic relationships, progressing from simple to complex structures; they obviously have phylogenetic implications, but no attempt has been made to treat these rigorously.

Keys are generally easier to use in the long run if they bear at least some resemblance to the classification adopted, but there are obvious difficulties with an anatomically based classification that is imperfectly correlated with external characters. Two possibilities are offered here. Firstly, to enter the initial key and pursue a somewhat tortuous course through the system. Alternatively, if the tribe is known, to go straight to the relevant tribal key, for each is complete in itself. Note that terms such as spikelet and lemma refer to the female-fertile form (conventionally abbreviated to 'fertile') unless otherwise stated.

Generic names, accompanied by selected additional references where relevant, are followed by the type species (and its currently accepted synonym if the epithet is different; only the latter for most invalid names). Generic delimitation is sensitive to the sample studied, and the diagnoses draw attention to aberrant and intermediate species whose accommodation presents difficulties. The section following the description gives the number of species, mainly based upon the Kew collections and likely to be an underestimate; also a brief indication of principal habitats, which should obviously be taken as no more than a rough approximation. Sectional keys are provided for some of the larger genera (with a common example species in parentheses) in order to indicate range of variation in more detail, but a critical appraisal at this level has not been attempted.

Any new combinations implied here should be regarded as provisional names pending a more detailed study at specific level.

REFERENCES

Anton, A.M. & Cocucci, A.E. (1984). The grass megagametophyte and its possible phylogenetic applications. Pl. Syst. Evol. 146: 117—121.

Auquier, P. (1963). Critères anciens et modernes dans la systématique des Graminées. Natura Mosana 16: 1—63.

Beetle, A.A. (1980). Vivipary, proliferation and phyllody in grasses. J. Range Manage. 33: 256—261.

Bogdan, A.V. (1962). Grass pollination by bees in Kenya. Proc. Linn. Soc. London 173: 57—60.

Brown, W.V. (1958). Apomixis as related to geographical distribution in Panicoid grass tribes. J.S. Afr. Bot. 24: 191—200.

Brown, W.V. (1960). The morphology of the grass embryo. Phytomorph. 10: 215—223.

Brown, W.V. (1975). Variations in anatomy, associations and origins of Kranz tissue. Amer. J. Bot. 62: 395—402.

Brown, W.V. (1977). The Kranz syndrome and its subtypes in grass systematics. Mem. Torr. Bot. Cl. 23: 1—97.

Brown, W.V. & Emery, H.P. (1958). Apomixis in the Gramineae: Panicoideae. Amer. J. Bot. 45: 253—263.

Brown, W.V., Harris, W.F. & Graham, J.D. (1959a). Grass morphology and systematics: I. The internode. Southw. Nat. 4: 115—125.

Brown, W.V., Pratt, G.A. & Mobley, H.M. (1959b). Grass morphology and systematics: II. The nodal pulvinus. Southw. Nat. 4: 126—133.

Burns, W. (1946). Corm and bulb formation in plants with special reference to the Gramineae. Trans. Proc. Bot. Soc. Edinb. 34: 316—347.

Campbell, C.S., Quinn, J.A., Cheplick, G.P. & Bell, T.J. (1983). Cleistogamy in grasses. Ann. Rev. Ecol. Syst. 14: 411—441.

Carnahan, H.L. & Hill, H.D. (1961). Cytology and genetics of forage grasses. Bot. Rev. 27: 1—162.

Clayton, W.D. (1972). Some aspects of the genus concept. Kew Bull. 27: 281—287.

Clayton, W.D. (1974). The logarithmic distribution of Angiosperm families. Kew Bull. 29: 271—279.

Clayton, W.D. (1975). Chorology of the genera of Gramineae. Kew Bull. 30: 111—132.

Clayton, W.D. (1976). The chorology of African mountain grasses. Kew Bull. 31: 273—288.

Clayton, W.D. (1981a). Evolution and distribution of grasses. Ann. Miss. Bot. Gard. 68: 5—14.

Clayton, W.D. (1981b). Early sources of tribal names in Gramineae. Kew Bull. 36: 483—485.

Clayton, W.D. (1983). The genus concept in practice. Kew Bull. 38: 149—153.

Clayton, W.D. & Cope, T.A. (1980a). The chorology of Old World species of Gramineae. Kew Bull. 35: 135—171.

Clayton, W.D. & Cope, T.A. (1980b). The chorology of North American species of Gramineae. Kew Bull. 35: 567—576.

Clifford, H.T. (1961). Floral evolution in the family Gramineae. Evolution 15: 455—460.

Connor, H.E. (1980). Breeding systems in the grasses — a survey. New Zealand J. Bot. 17: 547—574.

Connor, H.E. (1981). Evolution of reproductive systems in the Gramineae. Ann. Miss. Bot. Gard. 68: 48—74.

Cross, R.A. (1980). Distribution of subfamilies of Gramineae in the Old World. Kew Bull. 35: 279—289.

Daghlian, C.P. (1981). A review of fossil records of Monocotyledons. Bot. Rev. 47: 517—555.

Dahlgren, R. & Rasmussen, F.N. (1983). Monocotyledon evolution. Evol. Biol. 16: 255—395.

Decker, H.F. (1964). An anatomic-systematic study of the classical tribe Festuceae (Gramineae). Amer. J. Bot. 51: 453—463.

Dengler, W.G., Dengler, R.E. & Hattersley, P.W. (1985). Differing ontogenetic origins of PCR ("kranz") sheaths in leaf-blades of C_4 grasses (Poaceae). Amer. J. Bot. 72: 284—302.

Edwards, G. & Walker, D. (1983). C_3, C_4. Oxford.

Ellis, R.P., Vogel, J.C. & Fuls, A. (1980). Photosynthetic pathways and the geographical distribution of grasses in south west Namibia. South Afr. J. Sci. 76: 307—314.

Estes, J.R., Tyrl, R.J. & Brunken, J.N. (1982). Grasses and grasslands. Norman, Oklahoma.

Fedorov, A.A. (1969). Chromosome numbers of flowering plants. Leningrad.

Gould, F.W. (1983). Grass Systematics, ed. 2. College Station, Texas.

Grandbacher, F.J. (1963). The physiological function of the cereal awn. Bot. Rev. 29: 366—381.

Guignard, J.L. & Mestre, J.C. (1970). L'embryon des Graminées. Phytomorph. 20: 190—197.

Harberd, D.J. (1961). Observations on population structure and longevity of Festuca rubra. New Phytol. 60: 184—206.

Harberd, D.J. (1962). Some observations of natural clones in Festuca ovina. New Phytol. 61: 85—100.

Hartley, W. (1950). The global distribution of tribes of the Gramineae in relation to historical and environmental factors. Austr. J. Agric. Res. 1: 355—373.

Hattersley, P.W. (1983). The distribution of C_3 and C_4 grasses in Australia in relation to climate. Oecologia 57: 113—128.

Heslop-Harrison, J. (1982). Pollen-stigma interaction and cross-incompatibility in the grasses. Science 215: 1358—1364.

Jacques-Félix, H. (1962). Les Graminées d'Afrique tropicale. Paris.

Jirasek, V. & Jozifova, M. (1968). Morphology of lodicules, their variability and importance in the taxonomy of the Poaceae family. Bol. Soc. Arg. Bot. 12: 324—349.

Johnston, C.R. & Watson, L. (1983). Germination flaps in grass lemmas. Phytomorph. 31: 78—85.

Jones, M.D. & Newell, L.C. (1946). Pollination cycles and pollen dispersal in relation to grass improvement. Univ. Nebraska Agric. Exp. Sta., Res. Bull. 148.

Jones, M.D. & Newell, L.C. (1948). Longevity of stigmas and anthers in grasses. J. Amer. Soc. Agron. 40: 195—204.

Kimber, G. & Riley, R. (1963). Haploid angiosperms. Bot. Rev. 29: 480—531.

Kinges, H. (1961). Merkmale des Gramineenembryos. Bot. Jahrb. 81: 50—93.

Knobloch, I.W. (1968). A check list of crosses in the Gramineae. East Lancing, Michigan.

Kozlowski, T.T. & Ahlgren, C.E. (1974). Fire and ecosystems. New York, San Francisco & London.

Langer, R.H.M. & Ryle, G.J.A. (1958). Vegetative proliferation in herbage grasses. J. Brit. Grassl. Soc. 13: 29—33.

Linder, H.P. & Ferguson, I.K. (1985). On the pollen morphology and phylogeny of the Restionales and Poales. Grana 24: 65—76.

Lonsdale, W.M. & Watkinson, A.R. (1983). Plant geometry and self thinning. J. Ecol. 71: 285—297.

Metcalfe, C.R. (1960). Anatomy of the Monocotyledons. I. Gramineae. Oxford.

Mlada, J. (1977). The histological structure of the grass embryo and its significance for the taxonomy of the family Poaceae. Acta Univ. Carol. Biol. 1974: 51—156.

Moore, R.J. (1973). Index of plant chromosome numbers 1967—71. Reg. Veg. 90.

Muller, J. (1981). Fossil pollen records of extant Angiosperms. Bot. Rev. 47: 1—145.

Negbi, M. (1984). The structure and function of the scutellum of the Gramineae. Bot. J. Linn. Soc. 88: 205—222.

Newton, J.E. & Blackman, G.E. (1970). The penetration of solar radiation through canopies of different structure. Ann. Bot. n.s. 34: 329—348.

Nygren, A. (1954). Apomixis in the Angiosperms. Bot. Rev. 20: 577—644.

Page, J.S. (1978). A scanning electron microscope survey of grass pollen. Kew Bull. 32: 313—319.

Parsons, J.J. (1970). The Africanization of the New World tropical grasslands. Tüb. Geogr. Stud. 34: 141—153.

Peart, M.H. (1984). The effects of morphology, orientation and position of grass diaspores on seedling survival. J. Ecol. 72: 437—453.

Philipson, W.R. (1935). The development and morphology of the ligule in grasses. New Phytol. 34: 310—325.

Pissarek, H.P. (1971). Untersuchungen über Bau und Funktion der Gramineen-Lodiculae. Beitr. Biol. Pfl. 47: 313—370.

Prat, H. (1960). Revue d'agrostologie. Bull. Soc. Bot. Fr. 107: 32—79 (1960).

Reeder, J.R. (1957). The embryo in grass systematics. Amer. J. Bot. 44: 756—768.

Reeder, J.R. (1962). The bambusoid embryo: a reappraisal. Amer. J. Bot. 49: 639—641.

Schantz, H.L. (1954). The place of grasslands in the earth's cover of vegetation. Ecology 35: 143—145.

Scholz, H. (1975). Grassland evolution in Europe. Taxon 24: 81—90.

Shields, L.M. (1951). The involution mechanism in leaves of certain xeric grasses. Phytomorph. 1: 225—241.

Stebbins, G.L. (1956). Cytogenetics and evolution of the grass family. Amer. J. Bot. 43: 890—905.

Stebbins, G.L. (1981). Coevolution of grasses and herbivores. Ann. Miss. Bot. Gard. 68: 75—86.

Tateoka, T., Inoue, S. & Kawano, S. (1959). Systematic significance of bicellular microhairs of leaf epidermis. Bot. Gaz. 121: 80—91.

Thomasson, J.R. (1980). Paleoagrostology: a historical review. Iowa State J. Res. 54: 301—317.

Throne, G.N. (1959). Photosynthesis of lamina and sheaths of barley leaves. Ann. Bot. n.s. 23: 365—370.

Toole, E.H. & Brown, E. (1946). Final results of the Duvel buried seed experiments. J. Agric. Res. 72: 201—210.

Tran, V.N. (1971). La ligule dorsale des Graminées. Bull. Soc. Bot. France 118: 639—657.

Tran, V.N. (1972). Les oreillettes des Graminées. Bull. Soc. Bot. France 119: 441—461.

Tran, V.N. (1973). Sur la valeur morphologique des lemmes de Graminées. Bull. Mus. Hist. Nat. sér. 3, 128, Bot. 8: 33—57.

Troughton, A. (1957). The underground organs of herbage grasses. Comm. Bur. Past. Field Crops, Bull. 44.

Twiss, P.C. (1969). Morphological classification of grass phytoliths. Proc. Soil Sci. Soc. Amer. 33: 109—115.

Watson, L. & Knox, R.B. (1976). Pollen wall antigens and allergens; taxonomically ordered variation among grasses. Ann. Bot. 40: 399-408.

de Wet, J.M.J. (1981). Grasses and the culture history of man. Ann. Miss. Bot. Gard. 68: 87—104.

Youngner, V.B. & McKell, C.M. (1972). The biology and utilization of grasses. New York & London.

Table 2. Synopsis of subfamilies, tribes & subtribes.

PART 2. ENUMERATION OF GENERA

GRAMINEAE Juss., Gen. Pl.: 28 (1789); Benth. & Hook., Gen. Pl. 3: 1074—1215 (1883); Hack. in Engl. & Prantl, Nat. Pfl.-Fam. 2, 2: 1—97 (1887), translated by Lam.-Scrib. & Southw. as The True Grasses (1896); Bews, The World's Grasses (1929); Roshev., Zlaki (1937); Pilger, Nat. Pfl.-Fam. ed. 2, 14e (1940) & 14d (1956); Pilger in Bot. Jahrb. 76: 271—409 (1954). *Poaceae* Barnh. in Bull. Torr. Bot.Cl. 22: 7 (1895) nom altern. *Anomochloaceae* Nakai, Ord. Fam. etc.: App. 222 (1943). *Parianaceae* Nakai l.c. *Streptochaetaceae* Nakai l.c. *Bambusaceae* Nakai l.c. 223.

651 Genera; ± 10,000 species.

KEY TO TRIBES

1   Bamboos with woody culms   **1 Bambuseae** (p 35)
1   Herbs (cane-like, reed-like or suffrutescent in a few genera):
  2   Spikelets 1—many-flowered, if 2-flowered then both bisexual or the upper barren:
    3   Spikelets with 1 fertile floret, with or without additional ♂ or barren florets:
      4   Inflorescence branches subtended by spathes
               2 Anomochloeae (p 57)
      4   Inflorescence not spathate:
        5   Spikelets with a whorl of 5 empty scales at base, a long coiled awn, and borne in a raceme   **3 Streptochaeteae** (p 58)
        5   Spikelets not as above:
          6 Palea 1-keeled glumes absent or minute   **9 Oryzeae** (p 70)
          6 Palea 2-keeled, rarely 0—1-keeled and then glumes well developed:
            7   Spikelets unisexual (or leaf-blades sagittate); lemma entire:
              8   Spikelets not in verticels (but see *62 Froesiochloa* which has glumeless ♂ spikelets):
                9   Leaf-blades parallel nerved   **4 Olyreae** (p 59)
                9   Leaf-blades obliquely nerved   **6 Phareae** (p 67)
              8   Spikelets in verticels of 5 ♂ surrounding 1 ♀; ♂ spikelets with glumes
                     5 Parianeae (p 66)
            7   Spikelets bisexual, sometimes unisexual but then lemmas 3-awned or 3-toothed:
            10   Leaf-blades with distinct cross-nerves, broadly linear to ovate:
              11   Lowest floret ♂ or empty.   **1 Bambuseae** (p 35)
              11   Lowest floret bisexual:
                12   Grain globose with thick pericarp; spikelets falling entire
                    7 Phaenospermateae (p 68)
                12   Grain ellipsoid to trigonous; lemma 3—9-nerved (if 1-nerved see *550 Sphaerocaryum*)   **24 Centotheceae** (p 159)

10 Leaf-blades without evident cross-nerves:
13 Inflorescence a panicle (reduced to a single spikelet in some *Aciachne, Ehrharta, Zoysia*):
14 Ligule membranous, or spikelet with barren florets below the fertile:
15 Lemma terete to gibbous, firmly membranous to coriaceous, usually enfolding and concealing palea; spikelets 1-flowered without rhachilla extension; awn terminal, rarely absent
16 Stipeae (p 82)
15 Lemma not indurated and clasping palea, or if so then accompanied by rhachilla extension, dorsal awn or sterile florets:
16 Spikelets with at most 1 barren floret below the fertile:
17 Glumes shorter than floret, this with or without a straight terminal awn:
18 Glumes tiny, the lower ± suppressed; rhachilla extension a bristle almost as long as floret **13 Brachyelytreae** (p 78)
18 Glumes well developed, rarely reduced and then no rhachilla extension **17 Poeae** (p 87)
17 Glumes longer than floret, or lemma with dorsal or geniculate awn:
19 Fertile spikelets deciduous in triads, or accompanied by sterile spikelets **17 Poeae** (p 87)
19 Fertile spikelets not as above **21 Aveneae** (p 116)
16 Spikelets with 2 ♂ or barren florets below the fertile:
20 Spikelets disarticulating above glumes (if awns ciliate see *336 Blepharidachne*; if palea coriaceous see *9 Neurolepis*):
21 Lower lemmas coriaceous, barren, at least the upper longer than fertile floret **11 Ehrharteae** (p 76)
21 Lower lemmas membranous or subulate, sometimes coriaceous and then ♂ **21 Aveneae** (p 116)
20 Spikelets falling entire (if awnless see *455 Lasiacis & 457 Panicum*) **20 Brylkinieae** (p 115)
14 Ligule a line of hairs; lowest floret fertile:
22 Lemma cleft into 7—9 awns or deep lobes
29 Pappophoreae (p 188)
22 Lemma 0—3 awned (sometimes 5-lobed in *Amphipogon*):
23 Spikelets disarticulating above glumes, rarely falling entire and then strongly laterally compressed:
24 Lemma (1—)3-awned (*Amphipogon* sometimes merely tridentate), involute or convolute and concealing palea; spikelets strictly 1-flowered:
25 Palea as long as lemma **25 Arundineae** (p 164)
25 Palea less than ½ length of lemma **27 Aristideae** (p 184)
24 Lemma awnless, rarely 1-awned and then either accompanied by sterile florets or palea not concealed
31 Eragrostideae (p 191)
23 Spikelets falling entire, subterete (if panicle reduced to 1 spikelet see *435 Zoysia*) **39 Arundinelleae** (p 313)
13 Inflorescence composed of racemes:
26 Racemes single, the spikelets edgeways on and ± sunk in rhachis; lower glume suppressed:

27   Upper glume suppressed or almost so   **14 Nardeae** (p 81)
27   Upper glume longer than lemma   **32 Leptureae** (p 228)
26   Racemes several, or if single then spikelets broadside on:
  28   Body of lemma 5—9-nerved, or leaf-blades auriculate (*Henrardia*):
    29   Spikelets with 2 sterile lemmas below fertile floret
                         11 Ehrharteae (p 76)
    29   Spikelets without (rarely with 1) sterile lemmas:
      30   Raceme unilateral, or irregular and then awn geniculate (if
          lemma transversely bearded see *280 Danthonidium*)
                                21 Aveneae (p 116)
      30   Raceme bilateral; awn never geniculate
                                23 Triticeae (p 146)
  28   Body of lemma 3-nerved; leaf-blades not auriculate:
    31   Racemes single, bilateral, the spikelets strictly 1-flowered and
        in 2 opposite rows   **18 Hainardeae** (p 109)
    31   Racemes 1—many, unilateral or bottle-brush
                            33 Cynodonteae (p 229)
3   Spikelets with 2 or more fertile florets:
  32   Leaves short, imbricate, spirally arranged; plant moss-like
                        28 Micraireae (p 183)
  32   Leaves 2-rowed, not moss-like:
  33   Spikelet urn-like, of 2 opposing lemmas fused into a tube
                            15 Lygeae (p 81)
  33   Spikelet with free lemmas:
  34   Lemma margins clasping palea keels, both scales usually ± indurated;
      spikelets strictly 2-flowered (if lemma bilobed see *272 Pseudo-
      pentameris*):
    35   Lemma at most puberulous, never awned   **35 Isachneae** (p 308)
    35   Lemma pilose or awned   **37 Eriachneae** (p 311)
  34   Lemma margins not clasping palea keels:
  36   Lemmas 5 or more nerved:
    37   Inflorescence of several racemes:
      38   Leaf-blades with distinct cross-nerves, or lowest floret sterile
                        24 Centotheceae (p 159)
      38   Leaf-blades without cross-nerves or apparently so; lowest
         floret fertile   **31 Eragrostideae** (p 191)
    37   Inflorescence a panicle or single raceme:
      39   Leaves without ligules; lemmas prominently 13—15-nerved
                        30 Orcuttieae (p 190)
      39   Leaves with ligules:
      40   Ligule membranous, rarely with a ciliolate margin:
        41   Inflorescence a panicle, sometimes a raceme and then
          unilateral or spikelets edgeways on or lemma geniculately
          awned:
          42   Stigmas retrorsely barbed and tangled; inflorescence a
            raceme   **8 Streptogyneae** (p 69)
        42   Stigmas plumose:
          43   Upper glume shorter than adjacent floret or almost so;
            lemma with or without terminal or subterminal awn:
            44   Ovary rarely hairy or appendaged, and then the
              stigmas terminal:
            45   Glumes not side by side:

46   Leaf-blades without cross-nerves (or these indistinct in
      some *Festuca*)   **17 Poeae** (p 87)

46   Leaf-blades broad with prominent cross-nerves on the
      underside   **24 Centotheceae** (p 159)

45   Glumes side by side; spikelets sunk in rhachis of raceme
                       18 Hainardieae (p 109)

44   Ovary capped by a hairy lobed appendage, the stigmas
      subterminal   **22 Bromeae** (p 143)

43   Upper glume exceeding adjacent floret, or awn dorsal, or awn
      geniculate   **21 Aveneae** (p 116)

41 Inflorescence a simple or compound bilateral raceme, the
    spikelets broadside to rhachis; leaf-blades linear (if oblong see
    13 Guaduella); ovary hairy (if glabrous go to 45)
                       23 Triticeae (p 146)

40 Ligule a line of hairs, sometimes mounted on a brief scarious
    base:

47   Spikelets disarticulating between florets, rarely falling entire but
      then awn geniculate (*Chaetobromus*) or whole panicle deciduous
      (*Urochlaena*):

48   Leaf-blades herbaceous, or if pungent the plant tufted (if with
         7—11 straight awns see *303 Cottea*)   **25 Arundineae** (p 164)

48   Leaf-blades stiff, distichous, pungent; plant rhizomatous or
        stoloniferous   **31 Eragrostideae** (p 191)

47   Spikelets not disarticulating between florets:

49   Glumes falling with spikelet   **31 Eragrostideae** (p 191)

49   Glumes persistent on inflorescence:

50   Inflorescence a panicle; lemmas 2—19-awned (if 1-awned
         see *363 Ectrosia*)   **29 Pappophoreae** (p 188)

50   Inflorescence a raceme   **33 Cynodonteae** (p 229)

36 Lemmas 1—3-nerved:

51   Pericarp thickened into a pallid beak or knob at tip of grain
                       12 Diarrheneae (p 77)

51   Pericarp ± uniform in thickness:

52   Inflorescence a panicle or several racemes, if a single raceme
      then spikelets broadside on   **31 Eragrostideae** (p 191)

52   Inflorescence a single raceme, the spikelets edgeways on and
      sunk into its axis   **32 Leptureae** (p 228)

2 Spikelets 2-flowered, the lower floret ♂ or barren, the upper fertile, without
   rhachilla extension (except *Humbertochloa, Steyermarkochloa, Thysanolaena*
   and a few Paniceae):

53 Spikelets breaking up at maturity above the persistent glumes, or rarely
    falling in triads from a fragile hooked peduncle (if lower lemma dorsally
    awned see *172 Arrhenatherum*):

54   Glumes deciduous; fertile floret dorsally compressed; lower glume
      5—9-nerved (if 3-nerved see *455 Panicum*):

55   Paleas present   **35 Isachneae** (p 308)

55   Paleas absent   **36 Hubbardieae** (p 310)

54   Glumes persistent; fertile floret terete   **39 Arundinelleae** (p 313)

53 Spikelets falling entire at maturity:

56   Upper (rarely lower) lemma or palea cartilaginous to bony, thicker than
      lower glume; spikelets seldom paired and then similar in appearance
      (except *Cyphochlaena*); upper lemma awnless, rarely with a straight awn:

57 Spikelets falling singly with pedicel attached, very small, borne in a large panicle **26 Thysanolaeneae** (p 183)

57 Spikelets rarely falling with pedicel attached and then not as above:

 58 Inflorescence axis herbaceous, enfolding deciduous racemes; spikelets unisexual, the lower lemma indurated **10 Phyllorachideae** (p 75)

 58 Inflorescence axis seldom herbaceous, and then spikelets not as above:

  59 Leaf-sheath clasping stem **34 Paniceae** (p 256)

  59 Leaf-sheath cylindrical, culm-like; upper palea thickenened, convolute **38 Steyermarkochloeae** (p 312)

56 Both lemmas hyaline to membranous, thinner than lower glume, this usually indurated:

 60 Spikelets never paired, nor in fragile racemes, nor geniculately awned **34 Paniceae** (p 256)

 60 Spikelets paired, one sessile the other pedicelled, usually dissimilar, the pedicelled sometimes much reduced, rarely single and then either in fragile racemes or the upper lemma geniculately awned (some exceptions in *Dimeria*); lower glume as long as spikelet or almost so **40 Andropogoneae** (p 320)

I. SUBFAMILY BAMBUSOIDEAE

Asch. & Graeb., Syn. Mitteleur Fl. 2: 769 (1902); Cald. & Sod. in Smiths. Contrib. Bot. 44: 1—27 (1980). *Pharoideae* Beetle in Bull. Torr. Bot. Cl. 82: 197 (1955) sine descr lat. *Olyroideae* Pilger, Nat. Pfl.-Fam. ed. 2, 14d: 168 (1956). *Anomochlooideae* Potztal in Willdenowia 1: 772 (1957) *Parianoideae* (C.E. Hubbard) Butzin, Neue Unters. Blüte Gram.: 148 (1965). *Streptochaetoideae* (C.E. Hubbard) Butzin l.c. *Ehrhartoideae* Caro in Dominguezia 4: 11 (1982). *Oryzoideae* Caro l.c. 10.

Herbs, shrubs, tall trees or climbers, commonly with lanceolate tessellately nerved leaf-blades. Frequent external characters: membranous ligule; panicle or complex inflorescence; 1—many-flowered laterally compressed spikelets; several—many-nerved entire awnless lemmas.

Lodicules mostly 2—3, lanceolate, hyaline to membranous, acute; stamens 1—6, rarely more; stigmas 1—3. Caryopsis (rarely achene or berry) with embryo $\frac{1}{10}$—$\frac{1}{5}$ its length, and linear hilum; embryo bambusoid F+PP rarely F-PP, or oryzoid F+FP; mesocotyl not elongating (see also note under Bromeae).

Chlorenchyma irregularly arranged; bundle sheaths double; micro-hairs usually slender, occasionally absent; fusoid cells commonly present; stomatal subsidiary cells low-dome-shaped to triangular. Other common characters are papillose epidermal cells, transverse silica-bodies, palisade layer, invaginated chlorenchyma cells, stomata in lower epidermis and leaf midrib with the bundles triple or more complex. This is the non-kranz anatomy, including fusoid cell and palisade variants, shown in fig. 10. See also Renvoize in Kew Bull. 40: 509—535 (1985).

The extent of the subfamily may be broadly defined by the distribution of fusoid cells, whose specialized nature is indicated by the fact that they occur in no other family but the Gramineae. They are vertical plates with a very narrow lumen lying transversely in the mesophyll, and are often torn away in a thin section to leave an apparent cavity. The reason for their peculiar shape is unknown. Another bambusoid peculiarity is the occurrence of chlorenchyma cells with deeply invaginated walls projecting into the lumen; they are termed 'arm' cells. Fusoid and arm cells are not always present, but then the diagnosis may be extended by considering a suite of supplementary characters which occur frequently in Bambusoideae but only sporadically in other subfamilies; these are the epidermal papillae, a tendency to trimerous floral symmetry, and a bambusoid or oryzoid embryo. More controversial is a further extension to embrace a few small tribes of problematical affinity, whose claim to membership rests almost wholly upon their embryo.

The subfamily is markedly heterogeneous, and may be loosely divided into 5 groups:

1. Bambuseae. Bambusoid anatomy and embryo. Trees with complex branch and inflorescence architecture but simple, often trimerous, spikelets. A successful tribe of tropical and warm temperate forest and woodland.
2. Anomochloeae, Streptochaeteae. Leaf anatomy clearly bambusoid. Spikelets anomalous but apparently derived rather than primitive. Relict tribes of forest undergrowth in the New World tropics.

3. Olyreae, Parianeae, Phareae. Anatomy and embryo wholly bambusoid. Successful tribes of the forest ground layer, particularly in the New World tropics.
4. Oryzeae, Phyllorachideae, Streptogyneae. Fusoid cells often lacking and embryo usually oryzoid, but not clearly separable from the previous group. Some forest undergrowth plants, but successfully diversifying into swampy habitats of tropical and warm temperate regions.
5. Phaenospermateae, Ehrharteae, Diarrheneae, Brachyelytreae. A miscellany of warm temperate tribes with no clear relatives, but slightly more claim to bambusoid affinity than to any other; their placing in fig. 5 is frankly speculative. Three of them are isolated relics, but Ehrharteae is well established in the southern hemisphere.

The pattern that emerges is a puzzling mixture of advance and retreat: of isolated relics; of active adaptive radiation in forest, forest floor and aquatic habitats; and of a signal failure to compete in grassland. The ambiguity of the evidence, and a corresponding ambivalence in morphology where simple spikelets contrast with complex and often unique vegetative structures, have provoked much debate on the relative primitiveness of the subfamily. The paradox may be resolved by regarding Bambusoideae as heir to the original forest ecotone environment, still competitive in the moister and shadier habitats, but thrust aside in the open country by the mainstream of grassland evolution. In this sense, and in the sense that evolution has bypassed the spikelets of Bambuseae, the subfamily is primitive. In most other respects it is highly advanced. In particular it would seem fallacious to treat the specialized forest tribes, or their present habitats, as ancestral, and more realistic to envisage the common ancestor of the extant grasses as essentially grass like.

1. BAMBUSEAE

Nees, Agrost. Bras.: 520 (1829); Gamble in Ann. Bot. Gard. Calcutta 7: 1—133 (1896); E.G. Camus, Bambusées (1913); A. Camus in Arch. Mus. Hist. Nat. Paris sér. 6, 12: 601—603 (1935); Holttum in Gard. Bull. Singapore 1: 1—135 (1958); McClure, The Bamboos (1966); McClure in Smiths. Contrib. Bot. 9: 1—148 (1973); Suzuki, Index to Japanese Bambusaceae (1978); Keng in J. Bam. Res. 1: 1—19 (1982). *Arundinarieae* Aschers. & Graebn., Syn. Mitteleur. Fl. 2: 770 (1902). *Arthrostylideae* Camus, Bambusées: 16 (1913). *Chusqueae* Camus l.c. *Shibataeeae* Nakai in J. Jap. Bot. 9: 83 (1933). *Hikelieae* A. Camus in Arch. Mus. Hist. Nat. Paris sér. 6, 12: 601 (1935) sine descr lat. *Phyllostachideae* Keng, Fl. Ill. Pl. Prim. Sin. Gram.: 87 (1959) sine descr lat. *Atractocarpeae* Jac.-Fél., Gram. Afr. Trop.: 117 (1962) sine descr lat. *Dendrocalameae, Melocanneae & Puelieae* Potztal in Engl., Syllabus Pfl.-Fam. ed. 12, 2: 577 (1964) sine descr lat. *Chimonocalameae* Keng f. in J. Bam. Res. 1: 15 (1982) sine descr lat.

Perennial trees, shrubs or climbers; culms woody (except *Glaziophyton, Guaduella, Neurolepis, Puelia*), usually hollow, divided into cylindrical segments by the nodes (occasionally the lowest internode disproportionately elongated), the lower half clad in broad leaf-sheaths with rudimentary blade ('culm-sheaths'), the upper half copiously branched, one or more branches grouped at each node ('branch complement'); ligule membranous, an external ligule often present; leaf-blades linear to oblong, usually with cross-nerves and a short false petiole, deciduous from sheath, the sheath sometimes conspicuously setose at the mouth. Inflorescence a small panicle or raceme, the latter often reduced to a single spikelet, borne at the tips of branches but often aggregated in clusters or condensed about a node, the spikelets all alike. Spikelets of 1—many fertile florets, usually laterally compressed and disarticulating below each floret; glumes variable, usually 2—4, sometimes the lowest vestigial or the upper acquiring palea rudiments, mostly persistent, shorter than lemma, scarious to coriaceous; lemmas herbaceous to coriaceous, nearly always 5- or more nerved, entire, awnless or rarely with a short straight awn from tip; palea exposed or ± enfolded by lemma, usually several-nerved and 2-keeled, but if 1-flowered then rounded on back with a narrow sulcus if rhachilla extension present; lodicules usually 3 (more in *Ochlandra*, *Schizostachyum*), mostly large and supplied with vascular bundles; stamens 3—6 (except *Ochlandra*); stigmas 1—3, Fruit usually a caryopsis with linear hilum, rarely an achene (a berry in *Olmeca*, *Melocalamus*, *Dinochloa*, *Melocanna*, *Ochlandra*).

Genera 49; species ± 840; tropical and warm temperate regions.

Anatomy. Non-kranz, usually with slender microhairs and fusoid cells; papillae usually present on lower epidermis, occasionally on upper; transverse silica bodies usually present; arm cells present; midrib complex in ¼ of the genera; stomata mostly on lower epidermis.

Chromosomes. The basic number is 12.

2n	24	40	48	72
No of species	4	6	81	17

The tribe is defined by its copiously branched woody culms. Woodiness is generally considered to be a derived condition in Monocotyledons, and its occurrence in Gramineae is associated with a number of special features which necessitate some amplification of the general morphology discussed in the introduction.

The underground parts are well developed and of two kinds. Sympodial (or pachymorph) rhizomes turn upwards at the tip to produce an apical culm, the rhizome being continued by a lateral bud. They are usually short, clavate and closely packed into clumps, but sometimes the neck is elongated and the habit open. Monopodial (or leptomorph) rhizomes run indefinitely, producing culms from lateral buds. They are slender, elongated and spreading, but clumps can form by tillering at the base of the culm. A few species are amphipodial, possessing both kinds; they are normally included in the monopodial group, but are a source of ambiguity if the runners go unnoticed. *Chusquea* is the only genus containing both monopodial and strictly sympodial species.

The branch system is unique among Monocotyledons and a distinctive feature of bamboo architecture. Its developmental morphology is imperfectly understood, but it apparently arises from one axillary primordium which may form a single bud in the usual way or, by precocious subdivision may develop into a little group of nodal buds (the 'bud complement'); only in *Chusquea* do truly adventitious buds seem to take part. In either case the initial branch internodes may be so abbreviated that their lateral buds also appear to be sessile on the node. The number of apparent axillary branches, taken from the mid-culm region, is known as the branch complement. Leaves, though generally distinguishable from those of true grasses, are too uniform within the tribe to be of much taxonomic value.

The bamboo inflorescence is small and borne at the tips of the prolific lateral branches, but it often combines with its neighbours to form complex clusters. By analogy with the true grasses, whose inflorescence variants are regarded as derived from a panicle by the twin processes of compaction and reduction, the following sequence of intergrading forms may be postulated (fig. 2):
1. Simple (or semelauctant); a panicle or raceme, the latter occasionally reduced to a single spikelet. This is the standard form typical of most grasses. The branches are usually naked, but tiny subtending bracts occur in a few genera, where they presumably represent the vestiges of primitive subtending leaves.
2. Compound; racemes of one to few spikelets, more or less embraced by spathiform sheaths from the tip of the supporting branchlet, and aggregated into a fascicle or a false panicle. Compound inflorescences also occur in Andropogoneae, though this tribe seldom achieves the typical bambusoid reduction of the raceme to a single spikelet.
3. Iterauctant; a compound inflorescence of 1-spikelet racemes more or less condensed about a node by abbreviation of the supporting branches, coupled with reduction of the surrounding spathes to bracts at the base of the spikelet. The initial nodal branch is thus reduced to a short axis clad in glume-like bracts and tipped by a spikelet, its appearance being aptly indicated by the term pseudospikelet. Buds in the axils of the basal bracts develop into the next order of pseudospikelets, which then repeat the process, the sequential development of successive orders resulting in an inflorescence containing spikelets of mixed age; the ultimate order is often sterile or rudimentary. The ramification of the inflorescence is apparent when the basal bracts are distant, but they are more often contiguous and then the inflorescence becomes a congested mass of pseudospikelets concealing the node. The iterauctant contraction of flowering branches is peculiar to bamboos, and there is an evident homology with the precocious condensation of the branch complement.
4. Bare branched; iterauctant inflorescences borne alternately on the nodes of a bare branch or even entire culm, the leaves being reduced to insignificant bracts. This exaggeration of the reproductive phase is commonly associated with intermittent flowering. Simple and compound inflorescences often attain a similar effect by shedding the leaves.

The bamboo inflorescence is here interpreted as a highly advanced structure resulting from progressive contraction of a panicle and the branch bearing it, but two other theories on the derivation of the bamboo inflorescence should be mentioned. In the first it is contended that the compound inflorescence represents a primitive form of panicle with subtending leaves; but this theory does not satisfactorily account for the presence of brief racemes in *Decaryochloa*, *Semiarundinaria* and *Thamnocalamus*. In the second the pseudospikelet is seen as an intermediate stage in the derivation of the spikelet from an archetypal monocotyledonous spike; but the associated nodal condensation seems unlikely to be primitive, and it is difficult to envisage it subsequently expanding into the typical grass panicle.

The spikelet of bamboos is like that of the true grasses except that the lemma is never elaborate, the palea usually many-nerved, and the glumes not always clearly differentiated. There are commonly two glumes, but sometimes more and then the lowest may be rudimentary, while the upper tend to become increasingly lemma-like and occasionally contain a rudimentary palea. These are transitional scales of indefinite homology to which the term sterile lemma (applied in the true grasses to scales unlike glumes and apparently derived from florets) is difficult to apply consistently; it is best avoided by calling them all glumes. The number of floral parts also varies, sometimes approaching the liliaceous formula of P3 A6 G(3). Hence the bamboo spikelet can be seen as precursory to the standardization of spikelet structure in the true grasses. Its retarded evolutionary status stands in marked contrast to the complexity of most other bamboo structures.It should be added that the origin of the grass spikelet is a mystery. The assumption that it is derived from a spike of trimerous petaloid flowers is entirely reasonable, yet the fact remains that most monocotyledonous spikes lack prophylls, and cannot therefore account for the presence of paleas. Comparative studies on the inflorescence of Restionaceae may prove helpful.

Pseudospikelets closely imitate spikelets, but their branch derivation can be recognised by the fact that they are sessile within the basal bracts of older spikelets, and that branch prophylls are interpolated in the sequence of scales just below the true glumes.

Many bamboos flower annually and some seem to flower almost continuously throughout the year, but the most remarkable are those which flower periodically. When this phenomenon is well developed flowering occurs at intervals of 20—120 years according to species, though there is usually some sporadic flowering of individual culms or clumps in the interim; the flowering of each species is synchronized to within a few years over a wide geographical range; and the plants usually die after flowering. In practice flowering is seldom so neatly circumscribed, and in some species seems to be quite irregular. However, the records available, though numerous, are mostly a haphazard collection of anecdotal observations which afford a poor basis for precise analysis. Consequently most of the physiological questions posed by this strange phenomenon go unanswered, and the timing mechanism is unknown. Flowering has considerable biological repercussions as an important part of the vegetation cover dies out, and as predator populations surge in response to the sudden abundance of grain. In fact the function of periodic flowering may be to ensure regeneration by temporary satiation of the seed predators (Janzen in Ann. Rev. Ecol. Syst. 7: 347—391, 1976).

The fruit is usually a caryopsis, though sometimes with fairly thick and separable pericarp; in a few genera it is an achene with free pericarp. However, the fruit of most species is imperfectly known, and much confused by conflicting accounts of pericarp thickness taken from immature grains. The most interesting fruits are the berries with thick fleshy pericarp throughout (actually of a tough leathery consistency in dried specimens) whose endosperm is evanescent, food storage being transferred to a grossly enlarged scutellum.

One consequence of periodic flowering is that the spikelets of many bamboos are poorly known, and the classification of the tribe rests upon insecure foundations. It has become apparent that earlier classifications emphasizing stamens, palea keels and pericarp texture are unsatisfactory, and the system employed here takes up a suggestion by Holttum (Phytomorph. 6: 73—90, 1956) that the ovary appendage might be used as a primary criterion. Such a system is of little use for identification in the usual sterile condition, and many authors have turned to vegetative characters. Even here there are great difficulties since most specimens consist only of leafy shoots which are almost useless for taxonomy, and it is unfortunate that rhizomes, culm sheaths, and branch and bud complements have been consistently neglected by collectors. Hence both floral and vegetative classifications are severely hampered by enormous gaps in our knowledge, particularly in S.E. Asia where the last major revision dates back nearly 100 years. The present treatment of the tribe must therefore be seen as a provisional and somewhat speculative attempt to fit existing knowledge of the bamboos into the overall system of the family, pending the development of a more critical classification. Accordingly genera have been treated in a wide sense, and aberrant species largely ignored.

The bamboos are essentially plants of the forest and of the secondary vegetation derived from it, though a few have adapted to drier conditions. They are well represented in Asia and America but almost absent from Africa; it is possible that they were eliminated during a cool spell in the Pleistocene when a catastrophic contraction of the African rain forest is believed to have occurred.

Bamboos have a multitude of uses including construction and handicrafts (McClure in Econ. Bot. 10: 335—361, 1956; Soderstrom & Calderon in Biotropica 11: 161—172, 1979), edible shoots (Young in Econ. Bot. 8: 377—386, 1954) and paper making. Tabashir is a siliceous concretion deposited within the culm of several species, and credited with magical properties. The geographical range of bamboos has been greatly extended by the cultivation of timber species in the tropics, and of ornamentals in the north temperate zone.

1   Ovary appendage lacking or inconspicuous:
  2 Spikelet with 1 fertile floret invested by 2 large glumes, all deciduous together; two smaller glumes persistent, sometimes obsolete:
    3 Culm woody, branched   **8 Chusquea**
    3 Culm herbaceous, simple   **9 Neurolepis**
  2 Spikelet with 2 or more fertile florets, rarely 1-flowered but then not deciduous with 2 glumes:
    4 Rhizomes all sympodial:
      5 Branch complement 3 or more:
        6 Inflorescence simple, exserted, supported by narrow sheaths:
          7 Nodes 1-ridged   **1 Sinarundinaria**
          7 Nodes 2-ridged   **2 Colanthelia**
        6 Inflorescence compound, of spathate fascicles   **3 Thamnocalamus**
      5 Branch complement 1, or the culm unbranched:
        8 Culm woody:
          9 Leaf-blades not leathery:
            10 Fruit a caryopsis   **4 Aulonemia**
            10 Fruit fleshy   **5 Olmeca**
          9 Leaf-blades leathery, scarcely narrowed at base, imbricate above an elongated internode (scarcely so in *M. gracilis, M. steyermarkii* which have wiry culms up to 1 m high)   **6 Myriocladus**
        8 Culm herbaceous:
          11 Culms leafless   **7 Glaziophyton**
          11 Culms, or some of them, leafy   **13 Guaduella**
    4 Rhizomes, or some of them, monopodial:
      12 Branch complement 1, equalling culm:
        13 Stamens 6   **14 Sasa**
        13 Stamens 3:
          14 Stigmas 3   **15 Pseudosasa**
          14 Stigmas 2   **16 Indocalamus**
      12 Branch complement 3—7, thinner than culm:
        15 Stamens 6:
          16 Spikelets several-flowered:
            17 Inflorescence a scanty panicle or raceme   **17 Acidosasa**

17   Inflorescence compound, of single spikelets in loose fascicles
     18 Indosasa
  16   Spikelets 1-flowered:
  18   Lemma keeled   **11 Hitchcockella**
  18   Lemma rounded   **12 Perrierbambus**
 15   Stamens 3:
  19   Inflorescence simple   **10 Arundinaria**
  19   Inflorescence compound or weakly iterauctant:
    20   Culm nodes not swollen, without root thorns **19 Sinobambusa**
    20   Culm nodes conspicuously swollen, or with root thorns
     20 Chimonobambusa
1   Ovary with conspicuous apical appendage:
 21   Ovary appendage broadly conical and fleshy:
  22   Inflorescence simple or compound, borne at tips of branches (these
      sometimes loosely clustered about node):
  23   Stigmas 3:
   24   Rhizome sympodial; stamens 6:
    25   Spikelets several-flowered   **21 Racemobambos**
    25   Spikelets with 1 fertile floret:
     26   Culm branched:
      27   Inflorescence simple, exserted   **22 Nastus**
      27   Inflorescence compound:
       28   Palea not convolute   **23 Pseudocoix**
       28   Palea convolute   **25 Decaryochloa**
     26   Culm unbranched in vegetative state:
      29   Culm herbaceous   **26 Puelia**
      29   Culm woody   **27 Greslania**
   24   Rhizome monopodial; stamens 3:
    30   Culm cylindrical   **28 Semiarundinaria**
    30   Culm strongly flattened on one side:
     31   Leaf-sheaths developed   **29 Phyllostachys**
     31   Leaf-sheaths obsolete   **30 Shibataea**
  23   Stigmas 2:
   32   Branch complement clustered or horizontal:
    33   Spikelet with several fertile florets:
     34   Scrambler or climber; branch complement usually with 1 dominant
       branch   **31 Arthrostylidium**
     34   Shrub or small tree; branch complement subequal **32 Apoclada**
    33   Spikelet with 1 fertile floret:
     35   Lemma laterally compressed:
      36   Inflorescence fasciculate   **33 Elytrostachys**
      36   Inflorescence globose   **34 Athroostachys**
     35   Lemma terete   **35 Atractantha**
   32   Branch complement flabellate around a flat triangular space:
    37   Blade of culm-sheath not constricted at base **36 Rhipidocladum**
    37   Blade of culm-sheath constricted at base:
     38   Spikelets pedicelled   **37 Actinocladum**
     38   Spikelets sessile   **38 Merostachys**
  22   Inflorescence iterauctant, comprising 1 or more spikelets ± sessile on a
      branch node:
   39   Glumes dimorphic, the lower short and membranous, the 2 upper
      crustaceous and resembling the single fertile lemma   **24 Hickelia**

39   Glumes alike or gradually increasing in size:
  40   Pericarp thin; grain mainly composed of endosperm:
    41   Florets separated by a rhachilla internode, or if 1-flowered then rhachilla extension present:
      42   Paleas alike, not bifid:

43 Inflorescence tufted or stellate	**39 Bambusa**
43 Inflorescence cupuliform	**40 Oreobambos**
42 Paleas different, the lowest bifid	**41 Thyrsostachys**

    41   Florets arising at almost the same level and deciduous together, if 1-flowered then rhachilla extension absent:

44 Palea of all florets 2-keeled	**42 Gigantochloa**
44 Palea of sole or uppermost floret rounded on back	**43 Dendrocalamus**

  40   Pericarp fleshy; grain filled by enlarged scutellum:

45 Spikelets 2-flowered; palea 2-keeled	**44 Melocalamus**
45 Spikelets 1-flowered; palea rounded	**45 Dinochloa**

21   Ovary appendage long, stiff, tapering:
  46   Fruit a caryopsis with thin pericarp:

47 Spikelet disarticulating above glumes	**46 Schizostachyum**
47 Spikelet deciduous with 1—4 glumes attached	**47 Oxytenanthera**

  46   Fruit a berry with fleshy pericarp:

48 Stamens 6	**48 Melocanna**
48 Stamens 15—120	**49 Ochlandra**

a. ARUNDINARIINAE Benth. in J. Linn. Soc. Bot. 19: 31 (1881). *Perrierbambusinae* A. Camus in Arch. Mus. Hist. Nat. Paris sér. 6, 12: 603 (1935) sine descr lat. *Pleioblastinae* Keng, Fl. Ill. Pl. Prim. Sin. Gram.: 29 (1959) sine descr lat. *Sasainae* & *Thamnocalaminae* Keng f. in J. Bam. Res. 1: 15—18 (1982) sine descr lat.

Ovary appendage absent or inconspicuous. Inflorescence usually simple with pedicellate spikelets, rarely compound or weakly iterauctant. Culm-sheaths mostly persistent.

The most primitive subtribe, with simple inflorescence and ovary. It contains two compact generic clusters based on *Sasa* and *Chusquea*; a loose assemblage of broadly similar genera (including *Arundinaria, Sinarundinaria, Thamnocalamus* and *Chimonobambusa*) whose inter-relationships are sensitive to subjective preferences in character weighting; and an assortment of isolated peripheral genera whose placing is largely speculative (fig. 8). Mainly warm temperate and montane, but some tropical.

1. Sinarundinaria Nakai in J. Jap. Bot. 11: 1 (1935) — S. nitida (Mitf.) Nakai. *Yushania* Keng f. in Acta Phytotax. Sin. 6: 355 (1957) — Y. niitakayamensis (Hayata) Keng f. *Yushania subgen Otatea* McClure & Smith in Smiths. Contrib. Bot. 44: 21 (1980) — Y. aztecorum McClure & Smith. *Chimonocalamus* Hsueh & Yi in Acta Bot. Yunnan. 1: 75 (1979) — C. delicatus Hsueh & Yi. *Otatea* (McClure & Smith) Cald. & Sod. in Smiths. Contrib. Bot. 44: 21 (1980). *Ampelocalamus* Chen, Wen & Sheng in Acta Phytotax. Sin. 19: 332 (1981) — A. actinotrichus (Merr. & Chun) Chen, Wen & Sheng *Burmabambus* Keng f. in J. Bam. Res. 1: 173

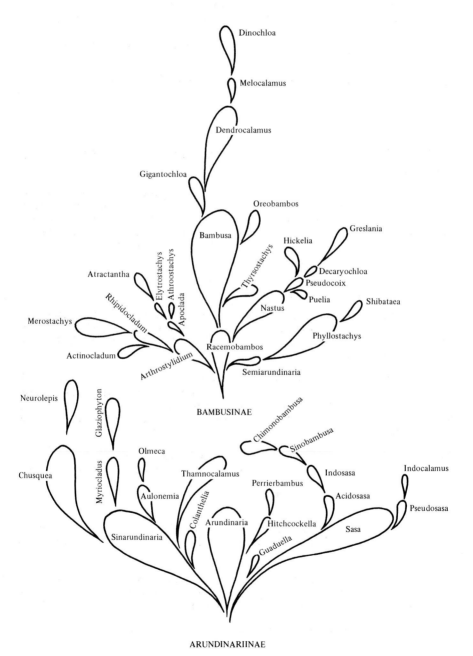

Fig. 8   Diagram of relationships in Bambuseae.

(1982) — B. elegans (Kurz) Keng f. *Drepanostachyum* Keng f. l.c. 2: 15 (1983) — D. falcatum (Nees) Keng f.

Shrub or small tree; sympodial, the neck sometimes elongated; culm hollow or solid, occasionally with thorns derived from adventitious roots at the nodes, sometimes the leafy and flowering culms separate; branch complement 3—7, subequal. Inflorescence a panicle, sometimes reduced to a raceme. Spikelets 1—several-flowered plus a sterile floret; glumes 2; lemma sometimes awned; stamens 3; stigmas 2.

Species ± 50. Mostly tropical Asia and Madagascar, but 1 species on tropical African mountains and 2 in Central America. Woodland or in the open, lowland to high mountains.

2. Colanthelia McClure & Smith in Smiths. Contrib. Bot. 9: 77 (1973) — C. cingulata (McClure & Smith) McClure.

Shrub or scrambler; sympodial; nodes with 2 ridges, one above and one below branch complement; culm-sheaths abscissing above their base, leaving a narrow persistent girdle on the culm; branch complement several, 1 branch dominant. Inflorescence a weak panicle or raceme, sometimes reduced to 1—2 spikelets. Spikelets few—many-flowered; glumes 1—3; stamens 3; stigmas 2.

Species 7. Eastern Brazil. Forest.

3. Thamnocalamus Munro in Trans. Linn. Soc. 26: 33 (1868) — T. spathiflorus (Trin.) Munro. *Fargesia* Franch. in Bull. Mens. Soc. Linn. Paris 2: 1067 (1893) —F. spathacea Franch. *Himalayacalamus* Keng f. in J. Bam. Res. 2: 23 (1983) — H. falconeri (Hook. f.) Keng f.

Bush or small tree; sympodial; branch complement 5—8, subequal. Inflorescence compound, comprising several racemes each of 1—several spikelets and subtended by a bract, these gathered into a fascicle subtended and partly enveloped by a spathe. Spikelets 1—several-flowered plus sterile floret; glumes 2; lemma often awned; stamens 3; stigmas 3.

Species 7. China and Himalayas; also South Africa. Forest.
The inflorescence of *T. falconeri*, with long racemes and short spathes, approaches the simple condition.

4. Aulonemia Goudot in Ann. Sci. Nat. Bot. ser. 3, 5: 75 (1846) — A. queko Goudot. *Matudacalamus* Maekawa in J. Jap. Bot. 36: 344 (1961) — M. laxus Maekawa.

Bush, tree or scrambler; sympodial; culm hollow or solid; branch complement 1. Inflorescence a panicle, usually open. Spikelets few—many-flowered; glumes 2—3; lemmas sometimes awned; stamens 3; stigmas 2.

Species 24. Mexico to Bolivia and Brazil. Montane forest.

5. Olmeca Soderstrom in Phytologia 51: 161 (1982) & Amer. J. Bot. 68: 1361—1373 (1981) — O. reflexa Soderstrom.

Tree; sympodial with greatly elongated neck (up to 8 m); culm solid or thick walled; branch complement 1. Inflorescence a panicle. Spikelets many-flowered; glumes 2; stamens 3; stigmas 2. Fruit fleshy, globose, 1.5—2.5 cm diam.; size of endosperm not known.

Species 2. Mexico. Rain forest.
Apparently related to *Aulonemia*, but the ovary type is uncertain.

6. Myriocladus Swallen in Fieldiana Bot. 28: 34 (1951); Swallen in Mem. New York Bot. Gard. 9: 237—249 (1957) — M. virgatus Swallen.

Cane or small tree; sympodial; culm simple or with few erect branches (complement 1), hollow or solid, the lowest internode elongated (*M. gracilis, M. steyermarkii* scarcely so), the upper crowded and bearing persistent imbricate leaf-sheaths with leathery blades. Inflorescence usually a tall terminal spire of unilateral racemes distributed along a central axis, the spikelets sessile or pedicelled, rarely (*M. gracilis, M. steyermarkii*) a solitary raceme of 3—5 spikelets borne laterally. Spikelets of 2 (rarely 1—5) fertile and 1 sterile floret, these sometimes deciduous together; glumes 3, sometimes awned; palea 2—several-nerved; stamens 3; stigmas 2.

Species 20. Venezuela. Thickets on sandstone.
A strange genus resembling a Bromeliad on top of a cane, and probably derived from *Aulonemia*. *M. gracilis* and *M. steyermarkii* with short wiry culms, subequal internodes and brief racemes are somewhat aberrant, but linked to the main body of the genus by *M. neblinaensis*.

7. Glaziophyton Franch. in J. Bot. Paris 3: 277 (1889) — G. mirabile Franch.

Reed-like; sympodial; culm simple, leafless (but little leafy tillers develop after burning), most of its length comprising a single elongated internode, this hollow with pithy septa, the upper nodes crowded. Inflorescence compound, the racemes comprising 1 spikelet subtended by bract and prophyll, and aggregated into a large terminal false panicle. Spikelets of 2 fertile florets plus a rudiment; glumes 0—3; palea 2-nerved; stamens 3; stigmas 2.

Species 1. Eastern Brazil. Dry mountain tops.
A weird genus with juncoid culms, paradoxically sprouting typical bamboo twigs from the base after burning. Apparently related to *Myriocladus*, particularly to those species with a reduced inflorescence.

8. Chusquea Kunth in J. Phys. Chim. Hist. Nat. Arts 95: 151 (1822) — C. scandens Kunth. *Rettbergia* Raddi, Agrost. Bras.: 17 (1823) — R. bambusoides Raddi. *Mustelia* Steud., Nom. Bot. ed. 2, 2: 168 (1841) non Spreng. (1801), nom superfl pro Chusquea. *Coliquea* Bibra in Denksch. Akad. Wiss. Wien Math. Naturw. 5: 115 (1853) nom nud — C. quila. *Dendragrostis* Jackson, Ind. Kew.: 727 (1893) in syn sub Chusquea. *Swallenochloa* McClure in Smiths. Contrib. Bot. 9: 106 (1973); Soderstrom & Calderon in Brittonia 30: 297—312 (1979) — S. subtesselata (Hitchc.) McClure.

Tree, shrub or climber; mostly sympodial, but sometimes monopodial or mixed; culm solid, rarely with an irregular lumen; branch complement (partly derived from adventitious buds) several to many in a cluster and often wreathing the nodes (arising below node in *C. bambusoides*), the central bud much larger and either remaining dormant or producing a culmlike branch. Inflorescence an open or condensed or rarely capitate panicle, sometimes reduced to a scanty raceme. Spikelets of 1 fertile floret without rhachilla extension; glumes 4, rarely awned, the 2 lower small or rudimentary, the 2 upper shorter than or equalling the floret and deciduous with it; stamens 3; stigmas 2.

Species ± 100. Central and South America. Montane woodlands.
A large and difficult genus for which no adequate revision is available (but see check-list in Smiths. Contrib. Bot. 9: 74—77, 1973). It refutes the usual maxim that sympodial and monopodial species are not congeneric. The lower pair of glumes are sometimes reduced to obscure lips on the pedicel tip, and are then easily overlooked. It is one of the few bamboo genera in which a distinction between glumes and sterile lemmas would be appropriate; note the parallel with *Oryza*.

9. Neurolepis Meisner, Pl. Vasc. Gen. 2: 325 (1843); Soderstrom in Mem. New York Bot. Gard. 18, 2: 13—21 (1969) — nom nov pro seq. *Platonia* Kunth, Rév. Gram. 1: 139 (1829) nom rejic non Mart. (1832) — P. elata Kunth. *Planotia* Munro in Trans. Linn. Soc. 26: 70 (1868) nom superfl pro Neurolepis.

Tall reed; sympodial; culm simple; leaf-blades linear, with or without cross-nerves, often very large. Inflorescence a large terminal panicle. Spikelets like *Chusquea*, but lemma 3—7-nerved and palea 2-nerved.

Species 9. Trinidad and Venezuela to Peru. High Andean shrub forest.
Grass-like plants with long leathery leaf-blades; those of *N. elata* can be enormous, up to 5 m long and 30 cm wide. Some species have a peculiar double ligule, the usual short membrane being backed by a larger lacerate membrane. Despite its unusual habit, the spikelets link the genus to *Chusquea*.

10. Arundinaria Michaux, Fl. Bor. Am. 1: 73 (1803); Nakai in J. Arn. Arb. 6: 145—153 (1925) — A. macrosperma Michaux (= A. gigantea). *Miegia* Pers., Syn. Pl. 1: 101 (1805) non Schreb. (1791) & *Ludolphia* Willd. in Ges. Nat. Freunde Berlin 2: 230(1808) non Adans. (1763) & *Macronax* Raf. in Med. Repos. ser. 2, 5: 353 (1808) — nom superfl pro Arundinaria. *Triglossum* Roem. & Schult., Syst. Veg. 2: 55, 846 (1817) — T. bambusinum Roem. & Schult. (= A. gigantea). *Tschompskia* Aschers. & Graebn., Syn. Mitteleur. Fl. 2, 1: 772 (1902) nom nud — A. simonii. *Pleioblastus* Nakai in J. Arn. Arb. 6: 145 (1925) — P. communis (Mak.) Nakai (= P. chino). *Nipponocalamus* Nakai in J. Jap. Bot. 18: 350 (1942) — N. simonii (Carr.) Nakai. *Oligostachyum* Wang & Ye in Nanjing Univ. J. Nat. Sci. 1982: 95 (1982) — O. sulcatum Wang & Ye. *Bashania* Keng f. & Yi in J. Bam. Res. 1: 171 (1982) — B. quingchengsanensis Keng f. & Yi. *Butania* Keng f. l.c. 175 — B. pantlingii

(Gamble) Keng f. *Omeiocalamus* Keng f. l.c. 2: 20 (1983) in syn sub A. fangiana. *Clavinodum* Wen in J. Bam. Res. 3: 23 (1984) — C. oedogonatum (Wang & Ye) Wen.

Shrub or small tree; monopodial; branch complement 3—7, subequal, thinner than culm. Inflorescence a scanty panicle or raceme, sometimes reduced to 1 spikelet, the branches naked or occasionally subtended by tiny bracts. Spikelets several—many-flowered; glumes 1—3 (lemma shortly awned in *A. pantlingii*); stamens 3; stigmas 3 (2 in *Bashania*).

Species ± 50. Northern India to Japan; North America. Forming thickets in forest, grassland and inhabited places.

A curious feature of *A. simonii*, and some other bamboos, is that the lower surface of the leaf is darker green on one side of the midrib than the other (Jones & Hermes in Ann. Bot. 48: 407—410, 1981). The darker side bears more papillae, and was outside when the leaf was rolled in the bud.

11. Hitchcockella A. Camus in Compt. Rend. Acad. Sci. 181: 253 (1925) — H. baronii A. Camus.

Shrub; rhizome unknown; branch complement several. Inflorescence a raceme of 1—3 spikelets, concealed by surrounding leaves. Spikelets 1-flowered without rhachilla extension; glumes 3—4, the uppermost lemma-like and falling with floret; lemma laterally compressed and keeled; stamens 6; stigmas 2.

Species 1. Madagascar.

12. Perrierbambus A. Camus in Bull. Soc. Bot. France 71: 669 (1924) — P. madagascariensis A. Camus.

Shrub; monopodial; branch complement several; leaves annually deciduous. Inflorescence a brief raceme of 1—3 spikelets, concealed within an involucre-like cluster of diminished leaf-blades. Spikelets 1-flowered without rhachilla extension; glumes 1—2; lemma rounded on back; stamens 6; stigmas 2—3.

Species 2. Madagascar. Dry woodland.

In this genus, and to a lesser extent in *Hitchcockella*, the inflorescence is protected by involucral leaf-blades instead of the more usual development of spathiform sheaths. The two genera are rather isolated and their relatives uncertain.

13. Guaduella Franch. in Bull. Mens. Soc. Linn. Paris 1: 676 (1887) as 'Guadella' emend in J. Bot. Paris 3: 305 (1889); Clayton in Kew Bull. 16: 247—250 (1962) —G. marantifolia Franch. *Microbambus* K. Schum. in Bot. Jahrb. 24: 336 (1897) —M. macrostachys K. Schum.

Perennial herb; rhizome sympodial; culm simple to sparsely branched (complement 1), sometimes the leaves and inflorescence on separate culms; leaves large. Inflorescence a scanty panicle often reduced to a raceme. Spikelets many-flowered, shortly pedicelled or sessile; glumes 2—4; stamens 6; stigmas 2.

Species 6. Sierra Leone to Angola. Forest shade.
A grass of rain forest undergrowth, easily mistaken for *Aframomum* (Zingiberaceae).

14. Sasa Mak. & Shib. in Bot. Mag. Tokyo 15: 18 (1901); Suzuki in Jap. J. Bot. 18: 289—307 (1964) & l.c. 19: 99—125 (1965) & l.c.: 419—457 (1967) — S. albo-marginata (Miq.) Mak. & Shib. (= S. veitchii). *Sasaella* Mak. in J. Jap. Bot. 6: 15 (1929); Suzuki in J. Jap. Bot. 51: 97—103, 151—158, 220—224, 269—277 (1976) —S. ramosa (Mak.) Mak. *Sasamorpha* Nakai in J. Fac. Agric. Hokkaido Univ. 26: 180 (1931); Suzuki in J. Jap. Bot. 50: 129—142 (1975) — S. borealis (Hack.) Nakai. *Neosasamorpha* Tatewaki in Trans. Hokkaido For. Soc. 38, 2: 8 (1940) — N. asagishiana (Mak. & Uch.) Tatewaki (= S. shimidzuana). *Nipponobambusa* Muroi in Hyogo Pref. J. Sci. Ed. Nat. Hist. 6: 89 (1940) — N. sawadai (Mak.) Muroi.

Small to medium shrub; monopodial or amphipodial; branch complement 1, exceptionally 3 and then 1 dominant; leaves large. Inflorescence a small panicle, the branches naked or subtended by tiny bracts. Spikelets several-flowered; glumes 2; stamens 6; stigmas 3.

Species ± 50. Mainly Japan, extending to Korea, adjacent parts of China and Kuriles. Woodland and inhabited places.

15. Pseudosasa Nakai in J. Arn. Arb. 6: 150 (1925) — P. japonica (Steud.) Nakai. *Yadakeya* Mak. in J. Jap. Bot. 6: 16 (1929) nom superfl pro Pseudosasa.

Shrub. Like *Sasa* but stamens 3(—4).

Species 4. Japan and Taiwan. Woodland and roadside.

16. Indocalamus Nakai in J. Arn. Arb. 6: 148 (1925), emend Chao, Chu & Hsiung in Acta Phytotax. Sin. 18: 25 (1980) — I. sinicus (Hance) Nakai. *Gelidocalamus* Wen in J. Bam. Res. 1: 21 (1982) — G. stellatus Wen. *Ferrocalamus* Hsueh & Keng f. l.c.: 137 — F. strictus Hsueh & Keng f.

Shrub. Like *Sasa* but stamens 3, stigmas 2.

Species ± 10. Southern China. Woodland and forming thickets in open country.

17. Acidosasa Chu & Chao in J. Nanjing Coll. For. Prod. 1979: 142 (1979) — A. chinensis Chu & Chao.

Shrub; monopodial; branch complement 3, subequal; leaves large. Inflorescence a scanty panicle or raceme. Spikelets several-flowered; glumes 4; stamens 6; stigmas 3.

Species 1. Southern China.

18. Indosasa McClure in Lingnan Univ. Sci. Bull. 9: 28 (1940); Chao & Chu in Acta Phytotax. Sin. 21: 60—75 (1983) — I. crassiflora McClure.

Shrub; monopodial; nodes 2-ridged; branch complement 3, subequal; leaves large. Inflorescence weakly iterauctant with short espathate branches loosely grouped about a node (but in *I. hispida* the basal bracts spathiform, and the inflorescence closer to compound). Spikelets several—many-flowered; glumes 2; lemmas coriaceous; stamens 6; stigmas 3.

Species 10. China and Viet Nam. Forest and roadside.

19. Sinobambusa Nakai in J. Arn. Arb. 6: 152 (1925); Wen in J. Bam. Res. 1: 140—164 (1982) — S. tootsik (Sieb.) Mak. *Neobambus* Keng f. in Tech. Bull. Nat. For. Res. Bur. China 8: 15 (1948) nom nud — S. dolichantha.

Shrub or small tree. Like *Indosasa* but stamens 3, stigmas 2—-3.

Species 16. China and Taiwan. Forest.

20. Chimonobambusa Mak. in Bot. Mag. Tokyo 28: 153 (1914) — C. marmorea (Mitf.) Mak. *Oreocalamus* Keng in Sunyatsenia 4: 146 (1940) — O. szechuanensis (Rendle) Keng. *Quiongzhuea* Hsueh & Yi in Acta Bot. Yunnan. 2: 91—92 (1980) —Q. tumidinoda Hsueh & Yi.

Shrub; monopodial; culm nodes 2-ridged, swollen, with root-thorns between ridges; branch complement 3—7, subequal. Inflorescence compound, comprising 1—3 single-spikelet racemes grouped in loose espathate fascicles. Spikelets many-flowered, the florets distant; glumes 2; lemmas membranous; anthers 3; stigmas 2.

Species 6. China and Japan. Forest.
The culm of *C. quadrangularis* is square in section.

b. BAMBUSINAE Presl, Rel. Haenk. 1: 256 (1830). *Dendrocalaminae* Benth. in J. Linn. Soc. Bot. 19: 31 (1881). *Hickeliinae* A. Camus in Compt. Rend. Acad. Sci. 179: 480 (1924). *Pseudocoicinae* A. Camus in Arch. Mus. Hist. Nat. Paris sér. 6, 12: 603 (1935) sine descr lat.

Ovary appendage broadly conical and usually hairy. Inflorescence rarely simple, usually compound or iterauctant. Culm-sheaths mostly deciduous.

The subtribe is defined by precocious growth of the pericarp at the tip of the ovary soon after fertilization, when it forms a broadly conical or even toadstool-like cap. By maturity this has become incorporated in the pericarp and is then no more than an apical thickening. The genera progress from simple to complex inflorescence structures along a number of parallel lines (fig. 8). Mainly tropical.

21. Racemobambos Holttum in Gard. Bull. Singapore 15: 268 (1956); Dransfield in Kew Bull. 37: 661—679 (1983) — R. gibbsiae (Stapf) Holttum. *Microcalamus* Gamble in J. As. Soc. Bengal, Nat. Hist. 59: 207 (1890) non Franch. (1889) — M. prainii Gamble. *Neomicrocalamus* Keng f. in J. Bam. Res. 2: 146 (1983) nom nov pro Microcalamus.

Climber or scrambler; sympodial with long neck; branch complement several—many, 1 dominant. Inflorescence a small panicle or raceme, each spikelet usually subtended by a tiny bract (this glume-like with rudimentary blade in *R. prainii*). Spikelets several-flowered; glumes 2—3; stamens 6; stigmas 3.

Species 17. Assam and southern China, through Malesia to the Solomon Is. Mountain forest.
Note the unusually well developed bracts in the inflorescence of *R. prainii*.

22. Nastus Juss., Gen. Pl.: 34 (1789); Holttum in Kew Bull. 10: 591—594 (1956) & 21: 283—292 (1967) — N. borbonicus Gmel. *Stemmatospermum* P. Beauv., Ess. Agrost.: 144 (1812) — S. verticillatum P. Beauv. (= N. borbonicus). *Chloothamnus* Büse in Miq., Pl. Jungh.: 386 (1854) — C. chilianthus Büse (= N. elegantissimus). *Oreiostachys* Gamble in Versl. Wis. Nat. Akad. Wet. Amsterdam 10: 685 (1908) —O. pullei Gamble (= N. elegantissimus).

Tree or scrambler; sympodial; branch complement many, subequal (arising below node in *N. productus* and a few others). Inflorescence an open or contracted panicle or reduced to a raceme (often a single spikelet in *N. aristatus*), exserted. Spikelets of 1 fertile floret with or without rhachilla extension bearing a rudiment; glumes 4—6, of increasing size, 2—3 of them deciduous with the floret; lemma firmly membranous; stamens 6; stigmas 3.

Species 18. Madagascar, Reunion, Sumatra to Solomons. Montane forest.
N. hooglandii, with well developed sheath subtending a small contracted panicle, verges on a compound inflorescence; it has retrorsely scabrid upper nodes to assist climbing.

23. Pseudocoix A. Camus in Compt. Rend. Acad. Sci. 179: 478 (1924) & Bull. Soc. Bot. France 71: 903—906 (1925) — P. perrieri A. Camus.

Shrub or scrambler; branch complement several. Inflorescence compound, of single spikelets each subtended by a leaf or bract and gathered into a fascicle. Spikelets 1-flowered plus rhachilla extension, deciduous with the glumes; glumes 2—3 membranous, plus 1—2 indurated and lemma-like; lemma crustaceous, smooth, shiny; palea sulcate; lodicules well developed; stamens 6, free; stigmas 3.

Species 1. Madagascar and Tanzania. Forest.

24. Hickelia A. Camus in Compt. Rend. Acad. Sci. 179: 479 (1924) & Bull. Soc. Bot. France 71: 899 (1925) — H. madagascariensis A. Camus.

Climber. Like *Pseudocoix* but inflorescence iterauctant, of stellate spikelet clusters around the nodes.

Species 1. Madagascar. Forest.

25. Decaryochloa A. Camus in Bull. Soc. Bot. France 93: 242 (1946) — D. diadelpha A. Camus.

Climber; branch complement several. Inflorescence compound, comprising racemes of 1—3 spikelets supported by a subspathiform sheath and grouped in fascicles. Spikelets 1-flowered with or without a rhachilla extension; glumes 2—4; lemma coriaceous, not shiny; palea coriaceous, convolute; lodicules small; stamens 6, in 2 groups of 3; stigmas 3. Fruit with fleshy pericarp.

Species 1. Madagascar. Forest.

26. Puelia Franch. in Bull. Mens. Soc. Linn. Paris 1: 674 (1887); Clayton in Hook. Ic. Pl. 37: t 3642 (1967) — P. ciliata Franch. *Atractocarpa* Franch. in Bull. Mens. Soc. Linn. Paris 1: 675 (1887) — P. olyriformis Franch.

Perennial herb; sympodial; culm simple, sometimes leaves and inflorescence on separate culms. Inflorescence a narrow panicle (branches subtended by little bracts in *P. ciliata*). Spikelets with 1 fertile floret; glumes 2—3(—7); lower 3—6 florets ♂, herbaceous to coriaceous, deciduous with fertile floret, the rhachilla reduced to a rounded callus; uppermost floret ♀, softly leathery, borne upon a distinct internode, this slightly prolonged into a horn or frill at base of floret; stamens 6, the filaments united; stigmas 3. Fruit an achene.

Species 5. Sierra Leone to Angola. Forest shade.
A genus with many odd features including external ligules, dimorphic florets and peculiar rhachilla extension. *P. coriacea* has root tubers. *P. schumanniana* has only one large leaf, perched on the tip of a slender culm.

27. Greslania Balansa. in Bull. Soc. Bot. France 19: 319 (1873) — G. montana Balansa.

Woody cane 1—3 m high; sympodial; culms unbranched in vegetative state, leafy. Inflorescence compound, of 1-spikelet racemes each subtended by bract and prophyll, these aggregated into a large terminal false panicle. Spikelets 1-flowered plus rhachilla extension; glumes 2; stamens 6; stigmas 3. Fruit with fleshy pericarp.

Species 4. New Caledonia. Mountain slopes and riversides.
A strange plant, superficially reminiscent of *Myriocladus* and *Glaziophyton*.

28. Semiarundinaria Nakai in J. Arn. Arb. 6: 150 (1925) — S. fastuosa (Mitf.) Nakai. *Brachystachyum* Keng in Sunyatsenia 4: 151 (1940) — S. densiflorum (Rendle) Keng.

Shrub or small tree; monopodial; culms cylindrical; branch complement 3—many. Inflorescence compound, comprising racemes of 1—3 spikelets subtended by a spatheole and grouped in fascicles. Spikelets several-flowered; glumes 0—3; stamens 3; stigmas 3.

Species ± 5. China and Japan. Light woodland.

29. Phyllostachys Sieb. & Zucc. in Abh. Math.-Phys. Kön. Bayer. Akad. 3: 745 (1843) nom conserv; McClure, U.S. Dept. Agric. Handb. 114: 1—69 (1957); Wang et al in Acta Phytotax. Sin. 18: 15—19, 48—92 (1980) — P. bambusoides Sieb. & Zucc. *Sinoarundinaria* Ohwi in Mayebara, Fl. Austro-Higo.: 86 (1931) nom superfl pro Phyllostachys.

Shrub or tree; monopodial; culm flattened on one side; branch complement 2, unequal, rarely with a small third central branch. Inflorescence compound, of 1-spikelet racemes gathered into spathate fascicles or capitulae. Spikelets 1—3-flowered plus rhachilla extension; glumes 0—3; stamens 3; stigmas 3.

Species ± 45. Himalaya to Japan. Woodland.

30. Shibataea Nakai in J. Jap. Bot. 9: 83 (1933) — S. kumasaca (Steud.) Nakai.

Small shrub; monopodial; culm flattened on one side; nodes 2-ridged; branch complement 3—5, subequal; leaf-sheaths obsolete. Inflorescence compound, of 1-spikelet racemes gathered into spathate fascicles. Spikelets 2-flowered plus rhachilla extension; glumes 2—3; lemma chartaceous; stamens 3; stigmas 3.

Species 3. China and Japan. Woodland.

31. Arthrostylidium Rupr. in Mém. Acad. Sci. Petersb. sér. 6, 3: 117 (1840) — A. cubense Rupr.

Scrambler or climber; sympodial; culms thick walled or almost solid; branch complement numerous, clustered, 1 branch dominant (but sometimes dormant), this slightly decurrent towards the nodal ridge as a low bulge which is naked or flanked (and sometimes obscured) by lateral buds. Inflorescence a slender raceme (sometimes only 1—3 spikelets in A. *capillifolium*; short racemes on a central axis in A. *angustifolium*), the rhachis sometimes zigzag. Spikelets few—several-flowered, sessile; glumes 2—3; stamens 3; stigmas 2.

Species 20. West Indies to Brazil. Forest.
The decurrent bulge foreshadows the more extreme branch complement of *Rhipidocladum*. A few species have the branch tips retrorsely scabrid as an aid to climbing. A. *capillifolium* has filiform leaf-blades.

32. Apoclada McClure in Reitz, Fl. Ill. Cat. Gram. Supl.: 57 (1967) — A. simplex McClure & Smith.

Shrub or small tree; sympodial; culms solid or hollow; branch complement typically 5, in a horizontal line, subequal. Inflorescence reduced to a single spikelet (raceme of 1—4 spikelets in *A. arenicola*), solitary at tip of slender leafy supporting branch. Spikelets several—many-flowered, large compared to adjacent genera; glumes 0, but spikelet embraced below by leaves of supporting branch; stamens 3 (*A. diversa* 3—6); stigmas 2.

Species 4. Brazil. Open woodland.

33. Elytrostachys McClure in J. Wash. Acad. Sci. 32: 173 (1942) — E. typica McClure.

Scrambler; sympodial; branch complement numerous, 1 dominant. Inflorescence compound, of stoutly pedunculate 1-spikelet racemes supported by spathiform sheaths and gathered into a fascicle. Spikelets 1-flowered plus rhachilla extension; glumes 2; lemma lanceolate in profile, laterally compressed; stamens 6; stigmas 2.

Species 2. Honduras to Venezuela. Rain forest.

34. Athroostachys Benth. in Benth. & Hook., Gen. Pl. 3: 1208 (1883) & J. Linn. Soc. Bot. 19: 134 (1881) sine descr as 'Achroostachys' — A. capitata (Hook.) Benth.

Scrambler; sympodial; branch complement 3, subequal. Inflorescence compound, of 1-spikelet racemes arranged in a globose head, its branchlets mostly subtended by little bracts. Spikelets with 1 fertile and 1 sterile floret; glumes 2; stamens 3; stigmas 2. Ovary type uncertain.

Species 1. Eastern Brazil. Forest.

35. Atractantha McClure in Smiths. Contrib. Bot. 9: 42 (1973) — A. radiata McClure.

Climber; sympodial; culm solid; branch complement several, approximately horizontal, 1 dominant. Inflorescence compound, of stoutly pedunculate 1-spikelet racemes supported by narrow sheaths or bracts, these aggregated in a fascicle or globose head. Spikelets 1-flowered plus rhachilla extension; glumes 0; lemma terete, convolute, thorn-like; stamens 3; stigmas 2.

Species ± 10. Eastern Brazil. Rain forest.

36. Rhipidocladum McClure in Smiths. Contrib. Bot. 9: 101 (1973) — R. harmonicum (Parodi) McClure.

Slender tree or scrambler; sympodial; blade of culm sheath the same width as sheath, erect; branch complement flabellate around a smooth triangular space, subequal. Inflorescence a lax unilateral raceme (*R. harmonicum* bilateral with zig-zag rhachis), the spikelets single (*R. geminatum* paired) and sessile. Spikelets of few to several fertile florets with depauperate florets above; glumes 2—3; stamens 3; stigmas 2. Fruit a caryopsis.

Species 10. Mexico to Brazil and Bolivia. Forest.

37. Actinocladum Soderstrom in Amer. J. Bot. 68: 1201 (1981) — A. verticillatum (Nees) Soderstrom.

Small tree; sympodial; blade of culm sheath horizontal with upwardly curved tip, constricted at base. Inflorescence a sparse panicle or raceme with pedicelled spikelets. Fruit an achene. Otherwise like *Rhipidocladum*.

Species 1. Brazil. Savanna.
The plant is conditioned to destruction of its culms by savanna fires, regenerating from dormant bud complements at two special ground-level nodes.

38. Merostachys Spreng., Syst. Veg. 1: 132, 249 (1824) — M. speciosa Spreng. *Brasilocalamus* Nakai in J. Jap. Bot. 9: 10 (1933) — B. pubescens (Doell) Nakai (= M. pluriflora).

Tree, shrub or scrambler; sympodial; blade of culm sheath constricted and ± petiolate at base, reflexed; branch complement like *Rhipidocladum*. Inflorescence a dense unilateral pectinate raceme, the spikelets single (rarely 2—3), sessile, becoming rudimentary on the excurrent tip. Spikelets of 1—2 fertile florets (*M. pluriflora, M. polyantha* 2—10) plus rhachilla extension and vestigial floret; glumes 2; stamens 3; stigmas 2. Fruit an achene.

Species ± 40. Argentina to Guatemala, but mainly Brazil. Forest.

39. Bambusa Schreb., Gen. Pl. 1: 236 (1789) nom conserv pro seq. *Bambos* Retz., Obs. Bot. 5: 24 (1788) nom rejic — B. arundinacea Retz. *Bambusa* Caldas, Seman. Nueva Grenada: 131 (1809) non Schreb. (1789) — B. aculeata Caldas. *Guadua* Kunth in J. Phys. Chim. Hist. Nat. 95: 150 (1822) — G. angustifolia Kunth. *Ischurochloa* Büse in Miq., Pl. Jungh.: 389 (1854) — I. spinosa (Roxb.) Büse. *Bonia* Balansa in J. Bot. Paris 4: 29 (1890) — B. tonkinensis Balansa. *Arundarbor* Kuntze, Rev. Gen. Pl. 2: 760 (1891) nom superfl pro Bambusa. *Leleba* Nakai in J. Jap. Bot. 9: 9 (1933) — L. floribunda (Büse) Nakai. *Tetragonocalamus* Nakai l.c.: 88 — T. angulatus (Munro) Nakai. *Lingnania* McClure in Lingnan Univ. Sci. Bull. 9: 34 (1940) — L. chungii (McClure) McClure. *Bambusa subgen Dendrocalamopsis* Chia & Fung in Acta Phytotax. Sin. 18: 214 (1980) — B. oldhamii Munro. *Dendrocalamopsis* (Chia & Fung) Keng f. in J. Bam. Res. 2: 11 (1983).

Tree, shrub or scrambler; sympodial; branch complement several to many, 1 dominant, sometimes with recurved branch-thorns at the node. Inflorescence iterauctant, comprising an untidy tuft or stellate cluster of 1—many pseudospikelets sessile on a node, the primary subtending scale usually glumaceous but sometimes spathaceous. Spikelets 2—many-flowered (1-flowered plus rhachilla extension in *B. wrayi* and a few others), the rhachilla internodes distinct and florets separately deciduous; glumes 1—3; lemmas subequal; palea 2-keeled; lodicules 2—3; stamens 6, free (filaments connate in *B. heterostachya*); stigmas usually 3.

Species ± 120. Tropical Asia and America. Forest. *B. vulgaris* is perhaps the commonest bamboo grown around villages for general constructional work.

40. Oreobambos K. Schum. in Not. Bot. Gart. Berlin 1: 178 (1896) — O. buchwaldii K. Schum.

Tree; sympodial; branch complement several, 1 dominant. Inflorescence iterauctant, comprising a cupuliform cluster of pseudospikelets surrounded by involucre-like bracts, on bare branches. Spikelets 2-flowered usually plus rhachilla extension, deciduous with the glume, the rhachilla internode distinct; glume 1; lemmas subequal; palea 2-keeled; lodicules 0; stamens 6; stigma 1.

Species 1. Uganda to Zimbabwe. Forest.

41. Thyrsostachys Gamble in Indian For. 20: 1 (1894) — T. oliveri Gamble.

Tree; sympodial; branch complement several. Inflorescence iterauctant, comprising a cluster of 1—3 pseudospikelets embraced by a spathiform sheath, these sessile upon a branch node. Spikelets of 1—2 ♂ florets followed by 1 fertile floret and a rhachilla extension, these deciduous together; glumes 1—2; lemma chartaceous; palea of lowest floret bifid for ± ⅓ its length; lodicules 0—3; stamens 6; stigmas 3.

Species 2. Burma and Thailand. Rain forest.

42. Gigantochloa Munro in Trans. Linn. Soc. 26: 123 (1868) — G. atter Munro.

Tree; sympodial; branch complement several, 1 dominant. Inflorescence iteraucant, a dense stellate cluster, on bare branches. Spikelets 2—5-flowered terminating in a long narrow empty lemma, the rhachilla internodes abbreviated and obscure; glumes 2—4; lemmas increasing in length upwards; palea strongly 2-keeled; lodicules 0; stamens 6, the filaments united into a firm tube; stigma 1.

Species ± 15. Assam to Malaya. Forest.

43. Dendrocalamus Nees in Linnaea 9: 476 (1835) — D. strictus (Roxb.) Nees. *Klemachloa* Parker in Indian For. 58: 7 (1932) — K. detinens Parker. *Sinocalamus* McClure in Lingnan Univ. Sci. Bull. 9: 66 (1940); Chia & Fung in Acta Phytotax. Sin. 18: 211—216 (1980) — S. latiflorus (Munro) McClure. *Neosinocalamus* Keng f. in J. Bam. Res. 2: 148 (1983) — N. affinis (Rendle) Keng f.

Tree; sympodial; branch complement several, 1 dominant. Inflorescence iterauctant, a congested soft or spiky globose mass, on bare branches. Spikelets 1—6-flowered with or without rhachilla extension and rudiment (always without when 1-flowered), mostly 5—20 mm long, the rhachilla internodes abbreviated and obscure; glumes 2—3; lemmas increasing in length upwards, sometimes with an awn-point; palea of lower florets 2-keeled, of the uppermost rounded (or imperfectly keeled when rhachilla extension present); lodicules 0; stamens 6, the filaments free or united into a flimsy tube; stigmas 1(—3).

Species ± 35. India and Sri Lanka to China and the Philippines. *D. strictus*, with its solid culms, is one of the most important timber bamboos.
D. giganteus is probably the largest of all grasses, attaining 30—35 m.

44. Melocalamus Benth. in Benth. & Hook., Gen. Pl. 3: 1212 (1883); McClure in Kew Bull. 1936: 251—254 (1936) — M. compactiflorus (Kurz) Benth.

Climber; vegetative parts and inflorescence like *Dinochloa*. Spikelets 2-flowered plus rhachilla extension, small (up to 4 mm); glumes 2; lemmas subequal; paleas both 2-keeled; lodicules 3; stamens 6; stigmas 2—3. Fruit globose (1.5—2 cm) with fleshy pericarp, without endosperm, sometimes viviparous.

Species 1. Assam and Bangladesh to Indo-China. Forest.

45. Dinochloa Büse in Miq., Pl. Jungh.: 387 (1854); Dransfield in Kew Bull. 36: 613—633 (1981) — D. tjankorreh Büse (= D. scandens).

Climber; sympodial; culms zig-zag; culm sheaths with rugose girdle at base; branch complement several to many, the primary bud dormant but capable of replacing culm following damage. Inflorescence iterauctant, glomerate, on a huge fan of bare branches up to 3 m long. Spikelets 1-flowered without rhachilla extension, very small (mostly 2—4 mm); glumes 2—3; palea rounded on back; lodicules 0; stamens 6; stigmas 3. Fruit a berry, globose to ovoid (2—30 mm) with fleshy pericarp, without endosperm.

Species ± 25. Burma to Philippines, but mainly Malesia. Forest.
The zig-zag culm and roughened sheath girdle are aids to climbing.

c. MELOCANNINAE Reichenb., Deutsch. Fl. 6: 6 (1846).

Ovary appendage long, stiff, tapering. Inflorescence iterauctant, sometimes laxly so. Rhizome sympodial; branch complement several to many; culm-sheaths mostly deciduous.

A small subtribe with hollow steeple-like ovary appendage. It is relatively advanced, perhaps with an origin somewhere in the *Bambusa* complex. Tropical.

46. Schizostachyum Nees, Agrost. Bras.: 535 (1829); Vriese, Pl. Ind. Bat. Or.: 116

(1857) as 'Schirostachyum'; McClure in Lingnan Sci. J. 14: 567—602 (1935) — S. blumii Nees. *Cephalostachyum* Munro in Trans. Linn. Soc. 26: 138 (1868) — C. capitatum Munro. *Pseudostachyum* Munro l.c. 141 — P. polymorphum Munro. *Teinostachyum* Munro l.c. 142 — T. griffithii Munro. *Neohouzeaua* A. Camus in Bull. Mus. Hist. Nat. 28: 100 (1922) & Bull. Soc. Linn. Lyon 9: 185—188 (1945) —N. mekongensis A. Camus. *Dendrochloa* Parkinson in Indian For. 59: 707 (1933) — D. distans Parkinson. *Leptocanna* Chia & Fung in Acta Phytotax. Sin. 19: 212 (1981) — L. chinensis (Rendle) Chia & Fung.

Shrub or tree; culm thin-walled (*S. caudatum* thick) and usually drooping at tip. Inflorescence iterauctant, of untidy and sometimes lax tufts of few to many spikelets, spathate or on bare branches, rarely a capitulum at branch tip. Spikelets 1—several-flowered usually plus rudiment; glumes 0—4, persistent; lemmas acute to pungent; uppermost palea rounded or sulcate, convolute, exceeding lemma; lodicules (0—)3(—10); stamens (4—)6, usually free but sometimes united; stigmas (2—)3; ovary appendage with free central strand. Fruit a caryopsis, or achene with thin crustaceous pericarp separable from seed, oblong to ovoid (*S. polymorphum* globose).

Species ± 60. Madagascar, India and Malesia, extending to China and Hawaii. Forest.

A variable genus, but with no sharp distinctions between the segregates proposed. A few species, notably *S. latifolium*, have up to 10 lodicules, the upper grading into staminodes.

47. Oxytenanthera Munro in Trans. Linn. Soc. 2: 126 (1868) — O. abyssinica (A. Rich.) Munro. *Scirpobambus* Kuntze in Post, Lexicon: 509 (1903) nom superfl pro Oxytenanthera. *Houzeaubambus* Mattei in Boll. Soc. Ort. Mut. Soccor. Palermo 8, 6: 84 (1810) — H. borzii (Mattei) Mattei (= O. abyssinica).

Shrub or small tree; culm solid or thick-walled. Inflorescence iterauctant, of spiky globose clusters on bare branches, the clusters sometimes confluent or condensed into a capitulum at the branch tip. Spikelets 1—2-flowered usually without rhachilla extension; glumes of increasing size, 2—4 persistent plus 1—4 deciduous with floret; lemmas pungent; uppermost palea rounded or shallowly sulcate; lodicules 0; stamens 6, the filaments united; stigmas 3; ovary appendage hollow without central strand. Fruit a caryopsis.

Species 1. Tropical Africa. Savanna woodland. *O. abyssinica* is tapped for wine in Tanzania by slicing the top off young shoots about 1 m high (Mgeni in Indian For. 109: 306—308, 1983).

48. Melocanna Trin. in Spreng., Neue Ent. 2: 43 (1820); Petrova in Bot. Zh. 50: 1288—1304 (1965) — M. bambusoides Trin. (= M. baccifera). *Beesha* Kunth in J. Phys. Chim. Hist. Nat. 95: 151 (1822) nom superfl pro Melocanna.

Shrub or tree. Inflorescence iterauctant, of few to several spikelets tightly appressed in an oblong bundle, these spathate and imbricate on secund raceme-like branches. Spikelets 1-flowered with or without rhachilla extension; glumes 2—4; lemma pungent; palea rounded; lodicules 2; stamens 6, free or irregularly united; stigmas 3. Fruit pyriform (7—12 cm long) with fleshy pericarp, without endosperm.

Species 2. Eastern India to Burma. Forest.
The fruit is the largest in the family and its peculiarities have been discussed by Stapf (Trans. Linn. Soc. 6: 401—425, 1904), Petrova & Yakovlev (Bot. Zh. 53: 1688—1703, 1968) and Yakovlev (Ann. Bogor. 5: 109—115, 1970). Some of the fruits germinate while still attached to the branch, a rare example of true vivipary (Vaid in J. Bombay Nat. Hist. Soc. 59: 696—697, 1962).

49. Ochlandra Thw., Enum. Pl. Zeyl.: 376 (1864); A. Camus in Bull. Soc. Linn. Lyon 9: 185—188 (1945) — O. stridula Thw. *Beesha* Munro in Trans. Linn. Soc. 26: 144 (1868) non Kunth (1822), nom superfl pro Ochlandra. *Irulia* Bedd., For. Man. Bot.: 235 (1873) in syn sub O. travancorica.

Shrub or reed. Inflorescence iterauctant, of untidy stellate clusters, spathate or on bare branches. Spikelets 1-flowered; glumes 2—5, deciduous with floret; palea rounded; lodicules 1—15; stamens 15—120, the filaments free or united; stigmas 4—6. Fruit ovoid to pyriform (2—5 cm long) with fleshy pericarp, without endosperm.

Species 7. Southern India and Sri Lanka. Thickets in forest.
The genus is remarkable for its numerous stamens and lodicules, the latter up to 1.5 cm long.

2. ANOMOCHLOEAE

C.E. Hubbard in Hutch., Fam. Fl. Pl. 2: 219 (1934).

Herbaceous; ligule a band of hairs; leaf-blades ovate, with cross-nerves and long false petiole. Inflorescence leafy, compactly spiciform, of 3—6 spathes each subtending a dwarf branch system, this with appropriate prophyll and subtending scales supporting 1—3 pedicels tipped by a 'spikelet'. Spikelets 1-flowered without rhachilla extension, laterally compressed, falling entire; bract 1 spathe-like, chartaceous, many-nerved, with cross-nerves; bract 2 raised upon a stout internode, rounded on back, coriaceous, many-nerved, the tip produced into a long herbaceous tail; lodicules 0, their place taken by a dense ring of hairs; stamens 4; stigma 1, papillose. Caryopsis ellipsoid.
Genus 1; species 1. New World tropics.

Anatomy. Non-kranz, the microhairs short with inflated apical cell, and fusoid cells separated by several large clear thin walled cells; upper epidermis with unusually large intercostal silica bodies; arm cells present; midrib complex; stomata mainly in lower epidermis. Embryo not known.

Chromosomes. Not known.

A rare tribe, formerly known only from seeds cultivated at Paris, but recently rediscovered in its native habitat. It resembles Marantaceae, but earlier doubts regarding its inclusion in Gramineae have been resolved by its bambusoid leaf anatomy. The floral parts are considerably modified, suggesting that this is also likely to be true of the spikelet as a whole. Its peculiar structure may be interpreted as the reduction of the true spikelet scales to a ring of hairs, and their replacement by two bracts derived anew from spathiform leaf-sheaths. The compound inflorescence is reminiscent of some woody bamboos, but ligular hairs are unusual in the subfamily, and the structure of the so-called spikelets finds no parallel amoung the bamboos.

50. Anomochloa Brongn. in Ann. Sci. Nat. Bot. sér 3, 16: 368 (1851) — A. marantoidea Brongn.

Perennial. Description as for tribe.

Species 1. Brazil. Forest shade.

3. STREPTOCHAETEAE

C.E. Hubbard in Hutch., Fam. Fl. Pl. 2: 205 (1934). *Streptochaetinae* Nees in Lindley, Nat. Syst. ed. 2: 378 (1836), based on description in Linnaea 9: 467 (1835).

Herbaceous; ligule a line of hairs; leaf-blades lanceolate to ovate, with cross-nerves. Inflorescence a tough many-sided raceme, the 'spikelets' alike. Spikelets 1-flowered without rhachilla extension, slenderly conical, falling entire, composed of coriaceous many-nerved bracts; bracts 1—5 whorled, very rarely with axillary bud rudiments, dentate; bract 6 produced into a very long coiled awn; bracts 7—8 side by side and opposing bract 6, the tips reflexed; bracts 9—11 as long as spikelet (up to 2 cm), whorled, forming a cone; lemma, palea and lodicules absent; stamens 6, the filaments united; stigmas 3, scaberulous. Caryopsis linear, terete, the pericarp separable with difficulty when wet.
Genus 1; species 3. New World tropics.

Anatomy. Non-kranz with slender microhairs and fusoid cells; transverse silica bodies present; midrib simple; stomata confined to lower epidermis, their subsidiary cells parallel-sided. Embryo bambusoid, but without epiblast.

Chromosomes. 2n = 22 (2 species).

The spikelets are highly modified to form a specialized hair trap and their structure has long been a puzzle, for the usual interpretation of bract 6 as a lemma forces unnatural homologies on the other scales, which then appear to be grossly anomalous within the family. The interpretation given here is due to Soderstrom (ref below), though his equation of the *Streptochaeta* 'spikelet' with a bamboo pseudospikelet is doubtful since the inflorescence is clearly not iterauctant. It seems more likely that *Anomochloa* and *Streptochaeta*, both with ligular hairs, lie on an independent evolutionary line in which the spikelet scales have been suppressed in favour of spathiform bracts.

51. Streptochaeta Schrad. in Nees, Agrost. Bras. : 536 (1829); Page in Bull. Torr. Bot. Cl. 78 : 22—37 (1951); Soderstrom in Ann. Miss. Bot. Gard. 68 : 29—41 (1981) — S. spicata Nees. *Lepideilema* Trin. in Mém. Acad. Sci. Petersb. sér. 6, 1: 93 (1830) — L. lancifolium Trin. (= S. spicata).

Perennial. Description as for tribe.

Species 3. Mexico to Argentina. Forest shade.
The spikelets, dangling from their coiled awns, form a very efficient hair trap; hairs are deflected by the central cone into the cleft between bracts 7 and 8, becoming wedged between their overlapping margins.

4. OLYREAE

Spenner, Fl. Friburg. 1: 172 (1825); Soderstrom & Zuloaga in Brittonia 37: 22—35 (1985). *Buergersiochloeae* Blake in Blumea, Suppl. 3: 62 (1946).
Olyrinae Reichenb., Deutsch. Fl. 6: 5 (1846).

Herbaceous or sometimes cane-like; ligule scarious; leaf-blades lanceolate to oblong or ovate (*Ekmanochloa* narrower), the nerves parallel to midrib, with cross-nerves (sometimes indistinct) and false petiole. Inflorescence a raceme or panicle bearing unisexual spikelets, the sexes mixed or on separate monoecious inflorescences, terminal or axillary, in the latter case often several together on a short branch and subtended by prophylls. Female spikelets 1-flowered without rhachilla extension, dorsally compressed (except *Lithachne*), disarticulating below floret or rarely falling entire; glumes 2, mostly 3—7-nerved, not persistent, nearly always longer than floret, entire; lemma cartilaginous to bony usually with germination flap at base, mostly 5—7-nerved, subacute, awnless (except *Buergersiochloa, Ekmanochloa*); palea 2—9-nerved; lodicules 3; stigmas 2(—3), usually plumose. Caryopsis ovoid to lanceolate. Male spikelets 1-flowered, small, fusiform, readily deciduous; glumes lacking or minute; lemma membranous, 3-nerved (except *Maclurolyra*), acute to acuminate (*Olyra* often awned); lodicules 3; stamens (2—)3, the filaments free (except *Buergersiochloa, Froesiochloa*).
Genera 16; species ± 100. Tropical America; Africa, but probably introduced there; 1 genus in New Guinea.

Anatomy. Non-kranz with slender microhairs and fusoid cells (these lacking in *Ekmanochloa, Raddiella*); papillae and sometimes transverse silica bodies present; midrib simple or triple; stomata confined to lower epidermis (except *Buergersiochloa, Olyra, Raddia*); palisade layer present in *Lithachne, Raddiella, Sucrea.* Embryo bambusoid.

Chromosomes. Basic number usually 11.

2n	20	22	44
No of species	4	14	2

A homogeneous tribe of closely related and narrowly defined genera (fig. 9). Perhaps too narrowly defined, but it is difficult to broaden the genera without creating a grossly variable *Olyra*. In fact generic concepts are currently rather

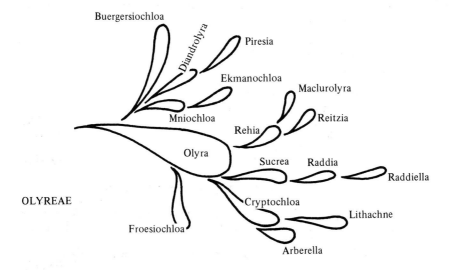

OLYREAE

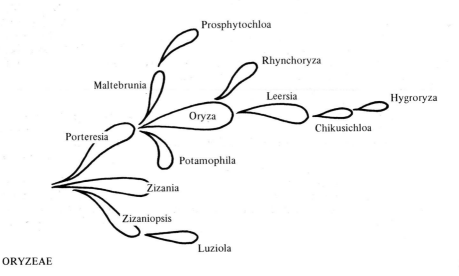

ORYZEAE

Fig. 9   Diagram of relationships in Olyreae and Oryzeae.

fluid, as they attempt to accommodate the new species that are continually being discovered in South American forests.

The tribe is unusual in that it has not only successfully occupied the special environment of the forest floor, but it also seems to be undergoing adaptive radiation there. The lower epidermis of the leaf is often purplish, and this is thought to be a shade adaptation concerned with reflecting back any unused light passing through the leaf (Soderstrom in Brittonia 34: 25—29, 1982). The tribe is usually easy to recognize, but there is a slight risk of confusing the bony lemma with that of Paniceae.

1 Inflorescence always borne on leafy culms:
  2 Spikelets not falling in clusters:
    3 Female floret without distinct callus:
      4 Sexes mixed in the same inflorescence:
        5 Glumes without cartilaginous margins:
          6 Inflorescence an open panicle (except *Olyra longifolia*):
            7 Floret herbaceous   *254 Pohlidium*
            7 Floret indurated   **52 Olyra**
          6 Inflorescence racemelike:
            8 Basal culm internode swollen   **53 Rehia**
            8 Basal culm internode not swollen:
              9 Lemma of ♂ spikelet 7-nerved; ♀ glumes herbaceous
                            54 Maclurolyra
              9 Lemma of ♂ spikelet 3-nerved; ♀ glumes coriaceous   **55 Reitzia**
        5 Glumes with a cartilaginous strip along the margin   **56 Sucrea**
      4 Sexes in separate inflorescences:
        10 Female spikelets disarticulating above glumes, without a callus
                            57 Raddia
        10 Female spikelets falling entire, with a little swollen callus at their base
                            58 Raddiella
    3 Female floret on a short columnar callus (except *Arberella lancifolia*):
      11 Female lemma dorsally compressed:
        12 Glumes 3—5-nerved   **59 Cryptochloa**
        12 Glumes 9—11-nerved   **60 Arberella**
      11 Female lemma laterally compressed, truncate   **61 Lithachne**
  2 Spikelets falling in clusters   **62 Froesiochloa**
1 Inflorescence borne on specialized culms, these bladeless or with a single protective blade, rarely also on leafy culms:
  13 Inflorescence raceme-like:
    14 Sexes mixed:
      15 Fertile culm erect, bearing a single leaf-blade and terminal raceme
                          63 Diandrolyra
      15 Fertile culm decumbent, bladeless, with axillary inflorescences
                          64 Piresia
    14 Sexes on separate racemes of a pair:
      16 Female lemma awnless   **65 Mniochloa**
      16 Female lemma awned   **66 Ekmanochloa**
  13 Inflorescence a contracted pancle; lemma awned (otherwise see *Olyra ecaudata*)   **67 Buergersiochloa**

52. Olyra L., Syst. Nat. ed. 10: 1261 (1759) — O. latifolia L. *Mapira* Adans., Fam. Pl. 2: 39, 574 (1763) nom superfl pro Olyra.

Perennial, often with clambering cane-like culms. Inflorescence a panicle, open or somewhat contracted, terminal or also from a few nodes immediately below (*O. longifolia* spiciform and axillary), the branches with 1—several ♀ spikelets above and several—many ♂ spikelets below, sometimes the lower branches all ♂. Female spikelet elliptic to ovate, the pedicel clavate (except *O. lateralis, O. ramosissima, O. micrantha* which have the lowest rhachilla internode swollen into a callus; *O. lateralis* sheds the spikelet entire); glumes papery, caudate to awned (*O. lateralis, O. ramosissima* herbaceous and acute); lemma bony, smooth or rarely tessellate. Male spikelet usually shortly awned.

Species 23. Mexico to Argentina; *O. latifolia* also in Africa and Madagascar, probably introduced as it is a weedy species of pathsides and forest margins. Forest.

53. Rehia Fitjen in Blumea 22: 416 (1975) nom nov pro seq. *Bulbulus* Swallen in Phytologia 11: 154 (1964) nom inval, coincident with technical term — B. nervatus Swallen.

Perennial; basal culm internode swollen, corm-like. Inflorescence a reduced raceme-like panicle of 2—5 ♀ spikelets each accompanied by 1—2 ♂, the panicles borne singly or several together and barely emergent from uppermost leaf-sheath. Female spikelet lanceolate; glumes papery, acute; lemma bony, pubescent.

Species 1. Brazil and Guiana. Forest shade.

54. Maclurolyra Cald. & Sod. in Smiths. Contrib. Bot. 11: 6 (1973) — M. tecta Cald. & Sod.

Perennial. Inflorescence like *Rehia*. Female spikelet lanceolate; glumes herbaceous, acute; lemma bony, pubescent; stigma not plumose. Male spikelet with 7-nerved lemma.

Species 1. Panama. Forest.

55. Reitzia Swallen in Sellowia 7: 7 (1956) — R. smithii Swallen.

Perennial. Inflorescence like *Rehia*. Female spikelet lanceolate; glumes coriaceous, acuminate; lemma cartilaginous, 5-nerved, with purple mottling.

Species 1. Brazil. Forest.
Genera 53—55 are barely distinct, and are not much different from *Olyra*.

56. Sucrea Soderstrom in Brittonia 33: 200 (1981) — S. monophylla Soderstrom.

Perennial. Inflorescence an open or spiciform panicle, terminal, ♀ above and ♂ below. Female spikelet elliptic to ovate; glumes membranous with cartilaginous margins, acute to acuminate; lemma bony.

Species 3. Brazil. Forest shade.
The genus lies between *Olyra* and *Raddia*. Sterile culms of *S. monophylla* bear a single large leaf at the tip. *S. sampaiana* has root tubers.

57. Raddia Bertoloni, Opusc. Sci. 3: 410 (1819) — R. brasiliensis Bertoloni. *Strephium* Nees, Agrost. Bras.: 298 (1829) — S. distichophyllum Nees. *Hellera* Doell in Mart., Fl. Bras. 2, 2: 314 (1877) nom nud — R. distichophylla.

Perennial, often fern-like; leaf tip asymmetrically apiculate. Inflorescence of two kinds, a ♂ panicle which is usually terminal, and axillary ♀ racemes. Female spikelet elliptic to narrowly ovate; glumes firmly membranous with cartilaginous margins, acuminate; lemma coriaceous.

Species ± 12. Brazil and Guiana. Forest.

58. Raddiella Swallen in Maguire in Bull. Torr. Bot. Cl. 75: 89 (1948); Soderstrom in Mem. New York Bot. Gard. 12, 3: 5—7 (1965) — R. nana (Doell) Swallen (= R. esenbeckii).

Delicate perennial, the culms weak or trailing; leaf tip asymmetrically apiculate. Inflorescence of two kinds, the ♂ terminal, the ♀ axillary, both consisting of an impoverished raceme-like panicle sometimes reduced to only 2 spikelets. Female spikelet elliptic, falling entire, mounted on a little callus formed from swollen lowest rhachilla internode and adherent base of lower glume; glumes herbaceous, acute; lemma bony.

Species 8. Panama to Brazil. Damp depressions, wet cliffs and near waterfalls.

59. Cryptochloa Swallen in Ann. Miss. Bot. Gard. 29: 317 (1942); Soderstrom in Brittonia 34: 199—209 (1982) — C. variana Swallen.

Perennial, sometimes fern-like. Inflorescence a panicle, terminal and axillary, often impoverished and raceme-like, bearing 1—several ♀ spikelets above and ♂ spikelets below. Female spikelet elliptic; glumes herbaceous, 3—5(—7)-nerved, acute to acuminate; lemma bony, usually glabrous, bluntly acute, raised on a short columnar callus.

Species ± 15. Mexico to Brazil. Forest.
Linked to *Olyra* through *O. longifolia*.

60. Arberella Sod. & Cald. in Brittonia 31: 433 (1979) — A. dressleri Sod. & Cald.

Like *Cryptochloa* but inflorescence bearing only one ♀ spikelet with ♂ spikelets below (rarely all ♂), glumes (5—)9—11-nerved, lemma pubescent on a shorter callus (*A. lancifolia* without callus).

Species 5. Costa Rica to Brazil. Forest.
Barely separable from *Cryptochloa*.

61. Lithachne P. Beauv., Ess. Agrost.: 135 (1812); Soderstrom in Brittonia 32: 495—501 (1980) — L. axillaris P. Beauv. (= L. pauciflora).

Perennial. Inflorescence of two kinds, a terminal ♂ panicle, and axillary inflorescences reduced to a single ♀ spikelet (with ♂ spikelets below it in *L. pauciflora*). Female spikelet laterally compressed, triangular; glumes papery, acuminate to caudate; lemma bony, gibbous, truncate, raised above glumes on a short columnar internode.

Species 4. Mexico to Argentina. Moist forest.
Soderstrom (l.c.) observes that the leaves droop downwards at night. Nocturnal movements have also been recorded from *Raddia* and *Cryptochloa*, whose leaves move upwards and fold together.

62. Froesiochloa G.A. Black in Bol. Tec. Inst. Agron. Norte 20: 29 (1950) — F. boutelouoides G.A. Black.

Perennial. Inflorescence of 2—4 short deciduous clusters on a central axis, each cluster comprising 1 ♀ spikelet surrounded by 6—10 ♂ spikelets. Female spikelet lanceolate; glumes herbaceous, acuminate; lemma coriaceous. Male spikelet: filaments united.
Species 2. Brazil and Guiana. Forest shade.

63. Diandrolyra Stapf in Kew Bull. 1906: 204 (1960) — D. bicolor Stapf.

Low growing perennial. Inflorescence a short raceme of paired ♂ and ♀ spikelets, terminal on a special culm whose single leaf-blade shields the raceme (sometimes also terminating an ordinary leafy culm). Female spikelet elliptic; glumes herbaceous, cuspidate; lemma coriaceous, glabrous; staminodes 3; stigmas 2. Male spikelet: stamens 2—3; ovary sterile with 3 stigmas.

Species ± 6. Brazil. Forest ground layer.
The inflorescence leaf seems to serve a protective function, its petiole turning (without inversion of surfaces) until the blade lies immediately above the ± horizontal raceme. By contrast the spikelet is relatively primitive with incomplete sexual separation, displayed also to a lesser extent in *Piresia* and *Buergersiochloa* (Sod. & Cald. in Biotropica 6: 141—153, 1974).

64. Piresia Swallen in Phytologia 11: 152 (1964); Soderstrom in Brittonia 34: 199—209 (1982) — P. goeldii Swallen.

Low growing fern-like perennial. Inflorescence a short impoverished raceme-like panicle of mixed ♂ and ♀ spikelets, terminal and axillary on a special bladeless decumbent culm (rarely also terminating a leafy culm). Female spikelet narrowly elliptic; glumes herbaceous, acute; lemma coriaceous, pubescent; staminodes 0 or 3; stigmas 2. Male spikelet: stamens 3; sterile ovary with 1 stigma sometimes present.

Species ± 7. Venezuela and Trinidad to Brazil. Forest shade.
The flowering culms lie among leaf litter, or even burrow through it.

65. Mniochloa Chase in Proc. Biol. Soc. Wash. 21: 185 (1908) — M. pulchella (Griseb.) Chase.

Low growing perennial; leaf-blades lanceolate to ovate. Inflorescence a pair of racemes, one ♂ the other ♀, terminating a special bladeless culm. Female spikelet narrowly elliptic; glumes herbaceous, acute (shorter than lemma in *M. pulchella*); lemma cartilaginous, acute or obtuse.
Species 2. Cuba. Shady rocks.

66. Ekmanochloa Hitchc., Man. Grasses W. Ind.: 374 (1936) — E. subaphylla Hitchc.

Erect caespitose perennial; leaf-blades narrowly lanceolate or suppressed. Inflorescence like *Mniochloa*. Female spikelet lanceolate; glumes herbaceous (shorter than lemma and emarginate in *E. subaphylla*); lemma coriaceous, slenderly awned.

Species 2. Cuba. Rocky hills and pineland.
Superficially unlike most of the tribe, due to its caespitose habit and narrow leaves. The leaf-blades of *E. subaphylla* may be altogether suppressed, photosynthetic function being transferred to the culm.

67. Buergersiochloa Pilger in Bot. Jahrb. 52: 167 (1914); Fitjen in Blumea 22: 415—418 (1975) — B. bambusoides Pilg.

Perennial. Inflorescence a contracted panicle, the sexes mixed but predominantly ♀ above and ♂ below, terminal on a special leafless culm. Female spikelet lanceolate; glumes membranous, shorter than spikelet, obtuse; lemma coriaceous, pubescent, awned; staminodes 3; stigmas 2. Male spikelet: lemma acuminate to awned; stamens 2—3, the filaments united.

Species 1. New Guinea. Forest.
The geographical disjunction is reflected in its leaf anatomy, but this is not sufficiently different to justify removal from the tribe.

5. PARIANEAE.

C.E. Hubbard in Hutch., Fam. Fl. Pl. 2: 219 (1934). *Parianinae* Hack., Nat. Pfl.-Fam. 2, 2: 88 (1887).

Herbaceous, sometimes with leaves and inflorescence borne on different culms; ligule membranous, the sheaths often with fimbriate shoulders; leaf-blades linear to oblong, with obscure cross-nerves, narrowed to a short false petiole. Inflorescence spiciform with fragile rhachis, bearing verticels of 5 (rarely 4 or 6) ♂ spikelets surrounding a ♀ spikelet, these shed together. Spikelets 1-flowered without rhachilla extension, the ♀ eventually disarticulating below floret. Female spikelet sessile, plump, slightly laterally compressed; glumes 2, as long as spikelet, membranous, 1—3-nerved, entire; lemma coriaceous, 3-nerved, entire; palea 3-nerved, resembling lemma; lodicules 3; stigmas 2, usually plumose. Male spikelets borne upon a flattened pedicel, strongly dorsally compressed; glumes 2, lateral, mostly shorter than lemma, coriaceous (sometimes pedicels fused along margins in groups of 2 or 3, and then middle glumes often suppressed); lemma and palea coriaceous, 3(—5)-nerved; stamens sometimes numerous.
Genera 2; species ± 40. Tropical S. America.

Anatomy. Non-kranz with slender microhairs and fusoid cells; arm cells present; midrib simple or triple; stomata mainly in lower epidermis. Embryo bambusoid.

Chromosomes. 2n = 22, 44, 48.

A small tribe allied to Olyreae in which male spikelets with enlarged pedicels have developed into an involucre, surrounding or completely enclosing the female spikelet. *Pariana* shows an unusual trend towards multiple stamens, encountered elsewhere only in *Ochlandra* and *Luziola*. There is evidence that pollination is largely entomophilous as an adaptation to the forest floor habitat (Sod. & Cald. in Biotropica 3: 1—16, 1971). *Eremitis* has taken an opposite course by reducing the inflorescence and developing cleistogamy.

Inflorescence of several deciduous verticels, exserted   **68 Pariana**
Inflorescence of 1 deciduous verticel, enclosed by a spathe   **69 Eremitis**

68. Pariana Aubl., Hist. Pl. Guiane: 876 (1775); Tutin in J. Linn. Soc. Bot. 50: 337—362 (1936) — P. campestris Aubl.

Perennial. Inflorescence exserted from uppermost sheath, of numerous deciduous verticels. Pedicels not exceeding ♂ spikelets, partially connate along the margins, involucre-like; stamens 6—30, the filaments often united in bundles. Glumes of ♀ spikelet covering floret.

Species ± 30. Amazon basin; Costa Rica. Forest.
P. lanceolata and *P. parvispica* have pedicels 3—5 times longer than ♂ spikelets and only 2—3 stamens. They connect *Pariana* to *Eremitis* and may constitute a separate genus.

69. Eremitis Doell in Mart., Fl. Bras. 2, 2: 338 (1877) — E. monothalamia Doell (= E. parviflora).

Perennial. Inflorescence enclosed by spathiform uppermost sheath, of 1 deciduous verticel with 1 or more rudimentary whorls below it. Pedicels 3 times longer than ♂ spikelet, fused along margins in groups, together forming a cylindrical flask; stamens 2, the filaments fused. Glumes of ♀ spikelet linear. Cleistogamous inflorescences also present, either decumbent in leaf litter or burrowing underground.

Species ± 7. Eastern Brazil. Forest.

6. PHAREAE

Stapf in Fl. Cap. 7: 319 (1898). *Pharinae* Prodoehl in Bot. Arch. 1: 212 (1922).

Herbaceous; ligule scarious, the margin sometimes ciliolate; leaf-blades linear to oblong, the nerves slanting obliquely from the midrib, with cross-nerves and a false petiole, this twisted to bring the abaxial leaf surface uppermost. Inflorescence a panicle, the ultimate branchlets bearing 1—2 ♀ and a terminal ♂ spikelet. Female spikelet 1-flowered without rhachilla extension, terete to inflated, disarticulating below floret; glumes 2, persistent or not, shorter than floret, scarious, entire; lemma chartaceous becoming coriaceous, involute or utriculate, 5 or more nerved, clothed in minute hairs, entire; palea 2-nerved; lodicules 0; stigmas 3, puberulous. Caryopsis oblong to linear. Male spikelets like ♀, but much smaller and soon deciduous; stamens 6.
Genera 3; species 11. Tropics.

Anatomy. Non-kranz without microhairs but with fusoid cells; intercostal zone of upper epidermis with isolated fibres containing many small silica bodies; midrib simple or complex; stomata mainly in anatomically upper epidermis (becoming the underside after inversion). Embryo bambusoid.

Chromosomes. 2n = 24 (4 species counted)

Related to Olyreae, but the leaf-blades inverted and with a curious quasi-pinnate venation. A forest tribe, whose adherent lemma hairs provide an effective means of animal dispersal. *Suddia* is provisionally included, but its characters have been omitted from the tribal description.

1   Leaf-blades not sagittate:
2   Lemma open along one side   **70 Pharus**
2   Lemma closed except for an apical pore   **71 Leptaspis**
1   Leaf-blades sagittate   **72 Suddia**

70. Pharus P. Browne, Civ. Nat. Hist. Jamaica: 344 (1756) — P. latifolius L.

Perennial. Panicle fragile, branches or the whole panicle readily breaking away. Female lemma cylindrical (*P. cornutus* almost thorn-like), involute, clasping palea keels.

Species 5. New World Tropics. Forest shade.

71. Leptaspis R. Br., Prodr. Fl. Nov. Holl.: 211 (1810); Jansen in Reinwardtia 2: 305 (1953) — L. banksii R. Br. *Scrotochloa* Jud. in Phytologia 56: 299—304 (1984) — S. urceolata (Roxb.) Jud.

Perennial. Panicle tough or shed as a whole. Female lemma inflated, cockle-shell or urn-like, closed except for an apical or excentric pore through which stigmas and tip of a slender linear palea protrude.

Species 5. Old World tropics. Forest shade.
Inflorescence branchlets of *L. cochleata* are sometimes subtended by setiform bracts.

72. Suddia Renvoize in Kew Bull. 39: 455 (1984) — S. sagittifolia Renvoize.

Rhizomatous perennial; leaf-blades with a false petiole up to 1 m long, conspicuously sagittate, ± erect, with slanting venation and cross-nerves. Panicle tough. Spikelets 1-flowered, falling entire, apparently bisexual; glumes as long as floret, prominently nerved; lemma 3-nerved?
Anatomy: fusoid cells, microhairs and complex midrib present, but no fibres.

Species 1. Sudan. Swamps.
The genus is readily recognized by its extraordinary leaves. The only panicles collected have been damaged by a smut fungus, leaving details of the spikelet structure in doubt. Hence the tribal relationships cannot be elucidated, though Phareae seems to contain the nearest relatives.

7. PHAENOSPERMATEAE

Renvoize & Clayton in Kew Bull. 40: 478 (1985). *Phaenospermatinae* Ohwi in Acta Phytotax. Geobot. 11: 183 (1942) nom nud.

Herbaceous; ligule membranous; leaf-blades broadly linear, the nerves slanting obliquely from midrib, with cross-nerves and a narrow or falsely petiolate base, this twisted to bring the abaxial side uppermost. Inflorescence a panicle, the spikelets alike. Spikelets 1-flowered without rhachilla extension, dorsally compressed, falling entire; glumes 2, shorter than floret, membranous; lemma membranous, 3—7-nerved, entire; palea resembling lemma but 2-nerved; lodicules 3; stamens 3; stigmas 2, plumose. Grain globose with small apical knob, the thick pericarp softening and peeling away when wet.
Genus 1; species 1. East Asia.

Anatomy. Non-kranz without microhairs or fusoid cells; midrib triple; stomata mainly on anatomically upper epidermis. Embryo bambusoid.

Chromosomes. 2n = 24.

An isolated tribe of bambusoid affinity, and some claim to similarity with Phareae through the unusual leaf venation and inversion.

73. Phaenosperma Benth. in J. Linn. Soc. Bot. 19: 59 (1881); Tateoka in Bot. Mag. Tokyo 69: 311—315 (1956); Conert in Bot. Jahrb. 78: 195—207 (1959) — P. globosa Benth.

Perennial. Description as for tribe.

Species 1. Assam to Japan. Warm temperate forest.

8. STREPTOGYNEAE

Cald. & Sod. in Smiths. Contrib. Bot. 44: 18 (1980). *Streptogyninae* Pilger in Bot. Jahrb. 76: 311 (1954) sine descr lat.

Herbaceous; ligule membranous; leaf-blades linear to lanceolate, with cross-nerves and often a short false petiole. Inflorescence a tough unilateral raceme, the spikelets alike. Spikelets several-flowered, the lower florets fertile the upper reduced, subterete, disarticulating below each floret; glumes 2, persistent, chartaceous, entire, the upper a little shorter than lowest lemma and 6—17-nerved; lemma coriaceous and convolute at maturity, 7—13-nerved, bidentate, with a straight awn; palea 2-nerved, these contiguous and median; lodicules 3; stamens 2; stigmas 2—3, after fertilization growing into tendrils (these retrorsely spinulose in *S. crinita*). Caryopsis linear.
Genus 1; species 2. Tropics.

Anatomy. Non-kranz without microhairs but with fusoid cells; midrib double; stomata more frequent in lower epidermis. Embryo oryzoid.

Chromosomes. 2n = 24.

A forest tribe without close relatives, and differing from most other bamboo allies in the possession of many-flowered spikelets; these are equipped with a novel device for animal dispersal. See also *Streblochaete* and *Streptochaeta*, where similar mechanisms have evolved from different spikelet parts.

74. Streptogyna P. Beauv., Ess. Agrost.: 80 (1812); Hubbard in Hook. Ic. Pl. 36: t 3572 (1956) — S. crinita P. Beauv. *Streptia* Doell in Mart., Fl. Bras. 2, 3: 171 (1880) in syn sub Streptogyna.

Perennial. Description as for tribe.

Species 2. West Africa to southern India and Sri Lanka; Mexico to Brazil. Forest shade.
At maturity the disarticulated florets dangle from the raceme by their long tangled stigmas, with the springy rhachilla-internode appressed to the base of each lemma forming a tenacious trap for hairs. Another unusual feature is the short membranous external ligule (Tran in Bull. Soc. Bot. France 118: 657, 1973).

9. ORYZEAE

Dumort., Obs. Gram. Belg.: 83 (1824). *Zizanieae* Hitchc., Gen. grasses U.S.: 18 (1920).
Oryzinae Reichenb., Deutsch. Fl. 6: 5 (1846). *Zizaniinae* Benth. in J. Linn. Soc. Bot. 19: 54 (1881). *Chikusichloinae* Honda in J. Fac. Sci. Univ. Tokyo 3: 303 (1930). *Luziolinae* Terr. & Rob. in Bull. Torr. Bot. Cl. 101: 244 (1974).

Herbaceous; ligule membranous; leaf-blades usually linear and without cross-nerves or false petiole. Inflorescence a panicle, occasionally with simple raceme-like primary branches, the spikelets all alike or the sexes separate. Spikelets 1-flowered, or 3-flowered with the 2 lower florets reduced to sterile lemmas, without rhachilla extension, mostly laterally compressed, disarticulating above glumes; glumes absent, or just discernible as obscure lips at tip of pedicel; lemma membranous to coriaceous, 5—10-nerved, entire, with or without a straight awn; palea resembling lemma, 3—7-nerved; lodicules 2; stamens usually 6; stigmas 2, plumose. Caryopsis linear to ovoid (pericarp free in *Luziola, Zizaniopsis*).
Genera 12; species ± 70. Tropical and warm temperate regions.

Anatomy. Non-kranz with slender microhairs (short with inflated apical cell in *Hygroryza* & *Zizaniopsis,* absent in *Luziola* & *Porteresia*) with or without fusoid cells; papillae (except *Chikusichloa*) and transverse silica bodies (*Chikusichloa* & *Potamophila* longitudinal, *Porteresia* none) present; arm cells sometimes present; midrib complex with air spaces and sometimes stellate aerenchyma (*Chikusichloa, Hygroryza, Porteresia, Prosphytochloa* simple), the secondary bundles double in *Luziola* & *Porteresia*; stomata in both surfaces (lower only in *Maltebrunia, Prosphytochloa*). Embryo oryzoid (*Porteresia, Zizania* bambusoid). See also under *Porteresia.*

Chromosomes. The basic number is 12, except *Zizania* where x = 15.

2n	24	30	48
No of species	32	3	20

The tribe is characterized by highly modified spikelets in which:
a. Glumes are reduced to two tiny lobes on the pedicel tip; usually obscure, but easily seen in a few species, particularly *Oryza australiensis.*
b. Two little scales or bristles are attached to the base of the fertile floret in the *Oryza* group. They are regarded as sterile florets reduced to empty lemmas.
c. The palea is 3—7-nerved with a central keel, apparently an elaboration of the multi-nerved palea found in Bambuseae, Olyreae and Parianeae.
The precise homology of the parts is still open to argument, and the various theories are reviewed by Núñez in Bol. Soc. Arg. Bot. 12: 57—97 (1968). The most usual alternative is to interpret both principal scales as lemmas, the anthoecium then being a compound structure derived from 2 modified florets.
The anatomy is variable but clearly bambusoid, diverging from the main line by suppression of fusoid cells in some genera and of the scutellum cleft in most. A few genera occupy typically bambusoid forest habitats, but most have specialized in aquatic environments. Relationships between the genera are suggested in fig. 9.
The tribe is recognized by its lack of glumes. Few other genera share this

character and they have normal 2-keeled paleas. There may be some difficulty with the *Oryza* group, whose sterile lemmas are often mistaken for glumes.

1   Spikelets with 2 sterile lemmas below the fertile floret (if these long-awned see *89 Ehrharta*), bisexual (except *Potamophila*):
2   Fertile lemma coriaceous, strongly keeled:
  3 Leaf-margins tuberculate-spiny   **75 Porteresia**
  3 Leaf-margins smooth or scabrid:
    4 Fertile lemma coriaceous throughout   **76 Oryza**
    4 Fertile lemma with a long herbaceous beak   **77 Rhynchoryza**
2   Fertile lemma membranous to chartaceous, scarcely keeled:
  5 Plant erect:
    6 Leaf-blades linear, not petiolate   **78 Potamophila**
    6 Leaf-blades lanceolate to narrowly ovate, usually petiolate
                                    79 Maltebrunia
  5 Plant climbing, with clinging filiform leaf tips   **80 Prosphytochloa**
1   Spikelets strictly 1-flowered:
7   Spikelets bisexual:
  8 Leaf-blades linear:
    9 Floret strongly laterally compressed, seldom stipitate (if glumes present see *200 Simplicia*)   **81 Leersia**
    9 Floret plump, slightly dorsally compressed, stipitate   **82 Chikusichloa**
  8 Leaf-blades elliptic; floret stipitate   **83 Hygroryza**
7   Spikelets unisexual:
  10 Fruit a linear caryopsis   **84 Zizania**
  10 Fruit an ovoid achene:
    11 Female lemma awned   **85 Zizaniopsis**
    11 Female lemma awnless   **86 Luziola**

75. Porteresia Tateoka in Bull. Nat. Sci. Mus. Tokyo 8: 406 (1965) nom nov pro seq. *Sclerophyllum* Griff., Not. Pl. As. 3: 8 (1851) non Gaud. (1829); Tateoka in Amer. J. Bot. 51: 539—543 (1964); Sharma & Shastry in Bull. Bot. Surv. India 8: 42—44 (1966) — S. coarctatum (Roxb.) Griff. *Indoryza* Henry & Roy in Bull. Bot. Surv. India 10: 274 (1969) nom superfl pro Porteresia.

Perennial. Like *Oryza*, but leaf-blades coriaceous with tuberculate prickly margins.

Species 1. India, Burma. Brackish water of deltas and tidal swamps.
Outwardly resembling *Oryza*, but with a bambusoid embryo, and unusual leaf anatomy having 2 superposed bundles in each rib, air spaces within the lamina and some papillae with bifurcate tips. Moreover the upper bundle of each pair is inverted with phloem uppermost (this is not so in *Luziola* nor in the complex midrib of other bambusoid genera).

76. Oryza L., Sp. Pl.: 333 (1753); Tateoka in Bot. Mag. Tokyo 76: 165—173 (1963); Sharma & Shastry in Kachroo, Adv. Front. Cytogen.: 5—20 (1974) — O. sativa L. *Padia* Moritzi, Syst. Verzeich. Zoll.: 103 (1845) — P. meyeriana Zoll. & Mor.

Annual or perennial; leaf-blades linear to narrowly lanceolate, herbaceous, with smooth or scabrid margins. Panicle often with simple raceme-like primary branches. Spikelets with 1 fertile floret above 2 sterile lemmas, strongly laterally compressed; sterile lemmas ⅛—½ length of spikelet (*O. grandiglumis, O. longiglumis* longer), subulate to narrowly ovate (*O. grandiglumis* broader and resembling palea), coriaceous; fertile lemma coriaceous, strongly keeled, clasping lateral nerves of palea, awned or awnless; stamens 6.

Species ± 20. Tropics & subtropics. Humid forests and open swamps. *O. sativa* (Rice) is cultivated throughout the area of the genus, usually in flooded fields though some races are grown on dry land. It was probably derived from wild *O. rufipogon* in the Nepal—Yunnan area some 2500 years ago, with some evidence that the two major races, tropical Indica and cool-tolerant Japonica, were domesticated independently. A second cultivated species, *O. glaberrima,* was domesticated in west Africa from *O. barthii* (Chang in Euphytica 25: 425—441, 1976; Second in Genet. Sel. Evol. 17: 89—114, 1985).

77. Rynchoryza Baillon, Hist. Pl. 12: 291 (1893) — R. subulata (Nees) Baillon.

Perennial. Like *Oryza* except: sterile lemmas $\frac{1}{10}$ length of spikelet, broadly ovate, cuspidate; fertile lemma coriaceous below, the tip extended beyond the palea as a conical herbaceous beak composed of aerenchyma with transverse septa, eventually tapering to an awn.

Species 1. Paraguay to Argentina. Swamps.
A segregate from *Oryza,* distinguished by the flotation device built into the spikelet.

78. Potamophila R. Br., Prodr. Fl. Nov. Holl.: 211 (1810) — P. parviflora R. Br.

Tufted perennial; leaf-blades linear. Panicle of mixed unisexual and bisexual spikelets, these all alike. Spikelets with 1 fertile floret above 2 sterile lemmas, weakly compressed; sterile lemmas ⅛ length of spikelet, ovate, membranous, nerveless; fertile lemma thinly chartaceous, awnless, not clasping palea; stamens 6.

Species 1. Australia, New South Wales. Gravel banks in streams.
Potamophila, Maltebrunia and *Prosphytochloa* share a very similar spikelet structure, but differ considerably in their habit.

79. Maltebrunia Kunth, Rév. Gram. 1: 6 (1829); Hubbard in Hook. Ic. Pl. 36: t 3595 (1962) — M. leersioides Kunth.

Erect perennial; leaf-blades lanceolate to narrowly ovate, with cross-nerves and usually a false petiole. Spikelets bisexual, with 1 fertile floret on a short callus above 2 sterile lemmas, weakly compressed; sterile lemmas $\frac{1}{10}$—$\frac{1}{5}$ length of spikelet (*M. letestui* shorter), subulate; fertile lemma firmly chartaceous, awnless, the margins clasping lateral nerves of palea; stamens 6.

Species 3—5. Gabon, Tanzania and Madagascar. Forest.
M. letestui, with insignificant sterile lemmas, verges upon the condition found in *Chikusichloa mutica*; the latter has a longer callus and linear leaf-blades.

80. Prosphytochloa Schweick. in Züchter 31: 193 (1961); de Winter in Bothalia 6: 117—137 (1951) — P. prehensilis (Nees) Schweick.

Climbing perennial; leaf-blades not petiolate, the lower narrowly lanceolate, the upper on each sterile shoot linear, retrorsely scabrid and extended into a long tendril-like filiform tip. Spikelets like *Maltebrunia*.

Species 1. South Africa. Shady forest.
A most unusual grass, capable of climbing to a height of 10 m. The leaf tips do not seem to be actively prehensile, but rather to rely upon gentle wind movements brushing them against supports to which their retrorse scabridity then clings tenaciously.

81. Leersia Sw., Prod. Veg. Ind. Occ.: 21 (1788) nom conserv; Launert in Senck. Biol. 46: 129—153 (1965); Pyrah in Iowa St. J. Sci. 44: 215—270 (1969) — L. oryzoides (L.) Sw. *Homalocenchrus* Mieg in Acta Helv. Phys. Math. 4: 307 (1760) nom rejic — H. oryzoides (L.) Poll. *Ehrhartia* Weber in Wigg., Prim. Fl. Hols.: 63 (1780) nom superfl pro Homalocenchrus. *Asprella* Schreb., Gen. Pl.: 45 (1789) nom superfl pro Homalocenchrus. *Laertia* Gromov in Trudy Obsh. Nauk Khark. Univ. 1: 141 (1817) nom superfl pro Leersia. *Endodia* Raf., Neogenyton: 4 (1825) — L. lenticularis Michaux. *Aplexia* Raf. l.c. — L. virginica Willd. *Blepharochloa* Endl., Gen. Pl.: 1352 (1840) — L. ciliata (Retz.) Roxb. (= L. hexandra). *Turraya* Wall., Cat.: 8637d (1847) nom nud — L. hexandra. *Pseudoryza* Griff., Ic. Pl. As. 3: t 144 (1851) nom superfl pro Blepharochloa.

Perennial, rarely annual. Panicle branches sometimes simple and raceme-like. Spikelets 1-flowered, strongly laterally compressed, not stipitate (or shortly so in *L. perrieri, L. stipitata*); lemma chartaceous to coriaceous, awnless (*L. nematostachya, L. perrieri, L. stipitata, L. tisserantii* awned); stamens 1, 2, 3 or 6.

Species 18. Tropical and warm temperate regions. Marshland, stream banks and shallow water; a few species in woodland. *L. hexandra* is a serious rice field weed.
The genus is distinguished from *Oryza* only by the absence of sterile lemmas, and is linked to *Chikusichloa* by the species with shortly stipitate florets.

82. Chikusichloa Koidzumi in Bot. Mag. Tokyo 39: 23 (1925) — C. aquatica Koidzumi.

Perennial; leaf-blades linear. Spikelets 1-flowered, slightly dorsally compressed, the floret borne upon a long slender stipe and falling with it; lemma membranous, strongly nerved, at most scaberulous, acute to awned; stamen 1.

Species 3. Sumatra to Japan. Wet places in forest.

The stipe of *C. mutica* may have 2 minute lemma vestiges at its base, and is evidently formed from the callus of the fertile floret. The genus is barely separable from *Leersia*.

83. Hygroryza Nees in Edinb. New Phil. J. 15: 380 (1833); Benth. in J. Linn. Soc. Bot. 19: 55 (1881) as "Hygrorhiza" — H. aristata (Retz.) Nees. *Potamochloa* Griff. in J. As. Soc. Bengal 5: 571 (1836) nom superfl pro Hygroryza.

Stoloniferous perennial with aquatic adventitious roots; leaf-blades elliptic, floating, the sheaths inflated. Spikelets 1-flowered, the floret borne upon a long slender stipe and falling with it; lemma firmly membranous, awned; stamens 6.

Species 1. India to Sri Lanka. Floating in water.

84. Zizania L., Sp. Pl.: 991 (1753); Dore, Canad. Dept. Agric. Pub. 1393 (1960); de Wet & Oelke in J. Agric. Trad. Bot. Appl. 25: 67—84 (1978) — Z. aquatica L. *Fartis* Adans., Fam. Pl. 2: 37 (1763) nom superfl pro Zizania. *Elymus* Mitchell, Diss. Brev. Bot. Zool.: 32 (1769) non L. (1753) — specimen of Z. aquatica. *Hydropyrum* Link, Hort. Berol. 1: 252 (1827) — H. esculentum Link (= Z. aquatica). *Melinum* Link, Handb. Erk. Gew. 1: 96 (1829) non Medik (1791) — M. palustre (L.) Link (= Z. aquatica). *Ceratochaete* Lunell in Amer. Midl. Nat. 4: 214 (1915) nom superfl pro Zizania.

Tall annual or perennial. Panicle branches unisexual, the lower all ♂, the upper all ♀. Female spikelet: lemma coriaceous, tightly clasping keels of palea, awned from tip. Caryopsis linear, with elongated embryo ½ to as long as itself. Male spikelet: lemma membranous, acuminate to shortly awned; stamens 6.

Species 3. Eastern Asia from Russian Far East to Indo-China; North America. Marshes and shallow water. The grain of Z. *aquatica* (Wildrice) is gathered from wild stands, and the selection of domesticated non-shattering forms is giving it some potential as a minor crop. The young shoots of Z. *latifolia*, swollen by infection with *Ustilago esculenta*, are cultivated as a vegetable in China (Terrell & Batra in Econ. Bot. 36: 274—285, 1982).

85. Zizaniopsis Doell & Asch. in Mart., Fl. Bras. 2, 2: 12 (1871); Quarin in Hickenia 1, 8: 39—42 (1976) — Z. microstachya (Nees) Doell & Asch.

Tall reed-like annual or perennial. Panicle branches bisexual, each primary branch bearing ♂ spikelets below and ♀ above. Female spikelet: lemma chartaceous, not clasping palea keels nor with prominent nerves, shortly awned. Achene ovoid, beaked with the persistent style, the pericarp free and indurated. Male spikelet resembling ♀ but awnless; stamens 6.

Species 5. Southern USA to Argentina. Swamps and stream banks.

86. Luziola Juss., Gen. Pl.: 33 (1789); Swallen in Ann. Miss. Bot. Gard. 52: 472—475 (1966) — L. peruviana Gmel. *Hydrochloa* P. Beauv., Ess. Agrost.: 135

(1812) — H. caroliniensis P. Beauv. (= L. fluitans). *Caryochloa* Trin., Gram. Pan.: 54 (1826) — C. brasiliensis Trin. *Arrozia* Kunth, Enum. Pl. 1: 11 (1833) nom superfl pro Caryochloa.

Low growing perennial. Panicle unisexual, the ♂ terminal the ♀ axillary (but *L. brasiliensis, L. caespitosa* of mixed sex with ♂ spikelets uppermost), often small (only a few spikelets in *L. fluitans, L. fragilis*). Female spikelet: lemma thinly membranous with thickened nerves, sometimes shredding into fibres at maturity, awnless. Achene ovoid, the pericarp free and coriaceous. Male spikelet: lemma membranous; stamens 6—16.

Species 11. Southern USA to Argentina. Ponds, marshes and stream banks.

10. PHYLLORACHIDEAE

C.E. Hubbard in Hook. Ic. Pl. 34: t 3386 (1939); Tateoka in Bot. Mag. Tokyo 69: 83—86 (1956).

Suffrutescent, with slender canelike culms ± 1 m high; ligule a very short membrane with ciliate fringe; leaf-blades lanceolate to ovate, with inconspicuous cross-nerves, the base cordate to sagittate, constricted or shortly petiolate. Inflorescence terminal, exserted, with herbaceous primary axis whose leafy margins enfold short cuneate racemes borne along the midrib; racemes falling entire, of 1—4 unisexual spikelets (and often additional vestiges) on a flattened rhachis; sometimes also with axillary inflorescences almost enclosed by subtending sheath and comprising 1—2 elongated ♀ spikelets on a terete axis. Female spikelet 2-flowered, with (*Humbertochloa*) or without (*Phyllorachis*) rhachilla extension, laterally compressed; lower glume subulate, the upper shorter than spikelet and membranous; lower floret reduced to a lemma, this many-nerved, becoming thickened and wrapped around upper floret; upper lemma thinly coriaceous, 7—11-nerved, awnless; palea 2-keeled (*Phyllorachis* with 6—10 additional nerves); lodicules 2; stigmas 2. Caryopsis ellipsoid. Male spikelet similar but smaller; stamens 3 or 6.
Genera 2; species 3. Africa and Madagascar.

Anatomy. Non-kranz with slender microhairs but no fusoid cells; transverse silica bodies sometimes present; arm cells present; midrib simple; stomata on both sides or mainly the lower; palisade layer present. Embryo bambusoid.

Chromosomes. 2n = 24 (*Phyllorachis sagittata*).

A small specialized tribe, loosely related to Oryzeae.

Inflorescence bisexual; lower lemma of ♀ spikelet grooved   **87 Phyllorachis**
Inflorescence unisexual; lower lemma of ♀ spikelet rounded
88 Humbertochloa

87. Phyllorachis Trimen in J. Bot. 17: 353 (1879) — P. sagittata Trimen.

Perennial. Inflorescence bisexual, each raceme with 1 ♀ spikelet below and 2—3 ♂ above. Lower lemma of ♀ spikelet with a median groove.

Species 1. Tanzania to Zimbabwe and Angola. Riverine forest.

88. Humbertochloa A. Camus & Stapf in Bull. Soc. Bot. France 81: 467 (1934) —H. bambusiuscula A. Camus & Stapf

Perennial. Inflorescence unisexual, the ♀ with 1 spikelet per raceme, the ♂ with 1—4. Lower lemma of ♀ spikelet rounded across back.

Species 2. Tanzania and Madagascar. Forest shade.

11. EHRHARTEAE

Nevski in Trudy Bot. Inst. Akad. Nauk SSSR 4: 227 (1937); Tateoka in Bot. Gaz. 124: 264—270 (1963).

Herbaceous; ligule usually membranous, sometimes represented by a brief rim or a line of hairs; leaf-blades linear to convolute, without cross-nerves or false petiole. Inflorescence a panicle or sometimes a unilateral raceme (only 1—2 spikelets in *E. dodii, E. uniflora*). Spikelets 3-flowered with the 2 lower florets reduced to sterile lemmas, with or more often without rhachilla extension, laterally compressed, disarticulating above glumes; glumes 2, persistent, shorter than (almost suppressed in *E. stipoides*) or exceeding floret, membranous; sterile lemmas or at least the upper as long as fertile floret, coriaceous, awned or awnless; fertile lemma firmly cartilaginous to coriaceous, 5—7-nerved, entire, awnless; palea 0,1,2 or rarely 3—5-nerved; lodicules 2; stamens 1,2,3,4 or 6; stigmas 2. Caryopsis ellipsoid.
Genus 1; species ± 35. South temperate regions of Old World.

Anatomy. Non-kranz with microhairs slender or the apical cell short and inflated, without fusoid cells; midrib simple; stomata on both sides. Embryo bambusoid, but without epiblast.

Chromosomes. The basic number is 12.

2n	24	40	48
No of species	3	1	2

A tribe of arguable affinity, but the membranous lodicules, *Oryza*-like spikelets and bambusoid embryo all point to a link with Oryzeae. However it has diverged from the typical oryzoid life style by its occupation of open hillside habitats. It may be a bambusoid relic which has survived extinction by retreating to the southern hemisphere, and is now undergoing a bout of speciation following adaptation to the winter rainfall regime of the South African Cape.
It could be confused with *Oryza* or with the *Hierochloe* group of genera, but the large coriaceous sterile lemmas of *Ehrharta* are usually sufficiently diagnostic.

89. Ehrharta Thunb. in Vet. Acad. Handl. Stockholm 40: 217 (1779) nom conserv; Willemse in Blumea 28: 181—194 (1982) — E. capensis Thunb. *Trochera* L. Rich. in Rozier, J. Phys. 13: 225 (1779) nom rejic — T. striata L. Rich. (= E. bulbosa). *Tetrarrhena* R. Br., Prodr. Fl. Nov. Holl.: 209 (1810) — T. distichophylla

(Labill.) R. Br. *Microlaena* R. Br., l.c.: 210 (1810); Kuntze in Post, Lexicon: 364 (1903) as "Microchlaena" — M. stipoides (Labill.) R. Br. *Diplax* Bennett in Pl. Jav. Rar.: 11 (1838) — D. avenacea Raoul (= E. diplax). *Petriella* Zotov in Trans. Roy. Soc. New Zealand 73: 235 (1943) non Curzi (1930) — P. colensoi (Hook.f.) Zotov.

Annual or perennial, rarely with tuberous basal internode. Spikelet: glumes tiny to large (reduced to obscure lips and separated from florets by a stipe in *E. stipoides*); sterile lemmas often transversely wrinkled, the upper often narrowed to a hook at the base, this sometimes appendaged (as in *E. calycina*), the lower sub-equal or shorter (reduced to a tiny scale in *E. dodii, E. rupestris, E. setacea, E. tricostata, E. uniflora*).

Species ± 35. About 25 species in South Africa, one of them extending to Ethiopia; the rest Indonesia to New Zealand. Habitat variable, from wet places and forest glades to rocky mountain sides; rarely on coastal sand dunes.

There is notable variation in such characters as glume length, lemma awns, palea nerves and stamen number, but these characters are not sufficiently well correlated with one another to justify recognition of segregate genera (Willemse l.c.). Cleistogenes occur in *E. stipoides* (Connor & Mathews in New Zealand J. Bot. 15: 531—534, 1977), where they have been mistaken for a distinct species.

12. DIARRHENEAE

(Ohwi) Campbell in J. Arn. Arb. 66: 188 (1985). *Diarrheninae* Ohwi in Acta Phytotax. Geobot. 10: 134 (1941).

Herbaceous; ligule membranous; leaf-blades narrowly lanceolate, without cross-nerves, narrowed at base. Inflorescence an open or contracted panicle, the spikelets all alike. Spikelets of 2—5 fertile florets plus a reduced uppermost floret, laterally compressed, disarticulating below each floret; glumes 2, shorter than lemmas; lemmas cartilaginous to thinly coriaceous, 3(—5)-nerved, obtuse or with an awn-point; palea 2-nerved; lodicules 2, large, membranous; stamens 1—3. Grain obliquely ellipsoid, the pericarp thick, enlarged at tip into a conspicuous pallid knob or beak bearing 2 terminal stigmas, softening and peeling away when wet.

Genus 1; species 4. North America and east Asia.

Anatomy. Non-kranz with obscure microhairs and without fusoid cells; midrib simple; stomata mostly on upper epidermis. Embryo bambusoid (Macfarlane & Watson in Taxon 29: 652—653, 1980).

Chromosomes. 2n = 38, 60; basic number probably 10.

The tribe is distinguished by its peculiar grain rather like that of Bambusinae. It is not easy to place, but has bambusoid embryo and lodicules. Unlike most of the bamboo allies it has several-flowered spikelets, imparting a resemblance to Poeae.

90. Diarrhena P. Beauv., Ess. Agrost.: 142 (1812) nom conserv — D. americana P. Beauv. *Korycarpus* Lag., Gen. Sp. Nov.: 34 (1816); Spreng., Syst. Veg. 1: 123 (1825) as "Corycarpus" — nom superfl pro Diarrhena. *Roemeria* Roem. & Schult., Syst.

Veg. 1: 61, 287 (1817) non Medik (1792) — R. zeae Roem. & Schult. (= D. americana). *Diarina* Raf. in J. Phys. Chim. 89: 104 (1819) nom superfl pro Diarrhena. *Onoea* Franch. & Sav., Enum. Pl. Jap. 2: 178 (1879) nom nud — D. japonica. *Neomolinia* Honda in J. Fac. Sci. Tokyo Bot. 3: 110 (1930) — N. faurei (Hack.) Honda.

Perennial. Description as for tribe.

Species 4. Eastern USA; eastern USSR to Japan. Woodland.

13. BRACHYELYTREAE

Ohwi in Bot. Mag. Tokyo 55: 361 (1941); Tateoka in J. Jap. Bot. 32: 111—114 (1957). *Brachyelytrinae* (Ohwi) Ohwi in Acta Phytotax. Geobot. 11: 183 (1942).

Herbaceous; ligule membranous; leaf-blades narrowly lanceolate, with or without indistinct cross-nerves, constricted at base. Inflorescence a scanty panicle, the spikelets all alike. Spikelets 1-flowered with bristle-like rhachilla extension, dorsally compressed, disarticulating above glumes; glumes 2, tiny, the lower ± suppressed, the upper subulate and $\frac{1}{10}$—$\frac{1}{4}$ length of floret; lemma herbaceous, 5-nerved, with straight awn from tip; palea 2-nerved, convolute; lodicules 2; stamens 2. Caryopsis linear, surmounted by a pallid pubescent beak bearing 2 terminal stigmas, the pericarp thick and separable with difficulty.
Genus 1; species 1. North America and east Asia.

Anatomy. Non-kranz without microhairs or fusoid cells; papillae present on interstomatal cells; midrib simple; stomata confined to lower epidermis, their subsidiary cells low dome shaped to parallel sided. Embryo oryzoid.

Chromosomes. 2n = 22.

An odd little tribe, with grain structure and geographical distribution very like those of Diarrheneae.

91. Brachyelytrum P. Beauv., Ess. Agrost.: 39 (1812); Koyama & Kawano in Canad. J. Bot. 42: 863—867 (1964) — B. erectum (Schreb.) P. Beauv.

Perennial. Description as for tribe.

Species 1. Eastern North America, and eastern China to Japan. Woodland.
The unusual disjunct distribution suggests that *Brachyelytrum* and *Diarrhena* may be relics of a widespread mid-Tertiary woodland flora (Koyama &Kawano l.c.). A similar caryopsis occurs in the unrelated genus *Urochondra*.

II. SUBFAMILY POOIDEAE

;Macfarlane & Watson in Taxon 29: 645—666 (1980) & 31: 178—203 (1982). *Festucoideae* Rouy, Fl. France 14: 28 (1913). *Hordeoideae* Rouy. l.c. 343. *Secaloideae* Rouy l.c. 298. *Agrostidoideae* Keng & Keng f. in Acta Bot. Sin. 9: 60 (1960).

Herbs, usually with linear leaf-blades. Frequent external characters: membranous ligule; panicle; 1—many-flowered laterally compressed spikelets with fragile rhachilla; several-nerved entire lemmas with or without an apical or dorsal awn.

Lodicules 2—3, membranous to hyaline, acute to asymmetrically bilobed; stamens 3, rarely fewer; stigmas 2 (but see *Megalachne, Pseudodanthonia, Stipa*). Caryopsis with embryo $\frac{1}{6}$—$\frac{1}{3}$ its length and linear to round hilum; embryo pooid F+FF, but the epiblast sometimes absent in Bromeae and Triticeae (*Avena, Brachypodium, Metcalfia* & *Triticum* have been reported as oryzoid F+FP).

Chlorenchyma irregularly arranged with more than 4 cells between vascular bundles; bundle sheaths double; microhairs absent (except *Nardus, Lygeum*); stomatal subsidiary cells triangular, domed or parallel sided; midrib simple. This is the standard form of non-kranz anatomy (fig. 10).

Pooideae are non-kranz grasses lacking microhairs and with a pooid embryo. The lodicules are thin, and the ligule is always membranous.

Inflorescence and spikelets are unspecialized and limited in their range of variation by comparison with other subfamilies, giving little insight into phyletic relationships between the tribes. This condition may signify a youthful stage of adaptive radiation, or it may indicate that selection pressures have been directed at internal physiology rather than external morphology. Certainly two important derived characters peculiar to the subfamily are of a cryptic nature, being modifications in the endosperm storage material (see Aveneae and Bromeae), and the development of large chromosomes. Pooideae are virtually limited to the temperate zones of both hemispheres, though bridging the tropics on the tops of high mountains, and it may therefore be supposed that the primary thrust of evolution has been physiological adjustment to a cold climate. A well marked secondary thrust has been a proliferation of annual genera adapted to the Mediterranean winter rainfall regime. The large proportion of Eurasian genera would seem to imply an origin on the northern land mass. The tribes show no obvious geographical or habitat preferences and seem, on the whole, to have advanced in parallel.

The possession of three lodicules, and very rarely of three stigmas, is taken to be primitive, denoting the remnants of a link with Bambusoideae though no intermediates have survived to confirm this relationship (except Diarrheneae?). Another primitive character is the retention of microhairs by Nardeae and Lygeae, two isolated relics tentatively included in the subfamily.

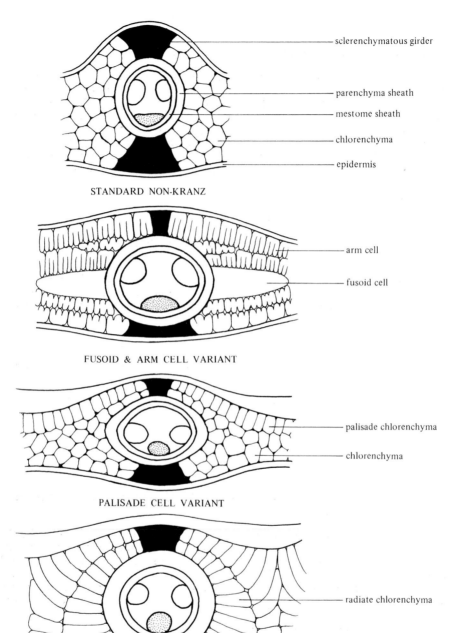

STANDARD NON-KRANZ

FUSOID & ARM CELL VARIANT

PALISADE CELL VARIANT

RADIATE CHLORENCHYMA VARIANT

sclerenchymatous girder

parenchyma sheath

mestome sheath

chlorenchyma

epidermis

arm cell

fusoid cell

palisade chlorenchyma

chlorenchyma

radiate chlorenchyma

Fig. 10 Leaf anatomy in transverse section: non-kranz types. From top to bottom the species are — *Poa trivialis, Gigantochloa verticillata, Centotheca lappacea* and *Isachne globosa.*

14. NARDEAE

Koch, Syn. Fl. Germ.: 830 (1837). *Nardinae* Reichenb., Deutsch. Fl. 6: 4 (1846).

Ligule membranous. Inflorescence a unilateral raceme, the spikelets alike and borne edgeways on with the lemma opposed to a shallow hollow in the tough rhachis but not embedded. Spikelets 1-flowered without rhachilla extension, dorsally compressed, disarticulating beneath floret; lower glume reduced to a cupular rim on the rhachis, the upper suppressed or almost so; lemma abaxial, 3-nerved, with a weak dorsal and 2 strong lateral keels, subcoriaceous, awned from tip; palea 2-nerved, shorter than lemma; lodicules 0; stamens 3; stigma 1, puberulous. Caryopsis fusiform; embryo $\frac{1}{6}$ its length; hilum linear.
Genus 1; species 1. Europe.

Anatomy. Non-kranz, with slender microhairs.

Chromosomes. 2n = 26, giving the unusual basic number of 13.

A little tribe whose unusual spikelets give no clue to its origin. The embryo structure, embryo length and ligule are pooid, but the microhairs bambusoid-arundinoid; the lodicules, unfortunately, contribute nothing to the solution of this conundrum. On balance it seems best to treat it as an early departure from the pooid line before the loss of microhairs.

92. Nardus L., Sp. Pl.: 53 (1753) — N. stricta L. *Natschia* Bub., Fl. Pyr. 4: 405 (1901) nom superfl pro Nardus.

Tufted perennial with filiform leaf-blades. Description as for tribe.

Species 1. Europe. Moorland.

15. LYGEEAE

Lange in Willk. & Lange, Prodr. Fl. Hisp. 1: 33 (1861). *Sparteae* Reichenb., Consp. Reg. Veg.: 55 (1828) nom inval.

Ligule membranous. Inflorescence a single spikelet enclosed by a spatheole. Spikelet large, 2(—3)-flowered, urn-like, falling entire; glumes 0; lemmas many-nerved, villous, fused below along opposing margins to form a cylindrical coriaceous tube, the upper half free and chartaceous; paleas fused back to back and forming a transverse septum within the lemma tube, free above; lodicules 0; stamens 3; stigma 1, glabrous. Caryopsis fusiform; embryo ¼ its length; hilum linear.
Genus 1; species 1. Mediterranean.

Anatomy. Non-kranz, with slender microhairs.

Chromosomes. 2n = 40.

A little tribe with extraordinary spikelets, but resembling Nardeae in its combination of pooid embryo and bambusoid-arundinoid microhairs.

93. Lygeum L., Gen. Pl. ed. 5: 27, 522 (1754); Parodi in Rev. Arg. Agron. 28: 81—99 (1961) — L. spartum L. *Linosparton* Adans., Fam. Pl. 2: 34, 571 (1763) nom superfl pro Lygeum. *Spartum* P. Beauv., Ess. Agrost.: 178 (1812) in syn sub Lygeum.

Tufted perennial with wiry leaf-blades. Description as for tribe.

Species 1. Mediterranean. Dry open places. *L. spartum* (Esparto grass) is a source of fibre for mats, ropes and sails.

16. STIPEAE

Dumort., Obs. Gram. Belg.: 83 (1824). *Milieae* Endl., Fl. Poson.: 109 (1830).
Miliinae Dumort., Obs. Gram. Belg.: 135 (1824). *Stipinae* Griseb., Fl. Roumel. Bithyn. 2: 470 (1844). *Aciachninae* Caro in Dominguezia 4: 41 (1982). *Ortachninae* Caro l.c.

Ligule membranous; mostly wiry bunch grasses with rolled or filiform leaf-blades. Inflorescence an open or contracted panicle (reduced to 1 spikelet in *Aciachne*), the spikelets all alike. Spikelets 1-flowered without rhachilla extension, terete to laterally compressed (except *Oryzopsis, Milium*), disarticulating above glumes; glumes persistent, usually longer than floret, hyaline to membranous (except *Aciachne*), 1—7-nerved, mostly acute to long acuminate; lemma rounded on back, 5—9-nerved (3-nerved in *Aciachne, Oryzopsis miliacea*), membranous to crustaceous, terete to lenticular and often enclosing palea, awned from entire or bidenticulate tip (*Trikeraia*, some *Stipa* bilobed; *Milium, Psammochloa* awnless); palea usually ± as long as lemma, hyaline to membranous (except *Milium, Oryzopsis, Piptochaetium*), mostly without keels, usually acute; lodicules usually 3. Caryopsis usually fusiform; hilum linear.
Genera 9; species ± 400. Temperate and warm temperate regions.

Anatomy. Non-kranz, without microhairs (Renvoize in Kew Bull. 40: 731—736, 1985). Johnston & Watson (Phytomorph. 26: 297—301, 1976) report microhairs in a few species of *Stipa*, but Scholz (Willdenowia 12: 235—240, 1982) points out that they are 1-celled, and thus not strictly comparable to the usual microhair; Renvoize proposes the term pylidial hair. It is possible that they represent an intermediate stage in the loss of microhairs. Barkworth (Taxon 31: 233—243, 1982) comments that the size and shape of the epiblast are of some taxonomic value.

Chromosomes. The tribe is unusual in possessing an extensive aneuploid series of chromosome numbers, apparently based on x = 11. Chromosomes small.

2n	22	24	28	32	34	36	40	42	44	66
No of species	11	7	6	5	8	11	9	7	25	6

The tribe is defined by its single terete or indurated floret without rhachilla extension, mostly with a terminal awn. It is probably an early offshoot from the pooid line, retaining a trace of the common bambusoid ancestry in its 1-celled hairs, enclosed rounded palea and 3 thin lodicules, though its specialized spikelets and complex cytology are far from primitive. Unlike Aristideae and other tribes with hard florets there is no germination flap in the lemma.

It comprises a single large genus surrounded by a number of imperfectly differentiated satellites. *Psammochloa* and *Trikeraia* are not entirely typical, and their inclusion rests largely upon their 3 lodicules and unkeeled palea. The tribe is conspicuously successful as a constituent of dry open steppe communities.

The tribe is often quite difficult to distinguish from 1-flowered Aveneae, *Dichelachne* and *Limnodea* being excellent examples of convergent evolution; also *Anisopogon* from Arundineae and *Monodia* from Eragrostideae. These genera have either a rhachilla extension or a dorsal awn, but not obviously so at first sight.

Fossilized florets have been found in Kansas, Nebraska and Colorado dating back to the Oligocene (Elias in Geol. Soc. Amer. Sp. Paper 41, 1942; MacGinitie in Publ. Carnegie Inst. Wash. 599, 1953; Thomasson in Kansas Geol. Surv. Bull. 218, 1979). Thomasson (Science 199: 975—977, 1978) has used characters from the lemma epidermis to suggest relationships between modern genera and the Miocene fossil *Berriochloa*.

1   Glumes longer than floret or almost so (except *Stipa papposa* whose floret is plumose above):
  2   Palea not sulcate; lemma margins flat, overlapping or leaving back of palea exposed:
    3   Lemma entire or bidentate, rarely bilobed and then lobes not bristle-like:
      4   Floret terete or laterally compressed:
        5   Palea 0—2-nerved:
          6   Floret fusiform, terete or slightly laterally compressed; awn central
          94 Stipa
          6   Floret gibbously ellipsoid, laterally compressed; awn excentric
          95 Nassella
        5   Palea 5—7-nerved, chartaceous, resembling lemma   **96 Psammochloa**
      4   Floret dorsally compressed:
        7   Lemma awned   **97 Oryzopsis**
        7   Lemma awnless   **98 Milium**
    3   Lemma bilobed, the lobes setiform; callus obtuse; lemma membranous
    99 Trikeraia
  2   Palea sulcate; lemma margins inrolled along median line
  100 Piptochaetium
1   Glumes much shorter than floret:
  8   Glumes and lemma membranous, the latter not covering back of palea
  101 Ortachne
  8   Glumes and lemma indurated   **102 Aciachne**

94. Stipa L., Sp. Pl.: 78 (1753); Aschers., Fl. Brandenb. l: 812 (1864) as "Stupa"; Freitag in Notes Roy. Bot. Gard. Edinb. 43: 355—489 (1985) — S. pennata L. *Jarava* Ruiz & Pavon, Prodr. Fl. Peru.: 2 (1794) — J. ichu Ruiz & Pavon. *Achnatherum* P. Beauv., Ess. Agrost.: 19 (1812) — A. calamagrostis (L.) P. Beauv. *Sparteum* P. Beauv. l.c. 178, in syn sub Stipa. *Lasiagrostis* Link, Hort. Berol. 1: 99 (1827) nom superfl pro Achnatherum. *Macrochloa* Kunth, Rév. Gram. 1: 58 (1829) — M. tenacissima (L.) Kunth. *Aristella* Bertol., Fl. Ital. 1: 690 (1833) — A. bromoides (L.) Bertol. *Trichosantha* Steud., Nom. Bot. ed. 2, 2: 702 (1841) nom nud — S. capillata. *Orthoraphium* Nees in Proc. Linn. Soc. 1: 94 (1841) — O. roylei Nees. *Ptilagrostis* Griseb. in Ledeb., Fl. Ross. 4: 447 (1852); Barker in Syst. Bot. 8: 395—419 (1983) — P. mongholica (Trin.) Griseb. *Timouria* Roshev. in Fedtsch., Fl. As. Ross. 12: 173 (1916) — T. saposhnikovi Roshev. *Patis* Ohwi in Acta Phytotax. Geobot. 11: 181 (1942) — P. coreana (Honda) Ohwi. *Anemanthele* Veldkamp in Acta Bot. Neerl. 34: 107 (1985) — A. lessoniana (Steud.) Veldkamp.

Perennial, very rarely annual (*S. annua, S. capensis, S. compressa* and a few others); leaves harsh and narrow, rarely wide and flat (as in *S. dregeana, S. milleana, S. sibirica*). Floret fusiform, terete or rarely slightly laterally compressed, not gibbous, the callus pungent or rarely obtuse, bearded (glumes shorter than floret in *S. papposa*); lemma firmly membranous to coriaceous, the margins usually overlapping but occasionally covering only flanks of palea, entire to shortly bilobed (bifid for $\frac{1}{3}$ of lemma in *S. gigantea*); in American species the lemma occasionally thickened apically into a brief pallid cylindrical rostrum, and often terminating in a corona around base of awn, the corona usually toroidal and hairy, rarely tubular (as in *S. charruana*); awn generally conspicuous (a subulate stump in *S. saltensis*), persistent or deciduous, arising centrally from lemma, 1—2-geniculate with twisted column (simple and curved in *S. bromoides* and a few others), sometimes plumose; palea hyaline to thinly coriaceous, 2(—4)-nerved without keels, sometimes reduced or rudimentary, obtuse or acute; lodicules 2—3; stigmas very rarely 3.

Species ± 300. Temperate and warm temperate regions of the world. Steppes and rocky slopes. *S. tenacissima* (Halfa) is used for making paper, mats and cordage. The genus has some reputation as a fodder, at least in arid climates where little else will grow, but the pungent callus may cause injuries; *S. robusta* is said to have a narcotic effect on grazing livestock.

A somewhat variable genus, whose subdivisions are not sharply defined and seem best treated at infrageneric level. Many infrageneric taxa have been proposed in regional accounts of the genus, but there is no contemporary overall classification.

Axillary cleistogenes are fairly common, and can be related to survival under drought conditions (Brown in Bot. Gaz. 113: 438—444, 1952); some of them will explode like pop-corn on heating (Eilberg in Bol. Soc. Arg. Bot. 11: 303—305, 1969). The leaf-blades are rudimentary in *S. aphylla* and *S. muelleri*. A few species have enormous plumose awns, up to 50 cm in *S. pulcherrima*.

95. Nassella Desv. in Gay, Hist. Chile Bot. 6: 263 (1854); Parodi in Darwiniana 7: 369—394 (1947) — N. pungens Desv.

Perennial. Floret gibbously ellipsoid, laterally compressed, the callus obtuse to bluntly acute; lemma coriaceous, with overlapping margins, without corona; awn deciduous though sometimes tardily so, excentric, curved or geniculate, the column twisted or not; palea shorter than lemma, 0—1-nerved; lodicules 2.

Species 15. South America, mainly in the Andes. Hillsides. *N. trichotoma* is establishing itself in the Old World as a weed; it is very effectively dispersed by its deciduous panicle.

A segregate from *Stipa*, with asymmetric laterally compressed florets.

96. Psammochloa Hitchc. in J. Wash. Acad. Sci. 17: 140 (1927); Bor in Kew Bull. 6: 186—192 (1951) — P. mongolica Hitchc. (= P. villosa).

Perennial with long rhizomes. Floret terete, slightly exceeding glumes, the callus obtuse; lemma chartaceous, villous, covering only flanks of palea, awnless; palea resembling lemma, 5—7-nerved without keels, acute.

Species 1. Mongolia. Sand dunes.
Very like *Ammophila* in growth and appearance, but the many-nerved palea and 3 lodicules point to a derivation from *Stipa*.

97. Oryzopsis Michaux, Fl. Bor. Am. 1: 51 (1803); Johnson in Bot. Gaz. 107: 1—32 (1945) — O. asperifolia Michaux. *Dilepyrum* Raf. in Med. Repos. ser. 2, 5: 353 (1808) non Michaux (1803), nom superfl pro Oryzopsis. *Piptatherum* P. Beauv., Ess. Agrost.: 17 (1812); Freitag in Notes Roy. Bot. Gard. Edinb. 33: 341—408 (1975) — P. caerulescens (Desf.) P. Beauv. *Eriocoma* Nutt., Gen. N. Am. Pl. 1: 40 (1818) — E. cuspidata Nutt. (= O. hymenoides). *Urachne* Trin., Fund. Agrost.: 109 (1822) nom superfl pro Piptatherum. *Fendleria* Steud., Syn. Pl. Glum. 1: 419 (1854) — F. rhynchelytroides Steud. (= O. hymenoides).

Perennial; leaf-blades rolled or flat. Floret narrowly lanceolate to ovate, dorsally compressed, the callus very short and obtuse (*O. hymenoides* acute); lemma coriaceous to bony (*O. miliacea* 3-nerved), usually dark in colour, the margins seldom overlapping (but always so in *O. asperifolia*); awn deciduous, short and inconspicuous, straight, not twisted (persistent geniculate and twisted in *O. canadensis, O. exigua*); palea coriaceous, 2-nerved without keels, mostly acute; lodicules 2—3.

Species 35. Temperate and subtropical regions of northern hemisphere, especially Middle East. Mainly dry mountain slopes, but a few species in woodland.
The genus merges with *Stipa,* its dorsally compressed floret being the main distinguishing feature. The Old World species are reasonably distinct, but some of the American species, particularly *O. canadensis* and *O. hymenoides,* occupy an intermediate position.

98. Milium L., Sp. Pl.: 61 (1753) — M. effusum L. *Miliarium* Moench, Meth.: 204 (1794) nom superfl pro Milium.

Annual or perennial; leaf-blades flat. Floret narrowly elliptic, dorsally compressed, the callus very short and obtuse; lemma coriaceous, the margins not overlapping, awnless; palea coriaceous, 2-nerved without keels, obtuse; lodicules 2.

Species 4. North temperate zone of the Old World; also eastern N. America. Woodlands.
The genus is little more than an awnless version of *Oryzopsis*. Though comprising only four species, it has basic chromosome numbers of 4, 5, 7 & 9 (Petrova in Bot. Zh. 60: 393—394, 1975).

99. Trikeraia Bor in Kew Bull. 9: 555 (1955) — T. hookeri (Stapf) Bor.

Perennial. Floret lanceolate, slightly dorsally compressed, the callus obtuse; lemma membranous, covering only flanks of palea, bilobed, the lobes setiform; central awn persistent, curved, not twisted; palea 2-nerved without keels, acute.

Species 2. Tibet; Himalayas. High altitude plains, by water.
Not easily recognized as stipoid, the palea and 3 lodicules being the best indication.

100. Piptochaetium Presl, Rel. Haenk. 1: 222 (1830) nom conserv; Parodi in Rev. Mus. La Plata Bot. 6: 213—310 (1944); Valencia & Costas in Bol. Soc. Arg. Bot. 12: 167—179 (1968) — P. setifolium Presl (= P. panicoides). *Podopogon* Raf., Neogenyton: 4 (1825) nom rejic — Stipa avenacea L. *Caryochloa* Spreng., Syst. Veg. 4, 2: 22, 30 (1827) non Trin. (1826) — C. montevidensis Spreng.

Perennial. Floret sometimes cylindrical, more often gibbously obovoid to subglobose or lenticular, the callus obtuse to pungent; lemma crustaceous, its margins inrolled along median line and tucked into palea groove, the tip formed into a little hairy corona around base of awn; awn deciduous or not, usually with twisted column, curved or 1—2-geniculate (reduced to a little stump in *P. cucullatum*); palea thinly coriaceous, grooved between the two closely spaced keels, often with an apical mucro projecting from lemma tip.

Species 30. USA to Argentina. Steppe.
The genus can imitate *Stipa* and *Nasella*, but is readily distinguished by its grooved palea.

101. Ortachne Steud., Syn. Pl. Glum. 1: 121 (1854) — O. retorta Steud. (= O. rariflora). *Parodiella* J. & C. Reeder in Bol. Soc. Arg. Bot. 12: 268 (1968) non Speg. (1880) — P. erectifolia (Swallen) J. & C. Reeder. *Lorenzochloa* J. & C. Reeder l.c. 11: 239 (1969) nom nov pro Parodiella.

Short tufted perennial; leaf-blades filiform. Panicle of 10 or more spikelets borne well above leaves. Glumes shorter than floret, membranous, 1-nerved, truncate or acute; floret cylindrical, the callus acute; lemma membranous, 5-nerved, covering only flanks of palea; awn persistent, straight or curved; palea membranous, 2-nerved without keels (lodicules 2 in *O. breviseta*).

Species 3. Costa Rica to Peru; Patagonia. Open places in stunted montane woodland.
Evidently related to *Stipa*; compare *O. erectifolia* and *S. obtusa*.

102. Aciachne Benth. in Hook. Ic. Pl. 14: t 1362 (1881); Reeder in Bol. Soc. Arg. Bot. 12: 268—283 (1968) — A. pulvinata Benth.

Perennial, forming low cushions; leaf-blades subulate. Panicle reduced to a single (rarely 2—3) spikelet, nestling among the leaves. Glumes shorter than floret, coriaceous, 3—5-nerved, obtuse; floret cylindrical, slightly gibbous on back, the callus brief and truncate; lemma coriaceous, 3-nerved, convolute with overlapping margins, tapering to a subulate point; palea coriaceous, 2-nerved without keels, emarginate.

Species 1. Venezuela to Peru. High altitude glassland.

17. POEAE

Festuceae Dumort., Obs. Gram. Belg.: 82 (1824); Tateoka in Bot. Mag. Tokyo 75: 336—343 (1962); Decker in Amer. J. Bot. 51: 453—463 (1964). *Cynosureae* Dumort., Obs. Gram. Belg.: 82 (1824). *Lolieae* Reichenb., Consp. Reg. Veg.: 47 (1828). *Seslerieae* Koch, Syn. Fl. Germ.: 788 (1837). *Psilureae* Ovchinnikov, Fl. Tadzhik. 1: 117 (1957) sine descr lat. *Dupontieae* Löve & Löve in Op. Bot. 5: 38 (1961) nom nud. *Scolochloeae* Tzvelev in Bot. Zh. 53: 309 (1968). *Ampelodesmeae* (Conert) Tutin in Bot. J. Linn. Soc. 76: 369 (1978).

Loliinae Dumort., Obs. Gram. Belg.: 95 (1824). *Festucinae* Presl, Rel. Haenk. 1: 257 (1830). *Cynosurinae* Nees, Fl. Afr. Austr. 1: 423 (1841). *Sesleriinae* Parl., Fl. Palerm. 1: 127 (1845). *Coleanthinae* Reichenb., Deutsch. Fl. 6: 4 (1846). *Dactylidinae* Stapf in Fl. Cap. 7: 317 (1898). *Gramininae* Krause in Beih. Bot. Centralbl. 25, 2: 487 (1909) nom nud. *Ampelodesminae* Conert, Syst. Anat. Arund.: 145 (1961). *Psilurinae* Potztal in Willdenowia 5: 471 (1969). *Brizinae* Tzvelev in Bot. Zh. 53: 310 (1968). *Ammochloinae* Tzvelev, Zlaki: 535 (1976). *Echinariinae* Tzvelev l.c.: 534.

Ligule membranous; sheath margins mostly free, sometimes connate. Inflorescence a panicle, or sometimes a single unilateral raceme with spikelets broadside to a tough rhachis (exceptions in *Castellia, Lolium, Micropyropsis, Micropyrum, Psilurus*), the spikelets all alike (except *Cynosurus, Lamarckia, Libyella*, dioecious species of *Festuca & Poa*). Spikelets of (1—)2—many fertile florets with imperfect florets above (regularly 1-flowered in *Arctagrostis, Coleanthus*, some *Colpodium, Lamarckia, Libyella, Phippsia, Podophorus, Psilurus*), mostly laterally compressed, disarticulating below each floret (except *Ammochloa, Lamarckia, Microbriza, Psilurus, Vulpia*); glumes persistent, not or scarcely exceeding lowest lemma (a few exceptions in *Colpodium, Cynosurus, Dupontia, Festuca, Lamarckia, Loliolum, Lolium, Sesleria*), mostly membranous; lemmas membranous to coriaceous, 5—7(—13)-nerved (3-nerved in *Arctagrostis, Arctophila, Catabrosa, Cutandia, Libyella, Lindbergella, Parafestuca, Phippsia, Psilurus, Vulpiella*, and in some species of *Colpodium, Dupontia, Festuca, Poa, Vulpia; Coleanthus* 1-nerved), with or without a straight or curved awn from tip or between teeth; ovary sometimes hairy, but not with a lobed appendage (unloded appendage in *Ammochloa, Ampelodesmos, Sclerochloa*); lodicules 2 (*Ampelodesmos* 3); stigmas 2 (*Megalachne* sometimes 3). Caryopsis mostly ellipsoid; hilum linear or round; endosperm soft in some *Briza* and *Dactylis*.

Genera 49; species ± 1200. Temperate and cold regions.

Anatomy. Non-kranz without microhairs.

Chromosomes. Chromosomes large; basic number 7. Aberrant basic numbers are *Ampelodesmos* 12; *Catabrosa* 10; *Colpodium* various, including 2; *Echinaria* 9; *Sphenopus* 6.

87

2n	14	21	28	35	42	49	56	63	70	84
No of species	184	9	218	7	153	10	79	10	25	10

Poeae mostly have simple spikelets with short glumes, several florets and 5-nerved lemmas. However, reduction to single florets occurs in some genera, and 3-nerved lemmas are by no means rare (reduction also occurs in depauperate spikelets which can be misleading). Even the glumes may occasionally be fairly long, though only in *Colpodium* and *Dupontia* do they approach the condition found in Aveneae.

The tribe is close-knit with only slight differences between genera, though *Ampelodesmos* stands alone as a putative link with *Stipeae*. Its taxonomy is complicated by the marked contrast between a few large continuously variable genera (*Poa, Festuca, Briza, Colpodium, Vulpia*) and a crowd of minor segregates, raising a conceptual conflict between lumping and splitting which is difficult to reconcile satisfactorily.

The genera divide into three main lines founded on *Festuca* (rounded lemma, linear hilum), *Poa* (keeled lemma, round or oval hilum) and *Sesleria* (capitate inflorescence), but these groups are insufficiently distinct to warrant formal recognition as subtribes (fig. 11). In the family as a whole the short hilum is generally associated with evolutionary advancement. There is also a progression, in each of the lines, from perennial genera of temperate grassland formations, to opportunistic annuals of the Mediterranean.

In their spikelet structure Poeae represent a parallel evolutionary line to the tropical Eragrostideae, but have not developed the racemose inflorescence to anything like the same degree. Lemma nervation is the most obvious discriminatory character, but there is some overlap. A combinaton of lemma texture, inflorescence type and geographical origin resolves most of the problems, but it is sometimes necessary to examine lodicules, embryo length or even leaf cross-section. *Muhlenbergia*, being so variable, is particularly difficult to key, though in practice it is not much like any pooid genera except perhaps *Arctagrostis* and *Zingeria*.

1   Spikelets 1-flowered without rhachilla extension; lemma 3-nerved; lodicules fleshy, truncate; spikelets mostly small, lanceolate, lightly compressed, with subequal glumes (*Blepharoneuron, Lycurus, Muhlenbergia, Pereilema*)

Eragrostideae (p 191)

1   Spikelets not with above character combination:
  2   Fertile spikelets intermixed with sterile spikelets:
    3   Fertile spikelet with 1 sterile companion, the latter persistent

117 Cynosurus

    3   Fertile spikelet with several sterile companions, falling together

118 Lamarckia

  2   Fertile spikelets not accompanied by sterile spikelets:
    4   Inflorescence an open to contracted panicle or an elongated raceme:
     5   Inflorescence a bilateral raceme, the spikelets edgeways on; lower glume absent   **109 Lolium**
     5   Inflorescence a panicle, or a raceme and then the spikelets broadside on:
      6   Palea keels with a dorsal tooth or awn   *159 Pleuropogon*
      6   Palea keels not toothed or awned:
       7   Plant perennial:
        8   Lemmas rounded on the back, at least towards base:

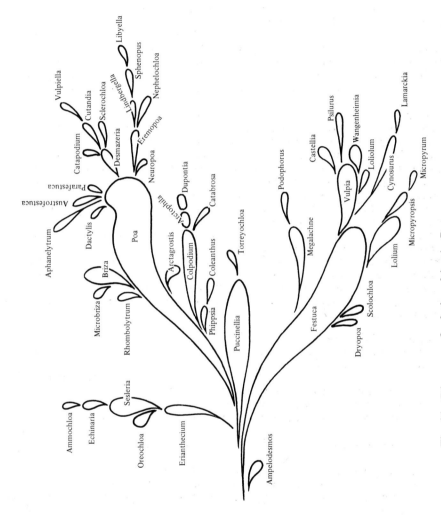

Fig. 11 Diagram of relationships in Poeae.

9 Leaf-blades short, stiff, distichous; dioecious *319 Reederochloa*
9 Leaf-blades flat to filiform, rarely pungent and then the plants not
  dioecious:
  10 Spikelets 1-flowered with rhachilla extension; lemma 3-nerved,
    coriaceous (if membranous see *104 Festuca africana*)
                    287 Dichaetaria
  10 Spikelets rarely 1-flowered and then lemma 5—7-nerved:
    11 Lodicules truncate, fleshy, usually connate; upper glume 1—5-
      nerved, often papery *Meliceae* (p 111)
    11 Lodicules lobed or pointed, hyaline, free; upper glume never
      1-nerved:
      12 Floret callus hairy:
        13 Spikelets several-flowered:
          14 Callus hairs long and conspicuous; lodicules 3
                    103 Ampelodesmos
          14 Callus hairs short; lodicules 2:
            15 Lemma smooth, thinly coriaceous (if hyaline to membranous
              see *187 Deschampsia*) **105 Scolochloa**
            15 Lemma scaberulous **106 Dryopoa**
        13 Spikelets 1-flowered:
          16 Lemma awned **108 Podophorus**
          16 Lemma awnless; palea 5—7-nerved (if 2-nerved see *197
            Agrostis zenkeri*) *96 Psammochloa*
      12 Floret callus glabrous:
        17 Lemma clearly bidentate with an awn-point from sinus
                    147 Erianthecium
        17 Lemma entire or obscurely bidenticulate:
          18 Inflorescence a bilateral raceme **110 Micropyropsis**
          18 Inflorescence a panicle:
            19 Tip of lemma firm, acute or awned; hilum oblong to linear
            (if glumes unequal and pedicel clavate see *112 Vulpia*)
                    104 Festuca
            19 Tip of lemma thinly scarious to hyaline, usually entire;
            hilum round to oval:
              20 Lemma indistinctly 5-nerved, quite smooth (if spikelets
              1-flowered see *197 Agrostis nipponensis*) **119 Puccinellia**
              20 Lemma prominently 5—7-nerved, these scaberulous
                    120 Torreyochloa
8 Lemmas keeled throughout (weakly in some *Briza*):
  21 Lemma orbicular to oblate with broad membranous margins
    appressed to lemma above **121 Briza**
  21 Lemma narrower, the margins less distinct and often inrolled:
    22 Lemma coriaceous and echinulose **122 Microbriza**
    22 Lemma not echinulose:
      23 Lateral nerves of lemma thickened below; rhachilla reduced to a
      callus **123 Rhombolytrum**
      23 Lateral nerves of lemma not thickened:
        24 Palea keels scaberulous to ciliolate:
          25 Spikelets falling entire (*Cinna, Sphenopholis*) *Aveneae* (p 116)
          25 Spikelets breaking up at maturity:
            26 Ovary glabrous:

27 Spikelets several-flowered (sometimes 1-flowered in small
    plants of *Poa*):
  28 Rhachilla glabrous:
    29 Glumes well developed:
      30 Lemma rarely acuminate and then not as below
                                            124 Poa
      30 Lemma acuminate, spinulose on keel; panicle secund,
          lobed   **125 Dactylis**
    29 Glumes vestigial   **126 Aphanelytrum**
  28 Rhachilla hairy:
    31 Lowest floret sterile   *251 Chasmanthium*
    31 Lowest floret fertile:
      32 Lemmas coriaceous:
        33 Lemmas 5—11-nerved   **127 Austrofestuca**
        33 Lemmas 3-nerved   **128 Parafestuca**
      32 Lemmas membranous with hyaline margins (if leaves
          filiform see *124 Poa variegata*)   Aveneae (p 116)
27 Spikelets 1-flowered; panicle well developed:
  34 Palea keels separated by flat membranous back; lemma
      3-nerved   **129 Arctagrostis**
  34 Palea keels approximate (*Ancistragrostis, Calamagrostis,
      Simplicia*)   Aveneae (p 116)
26 Ovary hairy:
  35 Floret callus glabrous   **104 Festuca**
  35 Floret callus bearded; spikelet long awned
                          107 Megalachne
24 Palea keels smooth or lanulose (*Phippsia concinna* hispidulous):
  36 Glumes well developed:
    37 Lemma indistinctly 3—5-nerved, obtuse to acute:
      38 Floret callus glabrous   **130 Colpodium**
      38 Floret callus with few to many stiff hairs:
        39 Glumes much shorter than adjacent lemmas
                          131 Arctophila
        39 Glumes longer than adjacent lemmas or almost so
                          132 Dupontia
    37 Lemma prominently 3-nerved, broadly obtuse to truncate
                       133 Catabrosa
  36 Glumes inconspicuous; spikelet 1-flowered   **134 Phippsia**
7 Plants annual:
  40 Inflorescence a bilateral raceme; glumes subequal
                          111 Micropyrum
  40 Inflorescence a panicle or unilateral raceme:
    41 Lemma awned, or spikelets borne in a pectinate raceme:
      42 Lower glume present, though sometimes small:
        43 Lemma 5-nerved:
          44 Inflorescence branches all fertile:
            45 Glumes shorter than adjacent lemmas:
              46 Inflorescence a panicle or open raceme, rarely pectinate and
                then the lower glume a little scale   **112 Vulpia**
              46 Inflorescence a pectinate raceme; glumes equal, the lower
                subulate   **113 Wangenheimia**

45 Glumes longer than adjacent lemmas, almost equalling
    spikelet   **114 Loliolum**
44 Inflorescence with lowest whorl of branches sterile
                              138 Nephelochloa
43 Lemma strongly 3-nerved   **146 Vulpiella**
42 Lower glume absent; spikelet with 1 fertile floret:
47 Inflorescence a raceme   **116 Psilurus**
47 Inflorescence a panicle   **135 Coleanthus**
41 Lemma awnless, at most mucronate; inflorescence never a
    pectinate raceme:
48 Lemma tuberculate   **115 Castellia**
48 Lemma not tuberculate:
49 Lemma 5—11-nerved:
50 Lemma rounded on back:
51 Lemma membranous (see also *190 Periballia*)**119 Puccinellia**
51 Lemma coriaceous   **143 Catapodium**
50 Lemma keeled:
52 Pedicels slender; inflorescence a panicle, open or contracted
    but not 1-sided:
53 Lemma orbicular to oblate   **121 Briza**
53 Lemma lanceolate to ovate:
54 Lemma with 9—11 prominently ribbed nerves
                        136 Neuropoa
54 Lemma with 5 flat nerves:
55 Panicle branches not usually whorled; lemmas narrowly
    ovate in side view   **124 Poa**
55 Panicle branches whorled, at least in larger panicles;
    lemmas lanceolate to narrowly oblong in side view
                        137 Eremopoa
52 Pedicels stout; inflorescence a 1-sided panicle with short stiff
    branches, or a raceme:
56 Lowest rhachilla internode not noticeably swollen; upper
    glume 3—5-nerved   **142 Desmazeria**
56 Lowest rhachilla internode swollen; upper glume 5—9-nerved
                        144 Sclerochloa
49 Lemma 3-nerved:
57 Spikelets several-flowered:
58 Panicle branches and pedicels slender, flexuous, persistent:
59 Glumes subequal (see also *190 Periballia*) **139 Lindbergella**
59 Glumes unequal, the lower small   **140 Sphenopus**
58 Panicle branches and pedicels stout, stiff, deciduous
                        145 Cutandia
57 Spikelets 1-flowered:
60 Inflorescence a brief raceme   **141 Libyella**
60 Inflorescence a diffuse panicle   *210 Zingeria*
4 Inflorescence a capitate to spiciform panicle or an ovoid raceme:
61 Inflorescence a raceme; perennial (if annual go to 7) **148 Oreochloa**
61 Inflorescence a panicle:
62 Lemma keeled, often shiny   *Aveneae* (p 116)
62 Lemma rounded on back, not shiny:

63 Perennial	**149 Sesleria**
63 Annual:	
64 Lemma mucronate	**150 Ammochloa**
64 Lemma spinously 5—7-awned	**151 Echinaria**

103. Ampelodesmos Link, Hort. Berol. 1: 136 (1827); Decker in Brittonia 16: 76—79 (1964) — A. tenax (Vahl) Link (= A. mauritanicus). *Ampelodonax* Lojac., Fl. Sic. 3: 282 (1909) — A. bicolor (Poir.) Lojac. (= A. mauritanicus).

Perennial; stem solid; leaf-blades harsh. Panicle large, loosely contracted. Spikelets several-flowered; glumes 3—5-nerved, firmly membranous, apiculate; lemmas coriaceous, rounded on back, 5—7-nerved, villous below, bidentate with a subulate point from sinus; floret callus and rhachilla bearded; lodicules 3, large, lanceolate; ovary with hairy apical appendage. Hilum linear. Chromosomes small, x = 12.

Species 1. Mediterranean. Dry places near coast. *A. mauritanicus* is used for rope making.

An anomalous genus, resembling *Festuca* but with small chromosomes and 3 lodicules. It hardly warrants a separate tribe, and is better regarded as a primitive member of Poeae.

104. Festuca L., Sp. Pl.: 73 (1753) — F. ovina L. *Festucaria* Fabric., Enum.: 207 (1759) nom superfl pro Festuca. *Schedonorus* P. Beauv., Ess. Agrost.: 99 (1812); Roem. & Schult., Syst. Veg. 2: 42 (1817) as "Schoenodorus" — S. pratensis (Huds.) P. Beauv. *Leucopoa* Griseb. in Ledeb., Fl. Ross. 4: 383 (1852) — L. sibirica Griseb. *Amphigenes* Janka in Linnaea 30: 619 (1860) — A. nutans (Host) Janka (= F. pulchella). *Drymonaetes* Fourr. in Ann. Soc. Linn. Lyon 17: 187 (1869) nom nud —F. gigantea. *Bucetum* Parnell, Grasses Scotland: 106 (1872) nom superfl pro Schedonorus. *Helleria* Fourn., Mex. Pl. 2: 128 (1886) non Nees & Mart. (1824) —H. livida (Kunth) Fourn. *Lojaconoa* Gand., Fl. Europ. 25: 341 (1891) — L. caerulescens (Desf.) Gand. *Pseudobromus* K. Schum. in Engl., Pfl. Ost-Afr. C: 108 (1895); de Winter in Bothalia 6: 139—151 (1951) — P. silvaticus K. Schum. (= F. africana). *Festuca subgen Hesperochloa* Piper in Contrib. U.S. Nat. Herb. 10: 10 (1906) — F. confinis Vasey (= F. kingii). *Hesperochloa* (Piper) Rydberg in Bull. Torr. Bot. Cl. 39: 106 (1912). *Wasatchia* M.E. Jones in Contrib. West. Bot. 14: 16 (1912) nom superfl pro Hesperochloa. *Gramen* Krause in Beih. Bot. Centralbl. 32, 2: 331 (1914) non Seguier (1754), nom nud — F. rubra. *Gnomonia* Lunell in Amer. Midl. Nat. 4: 224 (1915) non Ces. & De Not. (1863), nom superfl pro Festuca. *Anatherum* Nabelek in Spisy Prir. Fak. Masary. Univ. 111: 10 (1929) non P. Beauv. (1812) — A. tauricola Nabelek. *Leiopoa* Ohwi in Acta Phytotax. Geobot. 1: 66 (1932) — L. nuda (Hack.) Ohwi. *Nabelekia* Roshev., Zlaki: 254 (1937) nom nov pro Anatherum. *Hellerochloa* Rauschert in Taxon 31: 561 (1982) nom nov pro Helleria. *Drymochloa* Holub in Fol. Geobot. Phytotax 19:95 (1984) — D. drymeja (Mert. & Koch) Holub. *Argillochloa* Weber in Phytologia 55: 1 (1984) — A. dasyclada (Beal) Weber.

Perennial; occasionally dioecious; leaf-blades sometimes flat (with cross-nerves in F. *gigantea*, F. *africana* and allies) but mostly rolled to filiform, rarely pungent, the basal sheaths occasionally thickened into a bulb. Panicle open or contracted. Spikelets 2—several-flowered (*F. africana, F. monantha* 1-flowered plus rhachilla extension); upper glume 3-nerved (1-nerved in a few species with very short glumes), membranous to herbaceous (exceeding lemma in *F. livida*), acute; lemmas membranous to thinly coriaceous, rounded on back at least towards base (Subgen *Hesperochloa* keeled), 5-nerved (*F. africana, F. altissima, F. asthenica, F. engleri* 3-nerved), acute to shortly awned (Subgen *Obtusae* narrowly obtuse and coriaceous), the awn terminal or rarely subterminal (*F. subuliflora* and a few others obscurely bidenticulate); floret callus and rhachilla glabrous (callus minutely pubescent in *F. subuliflora*); palea keels ± scaberulous; stamens 3; ovary sometimes hairy on top. Hilum linear, rarely oblong.

Species ± 450. Temperate regions throughout the world, extending through tropics on mountain tops. Hills, plains and meadows. Most of the species provide good grazing, one of the best being *F. pratensis* (Meadow Fescue). *F. rubra* (Red Fescue) is an important constituent of fine lawns.

A large and variable genus for which no overall treatment is available, but the following simplified key indicates the main lines of variation.

Glumes membranous throughout:
  Lemma keeled; ovary hairy; often dioecious (F. sibirica)   Subgen *Hesperochloa*
  Lemma rounded; ovary glabrous (F. karatavica)   Subgen *Xanthochloa*
Glumes herbaceous, or membranous only on margins:
  Leaf-blades flat:
    Culm-base clad in papery scales; lemma keeled above; ovary hairy (F. altissima)   Subgen *Drymanthele*
    Culm-base not so clad; lemma rounded:
      Auricles present; ovary glabrous (F. pratensis)   Subgen *Schedonorus*
      Auricles absent; ovary hairy:
        Lemma acute:
          Floret with a short blunt callus (F. subulata)   Subgen *Subulatae*
          Floret stipitate (F. subuliflora)   Subgen *Subuliflorae*
        Lemma subacute to narrowly obtuse when flattened (F. subverticillata)
                        Subgen *Obtusae*
  Leaf-blades usually rolled; lemma rounded; ovary hairy or glabrous:
    Glumes shorter than adjacent lemma (F. rubra)   Subgen *Festuca*
    Glumes longer than adjacent lemma (F. livida)   Subgen *Helleria*

Subgen *Festuca* is the largest; it is taxonomically difficult, and identification often depends upon examining the disposition of sclerenchyma strands in a transverse section of the leaf. Spikelet proliferation occurs in a few species.

F. africana is somewhat aberrant, commonly having 1-flowered spikelets and 3-nerved lemmas, but it is linked through *F. engleri* to orthodox members of the genus such as *F. subulata* and *F. gigantea*. Species in this group are not always easy to distinguish from *Bromus* and *Bromuniola*

105. Scolochloa Link, Hort. Berol. 1: 136 (1837) nom conserv non Mert. & Koch (1823) — S. festucacea (Willd.) Link. *Fluminia* Fries, Summa Veg. Scand. 1: 247 (1846) — F. arundinacea Fries. (= S. festucacea).

Perennial. Panicle open. Spikelets several-flowered; upper glume 3—5-nerved, firmly membranous; lemmas thinly coriaceous, rounded on back, 5—7-nerved these smooth and not raised, indistinctly tridenticulate and sometimes mucronate; floret callus bearded with stiff hairs; ovary hairy on top. Hilum linear.

Species 1. North temperate zone. Lakes and river banks in shallow water.

106. Dryopoa Vickery in Contrib. New South Wales Herb. 3: 195 (1963) — C. dives (F. Muell.) Vickery.

Like *Scolochloa* but lemma nerves raised and scaberulous.

Species 1. South east Australia. Sclerophyll forest.
Dryopoa and *Scolochloa* are very similar, though probably of independent origin. They are both minor segregates, doubtfully worth separating from *Festuca*.

107. Megalachne Steud., Syn. Pl. Glum. 1: 237 (1854); Matthei in Bol. Soc. Biol. Concep. 48: 165—172 (1974) — M. berteroniana Steud. *Pantathera* Phil. in Bot. Zeit. 14: 649 (1856) — P. fernandeziana Phil. (= M. berteroniana).

Perennial. Panicle moderately open. Spikelets several-flowered; glumes ± as long as adjacent lemma, herbaceous, 3—5-nerved, aristulate to long awned; lemmas coriaceous, keeled, 5-nerved, with a long flexuous terminal awn; floret callus pubescent; stigmas 2—3; ovary hairy on top. Hilum linear.

Species 2. Juan Fernandez Is. Rocky slopes.
An island endemic, whose hairy ovary suggests a relationship with *Festuca*.

108. Podophorus Phil. in Bot. Zeit. 14: 648 (1856) — P. bromoides Phil.

Perennial? Panicle scanty. Spikelets 1-flowered plus awned rhachilla extension; glumes shorter than lemma, herbaceous, 5-nerved, acute; lemma coriaceous, subterete, 5-nerved, with a flexuous terminal awn; floret callus pubescent; ovary hairy on top. Hilum linear.

Species 1. Juan Fernandez Is.
A little known oddity, probably derived from *Megalachne*.

109. Lolium L., Sp. Pl.: 83 (1753); Terrell, U.S. Dept. Agric. Tech. Bull. 1392: 1—65 (1968) — L. perenne L. *Craepalia* Schrank, Baier. Fl. 1: 382 (1789) — C. temulenta (L.) Schrank. *Crypturus* Link in Linnaea 17: 387 (1843) — C. loliaceus (Bory) Link (= L. rigidum). *Arthrochortus* Lowe in Hook. J. Bot. 8: 301 (1856) — A. loliaceus Lowe (= L. rigidum).

Annual or perennial. Raceme with spikelets in 2 opposite rows edgeways on and partially sunk in rhachis. Spikelets several—many-flowered; lower glume absent (except terminal spikelet); upper glume abaxial, shorter than lemma to as long as spikelet, coriaceous; lemma membranous to coriaceous, with or without a subterminal awn. Hilum linear.

Species 8. Temperate Eurasia, introduced elsewhere. Meadows, pastures and weedy places. *L. perenne* (Perennial Rye grass) is one of the best pasture species in temperate regions, combining well with nitrogen-fixing *Trifolium*; it is also used for playing fields. Annual *L. multiflorum* (Italian Rye grass) is a good plant for temporary pastures. *L. temulentum* (Darnel) has an evil reputation as a weed for its grain sometimes becomes poisonous through fungal infection and, at least in primitive agriculture, is apt to get harvested along with the crop.

All the species are more or less interfertile; consequently they intergrade morphologically and are very difficult to separate. Most of them will hybridize readily with *Festuca arundinacea* and its allies. Nevertheless the two genera are so easily distinguished that it seems unrealistic to unite them.

110. Micropyropsis Romero-Zarco & Cabezudo in Lagascalia 11: 95 (1983) — M. tuberosa Romero-Zarco & Cabezudo.

Perennial, the basal internode thickened into a corm. Like *Micropyrum* but spikelet scales thinner and lemma with slender subterminal awn.

Species 1. Spain. Damp sands.

111. Micropyrum (Gaud.) Link in Linnaea 17: 397 (1844). *Triticum sect Micropyrum* Gaud., Fl. Helv. 1: 366 (1828) — T. tenellum L.

Annual. Raceme bilateral, the spikelets broadside on in two opposite rows. Spikelets several—many-flowered; glumes subequal, coriaceous, rounded on back, the upper strongly 3-nerved, obtuse to acute; lemmas coriaceous, rounded, 5-nerved, obtuse to emarginate, occasionally awned. Hilum linear.

Species 3. Mediterranean. Dry open places.

112. Vulpia Gmel., Fl. Bad. 1: 8 (1805); Cotton & Stace in Bot. Not. 130: 173—187 (1977) — V. myuros (L.) Gmel. *Zerna* Panzer, Id. Rev. Gräser: 46 (1813) nom superfl pro Vulpia. *Mygalurus* Link, Enum. Hort. Berol. 1: 92 (1821) nom superfl pro Vulpia. *Chloammia* Raf., Neogenyton: 4 (1825) — Festuca tenella Willd. (= V. octoflora). *Dasiola* Raf. l.c. — D. elliotea Raf. (= V. sciurea). *Brachypodium sect Nardurus* Bluff, Nees & Schauer, Comp. Fl. Germ. ed. 2, 1: 193 (1836) — B. tenellum (Lam.) Roem. & Schult. (= V. unilateralis). *Nardurus* (Bluff, Nees & Schauer) Reichenb., Nom.: 39 (1841). *Festucaria* Link in Linnaea 17: 398 (1844) non Fabric. (1759) — F. psilantha (Link) Link (= V. unilateralis). *Ctenopsis* De Not., Ind. Sem. Hort. Gen.:26 (1847); Paunero in Ann. Inst. Bot. Cav. 21: 357—386 (1963) — C. pectinella (Delile) De Not. *Prosphysis* Dulac, Fl. Hautes-Pyr.: 67 (1867) nom superfl pro Nardurus. *Distomomischus* Dulac l.c. 91, nom superfl pro Vulpia. *Loretia* Duval-Jouve in Rev. Sci Nat. sér. 2, 2: 38 (1880) — L. geniculata (L.)

Duval-Jouve. *Narduretia* Villar in Bull. Soc. Hist. Nat. Afr. Nord 16: 100 (1925) —N. delicatula (Lag.) Villar.

Annual (*V. sicula* perennial). Inflorescence a scanty ± secund panicle or a raceme (of several racemes disposed along an axis and deflexing at maturity in *V. microstachys*). Spikelets several-flowered (*V. inops* with only 1 fertile floret, a few other species sometimes so), disarticulating below each fertile floret and sometimes also below pedicel, this clavate or slender; glumes very unequal (*V. inops, V. octoflora* subequal) the lower sometimes minute, the upper 1—3-nerved, acute to awned; lemmas thinly coriaceous, rounded or occasionally keeled, faintly 5-nerved (*V. ciliata* sometimes 3-nerved), narrow, tapering into a long straight awn (*V. octoflora, V. unilateralis* and *sect Ctenopsis* shortly awned); floret callus glabrous (*V. fontquerana* pubescent and pungent); stamens 1—3, often small and cleistogamous; ovary sometimes hairy. Caryopsis linear; hilum linear.

Species 22. Temperate and subtropical regions of northern hemisphere; introduced to southern hemisphere, though perhaps a few endemic species in South America. Dry open places.
A surprisingly variable little genus, closely related to and hybridizing with *Festuca* but introducing a number of novel trends associated with its annual lifestyle. Variation is indicated in the following key to sections.

Spikelets ± appressed to branches:
  Spikelets single:
    Florets chasmogamous (V. ligustica)   Sect *Loretia*
    Florets cleistogamous:
      Upper florets smaller but not otherwise modified:
        Inflorescence a panicle (V. myuros)   Sect *Vulpia*
        Inflorescence a raceme (V. unilateralis)   Sect *Apalochloa*
      Upper florets reduced to a bunch of awns (V. fasciculata)   Sect *Monachne*
  Spikelets in deciduous triads (V. inops)   Sect *Spirachne*
Spikelets pectinate (V. pectinella)   Sect *Ctenopsis*

V. pectinella is very different in appearance, imitating *Ctenium*, but the other members of its section are less distinct.

113. Wangenheimia Moench, Meth.: 200 (1794) — W. disticha Moench (= W. lima)

Annual. Raceme oblong, the spikelets densely imbricate. Spikelets several-flowered; glumes equal in length, the lower subulate and turned inward to lie along face of spikelets, the upper boat-shaped, 2—3-nerved and strongly coriaceous with membranous margins; lemmas coriaceous with membranous margins, keeled all along or lowest rounded towards base, 5-nerved, obtuse to acuminate or mucronate. Hilum oblong.

Species 2. Spain and North Africa. Dry open places.
Related to *Vulpia pectinella*.

114. Loliolum Krecz. & Bobrov in Kom., Fl. SSSR 2: 766 (1934) — L. orientale (Boiss.) Krecz. & Bobrov (= L. subulatum).

Annual. Raceme unilateral. Spikelets several-flowered; glumes subequal, longer than adjacent lemmas and almost as long as spikelet; lemmas coriaceous, rounded, faintly 5-nerved, shortly awned. Hilum linear.

Species 1. Eastern Mediterranean to central Asia. Dry places.
Probably related to *Vulpia unilateralis*.

115. Castellia Tineo, Pl. Rar. Sic. 2: 17 (1846) — C. tuberculata Tineo (= C. tuberculosa).

Annual. Racemes single or scattered along a central axis. Spikelets several-flowered; lemmas membranous, densely tuberculate, rounded, 5-nerved, subacute. Hilum linear.

Species 1. Canary Is, Mediterranean, Sudan, Somalia and Pakistan. Dry open places.
Apparently widespread, but of very local occurrence and rarely collected.

116. Psilurus Trin., Fund. Agrost.: 93 (1822) — P. nardoides Trin. (= P. incurvus). *Asprella* Host, Gram. Austr. 4: 17 (1809) non Schreb. (1789) — A. nardiformis (= P. incurvus).

Annual. Raceme slender, tardily fragile, the spikelets distant on elongated internodes. Spikelets 1-flowered plus rhachilla extension or sometimes a sterile floret; lower glume 0, the upper very small; lemma coriaceous, keeled, 3-nerved, awned; stamen 1. Caryopsis linear; hilum linear.

Species 1. Mediterranean to Pakistan. Dry places.
An isolated genus, apparently related to *Vulpia*.

117. Cynosurus L., Sp. Pl.: 72 (1753); Jirasek & Chrtek in Novit. Bot. Prag. 1964: 23—27 (1964) — C. cristatus L. *Falona* Adans., Fam. Pl. 2: 496 (1763); Dumort., Obs. Gram. Belg.: 114 (1824) as "Phalona" — F. echinata (L.) Dumort.

Annual or perennial. Panicle spiciform or capitate, ± unilateral, bearing paired spikelets, the outer of each pair sterile and covering a fertile spikelet. Fertile spikelet (1—)2—5-flowered; glumes narrow (exceeding lemma in *C. coloratus, C. echinatus*); lemmas coriaceous, rounded, 5-nerved, scabrid above, acute narrowly obtuse or bidenticulate, muticous mucronate or awned. Sterile spikelet reduced to a pectinate cluster of sterile lemmas, persistent on panicle. Hilum oblong to linear.

Species 8. Europe, N. Africa, Middle East. Meadows and weedy places.
The species divide into two groups, short awned spiciform and long awned capitate, but they are not worth recognizing as separate genera. Immediate relatives of the genus are uncertain, but the spikelets bear some resemblance to *Loliolum*.

118. Lamarckia Moench, Meth.: 201 (1794) as "Lamarkia"; corr Koeler, Descr. Gram.: 376 (1802) nom conserv non Olivi (1792) — L. aurea (L.) Moench. *Achyrodes* Boehmer in Ludwig, Def. Gen. Pl. ed. 3: 420 (1760) nom rejic — L. aurea. *Chrysurus* Pers., Syn. Pl. 1: 80 (1805) nom superfl pro Lamarckia. *Pterium* Desv. in J. Bot. Agr. ser. 2, 1: 75 (1813) — P. elegans Desv. (= L. aurea). *Tinaea* Garzia in Rel. Accad. Zel. Aci-Reale Sci. 3—4: 24 (1838) non Tinea Spreng. (1820), nom superfl pro Lamarckia.

Annual. Panicle condensed, secund, bearing deciduous clusters of 3 sterile spikelets ± covering 2 smaller spikelets, one of them fertile and the other reduced. Fertile spikelet 1-flowered plus awned rudiment; glumes narrow, exceeding lemma; floret raised on a long rhachilla internode; lemma membranous, rounded, 5-nerved, scabrid above, bidentate, awned from sinus. Sterile spikelets many-flowered, linear; lemmas membranous, empty, obtuse. Hilum linear.

Species 1. Mediterranean and Middle East. Dry open places.

Most clusters are of the standard form described above, but Beddows (New Phytol. 37: 113—127, 1938) has shown that on occasion the number of spikelets can vary considerably. Moreover exceptional fertile spikelets attain 2—13 bisexual florets, thus confirming inclusion of the genus in Poeae.

119. Puccinellia Parl., Fl. Ital. 1: 366 (1848) nom conserv — P. distans (L.) Parl. *Poa sect Atropis* Trin. in Mém. Acad. Sci. Pétersb. sér. 6, 6: 68 (1836) — P. distans L. *Atropis* (Trin.) Griseb. in Ledeb., Fl. Ross. 4: 388 (1852) nom superfl.

Perennial (*P. rupestris, P. simplex* and a few others annual); sheath margins free. Panicle open or contracted (reduced and often raceme-like in *P. simplex*). Spikelets 2—several-flowered; upper glume 3-nerved; lemmas membranous becoming thinly scarious or hyaline at tip, rounded on back, weakly 5-nerved, smooth, obtuse or sometimes acute, ± erose; floret callus and rhachilla glabrous, but base of lemma often pubescent; palea keels scaberulous to ciliate; ovary glabrous. Hilum round to oval.

Species ± 80. Temperate regions throughout world, but principally Asia. Coastal and inland saline or alkaline soils; mountain grassland in Himalayas.

Allied to *Poa* but with a rounded lemma. Often difficult to distinguish from *Festuca* (acute lemma and elongated hilum) or *Glyceria* (1-nerved upper glume).

120. Torreyochloa Church in Amer. J. Bot. 36: 163 (1949) — T. pauciflora (Presl) Church.

Like *Puccinellia* but lemma with 5—7 prominent scaberulous nerves.

Species 4. North America and NE Asia. Shallow water and wet meadows.

121. Briza L., Sp. Pl.: 70 (1753); Matthei in Willdenowia, Beih. 8: 1—168 (1975); Nicora & Rugolo in Darwiniana 23: 279—309 (1981) — B. minor L. *Tremularia*

Fabric., Enum.: 207 (1759) nom superfl pro Briza. *Calosteca* Desv. in Nouv. Bull. Sci. Soc. Philom. 2: 190 (1810); P. Beauv., Ess. Agrost.: 85 (1812) as "Calotheca" —C. brizoides (Lam.) Desv. *Chascolytrum* Desv. l.c. — C. subaristatum (Lam.) Desv. *Chondrachyrum* Nees in Lindl., Nat. Syst. ed. 2: 449 (1836) — C. scabrum Steud. *Brizochloa* Jirasek & Chrtek in Novit. Bot. Prag. 1966: 40 (1967) — B. spicata (Sibth. & Sm.) Jirasek & Chrtek (= Briza humilis). *Lombardochloa* Ros. & Arril. in An. Fac. Quim. 9: 260 (1979) — L. rufa (Presl) Ros. & Arril.

Perennial, sometimes annual. Panicle open to loosely contracted. Spikelets several—many-flowered, ovate to rotund, laterally compressed or globose, glumes cordate to narrowly ovate; lemmas orbicular to oblate, folded or flattened, chartaceous to coriaceous with broad membranous margins on upper half or all along, clasping floret above and sometimes elaborated into basal auricles or lateral wings (*B. rufa* with basal glands), gibbous on the back and keeled though sometimes indistinctly so (*B. rufa* rounded), 5—11-nerved, obtuse cuspidate or bilobed, with or without a mucro (*B. brizoides* shortly awned); palea sometimes much shorter than lemma, lanceolate to orbicular; stamens 1—3. Hilum round to elliptic (*B. maxima* linear); endosperm sometimes soft.

Species 20. Temperate Eurasia and South America. Grassland and open places, dry or moist soils. *B. maxima* and other species with delicate trembling panicles are grown as ornamentals.

Briza can usually be recognized by its very broad lemmas whose membranous margins are appressed to the flanks of the floret above, but its proximity to *Poa* can be seen in the intermediate species *B. monandra* and *P. poidium*. The lemma margins of *B. rufa* are at first appressed, but tend to inroll at maturity suggesting a link with *Microbriza*. Lemma shape is very variable and often ornate, but there are no subdivisions sufficiently distinct to justify splitting the genus.

122. Microbriza Nicora & Rugolo in Darwiniana 23: 292 (1981) — M. poimorpha (Presl) Nicora & Rugolo. *Monostemon* Henr. in Med. Herb. Leiden 40: 72 (1921) in syn sub Briza poimorpha.

Perennial. Panicle condensed about main branches. Spikelets 2(—3)-flowered, broadly ovate to orbicular, the florets arising at about the same level and usually falling as a pair; glumes about as long as lemmas; lemmas broadly ovate, thinly coriaceous with inflexed margins, keeled, 5-nerved, echinulose, obtuse. Hilum round.

Species 2. Brazil to Argentina. Moist or marshy soil.
The genus could be mistaken for *Isachne* at first glance, but the latter has a ligular line of hairs.

123. Rhombolytrum Link, Hort. Berol. 2: 296 (1833); Nicora & Rugolo in Darwiniana 23: 298—302 (1981) — R. rhomboideum Link. *Gymnache* Parodi in Not. Mus. La Plata 3: 29 (1938) — G. jaffuelii Parodi.

Perennial. Panicle loosely contracted. Spikelets several-flowered, the rhachilla very short; lemmas dorsally compressed, keeled, 5-nerved, the margins thickened and indurated in lower third, entire or bidentate, mucronate or not; stamen 1. Hilum round.

Species 3. Southern Brazil, Uruguay and Chile. Stony slopes.

124. Poa L., Sp. Pl.: 67 (1753) — P. pratensis L. *Panicularia* Fabric., Enum.: 207 (1759) nom superfl pro Poa. *Poidium* Nees in Lindl., Nat. Syst. ed. 2: 450 (1836); Nicora & Rugolo in Darwiniana 23: 303—306 (1981) — P. brasiliense Steud. (= Poa poidium). *Poagris* Raf., Fl. Tell. 1: 18 (1837) nom superfl pro Poa. *Glyceria sect Arctopoa* Griseb. in Ledeb., Fl. Ross. 4: 392 (1852) — G. glumaris (Trin.) Griseb. (= P. eminens). *Oreopoa* Gand., Fl. Eur. 26: 186 (1891) nom nud — P. alpina. *Dasypoa* Pilger in Bot. Jahrb. 25: 716 (1898) — D. tenuis Pilger (= P. scaberula). *Paneion* Lunell in Amer. Midl. Nat. 4: 221 (1914) nom superfl pro Poa. *Bellardiochloa* Chiov., Stud. Veg. Piemonte: 60 (1929) — B. violacea (Bell.) Chiov. (= P. variegata). *Arctopoa* (Griseb.) Probat. in Nov. Sist. Vysh. Rast. 11: 49 (1974). *Parodiochloa* C.E. Hubbard in Bull. Brit. Mus. 8: 395 (1981) — P. flabellata (Lam.) C.E. Hubbard.

Perennial, ± 15 species annual; sometimes dioecious; leaf-blades flat or setaceous, rarely pungent, the basal sheaths occasionally thickened into a bulb. Panicle open or contracted. Spikelets 2—several-flowered (*P. epileuca* and allies 1—2-flowered); upper glume nearly always 3-nerved; lemmas herbaceous or membranous often with hyaline margins which tend to inflex at maturity, keeled throughout, the keel glabrous or sometimes ciliate, 5—7-nerved but occasionally the intermediate nerves obscure or obsolescent, obtuse to acute, awnless (*P. variegata* mucronate; *P. flabellata* and allies acuminate to shortly awned); floret callus often with a web of fine cottony hairs, the rhachilla glabrous (*P. variegata* shortly pilose; *P. sandvichensis* hispidulous); palea keels scaberulous to stiffly ciliolate (almost smooth in some annual species); stamens 3, rarely 1; ovary glabrous. Hilum round to oval.

Species ± 500. Cool temperate regions throughout the world, extending through the tropics on mountain tops (mapped by Hartley in Austral. J. Bot. 9: 152—161, 1961). Habitat variable, but typically meadowland from sea level to above tree line. The genus includes many valuable forage species, particularly *P. pratensis* (Meadow or Blue grass). The weedy ephemeral *P. annua* is probably the most cosmopolitan of all grass species.

Poa is an extremely uniform genus for which there is no satisfactory infrageneric classification. Its taxonomy is rendered difficult by the dearth of useful discriminatory characters, and complicated by the widespread occurrence of apomixy and introgression.

About 30 diclinous species occur in America, mainly in the far south; most are dioecious with the two sexes dissimilar, but some are gynodioecious with the spikelets almost alike. Spikelet proliferation is fairly common, particularly among the high mountain species. When present, the callus hairs are at first tightly packed, but spread after abscission into a fine clinging web that presumably aids dispersal.

In the southern hemisphere there is a tendency towards acuminate or even briefly awned lemmas, exemplified by *P. cookii, P. flabellata* and *P. novae-zeylandiae*, but they are closely linked to the main body of the genus by intermediates. *P. variegata* from Europe is also somewhat aberrant, but the shape and texture of its lemmas are typical of *Poa*.

The genus differs from *Festuca* mainly in its keeled lemma and round hilum, but there is some overlap. Species with obsolescent marginal nerves may be confused with Eragrostideae, though usually a few lemmas with more than 3 nerves can be found. The few-flowered New Guinea species allied to *P. epileuca* are also difficult to identify when reduced to 1 floret, but their well spread palea keels distinguish them from *Calamagrostis*.

125. Dactylis L., Sp. Pl.: 71 (1753); Domin in Acta Bot. Bohem. 14: 1—147 (1943); Stebbins & Zohary in Univ. Calif. Publ. Bot. 31: 1—40 (1959); Borrill in J. Linn. Soc. Bot. 56: 441—452 (1961) & Ann. Rep. Welsh Pl. Br. Sta. 1977: 190—209 (1978) — D. glomerata L. *Amaxitis* Adans., Fam. Pl. 2: 34, 515 (1763) nom superfl pro Dactylis. *Trachypoa* Bub., Fl. Pyr. 4: 359 (1901) nom superfl pro Dactylis.

Tufted perennial, the vegetative shoots strongly laterally compressed. Panicle contracted, lobed, 1-sided, the spikelets crowded in compact fascicles at the end of short main branches. Spikelets 2—5-flowered, strongly laterally compressed; glumes keeled; lemmas thinly coriaceous, keeled, 5-nerved, spinously ciliate on keel, entire or bidentate, mucronate to briefly awned. Hilum round; endosperm soft.

Species 1. Temperate Eurasia, introduced elsewhere. Habitat variable, including meadows, woodlands, waste land and stony hills. *D. glomerata* (Cocksfoot, Orchard grass) is a valuable forage grass.
The genus mainly consists of a large and extremely variable tetraploid complex, but there are a dozen or so little enclaves of diploids particularly around the Mediterranean. Numerous segregates have been described, but they intergrade to such an extent that they warrant no more than infraspecific status.
Dactylis is a segregate from *Poa*, sharing most of its characters with species of the *P. flabellata* group, though there is no evidence of direct relationship with the latter.

126. Aphanelytrum Hack. in Oest. Bot. Zeitschr. 52: 12 (1902); Chase in Bot. Gaz. 61: 340—343 (1916) — A. procumbens Hack.

Perennial. Panicle lax. Spikelets 2—3-flowered plus rhachilla extension, the rhachilla internodes filiform and up to ¾ length of floret; glumes mostly vestigial, rarely up to 1 mm; lemmas herbaceous, keeled throughout, 5-nerved, acuminate to a filiform tip; palea keels minutely scaberulous; ovary glabrous. Hilum oval.

Species 1. Colombia, Bolivia, Ecuador. Humid montane forest, scrambling over rocks and other vegetation.

127. Austrofestuca (Tzvelev) Alexeev in Byull. Mosk. Obsh. Ispyt. Prirody 81, 5: 55 (1976). *Festuca subgen Austrofestuca* Tzvelev in Bot. Zh. 56: 1257 (1971) — F. littoralis Labill.

Perennial; leaf-blades flat to subterete. Panicle open or contracted. Spikelets several-flowered; upper glume 3—7-nerved; lemmas coriaceous, keeled throughout, 5—11-nerved, subacute to shortly awned (*A. hookeriana* bidenticulate); floret callus and rhachilla shortly pilose; palea keels ciliolate to scaberulous; ovary glabrous. Hilum oval.

Species 4. Australia, New Zealand. Coastal dunes and inland woodland.

An enigmatic genus, commonly included in *Festuca*, but with a greater resemblance to the southern variant of *Poa*.

128. Parafestuca Alexeev in Byull. Mosk. Obsh. Ispyt. Prirody 90: 107 (1985) — P. albida (Lowe) Alexeev.

Perennial. Like *Austrofestuca* but lemmas 3-nerved.

Species 1. Madeira. Hill slopes.

129. Arctagrostis Griseb.in Ledeb., Fl. Ross. 4: 434 (1852) — A. latifolia (R. Br.) Griseb.

Perennial. Panicle contracted. Spikelets 1-flowered with or without rhachilla extension; glumes mostly equal, shorter than lemma, acute; lemmas membranous with hyaline tip, keeled, 3-nerved, obtuse to acute or mucronate; floret callus glabrous; palea keels scaberulous.

Species 1. Arctic. Marshy tundra.

The genus is often placed in Aveneae, but seems to have more in common with *Colpodium*.

130. Colpodium Trin., Fund. Agrost. : 119 (1822); Tzvelev in Nov. Sist. Vysh. Rast. 1: 5—19 (1964); Alexeev l.c. 17: 4—10 (1980) — C. stevenii Trin. (= C. versicolor). *Keniochloa* Meld. in Svensk Bot. Tid. 50: 538 (1956) — K. chionogeiton (Pilger) Meld. *Colpodium subgen Hyalopoa* Tzvelev, Arkt. Fl. SSSR 2: 172 (1964) — C. ponticum (Bal.) Woronov. *Colpodium subgen Paracolpodium* Tzvelev in Nov. Sist. Vysh. Rast. 1: 9 (1964) — C. altaicum Trin. *Colpodium subgen Catabrosella* Tzvelev l.c. : 12 — C. humile (Bieb.) Griseb. *Catabrosella* (Tzvelev) Tzvelev in Bot. Zh. 50: 1320 (1965). *Hyalopoa* (Tzvelev) Tzvelev l.c: *Paracolpodium* (Tzvelev) Tzvelev l.c.; Alexeev in Nov. Sist. Vysh. Rast. 18: 86—95 (1981).

Perennial. Panicle open or sometimes contracted. Spikelets 1—4-flowered; glumes unequal to subequal, the upper ½ to as long as lemma (exceeding it in *C. chionogeiton, C. oreades, C. tibeticum*), obtuse to acute; lemmas thinly membranous becoming hyaline at tip, keeled throughout, indistinctly 3—5-nerved below (nerves somewhat raised in *C. nutans*) but almost nerveless in upper half, obtuse to acute (*C. lanatiflorum* sometimes mucronate); floret callus glabrous or with a web of cottony hairs; palea smooth or with fine hairs but never scaberulous. Hilum oblong.

Species 19. Turkey and Caucasus to Nepal and eastern Siberia; Mts Kenya and Kilimanjaro; Lesotho. High mountains.

Colpodium is a high altitude segregate from *Poa*, very similar to the *P. alpina* group but differing in fewer florets, thinner lemmas and non-scabrid palea keels.

The basic chromosome number is usually 7, but there are some irregularities: *C. humile* & *C. variegatum* 2n = 10; *C. chionogeiton* & *C. hedbergii* 2n = 8; *C. versicolor* 2n = 4 (Sokolovskaya & Probatova in Bot. Zh. 62: 241—245, 1977). Reported counts of *C. fibrosum* 2n = 18 and *C. humile* 2n = 12 may be erroneous.

131. Arctophila (Rupr.) Anderss., Pl. Scand. Gram. : 48 (1852). *Poa subtaxon Arctophila* Rupr., Beitr. Pfl. Russ. Reich. 2: 64 (1846) — P. fulva Trin.

Like *Colpodium* but floret callus bearded with few to many stiff hairs; spikelets 2—6-flowered with glumes shorter than adjacent lemma; lemmas weakly keeled, 3-nerved.

Species 1. Arctic. Wet places.

132. Dupontia R. Br., Chlor. Melv. : 32 (1823) — D. fisheri R. Br.

Like *Arctophila* but glumes longer than adjacent lemma or almost so; spikelets (1—)2(—4)-flowered; lemmas 3—5-nerved.

Species 1. Arctic. Wet places.
Colpodium, Arctophila and *Dupontia* are barely distinct; the two latter hybridize.

133. Catabrosa P. Beauv., Ess. Agrost.: 97 (1812); Nicora & Rugolo in Darwiniana 23: 181—185 (1981) — C. aquatica (L.) P. Beauv.

Perennial. Panicle open. Spikelets (1—)2(—3)-flowered; glumes unequal, the upper less than $^2/_3$ lemma length, the lower less than $^1/_3$, broadly obtuse to truncate; lemmas thinly membranous becoming hyaline at tip, keeled, prominently 3-nerved with raised nerves, broadly obtuse to truncate, erose; floret callus glabrous. Hilum oblong.

Species 2. North temperate zone; Chile. Marshes and shallow water from sea level to high altitudes.
Catabrosa shows some similarity to *Colpodium nutans* and the two genera are evidently related. Despite its chromosome number (2n = 20) it has little in common with *Glyceria*.

134. Phippsia (Trin.) R. Br., Chlor. Melv. : 27 (1823). *Vilfa subgen Phippsia* Trin. in Spreng., Neue Ent. 2: 37 (1820) — V. algida (Soland.) Trin.

Dwarf perennial. Panicle contracted. Spikelets 1-flowered without rhachilla extension; glumes small, up to $^1/_3$ length of lemma, narrowly ovate, readily deciduous; lemma membranous, keeled, 3-nerved, acute or obtuse; palea keels smooth (*P. concinna* hispidulous); stamens 1—3. Caryopsis elliptic, protruding from floret at maturity; hilum oval.

Species 3. Arctic; high Andes of Argentina. Damp open places.

Phippsia hybridizes with *Puccinellia*, and is distinguished from *Catabrosa* mainly by its obsolescent glumes. The protruding grains give it a superficial resemblance to *Sporobolus*.

135. Coleanthus Seidel in Roem. & Schult., Syst. Veg. 2: 11, 276 (1817) nom conserv — C. subtilis (Tratt.) Seidel. *Schmidtia* Tratt., Fl. Oest. Kaiserth. 1: 12 (1816) nom rejic non Steud. (1852) — S. subtilis Tratt. *Wilibalda* Roth, Enum. 1, 1: 92 (1827) & *Smidetia* Raf., Aut. Bot. : 187 (1840) & l.c. "Schmiedtia" — nom superfl pro Coleanthus.

Dwarf annual. Panicle with spikelets in globular clusters on its scanty branches, embraced below by inflated upper sheath. Spikelets 1-flowered without rhachilla extension; glumes absent; lemma hyaline, keeled, 1-nerved, with a short subulate awn; palea keels smooth; lodicules 0; stamens 2. Caryopsis elliptic, protruding from floret; hilum oval.

Species 1. Central Europe and northern Asia; north America. Pond margins.
An uncommon little grass with umbel-like spikelet clusters; perhaps related to *Phippsia*.

136. Neuropoa Clayton in Kew Bull. 40: 728 (1985) — N. fax (Willis & Court) Clayton.

Annual. Panicle usually contracted, scanty, subracemose. Spikelets several—many-flowered; upper glume 3—5-nerved, membranous, obtuse; lemma chartaceous with hyaline margins, keeled, with 9—11 (rarely fewer) prominently ribbed nerves, obtuse to emarginate. Hilum round.

Species 1. Australia. Sandy or saline soils.
A minor segregate from *Poa*, comparable to corresponding annual genera from the Mediterranean.

137. Eremopoa Roshev. in Kom., Fl. SSSR 2: 756 (1934) — E. persica (Trin.) Roshev.

Annual. Panicle branches whorled, the lower sometimes sterile. Spikelets like *Poa* but lemmas lanceolate to narrowly oblong in side view, and obtuse to acuminate or mucronate.

Species 4. Eastern Mediterranean to western China.
There is a good deal of minor variation, and several more species are sometimes distinguished. The genus has a recognizable facies but otherwise is barely distinct from *Poa*, whose few annual species have the lemmas narrowly ovate in side view and the panicle branches not whorled; but there are intermediates such as *P. bolandieri*.

138. Nephelochloa Boiss., Diagn. Pl. Or. 1, 5: 72 (1844) — N. orientalis Boiss.

Annual. Panicle branches whorled, the lower sterile. Spikelets several-flowered; lemmas membranous, rounded, 5-nerved, bilobed, shortly awned; rhachilla internode tipped by a ring of hairs. Hilum round.

Species 1. Turkey. Dry places.
Linked to *Eremopoa* through *E. nephelochloides*.

139. Lindbergella Bor in Svensk Bot. Tid. 63: 368 (1969) nom nov pro seq. *Lindbergia* Bor l.c. 62: 467 (1969) non Kindberg (1897) — L. sintenisii (Lindb.) Bor.

Annual. Panicle branches indistinctly whorled. Spikelets 2—several-flowered on terete pedicels; glumes subequal, the upper 5-nerved; lemmas coriaceous, keeled, 3-nerved, asperulous, appressed pubescent on keel and nerves, obtuse to acute or mucronate. Hilum rounded.

Species 1. Cyprus. Rocky slopes.
Related to *Eremopoa*, but easily mistaken for *Eragrostis* from which it is best distinguished by the lemma hairs.

140. Sphenopus Trin., Fund. Agrost.: 135 (1822) — S. gouanii Trin. (= S. divaricatus).

Annual. Panicle open, divaricate. Spikelets several-flowered, on long pedicels gradually widening upwards; glumes unequal, the lower very small, the upper membranous and 1-nerved; lemmas membranous, keeled, 3-nerved, obtuse to subacute. Hilum round.

Species 2. Mediterranean to Iran. Saline soils.
Chromosome numbers of 2n = 12 & 24 have been recorded.

141. Libyella Pamp. in Bull. Soc. Bot. Ital. 1925: 151 (1925) — L. cyrenaica (Dur. & Barr.) Pamp.

Tiny annual 2—5 cm high. Raceme sparse, the lowest spikelet ♀ and hidden within the uppermost leaf-sheath, distant from the rest which are bisexual and well exserted. Spikelets 1-flowered without rhachilla extension; glumes very small (absent from ♀ spikelet); lemma thinly membranous, rounded, faintly 3-nerved, erose; lodicules 0. Hilum oval.

Species 1. Libya. Sandy places near the coast.
The female spikelets resemble cleistogenes, but have long emergent stigmas. The genus seems to be a midget derivative of the *Poa*-like annuals.

142. Desmazeria Dumort., Comm. Bot.: 26 (1822) as "Demazeria"; corr Dumort., Obs. Gram. Belg.: 46 (1824); Scholz in Bot. Jahrb. 94: 556—561 (1974); Stace in Bot. J. Linn. Soc. 76: 351 (1978) — D. sicula (Jacq.) Dumort. *Brizopyrum* Link, Hort. Berol. 1: 159 (1827) nom superfl pro Desmazeria.

Annual. Panicle 1-sided with short stiff branches, or reduced to a raceme. Spikelets several—many-flowered on stout pedicels; glumes subequal, coriaceous, 3—5-nerved; lemmas narrowly ovate in side view, coriaceous, keeled, 5-nerved but the intermediates sometimes faint, capitate hairy below, subacute. Hilum round.

Species 4. Mediterranean. Dry sandy places.
D. philistaea provides a link with *Cutandia*.

143. Catapodium Link, Hort. Berol. 1: 44 (1827); Paunero in An. Bot. Cav. 25: 207—241 (1967) — C. loliaceum (Huds.) Link (= C. marinum). *Scleropoa* Griseb., Fl. Rumel. Bithyn. 2: 431 (1846) — S. rigida (L.) Griseb. *Synaphe* Dulac, Fl. Hautes-Pyr.: 90 (1867) nom superfl pro Scleropoa.

Like *Desmazeria*, but lemmas rounded at least towards the base and glabrous.

Species 2. Europe and North Africa to Iran. Dry places.
The genus is only marginally distinct from *Desmazeria*, the most reliable distinguishing character being the glabrous lemmas. It differs from annual *Puccinellia* by little more than the lemma texture, but is probably not directly related.

144. Sclerochloa P. Beauv., Ess. Agrost.: 97 (1812) — S. dura (L.) P. Beauv. *Amblychloa* Link in Linnaea 17: 399 (1844) nom prov pro Sclerochloa. *Crassipes* Swallen in Amer. J. Bot. 18: 684 (1931) — C. annuus Swallen (= S. dura).

Annual. Panicle contracted, 1-sided, with very short stout branches, often reduced to an oblong raceme, the spikelets tardily disarticulating between florets and below pedicel. Spikelets several-flowered, the lowest rhachilla internode enlarged; glumes unequal, herbaceous with membranous margins, obtuse, the lower 3—5-nerved, the upper 5—9; lemma coriaceous with membranous margins, keeled, 5—7-nerved, obtuse. Caryopsis with a beak formed from persistent style base; hilum round.

Species 2. Southern Europe and Middle East. Dry weedy places and saline soils.

145. Cutandia Willk. in Bot. Zeit. 18: 130 (1860); Stace in Bot. J. Linn. Soc. 76: 351—352 (1978) — C. scleropoides Willk. (= C. memphitica).

Annual. Panicle sparse with stiffly divergent branches, these stout and deciduous after spikelets commence to break up (rarely the smallest inflorescences of *C. maritima* reduced to a raceme). Spikelets several-flowered; glumes slightly to very unequal; lemmas narrowly lanceolate in side view, membranous to subcoriaceous, keeled, prominently 3-nerved, entire or emarginate, with or without a mucro. Caryopsis narrow, with appendage formed from persistent style base; hilum oval.

Species 6. Mediterranean and Middle East. Maritime sands and stony hillsides.

A 3-nerved lemma is not common in Poeae, but the characteristic panicle should prevent confusion with *Eragrostis*.

146. Vulpiella (Batt. & Trab.) Burollet in Ann. Serv. Bot. Tunis 4: 68 (1927). *Cutandia subgen Vulpiella* Batt. & Trab., Fl. Alg. Monocot. : 238 (1895) — C. incrassata (Loisel.) Batt. & Trab. (= V. tenuis).

Like *Cutandia* but panicle branches neither divaricate nor deciduous; lemmas awned.

Species 1. Western Mediterranean. Dry sandy places.

147. Erianthecium Parodi in Not. Mus. La Plata 8: 75 (1943) — E. bulbosum Parodi.

Perennial; culm base bulbous. Panicle dense. Spikelets 3—4-flowered; glumes almost as long as lemma; lemmas coriaceous, rounded, densely pubescent, bidentate with an awn-point from sinus; palea pubescent, the keels long ciliate; stigmas pubescent, terminally exserted. Endosperm soft.

Species 1. Uruguay and southern Brazil. Stony slopes.
The lemma tip and stigmas suggest a relationship with *Sesleria*.

148. Oreochloa Link, Hort. Berol. 1: 44 (1827); Deyl in Op. Bot. Cech. 3: 239—247 (1946) — O. disticha (Wulfen) Link.

Perennial. Raceme unilateral, the imbricate spikelets crowded into an ovoid head, without basal bracts. Spikelets 3—7-flowered; lemmas membranous, keeled, obtuse acute or mucronate. Hilum oval.

Species 4. Southern Europe. Mountain rocks.

149. Sesleria Scop., Fl. Carn. : 189 (1760); Deyl in Op. Bot. Cech. 3: 1—238 (1946) — S. caerulea (L.) Ard. *Psilathera* Link, Hort. Berol. 1: 121 (1827) — P. tenella (Host) Link (= S. ovata). *Diptychum* Dulac, Fl. Hautes-Pyr. : 81 (1867) nom superfl pro Sesleria. *Sesleriella* Deyl in Op. Bot. Cech. 3: 230 (1946) — S. sphaerocephala (Ard.) Deyl.

Perennial. Panicle capitate or sometimes spiciform, its base subtended by usually 2 scarious bracts. Spikelets 2—5-flowered; glumes shorter than or slightly exceeding lowest lemma; lemmas membranous, rounded, 2—5-toothed, the teeth often produced into short awns; palea muticous or 2-awned; stigmas pubescent, terminally exserted. Hilum oval.

Species 27. Europe, especially Balkans. Mountain rocks.
A difficult genus of closely related intergrading species. The subtending bracts

are probably derived from the glumes of a sterile spikelet. A comparable modification occurs in *Ammochloa pungens*, a few of whose outer spikelets are sometimes sterile with reduced florets but retain their full-size glumes.

150. Ammochloa Boiss., Diagn. Pl. Or. 1, 13: 51 (1854) — A. palaestina Boiss. *Cephalochloa* Coss. & Dur. in Ann. Sci. Nat. Bot. sér. 4, 1: 229 (1854) nom nud — A. pungens. *Ammochloa sect Dictyochloa* Murbeck in Acta Univ. Lund 36, 4: 12 (1900) — A. involucrata Murbeck. *Dictyochloa* (Murbeck) E.G. Camus in Act. Congr. Int. Bot. 1900: 344 (1901).

Annual. Panicle capitate, exserted or nestling among basal leaf-sheaths or (*A. involucrata*) enveloped by an inflated net-veined leaf-sheath and falling as a whole. Spikelets 7—15-flowered (*A. involucrata* (1—)2—3-flowered); glumes asymmetrically winged from keel; lemmas coriaceous (*A. involucrata* membranous between nerves) with broad membranous margins, rounded, mucronate; lodicules 0. Caryopsis capped by persistent style base (forming a membranous beak as long as grain in *A. palaestina*); hilum round.

Species 3. Mediterranean and Middle East. Dry sandy places.
Although considerably modified, *A. involucrata* is closely related to the other species and best treated as congeneric with them.

151. Echinaria Desf., Fl. Atlant. 2: 385 (1799) nom conserv non Fabric. (1759) —E. capitata (L.) Desf. *Panicastrella* Moench, Meth.: 205 (1794) nom rejic — P. capitata (L.) Moench.

Annual. Panicle capitate, exserted, prickly. Spikelets (1—)3—4-flowered; glumes mucronate, the lower 2-nerved; lemmas coriaceous, rounded, the 5—7 strong nerves prolonged as spinous awns; palea spinously 2-awned. Hilum oval.

Species 1. Mediterranean and Middle East. Dry open places.

18. HAINARDIEAE

Greuter in Boissiera 13: 178 (1967); Hubbard in Blumea, Suppl. 3: 10—21 (1946).
Pholiurinae Janchen in Phyton 5: 60 (1953) nom nud. *Parapholinae* Caro in Dominguezia 4: 41 (1982).

Ligule membranous, glabrous; leaf-blades not auriculate. Inflorescence a single cylindrical bilateral (except *Narduroides*) raceme, tough or fragile, the spikelets alternate in 2 opposite rows, sessile and ± sunk in the rhachis, broadside on (except *Hainardia*), all alike. Spikelets 1—2-flowered with or without a minute rhachilla extension (*Agropyropsis, Narduroides* 3—6-flowered); glumes appressed to rhachis, subequal and side by side (except *Hainardia*), usually exceeding and covering the floret, coriaceous, strongly 3—7-nerved, obtuse or acute; lemma usually hyaline, 3—5-nerved, entire and awnless (except *Scribneria*). Caryopsis narrowly oblong, the hilum round to narrowly oblong; endosperm soft in *Parapholis, Pholiurus*.

Genera 6; species ± 10. Mediterranean and north-west America.

Anatomy. Non-kranz without microhairs.

Chromosomes. Chromosomes large; basic number 7.

2n	14	28	36
No of species	4	2	2

A small group of genera in which the rhachis internode is progressively integrated with the spikelet. They are best recognized by the collateral glumes, but are otherwise fairly close to annual members of Poeae with a short hilum such as *Catapodium.* They have specialized in adaptation to saline soils.

Comparable rat-tail racemes have evolved many times, and examples are to be found in most tribes. Their similarity in *Hainardia, Henrardia* and *Lepturus* is particularly striking.

1 Glumes 2; spikelets broadside to rhachis:		
2 Spikelets 2—6-flowered:		
3 Raceme unilateral	**152 Narduroides**	
3 Raceme bilateral:		
4 Lemma 5-nerved	**153 Agropyropsis**	
4 Lemma 3-nerved	**154 Pholiurus**	
2 Spikelets 1-flowered:		
5 Lemma awnless	**155 Parapholis**	
5 Lemma awned	**156 Scribneria**	
1 Glume 1; spikelets edgeways to rhachis	**157 Hainardia**	

152. Narduroides Rouy, Fl. France 14: 301 (1913) — N. salzmannii (Boiss.) Rouy.

Annual. Raceme rhachis unilateral, tough, the spikelets disarticulating beneath each floret. Spikelets 4—6-flowered with distinct rhachilla internodes, exserted from the glumes; lemmas thinly coriaceous, faintly 5-nerved.

Species 1. Mediterranean. Dry places.

153. Agropyropsis (Batt. & Trab.) A. Camus in Bull. Soc. Bot. Fr. 82: 11 (1935). *Catapodium sect Agropyropsis* Batt. & Trab., Fl. Alg. Monocot.: 233 (1895) — C. lolium Batt. & Trab.

Perennial. Raceme rhachis fragile. Spikelets 3—6-flowered with distinct rhachilla internodes, shortly exserted from the glumes; lemmas membranous, 5-nerved (or the lowest 1—3-nerved).

Species 1. Algeria. Damp saline soils.

154. Pholiurus Trin., Fund. Agrost.: 131 (1820) — P. pannonicus (Host) Trin.

Annual. Raceme rhachis tough, the spikelets falling entire. Spikelets 2-

flowered, the florets sessile and adjacent; lemmas hyaline, 3-nerved, the lateral nerves extending almost to apex. Endosperm soft.

Species 1. Eastern Europe and central Asia. Saline soils.

155. Parapholis C.E. Hubbard in Blumea, Suppl. 3: 14 (1946); Runemark in Bot. Not. 115: 1—17 (1962) — P. incurva (L.) C.E. Hubbard. *Lepidurus* Janchen in Wiener Bot. Zeitschr. 93: 85 (1944) nom prov — P. incurva.

Annual. Raceme rhachis fragile. Spikelets 1-flowered; lemma hyaline, 3-nerved, the laterals very short. Endosperm liquid.

Species 6. Middle East and Mediterranean, northwards along Atlantic coast of Europe to Baltic; introduced to most other temperate regions. Sandy soils near sea, and salt marshes.
Barely worth distinguishing from *Pholiurus*.

156. Scribneria Hack. in Bot. Gaz. 11: 105 (1886) — S. bolanderi (Thurber) Hack.

Annual. Raceme rhachis tough, the spikelets disarticulating above glumes. Spikelets 1-flowered; lemma membranous, 3-nerved the laterals short, bidentate with a straight awn from sinus; stamen 1.

Species 1. USA, Washington to California. Damp sandy soils in mountains.

157. Hainardia Greuter in Boissiera 13: 178 (1967) — H. cylindrica (Willd.) Greuter.

Annual. Raceme rhachis fragile, the spikelets edgeways on. Spikelets 1-flowered; lower glume suppressed (except terminal spikelet), the upper abaxial; lemma hyaline, 3-nerved, the laterals very short.

Species 1. Mediterranean. Meadows and roadsides in coastal districts.
Commonly known as *Monerma*, but this is actually a superfluous name for *Lepturus*.

19. MELICEAE

Reichenb., Consp. Reg. Veg.: 53 (1828). *Glycerieae* Endl., Fl. Poson.: 117 (1830). *Melicinae* Fries, Summa Veg. Scand.1: 78 (1846). *Glyceriinae* Dumort. in Bull. Soc. Bot. Belg. 7: 67 (1868).

Ligule membranous; sheath margins connate. Inflorescence a panicle or raceme, the spikelets all alike. Spikelets of several to many fertile florets (except *Triniochloa*, some *Melica*) with imperfect florets above, these distinct or more often gathered into a clump of rudimentary lemmas, laterally compressed (except *Triniochloa*), disarticulating below each floret (except *Lycochloa, Melica*);

glumes persistent, not exceeding adjacent lemma (except *Triniochloa*, some *Melica*), often papery; lemmas herbaceous to coriaceous, distinctly 5—9(—13)-nerved, rounded on back, with or without a straight or curved awn (*Triniochloa* geniculate) from tip or back; lodicules 2, usually connate, short, fleshy, truncate. Caryopsis ellipsoid to terete; hilum linear.

Genera 8; species ± 130. Temperate regions.

Anatomy. Non-kranz without microhairs.

Chromosomes. Chromosomes small; basic number variable, mainly 9 or 10.

2n	18	20	36	40
No of species	35	16	8	14

A little group of genera (fig 13) with variable external morphology, but united by their connate sheath margins, peculiar lodicules and atypical chromosome number. Despite the chromosomes, they seem derived from, rather than ancestral to, Poeae. They occupy a wide range of habitats, but generally omit the competitive environment of plains and steppe.

The spikelets are easily confused with Poeae; the clavate rhachilla termination is sometimes helpful, but it is often necessary to seek confirmation from the lodicules.

1   Floret callus glabrous:
  2   Palea keels dorsally notched or awned   **159 Pleuropogon**
  2   Palea keels entire:
    3   Upper glume 1-nerved   **158 Glyceria**
    3   Upper glume 3—5-nerved:
      4   Lemma not flabellate; palea unlobed   **160 Melica**
      4   Lemma flabellate; palea lobed   **161 Anthochloa**
1   Floret callus hairy:
  5   Spikelets several-flowered:
    6   Callus oblong, blunt:
      7   Rhachilla fragile; awn subterminal   **162 Schizachne**
      7   Rhachilla tough; awn clearly dorsal   **163 Lycochloa**
    6   Callus linear, pungent   **164 Streblochaete**
  5   Spikelets 1-flowered   **165 Triniochloa**

158. Glyceria R. Br., Prodr. Fl. Nov. Holl.: 179 (1810) nom conserv; Church in Amer. J. Bot. 36: 155—165 (1949) — G. fluitans (L.) R. Br. *Nevroloma* Raf. in J. Phys. Chim. 89: 106 (1819) — Briza canadensis Michaux. *Hydrochloa* Hartm., Gen. Gram. Scand.: 8 (1819) non P. Beauv. (1812), nom superfl pro Glyceria. *Poa sect Hydropoa* Dumort., Obs. Gram. Belg.: 111 (1824) — P. aquatica L. (= G. maxima). *Exydra* Endl., Fl. Poson.: 119 (1830) — E. aquatica (L.) Endl. (= G. maxima). *Devauxia* Kunth, Enum. Pl. 1: 367 (1833) non R. Br. (1810), in syn sub G. fluitans. *Heleochloa* Fries, Fl. Scan.: 202 (1835) nom nud non Roem. (1807) — G. maxima. *Plotia* Steud., Nom. Bot. ed. 2, 2: 356 (1841) nom nud non Adans. (1763) — G. obtusa. *Porroteranthe* Steud., Syn. Pl. Glum. 1: 287 (1854) — P. drummondii Steud. *Hemibromus* Steud. l.c.: 317 — H. japonicus Steud. (= G. acutiflora). *Hydropoa* (Dumort.) Dumort. in Bull. Soc. Bot. Belg. 7: 67 (1868) nom superfl pro Exydra.

Perennial; leaves with cross-nerves in the larger species. Panicle copious, or narrow and almost raceme-like. Spikelets several—many-flowered, terminating in a small floret (this clavate in *G. melicaria*); glumes very small to almost as long as adjacent lemma and of similar texture, 1-nerved; lemma herbaceous, membranous or thinly coriaceous, 5—11-nerved, acute, obtuse or 3—5-toothed; stamens 2—3. x = 10 (reports of 2n = 28 are unconfirmed).

Species ± 40. Temperate regions throughout the world. Wet places and shallow water.

A homogeneous genus often difficult to distinguish from *Puccinellia*, its 1-nerved upper glume being the most obvious difference. Species with plump ovate spikelets could be mistaken for *Briza*.

159. Pleuropogon R. Br., Chlor. Melv.: 31 (1823); Benson in Amer. J. Bot. 28: 358—360 (1941) — P. sabinii R. Br. *Lophochlaena* Nees in Ann. Nat. Hist. 1: 283 (1838); Löve & Löve in Bol. Soc. Brot. ser.2, 53: 563—585 (1980) — L. californica Nees. *Lepitoma* Steud., Nom. Bot. ed. 2, 2: 29 (1841) nom nud — P. californicus.

Perennial (*P. californicus* weakly so). Raceme open with large, distant and often deflexed spikelets on short pedicels. Spikelets several—many-flowered, terminating in a small floret; glumes membranous, the upper 1(—3)-nerved, erose; lemmas membranous to thinly coriaceous, 7-nerved, obtuse and erose to irregularly toothed, with or without a terminal awn; palea keels narrowly winged, each bearing a dorsal tooth or awn (often 2 awns in *P. sabinii*). x = 9, 10.

Species 5. Circumarctic, extending down Pacific coast of America to California; also in Russian Altai. Wet meadows and stream banks.

There is a chromosomal difference between Arctic (2n = 40) and Pacific coast (2n = 18, 36) species, but sufficient similarity in their unusual inflorescence and palea to afford no justification for splitting the genus.

160. Melica L., Sp. Pl.: 66 (1753); Hempel in Feddes Rep. 81: 131—145 (1970), 657—686 (1971) & 84: 533—568 (1973) — M. nutans L. *Dalucum* Adans., Fam. Pl. 2: 34, 548 (1763) nom superfl pro Melica. *Beckeria* Bernh., Syst. Verz. Pfl.: 20, 40 (1800) — B. ciliata (L.) Bernh. *Claudia* Opiz in Lotos 3: 67 (1853) nom superfl pro Beckeria. *Melica subgen Bromelica* Thurber in Watson, Bot. Calif. 2: 304 (1880) —M. geyeri Munro. *Verinea* Merino in An. Soc. Esp. Hist. Nat. 28: 8 (1899) non Pomel (1860) — V. pterostachys Merino (= M. ciliata). *Bromelica* (Thurber) Farwell in Rhodora 21: 77 (1919).

Perennial; lowest culm internode often thickened into a storage organ and sometimes bulbous; leaf-blades occasionally with cross-nerves. Panicle loose or dense, usually narrow, often scanty and sometimes raceme-like. Spikelets 1—several-flowered, terminating in a clavate clump of 2—3 rudiments or rarely in a little floret, disarticulating below glumes or below lowest floret, reluctantly between florets; glumes shorter than lemma or as long as spikelet, papery with hyaline tips, often colourful (the lower much enlarged in *M. brasiliana* and allies), 3—5-nerved, obtuse or acute; lemmas mostly coriaceous but sometimes membranous, often hyaline towards tip, 5—9(—13)-nerved, notched obtuse or acute, sometimes mucronate (*M. aristata, M. harfordii, M. smithii* straight awned from below tip); floret callus glabrous. x = 9.

Species ± 80. Temperate regions throughout the world, except Australia. Woodland shade to dry stony slopes.

A very variable genus, divisible into 2 subgenera and many sections:

Spikelets mostly 2—6-flowered, disarticulating above glumes; pedicel glabrous; basal internode thickened (M. bulbosa)   Subgen *Bromelica*
Spikelets mostly 1—2-flowered, disarticulating below glumes; pedicel hairy; basal internode not thickened (M. nutans)   Subgen *Melica*

It is usually easy enough to recognize by its papery glumes, clavate rudiments and unusual disarticulation. However, none of these characters is entirely reliable, and some primitive N. American members of Subgen *Bromelica* are very similar to *Festuca*; the lodicules then provide the best distinguishing character. The most flamboyant variation occurs in the Eurasian *M. ciliata* group with its long-hairy spikelets; and the S. American *M. brasiliana* group with its huge flabellate lower glume. *M. sarmentosa* can climb to a height of 6 m with the aid of filiform retrorsely scabrid leaf tips.

161. Anthochloa Nees & Meyen in Meyen, Reise 2: 14 (1834) — A. lepidula Nees & Meyen.

Dwarf perennial. Panicle short, dense, embraced by subtending sheath. Spikelets several-flowered, terminating in a clavate clump of rudiments; glumes shorter than spikelet, orbicular, hyaline, the upper 3-nerved; lemmas flabellate, 5-nerved, herbaceous below, broadly expanded and hyaline above; palea expanded into 4 hyaline lobes. 2n = 42.

Species 1. Peru to Chile. High montane region.
A derivative of *Melica* with grossly broadened papery white lemmas.

162. Schizachne Hack. in Feddes Rep. 7: 322 (1909); Swallen in J. Wash. Acad. Sci. 18: 203—206 (1928); Koyama & Kawano in Canad. J. Bot. 42: 860—862 (1964) — S. fauriei Hack. (= S. purpurascens).

Perennial. Panicle scanty. Spikelets several-flowered, terminating in 1 or a pair of sterile florets; glumes membranous, the lower 3- the upper 5-nerved, acute; lemmas herbaceous, 7-nerved, straight awned from just below bifid tip; floret callus oblong, bearded; palea keels ciliate above. 2n = 20.

Species 1. North America; Urals to Japan. Woodland.
Differs from *Melica subgen Bromelica* mainly in the hairy callus.

163. Lycochloa Samuels. in Ark. Bot. 25, 8: 4 (1933) — L. avenacea Samuels.

Perennial. Raceme lax, the spikelets distant and shortly pedicelled. Spikelets 2-flowered plus a narrowly lanceolate cluster of rudiments, disarticulating above glumes only; glumes papery, 5-nerved, acute; lemmas coriaceous, 11-nerved these forming ribs, bidentate, with a curved awn from upper third of back; floret callus bearded.

Species 1. Syria. Among rocks.
An evident derivative from *Schizachne.*

164. Streblochaete Pilger in Bot. Jahrb. 37, Beibl. 85: 61 (1906); Tateoka in Bot. Mag. Tokyo 78: 289—293 (1965) — S. nutans Pilger (= S. longiarista). *Koordersiochloa* Merr. in Philipp. J. Sci. Bot. 12: 67 (1917) — K. javanica Merr. (= S. longiarista). *Pseudostreptogyne* A. Camus in Bull. Soc. Bot. Fr. 77: 476 (1930) — P. richardii A. Camus (= S. longiarista).

Perennial. Panicle narrow. Spikelets several-flowered, terminating in a lanceolate cluster of rudiments; glumes membranous, 3—5-nerved, acute; lemmas herbaceous, 7-nerved, bidentate, with a filiform awn from upper third of back, this coiling and entanglng its neighbours; floret callus pubescent, pungent; lodicules free. 2n = 20.

Species 1. Tropical Africa, Réunion, Indonesia, Philippines. Glades in montane forest.
Coiling of the awn draws out the floret and exposes its callus; this readily adheres to animals and a tangle of florets is carried away with it.

165. Triniochloa Hitchc. in Contrib. U.S. Nat. Herb. 17: 303 (1913); Reeder in Amer. J. Bot. 55: 735 (1968) — T. stipoides (Kunth) Hitchc.

Perennial. Panicle open. Spikelets 1-flowered without rhachilla extension, dorsally compressed; glumes membranous, shorter than or equalling spikelet, 1-nerved, acuminate; lemma subcoriaceous, 5-nerved, setaceously bilobed, bearing a geniculate awn with twisted column from upper ¼ of back; floret callus blunt, bearded; palea sulcate with closely spaced keels, these not covered by lemma margins, setaceously bilobed. 2n = 32.

Species 4. Mexico to Bolivia. Stony hillsides.
An odd little genus imitating *Stipa*, yet the entire sheaths and melicoid lodicules indicate a relationship with *Schizachne.*

20. BRYLKINIEAE

Tateoka in Canad. J. Bot. 38: 962 (1960). *Brylkiniinae* Ohwi in Acta Phytotax. Geobot. 10: 107 (1941).

Ligule membranous; sheath margins connate. Inflorescence a raceme, the spikelets all alike. Spikelets of 1 fertile floret with 2 sterile lemmas below and a short rhachilla extension above, laterally compressed, falling entire together with the pedicel; glumes shorter than lemma, herbaceous, 3—5-nerved, acuminate; lemmas thinly coriaceous, 5—7-nerved, keeled, the sterile acuminate, the fertile terminally awned; palea keels closely adjacent; lodicules 2, free, well-developed, hyaline, rectangular. Caryopsis narrowly ellipsoid, with a glossy umbonate cap; hilum linear.
Genus 1; species 1. China and Japan.

Anatomy. Non-kranz without microhairs.

Chromosomes. 2n = 40

An oddment which is undoubtedly pooid, but its combination of sterile florets, chromosome number, large lodicules and ovary cap are awkward to accommodate. It seems best to treat it as a separate tribe allied to Meliceae.

166. Brylkinia Schmidt in Mém. Acad. Sci. Pétersb. sér. 7, 12: 199 (1868) — B. caudata (Munro) Schmidt.

Perennial. Description as for tribe.

Species 1. China and Japan. Woodland.

21. AVENEAE

Dumort., Obs. Gram. Belg. : 82 (1824). *Agrostideae* Dumort. l.c. 83. *Phleeae* Dumort. l.c. *Phalarideae* Dumort., Anal. Fam.: 64 (1829). *Anthoxantheae* Endl., Fl. Poson.: 113 (1830). *Alopecureae* Bluff, Nees & Schauer, Comp. Fl. Germ. ed 2, 1: 47 (1836). *Airopsideae* Gren. & Godr., Fl. France 3: 435 (1855). *Triseteae* Gren. & Godr. l.c. *Gaudinieae* Rouy, Fl. France 14: 336 (1913). *Cinneae* Ohwi in Bot. Mag. Tokyo 55: 360 (1941). *Beckmannieae* (Nevski) Dostal, Kvetena CSR: 1986 (1950). *Graphephoreae* (Asch. & Graeb.) Hylander, Nord. Karlvaxtfl. 1: 278 (1953).

Ligule membranous. Inflorescence a panicle (racemes in *Beckmannia, Duthiea, Gaudinia, Mibora*; and sometimes in *Helictotrichon, Metcalfia*), the spikelets all alike (except some *Phalaris*). Spikelets of 1—several fertile florets, laterally compressed (*Euthryptochloa, Zingeria* dorsally), disarticulating below each floret though with numerous exceptions; glumes persistent (except *Ventenata*), usually longer than adjacent lemmas and often as long as spikelet, commonly membranous and shining with thin hyaline margins; lemmas hyaline to coriaceous often with thin shiny margins, 5—11-nerved (3-nerved in *Airopsis, Antinoria, Chaetopogon, Cinna, Euthryptochloa, Limnodea, Periballia, Zingeria,* and in some species of *Agrostis, Calamagrostis, Koeleria, Phleum, Trisetaria*), typically with a dorsal awn (but see Duthieinae) this often geniculate with twisted column; lodicules 2 (except *Metcalfia, Stephanachne*); stigmas 2 (except *Pseudodanthonia*). Caryopsis mostly ellipsoid; hilum usually round or oval; endosperm sometimes soft, occasionally liquid.

Genera 57; species ± 1050. Temperate and cold regions.

Anatomy. Non-kranz without microhairs.

Chromosomes. Chromosomes large; basic number 7. Aberrant basic numbers are *Airopsis, Antinoria, Periballia* 4 & 9; *Anthoxanthum* 5; *Zingeria* 2.

2n	10	14	26	28	35	42	56	70	84	98
No of species	6	159	7	206	9	95	57	12	5	6

The tribe is characterized by long glumes of a somewhat scarious texture (contrasting with the short herbaceous or membranous glumes of Poeae) and by

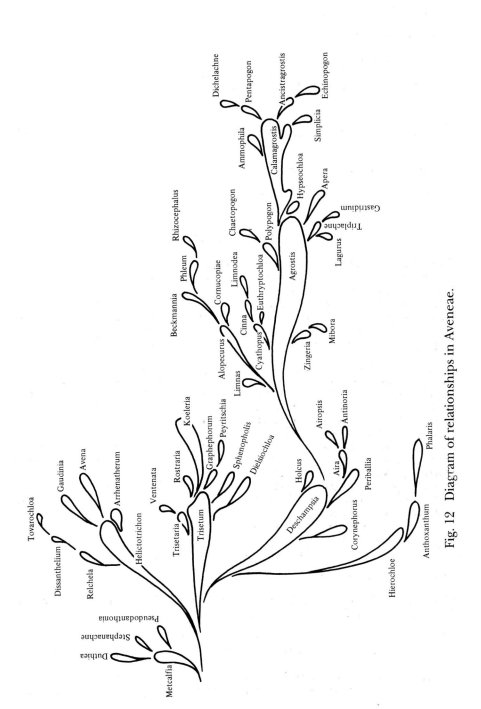

Fig. 12 Diagram of relationships in Aveneae.

geniculate dorsal awns, but these characters do not necessarily occur together. A curious feature is the occurrence of soft or liquid endosperm, the latter remaining fluid in herbarium specimens for 50 years or more (Terrell in Bull. Torr. Bot. Cl. 98: 264—268, 1971). It has a high content of lipids, with obvious adaptive implications for, weight for weight, lipids have about twice the energy value of carbohydrates. Soft endosperms are also found in a few genera of Poeae and Hainardieae; lipids in firm endosperms are more widely distributed, though confined to Pooideae (Rosengurtt et al in Adansonia sér 2, 11: 383—391, 1971).

The endosperm, the elaborate awn, and its unusual dorsal position all suggest that the tribe is more advanced than Poeae. It is somewhat heterogeneous, and has been divided into 4 facies designated as subtribes. Apart from the anomalous Duthieinae, these represent a progression from several-flowered to 1-flowered spikelets (fig 12). There is the usual contrast between large perennial grassland genera and small annual Mediterranean genera, though less pronounced than in Poeae.

Problems of identification mainly concern awnless species with atypically short glumes (notably *Koeleria*), which are difficult to distinguish from Poeae. *Muhlenbergia* is the most troublesome stranger, and there seems to be no easy way to exclude it.

1 Lemma awned from sinus of bilobed tip:
  2 Spikelets falling entire   *558 Garnotia*
  2 Spikelets breaking up at maturity:
    3 Floret callus pungent   *281 Anisopogon*
    3 Floret callus obtuse or acute:
      4 Lemma glabrous or hairy, but not conspicuously hairier at the top:
        5 Inflorescence a spiciform or capitate panicle; lemmas 3—5-toothed
                                         149 Sesleria
        5 Inflorescence a scanty panicle or raceme:
          6 Lodicules 3; stigmas 2, sessile:
            7 Spikelets 1-flowered   *99 Trikeraia*
            7 Spikelets several-flowered   **167 Metcalfia**
          6 Lodicules 2 or absent:
            8 Stigmas 3, sessile   **168 Pseudodanthonia**
            8 Stigmas 2, raised upon a style   **170 Duthiea**
      4 Lemma with a crown or fringe of hairs arising from base of lobes:
        9 Spikelets 1-flowered   **169 Stephanachne**
        9 Spikelets several-flowered   *275 Monachather*
1 Lemma awned from back, from tip, or awnless:
  10 Spikelets with 2 or more fertile florets:
    11 Ovary hairy:
      12 Inflorescence a panicle or raceme with tough axis:
        13 Perennial:
          14 Lemmas awned   **171 Helictotrichon**
          14 Lemmas awnless   **175 Relchela**
        13 Annual   **173 Avena**
      12 Inflorescence a fragile raceme   **174 Gaudinia**
    11 Ovary glabrous (except *Trisetum glaciale*):
      15 Lemmas keeled:
        16 Lemmas 3-nerved, enclosing palea; dwarf plants   **176 Dissanthelium**
        16 Lemmas 5- or more-nerved, rarely 3-nerved and then palea gaping:
          17 Spikelets breaking up at maturity:
            18 Plants perennial:

19 Lemma dorsally awned, the palea gaping:
  20 Spikelets disarticulating between florets (if awned from below middle see *184 Peyritschia*)   **178 Trisetum**
  20 Spikelet disarticulating only above glumes, the upper florets sterile   **186 Dielsiochloa**
19 Lemma awnless or with a subapical awn-point:
  21 Panicle spiciform, the branches hispidulous; palea gaping   **181 Koeleria**
  21 Panicle open or contracted, the branches scaberulous; palea not gaping:
    22 Lemma obtuse to acute   **183 Graphephorum**
    22 Lemma bilobed   **184 Peyritschia**
18 Plants annual:
  23 Lemmas bisetulate, sometimes minutely so, or bidentate   **179 Trisetaria**
  23 Lemmas obtuse to acute   **182 Rostraria**
17 Spikelets falling entire at maturity   **185 Sphenopholis**
15 Lemmas rounded on back:
24 Awn with a ring of hairs at junction of column and limb   **189 Corynephorus**
24 Awn without a ring of hairs or spikelets muticous:
  25 Plants perennial, tufted (if reed-like see *290 Arundo*):
    26 Floret callus pungent, or lemmas strongly ribbed, or apical florets forming a clavate clump (*Streblochaete, Lycochloa, Melica*)
      Meliceae (p 111)
    26 Floret callus blunt, lemmas not strongly ribbed, apical florets not clumped (if lemma with terminal awn see *104 Festuca livida*):
      27 Lemmas herbaceous to subcoriaceous, stoutly awned, well exserted from glumes   **171 Helictotrichon**
      27 Lemmas membranous to cartilaginous, inconspicuously awned, seldom much exserted   **187 Deschampsia**
  25 Plants annual (*Antinoria* sometimes perennial), but if sterile spikelets present see *117 Cynosurus*:
    28 Lowest floret persistent   **180 Ventenata**
    28 Lowest floret deciduous like the rest:
      29 Inflorescence a raceme (*Lolium, Loliolum*)   *Poeae* (p 87)
      29 Inflorescence a panicle:
        30 Florets separated by an internode:
          31 Lemma bisetulate, sometimes minutely so   **179 Trisetaria**
          31 Lemma obtuse to 4-toothed:
            32 Rachilla extension present, hairy; lemmas dorsally awned   **187 Deschampsia**
          32 Rachilla extension absent:
            33 Glumes a little shorter than floret   **190 Periballia**
            33 Glumes exceeding and enclosing florets   **193 Antinoria**
        30 Florets arising at about the same level:
          34 Lemma awned   **191 Aira**
          34 Lemma awnless   **192 Airopsis**
10 Spikelets with 1 fertile floret:
35 Inflorescence of several racemes along a central axis   **221 Beckmannia**
35 Inflorescence a panicle, or very rarely a single raceme:

36　Fertile floret accompanied by ♂ or barren florets:
37　Spikelets 2-flowered:
38　Spikelet disarticulating above glumes; lower floret ♂
172 Arrhenatherum
38　Spikelet disarticulating below glumes; upper floret ♂　**188 Holcus**
37　Spikelets 3-flowered, the 2 lower ♂ or barren, these sometimes obscure in *Phalaris*:
39　Lower lemmas well developed:
40　Glumes subequal; lower florets ♂; lodicules 2　　**194 Hierochloe**
40　Glumes unequal; lower florets reduced to empty lemmas (rarely ♂), awned; lodicules 0　　**195 Anthoxanthum**
39　Lower lemmas rudimentary, awnless　　**196 Phalaris**
36　Fertile floret solitary, with or without a rhachilla extension:
41　Rhachilla terminating in a little clump of sterile lemmas　*160 Melica*
41　Rhachilla, when present, usually naked but never as above:
42　Spikelets disarticulating above glumes:
43　Lodicules fleshy, truncate:
44　Lemma 3-nerved, laterally compressed, with or without a terminal awn　*381 Muhlenbergia*
44　Lemma 5-nerved, dorsally compressed, with dorsal geniculate awn
165 Triniochloa
43　Lodicules thin:
45　Plants perennial:
46　Spikelet neither fusiform nor with a long wavy awn:
47　Lemma 0—3-awned:
48　Awn dorsal or absent:
49　Palea 2-keeled:
50　Floret hyaline to cartilaginous, its callus beardless or rarely with hairs up to ½ its length:
51　Lemma keeled or upper glume 3-nerved (if lemma tip setiform see *290 Arundo*)　　*Poeae* (p 87)
51　Lemma rounded; upper glume 1-nerved　　**197 Agrostis**
50　Floret firmly membranous to coriaceous, rarely hyaline and then with a callus beard as long as itself:
52　Lemma rounded to moderately keeled:
53　Ovary glabrous　　**198 Calamagrostis**
53　Ovary hairy on tip; lemma crustaceous, awnless
175 Relchela
52　Lemma strongly laterally compressed and keeled; panicle spiciform; leaf-blades convolute, rigid　**199 Ammophila**
49　Palea 1-keeled; glumes much shorter than floret; lemma 3-nerved　　**200 Simplicia**
48　Awn apical or subapical, stiff, straight or hooked (if lemma deeply bilobed see *170 Duthiea*):
54　Panicle contracted　　**201 Ancistragrostis**
54　Panicle spiciform to capitate　　**202 Echinopogon**
47　Lemma 5-awned　　**203 Pentapogon**
46　Spikelet fusiform with a long wavy awn 2—6 times its own length; callus pubescent　　**204 Dichelachne**
45　Plants annual:
55　Inflorescence a panicle:
56　Panicle spiciform or capitate:

a. DUTHIEINAE Potztal in Willdenowia 5: 472 (1969).

Spikelets of 1—several fertile florets; lemmas rounded on back, bidentate to bifid, geniculately awned from sinus. Hilum linear.

The occurrence of 3 lodicules and 3 stigmas suggests that this is the most primitive subtribe of Aveneae. The spikelets imitate Arundineae, but are contradicted by the membranous ligules and thin lodicules.

167. Metcalfia Conert in Willdenowia 2: 417 (1960); Tateoka in Bot. Mag. Tokyo 77: 69—72 (1964) — M. mexicana (Scribn.) Conert. *Helictotrichon subgen Danthoniastrum* Holub in Nemec, Klastersky et al, P.M. Opiz Bedeutung Pflanzentax.: 124 (1958) — H. compactum (Boiss. & Heldr.) Henr. *Danthoniastrum* (Holub) Holub in Fol. Geobot. Phytotax. 5: 435 (1970).

Perennial. Panicle narrow, scanty, often reduced to a ± bilateral raceme. Spikelets several-flowered; glumes unequal, shorter than lemma to as long as spikelet, membranous to herbaceous, 5—9-nerved, with scaberulous keel; lemmas thinly coriaceous, hairy below, bifid; lodicules 3; stigmas 2, plumose, sessile. Ovary hairy.

Species 2. Balkans and Caucasus; Mexico. Stony hills.
Sometimes mistaken for *Danthonia*, but the ligule is membranous, the embryo oryzoid and leaf anatomy pooid (Tateoka l.c.). In facies, and particularly in the hairy ovary, there is a resemblance to *Helictotrichon*. Its two species seem to be congeneric despite their wide geographic separation.

168. Pseudodanthonia Bor & Hubbard in Kew Bull. 12: 425 (Jan. 1958) —P. himalaica (Hook.f.) Bor & Hubbard. *Sinochasea* Keng in J. Wash. Acad. Sci. 48: 115 (May 1958) —S. trigyna Keng.

Perennial. Like *Metcalfia* except (*P. trigyna* 1-flowered): lodicules 2; stigmas 3, plumose, sessile.

Species 2. NW Himalaya and western China. Mountain slopes.

169. Stephanachne Keng in Contrib. Biol. Lab. Sci. Soc. China, Bot. 9: 134 (1934) — S. nigrescens Keng. *Pappagrostis* Roshev. in Kom., Fl. SSSR 2: 749 (1934) — P. pappophorea (Hack.) Roshev.

Perennial. Panicle contracted to spiciform. Spikelets 1-flowered without rhachilla extension; glumes subequal, exceeding lemma, membranous to herbaceous, 1—5-nerved, with scaberulous keel; lemma thinly coriaceous, hairy, bifid, the lobes acuminate or produced into an awn and with a crown of long hairs from their base; palea hairy on back; lodicules 2 (*S. nigrescens* 3); stigmas 2, plumose, sessile. Ovary glabrous.

Species 2. Central Asia and western China. Hill slopes.

170. Duthiea Hack. in Verh. Bot. Ges. Wien 45: 200 (1895); Bor in Kew Bull. 8: 547—553 (1954) — D. bromoides Hack. *Triavenopsis* Candargy in Arch. Biol. Veg. 1: 64 (1901) — T. brachypodium Candargy. *Thrixgyne* Keng in Sunyatsenia 6: 80 (1941) — T. dura Keng (= D. brachypodium).

Perennial. Inflorescence scanty, reduced to a compact or elongated, unilateral raceme, the lowest pedicel and rarely some of the others subtended by a little scarious bract. Spikelets 2—3-flowered (*D. oligostachya* 1-flowered); glumes sub-equal, shorter than lemma to as long as spikelet, herbaceous with hyaline margins, 5—9-nerved, rounded on back; lemmas membranous to coriaceous, bidentate to bifid; palea bisetulate or not; lodicules 0; stigmas 2, papillose, borne on a long pubescent style. Ovary hairy; caryopsis tipped by a subulate beak formed from persistent style.

Species 3. Himalayas, from Afghanistan to western China. Mountain slopes.
Evidently related to *Metcalfia* despite the unusual ovary. The homology of the inflorescence bract is uncertain, but it may represent a reduced panicle branch.

b. AVENINAE Presl, Rel. Haenk. 1: 246 (1830). *Airinae* Fries, Summa Veg. Scand. 1: 77 (1846). *Holcinae* Dumort. in Bull. Soc. Bot. Belg. 7: 68 (1868). *Graphephorinae* Asch. & Graeb., Syn. Mitteleur. Fl. 2, 1: 342 (1900). *Koeleriinae* Asch. & Graeb. l.c. *Airopsidinae* Rouy, Fl. France 14: 99 (1913). *Corynephorinae* Jirasek & Chrtek in Preslia 34: 381 (1962). *Aristaveninae* Albers & Butzin in Willdenowia 8: 82 (1977).

Spikelets with 2—several fertile florets plus a rudimentary floret or rhachilla extension (except *Arrhenatherum, Aira* & allies, *Holcus, Trisetaria linearis*); glumes equal or unequal, the upper sometimes a little shorter than lemma and seldom enclosing spikelet.

A large subtribe broadly divisible into 3 groups of genera:
Helictotrichon group. Ovary hairy.
Trisetum group. Lemma keeled; palea often gaping free from lemma, hyaline, and imparting a silvery sheen to the spikelet.
Deschampsia group. Lemma rounded; palea not gaping; spikelets 2-flowered.

171. Helictotrichon Schult., Syst. Veg. Mant. 3: 526 (1827); Holub in Nemec, Klastersky et al, P.M. Opiz Bedeutung Pflanzentax.: 103—133 (1958); Sevenster & Veldkamp in Blumea 28: 329—342 (1983) — H. sempervirens (Vill.) Pilger. *Danthorhiza* Ten., Fl. Nap. 1: x (1810) nom gen-sp inval — D. versicolor (Vill.) Ten. *Trisetum sect Avenula* Dumort., Obs. Gram. Belg.: 122 (1824) — T. pratense (L.) Dumort. *Avena sect Avenastrum* Koch, Syn. Fl. Germ.: 795 (1837) non Dumort. (1827), nom superfl pro sect Avenula. *Amphibromus* Nees in London J. Bot. 2: 420 (1843); Swallen in Amer. J. Bot. 18: 411—415 (1931) — A. neesii Steud. *Avenastrum* Opiz, Seznam: 20 (1852) based on sect Avenastrum Koch, which included A. sempervirens therefore nom superfl pro Helictotrichon. *Heuffelia* Schur, Enum. Pl. Transsilv.: 760 (1866) non Opiz (1845), nom superfl pro Helictotrichon. *Avenula* (Dumort.) Dumort. in Bull. Soc. Bot. Belg. 7: 68 (1868). *Stipavena* Vierh. in Halac. in Verh. Bot. Ges. Wien 56: 369 (1906) nom superfl pro Helictotrichon. *Avenochloa* Holub in Acta Horti Bot. Prag. 1962: 82 (1963) nom superfl pro Avenula.

Perennial. Panicle usually narrow and erect, sometimes lax, rarely simple and raceme-like. Spikelets with 2—several fertile florets plus 1—2 reduced florets, disarticulating above glumes and usually also between florets, the rhachilla pilose; glumes unequal the upper usually shorter than spikelet and often shorter than lemma, hyaline to membranous, 1—5-nerved with scaberulous keel; lemmas firmly membranous to coriaceous, rounded or weakly keeled, glabrous (some S. American species hairy), bidentate, rarely 4-dentate or bisetulate, dorsally awned from above the middle, the awn usually geniculate, rarely recurved or straight; palea enclosed by lemma. Ovary hairy (Australian species glabrous); hilum linear; endosperm sometimes liquid.

Species ± 100. Mainly temperate Eurasia, but extending across the tropical mountains to temperate regions throughout the world. Dry hillsides; meadows and wood margins; a few species in or near water.

A fairly uniform genus in Eurasia, though sometimes partitioned on the basis of anatomical characters (Potztal in Bot. Jahrb. 75: 321—332, 1951; Holub in Acta Horti Bot. Prag. 1962: 75—86, 1963). It is more variable in the southern hemisphere, and the Australian species are sometimes segregated as *Amphibromus* on account of their glabrous ovary, but this alone seems an inadequate basis for generic separation.

172. Arrhenatherum P. Beauv., Ess. Agrost.: 55 (1812) — A. avenaceum P. Beauv. (= A. elatius). *Thorea* Rouy, Fl. France 14: 142 (1913) non Bory (1808) — T. longifolia (Thore) Rouy. *Pseudarrhenatherum* Rouy in Bull. Soc. Bot. Fr. 68: 401 (1921); Romero Zarco in Lagascalia 13: 255—273 (1985) — nom nov pro Thorea. *Thoreochloa* Holub in Acta Univ. Carol. Biol. 1962: 154 (1963) nom superfl pro Pseudarrhenatherum.

Perennial; basal internodes often swollen into globose corms. Panicle moderately dense. Spikelets 2-flowered with or without an additional rudiment, the lower floret ♂ and stoutly awned, the upper bisexual and weakly awned or awnless (rarely a few spikelets with both florets bisexual and alike), disarticulating above glumes and falling together; glumes unequal the upper as long as spikelet, 1—3-nerved with scaberulous keel; lemmas firmly membranous to subcoriaceous, rounded, bidenticulate, at least the lower geniculately awned from the back. Ovary hairy; hilum linear.

Species 6. Europe, Mediterranean and Middle East. Weedy places and dry grassland.

A segregate from *Helictotrichon* with dimorphic florets. However, the degree of dimorphism varies considerably, even within the same panicle, and the distinction is barely tenable.

173. Avena L., Sp. Pl.: 79 (1753); Malzew in Trudy Prikl. Bot. Genet. Selek., Suppl. 38: 1—522 (1930); Baum in Canad. J. Bot. 46: 122—132 (1968) & Oats, Wild and Cultivated (1977) — A. sativa L. *Preissia* Opiz, Seznam: 79 (1852) nom nud non Corda (1829) — A. strigosa. *Anelytrum* Hack. in Feddes Rep. 8: 519 (1910) — A. avenaceum Hack. (= deformed Avena fatua).

Annual. Panicle loose, nodding. Spikelets large (10—40 mm), 2—several-flowered, disarticulating below each floret or only above glumes (cultivated species persistent); glumes herbaceous to membranous, usually equal and as long as spikelet (shorter than lemma in *A. nuda*, some *A. sativa*), 3—11-nerved, rounded on back, smooth; lemmas coriaceous (*A. nuda*, some *A. sativa* membranous), rounded, bidentate to biaristulate the latter rarely with 2 additional setae, geniculately awned from the back (awn often reduced or absent in cultivated species); floret callus, when deciduous, acute to pungent. Ovary hairy; hilum linear.

Species ± 25. Mainly Mediterranean and Middle East, extending to northern Europe, and widely introduced to other temperate regions; 2 species in Ethiopia. Weedy places. There are 6—7 cultivated species including *A. sativa* (Oats). The genus first appears in archaeological records from the Middle East as a wheat field weed, but as agriculture spread northwards its adaptability to the damp climate of NW Europe led to its domestication there in about 2000 BC (Sampson in Bot. Mus. Leafl. Harvard 16: 265—303, 1954). Meanwhile the weedy forms continued to evolve, and *A. fatua* (Wild Oats) is now one of the world's worst weeds.

A uniform genus, varying mainly in lemma tip and mode of spikelet disarticulation. It is distinguished from *Helictotrichon* by the annual habit and smooth rounded glumes; *H. macrostachyum* is intermediate.

174. Gaudinia P. Beauv., Ess. Agrost.: 95 (1812) — G. fragilis (L.) P. Beauv. *Arthrostachya* Link, Hort. Berol.1: 151 (1827) — A. coarctata Link. *Falimiria* Reichenb., Consp. Reg. Veg.: 54 (1828) nom superfl pro Arthrostachya. *Cyclichnium* Dulac, Fl. Hautes-Pyr.: 68 (1867) nom superfl pro Gaudinia.

Annual or biennial. Inflorescence a fragile bilateral raceme, fracturing at base of each internode, the spikelets sessile in opposite rows and broadside on. Spikelets several-flowered, falling entire; glumes equal or not, shorter than lemma, herbaceous, with 3—7(—11) ribbed nerves; lemmas thinly coriaceous, weakly keeled, acute, with dorsal geniculate awn (*G. hispanica* awnless). Ovary hairy; hilum round; endosperm liquid.

Species 4. Mediterranean. Weedy places.
The genus has an unusual inflorescence for Aveneae, but the geniculate awn and compound starch grains exclude it from Triticeae. Awnless *G. hispanica*, a difficult species to identify, is linked to the genus by shortly awned *G. maroccana*.

175. Relchela Steud., Syn. Pl. Glum. 1: 101 (1854), also as *Lechlera* in note; Muñoz in J. Arn. Arb. 22: 209—218 (1941) — R. panicoides Steud.

Perennial. Panicle contracted. Spikelets 1—2-flowered plus brief rhachilla extension, the rhachilla pubescent; glumes equal, longer than lemma, membranous; lemmas crustaceous, rounded, obtuse; palea coriaceous, covered by overlapping margins of lemma; callus pubesent. Ovary hairy on top; hilum oval; endosperm solid.

Species 1. Argentina and Chile. Woodland margins.
A genus of uncertain affinity, but the hairy ovary hints at a link with *Helictotrichon*. It could be mistaken for *Calamagrostis*, but is often 2-flowered; or even *Stipa*, but it has a rhachilla extension.

176. Dissanthelium Trin. in Linnaea 10: 305 (1836); Swallen & Tovar in Phytologia 11: 361—376 (1965) — D. supinum Trin. (= D. calycinum). *Phalaridium* Nees & Meyen in Nova Acta Acad. Leop.-Carol. Nat. Cur. 19, Suppl.: 161 (1843) — P. peruvianum Nees & Meyen. *Stenochloa* Nutt in Proc. Acad. Nat. Sci. Philad. 4: 25 (1848) — S. californica Nutt. *Graminastrum* Krause in Beih. Bot. Centralbl. 32, 2: 348 (1914) — G. macusaniense Krause (= D. minimum).

Perennial, a few annual, mostly dwarf. Panicle contracted to spiciform. Spikelets 2-flowered, the rhachilla very short without extension; glumes equal, as long as spikelet (barely exceeding lemma in *D. brevifolium*, *D. rauhii*), firmly membranous to herbaceous, 3-nerved; lemmas membranous, keeled, 3-nerved, obtuse to acute; palea enclosed by lemma. Endosperm solid.

Species 16. Peru and Bolivia, extending to Mexico and California. Mainly high Andean puna.
A homogeneous genus of uncertain affinity, perhaps related to *Relchela*. The species with short glumes might be mistaken for depauperate *Poa*.

177. Tovarochloa Macfarlane & But in Brittonia 34: 478 (1982) — T. peruviana Macfarlane & But.

Tiny annual; leaf-sheaths inflated, continuous with the short triangular blade. Panicle capitate, hidden among sheaths. Spikelets 1-flowered without rhachilla extension; glumes a little shorter than spikelet, with single thickened nerve; lemma 1-nerved, keeled, abruptly narrowed to a subulate tip; palea resembling lemma.

Species 1. Peru. High Andes.
A rare genus of uncertain affinity.

178. Trisetum Pers., Syn. Pl. 1: 97 (1805) nom conserv; Chrtek in Bot. Not. 118: 210—224 (1965) — T. pratense Pers. (= T. flavescens). *Trisetarium* Poir., Encycl. Suppl. 5: 365 (1817) & *Acrospelion* Schult., Syst. Veg. Mant. 3: 526 (1827) & *Rebentischia* Opiz in Lotos 4: 104 (1854) — nom superfl pro Trisetum. *Rupestrina* Prov., Fl. Canad.: 689 (1862) — R. pubescens Prov. (= T. spicatum).

Perennial. Panicle moderately dense to spiciform, rarely open. Spikelets 2— several-flowered, the rhachilla hairy; glumes mostly unequal and shorter than spikelet; lemmas membranous to thinly coriaceous, strongly compressed and distinctly keeled, bidentate or sometimes bisetulate (*T. tonduzii* 4-setulate), dorsally awned from below middle, the awn geniculate or merely reflexed; palea gaping, silvery. Ovary glabrous (*T. glaciale* hairy); endosperm sometimes liquid.

Species ± 70. All temperate regions except Africa. Weedy places, meadows, mountain slopes and alpine grassland.
Trisetum resembles *Helictotrichon*, but the ovary is glabrous, the lemma keeled and of thinner texture, and the palea free.
Trisetum and *Koeleria* belong to a dense cluster of inter-related genera. None of them is clearly disjunct though each has a recognizable facies, leaving a choice between numerous splits or an unwieldy lump.

179. Trisetaria Forssk., Fl. Aegypt.-Arab.: lx, 27 (1775) — T. linearis Forssk. *Trichaeta* P. Beauv., Ess. Agrost.: 86 (1812) — T. ovata (Cav.) P. Beauv. *Avellinia* Parl., Pl. Nov.: 59 (1842) — A. michelii (Savi) Parl. *Sennenia* Sennen in Bull. Acad. Geogr. Bot. 18: 468 (1908) nom nud — T. scabriuscula. *Parvotrisetum* Chrtek in Preslia 37: 201 (1965) — P. myrianthum (Bertol.) Chrtek.

Annual. Panicle contracted to spiciform (*T. myriantha, T. parviflora* open; *T. ovata* capitate). Spikelets 2—several-flowered (*T. linearis* 1-flowered); upper glume as long as spikelet; lemmas membranous to thinly coriaceous, narrowly oblong to linear in side view (*T. michelii* 3-nerved), weakly keeled or rounded, bisetulate but sometimes minutely so, with a straight or geniculate dorsal awn from above the middle (this sometimes absent in *T. koelerioides*, below middle in *T. glumacea*); palea gaping, hyaline, but sometimes narrow and inconspicuous. Ovary like *Trisetum*.

Species ± 15. Mediterranean to western Himalayas. Dry open places.
A somewhat heterogeneous cluster of annual species related to *Trisetum*. The genus is very close to *Rostraria*, being distinguished mainly by the bisetulate lemma. *T. linearis* resembles *Triplachne* but the upper glume is 3-nerved and the palea gaping.

180. Ventenata Koel., Descr. Gram.: 272 (1802) nom conserv — V. avenacea Koel. *Heteranthus* Borkh. in Botaniker 16—18: 71 (1796) nom rejic — H. tenuis (Moench) Dumort. (= V. dubia). *Heterochaeta* Schult., Syst. Veg. 2, Add. 1: 526 (1827) nom superfl pro Heteranthus. *Malya* Opiz, Seznam: 62 (1852) nom superfl pro Ventenata. *Ventenata sect Gaudinopsis* Boiss., Fl. Or. 5: 540 (1884) — V. macra (Bieb.) Boiss. *Pilgerochloa* Eig in Feddes Rep. 26: 71 (1929) — P. blanchei (Bois) Eig. *Gaudinopsis* (Boiss.) Eig. l.c. 74.

Annual. Panicle lax, or spiciform and then sometimes reduced to a raceme. Spikelets 2—several-flowered, the lowest floret persistent and eventually falling together with glumes and pedicel; glumes herbaceous, shorter than lemma, prominently nerved; lemmas thinly coriaceous, rounded, all bisexual, the lowest acute or setulate but otherwise awnless (*V. blanchei* dorsally awned), the rest bidentate to bisetulate and bearing a geniculate dorsal awn; palea not gaping. Ovary like *Trisetum*.

Species 5. Southern Europe to Iran. Dry places.
Linked to *Trisetaria* through *V. blanchei*.

181. Koeleria Pers., Syn. Pl. 1: 97 (1805); Domin in Bibl. Bot. 14: 1—354 (1907) —K. gracilis Pers. (= K. macrantha). *Airochloa* Link, Hort. Berol. 1: 126 (1827); Jackson in Ind. Kew.: 25 (1895) as "*Achrochloa* " — A. cristata (L.) Link (= K. macrantha). *Brachystylus* Dulac, Fl. Hautes-Pyr.: 85 (1867) nom superfl pro Airochloa. *Leptophyllochloa* Cald. in Nicora, Fl. Patag. 3: 69 (1978) — L. micrathera (Desv.) Cald.

Perennial, the basal sheaths sometimes swollen into bulbs. Panicle spiciform, the branches hispidulous. Spikelets 2—several-flowered, the rhachilla glabrous to puberulous; glumes unequal or subequal, usually shorter than lemma; lemmas membranous, strongly compressed and distinctly keeled (*K. micrathera* and sometimes a few other species 3-nerved), obtuse to acuminate, awnless or with a subapical mucro up to 1 mm long; palea gaping. Ovary glabrous; endosperm sometimes liquid.

Species ± 35. Temperate regions throughout the world. Dry grassland and rocky places.

A genus of closely intergrading species, whose critical taxonomy has still to be worked out. It seems likely that the simple spikelet structure is derived from *Trisetum* rather than ancestral to it; certainly the two genera are very close, with the briefly awned species *K. bergii*, *K. litvinowii* and *K. micrathera* as intermediates. It is easily mistaken for *Poa*, but that genus never has spiciform panicles, hispidulous branches and shining spikelets occurring together in the same species.

182. Rostraria Trin., Fund. Agrost.: 149 (1822) — R. pubescens Trin. *Aegialitis* Trin. l.c. 127, non R. Br. (1810) — A. tenuis Trin. (= R. pubescens). *Aegialina* Schult., Syst. Veg. Mant. 2: 13 (1824) nom nov pro Aegialitis. *Poarion* Reichenb., Consp. Reg. Veg.: 51 (1828) nom superfl pro Aegialina. *Lophochloa* Reichenb., Fl. Germ. Exc.: 42 (1830) — L. phleoides (L.) Reichenb. (= R. cristata). *Wilhelmsia* Koch in Linnaea 21: 400 (1848) — W. caucasica Koch (= R. cristata). *Ktenosachne* Steud., Syn. Pl. Glum. 1: 150 (1854) — K. tenerrima Steud. (= R. pubescens).

Annual. Lemmas membranous, narrowly oblong in side view, obtuse to acute, with a straight awnlet up to 3 mm long mounted high on the back or just below tip, occasionally muticous. Otherwise like *Koeleria*.

Species ± 10. Mediterranean and Middle East. Dry weedy places.
An annual derivative of *Koeleria* with somewhat better development of the awn.

183. Graphephorum Desv. in Nouv. Bull. Sci. Soc. Philom. 2: 189 (1810) — G. melicoideum (Michaux) Desv.

Perennial. Panicle open to moderately contracted. Spikelets 2—several-flowered, the rhachilla copiously pilose; upper glume as long as lemma; lemmas membranous with hyaline margins, keeled, obtuse to acute, awnless or rarely with a dorsal mucro; palea not gaping. Ovary like *Koeleria*.

Species 3. North and central America. Lowland meadows and near water; also high mountains.
An American segregate which fits neither *Trisetum* nor *Koeleria*.

184. Peyritschia Fourn., Mex. Pl. 2: 109 (1886); Koch in Taxon 28: 225—235 (1979) — P. koelerioides (Peyr.) Fourn.

Perennial. Panicle slender, contracted. Spikelets 2-flowered with or without rhachilla extension; rhachilla glabrous to pubescent; glumes subequal, as long as spikelet; lemmas obtusely bilobed, muticous or mucronate near tip (*P. pringlei* geniculately awned from lower half); stamens 2. Otherwise like *Graphephorum*.

Species 2. Mexico and Costa Rica. Mountain slopes in woodland.
A heterogeneous genus with distinctive lemma tip. *P. pringlei* is somewhat aberrant, being superficially similar to *Deschampsia* but has the lemma keeled above the awn insertion and liquid endosperm.

185. Sphenopholis Scribn. in Rhodora 8: 142 (1906) nom nov pro Colobanthus; Erdman in Iowa State J. Sci. 39: 289—336 (1965). *Trisetum sect Colobanthus* Trin. in Mém. Acad. Sci. Pétersb. sér. 6, 1: 66 (1830) — T. pennsylvanicum (Spreng.) Trin. (= S. nitidum). *Reboulea* Kunth, Rév. Gram. 1: 341 (1830) non Reboulia Raddi (1818) — R. gracilis Kunth (= C. obtusatum). *Colobanthus* (Trin.) Spach, Hist. Nat. Veg. Phan. 13: 163 (1841) non Bartling (1830). *Trisetum subgen Colobanthium* Reichenb., Deutsche Bot. 1, 2: 149 (1841) nom nov pro sect Colobanthus. *Colobanthium* (Reichenb.) Taylor in Ind. Kew. 13: 33 (1966) nom superfl pro Sphenopholis.

Perennial, sometimes short-lived (*S. interruptum* annual). Panicle open to spiciform. Spikelets 2(—3)-flowered, falling entire; glumes unequal, shorter than lemma, the upper often much broader than lower, firmly membranous; lemmas membranous, keeled, muticous or mucronate or with a reflexed or geniculate dorsal awn; palea gaping. Ovary like *Trisetum*.

Species 5. Canada to Mexico. Woodland, prairie and marshy places.
S. pennsylvanicum has a well-developed awn and links the genus to *Trisetum*.

186. Dielsiochloa Pilger in Bot. Jahrb. 73: 99 (1943) — D. floribunda (Pilger) Pilger.

Perennial. Panicle oblong, compact. Spikelets 6—10-flowered, the lower 2—3 florets fertile, the rest smaller and sterile; rhachilla wavy, disarticulating only above glumes; glumes shorter than lemma; lemmas firmly membranous, keeled, bilobed, with straight dorsal awn; palea gaping. Ovary glabrous; hilum linear; endosperm solid.

Species 1. Peru, Bolivia and Chile. High altitude grassland.
A distinctive genus with the spikelets highly modified for dispersal. Presumably related to *Trisetum*, though with a different caryopsis.

187. Deschampsia P. Beauv., Ess. Agrost.: 91 (1812) — D. cespitosa (L.) P. Beauv. *Campella* Link, Hort. Berol. 1: 122 (1827); Kunth, Enum. Pl. 1: 286 (1833) as "Campelia" — nom superfl pro Deschampsia. *Vahlodea* Fries in Bot. Not. 1842: 141, 178 (1842) — V. atropurpurea (Wahl.) Fries. *Avenella* Parl., Fl. Ital. 1: 246 (1848) — A. flexuosa (L.) Parl. *Czerniaevia* Ledeb., Fl. Ross. 4: 422 (1853) in syn sub D. bottnica (= D. cespitosa). *Airidium* Steud., Syn. Pl. Glum. 1: 423 (1854) — A. elegantulum Steud. (= D. antarctica). *Monandraira* Desv. in Gay, Hist. Chile Bot. 6: 341 (1854) — M. berteroana (Kunth) Desv. *Lerchenfeldia* Schur, Enum. Fl.

Transsilv.: 753 (1866) nom superfl pro Avenella. *Podinapus* Dulac, Fl. Hautes-Pyr.: 82 (1867) nom superfl pro Deschampsia. *Erioblastus* Honda in J. Fac. Sci. Tokyo 3: 142 (1930) — E. flexuosus Honda (= *D.* atropurpurea). *Homoiachne* Pilger in Bot. Jahrb. 74: 556 (1949) — H. caespitosa (Boiss.) Pilger (= *D.* minor). *Aristavena* Albers & Butzin in Willdenowia 8: 83 (1977) — A. setacea (Hudson) Albers & Butzin.

Perennial, a few annual in America. Panicle usually open. Spikelets 2-flowered plus rhachilla extension, the lower floret sessile; rhachilla well developed and hairy (*D. chapmanii* glabrous); glumes mostly equal and as long as or much exceeding florets (*D. tenella* and allies shorter); lemmas hyaline to polished cartilaginous, rounded (*D. minor* 3-nerved), 4-toothed to denticulately truncate (rarely bilobed and then awned from below middle), with inconspicuous straight or weakly geniculate dorsal awn from base or lower half (*D. atropurpurea, D. media* and a few others above middle; *D. tenella* and allies mucronate to muticous); callus pubescent to conspicuously bearded. Endosperm solid.

Species ± 40. Temperate regions throughout world. Meadows, moorland and woodland.

A tolerably uniform genus sharing some of its characters with a number of other genera. It may be distinguished from *Helictotrichon* by its small delicate spikelets and slender awns; and from *Trisetum* by its rounded lemma back or, less reliably, by the lemma tip and awn insertion. The awnless short-glumed New Zealand species allied to *D. tenella* have a denticulate lemma tip which distinguishes them from *Poa*. The annual species are separated from *Aira* by their lemma texture and well developed rhachilla.

188. Holcus L., Sp. Pl.: 1047 (1753) nom conserv — H. lanatus L. *Sorgum* Adans., Fam. Pl. 2: 38, 606 (1763) & *Arthrochloa* R. Br., Chlor. Melv.: 35 (1823) & *Ginannia* Bub., Fl. Pyr. 4: 321 (1901) non Scop. (1777), & *Homalachna* Kuntze in Post, Lexicon: 285 (1903) based on Holcus sect Homalachne Benth. & Hook., Gen. Pl. 3: 1159 (1883) & *Notholcus* Hitchc. in Jepson, Fl. Calif. 1: 126 (1912) & *Nothoholcus* Nash in Britton & Brown, Ill. Fl. North. U.S. ed. 2, 1: 214 (1913) — nom superfl pro Holcus.

Annual or perennial. Panicle moderately dense. Spikelets 2-flowered often with brief rhachilla extension, the lower floret bisexual and usually raised upon a curved rhachilla internode, the upper ♂, falling entire; glumes subequal, enclosing florets, papery (awned in *H. setiglumis*); lemmas polished cartilaginous, rounded, indistinctly nerved, obtuse to bidentate, the lower awnless, the upper with geniculate or hooked or straight dorsal awn from upper third. Endosperm sometimes soft.

Species 6. Europe, North Africa and Middle East. Grassland, open woodland and waste land; *H. lanatus* (Yorkshire Fog) introduced as a weed to most temperate regions.

Holcus intergrades with *Deschampsia* through *D. minor* and *D. reuteri*. The relationship between the genera is akin to that between *Helictotrichon* and *Arrhenatherum*.

189. Corynephorus P. Beauv., Ess. Agrost.: 90 (1812) nom conserv —

C. canescens (L.) P. Beauv. *Weingaertneria* Bernh., Syst. Verz. Pfl. 1: 23, 51 (1800) nom rejic pro Corynephorus. *Anachortus* Jirasek & Chrtek in Preslia 34: 383 (1962) — A. macrantherus (Boiss. & Reut.) Jirasek & Chrtek.

Annual or perennial. Panicle open or contracted. Spikelets 2-flowered plus rhachilla extension; glumes equal, as long as spikelet; lemmas thinly membranous, rounded, minutely bidenticulate, with a basal awn, this divided into twisted column and clavate limb with a ring of hairs at the junction. Endosperm solid.

Species 5. Europe and Mediterranean to Iran. Littoral dunes and other sandy places.
A genus amply defined by its extraordinary awns.

190. Periballia Trin., Fund. Agrost.: 133 (1822); Paunero in An. Bot. Cav. 21: 343—348 (1963) — P. hispanica Trin. (= P. involucrata). *Molineria* Parl., Fl. Ital. 1: 236 (1850) non Colla (1826) — M. minuta (Loefl.) Parl. *Molineriella* Rouy, Fl. France 14: 102 (1913) nom nov pro Molineria.

Annual. Panicle open (lower branches sterile in *P. involucrata*). Spikelets 2-flowered without rhachilla extension, the florets separated by a short internode; glumes equal, a little shorter than lemma; lemmas lanceolate, membranous, 3—7-nerved, rounded, obtuse to denticulate, awnless or with a straight dorsal or subapical awn. Caryopsis narrowly oblong, flattened on one face; endosperm solid. 2n = 8, 14, 18.

Species 3. Mediterranean. Dry sandy places.
Somewhat heterogeneous, each species having a different chromosome number.

191. Aira L., Sp. Pl.: 63 (1853); Aschers., Fl. Brandenb. 1: 830 (1864) as "Aera" —A. praecox L. *Aspris* Adans., Fam. Pl. 2: 496 (1763) nom superfl pro Aira. *Aira sect Airella* Dumort., Obs. Gram. Belg.: 120 (1824) — A. caryophyllea L. *Fiorinia* Parl., Fl. Ital. 1: 232 (1850) — F. pulchella (Link) Parl. (= A. tenorii). *Caryophyllea* Opiz, Seznam: 27 (1852) & *Fussia* Schur, Enum. Pl. Transsilv.: 754 (1866) & *Airella* (Dumort.) Dumort. in Bull. Soc. Bot. Belg. 7: 68 (1868) & *Salmasia* Bub., Fl. Pyr. 4: 315 (1901) non Schreb. (1789) — nom superfl pro Aira.

Annual. Panicle open or contracted. Spikelets 2-flowered without rhachilla extension, the florets arising at about the same level; glumes equal, enclosing florets; lemmas lanceolate, thinly coriaceous, scaberulous, 5-nerved, rounded, acuminately bilobed, with geniculate dorsal awn from lower half (sometimes the lower and rarely both florets awnless). Caryopsis fusiform; endosperm solid. 2n = 14, 28.

Species 8. Europe and Mediterranean to Iran; now widespread as a weed. Open places on dry sandy soils.

192. Airopsis Desv. in J. Bot. Desv. 1: 200 (1809) — A. globosa (Thore) Desv.

(= A. tenella). *Aeropsis* Aschers. & Graebn., Syn. Mitteleur. Fl. 2, 1: 298 (1899) & *Sphaerella* Bub., Fl. Pyr. 4: 320 (1901) non Sommerfelt (1824) — nom superfl pro Airopsis.

Annual. Panicle contracted. Spikelets 2-flowered without rhachilla extension, the florets arising at about the same level; glumes equal, enclosing florets; lemmas gibbously orbicular, membranous, 3-nerved, rounded, obtusely tridentate, awnless. Caryopsis hemispherical; endosperm solid. 2n = 8.

Species 1. Mediterranean. Open sandy places.

193. Antinoria Parl., Fl. Palerm. 1: 92 (1845) — A. agrostidea (DC.) Parl.

Annual (*A. agrostidea* sometimes perennial). Panicle open. Spikelets like *Airopsis* but florets separated by a short internode, lemma elliptic, and caryopsis obovoid. 2n = 18.

Species 2. Mediterranean. Damp places.

c. PHALARIDINAE Reichenb., Consp. Reg. Veg.: 51 (1828). *Anthoxanthinae* Reichenb., Deutsch. Fl. 6: 4 (1846). *Foenodorinae* Krause in Beih. Bot. Centralbl. 25, 2: 487 (1909) nom nud.

Spikelets 3-flowered, the two lower florets ♂ or barren, the uppermost bisexual, disarticulating above glumes (except some *Phalaris*); glumes, or at least the upper, usually enclosing florets; fertile lemma rounded on back.

A little group with distinctive spikelet structure. Loosely related to *Deschampsia*.

194. Hierochloe R. Br., Prodr. Fl. Nov. Holl.: 208 (1810) nom conserv — H. odorata (L.) P. Beauv. *Savastana* Schrank, Baier. Fl. 1: 100, 337 (1789) non Savastania Scop. (1777) — S. hirta Schrank. *Torresia* Ruiz & Pavon, Prodr.: 125 (1794) nom rejic — T. utriculata Ruiz & Pavon. *Disarrenum* Labill., Nov. Holl. Pl. Spec. 2: 82 (1807) nom rejic — D. antarcticum Labill. (= H. redolens). *Dimesia* Raf. in Amer. Month. Mag. 1: 442 (1817) nom superfl pro Hierochloe. *Ataxia* R. Br., Chlor. Melv.: 35 (1823) — A. horsfieldii Kunth.

Perennial. Panicle open to dense. Spikelets urn-like at anthesis, the 2 lower florets ♂; glumes subequal, ± as long as florets or occasionally shorter, weakly keeled; sterile lemmas ± as long as fertile, firmly membranous to coriaceous, acute to bilobed, awnless or with subapical awnlet or with robust Anthoxanthum-like awns; fertile lemma cartilaginous, the margins convolute and covering palea, emarginate; palea 1—3-nerved, without keels; lodicules 2; stamens 2 (3 in ♂ florets); stigmas plumose. x = 7.

Species ± 30. Temperate and Arctic regions generally, except Africa. Woods, marshy places, open grassland and tundra.

195. Anthoxanthum L., Sp. Pl.: 28 (1753) — A. odoratum L. *Flavia* Fabric., Enum.: 206 (1759) nom superfl pro Anthoxanthum. *Xanthonanthus* St-Lager in Ann. Soc. Bot. Lyon 7: 119 (1880) & l.c. 8: 189 (1881) as "Xanthanthos" — nom superfl pro Anthoxanthum. *Foenodorum* Krause in Naturw. Wochenschr. 10: 220 (1911) nom superfl pro Anthoxanthum.

Annual or perennial. Panicle contracted to spiciform. Spikelets lanceolate, the 2 lower florets represented by empty lemmas (rarely 1 or even both ♂); glumes unequal, the upper usually exceeding and enclosing the florets, keeled; sterile lemmas longer than fertile, membranous, bilobed, the lower with a short straight awn from above middle, the upper geniculately awned from below middle; fertile lemma cartilaginous, the margins convolute and covering palea, emarginate; palea 1-nerved, without keels; lodicules 0; stamens 2; stigmas pubescent, protogynous. x = 5 (7 in American species).

Species ± 18. Temperate Eurasia and Africa including the tropical mountains, and in central America; introduced to other temperate regions. Meadows and dry grassland.
Anthoxanthum is adjacent to *Hierochloe* but, despite some intermediate species, is sufficiently distinct to justify generic status. Both genera are sweetly scented with coumarin.

196. Phalaris L., Sp. Pl.: 54 (1753); Anderson in Iowa State J. Sci. 36: 1—96 (1961) — P. canariensis L. *Phalaroides* Wolf, Gen. Pl. Vocab. Char. Def.: 11 (1776) — P. arundinacea (L.) Rausch. *Typhoides* Moench, Meth.: 201 (1794) & *Baldingera* Gaertn., Meyer & Scherb., Fl. Wetterau 1: 43, 96 (1799) & *Digraphis* Trin., Fund. Agrost.: 127 (1822) & *Endallex* Raf. in Bull. Bot. Genève 1: 220 (1830) & *Phalaridantha* St-Lager in Cariot, Etude Fleurs ed. 8, 2: 900 (1889) — nom superfl pro Phalaroides.

Annual, or perennial and then the lowest culm internode sometimes swollen into a corm. Panicle spiciform to capitate (*P. arundinacea* merely contracted). Spikelets ovate, the two lower florets reduced to rudimentary lemmas (gathered into deciduous clusters of 1 fertile and up to 6 ± deformed sterile spikelets in *P. paradoxa, P. caerulescens*); glumes equal, exceeding and enclosing lemma, keeled, the keel usually winged; sterile lemmas usually subulate and up to ½ length of fertile lemma, rarely chaffy or little fleshy scales, sometimes the lower reduced to an obscure knob (both obscure in *P. paradoxa, P. caerulescens*); fertile lemma polished coriaceous, the margins not overlapping, acute, awnless; palea coriaceous, 2-nerved, without keels. Hilum linear. x = 7 (6 in 3 species).

Species 15. North temperate zone, but mainly Mediterranean with a secondary centre in California; also in South America. Dry weedy places and on damp soils.
P. canariensis (Canary grass) is cultivated, mainly for bird seed.

d. ALOPECURINAE Dumort., Anal. Fam.: 64 (1829). *Calamagrostidinae* Lindley, Nat. Syst. ed. 2: 380 (1836) nom nud. *Agrostidinae* Griseb., Fl. Roumel. Bithyn. 2:

460 (1844). *Vilfinae* Steud., Syn. Pl. Glum. 1: 146 (1854). *Miborinae* Asch. & Graeb., Syn. Mitteleur. Fl. 2, 1: 118 (1899). *Phleinae* Asch. & Graeb. l.c. *Beckmanniinae* Nevski in Trudy Bot. Inst. Acad. Nauk SSSR 4: 228 (1937). *Cinninae* (Ohwi) Ohwi in Acta Phytotax. Geobot. 11: 183 (1942).

Spikelets 1-flowered; glumes commonly enclosing florets; palea not gaping.

The 1-flowered genera were formerly accommodated in a separate tribe Agrostideae, which included some genera with close relatives in Poeae, and a few extraneous elements such as *Muhlenbergia*. It is now recognized that this was an artificial assemblage, and that the gap between, for example, *Agrostis* and *Deschampsia* is so narrow that tribal status was unwarranted. It must be conceded, however, that a few genera have such simple spikelets that positive tribal indications are lacking and their assignment is somewhat arbitrary.

197. Agrostis L., Sp. Pl.: 61 (1753); Bjorkman in Symb. Bot. Ups. 17, 1: 1—112 (1960) — A stolonifera L. *Vilfa* Adans., Fam. Pl. 2: 495 (1763) — V. alba (L.) P. Beauv. (= A. stolonifera). *Trichodium* Michaux, Fl. Bor. Am. 1: 41 (1803) — T. laxiflorum Michaux (= A. scabra). *Decandolia* Batard, Ess. Fl. Maine Loire: 15, 28 (1809) nom superfl pro Agrostis. *Agraulus* P. Beauv., Ess. Agrost.: 5 (1812) — A. caninus (L.) P. Beauv. *Lachnagrostis* Trin., Fund. Agrost.: 128 (1822) — L. filiformis (Forst.) Trin. (= A. avenacea). *Notonema* Raf. in Bull. Bot. Genève 1: 220 (1830) — A. arachnoides Elliott (= A. elliottiana). *Candollea* Steud., Nom. Bot. ed. 2, 1: 273 (1840) non Mirbel (1802), nom superfl pro Decandolia. *Bromidium* Nees & Meyen in Meyen in Nova Acta Acad. Leop.-Carol. Nat. Cur. 19, suppl. 1: 154 (1843); Rugolo in Darwiniana 24: 187—210 (1982) — B. hygrometricum (Nees) Nees & Meyen. *Agrostis sect Podagrostis* Griseb. in Ledeb., Fl. Ross. 4: 436 (1852) —A. aequivalvis Trin. *Anomalotis* Steud., Syn. Pl. Glum. 1: 198 (1854) — A. quinqueseta Steud. *Didymochaeta* Steud. l.c.: 185 — D. chilensis Steud. *Agrestis* Bub., Fl. Pyr. 4: 281 (1901) nom superfl pro Agrostis. *Podagrostis* (Griseb.) Scribn. & Merr. in Contrib. U.S. Nat. Herb. 13: 58 (1910). *Pentatherum* Nabelek in Spisy Prir. Fak. Masary. Univ. 111: 8 (1929) — P. olympicum (Boiss.) Nabelek. *Senisetum* Honda in Bot. Mag. Tokyo 46: 371 (1932) — S. hideoi (Ohwi) Honda. *Heptaseta* Koidz. l.c. 47: 146 (1933) in syn sub Senisetum. *Neoschischkinia* Tzvelev in Bot. Zh. 53: 309 (1968) — N. elegans (Thore) Tzvelev (= A. tenerrima).

Annual or perennial. Panicle diffuse to contracted, rarely spiciform (much reduced and hidden among leaves in cushion-like *A. muscosa*). Spikelets usually without rhachilla extension; glumes equal or unequal, as long as to much longer than floret (shorter in *A. nipponensis, A. zenkeri*), membranous and shiny, 1-nerved, mostly acute to acuminate (*A. ampla, A. aristiglumis* awned); lemma hyaline to cartilaginous, thinner than glumes, glabrous or hairy, rounded, mostly 5- but sometimes 3-nerved, truncate to 4-dentate often with the nerves excurrent and the outer sometimes forming distinct lateral awns (*A. hideoi* 4-awned), with a geniculate, rarely flexuous, dorsal awn or awnless; palea usually shorter than lemma and often minute, largely covered by continuous inrolled margins of lemma; callus glabrous to shortly pubescent, rarely with a beard up to ½ its length and then the lemma hyaline. Endosperm sometimes liquid.

Species ± 220. Temperate regions throughout world, and on tropical mountains. Open places, grassland and light woodland. The genus includes many important species of second grade pastures. *A. capillaris* (Bent grass) and other fine-leaved species are used for lawns.

A large genus for which no adequate comprehensive treatment is available. Though variable it offers no obvious opportunities for subdivision. Reduction of the palea is correlated with the presence of thickened transverse ridges inside the outer wall of the epidermal cells of the lemma, producing a reticulate pattern known as the Trichodium Net. This also occurs in *Polypogon*, but seems to be of limited taxonomic significance at generic level.

Agrostis and *Calamagrostis* differ in habit, the former typically with an open panicle of smaller spikelets and a preference for drier sites. However, they intergrade completely and the boundary between them is almost arbitrary, though in practice the uncertainty is limited to a fairly small number of species. *Agrostis* is best distinguished by its thinner lemmas; the beardless callus is a useful but unreliable supporting character; the absence of a rhachilla extension has only slight diagnostic value.

198. Calamagrostis Adans., Fam. Pl. 2: 31, 530 (1763); Wasiljew in Feddes Rep. 63: 229—251 (1960) — Arundo calamagrostis L. (= C. canescens). *Deyeuxia* P. Beauv., Ess. Agrost.: 43 (1812); Weddell in Bull. Soc. Bot. Fr. 22: 173—180 (1875); Vickery in Contrib. New South Wales Herb. 1: 43—82 (1940) — D. montana (Gaud.) P. Beauv. (= C. arundinacea). *Amagris* Raf., Princ. Somiol.: 27 (1814) nom superfl pro Calamagrostis. *Chamaecalamus* Meyen, Reise 1: 456 (1834) — C. spectabilis Meyen (= C. rigescens). *Pteropodium* Steud., Nom. Bot. ed. 2, 2: 414 (1841) non DC. & Meisner (1840), nom nud — C. effusa. *Athernotus* Dulac, Fl. Hautes-Pyr.: 74 (1867) nom superfl pro Calamagrostis. *Cinnagrostis* Griseb. in Abh. Ges. Wiss. Gött. 19: 256 (1874) — C. polygama Griseb. *Achaeta* Fourn., Mex. Pl. 2: 109 (1886) — A. plumosa Fourn. (= C. eriantha). *Aulacolepis* Hack. in Feddes Rep. 3: 241 (1907) non Ettingsh. (1893) — A. treutleri (Kuntze) Hack. *Aniselytron* Merr. in Philipp. J. Sci. Bot. 5: 328 (1910); Korthof & Veldkamp in Gard. Bull. Singapore 37: 213—223 (1984) — A. agrostoides Merr. *Stylagrostis* Mez in Bot. Arch. 1: 20 (1922) — S. ovata (Presl) Mez. *Ancistrochloa* Honda in J. Jap. Bot. 12: 18 (1936) — A. fauriei (Hack.) Honda. *Stilpnophleum* Nevski in Trudy Bot. Inst. Akad. Nauk SSSR 3: 143 (1936) — S. anthoxanthoides (Munro) Nevski. *Sclerodeyeuxia* Pilger in Bot. Jahrb. 74: 19 (1947) — S. sclerophylla (Stapf) Pilger. *Anisachne* Keng in J. Wash. Acad. Sci. 48: 117 (1958) — A. gracilis Keng. *Neoaulacolepis* Rauschert in Taxon 31: 561 (1982) nom nov pro Aulacolepis.

Perennial. Panicle contracted to spiciform or capitate, rarely open. Spikelets with or without rhachilla extension; glumes equal or unequal, as long as or exceeding floret (shorter in *C. treutleri* and allies), membranous, 1(—3)-nerved, acute to acuminate; lemma membranous to coriaceous, sometimes hyaline but then callus hairs over ½ its length, usually firmer than glumes, rounded or keeled, (3—)5-nerved, bilobed to irregularly denticulate and sometimes the nerves excurrent, with inconspicuous straight or geniculate dorsal awn up to twice length of lemma (very rarely more but then with long callus hairs) but occasionally reduced to a subapical mucro or absent; palea ⅓ to as long as lemma, the keels distant or approximate; callus bearded with hairs from ⅕ (rarely shorter, *C. nudiflora* glabrous) to much longer than floret. Endosperm sometimes soft.

Species ± 270. Temperate regions throughout the world and on tropical mountains. Mainly damp places, but also in woods, heaths and mountain grassland.

Calamagrostis is variable and is sometimes divided into three genera:

Glumes longer than lemma:
Lemma hyaline, ½—⅔ as long as glumes; callus hairs ½ to much exceeding lemma   *Calamagrostis*
Lemma indurated, at least ¾ length of glumes; callus hairs shorter than lemma
                                                                                                                               Deyeuxia
Glumes shorter than lemma, this coriaceous and keeled; callus pubescent; palea keels contiguous above a narrow groove   *Aniselytron*

However, the characters supposedly separating *Calamagrostis* and *Deyeuxia* fail so often that the distinction is untenable at generic level. *Aniselytron* is distinct enough in SE Asia, but merges with *Calamagrostis* in Australia through such species as *C. mckiei*. Its short glumes and awnless keeled lemma imitate *Poa*, from which it is distinguished by the close-set palea keels.

The taxonomy of the genus is complicated by extensive interspecific hybridization and apomixy (Nygren in Symb. Bot. Ups. 17, 3: 1—105, 1962).

199. Ammophila Host, Gram. Austr. 4: 24 (1809) — A. arundinacea Host (= A. arenaria). *Psamma* P. Beauv., Ess. Agrost.: 143 (1812) — P. littoralis P. Beauv. (= A. arenaria).

Rhizomatous perennial; leaf-blades rigid, inrolled, pungent. Panicle spiciform. Spikelets with rhachilla extension; glumes equal, a little longer than floret, chartaceous, the upper 3-nerved, acute; lemma thinly coriaceous, sharply keeled, bidenticulate with subapical mucro; floret callus bearded. Hilum linear.

Species 2. Europe and North Africa, east coast of North America. Maritime sand dunes. An effective binder of drifting sand and often planted for this purpose; introduced to most temperate countries.

Hybridizes with *Calamagrostis*, differing mainly in its adaptation to a special environment.

200. Simplicia T. Kirk in Trans. Proc. New Zealand Inst. 29: 497 (1897); Zotov in New Zealand J. Bot. 9: 539—544 (1971) — S. laxa T. Kirk.

Perennial. Panicle open or contracted. Spikelet with rhachilla extension; glumes unequal, the upper less than ¼ length of floret, membranous, acute; lemma herbaceous, 3-nerved, keeled, acute, with or without a subapical awnlet; palea 1-keeled, 1—2-nerved; stamens 2—3.

Species 2. New Zealand. Grassland.
The genus is distinguished from short-glumed species of *Calamagrostis* mainly by its 3-nerved lemma. It resembles *Poa* but has a 1-keeled palea; also Oryzeae but has distinct glumes and fewer palea nerves.

201. Ancistragrostis S.T. Blake in Blumea, Suppl. 3: 56 (1946) — A. uncinioides S.T. Blake.

Perennial. Panicle contracted. Spikelets with rhachilla extension; glumes subequal, shorter than floret, membranous to thinly coriaceous, 1-nerved, obtuse to acute; lemma firmly membranous to coriaceous, keeled, 5-nerved, emarginate, with a short subulate subapical awn, this hooked or not at tip; callus shortly bearded.

Species 2. New Guinea and Australia. Damp places and mountain grassland. Related to the short-glumed species of *Calamagrostis*.

202. Echinopogon P. Beauv., Ess. Agrost.: 42 (1812); Hubbard in Hook. Ic. Pl. 33: t 3261 (1935) — E. ovatus (Forst.) P. Beauv. *Hystericina* Steud., Syn. Pl. Glum. 1: 35 (1854) — H. alopecuroides Steud. (= E. ovatus).

Perennial. Panicle spiciform to capitate. Spikelets with rhachilla extension; glumes equal, membranous, 1-nerved, as long as floret or a little shorter, acute to acuminate; lemma thinly coriaceous, distinctly 5—11-nerved, keeled, bidentate or setaceously bilobed, rarely entire, with stiff terminal or subapical awn (*E. phleoides* mucronate); callus shortly bearded. Hilum linear.

Species 7. New Guinea, Australia, New Zealand. Open woodland. Related to *Calamagrostis* through *Ancistragrostis*.

203. Pentapogon R. Br., Prodr. Fl. Nov. Holl.: 173 (1810) — P. billardieri R. Br. (= P. quadrifidum).

Perennial. Panicle moderately dense. Spikelets without rhachilla extension; glumes equal, longer than floret, thinly membranous, 1-nerved, acuminate to a short awn; lemma coriaceous, rounded, the margins overlapping and enclosing the 2-keeled palea, 4-awned at tip and with a long geniculate dorsal awn from upper third; callus bearded with hairs ¼ length of lemma. Endosperm soft.

Species 1. SE Australia. Open woodland. A segregate from *Calamagrostis*, reminiscent of the parallel but less extreme development in *Agrostis hideoi*.

204. Dichelachne Endl., Prodr. Fl. Ins. Norf.: 20 (1833); Veldkamp in Blumea 22: 5—12 (1974) — D. montana Endl. (= D. micrantha).

Perennial. Panicle contracted. Spikelets small, with or without minute rhachilla extension; glumes equal, longer or a little shorter than floret, hyaline to membranous, 1-nerved, acuminate; lemma linear to narrowly lanceolate, terete, thinly coriaceous, margins involute, lightly keeled, acute but easily splitting into 2 teeth, with long wavy dorsal to subapical awn 2—6 times its length; stamens 1—3; callus obtuse, pubescent. Endosperm liquid.

Species 5. New Guinea, Australia and New Zealand. Forest clearings to subalpine grassland.

A small homogeneous genus often mistaken for *Stipa*, but the subapical awn and liquid endosperm point to a relationship with *Calamagrostis*. It differs from the latter in its fusiform floret, short callus hairs and long wavy awn.

205. Triplachne Link, Hort. Berol. 2: 241 (1833) — T. nitens (Guss.) Link.

Annual. Panicle spiciform. Spikelets with rhachilla extension; glumes equal, longer than floret, membranous, 1-nerved, acute; lemma hyaline, gibbously ovate in side view, rounded, truncate, with 2 lateral awns and a geniculate dorsal awn; palea almost as long as lemma.

Species 1. Mediterranean. Open places near sea.

Triplachne is quite distinct in Europe, but its claim to generic rank is weakened by the parallel evolution of a similar facies in America which is not disjunct from *Agrostis*. These species, allied to *A. koelerioides* and sometimes placed in the genus *Bromidium*, are annuals with spiciform panicles and laterally awned lemmas, but the latter are lanceolate in side view and lack a palea.

206. Gastridium P. Beauv., Ess. Agrost.: 21 (1812) — G. australe P. Beauv. (= G. ventricosum).

Annual. Panicle spiciform. Spikelets with or without minute rhachilla extension; glumes unequal, membranous above, indurated and gibbously swollen below to accommodate the much shorter floret, 1-nerved, acuminate; lemma cartilaginous, rounded, truncate and denticulate, with a geniculate dorsal awn or awnless.

Species 2. Europe and North Africa eastwards to Iran. Grassy places and arable land.

Linked to *Agrostis* through *Triplachne*.

207. Lagurus L., Sp. Pl.: 81 (1753) — L. ovatus L. *Avena* Scop., Introd.: 74 (1777) non L. (1753), nom superfl pro Lagurus.

Annual. Panicle spiciform, ovoid. Spikelets with rhachilla extension; glumes equal, longer than floret, narrowly lanceolate, membranous, 1-nerved, white villous, acuminate to a slender awn; lemma membranous, rounded, 2-awned at tip and with a geniculate dorsal awn from upper third. Endosperm soft.

Species 1. Mediterranean. Maritime sands. Cultivated as an ornamental.

208. Apera Adans., Fam. Pl. 2: 495 (1763) — A. spica-venti (L.) P. Beauv. *Anemagrostis* Trin., Fund. Agrost.: 128 (1822) nom superfl pro Apera.

Annual. Panicle open or contracted. Spikelets with rhachilla extension; glumes unequal, the upper as long as or a little longer than floret and 3-nerved, hyaline to membranous and shining, acute to shortly awned; lemma firmly membranous, 5-nerved, rounded, with a long flexuous subapical awn. Endosperm liquid.

Species 3. Europe to Afghanistan. In dry sandy soils and as a weed of arable land.

209. Hypseochloa C.E. Hubbard in Kew Bull. 1936: 300 (1936) — H. cameroonensis C.E. Hubbard.

Annual. Panicle open. Spikelets with minute rhachilla extension; glumes equal, longer than floret, membranous, 5-nerved, acuminate; lemma thinly coriaceous including margins which are inrolled and clasping palea keels, rounded, bidentate, with dorsal geniculate awn.

Species 2. Cameroon Mt and Tanzania. Mountain grassland.

210. Zingeria Smirnov in Byull. Mosk. Obsh. Ispyt. Prirody 51, 2: 67 (1946) — Z. biebersteiniana (Claus) Smirnov. *Zingeriopsis* Probat. in Nov. Sist. Vysh. Rast. 14: 12 (1977) — Z. verticillata (Boiss. & Bal.) Probat.

Annual. Panicle diffuse, delicate. Spikelets without rhachilla extension, dorsally compressed; glumes equal (*Z. verticillata* unequal), as long as or a little shorter than floret, membranous, the upper 3-nerved, obtuse to acute; lemma membranous, 3-nerved, rounded on back, obtuse, awnless; palea 2-nerved, rounded.

Species 4. Roumania and Turkey to southern Russia and Iran. Meadows and stream sides.
The dorsally compressed spikelet bears some resemblance to *Milium*. Chromosome numbers are 2n = 4 (*Z. biebersteiniana*), 8 & 12, giving the very low basic number of 2 (Tzvelev & Zhukova in Bot. Zh. 59: 265—269, 1974).

211. Mibora Adans., Fam. Pl. 2: 495 (1763) — M. minima (L.) Desv. *Rothia* Borkh., Tent. Disp. Pl. Germ.: 43 (1792) nom rejic non Pers. (1807) & *Chamagrostis* Borkh. in Wibel, Prim. Fl. Werth.: 126 (1799) & *Sturmia* Hoppe in Sturm, Deutsch. Fl. 1, 7: (1799) & *Knappia* Sm. in Sm. & Sow., Engl. Bot. 16: 1127 (1803) — nom superfl pro Mibora. *Micagrostis* Juss. in Dict. Sci. Nat. 31: 17 (1824) in syn sub Mibora.

Dwarf annual. Inflorescence a unilateral raceme. Spikelets without rhachilla extension; glumes longer than floret, membranous, 1-nerved, obtuse; lemma hyaline, rounded, hairy, obtuse; lodicules 0; stigmas pubescent.

Species 2. Western Europe and North Africa. Damp sandy soils.

212. Polypogon Desf., Fl. Atlant. 1: 66 (1798) — P. monspeliensis (L.) Desf. *Santia* Savi in Mem. Soc. Ital. Modena 8: 479 (1799) — S. plumosa Savi

(= P. monspeliensis). *Chaetotropis* Kunth, Rév. Gram. 1: 72 (1829) — C. chilensis Kunth. *Raspailia* Presl, Rel. Haenk. 1: 238 (1830) nom prov pro seq. *Nowodworskya* Presl l.c.: 351 — N. agrostoides Presl (= P. elongatus).

Annual or perennial. Panicle contracted to spiciform (*P. hissaricus, P. schimperianus* open). Spikelets without rhachilla extension, falling entire together with pedicel or part of it; glumes equal, longer than floret, chartaceous, ± scabrid, 1-nerved, entire to bilobed, often with a slender awn; lemma hyaline, 5-nerved, rounded, the nerves sometimes excurrent from the ± truncate tip, awnless or with a subapical awnlet or a geniculate dorsal awn; palea ½ to as long as lemma.

Species 18. Warm temperate regions of the world, and on tropical mountains. Damp places.
A heterogeneous genus without clear subdivisions. It closely approaches *Agrostis* and hybridises with it, but is distinguished by its deciduous spikelets with stipitate base.

213. Chaetopogon Janchen, Eur. Gatt. Farn. ed. 2: 33 (1913) nom nov pro seq. *Chaeturus* Link in J. Bot. Schrad. 1799, 2: 313 (1800) non Chaiturus Willd. (1787) — C. fasciculatus Link.

Annual. Panicle moderately dense. Spikelets without rhachilla extension, falling entire together with the short pedicel; glumes unequal, longer than floret, linear-lanceolate, membranous, 1-nerved, the lower produced into a long slender awn; lemma hyaline, 1—3-nerved, rounded, acute; palea ½ as long as lemma, nerveless.

Species 1. Mediterranean. Sandy places.

214. Cyathopus Stapf in Hook. Ic. Pl. 24: t 2395 (1895) — C. sikkimensis Stapf.

Perennial. Panicle open. Spikelets without rhachilla extension, falling entire; glumes equal, slightly exceeding floret, chartaceous, strongly 3-nerved, acute; lemma membranous, 5-nerved, weakly keeled, subacute, awnless; palea as long as lemma, 2-keeled.

Species 1. Sikkim. In woods.

215. Euthryptochloa Cope in Kew Bull. (ined) — E. longiligula Cope.

Perennial. Like *Cyathopus* except: panicle contracted; glumes unequal, thinly membranous, the lower 1-nerved; lemma 3-nerved; palea with median groove.

Species 1. SW China. Mountain slopes.

216. Cinna L., Sp. Pl.: 5 (1753) — C. arundinacea L. *Abola* Adans., Fam. Pl. 2: 31, 5ll (1763) nom superfl pro Cinna. *Blyttia* Fries, Nov. Fl. Suec. Mant. 2: 2 (1839) non Arn. (1838) — B. suaveolens (Blytt) Fries (= C. latifolia). *Cinnastrum* Fourn., Mex. Pl. 2: 90 (1881) — C. poiforme (Kunth) Fourn.

Perennial. Panicle open. Spikelets with or without rhachilla extension, falling entire; glumes subequal, a little longer or shorter than floret, thinly membranous, the upper 1—3-nerved, acute; lemma firmly membranous, 3-nerved, keeled, subacute, with or without short straight awnlet near tip; palea as long as lemma, 1-keeled; stamens 1—2. Endosperm liquid.

Species 3. North temperate zone, and Mexico to Peru. Damp woods.

217. Limnodea Dewey in Coulter in Contrib. U.S. Nat. Herb. 2: 518 (1894) nom nov pro seq. *Greenia* Nutt. in Trans. Amer. Phil. Soc. ser. 2, 5: 142 (1835) non Wallman (1791) — G. arkansana Nutt. *Sclerachne* Trin. in Mém. Acad. Sci Pétersb. sér. 6, 4: 273 (1845) non R. Br. (1838), nom nov pro Greenia. *Thurberia* Benth. in J. Linn. Soc. Bot. 19: 58 (1881) non Gray (1854), nom nov pro Greenia.

Perennial. Panicle loose. Spikelets with rhachilla extension, falling entire; glumes equal, longer than floret, coriaceous, 3-nerved, acute; lemma thinly coriaceous, 3-nerved, weakly keeled, bidentate, geniculatedly awned from upper ¼ of back; palea hyaline, shorter than and enclosed by lemma; stamens 3. Endosperm liquid.

Species 1. North America. Prairie.
A prairie version of *Cinna*, mimicking *Stipa*.

218. Limnas Trin., Fund. Agrost.: 116 (1822) — L. stelleri Trin.

Perennial. Like *Alopecurus*, but panicle moderately dense to contracted; palea ¼ length of lemma; lodicules present; stamens 2.

Species 2. Siberia. Open woods and stony slopes.
Barely worth separating from *Alopecurus*.

219. Alopecurus L., Sp. Pl.: 60 (1753) — A. pratensis L. *Tozzettia* Savi in Mem. Soc. Ital. Modena 8: 477 (1799) — T. pratensis Savi (= A. rendlei). *Colobachne* P. Beauv., Ess. Agrost.: 22 (1812) — C. vaginata (Willd.) P. Beauv. *Alopecuropsis* Opiz in Lotos 7: 84 (1857) — A. textilis (Boiss.) Opiz.

Annual or perennial (lowest culm internode corm-like in *A. bulbosus*). Panicle spiciform, cylindrical to capitate. Spikelets without rhachilla extension, falling entire; glumes equal, a little longer than and enclosing floret, membranous to thinly coriaceous, often connate along the margins below, strongly keeled this usually ciliate, obtuse acute or shortly awned; lemma membranous, the margins often connate below, keeled, truncate to acute, with a straight or geniculate dorsal awn (*A. borii* muticous); palea usually small or absent; lodicules 0; stigmas pubescent, protogynous. Endosperm sometimes liquid.

Species 36. North temperate zone and in South America. Damp meadows to stony slopes. *A. pratensis* (Meadow Foxtail) is a useful pasture grass, and *A. myosuroides* (Black grass) is a common weed.

220. Cornucopiae L., Sp. Pl. : 54 (1753) — C. cucullatum L.

Annual; culms branched, the upper sheaths inflated and subtending 1— several panicles. Panicle capitate, the peduncle tip expanded into a dentate cupuliform involucre, falling as a whole (peduncle arcuate and retrorsely scabrid in *C. cucullatum*). Spikelets like *Alopecurus* (but dorsal awn very brief in *C. cucullatum*).

Species 2. Eastern Mediterranean to Iraq. Ditches and wet places.

221. Beckmannia Host, Gram. Austr. 3: 5 (1805); Reeder in Bull. Torr. Bot. Cl. 80: 187—196 (1953) — B. eruciformis (L.) Host. *Joachima* Ten., Fl. Nap. 1: ix, 16 (1811) but replaced by Beckmannia in some issues of the Flora; Ten., Cat. Pl. Hort. Neap.: 53 (1813) as "Ioackima" — J. phalaroides Ten. (= B. eruciformis). *Bruchmannia* Nutt., Gen. N. Am. Pl. 1: 48 (1818) nom superfl pro Beckmannia.

Perennial with lowest culm internode tuberous, or annual. Inflorescence of unilateral racemes on a central axis, the orbicular spikelets imbricate. Spikelets 1-flowered with or without an additional ♂ floret, falling entire; glumes herbaceous, gibbously inflated, enclosing all but tip of floret; lemma cartilaginous, rounded on back, acute or tapering to an awn-point. Caryopsis with round hilum and soft endosperm.

Species 2. North temperate zone. Meadows and damp places.
The genus has much in common with *Phleum*, though its inflorescence is most unusual in Aveneae.

222. Phleum L., Sp Pl.: 59 (1753) — P. pratense L. *Stelephuros* Adans., Fam. Pl. 2: 31, 607 (1763) nom superfl pro Phleum. *Achnodonton* P. Beauv., Ess. Agrost.: 24 (1812) — A tenuis (Host) P. Beauv. (= P. subulatum). *Chilochloa* P. Beauv. l.c. 37 —C. boehmeri (Wib.) P. Beauv. (= P. phleoides). *Heleochloa* P. Beauv. l.c. 23, 164 non Roem. (1807) — H. phalaroides (Koel.) P. Beauv. (= P. phleoides). *Achnodon* Link, Hort. Berol. 1: 65 (1827) nom superfl pro Achnodonton. *Maillea* Parl., Pl. Nov.: 31 (1842) — M. urvillei Parl. (= P. crypsoides). *Phalarella* Boiss., Diagn. Pl. Or. 1, 5: 70 (1844) nom prov pro Pseudophleum. *Plantinia* Bub., Fl. Pyr. 4: 268 (1901) nom superfl pro Phleum. *Pseudophleum* Dogan in Notes Roy. Bot. Gard. Edin. 40: 75 (1982) — P. gibbum (Boiss.) Dogan.

Annual or perennial (lowest culm internode corm-like in *P. pratense*). Panicle spiciform, cylindrical to capitate (sessile among basal leaves in *P. crypsoides*). Spikelets with or without rhachilla extension, falling entire; glumes equal, longer than and enclosing floret (*P. gibbum* shorter), membranous, not connate, strongly keeled this often ciliate, truncate to acute, with stout mucro or short stiff awn; lemma membranous, 3—7-nerved (*P. crypsoides* 1-nerved), keeled, truncate to subacute (*P. gibbum* rostrate), awnless or mucronate.

Species 15. North temperate zone and South America. Meadows and dry grasslands. *P. pratense* (Timothy) is a valuable grazing and hay species.

Variation within the genus is summarized in the following key:

Panicle branches free; spikelet usually with rhachilla extension:
  Glumes longer than floret:
    Glumes not winged:

Caryopsis ovoid (P. arenarium)	Sect *Chilochloa*
Caryopsis laterally compressed (P. subulatum)	Sect *Achnodon*
Glumes winged; lemma 1-nerved (P. crypsoides)	Sect *Maillea*
Glumes shorter than floret, coriaceous, gibbous	*P. gibbum*
Panicle branches fused to rhachis; spikelet without rhachilla extension (P. pratense)	Sect *Phleum*

223. Rhizocephalus Boiss., Diagn. Pl. Or. 1, 5: 68 (1844); Hubbard in Hook. Ic. Pl. 35: t 3493 (1951) — R. orientalis Boiss.

Dwarf annual. Panicle capitate, almost sessile among the basal leaves. Spikelets without rhachilla extension, falling entire; glumes equal, shorter than lemma, thinly coriaceous, clavate hairy, acute; lemma subcoriaceous, strongly 5-nerved, keeled, mucronate; palea well developed; lodicules 0, protogynous; stamens 2. Caryopsis ellipsoid, rostrate.

Species 1. Eastern Mediterranean to Iran. Arid places.

Easily mistaken for *Crypsis* which has a 1-nerved lemma, but actually related to *Phleum*.

22. BROMEAE

Dumort., Obs. Gram. Belg.: 82 (1824). *Brominae* (Dumort.) Dumort. in Bull. Soc. Bot. Belg. 7: 67 (1868).

Ligule membranous. Inflorescence a panicle, the spikelets all alike. Spikelets of several to many fertile florets with imperfect florets above, laterally compressed, disarticulating below each floret (except *Boissiera*); glumes persistent, shorter than lowest lemma, entire; lemmas herbaceous to coriaceous, 5—13-nerved, ± 2-toothed, with straight or recurved subapical awn, rarely awnless (*Boissiera, Bromus danthoniae* several-awned; *B. trinii* geniculately awned); lodicules glabrous; ovary capped by a hairy lobed appendage bearing subterminal stigmas. Caryopsis narrowly ellipsoid to linear, hollowed on hilar face.

Genera 3; species ± 150. Temperate regions.

Anatomy. Non-kranz without microhairs. Starch grains of endosperm simple, rounded.

Chromosomes. Chromosomes medium to large; basic number 7.

2n	14	28	42	56	70
No of species	45	48	30	30	8

Bromeae is very similar to Poeae, its claim to tribal status resting mainly upon its unusual starch grains. In the rest of the family the starch grains of the endosperm are compound or angular, and too variable to be of much systematic value (Tateoka in Bot. Mag. Tokyo 75: 377—383, 1962). The simple rounded form is peculiar to Bromeae and Triticeae, and the two tribes evidently represent an off-shoot from some ancestral member of Poeae. The reported hybrid between *Bromus* and *Festuca*, implying a much closer relationship with Poeae, has never been confirmed.

Serological studies emphasize the close relationship between Bromeae and Triticeae, with a weaker link to Poeae. They also reveal the isolated position of *Brachypodium*, which reacts serologically with none of these tribes, though possessing rounded starch grains (Smith in Ann. Bot. 33: 591—612, 1969).

Similar evidence comes from the mesocotyl, the internode below the coleoptile whose elongation usually pushes the seedling shoot above ground. Bromeae and Triticeae (but not *Brachypodium*) are exceptional in that the mesocotyl is hardly evident, seedling emergence being accomplished by elongation above the coleoptile node (Harberd in Ann. Bot. 36: 599—603, 1972).

Most of the species are concentrated in one large genus adapted to a range of mesic habitats in the temperate zone.

The tribe is not easily separated from Poeae, the most useful distinguishing character being its ovary appendage which is apparent even in young specimens.

1   Margins of leaf-sheath overlapping; lemmas awnless   **224 Littledalea**
1   Margins of leaf-sheath connate for most of their length:
  2   Florets with or without 1 awn (more in *B. danthoniae*), falling separately
                                                   225 Bromus
  2   Florets with 5—9 well developed awns, falling in a cluster   **226 Boissiera**

224. Littledalea Hemsl. in Hook. Ic. Pl. 25: t 2472 (1896) — L. tibetica Hemsl.

Perennial; leaf-sheaths with margins free and overlapping almost to the base. Panicle loosely contracted, of few spikelets. Spikelets cuneate to oblong; glumes membranous, the lower 1-nerved; lemmas membranous to papery, large (12—28 mm long), rounded on back, obtuse to truncate and erose, muticous.

Species 3. Central Asia. Stony slopes.
Littledalea can be recognized by its large muticous papery lemmas, but is not unlike some species of *Bromus* such as *B. lanatus*. Its claim to generic rank is somewhat tenuous, resting largely upon the different leaf-sheaths.

225. Bromus L., Sp. Pl.: 76 (1753); Wagnon in Brittonia 7: 415—480 (1952); Tournay in Bull. Jard. Bot. Brux. 31: 289—299 (1961); Smith in Notes Roy. Bot. Gard. Edinb. 30: 361—375 (1970) — B. secalinus L. *Avenaria* Fabric., Enum.: 206 (1759) nom superfl pro Bromus. *Ceratochloa* P. Beauv., Ess. Agrost.: 75, 158 (1812) — C. festucoides P. Beauv. (= B. catharticus). *Bromus sect Bromopsis* Dumort., Obs. Gram. Belg.: 117 (1824) — B. asper Murray (= B. ramosus). *Bromus sect Genea* Dumort. l.c.: 116 — B. sterilis. *Michelaria* Dumort. l.c.: 77 — M. bromoidea (Lej.) Dumort. *Libertia* Lejeune in Nova Acta Acad. Leop.-Carol. Nat. Cur. 12: 755

(1825) non Spreng. (1824); Steud., Syn. Pl. Glum. 1: 319 (1854) as "Sibertia" —nom superfl pro Michelaria. *Aechmophora* Steud., Nom. Bot. ed. 2, 1: 29 (1840) nom superfl pro Michelaria. *Serrafalcus* Parl., Rar. Pl. Sic. 2: 14 (1840) — S. racemosus (L.) Parl. *Anisantha* Koch in Linnaea 21: 394 (1848) — A. pontica Koch (= B. tectorum). *Triniusa* Steud., Syn. Pl. Glum. 1: 328 (1854) — T. danthoniae (Trin.) Steud. *Genea* (Dumort.) Dumort. in Bull. Soc. Bot. Belg. 7: 67 (1868) non Vittadini (1831). *Bromopsis* (Dumort.) Fourr. in Ann. Soc. Linn. Lyon sér.2, 17: 187 (1869). *Forasaccus* Bub., Fl. Pyr. 4: 379 (1901) nom superfl pro Bromus. *Festuca subgen Stenofestuca* Honda, Monogr. Poac.: 54 (1930) — F. pauciflora Thunb. *Nevskiella* Krecz. & Vved. in Trudy Sredne-Az. Univ. ser. 8b, 17: 15, 22 (1934) — N. gracillima (Bunge) Krecz. & Vved. *Trisetobromus* Nevski l.c.: 15 — T. hirtus (Trin.) Nevski (= B. trinii). *Stenofestuca* (Honda) Nakai in J. Jap. Bot. 25: 6 (1950).

Annual or perennial; leaf-sheaths with margins connate for most of their length, usually hairy. Panicle open or contracted, ample or scanty (very rarely reduced to a single spikelet). Spikelets cuneate to ovate; glumes herbaceous; lemmas herbaceous to subcoriaceous sometimes with membranous margins, entire or bidenticulate to bilobed, mucronate to long awned (*B. brevis, B. briziformis*, some *B. inermis*, some *B. lanatus* muticous; *B. danthoniae* 3-awned often with 2 additional awnlets), the awn subapical though sometimes minutely so (*B. pauciflorus* terminal); stamens (1—)3.

Species ± 150. Temperate regions of both hemispheres but mainly in the north. Woodland, meadow and ruderal habitats. Several of the perennial species are important forage grasses in the open woodlands of mountain regions in western USA. *B. inermis* is cultivated for hay, but most of the annual species are weedy; those with a pungent callus and rough awn, such as *B. rigidus* (Ripgut), may cause injury to livestock by penetrating mouth, eyes or intestines. *B. mango*, a biennial, was formerly grown as a cereal in Chile.

Variation within the genus is indicated by the following key (which ignores a few exceptions to the usual glume nervation):

Awn geniculate; lower glume 1-nerved (B. trinii)   Sect *Neobromus*
Awn straight or curved:
  Lemmas keeled; lower glume 3—5-nerved; perennial (B. catharticus)
                                         Sect *Ceratochloa*
  Lemmas rounded on back:
    Lower glume 1-nerved the upper 3-nerved:
      Perennial; spikelets parallel-sided; awn shorter than lemma (B. erectus)
                                         Sect *Pnigma*
    Annual:
      Awn 1—2 times length of lemma; spikelets many-flowered, cuneate
      (B. sterilis)   Sect *Genea*
      Awn 3—6 times length of lemma; spikelets 3—5-flowered, ovate to oblong
      (B. gracillimus)   Sect *Nevskiella*
    Lower glume 3—5-nerved, the upper 5—7-nerved; spikelets ovate to lanceolate; annual (B. hordeaceus)   Sect *Bromus*

Bromus is easily confused with *Festuca*, particularly *F. gigantea*. For certainty it is necessary to examine the ovary, but hairy tubular leaf-sheaths and subapical lemma awns are useful supporting distinctions, though not entirely reliable. It is less easily confused with *Helictotrichon*, whose awns are clearly dorsal and mostly geniculate, but *B. trinii* can be deceptive. *B. carinatus* provides a nice example of facultative cleistogamy induced by adverse conditions (Harlan in Amer. J. Bot. 32: 66—72, 1945).

226. Boissiera Steud., Nom. Bot. ed. 2, 1: 213 (1840) nom nov pro seq. *Pappophorum sect Euraphis* Trin. in Mém. Acad. Sci. Pétersb. sér. 6, 1: 92 (1830) —P. pumilio Trin. (= B. squarrosa). *Schnizleinia* Steud., Nom. Bot. ed. 2, 1: 213 (1840) in syn sub B. bromoides Steud. (= B. squarrosa). *Euraphis* (Trin.) Lindley, Veg. Kingdom : 115 (1846). *Wiestia* Boiss., Fl. Or. 5: 559 (1884) non Schultz-Bip. (1841), in syn sub Boissiera.

Annual; leaf-sheaths with margins connate for most of their length. Panicle densely contracted, ± ovate. Spikelets narrowly lanceolate, disarticulating above glumes but not between florets, the upper florets reduced to a bunch of awns; glumes membranous, the lower 3-nerved; lemmas chartaceous to coriaceous, prominently 11—13-nerved, with a transverse row of 5—9 awns across the back.

Species 1. Turkey to Pakistan. Open places on dry stony soils.
Boissiera is serologically indistinguisable from *Bromus* and evidently related to *B. danthoniae* (Smith in Feddes Rep. 79: 337—345, 1969), but is sufficiently distinct morphologically to justify a separate genus. Note the superficial similarity to *Enneapogon*.

23. TRITICEAE.

Dumort., Obs. Gram. Belg.: 82 (1824); Nevski in Trudy Bot. Inst. Akad. Nauk SSSR 1: 9—32 (1933); Runemark & Heneen in Bot. Not. 121: 51—79 (1968); Sakamoto in Seiken Ziho 24: 11—31 (1973); Baum in Canad. J. Bot. 56: 27—56, 374—385, 2948—2954 (1978); Löve in Feddes Rep. 95: 425—521 (1984). *Hordeeae* Spenner, Fl. Friburg 1: 155 (1825). *Secaleae* Reichenb., Consp. Reg. Veg.: 48 (1828). *Brachypodieae* Harz in Linnaea 43: 15 (1880). *Frumenteae* Krause in Verh. Nat. Ver. Preuss. Rheinl. 59: 172 (1903) nom inval.
Hordeinae Dumort., Obs. Gram. Belg.: 91 (1824). *Aegilopinae* Bluff, Nees & Schauer, Comp. Fl. Germ. ed. 2, 1: 52 (1836). *Triticinae* Griseb., Fl. Rumel. Bithyn. 2: 422 (1844). *Elyminae* Benth. in J. Linn. Soc. Bot. 19: 133 (1881). *Brachypodiinae* Hack. in Engl. & Prantl, Nat. Pfl.-Fam. 2, 2: 75 (1887). *Agropyrinae* Nevski in Trudy Bot. Inst. Akad. Nauk SSSR 1: 27 (1933). *Clinelyminae* Nevski l.c.: 26 nom inval. *Roegneriinae* Nevski l.c. *Henrardiinae* C.E. Hubbard in Hook. Ic. Pl. 35: t 3453 (1948).

Ligule membranous; leaf-blades often auriculate. Inflorescence a single bilateral raceme or quasi-raceme, the spikelets alternate in two opposite rows, single or in groups of 2—3 (rarely more) at each node, broadside to rhachis and usually sessile, all alike (except *Aegilops, Heteranthelium, Sitanion*); rhachis tough, or fragile and then disarticulating at base of internode (except *Henrardia*, some *Aegilops*). Spikelets 1—many-flowered with the apical florets smaller, laterally compressed (dorsally if 1-flowered), disarticulating below each floret if rhachis tough; glumes persistent, shorter or narrower than lemma leaving much of it exposed (except *Henrardia, Triticum polonicum*, some *Elymus*), usually coriaceous,

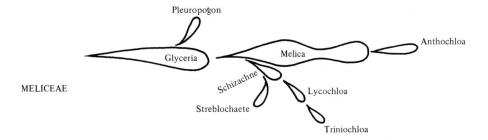

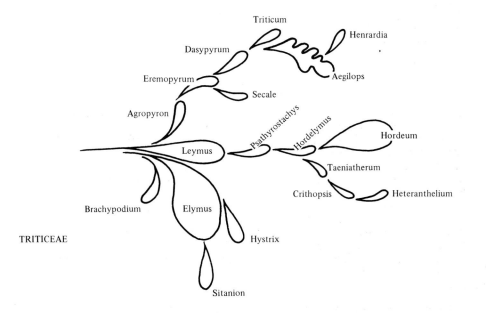

Fig. 13 Diagram of relationships in Meliceae and Triticeae.

sometimes awn-like; lemmas coriaceous (except some *Brachypodium*), 5—11-nerved (except *Henrardia*), with or without a straight or recurved awn from tip; lodicules ciliate; ovary tipped by a small fleshy hairy appendage. Caryopsis ellipsoid, hollowed on hilar face.

Genera 18; species ± 330. Temperate and warm temperate zones, principally in northern hemisphere.

Anatomy. Non-kranz without microhairs. Starch grains of endosperm simple, rounded.

Chromosomes. Chromosomes large; basic number 7 (but see *Brachypodium*).

2n	14	21	28	42	56
No of species	140	6	204	78	21

The tribe has a distinctive bilateral spicate inflorescence with the spikelets placed broadside to the rhachis. This is best termed a raceme, though it sometimes comes close to a spiciform panicle. Its derivation from a condensed panicle is well shown by *Leymus condensatus*, whose nodal spikelet cluster sometimes develops into a dwarf lateral branch. The racemes, when fragile, are unusual in that disarticulation occurs above each node, leaving the spikelet attached to the internode below it (outside Triticeae disarticulation is subnodal, leaving spikelet and internode side by side). This internode is analogous to the spikelet callus of other tribes, forming the tip of a cuneate dispersal unit which can propel itself along the ground by hygroscopic flexing of its awns.

Supporting characters are the coriaceous lemmas, hairy lodicules, hairy ovary tip and simple rounded starch grains. The latter point to a common origin with Bromeae, to which the anomalous genus *Brachypodium* bears some resemblance.

The taxonomy of the tribe is complicated by two special factors. Firstly the tribe shows an exceptional capacity for intergeneric hybridization involving most of its members, which creates problems both in the theoretical concept of generic rank, and in the practical construction of keys (hybrids have been ignored in the key below). It also implies a more close-knit reticulate pattern of relationships than the simplified trends shown in fig. 13 would suggest. Secondly cytogenetic research, attracted by the presence of 3 major cereal genera, has provided an unusually extensive knowledge of the tribe's genome constitution (summarized by Dewey in Estes et al, Grasses & Grasslands: 51—88, 1982 and in Gustafson, Gene Manipulation in Plant Improvement, 1984). However, the genome classification, though attractive in theory, is sometimes difficult to translate into practical morphological diagnoses. The net result of the two factors is that generic classification is currently in a state of flux, subject to major disagreements whose outcome is still uncertain.

Ecologically the tribe divides into two broad groups: annual genera of the Mediterranean region, and perennial genera of cool temperate plains and steppes.

Recognition of the tribe presents few problems, apart from *Henrardia*.

1   Lemma membranous, 3-nerved, enclosed by collateral glumes
244 Henrardia
1   Lemma ± coriaceous, 5—11-nerved:
 2   Spikelets in groups of 2 or more at each node of raceme:
  3   Spikelets sessile:
   4   Plants perennial:

5   Raceme rhachis tough:
 6   Glumes, or at least the upper, 3 or more nerved, usually broad, the lateral nerves ± rib-like:
   7   Spikelets pedicelled; lemma 7—9-nerved   **227 Brachypodium**
   7   Spikelets sessile, or if with a brief pedicel then lemma 5-nerved
                                                              228 Elymus
 6   Glumes 1(—5)-nerved, narrow with indistinct lateral nerves or awn-like, rarely absent:
   8   Glumes free to the base or absent:
     9   Leaf-blades flexible, herbaceous, mesic; glumes usually suppressed or much reduced   **229 Hystrix**
     9   Leaf-blades stiff, harsh, xeric; glumes well developed   **231 Leymus**
   8   Glumes connate for a short distance above base   **233 Hordelymus**
5   Raceme rhachis fragile:
   10   Lowermost floret in at least some of the spikelets represented by an awn, or the spikelets more than 2-flowered   **230 Sitanion**
   10   Lowermost floret always fertile; spikelets 1—2-flowered
                                                     232 Psathyrostachys
 4   Plants annual:
   11   Raceme rhachis tough   **234 Taeniatherum**
   11   Raceme rhachis fragile   **235 Crithopsis**
 3   Spikelets, or at least laterals in each triad, pedicelled (except cultivated species), 1-flowered; rhachis fragile   **237 Hordeum**
 2   Spikelets borne singly at each node:
   12   Glumes keeled to the base (*Triticum* sometimes rounded below but then annual):
   13   Glumes 1—2-keeled, without tufts of hair:
     14   Glumes acuminate, the nerves convergent in the tip:
       15   Lemma glabrous or pilose; raceme ± pectinate (otherwise see *231 Leymus*):
         16   Plant perennial; raceme tough   **238 Agropyron**
         16   Plant annual; raceme fragile or falling entire   **239 Eremopyrum**
       15   Lemma pectinately spinulose on keel   **240 Secale**
     14   Glumes obtuse to bidentate, the outer nerves separated at tip (if glumes markedly unequal see *174 Gaudinia*)   **242 Triticum**
   13   Glumes 2-keeled, with tufts of hair along the keels   **241 Dasypyrum**
   12   Glumes rounded on back, sometimes keeled above middle and then perennial:
   17   Plants annual:
     18   Glumes many-nerved (if palea keels pectinately spinulose see *227 Brachypodium distachyum*)   **243 Aegilops**
     18   Glumes awn-like   **236 Heteranthelium**
   17   Plants perennial   Go to 6

227. Brachypodium P. Beauv., Ess. Agrost.: 100, 155 (1812); Tateoka in Bol. Soc. Arg. Bot. 12: 44—56 (1968); Robertson in Genetica 56: 54—60 (1981) — B. pinnatum (L.) P. Beauv. *Tragus* Panzer, Id. Rev. Gräser: 40 (1813) non Haller (1768), nom superfl pro Brachypodium. *Trachynia* Link, Hort. Berol. 1: 42 (1827) — T. distachya (L.) Link. *Brevipodium* A. & D. Löve in Bot. Not. 114: 36 (1961) —B. sylvaticum (Huds.) A. & D. Löve.

Perennial (*B. distachyum* annual). Raceme linear, loose, its relatively few (rarely only 1) spikelets borne singly on a pedicel 0.5—2.5 mm long and divergent from a tough rhachis. Spikelets 5—20-flowered, elongated, subterete to lightly laterally compressed; glumes opposite, lanceolate, herbaceous to membranous, shorter than lowest lemma, distinctly 3—9-nerved, rounded on back, obtuse to shortly awned; lemmas herbaceous to firmly membranous but sometimes becoming coriaceous at maturity, 7—9-nerved, rounded on back, obtuse or shortly awned from tip.

Species 16. Temperate Eurasia, extending southwards on tropical mountains; Mexico to Bolivia. Woodland and open grassland.

The loose raceme and elongated spikelets give *Brachypodium* a recognizable and fairly uniform facies, but cytologically the genus is a hotch-potch. It contains species with basic chromosome numbers of 5, 7 and 9, also *B. mexicanum* with 2n = 38; moreover the chromosomes themselves are much smaller than in other genera of Triticeae or Bromeae. The situation is further complicated by a group of species with *Brachypodium*-like pedicels, but whose 5-nerved coriaceous lemmas and 2n = 14 fairly large chromosomes are better accommodated in *Elymus* (as *E. longearistatus* etc.). Cytology and serology point to an isolated position for *Brachypodium*, and it is often accommodated in an independent tribe. On the other hand it intergrades morphologically with *Elymus*, particularly *E. serpentini*, and on that account has here been treated as an aberrant member of Triticeae.

228. Elymus L., Sp. Pl.: 83 (1753); Gould in Madroño 9: 120—128 (1947); Bowden in Canad. J. Bot. 43: 1421—1448 (1965) — E. sibiricus L. *Sitospelos* Adans., Fam. Pl. 2: 36, 606 (1763) nom superfl pro Elymus. *Elytrigia* Desv. in Nouv. Bull. Sci. Soc. Philom. 2: 190 (1810) — E. repens (L.) Nevski. *Braconotia* Godr., Fl. Lorraine 3: 191 (1844) nom superfl pro Elytrigia. *Cryptopyrum* Heynh., Nom. Bot. Hort. 2: 174 (1846) nom nud — E. trachycaulus. *Roegneria* Koch in Linnaea 21: 413 (1848) — R. caucasica Koch. *Elymus sect. Clinelymus* Griseb. in Ledeb., Fl. Ross. 4: 330 (1852) nom superfl pro sect Elymus. *Anthosachne* Steud., Syn. Pl. Glum. 1: 237 (1854) — A. australasica Steud. (= E. scabrus). *Crithopyrum*Steud. l.c.: 344 in syn sub Triticum trachycaulum Link. *Goulardia* Husn., Gram. France Belg.: 83 (1899) — G. canina (L.) Husn. *Terrellia* Lunell in Amer. Midl. Nat. 4: 227 (1915) nom superfl pro Elymus. *Clinelymus* (Griseb.) Nevski in Isv. Bot. Sada Akad. Nauk SSSR 30: 640 (1932) nom superfl. *Elytrigia sect Pseudoroegneria* Nevski in Trudy Sredne-Az. Univ. ser. 8b, 17: 60 (1934) — E. strigosa (Bieb.) Nevski. *Brachypodium sect Festucopsis* C.E. Hubbard in Hook Ic. Pl. 33: t 3280 (1935) — B. serpentini C.E. Hubbard. *Campeiostachys* Drobov, Fl. Uzbek. 1: 300, 540 (1941) —C. schrenkiana (Schrenk.) Drobov. *Semeiostachys* Drobov l.c.: 281, 539 — S. turczaninovii (Drobov) Drobov (= E. gmelinii). *Festucopsis* (C.E. Hubbard) Melderis in Bot. J. Linn. Soc. 76: 317 (1978). *Lophopyrum* Löve in Taxon 29: 351 (1980) — L. elongatum (Host) Löve. *Pascopyrum* Löve l.c. 547 — P. smithii (Rydb.) Löve. *Pseudoroegneria* (Nevski) Löve l.c. 168. *Thinopyrum* Löve l.c. 351 —T. junceum (L.) Löve (= E. farctus).

Perennial. Raceme linear, dense, its many spikelets borne singly or occasionally in pairs (up to 4 in *E. canadensis*), sessile (*E. longearistatus* & allies, *E. sanctus, E. serpentini* briefly pedicelled) and appressed to a tough rhachis

(*E. farctus* fragile; *E. scribneri* tardily so). Spikelets 3—9-flowered, clearly laterally compressed; glumes opposite or side by side, lanceolate to narrowly oblong (linear in *E. sibiricus, E. canadensis* & allies), firmly membranous to coriaceous, the lower usually ½ length of lowest lemma, distinctly 3—9-nerved (very rarely the lower 1-nerved), the nerves parallel or convergent and commonly keeled in upper half, obtuse to shortly awned; lemmas coriaceous, 5-nerved, rounded on back or keeled only at tip, obtuse acute or bidentate, muticous or awned, the latter sometimes long and recurved.

Species ± 150. Best represented in Asia, but extending through temperate latitudes of northern and southern hemispheres. Wide range of meadow, woodland, upland and steppe habitats, also on dunes. The genus (Wheatgrass, Wildrye) includes a number of valuable forage species, particularly on the N American plains. The dune species include useful sand binders. *E. repens* (Couch grass) is a rampantly rhizomatous weed.

Elymus and *Leymus* are contiguous genera, whose separation has been contentious. The traditional criterion of single or paired spikelets is unsatisfactory, as it sometimes separates closely related species, and is ambiguous when both spikelet arrangements are mixed on the same plant. Glume nervation marks a more natural division, which seems worth upholding at generic level. Difficulties in identification may arise with species such as *E. nutans, E. schrenkianus* & *E. sibiricus* having narrow glumes less than ¼ the length of the lemma, whose lower glume may be very small and only 1-nerved; also with species such as *E. canadensis* whose glumes are long and linear, though the nerves are clearly ribbed.

E. farctus has fragile racemes, but is otherwise so close to *E. elongatus* that generic separation seems inappropriate. The tardily disarticulating racemes of *E. scribneri* may signify hybridization with *Sitanion*.

The spikelets of *Elymus* have a brief callus at the base, but in a few species there is also a pedicel. The latter, though often obscure or inconstant, can be quite well developed and then provides a link with *Brachypodium*.

229. Hystrix Moench, Meth.: 294 (1794) — H. patula Moench. *Asperella* Humboldt in Bot. Mag. Zürich 7: 5 (1790) non Asprella Schreb. (1789) — A. hystrix (L.) Humboldt (= H. patula). *Gymnostichum* Schreb., Beschr. Gräser 3: 127 (1810) nom superfl pro Hystrix. *Stenostachys* Turcz. in Bull. Soc. Imp. Nat. Moscou 35: 330 (1862) — S. narduroides Turcz. (= H. gracilis). *Cockaynea* Zotov in Trans. Roy. Soc. New Zealand 73: 233 (1943) — C. laevis (Petrie) Zotov.

Perennial; leafblades flexible, flat and broadly linear (*H. gracilis, H. laevis* slender and flaccid), herbaceous, the tip filiform. Raceme linear, the spikelets borne in groups of 2—4 (singly in *H. gracilis, H. laevis*) on a tough rhachis. Spikelets (1—)2—4-flowered; glumes typically reduced to subulate stumps or suppressed, occasionally some of them represented by filiform bristles seldom more than ½ length of lemma (especially *H. coreana, H. laevis*); lemmas rounded on back, awned.

Species 9. North America and temperate Asia; New Zealand. Woodland and meadows.

Hystrix has the same genome as *Elymus*, and the two genera are often united for that reason. It is not closely related to *Leymus*, though easy to confuse with it when the glumes are developed; the mesic leaves are then the best distinguishing character. *Cockaynea* may be an unrelated example of parallel evolution, but it is not well known.

230. Sitanion Raf. in J. Phys. Chim. 89: 103 (1819); Wilson in Brittonia 15: 303—323 (1963) — S. elymoides Raf. (= S. hystrix). *Polyantherix* Nees in Ann. Nat. Hist. 1: 284 (1838) — P. hystrix (Nutt.) Nees.

Perennial. Raceme linear to oblong, the spikelets borne in groups of 2(—3) on a fragile rhachis (the rhachilla also often fragile), sometimes 1(—2) of the spikelets in each group sterile and reduced to a bunch of awns. Spikelets with 1—several fertile florets plus a smaller sterile terminal floret, but the lowermost floret in one or both spikelets of a pair reduced to an awn (except *S. longifolium*); glumes side by side, 1—several-nerved, long, awn-like, entire or 2—many-cleft; lemma broadly rounded on back, long awned from tip or from between lateral awnlets.

Species 4. Western North America from Canada to Mexico. Wide habitat range from subdesert to alpine meadow.

A small genus of variable and intergrading species. The inflorescence is excessively bristly, acicular glumes and awned lemmas being supplemented by the reduced lowermost lemma and by reduced spikelets. *S. longifolium*, whose several-flowered spikelets have unmodified lemmas, provides a link with *Elymus*, and it has been shown that the two genera share the same genome.

231. Leymus Hochst. in Flora 3l: 118 (1848); Bowden in Canad. J. Bot. 42: 547—601 (1964); Barkworth & Atkins in Amer. J. Bot. 71: 609—625 (1984) — L. arenarius (L.) Hochst. *Triticum sect Anisopyrum* Griseb. in Ledeb., Fl. Ross. 4: 343 (1852) —T. ramosum Trin. *Anisopyrum* (Griseb.) Gren. & Duval, Fl. Mass. Adv. Suppl.: 24 (1859) nom prov. *Aneurolepidium* Nevski in Trudy Bot. Inst. Akad. Nauk SSSR 2: 69 (1934) — A. multicaule (Kar. & Kir.) Nevski. *Malacurus* Nevski in Trudy Sredne-Az. Univ. ser. 8b, 17: 38 (1934) — M. lanatus (Korj.) Nevski.

Perennial; leaf-blades stiff, flat or rolled, harsh and usually glaucous, the tip ± pungent. Raceme linear, the spikelets borne in pairs (3—6 or more in a few species such as *L. racemosus* & *L. condensatus*, the latter occasionally with dwarf side branches) or rarely singly, and appressed to a tough rhachis. Spikelets 3—7-flowered (*L. cappadocicus* 1—2-flowered); glumes opposite or side by side, mostly over ½ length of lemma (lower glume of *L. aemulans, L. innovatus, L. ramosus* sometimes less than ¼), typically 1-nerved and linear or awn-like, but sometimes narrowly lanceolate (especially *L. arenarius* & allies) and then coriaceous and 1—3(—5)-nerved the nerves not raised (except *L. mollis*), keel-less or keeled almost to base, acute to shortly awned; lemmas not keeled or only at tip, acute to shortly awned.

Species ± 40. North temperate zone; 1 species in Argentina. Stony slopes and steppes; often adapted to saline, alkaline or dune habitats. The dune species include a number of useful sand binders.

232. Psathyrostachys Nevski in Komarov, Fl. SSSR 2: 712 (1934) — P. lanuginosa (Trin.) Nevski.

Perennial. Raceme linear to oblong, the spikelets sessile in triads or sometimes in pairs, on a fragile rhachis. Spikelets 1—2-flowered plus rhachilla extension, dorsally compressed; glumes side by side, awn-like, entire; lemma broadly rounded on back, acuminate to awned.

Species 7. Urals to Siberia; Turkey to Afghanistan. Stony slopes.
The genus is intermediate between *Leymus* and *Hordeum*. It mimics *Sitanion*, which seems to be a parallel N American development from a different ancestry.

233. Hordelymus (Jessen) Harz, Samenkunde 2: 1147 (1885). *Cuviera* Koeler, Descr. Gram.: 328 (1802) nom rejic non DC (1807) — C. europaeus (L.) Koel. *Elymus sect Leptothrix* Dumort., Obs. Gram. Belg.: 92 (1824) — E. europaeus (L.) Dumort. *Orostachys* Steud., Nom. Bot. ed. 2, 2: 233 (1841) nom nud — H. europaeus. *Elymus sect Medusather* Griseb. in Ledeb., Fl. Ross. 4: 329 (1852) nom superfl pro sect Leptothrix. *Hordeum subgen Hordelymus* Jessen, Deutsch. Gräser: 202 (1863) — H. europaeus (L.) All. *Leptothrix* (Dumort.) Dumort. in Bull. Soc. Bot. Belg. 7: 66 (1868) non Kuetzing (1843). *Medusather* Candargy in Arch. Biol. Veg. 1: 38 (1901) nom superfl pro Hordelymus.

Perennial. Raceme oblong to linear, with triads of spikelets, all sessile and fertile or the central ♂, on tough rhachis. Spikelets 1(—2)-flowered plus bristle-like rhachilla extension, dorsally compressed; glumes side by side, awn-like, connate for a short distance from base; lemma rounded on back, acuminate to an awn.

Species 1. Europe and North Africa, eastward to the Caucasus. Woodland.

234. Taeniatherum Nevski in Trudy Sredne-Az. Univ. ser. 8b, 17: 38 (1934); Humphries in Bot. J. Linn. Soc. 76: 340—344 (1978) — T. crinitum (Schreb.) Nevski (= T. caput-medusae).

Annual. Raceme narrowly oblong, the spikelets paired on a tough glabrous rhachis. Spikelets 2-flowered, the upper ± rudimentary; glumes side by side, awn-like; lemma broadly rounded on back, with long recurved awn.

Species 1. Mediterranean and Middle East from Spain to Pakistan. Grassy slopes on dry stony soils.

235. Crithopsis Jaub. & Spach, Ill. Pl. Or. 4: 30 (1851) — C. rhachitricha Jaub. & Spach (= C. delileana).

Annual. Raceme narrowly oblong, the spikelets paired on a fragile hairy rhachis. Spikelets 2-flowered, the upper ± rudimentary; glumes opposite, linear, 1—5-nerved, awned; lemma broadly rounded on back, awned.

Species 1. Libya and Crete to Iran. Dry grassland.

236. Heteranthelium Jaub. & Spach, Ill. Pl. Or. 4: 24 (1851) — H. piliferum (Russell) Jaub. & Spach.

Annual. Raceme oblong, with single spikelets on a fragile rhachis, this breaking into several segments of 1—2 fertile nodes below and 1—3 sterile nodes above, the latter closely spaced with their spikelets reduced to a bunch of awns. Fertile spikelets 1—2-flowered, plus rhachilla extension crowned by a tuft of awns; glumes awn-like; lemma rounded on back, tuberculate, tapering to a long awn.

Species 1. Turkey to Pakistan. Dry slopes.
An unusual genus with highly evolved disseminules.

237. Hordeum L., Sp. Pl.: 84 (1753); Nevski in Trudy Bot. Inst. Akad. Nauk SSSR 5: 64—255 (1941); Bothmer, Jacobsen & Jorgenson in Proc. 4th Int. Barley Gen. Symp. Edinburgh: 13—21 (1981) — H. vulgare L. *Zeocriton* Wolf, Gen. Pl. Vocab. Char. Def.: 21 (1776) — Z. commune P. Beauv. (= H. distichon). *Critesion* Raf. in J. Phys. Chim. 89: 103 (1819) — C. geniculatum Raf. (= H. jubatum). *Critho* E. Meyer, Ind. Sem. Hort. Regiomont.: 5 (1848) — C. aegiceras (Royle) E. Meyer.

Annual or perennial. Raceme oblong to linear, with triads of 1 central bisexual spikelet and 2 ♂ or barren laterals, all pedicelled or the central sessile, on fragile rhachis (all sessile on tough rhachis in cultivated species). Central spikelet 1-flowered plus bristle-like rhachilla extension, dorsally compressed; glumes side by side, narrowly lanceolate weakly 3-nerved and flat, or more often awn-like, free to the base; lemma rounded on back, obscurely nerved, acuminate to a conspicuous awn (merely a short awn-point in *H. muticum* and some other S. American species). Lateral spikelets usually smaller than central and often reduced to a bunch of 3 awns.

Species ± 40. Temperate regions throughout the world. Open weedy places, usually on dry soils. *H. vulgare* (Barley) is an important cereal of temperate regions, whose short growing season has enabled it to extend into the arid and high altitude fringes of temperate agriculture; it also has some tolerance for saline soils. Wild *H. spontaneum* was domesticated in the Near East some time prior to 7000 BC, giving rise to the 2-rowed cultivated form *H. distichon*. This then underwent a mutation to form 6-rowed *H. vulgare*, in which all the spikelets in each triad are fertile (also a 4-rowed variant in which the central spikelet is sterile). An ealier hypothesis regarded *H. agriocrithon*, a 6-rowed barley with fragile rhachis, as the ancestral wild form, but this species is now considered to be a hybrid of *H. spontaneum* × *H. vulgare* (Helbaek in Econ. Bot. 20: 350—360, 1966; Staudt l.c. 15: 205—212, 1961; Zohary in Bull. Res. Counc. Israel 9D: 2—42, 1960). *H. aegiceras* is a strange cultivated form with the heritable abnormality of a lemma terminating in a trilobed appendage bearing rudimentary accessory spikelets.
A uniform genus of closely related taxa, currently undergoing some reappraisal of the rank to which the traditional species should be assigned; thus

all the species of the preceding paragraph are now commonly included in *H. vulgare* (Bowden in Canad. J. Bot. 37: 677—681, 1959). Butzin (Neue Untersuch. Blüte Gram.: 78, 1965) believes that the glumes are the product of a split lower glume, the true upper glume being suppressed.

238. Agropyron Gaertn., Novi Comm. Acad. Sci. Petrop. 14: 539 (1770) — A. cristatum (L.) Gaertn. *Kratzmannia* Opiz, Seznam: 56 (1852) nom nud — A. cristatum. *Costia* Willkomm in Bot. Zeit. 16: 377 (1858) nom superfl pro Agropyron. *Agropyron sect Australopyrum* Tzvelev in Nov. Sist. Vysh. Rast. 10: 35 (1973) — A. pectinatum (Labill.) P. Beauv. *Australopyrum* (Tzvelev) Löve in Feddes Rep. 95: 442 (1984).

Perennial. Raceme broadly linear to narrowly oblong, with single spikelets divergently or pectinately arranged on a tough rhachis. Spikelets 3—10-flowered; glumes linear to narrowly ovate, indurated, 1—5-nerved, 1-keeled to the base, tapering to an acuminate or shortly awned tip in which the nerves converge; lemmas keeled, glabrous or pilose, tip like that of glumes; palea ± spinulose on keels, sometimes bimucronate.

Species ± 15. Mediterranean, through the Middle East to China; also Australia and New Zealand. Open steppes on dry sandy soils.
Agropyron is here restricted to a minor segregate with keeled glumes and somewhat pectinate racemes, but it was formerly used in a much wider sense to include most of *Elymus*. Keeled glumes sometimes occur in *Leymus*, but these species usually have paired spikelets and are never pectinate.

239. Eremopyrum (Ledeb.) Jaub. & Spach in Ann. Sci. Nat. Bot. ser. 3, 14: 360 (1851); Schur, Enum. Pl. Transsilv.: 807 (1866) as "Cremopyrum". *Triticum sect Eremopyrum* Ledeb., Fl. Altaica 1: 112 (1829) — T. orientale (L.) Bieb.

Annual. Raceme oblong to orbicular, fragile (falling as a whole in *E. triticeum*). Otherwise like *Agropyron*.

Species 5. Turkey to central Asia and Pakistan. Stony slopes, steppes and semi-desert.
The genus is little more than an annual version of *Agropyron*.

240. Secale L., Sp. Pl.: 84 (1753); Roshevitz in Trudy Bot. Inst. Akad. Nauk SSSR 6: 105—163 (1947); Ivanov & Yakovlev in Trudy Prikl. Bot. Genet. Selek. 44: 3—38 (1971); Kobylyanski l.c. 79: 24—38 (1983) — S. cereale L. *Gramen* Séguier, Pl. Veron. 3: 145 (1754); Dandy in Reg. Veg. 51: 52 (1967) — nom superfl pro Secale.

Annual or perennial. Raceme oblong to linear, with single spikelets on fragile rhachis (except cultivated forms). Spikelets 2-flowered plus short rhachilla extension; glumes linear, membranous, 1-nerved, sharply keeled to the base, acuminate or awned; lemmas sharply keeled, pectinate spinulose on the keel, tapering to an awn.

Species 4. Eastern Europe to central Asia; also Spain and South Africa. Sandy soils and dry hillsides. *S. cereale* (Rye) is grown as a cereal in most temperate regions, tolerating cold climates and poor soils. It probably originated in Turkey as a weedy derivative of wild *S. montanum* infesting wheat and barley fields, eventually being itself taken into cultivation when agriculture spread northward into colder climates (Stutz in Amer. J. Bot. 59: 59—70, 1971; Sencer & Hawkes in Biol. J. Linn. Soc. 13: 299—313, 1980).

The taxonomy of *Secale* is complicated by a host of ill-defined weedy intermediates between *S. montanum* and *S. cereale*, originally assigned to 11 different species by Roshevitz (l.c.). These are now usually reduced to infraspecific level, but the taxonomy of the genus is still unsettled.

241. Dasypyrum (Coss. & Dur.) Dur., Ind. Gen. Phan.: 504 (1888); Humphries in Bot. J. Linn. Soc. 76: 361—362 (1978). *Secalidium* Schur in Verh. Siebenberg. Ver. Naturw. (Sert. Fl. Transsilv.): 91 (1853) in syn sub Triticum villosum (L.) Bieb. *Triticum sect Dasypyrum* Coss. & Dur., Expl. Alg. Phan.: 202 (1855) — T. villosum. *Triticum sect Pseudosecale* Godr. in Gren. & Godr., Fl. France 3: 599 (1856) nom superfl pro sect Dasypyrum. *Haynaldia* Schur, Enum. Pl. Transsilv.: 807 (June 1866) non Schulzer (May 1866) — H. villosa (L.) Schur. *Pseudosecale* (Godr.) Degen, Fl. Veleb. 1: 575 (1936).

Annual or perennial. Raceme narrowly oblong, with single spikelets on a fragile rhachis. Spikelets 2—4-flowered, usually only the 2 lowest florets bisexual; glumes oblong to cuneate, coriaceous with truncate membranous flanks, strongly 2-keeled, the keels adorned with hair tufts and convergent above, awned; lemmas keeled with hair tufts on keel, entire or bidentate, awned.

Species 2. Southeast Europe and Turkey; North Africa. Stony slopes.

242. Triticum L., Sp. Pl.: 85 (1753); Jakubziner in Proc. 1st Int. Wheat Gen. Symp.: 207—217 (1959); Briggle & Reitz, US Dept. Agric. Tech. Bull. 1278 (1963); McKey in Hereditas, Suppl. 2: 237—276 (1966) — T. aestivum L. *Spelta* Wolf, Gen. Pl. Vocab. Char. Def.: 22 (1776) — T. spelta L. *Bromus* Scop., Introd.: 74 (1777) nom superfl pro Triticum. *Crithodium* Link in Linnaea 9: 132 (1834) — C. aegilopoides Link (= T. boeoticum). *Gigachilon* Seidl in Bercht. & Seidl, Oek.-tech. Fl. Böhm. 1: 425 (1836) in syn sub T. polonicum L. *Nivieria* Ser. in Ann. Soc. Roy. Agric. Lyon. 5: 114 (1842) — N. monococca (L.) Ser. *Deina* Alefeld, Landwirt. Fl. : 335 (1866) —D. polonica (L.) Alefeld. *Frumentum* Krause in Bot. Centralbl. 73: 339 (1898) nom superfl pro Triticum. *Zeia* Lunell in Amer. Midl. Nat. 4: 226 (1915) non Zea L. (1753) — nom superfl pro Triticum.

Annual. Raceme linear, bearing single spikelets on a fragile rhachis (tardily so or tough in cultivated species). Spikelets 3—9-flowered (sometimes only 1 of the florets bisexual in *T. boeoticum*, *T. monococcum*); glumes oblong to ovate (longer than lemmas in *T. polonicum*), coriaceous, 5—11-nerved, 1—2-keeled (but sometimes becoming rounded below as grain expands), obtuse truncate or bidentate, the lateral nerves diverging into the teeth, mucronate or awned; lemmas rounded on back or keeled near tip, the tip similar to that of glumes.

Species 10—20. Eastern Mediterranean to Iran. Stony hillsides, dry grassland and weedy places; more than half the species cultivated. Wheat is the principal cereal of temperate regions. It was domesticated in the Near East some time prior to 7000 BC, and provides a classical example of evolution through polyploidy. There are three ploidy levels and within each level selection has proceeded from wild species, to hulled cultivated species whose grain is tightly invested by lemma and palea, and thence to free-threshing naked species. Thus at diploid level wild *T. boeoticum* gave rise to hulled *T. monococcum*; there are no naked diploids. The tetraploid line commenced with the assimilation of a modified genome from *Aegilops speltoides*, producing wild *T. dicoccoides*, hulled *T. dicoccon* (Emmer) and naked *T. turgidum* (Rivet wheat) & *T. durum* (Macaroni wheat). The hexaploids acquired their extra genome from *Aegilops tauschii*, giving rise to hulled *T. spelta* (Spelt) and naked *T. aestivum* (Bread wheat) — there are no wild hexaploids. *T. zhukovskyi*, a rare Caucasian hulled wheat, is the only example of an alternative route to hexaploidy, it being an amphidiploid from *T. monococcum* and wild tetraploid *T. timopheevii*. A number of other species are recognized in each group, but modern agriculture is virtually confined to *T. durum* and *T. aestivum* (Helbaek in Econ. Bot. 20: 350—360, 1966; Kuckuck in Frankel & Bennett, Genetic Resources in Plants: 249—266, 1970).

As with other cereal genera, there is a profusion of weakly defined minor segregates, and much disagreement on their taxonomic treatment. *Triticum* differs however in the large number of cultivated species generally recognized, a consequence of its complicated genetic history. Bearing in mind the genetic constitution of *T. aestivum*, its separation from *Aegilops* is a matter of some contention.

243. Aegilops L., Sp. Pl.: 1050 (1753); Zhukovski in Trudy Prikl. Bot. Genet. Selek. 18: 417—609 (1928); Eig in Feddes Rep., Beih. 55: 1—228 (1929); Kihara in Züchter 12: 49—62 (1940); Hammer in Feddes Rep. 91: 225—258 (1980) — A. triuncialis L. *Aegicon* Adans., Fam. Pl. 2: 36, 513 (1763) nom superfl pro Aegilops. *Perlaria* Fabric., Enum. ed. 2: 371 (1763) nom superfl pro Aegilops. *Aegilops subgen Comopyrum* Jaub. & Spach, Ill. Pl. Or. 4: 12 (1851) — A. comosa Sibth. & Sm. *A. subgen Cylindropyrum* Jaub. & Spach l.c. — A. cylindrica Host. *A. subgen Gastropyrum* Jaub. & Spach l.c.: 17 — A. ventricosa Tausch. *A. subgen Sitopsis* Jaub. & Spach l.c. 21 — A. bicornis (Forssk.) Jaub. & Spach. *Amblyopyrum* Eig in Agric. Rec. P.Z.E. Inst. Agric. Nat. Hist. 2: 199 (1929) — A. muticum (Boiss.) Eig. *Sitopsis* (Jaub. & Spach) Löve in Biol. Zentralbl. 101: 206 (1982). *Orrhopygium* Löve l.c. —O. caudatum (L.) Löve. *Patropyrum* Löve l.c. — P. tauschii (Coss.) Löve. *Comopyrum* (Jaub. & Spach) Löve l.c.: 207. *Chennapyrum* Löve l.c. — C. uniaristatum (Vis.) Löve. *Kiharapyrum* Löve l.c. — K. umbellulatum (Zhuk.) Löve. *Aegilemma* Löve l.c. — A. kotschyi (Boiss.) Löve. *Cylindropyrum* (Jaub. & Spach) Löve l.c. *Aegilopodes* Löve l.c. nom superfl pro Aegilops. *Gastropyrum* (Jaub. & Spach) Löve l.c.: 208. *Aegilonearum* Löve l.c. — A. juvenale (Thell.) Löve.

Annual. Raceme slenderly linear to ovoid, bearing single spikelets, usually falling as a whole but sometimes fragile at top of internodes (or at base of internodes in sect. *Sitopsis*; tardily fragile in sect. *Amblyopyrum*), often with 1—4 rudimentary spikelets at base and the apical spikelets also somewhat reduced. Spikelets 2—8-flowered; glumes oblong to broadly ovate, coriaceous, with 7—13 parallel or divergent nerves, rounded on back, truncate, dentate or 1—5-awned;

lemmas rounded on back though sometimes lightly keeled at tip, ± bidentate (except *A. mutica*), usually 1—3-awned.

Species 21. Mediterranean and Middle East to Pakistan. Stony slopes, dry grassland and weedy places.
The wide range of variation in the genus is summarized in the following key:

Lemmas awnless, obtuse; raceme linear (A. mutica)   Sect *Amblyopyrum*
Lemmas awned though sometimes only in terminal spikelet of raceme, rarely
  awnless and then toothed:
Raceme linear, ± cylindrical:
  Spikelets cylindrical:
    Glumes truncate, emarginate or bidentate (A. speltoides)   Sect *Sitopsis*
    Glumes, at least of terminal spikelet, awned:
      Terminal awn shorter than raceme; raceme fragile (A. cylindrica)
                  Sect *Cylindropyrum*
      Terminal awn longer than raceme; raceme falling entire, short with only
        2—7 fertile spikelets, these sometimes slightly inflated (A. comosa)
                  Sect *Comopyrum*
  Spikelets inflated, the raceme moniliform; glumes truncate or those of apical
    spikelets with a subulate tooth (A. ventricosa)   Sect *Vertebrata*
Raceme lanceolate to ovate; lower spikelets ± inflated, the upper often markedly
  smaller; glumes mostly 2—4-awned (A. triuncialis)   Sect *Aegilops*

The breeding system responsible for this variability has been investigated (Zohary & Feldman in Evolution 16: 44—61, 1962). About half the species are diploid, and it is supposed that these have produced occasional hybrids which have doubled their chromosome number to form amphidiploids. The buffering effect of shared genomes has then made possible an elaborate network of cross-fertilization at tetraploid level; but at the same time self-pollination has become the predominant breeding mode. The system thus combines versatility in the production of new forms, with genetic stability for those which prove successful, and it probably represents a fairly common model of evolutionary progress in grasses. Taxonomically the diploid species are reasonably distinct, but the tetraploids form a canopy of intergrading forms that are very difficult to partition satisfactorily. A later stage in this process, with the tetraploid canopy paramount, can be seen in *Dactylis*.

244. Henrardia C.E. Hubbard in Blumea, Suppl. 3: 15 (1946) & in Hook. Ic. Pl. 35: t 3453 (1947) — H. persica (Boiss.) C.E. Hubbard.

Annual; leaf-blades auriculate. Raceme slender, cylindrical, with single spikelets closely appressed to hollows in rhachis, this fragile and disarticulating at tip of internode. Spikelets 1-flowered plus rhachilla extension; glumes exceeding and enclosing lemma, side by side, 3—7-nerved, asymmetrical; lemma membranous, 3-nerved (rarely with 2 extra subsidiary nerves), awnless.

Species 2. Middle East. Dry slopes.
Superficially similar to Hainardieae, but differing in hairy ovary, ciliate lodicules and simple starch grains. These characters place it in Triticeae and, although seemingly aberrant, it is not far removed from *Aegilops sect Vertebrata*.

III. SUBFAMILY CENTOTHECOIDEAE

Soderstrom in Taxon 30: 615 (1981).

Herbs, usually with broad leaf-blades. Frequent external characters: membranous ligule; panicle or racemes; 1—many-flowered laterally compressed spikelets; 5 or more-nerved lemmas.

Lodicules 2, cuneate, fleshy, truncate; stamens usually 3; stigmas 2. Caryopsis with embryo $\frac{1}{4}$—$\frac{1}{3}$ its length, and oval hilum; embryo centothecoid P+PP (*Zeugites* bambusoid).

Chlorenchyma forming a palisade layer below upper epidermis (not *Chasmanthium*, *Megastachya*), otherwise irregular; bundle sheaths double, the lateral cells of outer sheath enlarged; microhairs usually slender with oblique joint between the cells; stomatal subsidiary cells triangular; midrib simple or containing 3 bundles. This is the palisade variant of non-kranz anatomy (fig. 10). See also Renvoize in Kew Bull. (ined).

A small subfamily justified mainly by its distinctive embryo, but also by a suite of leaf anatomical characters which, though not unique, set it apart from its neighbours. It is not unlike the herbaceous bamboos in external appearance, but the cuneate lodicules ally it to the Arundinoid line. An offshoot of specialized forest grasses from near the base of this line seems the most likely phylogenetic interpretation.

24. CENTOTHECEAE

Ridley, Mat. Fl. Malay Pen. 3: 122 (1907). *Centothecinae* Benth. in J. Linn. Soc. Bot. 19: 31 (1881). *Zeugitinae* Caro in Dominguezia 4: 41 (1982).

Ligule a short scarious rim, this sometimes ciliolate; leaf-blades broad, with cross-nerves (except *Chasmanthium*) and sometimes a false petiole. Inflorescence a panicle or of racemes, the spikelets alike (except *Pohlidium*). Spikelets 1—many-flowered with upper florets ± reduced, laterally compressed, disarticulating below each floret or falling entire; glumes persistent, shorter than lemmas, herbaceous, usually entire; lemmas usually 5—9-nerved, herbaceous, awnless or shortly awned from tip; palea 2-nerved. Caryopsis ellipsoid or trigonous.

Genera 10; species ± 30. Tropics.

Anatomy. Non-kranz with slender microhairs, the apical cell $\frac{1}{2}$—3 times as long as basal cell, the two cells often joined obliquely; but *Bromuniola*, *Centotheca* & *Megastachya* with a type of mushroom button hair. Hooked hairs present in *Orthoclada*, *Zeugites*. Lersten & Pohl in Amer. J. Bot. 56: 1054—1057 (1969).

Chromosomes. The basic number is 12.

2n	24	48
No of species	9	5

The tribe can usually be recognized by its broad leaves with cross-nerves.

These characters are admittedly relative, cross-nerves occurring in other tribes though not so readily apparent, but they are difficult to avoid in diagnosis as the spikelet characters are variable. Despite its small size the tribe has a widespread distribution, and the variability of its spikelets may reflect the isolation of its present genera in widely dispersed specialized niches. The least modified spikelets occur in *Megastachya*, whose similarity to some primitive Arundineae and Eragrostideae suggests a common origin with these tribes.

Centotheceae are tropical plants of forest shade, though *Chasmanthium* has extended into the temperate woodlands of north America.

1 Florets, or at least the lower, bisexual:
  2 Leaf-blades with distinct cross-nerves:
    3 Lemmas awnless:
      4 Rhachilla internodes free; plants annual (if perennial see Bambuseae p.39):
        5 Spikelets 8—20-flowered, the apical florets similar but smaller
          245 Megastachya
        5 Spikelets 1—4-flowered, the terminal floret rudimentary
          246 Centotheca
      4 Rhachilla internodes fused to keels of adjacent palea   **247 Orthoclada**
    3 Lemmas awned:
      6 Spikelets with 1 fertile floret:
        7 Sterile lemma 1, its awn antrorsely scaberulous   **248 Chevalierella**
        7 Sterile lemmas several, their awns retrorsely scaberulous
          249 Lophatherum
      6 Spikelets with several fertile florets; lemma keeled (if rounded see
        104 Festuca)   **250 Bromuniola**
  2 Leaf-blades without cross-nerves   **251 Chasmanthium**
1 Florets unisexual:
  8 Spikelets bisexual, the lowest floret ♀, the rest ♂:
    9 Inflorescence a panicle   **252 Zeugites**
    9 Inflorescence a raceme   **253 Calderonella**
  8 Spikelets unisexual, 1-flowered   **254 Pohlidium**

245. Megastachya P. Beauv., Ess. Agrost.: 74 (1812) — M. owariensis P. Beauv. (= M. mucronata).

Annual; leaf-blades narrowly lanceolate, amplexicaul. Inflorescence a panicle, or the primary branches reduced to racemes. Spikelets breaking up at maturity, 8—20-flowered, the florets alike though smaller at the apex; lemmas mucronate.

Species 1. Tropical Africa. Forest.

246. Centotheca Desv. in Nouv. Bull. Sci. Soc. Philom. 2: 189 (1810) as "Centosteca", nom conserv; Monod de Froideville in Blumea 19: 57—60 (1971) — C. lappacea (L.) Desv. *Ramosia* Merr. in Philip. J. Sci. Bot. 11: 2 (1916) — R. philippinensis Merr.

Annual; leaf-blades broadly linear to lanceolate, narrowed at base. Inflorescence a panicle, or the primary branches reduced to racemes. Spikelets breaking up at maturity, 1—4-flowered plus rhachilla extension bearing a rudimentary floret (*C. uniflora* strictly 1-flowered), the upper florets decreasing in size and often with reflexed bristles; lemmas apiculate; stamens 2.

Species 4. West Africa from Guinée to Angola; tropical Asia and Pacific islands. Forest.

A homogeneous genus of barely distinct species. The lemma bristles serve as a dispersal device.

247. Orthoclada P. Beauv., Ess. Agrost.: 69 (1812); Hubbard in Hook. Ic. Pl. 35: t 3419 (1940) — O. rariflora (Lam.) P. Beauv. (= O. laxa).

Perennial; leaf-blades narrowly elliptic, falsely petiolate. Inflorescence a lax panicle, or the primary branches reduced to open racemes. Spikelets falling entire, 1—4-flowered plus rhachilla extension bearing a rudimentary floret, the upper florets decreasing in size, the lower half of each rhachilla internode fused to keels of adjacent palea; lemmas acuminate (stamens 2 in *O. laxa*).

Species 2. Tropical America; Tanzania, Zaire, Zambia. Forest.

248. Chevalierella A. Camus in Rev. Bot. Appl. 13: 421 (1933) — C. congoensis A. Camus (= C. dewildemanii).

Perennial; leaf-blades elliptic, falsely petiolate, Inflorescence of numerous loose racemes on a common axis. Spikelets falling entire, 1-flowered plus rhachilla extension bearing a small sterile floret; lemmas weakly 3—5-nerved, with an antrorsely scaberulous awn.

Species 1. Zaire. Forest.

249. Lophatherum Brongn. in Duperr., Voy. Coq. Bot. Phan.: 49 (1831) — L. gracile Brongn. *Acroelytrum* Steud. in Flora 29: 20 (1846) — A. japonicum Steud. (= L. gracile). *Allelotheca* Steud., Syn. Pl. Glum. 1: 117 (1854) — A. urvillei Steud. (= L. gracile).

Perennial; leaf-blades narrowly lanceolate, falsely petiolate. Inflorescence of loose or dense unilateral racemes on a central axis. Spikelets falling entire, 1-flowered plus rhachilla extension bearing a bunch of up to 9 sterile lemmas; lemmas with a retrorsely scaberulous awn, those of the sterile lemmas developing into a fan of recurved hooks at maturity; stamens 2—3.

Species 2. Tropical Asia. Forest.
The awns of the sterile lemmas function as a dispersal device. An unusual feature is the occurrence of food-storing root tubers.

250. Bromuniola Stapf & Hubbard in Kew Bull. 1926: 366 (1926) — B. gossweileri Stapf & Hubbard.

Perennial; leaf-blades narrowly lanceolate, the base attenuate. Inflorescence a lax panicle. Spikelets breaking up at maturity, 4—9-flowered, the lowest floret usually reduced to an empty lemma, the rest alike though smaller at the apex; lemma awned; palea strongly gibbous on the back.

Species 1. Tanzania to Angola. Forest.

251. Chasmanthium Link, Hort. Berol. 1: 159 (1827); Yates in Southw. Nat. 11: 415—455 (1966) — C. gracile (Michaux) Link (= C. laxum). *Gouldochloa* Valdés, Morden & Hatch in Syst. Bot. 11: 112 (1986) — G. curvifolia Valdés et al.

Perennial; leaf-blades linear to narrowly lanceolate, without cross-nerves or constricted base. Inflorescence a panicle, or the primary branches reduced to racemes. Spikelets breaking up at maturity, cuneate, 2—10-flowered plus rhachilla extension bearing a rudimentary floret, increasing in size upwards the lowest 1—2 florets being sterile (*C. latifolium* with large ovate spikelets and subequal florets); lemmas 5—15-nerved, acute; palea keels narrowly winged, gibbous; stamen 1.

Species 6. Eastern USA, Mexico. Woodland and semiarid shrubland.
This is the only temperate member of the tribe, extending northwards to the Canadian border. It resembles the chloridoid genus *Uniola*, in which it was formerly placed. It is an awkward genus to identify due to variable ligule and inflorescence, the latter sometimes including a few spikelets each with only 1 fertile floret.

252. Zeugites P. Browne, Civ. Nat. Hist. Jamaica: 341 (1756) nom conserv — Z. americana Willd. *Senites* Adans., Fam. Pl. 2: 39, 604 (1763) nom superfl pro Zeugites. *Despretzia* Kunth, Rév. Gram. 2: 485 (1831) — D. mexicana Kunth. *Galeottia* Mart. & Gal. in Bull. Acad. Brux. 9, 2: 247 (1842) nom nud pro seq. *Krombholzia* Fourn. in Bull. Soc. Bot. Belg. 15: 464 (1876) — K. mexicana Fourn. (= ?).

Perennial; leaf-blades lanceolate to ovate, contracted or falsely petiolate. Inflorescence a panicle. Spikelets falling entire or the ♂ part shed separately, 2—15-flowered, the lowest floret ♀, the rest ♂; glumes with cross-nerves, truncate to dentate; female lemma 7—13-nerved, slightly gibbous, acute to truncate or dentate (*Z. americana, Z. pringlei* awned); male florets larger or smaller than ♀, straight-backed, acute.

Species ± 12. Mexico and West Indies to Peru. Shady places in ravines and bushy hillsides.
The ovate blades and long slender false petioles of species such as *Z. mexicana* and *Z. pringlei* bear an uncanny resemblance to dicotyledonous leaves. Despite these and the highly modified spikelets, the bambusoid embryo suggests a relatively primitive status within the tribe.

253. Calderonella Sod. & Deck. in Ann. Miss. Bot. Gard. 60: 427 (1973) — C. sylvatica Sod. & Deck.

Perennial; leaf-blades lanceolate, falsely petiolate. Inflorescence a single raceme. Spikelets falling entire, 3—5-flowered, the lowest floret ♀, the rest ♂; glumes with cross-nerves, acute; female lemma 15—19-nerved, strongly gibbous, obtuse; male florets smaller, lanceolate.

Species 1. Panama. Forest.

254. Pohlidium Davidse, Sod. & Ellis in Syst. Bot. 11: 131 (1986) — P. petiolatum Davidse, Sod. & Ellis.

Perennial. Leaf-blades ovate, falsely petiolate. Inflorescence a panicle, mainly of ♀ spikelets with ♂ spikelets on the periphery. Female spikelet falling entire, 1-flowered; glumes absent; lemma herbaceous, the palea similar. Male spikelet like ♀, but 2—3-flowered with larger lemmas and sometimes a linear upper glume.

Species 1. Panama. Shady rocks.

163

IV. SUBFAMILY ARUNDINOIDEAE

Tateoka in J. Jap. Bot. 32: 277 (1957); Renvoize in Kew Bull. 36: 85—102 (1981). *Micrairoideae* Pilger, Nat. Pfl.-Fam. ed. 2, 14d: 167 (1956). *Phragmitoideae* Caro in Dominguezia 4: 13 (1982). *Aristidoideae* Caro l.c. 16.

Herbs or occasionally large reeds, usually with linear leaf-blades. Frequent external characters: ciliate ligule; panicle; several-flowered laterally compressed spikelets with fragile rhachilla; several-nerved bilobed lemmas awned from sinus.

Lodicules 2 (except *Anisopogon*), cuneate, fleshy, truncate; stamens 3; stigmas 2. Caryopsis (rarely achene) with embryo $\frac{1}{4}$—$\frac{1}{3}$($-\frac{1}{2}$) its length, and elliptic to linear rarely punctiform hilum; embryo arundinoid P–PF (*Sartidia* with the unusual formula P–FF).

Chlorenchyma irregularly arranged (except *Centropodia*, Aristideae); bundle sheaths double; microhairs usually slender, rarely absent; stomatal subsidiary cells domed or triangular; epidermal papillae occasionally present; leaf midrib simple (except Thysanolaeneae). This is the standard non-kranz type (fig 10). See also Renvoize in Kew Bull. (ined).

Arundinoideae are typically non-kranz grasses with slender microhairs, cuneate lodicules and arundinoid embryo. Their origin is obscure, links with Bambusoideae and Pooideae being no more than speculative, but they are thought to represent the basic stock from which the tropical savanna grasses evolved. The notorious fragmentation of the principal tribe, Arundineae, is consistent with a subsequent history of decline.

The spikelets intergrade with Chloridoideae, but a boundary can be set at the transition from non-kranz to kranz anatomy. This somewhat arbitrary criterion is supported by microhair and embryo differences, except for *Centropodia* and Aristideae which seem better retained in Arundinoideae, thereby implying a polyphyletic origin for C$_4$ metabolism. There are no corresponding non-kranz genera in Chloridoideae, or at least no supporting characters sufficiently strong to compel their admittance (but see *Eragrostis*).

Strangely the criteria are reversed at the boundary with Panicoideae. Here the leaf anatomy is indistinguishable from non-kranz Paniceae, but the spikelets (supported by the embryo) provide a sharp distinction.

25. ARUNDINEAE

Dumort., Obs. Gram. Belg.: 82 (1824); Conert, Syst. Anat. Arund.: 1—208 (1961); Zotov in New Zealand J. Bot. 1: 78—136 (1963). *Elytrophoreae* Jac.-Fél. in J. Agr. Trop. Bot. Appl. 5: 304 (1958). *Cortaderieae* Zotov in New Zealand J. Bot. 1: 83 (1963). *Danthonieae* Zotov l.c. 86. *Molinieae* Jirasek in Preslia 38: 33 (1966).

Phragmitinae Horaninow, Char. Ess.: 33 (1847). *Arundininae* Miq., Fl. Ind. Bat. 3: 360 (1857). *Danthoniinae* Beck, Fl. Niederoest.: 64 (1890). *Moliniinae* Ohwi in Acta Phytotax. Geobot. 10: 266 (1941). *Cortaderiinae* Conert, Syst. Anat. Arund.: 72 (1961). *Crinipinae* Conert l.c. 132.

Ligule a line of hairs (except *Anisopogon, Arundo, Dichaetaria, Elytrophorus, Hakonechloa, Monachather*); mostly tussock-forming perennials with basal leaves. Inflorescence a panicle, sometimes spiciform, or scanty and then often raceme-like or even reduced to a single spikelet, rarely a true raceme, the spikelets alike (except *Cortaderia, Lamprothyrsus, Gynerium, Elytrophorus*). Spikelets usually of several fertile florets with imperfect florets above, sometimes strictly 2-flowered with minute or suppressed rhachilla extension, very rarely 1-flowered, laterally compressed, disarticulating between florets (except *Chaetobromus, Schismus, Urochlaena*), the floret callus usually bearded short and obtuse but sometimes elongated; glumes persistent (except *Gynerium, Schismus*), variable in length, usually membranous and acute to acuminate; lemmas usually rounded on back, (1—)3—11-nerved, hyaline to coriaceous, entire or bilobed, with or without a straight or geniculate awn from tip or sinus; palea 2-nerved, well-developed. Caryopsis usually ellipsoid, sometimes with free or separable pericarp (an achene in *Dregeochloa, Pentameris, Pyrrhanthera*); hilum narrowly oblong to linear.

Genera 40; species ± 300. Cosmopolitan, but best developed in southern latitudes.

Anatomy. Non-kranz, except for *Centropodia* which is unique in possessing kranz PS anatomy; microhairs slender or stout, their apical cell ± as long as the basal cell (replaced by long slender papillae in *Chionochloa, Pentameris, Pseudopentameris, Diplopogon, Cortaderia*; absent in *Amphipogon*). Chlorenchyma cells of *Gynerium* & *Phragmites* invaginated. Thomasson (Bot. Gaz. 145: 204—209, 1984) describes the anatomy of a Miocene phragmitoid fossil.

Chromosomes. The basic number is 12; but 9 is common in *Cortaderia, Molinia*; 7 in *Pentaschistis*.

2n	12	18	24	36	42	48	72	90	96
No of species	8	3	25	19	5	17	17	5	3

The tribe is defined by its embryo and its non-kranz anatomy with slender microhairs, generally associated with a fairly simple spikelet structure. It is otherwise difficult to characterize, for it is heterogeneous with numerous isolated or weakly linked genera whose relationships are largely conjectural (fig 14). It is also difficult to categorize any of its features as primitive or advanced, and hence to infer the direction evolution has taken. The problems involved in circumscribing the tribe may be examined further by dividing it into the following facies.

1. Primitive (genera 255—263). A heterogeneous assortment of genera, brought together by their short glumes and multinerved lemmas with entire tips. This is the basic form of unspecialized spikelet common to a number of unrelated tribes, and it is tentatively labelled as primitive. Tropics.

2. Long glumes and bilobed lemmas with geniculate central awn (genera 264—279). A sprawling agglomeration of closely related and narrowly defined genera whose taxonomy is still controversial (see Tomlinson in Aliso 11: 97—114, 1985). Southern hemisphere.

3. One-flowered spikelet with wrap-around lemma (genera 280—283). Such spikelets are typical of Aristideae, and it is apparent that the boundaries of the two tribes are contingent. *Danthonidium* and *Anisopogon* have close relatives in the previous group, and their possession of a rhachilla extension and multinerved lemma further discourages transfer to Aristideae. But *Diplopogon* and

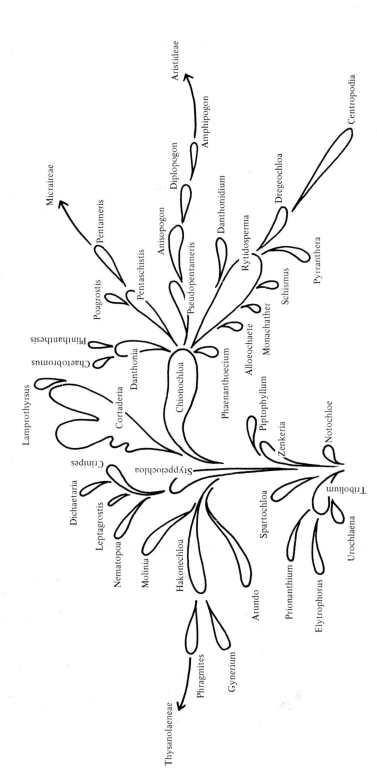

Fig. 14 Diagram of relationships in Arundineae.

Amphipogon are truly intermediate, being retained here somewhat arbitrarily because of their unreduced palea. The other 1-flowered genera are unrelated to this group. Australia.

4. Three-nerved lemmas (genera 284—287). This trend, which is also common in the two following groups, is apparently unrelated to parallel developments in Eragrostideae. Africa.

5. Dioecy (genera 288—289). This group is commonly placed among the tall reeds to form a separate tribe, but in fact seems more closely related to *Chionochloa*. Its megagametophyte has unusual haustorial synergids which also occur in group 2 (Philipson & Connor in Bot. Gaz. 145: 78—82, 1984). Dioecy has arisen independently in *Gynerium*. Southern hemisphere.

6. The reed habit (genera 290—294). The character brings together an otherwise somewhat heterogeneous collection of genera. Mainly north temperate.

It is worth noting that 6 genera have strictly 2-flowered spikelets; there is evidently some selection pressure favouring this structure, though its biological advantages are not clear. Achenes have arisen, apparently independently, in 3 genera; they have thick shell-like pericarps, quite unlike the thin membrane of chloridoid genera with a free pericarp. Finally there is the unexpected appearance of C_4 photosynthesis in *Centropodia*; its spikelets are so clearly related to *Rytidosperma* that it can scarcely be excluded from the tribe.

The generic groups are neither sufficiently homogeneous nor clearly defined to form a sound basis for the recognition of subtribes. It is possible that the weakly related genera of groups 1, 4 & 6 represent a primitive and once widespread Arundineae, now largely extinguished by competition from the more efficient physiology of later evolving tribes, and surviving only in specialized habitats or as isolated relicts. However the tribe has successfully adapted to the mountain grasslands south of Capricorn (or these have offered a refuge inaccessible to competitors), where active speciation has produced the close-knit genera of groups 2, 3 & 5.

Genera possessing long glumes and a lemma geniculately awned from the sinus are easy to recognize. For the rest the ciliate ligule will usually distinguish them from Pooideae, and the many-nerved lemma from Eragrostideae, but there is some overlap.

```
1  Spikelets 1-flowered:
 2  Lemma subentire:
  3  Leaf-blades pungent                            311 Monodia
  3  Leaf-blades not pungent:
   4  Lemma hairy; callus beardless; annual (if perennial see Arundo)
                                                   270 Poagrostis
   4  Lemma glabrous; callus long bearded          286 Leptagrostis
 2  Lemma 3-awned or 3-toothed:
  5  Lemma transversely bearded                     280 Danthonidium
  5  Lemma without a transverse line of hairs:
   6  Ligule membranous:
    7  Glumes longer than floret                    281 Anisopogon
    7  Glumes shorter than floret                   287 Dichaetaria
   6  Ligule a line of hairs:
    8  Central awn much longer than laterals        282 Diplopogon
    8  Central awn or tooth equal to laterals       283 Amphipogon
1  Spikelets 2—many-flowered:
```

9   Plants tufted with basal leaves:
 10   Plants all bisexual:
  11   Lemmas 5 or more-nerved:
   12   Lemma often hairy on back or flanks but not in tufts, sometimes glabrous:
    13   Lower glume shorter than lowest lemma:
     14   Lemma awnless:
      15   Leaf-blades pungent   *308 Triodia*
      15   Leaf-blades not pungent:
       16   Spikelets 3 or more-flowered (if with sterile florets below the fertile see *251 Chasmanthium*):
        17   Spikelets hairy   **255 Tribolium**
        17   Spikelets glabrous:
         18   Lemma tip entire:
          19   Leaf-blades well developed   **292 Molinia**
          19   Leaf-blades absent or much reduced   **259 Spartochloa**
         18   Lemma tip tridentate   **260 Notochloe**
       16   Spikelets strictly 2-flowered   **261 Zenkeria**
     14   Lemma awned:
      20   Panicle falling intact at maturity   **256 Urochlaena**
      20   Panicle shedding the florets at maturity; perennial (if annual see *555 Chandrasekharania*)
       21   Lodicules glabrous:
        22   Awn much longer than lemma   **262 Piptophyllum**
        22   Awn shorter than lemma   **263 Styppeiochloa**
       21   Lodicules ciliate   **264 Chionochloa**
    13   Lower glume longer than lowest lemma:
     23   Glumes persisting on panicle:
      24   Spikelets 3 or more-flowered, rarely 2-flowered and then with a well developed rhachilla extension:
       25   Fruit a caryopsis:
        26   Lodicules ciliate; spikelets awned; hilum $\frac{1}{2}$—$\frac{2}{3}$ length of grain (if shorter see *272 Rytidosperma*)   **264 Chionochloa**
        26   Lodicules glabrous:
         27   Lemma margins clavate hairy below, the tip entire
                                                              255 Tribolium
         27   Lemma margins with or without straight hairs, the tip nearly always bilobed or bidentate:
          28   Lemma tip cleft into 3 straight awns   *309 Plectrachne*
          28   Lemma tip awnless or with geniculate central awn:
           29   Palea at most puberulous on keels (if lemmas awnless and less than 3 mm long see *272 Rytidosperma*)   **265 Danthonia**
           29   Palea densely pubescent on back or flanks (if leaf-blades stiff and pungent see *308 Triodia irritans*)
                                                              267 Plinthanthesis
       25   Fruit an achene   **277 Pyrrhanthera**
      24   Spikelets strictly 2-flowered with minute rhachilla extension, or more than 3.5 cm long:
       30   Lemma membranous:
        31   Fruit a caryopsis   **268 Pentaschistis**
        31   Fruit an achene   **269 Pentameris**
       30   Lemma coriaceous, terete   **271 Pseudopentameris**

23 Glumes deciduous with spikelet:
  32 Lemma awned   **266 Chaetobromus**
  32 Lemma awnless   **276 Schismus**
12 Lemma with tufted hairs, or rarely with a transverse band of longer hairs:
  33 Floret callus obtuse, though sometimes narrowly so; lemma hairs very rarely in longitudinal lines:
    34 Ligule a line of hairs:
      35 Lowest floret similar to the rest:
        36 Glumes longer than lowest lemma, rarely shorter but then inflorescence not a raceme:
          37 Fruit a caryopsis   **272 Rytidosperma**
          37 Fruit with free pericarp   **278 Dregeochloa**
        36 Glumes shorter than lowest lemma; inflorescence a short raceme
              273 Phaenanthoecium
      35 Lowest floret different, persisting with the glumes, usually imperfect   **274 Alloeochaete**
    34 Ligule membranous   **275 Monachather**
  33 Floret callus pungent; lemma hairs in longitudinal lines
              279 Centropodia

11 Lemmas 1—3-nerved:
  38 Inflorescence strongly condensed:
    39 Panicle of globular clusters   **257 Elytrophorus**
    39 Panicle spiciform or reduced to a raceme   **258 Prionanthium**
  38 Inflorescence open or loosely contracted:
    40 Lemmas awned:
      41 Awn shorter than lemma   **263 Styppeiochloa**
      41 Awn longer than lemma:
        42 Palea $\frac{1}{2}$—$\frac{2}{3}$ length of lemma   **284 Crinipes**
        42 Palea almost as long as lemma   **285 Nematopoa**
    40 Lemmas awnless   **292 Molinia**
10 Plants gynodioecious; lodicules hairy:
  43 Lemmas with or without short lateral lobes up to 7 mm long; glumes 1 (—3)-nerved   **288 Cortaderia**
  43 Lemmas with well developed awned lateral lobes 2—4 cm long; glumes often nerveless   **289 Lamprothyrsus**
9 Plants reed-like with cauline leaves:
  44 Inflorescence bisexual:
    45 Lowest floret bisexual:
      46 Glumes as long as spikelet   **290 Arundo**
      46 Glumes much shorter than spikelet   **291 Hakonechloa**
    45 Lowest floret ♂ or empty   **293 Phragmites**
  44 Inflorescence unisexual   **294 Gynerium**

255. Tribolium Desv., Opusc.: 64 (1831); Renvoize in Kew Bull. 40: 795—799 (1985) — T. hispidum (Thunb.) Desv. *Lasiochloa* Kunth, Rév. Gram: 2: 556 (1832) — L. longifolia (Schrad.) Kunth (= T. hispidum). *Allagostachyum* Steud., Nom. Bot. ed. 2, 1: 50 (1840) nom nud — T. alternans. *Hystringium* Steud., l.c. 2: 11 (1841) in syn sub T. echinatum. *Brizopyrum* Stapf in Fl. Cap. 7: 318 (1898) non Link (1827) — B. capense (Spreng.) Nees (= T. uniolae). *Plagiochloa* Adamson & Sprague in J. S. Afr. Bot. 7: 89 (1941) nom nov pro Brizopyrum.

Annual or perennial. Panicle spiciform or lobed, reduced to a unilateral raceme in *T. uniolae* and allies, the spikelets densely imbricate. Spikelets broadly cuneate to orbicular, tardily disarticulating beneath each floret; glumes shorter than lemma or equalling spikelet, coriaceous, 3—7-nerved, glabrous or tuberculate bristly, acute to shortly awned; lemmas coriaceous, 5—9-nerved, clavate hairy on margins, emarginate to acute, rarely with a brief awn-point; palea keels sometimes winged. Grain with pericarp reluctantly separable.

Species ± 10. South Africa. Dry bushland.
At first sight the racemose species seem distinct, but their separation is insufficiently sharp to warrant generic status. The genus is somewhat detached from the main body of the tribe, and has at least a superficial similarity to *Coelachyrum* and *Uniola* in Eragrostideae.

256. Urochlaena Nees, Fl. Afr. Austr.: 437 (1841) — U. pusilla Nees.

Annual. Panicle spiciform to capitate, embraced by inflated uppermost leaf-sheath and falling intact with it at maturity. Spikelets: glumes shorter than lemma, herbaceous, 4—7-nerved, tuberculate bristly, with a recurved awn; lemmas herbaceous, 7—9-nerved, clavate hairy on back, tapering to a curved awn. Grain with free pericarp.

Species 1. South Africa. Dry bushland.
Related to *Tribolium utriculosum*.

257. Elytrophorus P. Beauv., Ess. Agrost.: 67 (1812); Schweickerdt in Ann. Natal Mus. 10: 191—214 (1942) — E. articulatus P. Beauv. (= E. spicatus). *Echinalysium* Trin., Fund. Agrost.: 142 (1822) nom superfl pro Elytrophorus.

Annual; ligule membranous. Panicle of dense globular spikelet clusters borne at intervals along a central axis and sometimes confluent, the outer spikelets of each cluster with enlarged lower glume and lower or all lemmas empty and glume-like, thus forming a chaffy involucre. Spikelets strongly laterally compressed; glumes shorter than lemma, narrow, membranous, 1-nerved, acuminate to a short awn-point; lemmas keeled, membranous, 3-nerved, ciliate on margins, entire, ± awned; palea narrowly or conspicuously winged; lodicules 1—2; stamens 1—3. Grain with embryo ½ its length and pericarp free.

Species 2. Tropical Africa, India and Australia. Wet places.
An isolated genus of uncertain affinity, but with some resemblance to *Tribolium*.

258. Prionanthium Desv., Opusc.: 64 (1831) — P. rigidum Desv. (= P. dentatum). *Prionachne* Nees in Lindley, Nat. Syst. ed. 2: 447 (1836) — P. ecklonii Nees. *Chondrolaena* Nees, Fl. Afr. Austr.: 133 (1841); Kuntze in Post, Lexicon: 122 (1903) as "Chondrochlaena" — nom superfl pro Prionachne.

Annual. Panicle spiciform (*P. dentatum*) or reduced to a unilateral raceme bearing single or paired spikelets. Spikelets strictly 2-flowered plus minute rhachilla extension; glumes subequal, as long as spikelet, rigidly herbaceous, prominently 5—8-nerved (*P. dentatum* 3—4-nerved, the laterals close to keel), strongly keeled and usually tuberculate-pectinate there, blunt; lemmas hyaline, faintly 3-nerved, glabrous or thinly pilose, acute.

Species 3. South Africa. Seasonally wet flats.
P. dentatum hints at a distant relationship with *Tribolium*.

259. Spartochloa C.E. Hubbard in Kew Bull. 7: 308 (1952) — S. scirpoidea (Steud.) C.E. Hubbard.

Perennial; culms terete; leaf-blades much reduced or absent. Panicle slender, contracted. Spikelets: glumes shorter than lemma, thinly coriaceous, 1—3-nerved; lemmas thinly coriaceous, 5—9-nerved, glabrous, entire.

Species 1. SW Australia. Arid places.
A rare genus with a habit reminiscent of *Triodia*, and spikelets hinting at a possible relationship with *Tribolium uniolae*. It is notable for extreme reduction of the leaf-blades, photosynthetic function being transfered to culm and sheath.

260. Notochloe Domin in Feddes Rep. 10: 117 (1911) — N. microdon (Benth.) Domin.

Perennial. Panicle lax. Spikelets: glumes shorter than lemma, thinly coriaceous, 3—5-nerved; lemmas thinly coriaceous, 7-nerved, the nerves forming ridges, glabrous, tridentate.

Species 1. Australia (New South Wales). Upland swamps.
A rare but unremarkable *Triodia*-like genus.

261. Zenkeria Trin. in Linnaea 11: 150 (1837); Bor in Hook. Ic. Pl. 36: t. 3597 (1962) — Z. elegans Trin.

Perennial, with fibrous base; leaf-blades flat or rolled: Spikelets strictly 2-flowered plus minute rhachilla extension; glumes shorter than lemma, 1-nerved to faintly 5-nerved; lemmas membranous, 7—9-nerved, pilose, acute to acuminate; lodicules glabrous.

Species 4. India and Sri Lanka. Upland grassland.

262. Piptophyllum C.E. Hubbard in Kew Bull. 12: 53 (1957) — P. welwitschii (Rendle) C.E. Hubbard.

Perennial, with tomentose fibrous base; leaf-blades setaceous, deciduous. Panicle delicate, with capillary branches. Spikelets strictly 2-flowered plus minute rhachilla extension; glumes shorter than lemma, 1-nerved, with a short awn-point; lemmas membranous, 5—9-nerved, pilose on margins, with 2 setiform lobes and a long flexuous central awn slightly twisted at base.

Species 1. Angola. Damp rocky places.

An isolated genus possibly related to *Zenkeria*, but also with some resemblance to *Nematopoa* and *Pentaschistis*.

263. Styppeiochloa de Winter in Bothalia 9: 134 (1966) — S. gynoglossa (Goossens) de Winter.

Perennial, with tomentose fibrous base; leaf-blades filiform, convolute, stiff, pungent. Spikelets 2—5-flowered: glumes shorter than lemma, both 1-nerved or the upper 3-nerved, with a short awn-point; lemmas membranous, 3—5(—7)-nerved, glabrous or pubescent on margins, bidentate, with a short straight awn, sometimes the teeth also briefly awned; palea as long as lemma; lodicules glabrous.

Species 2. Southern Africa and Madagascar. Seepage zones among rocks.

The genus is barely distinct from *Zenkeria*; *S. hitchcockii*, with 2-flowered spikelets and 3-nerved awned lemmas, lies midway between the two.

264. Chionochloa Zotov in New Zealand J. Bot. 1: 87 (1963) — C. rigida (Raoul) Zotov.

Perennial, forming dense tussocks clothed below with old leaf-sheaths; blades harsh, strongly ribbed, often pungent. Panicle scanty to copious. Spikelets: glumes mostly shorter than spkelet, often shorter than lemma, membranous, usually 1-nerved but sometimes 3—5-nerved in lower half; floret callus oblong to linear, blunt; lemmas membranous, 7—9-nerved, pilose on margins or all over, narrowly bilobed, the lobes often awned, with a straight or geniculate central awn; palea pilose on flanks; lodicules ciliate. Caryopsis with hilum $\frac{1}{2}$—$\frac{2}{3}$ its length.

Species ± 20. New Zealand; 1 species in SE Australia. Mainly alpine grassland, but a few species descend to sea level.

A homogeneous genus of New Zealand tussock grasses, intergrading with *Cortaderia* and *Rytidosperma*.

265. Danthonia DC. in Lam. & DC., Fl. Franç. ed. 3, 3: 32 (1805) nom conserv —D. spicata (L.) Roem. & Schult. *Sieglingia* Bernhardi, Syst. Verz. Pfl.: 20 (1800) nom rejic — S. decumbens (L.) Bernhardi. *Brachatera* Desv. in Nouv. Bull. Sci. Soc. Philom. 2: 189 (1810) nom superfl pro Sieglingia. *Merathrepta* Raf. in Bull. Bot. Genève 1: 221 (1830) nom superfl pro Danthonia. *Wilibald-Schmidtia* Conrad in Friedrich, Pfl. Gebirgs. Marienbad: 38 (1837) nom superfl pro Sieglingia. *Brachyathera* Kuntze in Post, Lexicon: 77 (1903) nom superfl pro Sieglingia.

Perennial; leaf-blades flat or rolled; cleistogenes usually present in culm sheaths. Panicle open or contracted, of few spikelets and sometimes reduced to a raceme (often only 1 spikelet in *D. unispicata*). Spikelets with rhachilla internodes $\frac{1}{10}$—$\frac{1}{5}$ length of lemma: glumes as long as spikelets (sometimes shorter in *D. decumbens, D. domingensis*), papery, (1—)3—9-nerved; floret callus short to narrowly oblong, blunt; lemmas firmly membranous, 7—9-nerved, pilose on margins or all over, bilobed the lobes often awned, with geniculate central awn (*D. decumbens* bidentate and mucronate); palea glabrous, or puberulous on keels; lodicules glabrous. Caryopsis with hilum ($\frac{1}{4}$—)$\frac{1}{3}$—$\frac{2}{3}$ its length.

Species 20. Europe, North and South America. Grasslands and open woodlands, often in hilly districts.

Despite its lack of an awn, *D. decumbens* is so closely related to *D. alpina* that it does not deserve generic separation (Conert in Jb. nass. Ver. Naturk. 100: 54—72, 1969). Cleistogenes are discussed by Dobrenz & Beetle in J. Range Manage. 19: 292—296 (1966).

Danthonia is commonly treated in a wide sense to include *Chionochloa*, *Rytidosperma* and a number of lesser satellite genera, since they are all closely related and difficult to separate. By using a combination of lemma indumentum, lodicule hairs and hilum length, these genera can be tolerably well defined, and their recognition has the advantage of throwing some light on the taxonomy of an otherwise unwieldy agglomeration of species. On the other hand the characters employed are of marginal significance at generic level and even then boundaries are sometimes blurred by awkward intermediates, implying that splitting has proceeded too far. In either case generic concepts in this group are highly controversial.

266. Chaetobromus Nees in Lindley, Nat. Syst. ed. 2: 449 (1836) — C. involucratus (Schrad.) Nees.

Perennial. Panicle usually contracted. Spikelets (2—)3—4-flowered, falling entire together with a linear bearded callus, subsequently disarticulating; glumes as long as spikelet, papery, the lower 5—10-nerved, the upper narrower and 3—5-nerved; lowest floret callus short and glabrous, the rest linear bearded and pungent; lemmas firmly membranous, 7—9-nerved, glabrous or hairy, 2-lobed with slenderly awned lobes (those of lowest lemma often awnless), geniculately awned from sinus; lodicules glabrous. Caryopsis with hilum ⅞ its length.

Species 3. South Africa. Dry sandy and stony soils.

267. Plinthanthesis Steud., Syn. Pl. Glum. 1: 14 (1854); Hubbard in Hook. Ic. Pl. 35: t 3439 (1943); Blake in Contrib. Queensl. Herb. 14: 1—4 (1972); Connor & Edgar in Taxon 30: 657—660 (1981) — P. urvillei Steud. *Blakeochloa* Veldkamp in Taxon 30: 478 (1981) nom superfl pro Plinthanthesis.

Perennial; leaf-blades filiform. Panicle moderately open. Spikelets (3—)5-flowered or 2-flowered plus rhachilla extension, the rhachilla internodes ⅓ length of lemma; glumes as long as spikelet, 1-nerved becoming 3-nerved below; floret callus short, obtuse; lemmas membranous, 7—9-nerved, densely pubescent in lines between nerves below, bidentate to bilobed, mucronate or with a geniculate central awn; palea densely pubescent below; lodicules glabrous. Caryopsis with hilum ½ its length.

Species 3. Australia. Upland heaths.

268. Pentaschistis (Nees) Spach, Hist. Nat. Veg. Phan. 13: 164 (1846); McClean in S. Afr. J. Sci. 23: 273—282 (1926). *Danthonia subgen Pentaschistis* Nees, Fl. Afr. Austr. 1: 280 (1841) — D. curvifolia Schrad. *Achneria* Benth. in Benth. & Hook., Gen. Pl. 3: 1158 (1883) non P. Beauv. (1812) — Eriachne steudelii Nees (= P. malouinensis). *Afrachneria* Sprague in J. Bot. 60: 138 (1922) nom nov pro Achneria.

Perennial (*P. airoides* and a few others annual); leaves harsh, mostly filiform or rolled, sometimes pungent. Panicle open, contracted or spiciform, often glandular. Spikelets 2-flowered plus minute rhachilla extension; glumes as long as spikelet, papery and often colourful, apparently 1-nerved but often closely 3—5-nerved at base of keel; floret callus short and obtuse to narrowly oblong (conical and pungent in *P. triseta*); lemmas membranous, 5—11-nerved, usually hairy, 2-lobed, each lobe finely awned from inner side (*P. heptamera* 2—4 awns per lobe; *P. humbertii* none) or sometimes represented only by an awn, the central awn geniculate, rarely the lemma acute to truncate and awnless (in several species the awns of the lower floret are occasionally reduced; in *P. imperfecta* the awns of both florets may be reduced; conversely the normally muticous *P. galpinii*, *P. pilosogluma*, *P. setifolia* may sometimes be awned); palea glabrous or almost so; lodicules glabrous. Caryopsis with hilum ½ its length.

Species ± 65. Mainly South Africa; 6 species Cameroun to Yemen and Tanzania; 3 species Madagascar. Mountain heath.

A homogeneous genus whose many species are difficult to distinguish. Ten of the species are normally awnless. However the evident plasticity of the awn character, and the fact that they do not form an obviously natural group among themselves, tell against their accommodation in a separate genus, *Afrachneria*.

269. Pentameris P. Beauv., Ess. Agrost.: 92 (1812) — P. thuarii P. Beauv.

Like *Pentaschistis*, but lemma with lobes, lateral awns and central awn always well developed; palea hairy. Fruit an achene with free brittle shell-like pericarp.

Species 5. South Africa. Mountain grassland.

It is not easy to distinguish from *Pentaschistis* without the fruit, but the spikelets are longer (12—25 mm) than is usual in that genus, and the palea is conspicuously hairy.

270. Poagrostis Stapf in Fl. Cap. 7: 760 (1899) — P. pusilla Stapf.

Short annual. Panicle delicate, with capillary branches, sometimes reduced to a few spikelets. Spikelets 1-flowered without rhachilla extension; glumes exceeding lemma, membranous, 1 or closely 3-nerved; lemma membranous, 7-nerved, finely pubescent, denticulate.

Species 1. South Africa. Damp mountain slopes in shade.
Presumably derived from *Pentaschistis*.

271. Pseudopentameris Conert in Mitt. Bot. Staats. Münch. 10: 303 (1971) — P.

macrantha (Schrad.) Conert.

Perennial; leaf-blades flat or rolled. Panicle contracted, often scanty and sometimes raceme-like. Spikelets large (35—55 mm), 2-flowered, sometimes with rhachilla extension and rarely a third floret; glumes much longer than florets, 3—7-nerved; floret callus linear, narrowly truncate; lemma terete, the margins clasping palea keels, coriaceous, 9-nerved, with 2 awned lobes and geniculate central awn. Caryopsis terete, with hilum ⅖ its length.

Species 2. South Africa. Rocky slopes.

272. Rytidosperma Steud., Syn. Pl. Glum. 1: 425 (1854); Vickery in Contrib. New South Wales Herb. 2: 249—325 (1956); Connor & Edgar in New Zealand J. Bot. 17: 311—337 (1979) — R. lechleri Steud. *Monostachya* Merrill in Philipp. J. Sci. Bot. 5: 330 (1910); Jacobs in Taxon 31: 737—743 (1982) — M. centrolepidoides Merrill (= R. oreoboloides). *Erythranthera* Zotov in New Zealand J. Bot. 1: 124 (1963) — E. australis (Petrie) Zotov. *Notodanthonia* Zotov. l.c. 104 — N. unarede (Raoul) Zotov. *Karroochloa* Conert & Türpe in Senck. Biol. 50: 290 (1969) — K. curva (Nees) Conert & Türpe. *Merxmuellera* Conert l.c. 51: 129 (1970) — M. davyi (C.E. Hubbard) Conert.

Perennial (*R. schismoides, R. tenellum* annual); leaf-blades flat or rolled, sometimes pungent. Panicle contracted, occasionally capitate, often scanty and then sometimes raceme-like (true raceme in *R. distichum*) or reduced to a few spikelets. Spikelets: glumes as long as spikelet or almost so (shorter than lemma in *R. craigii, R. oreoboloides*) narrow to boat-shaped, papery, 1—13-nerved; floret callus short to narrowly oblong, rarely linear, obtuse but sometimes narrowly so; lemmas membranous to coriaceous, 5—9-nerved, bearing hair tufts arranged in 2 transverse series, these often incomplete and sometimes reduced to 2 marginal tufts, rarely represented by a transverse band of longer hairs (*R. arundinaceum, R. curvum, R. pallidum* uniformly hairy; *R. australe* glabrous; *R. distichum, R. pumilum, R. schneideri* variable), bilobed the lobes usually awned (*R. craigii, R. oreoboloides* subentire), with a straight or more often geniculate central awn (awn-point or mucro in *R. australe, R. nivicola, R. nudum, R. oreoboloides, R. pumilum, R. thomsonii*); palea glabrous or less often pilose; lodicules ciliate (glabrous in *R. australe, R. pumilum* and a few others). Caryopsis with hilum ¼—⅓ its length.

Species ± 90. Mainly Australia, New Zealand and southern Africa; but also Indonesia, Himalaya, Arabia, Ethiopia, Madagascar and Argentina. Mountain grassland, a few species descending to the lowlands.

A large and somewhat heterogeneous genus; perhaps subdivisible, but the segregates proposed are not clearly circumscribed and a thorough worldwide revision is required. A few species with uniformly hairy lemmas are placed here because of their short hilum and ciliate lodicules; *R. pallidum* affords a link with *Chionochloa*. *R. oreoboloides* is a cushion plant with the inflorescence reduced to a single spikelet; although unusual, it is linked to the body of the genus through species such as *R. nudum*; *R. australe* and *R. pumilum* also belong with this alliance.

273. Phaenanthoecium C.E. Hubbard in Kew Bull. 1936: 329 (1936) — P. kostlinii (A. Rich.) C.E. Hubbard.

Perennial, with slender trailing culms. Inflorescence a single short raceme. Spikelets: glumes shorter than lowest lemma, membranous, the upper 3—4-nerved, obtuse or emarginate; floret callus very short; lemmas membranous, 9-nerved, glabrous except for tufts of hair along margin, bilobed with long-awned lobes, geniculately awned from sinus; lodicules ciliate. Caryopsis with hilum ⅘ its length.

Species 1. Yemen and Ethiopia. Shady cliffs.
Evidently a segregate from *Rytidosperma* with short glumes and long hilum.

274. Alloeochaete C.E. Hubbard in Hook. Ic. Pl. 35: t 3418 (1940); Kabuye & Renvoize in Kew Bull. 30: 569—577 (1975) — A. andongensis (Rendle) C.E. Hubbard.

Perennial. Panicle open or contracted. Spikelets: glumes shorter than lowest lemma, membranous, 3—5-nerved, acute to shortly awned; floret callus oblong; lowest floret ♂ or with an imperfect ovary (bisexual in *A. gracillima*, sometimes *A. geniculata*), persisting on panicle with the glumes, membranous, often with reduced awns; remaining lemmas firmer in texture, 5-nerved, glabrous except for tufts of hairs midway along each margin, bilobed with awned lobes, geniculately (*A. uluguruensis* merely reflexed) awned from sinus; lodicules glabrous. Fruit not seen.

Species 6. Tanzania, Mozambique, Malawi, Angola. Mountains, on shallow soils over rock.
The tussocks of *A. oreogena* are perched upon an extraordinary 'tree-trunk' up to 1.5 m high, formed from a compact mass of culms, dead fibrous leaf-sheaths and woolly hairs.

275. Monachather Steud., Syn. Pl. Glum. 1: 247 (1854) — M. paradoxus Steud.

Perennial with tomentose basal sheaths; ligule membranous. Panicle scanty, raceme-like. Spikelets: glumes as long as spikelet, papery, 13-nerved; floret callus short, narrowly obtuse; lemma coriaceous, 9—13-nerved, hairy on back and in a transverse fringe below sinus, deeply bilobed, the central awn scarcely exceeding lobes; palea coriaceous, glabrous; lodicules glabrous. Caryopsis with hilum ¼ its length.

Species 1. Australia. Arid grassland.

276. Schismus P. Beauv., Ess. Agrost.: 73 (1812); Conert in Abh. Senck. Nat. Ges. 532: 1—81 (1974) — S. barbatus (L.) Thell. *Electra* Panz., Id. Rev. Gräser: 49 (1813) — E. calycina (Loefl.) Panz. (= S. barbatus). *Hemisacris* Steud. in Flora 12: 490 (1829) — H. gonatodes Steud. (= S. barbatus).

Annual or weakly perennial. Panicle contracted or spiciform. Spikelets falling entire, or upper florets falling singly and then lower florets, glumes and pedicel tardily deciduous together; glumes as long as spikelet or almost so, membranous with hyaline margins, prominently 5—7-nerved; floret callus short; lemmas membranous, 7—9-nerved, pilose on back or margins, bilobed or merely notched, ± mucronate (up to 1.5 mm in *S. pleuropogon*); lodicules ciliate. Caryopsis with hilum ⅕ its length.

Species 5. South Africa; Mediterranean and Middle East. Dry open places. The genus is linked through *S. pleuropogon* to *Rytidosperma curvum*.

277. Pyrrhanthera Zotov in New Zealand J. Bot. 1: 125 (1963) — P. exigua (Kirk) Zotov.

Short mat-forming perennial; leaf-blades filiform. Panicle of 1—3 spikelets. Spikelets 3-flowered, the third floret sometimes rudimentary; glumes as long as spikelet, 7—9-nerved; floret callus very short; lemmas coriaceous, 9-nerved, sparsely pilose, tridentate; lodicules ciliate. Fruit an achene with free coriaceous pericarp and hilum ⅕ its length.

Species 1. New Zealand. Upland grassy plains. Allied to *Rytidosperma pumilum*.

278. Dregeochloa Conert in Senck. Biol. 47: 335 (1966) — D. pumila (Nees) Conert.

Perennial, the stiff acicular leaves forming low cushions. Panicle short, raceme-like. Spikelets like *Rytidosperma*, with 5—7-nerved glumes, long narrowly obtuse floret callus and glabrous lodicules. Fruit an achene with thick free pericarp and hilum ⅓ its length.

Species 2. South Africa. Dry rocky places. Imitates *Rytidosperma oreoboloides* in habit, and differs from that genus in little more than the free pericarp.

279. Centropodia Reichenb., Consp. Reg. Veg.: 212a (1828) nom nov pro seq. *Danthonia sect Centropodia* R. Br. in Den. & Clapp., Narr. Trav. Discov. N. & C. Africa: App. 244 (1826) nom prov — D. forskalii (Vahl) Trin. *Asthenatherum* Nevski in Trudy Sredne-Az. Univ. ser. 8b, 17: 8 (1934); Conert in Senck. Biol. 43: 239—266 (1962) — nom superfl pro Centropodia.

Perennial from a woody rootstock, facultatively annual; leaf-blades stiff, flat or rolled, pungent. Panicle contracted. Spikelets: glumes as long as spikelet, strongly 7—11-nerved; floret callus pungent; lemmas coriaceous, 9-nerved, with lines of short hairs between nerves and terminating above in a long tuft, bilobed, with a straight or geniculate awn from sinus; lodicules glabrous. Caryopsis with hilum ¼ its length.

Species 4. North Africa through Middle East to northern India; southern Africa. Desert.

The genus is apparently derived from *Dregeochloa*, and is best accommodated in Arundineae despite the possession of well developed kranz anatomy (Ellis in Bothalia 15: 153—159, 1984).

280. Danthonidium C.E. Hubbard in Hook. Ic. Pl. 34: t 3331 (1937) — D. gammiei (Bhide) C.E. Hubbard.

Annual. Inflorescence a short many-sided raceme. Spikelets 1-flowered plus rhachilla extension; glumes much longer than floret, 3—5-nerved; floret callus narrowly truncate; lemma cylindrical, convolute and enfolding palea, coriaceous, 9-nerved, transversely bearded above, with 2 awned lobes and geniculate central awn. Grain not known.

Species 1. India. Stony places.

The affinities of the genus are not entirely clear, for it shares characters with both *Rytidosperma* and *Anisopogon*.

281. Anisopogon R.Br., Prodr. Fl. Nov. Holl.: 176 (1810) — A. avenacea R.Br.

Perennial; ligule membranous; leaf-blades harsh, rolled, pungent. Panicle loose. Spikelets large, 1-flowered plus rhachilla extension; glumes much longer than floret, 7—11-nerved; floret callus long, pungent; lemma terete, involute and enfolding palea, coriaceous, 7-nerved, with 2 awned lobes flanked by membranous teeth, and geniculate central awn; lodicules 3, large (4 mm). Caryopsis with separable pericarp.

Species 1. SE Australia. Eucalyptus forest and heathland.

Closely resembling and apparently related to *Pseudopentameris*. The leaf anatomy is typical of Arundineae, though the amino acid composition of the endosperm resembles that of Stipeae (Yoeh & Watson in Phytochem. 20: 1041—51, 1981).

282. Diplopogon R. Br., Prod. Fl. Nov. Holl.: 176 (1810); Poir., Encycl. Suppl. 2: 489 (1812) as "Diplogon" — D. setaceus R. Br. *Dipogonia* P. Beauv., Ess. Agrost.: 125 (1812) nom superfl pro Diplopogon.

Perennial. Panicle capitate. Like *Amphipogon*, but central awn of lemma much longer than laterals and twisted.

Species 1. Australia. Wet places.

283. Amphipogon R. Br., Prodr. Fl. Nov. Holl.: 175 (1810); Vickery in Contrib. New South Wales Herb. 1: 281—295 (1950) — A. laguroides R. Br. *Gamelythrum* Nees in Hook. J. Bot. 2: 415 (1843) — G. turbinatum (R. Br.) Nees. *Pentacraspedon* Steud., Syn. Pl. Glum. 1: 151 (1854) — P. amphipogonoides Steud.

Tufted perennial; leaf-blades convolute, pungent. Panicle spiciform, or capitate and then sometimes with involucral sterile spikelets at base. Spikelets 1-flowered without rhachilla extension; glumes exceeding body of lemma, 3-nerved, acute or shortly awned (*A. debilis* tridentate); lemma narrowly ovoid, involute and enfolding palea, thinly coriaceous, 3-nerved, 3-lobed, each lobe tapering to a glabrous or ciliate awn (*A. amphipogonoides* tridentate awnless), sometimes with an extra membranous deciduous lobe on each flank; palea as long as lemma, without keels, rounded on flanks, bifid and 2-awned (*A. amphipogonoides* bidentate). Fruit with thin free pericarp.

Species 5. Australia. Dry grassland.

284. Crinipes Hochst. in Flora 38: 279 (1855); Hubbard in Kew Bull. 12: 54—58 (1957) — C. abyssinicus (A. Rich.) Hochst.

Perennial. Spikelet: glumes $\frac{1}{2}$—$\frac{3}{4}$ length of lemma, 1-nerved, acuminate or shortly awned; floret callus narrowly oblong, bearded; lemmas membranous, 3-nerved, hairy only on margins, entire or bidenticulate, with a long straight or flexuous awn; palea $\frac{1}{2}$—$\frac{2}{3}$ length of lemma, glabrous; lodicules glabrous.

Species 2. Sudan, Ethiopia and Uganda. Moist places among rocks.

285. Nematopoa C.E. Hubbard in Kew Bull. 12: 51 (1957) — N. longipes (Stent & Hubbard) C.E. Hubbard.

Perennial; leaf-blades filiform, but flexuous and not pungent. Spikelets: glumes short, $\frac{1}{4}$—$\frac{1}{2}$ length of lemma, hyaline, 0—1-nerved, obtuse to acute; floret callus oblong, villous; lemmas membranous, 3-nerved, pilose on back and margins, with 2 setaceous teeth and a long flexuous central awn; palea $\frac{4}{5}$ length of lemma.

Species 1. Zimbabwe. Moist places.

286. Leptagrostis C.E. Hubbard in Kew Bull. 1937: 63 (1937) — L. schimperiana (Hochst.) C.E. Hubbard.

Perennial. Spikelets 1-flowered plus rhachilla extension; glumes 1—3-nerved, acuminate, the upper as long as floret, the lower half as long; floret callus obtuse with a beard half as long as lemma; lemma membranous, 3-nerved, glabrous, entire or bidenticulate, with a short straight awn; palea as long as lemma; lodicules glabrous.

Species 1. Ethiopia.
A rare genus, apparently related to *Crinipes*.

287. Dichaetaria Steud., Syn. Pl. Glum. 1: 145 (1845) — D. wightii Steud.

Perennial; ligule membranous with ciliate fringe. Inflorescence a long lax panicle with raceme-like primary branches. Spikelets with 1 fertile floret, the rhachilla terminating in an awn-like sterile lemma; glumes 3-nerved, shorter than floret; floret callus acute, shortly bearded; lemma coriaceous, 3-nerved, scaberulous, setaceously bidentate, straight awned. Caryopsis linear.

Species 1. Southern India and Sri Lanka. Woodland shade.

An isolated genus with some resemblance to *Gymnopogon*, but possessing arundinoid leaf anatomy and embryo.

288. Cortaderia Stapf in Gard. Chron. ser. 3, 22: 396 (1897) nom conserv; Acevedo in Bol. Mus. Nac. Hist. Nat. 27: 205—246 (1959); Connor & Edgar in Taxon 23: 595—605 (1974) — C. selloana (Schult.) Asch. & Graeb. *Moorea* Lemaire in Ill. Hort. 2: Misc. 15 (1855) nom rejic non Rolfe (1890) — M. argentea (Nees) Lemaire (= C. selloana).

Perennial, often tall (leaf-blades convolute and pungent in *C. pungens, C. sericantha*); gynodioecious, the two forms similar or not. Panicle commonly large and plumose, sometimes small. Spikelets: glumes longer than lowest lemma, ⅔ to as long as spikelet, narrow, hyaline, 1-nerved (*C. pungens, C. sericantha* 3-nerved); floret callus linear, hairy; lemmas hyaline, 3—5(—7)-nerved, plumose on back, entire or with 2 filiform teeth, with or without a straight awn; palea glabrous or sometimes pilose; lodicules hairy; female plant with minute or well developed sterile anthers.

Species 24. Mainly South America, but 4 species in New Zealand and 1 in New Guinea. Hillsides, scrubland and ruderal sites. *C. selloana* (Pampas grass) is commonly grown as an ornamental.

The genus is best known for its large tussocks and handsome plumose panicle, but it can be small and *Chionochloa*-like. Connor & Edgar (l.c.) provide a sectional classification.

Sexes similar, all spikelets hairy, the female with well developed sterile anthers:
  Lemmas with 2 filiform teeth, awned from sinus; palea ⅔—⅘ length of lemma;
    lemma 3—7-nerved (C. richardii)   Sect *Bifida*
  Lemmas entire or bidenticulate; palea fully as long as lemma:
    Lemma with an awn 4—8 mm long, 3-nerved (C. pilosa)   Sect *Monoaristata*
    Lemma with a very brief awn, 3—5-nerved (C. modesta)   Sect *Mutica*
Sexes dissimilar, the bisexual spikelets glabrous or almost so, the female with
    minute staminodes; lemmas 3-nerved, entire, long drawn out into an acute or
    filiform tip; palea up to ½ length of lemma (C. selloana)   Sect *Cortaderia*

Gynodioecism (female and bisexual plants) encourages outbreeding, the sex ratios being maintained by poorer seed set and viability in bisexual plants. The sexes may be externally indistinguishable in the primitive sect *Bifida*, but strongly divergent in sect *Cortaderia*. In fact viability is so reduced in the bisexual plants of *C. selloana* that they function mainly as pollen parents, and the species is virtually dioecious. Other members of the section have adopted apomixy in the female plants, with a consequent decline in the bisexual form which may be very rare or unknown (Connor in Evolution 27: 663—678, 1973).

The genus intergrades with *Chionochloa*, and may be difficult to distinguish from it if only bisexual plants are available; consequently the placing of the intermediate *Cortaderia archboldii* is open to dispute.

289. Lamprothyrsus Pilger in Bot. Jahrb. 37, Beibl. 85: 58 (1906) — L. hieronymi (Kuntze) Pilger.

Perennial; gynodioecious, the two forms similar. Spikelets: glumes a little longer than lemma, $\frac{1}{2}$—$\frac{2}{3}$ length of spikelet, hyaline, 0—1-nerved, acuminate to an awn point; floret callus linear, villous; lemmas hyaline, 5-nerved, villous, bifid with awned lobes 20—40 mm long and a recurved central awn, this flat and sometimes slightly twisted at base; palea longer than body of lemma, pilose; lodicules hairy; female spikelets with minute staminodes.

Species 3. Bolivia to Argentina. Hill slopes.

290. Arundo L., Sp., Pl.: 81 (1753) — A. donax L. *Donax* P. Beauv., Ess. Agrost.: 77, 152 (1812) non Lour. (1790), nom superfl pro Arundo. *Scolochloa* Mert. & Koch in Roehl., Deutschl. Fl. ed. 3, 1: 528 (1823) nom superfl pro Arundo. *Amphidonax* Nees in Lindley, Nat. Syst. ed. 2: 449 (1836) — A. bengalensis (Retz.) Nees (= A. donax). *Donacium* Fries in Bot. Not. 1843: 132 (1843) & *Eudonax* Fries l.c. — nom superfl pro Donax.

Tall rhizomatous perennial reed (A. *formosana* of modest size); leaves cauline; ligule membranous with minutely ciliolate margin. Panicle large, plumose. Spikelets (sometimes 1-flowered in A. *plinii*): glumes as long as spikelet, 3—5-nerved; floret callus short; lemmas membranous, 3—7-nerved, plumose below middle, entire or bidentate, with a straight awnlet; palea $\frac{1}{2}$—$\frac{2}{3}$ length of lemma.

Species 3. Mediterranean to China; widely introduced elsewhere. River banks and damp places. A. *donax* is a useful source of canes for light construction; the reeds for modern wood-wind instruments are cut from its culms.

It is related to *Phragmites,* but probably not as closely as the similarity in habit would suggest.

291. Hakonechloa Honda in J. Fac. Sci. Tokyo Bot. 3: 113 (1930) —H. macra (Munro) Honda.

Short rhizmatous perennial; leaves cauline; ligule membranous with minutely ciliolate margin. Panicle small. Spikelets: glumes shorter than lemma, 3-nerved; floret callus slender, villous; lemmas membranous, 3-nerved, margins pilose, entire, with a straight awn almost as long as itself; palea $\frac{4}{5}$ length of lemma. Fruit with free pericarp.

Species 1. Japan. Wet cliffs.
Although *Hakonechloa* is only 50—90 cm high, its rhizomatous habit and free-standing culms suggest that it is related to the tall reeds.

292. Molinia Schrank, Baier. Fl. 1: 100, 334 (1789); Gray, Nat. Arr. Brit. Pl. 2: 110 (1821) as "Monilia"; Jirasek in Acta Univ. Carol. Biol. 1965: 227—243 (1965) & Preslia 38: 22—35 (1966); Frey in Frag. Fl. Geobot. 21: 21—50 (1975) — M. varia Schrank (= M. caerulea). *Enodium* Gaud., Agrost. Helv. 1: 145 (1811) & *Amblytes*

Dulac., Fl. Hautes-Pyr.: 80 (1867) — nom superfl pro Molinia. *Moliniopsis* Hayata in Bot. Mag. Tokyo 39: 258 (1925) — M. japonica (Hack.) Hayata.

Tufted perennial; culm internodes unequal, the lowest short clavately swollen and persisting for several years, the intermediate reduced to a stack of closely spaced leaf-bearing nodes, the topmost comprising most of the culm; leaf-blades deciduous from sheath. Panicle open or contracted. Spikelets 2—5-flowered (or a few spikelets in panicle 1-flowered), the rhachilla internodes usually ⅓—½ length of lemma; glumes shorter than lemma, 1—3-nerved; floret callus short, truncate, bearded (*M. caerulea* glabrous); lemmas membranous, 3(—5)-nerved, glabrous, acute; palea almost as long as lemma. Fruit with reluctantly free pericarp.

Species 2—4. Europe, western Russia, Turkey; China, Japan. Wet moorlands and heaths.
The genus is related to *Hakonechloa* through *M. japonica*. It is not easy to distinguish from *Eragrostis* though the long rhachilla internodes are usually diagnostic; fortunately the two genera are seldom sympatric. The basal culm internodes function as storage organs.

293. Phragmites Adans., Fam. Pl. 2: 34, 559 (1763); Clayton in Kew Bull. 21: 113—117 (1967) & in Taxon 17: 168—169 (1968) — Arundo phragmites L. (= P. australis). *Trichoon* Roth in Arch. Bot. 1, 3: 37 (1798); Benth. in J. Linn. Soc. Bot. 19: 112 (1881) as "Trichodon" — T. karka (Retz.) Roth. *Xenochloa* Roem. & Schult., Syst. Veg. 2: 501 (1817) — X. arundinacea Licht. (= P. australis). *Czernya* Presl, Cyp. Gram. Sic.: 22 (1826) — C. arundinacea Presl (= P. australis). *Oxyanthe* Steud., Syn. Pl. Glum. 1: 197 (1854) — O. japonica (Steud.) Steud. (= P. karka). *Miphragtes* Nieuwland in Amer. Midl. Nat. 3: 332 (1914) nom prov pro Phragmites.

Tall rhizomatous perennial reed; leaves cauline, the blades deciduous; ligule a very short membrane with long ciliate margin. Panicle large, plumose. Spikelets with lowest floret ♂ or empty; glumes shorter than lowest lemma, 3—5-nerved; floret callus linear, plumose; lemmas hyaline, 1—3-nerved, glabrous, long caudate, entire; palea ⅔ length of lemma.

Species 3—4. Cosmopolitan. Marshes and riversides. Used for mats and thatching.
A uniform genus of barely separable species. The spikelets emerge in a juvenile state and mature on the panicle. *Trichoon* is an example of a genus based on an imaginary character, the spikelet hairs supposedly arising from the ovary.

294. Gynerium P. Beauv., Ess. Agrost.: 138 (1812) — G. sagittatum (Aubl.) P. Beauv.

Giant rhizomatous perennial reed; dioecious; leaves clustered toward top of culm. Panicle large. Female spikelet usually 2-flowered without rhachilla extension; glumes not persistent, the upper much longer than lemma, membranous, 3—5-nerved, caudate, recurved; floret callus linear, glabrous or hairy; lemmas plumose, long caudate, entire; palea ¼ length of lemma. Male spikelet glabrous, the glumes and lemmas hyaline, without tails; stamens 2.

Species 1. Streamsides and damp places. Mexico and West Indies to Peru and Brazil. Used for constructional work, basketry and suchlike.

A gigantic grass up to 10 m tall. The leaves have a very short external ligule.

26. THYSANOLAENEAE

C.E. Hubbard in Hutch., Fam. Fl. Pl. 2: 222 (1934).

Ligule scarious. Inflorescence a large panicle contracted about primary branches, the spikelets all alike, immature at emergence. Spikelets tiny, 2-flowered plus rhachilla extension which sometimes bears a reduced floret, laterally compressed, falling entire with pedicel attached though subsequently disarticulating; glumes much shorter than spikelet, hyaline, 0—1-nerved, obtuse; lower floret barren without a palea, its lemma membranous, 1—3-nerved, glabrous, acuminate; upper floret bisexual, its lemma thinly 3-nerved, ciliate on margins, acuminate; stamens 2—3. Caryopsis subglobose, the hilum punctiform.

Genus 1; species 1. Tropical Asia.

Anatomy. Non-kranz with slender microhairs, the chlorenchyma cells with invaginated cell walls; midrib complex.

Chromosomes. 2n = 24

The tribe is distinguished by its spikelets with dimorphic florets disarticulating below the pedicel. It is evidently related to *Phragmites*, and tribal status probably overstates the degree of difference.

295. Thysanolaena Nees in Edinb. New Phil. J. 18: 180 (1835) — T. agrostis Nees (= T. maxima). *Myriachaeta* Moritzi, Syst. Verz.: 101 (1846) — M. arundinacea Zoll. & Mor. (= T. maxima).

Tall tufted perennial. Description as for tribe.

Species 1. Tropical Asia. Shrubby hillsides.

27. MICRAIREAE

Pilger, Nat. Pfl.-Fam. ed. 2, 14d: 167 (1956). *Micrairinae* Pilger in Bot. Jb. 74: 19 (1945) sine descr lat.

Ligule a line of hairs; leaves spirally arranged with ⅜ phyllotaxy; blades short, imbricate, sometimes pungent, eventually deciduous from sheath. Inflorescence a scanty panicle, sometimes reduced to a compact raceme, the spikelets alike. Spikelets 2-flowered without rhachilla extension, laterally compressed, disarticulating below each floret; glumes persistent, longer or shorter than florets, subequal, keeled, membranous, 1—3(—5)-nerved, obtuse to spinously acuminate; lemmas keeled or not, hyaline to thinly membranous, 1—3-nerved (*M. multinervia, M. subulifolia* prominently 5—9-nerved), obtuse to truncate or emarginate; palea 2-nerved, bifid to the base (*M. multinervia, M. subulifolia* undivided, 4—7-nerved, 2-keeled); lodicules 0; stamens 2. Caryopsis ellipsoid, the hilum oblong to linear.

Genus 1; species 13. Australia.

Anatomy. Non-kranz with stout finger-like microhairs. *M. subspicata* with simple to branched epidermal papillae. Embryo incompletely known, but apparently arundinoid.

Chromosomes. 2n = 20.

Micraireae is unique in the spiral arrangement of its leaf primordia; in all other grasses these are distichous, though subsequent twisting of the sheath may alter the orientation of mature leaves. It also has a peculiar palea, either multinerved or divided into two halves.

It occupies inhospitable rock outcrops with very shallow soils, and has the property of revival from the dried state.

Its anatomy (and embryo?) are arundinoid. Its unusual characters are not shared by primitive members of the subfamily. It seems therefore that it is best regarded as a derivative of Arundineae adapted to a specialized habitat.

296. Micraira F. Muell., Fragm. 5: 208 (1867); Blake in Proc. Roy. Soc. Queensland 74: 45—52 (1964); Clifford in Univ. Queensland Papers 4: 87—93 (1964); Lazarides in Brunonia 2: 67—84 (1979) & in Nuytsia 5: 273—303 (1985) — M. subulifolia F. Muell.

Perennial, forming a moss-like carpet. Description as for tribe.

Species 13. Australia. Shallow soils on rocks.

28. ARISTIDEAE

C.E. Hubbard in Bor, Grasses Burma Ceylon India Pak.: 685 (1960); Henrard in Med. Rijks Herb. Leiden 54 (1926), 54a (1927), 54b (1928), 58 (1929), 58a (1932), 58b (1933) 54c (1933); de Winter in Bothalia 8: 201—404 (1965). *Aristidinae* Maire & Weiler, Fl. Afr. Nord 2: 29 (1953) sine descr lat.

Ligule a line of hairs. Inflorescence an open to densely contracted panicle, the spikelets alike. Spikelets 1-flowered without rhachilla extension, laterally compressed or terete, disarticulating above glumes; glumes persistent, longer than body of lemma (rarely shorter in *Aristida*), membranous to scarious, mostly acute to acuminate; lemma terete, 1—3-nerved, ± coriaceous and usually with germination flap at base, wrapped around and concealing palea, 3-awned, these ± connate at the base and often raised upon a twisted column, the laterals sometimes reduced or rarely suppressed; palea less than ½ lemma length, sometimes little longer than lodicules; lodicules 2, rarely 0; stamens 3, rarely 1. Caryopsis usually fusiform, the hilum linear.

Genera 3; species ± 300. Tropics and subtropics.

Anatomy. Microhairs slender. Leaf section progresses from non-kranz (*Sartidia*) to kranz PS (*Stipagrostis*), and thence to a special form of kranz in *Aristida* (fig 18).

The latter resembles the PS form in the radial arrangement of its chlorenchyma, but the inner sheath is larger than the outer and both form starch; paradoxically the decarboxylating enzyme is NADP-ME, characteristic of MS grasses. It cannot plausibly be postulated as precursory to either of the two main forms, and is best regarded as a third form peculiar to *Aristida*.

Chromosomes. The basic number is 11.

2n	22	44
No of species	48	31

Aristideae is characterized by 1-flowered spikelets with terete enfolding lemma and a distinctive triple awn. It has achieved a pantropical distribution in dry or pioneer habitats, presumably owing much of its success to the acquisition of C_4 photosynthesis and a floret structure adapted to efficient dispersal.

The tribe is not easy to separate from Arundineae, to which it is linked through *Amphipogon*. The unusual short palea marks a sharp, though perhaps somewhat arbitrary, boundary between the tribes. There is some risk of confusing 1-awned species with Stipeae, a pooid tribe showing parallel development of terete lemmas but distinguished by its membranous ligule.

Awns glabrous:
  Upper glume 3-nerved, the lower 3—7-nerved   **297 Sartidia**
  Upper glume 1-nerved, the lower nearly always also 1-nerved   **299 Aristida**
Awns, or at least the central one, plumose   **298 Stipagrostis**

297. Sartidia de Winter in Kirkia 3: 137 (1963) — S. angolensis (C.E. Hubbard) de Winter.

Perennial. Spikelet: lower glume 3—7-nerved, upper 3-nerved; floret callus long, pungent; lemma involute; awns with or without a column, persistent, the branches glabrous and gyrate. Caryopsis with ventral groove and embryo less than ¼ its length; no scutellum cleft.

Species 4. Southern Africa and Madagascar. Savanna.
A primitive non-kranz genus, distinguished from *Aristida sect Aristida* by its 3-nerved upper glume supported by embryo differences.

298. Stipagrostis Nees in Linnaea 7: 290 (1832) — S. capensis Nees (= S. obtusa). *Schistachne* Fig. & De Not. in Mem. Acc. Sci. Torino ser. 2, 12: 252 (1852) — S. ciliata (Desf.) Fig. & De Not.

Perennial, sometimes with a knotty rhizomatous base or suffrutescent (*S. hermannii, S. namibensis, S. subacaulis* ephemeral); leaf-blades mostly convolute, occasionally pungent (especially *S. pungens, S. vulnerans*). Spikelet: glumes 1—11-nerved; floret callus long, pungent; lemma convolute (*S. anomala* involute); awns with or without a column, deciduous (*S. zeyheri subsp sericans* persistent), at least the central branch plumose (but see *S. anomala* below).

Species ± 50. Africa, Middle East, Central Asia and Pakistan. Desert and semi-desert; some species on shifting dunes.

The genus is adapted to arid conditions, having harsh, narrow leaves with thickened outer epidermis; the blades are sometimes short and soon deciduous, leaving culms and sheaths as the principal photosynthetic organs. A convenient, though slightly artificial, sectional classification is derived from the awn:

Awn 3-branched:
  Articulation near middle of lemma body (S. ciliata)　　　Sect *Schistachne*
  Articulation at tip of lemma (S. uniplumis)　　　Sect *Stipagrostis*
Awn unbranched, hairy only at base of column; articulation at tip of lemma (S. anomala)　　　Sect *Anomala*

Stipagrostis is sometimes included in *Aristida*, but has plumose awns, normal kranz PS anatomy, and a preference for drier habitats.

299. Aristida L., Sp. Pl.: 82 (1753); Lazarides in Brunonia 3: 271—333 (1980) —A. adscensionis L. *Kielboul* Adans., Fam. Pl. 2: 31, 539 (1763) nom superfl pro Aristida. *Streptachne* R. Br., Prodr. Fl. Nov. Holl.: 174 (1810); Blake in Proc. Roy. Soc. Queensland 56: 11—17 (1945) — S. stipoides R. Br. (= A. utilis). *Arthratherum* P. Beauv., Ess. Agrost.: 32 (1812) nom superfl pro Streptachne. *Chaetaria* P. Beauv. l.c. 30, nom superfl pro Aristida. *Curtopogon* P. Beauv. l.c. 32; Spreng., Syst. Veg. ed. 16, 1: 266 (1824) as "Cyrtopogon" — C. dichotomus (Michaux) P. Beauv. *Moulinsia* Raf. in Bull. Bot. Genève 1: 221 (1830) non Camb. (1829) — M. lanosa (Muhl.) Jacks. *Trixostis* Raf. l.c. — T. gracilis (Ell.) Jacks. (= A. longespica). *Aristopsis* Catasus in Fol. Geobot. Phytotax. 16: 439 (1981) — A. bissei Catasus (= immature Aristida sp.).

Annual or perennial; leaf-blades flat or rolled. Spikelet: glumes 1-nerved, or rarely the lower 3—5(—7)-nerved; floret callus obtuse to pungent or bidentate; lemma convolute or involute; awns with or without a column, persistent or deciduous, the branches glabrous, flat (especially *A. jemenica*) or terete, sometimes the laterals reduced or rarely suppressed (some New World species with branches gyrate, reflexed, or the central twisted). Caryopsis terete, or grooved when lemma involute, the embryo $\frac{1}{3}$ its length.

Species ± 250. Tropics and subtropics. Dry or weedy places.
A large homogeneous genus, subdivided according to its awn characters. The marked difference between convolute and involute lemmas cuts across this classification, and suggests that it is at least partly artificial. Sect *Aristida* is by far the largest, with some 200 species.

Awns persistent, with or without a column, rarely the lateral branches suppressed; lemma convolute or involute (A. adscensionis)　　　Sect *Aristida*
Awns deciduous:
 Awn single, bigeniculate; callus hairs ½ as long as the convolute lemma (A. parvula)　　　Sect *Schizachne*
 Awns three; callus at most bearded:
  Column absent; lemma involute (A. hordeacea)　　　Sect *Pseudochaetaria*
  Column present:
   Articulation at top of column; lemma usually involute (A. mutabilis)
　　　Sect *Pseudarthratherum*
   Articulation at base of column; lemma convolute (A. meridionalis)
　　　Sect *Arthratherum*

Axillary cleistogenes occur in *A. basiramea*. A remarkable mode of dispersal, observed in the desert near Khartoum, is the agglomeration of *A. funiculata* florets into balls up to 25 cm diameter, which are rolled along by the wind.

V. SUBFAMILY CHLORIDOIDEAE

Rouy, Fl. France 14: 2 (1913). *Eragrostoideae* Pilger, Nat. Pfl.-Fam. ed. 2, 14d: 167 (1956).

Herbs, usually with linear or convolute leaf-blades, often xeromorphic. Frequent external characters: unilateral racemes; 1—many-flowered laterally compressed spikelets with fragile rhachilla; 1—3-nerved lemmas.

Lodicules 2, cuneate, fleshy, truncate; stamens 3, rarely fewer; stigmas 2. Caryopsis (or utricle) with large embryo commonly $\frac{1}{3}$—$\frac{3}{4}$ its length, and punctiform or occasionally elliptic hilum; embryo chloridoid P+PF (*Cottea, Schmidtia, Entoplocamia, Fingerhuthia* centothecoid; *Myriostachya, Orcuttia, Cynodon, Uniola paniculata* arundinoid — other *Uniola spp* chloridoid).

Chlorenchyma clearly or obscurely radiate, generally limited to a discrete layer around bundle; bundle sheaths double; little variation in size between secondary and tertiary bundles; microhairs short and stout, typically egg-shaped with the apical cell shorter than the basal, occasionally finger-like with the apical cell as long as or longer than the basal (but see Pappophoreae); stomatal subsidiary cells domed or triangular; midrib simple or complex; long cells often papillate. See kranz PS type in fig 17.

The subfamily is characterized by its well developed kranz anatomy, distinctive swollen microhairs and usually 1—3-nerved lemmas. The tribes Eragrostideae, Leptureae, and Cynodonteae form a coherent group; Pappophoreae and Orcuttieae stand somewhat aloof, but are linked to the other tribes by the chloridoid microhairs of *Pappophorum*. The subfamily can thus be envisaged as a monophyletic line, whose adoption of efficient C$_4$ photosynthesis has led to its successful proliferation in the tropics. The anatomy shows little variation throughout the subfamily, a marked contrast with Panicoideae.

There is sufficient similarity between primitive members of Eragrostideae and Arundineae to suggest a common ancestry; indeed demarcation between the tribes at this level is probably not as sharp as the anatomical criterion makes it appear. There is also evidence for a direct link to Centotheceae, seen in the spikelet comparisons *Megastachya–Eragrostis* or *Chasmanthium–Uniola*, the occasional occurrence of centothecoid embryos, and the hooked hairs of Orcuttieae.

The subfamily contains few large genera but a host of very small ones, and its development has apparently been dominated by vigorous adaptive radiation into a wide range of specialized, often stressful, habitats. Indeed it is likely that physiological differences may often outweigh the morphological distinctions between genera.

The ligule is exceptionally variable and intermediate forms, membranous with ciliate margin, are common. An unusual feature is that the pericarp often loosens when the grain is soaked in water. At best it is a hyaline or mucilaginous skin from which the seed is readily shed and the fruit may be termed a utricle; at worst it may be peeled away only by careful dissection and is not easily distinguished from the pericarp of a true caryopsis. This variability greatly reduces its value as a taxonomic character. Another oddity is that a few species adapted to life on rock outcrops have the ability to revive from an air-dried state (Gaff & Ellis in Bothalia 11: 305—308, 1974). Liphschitz & Waisel (New Phytol. 73: 507—513, 1974) ascribe a salt-secreting function to the microhairs.

29. PAPPOPHOREAE

Kunth, Rév. Gram. 1: 82 (1829). *Pappophorinae* Dumort., Anal. Fam.: 63 (1829). *Cotteinae* Reeder in Madroño 18: 25 (1965).

Ligule a line of hairs. Inflorescence a dense often narrow panicle, the spikelets all alike. Spikelets several-flowered, slightly laterally compressed, the lower 2 or more florets bisexual (sometimes only 1 in *Enneapogon, Pappophorum*), the upper progressively reduced, disarticulating above glumes but not between florets (except *Cottea*); glumes persistent, thinly membranous, distinctly (1—)7—11-nerved, as long as body of lowest lemma to as long as spikelet, entire; lemma 9—11-nerved, broad, rounded on back, the nerves produced into 7—19 awns or hyaline lobes (except *Kaokochloa*); palea keels ciliate.
Genera 5; species 41. Tropics.

Anatomy. Kranz PS type. *Pappophorum* has microhairs of the usual chloridoid type, but the other genera have slender bulbous-tipped microhairs long enough to be visible under a × 10 lens. Renvoize in Kew Bull. 40: 737—744 (1985).

Chromosomes. The basic number is 9 or 10.

2n	18	20	22	36	40	60	100
No of species	1	3	1	5	3	3	1

A small tribe distinguished by its many awns and unusual microhairs, supported by the many-nerved glumes and tough rhachilla, though none of these characters is constant throughout. The genera are all closely related, but *Pappophorum* stands a little apart from the rest (Reeder, l.c.). Presumably there is a distant relationship between Pappophoreae and Eragrostideae, but there are no direct and obvious links between the two tribes.

1	Glumes 1-nerved	**300 Pappophorum**
1	Glumes 7—11-nerved:	
2	Lemmas with 7—11 awns or lobes:	
3	Rhachilla tough between florets:	
4	Lemma 9-awned, not lobed	**301 Enneapogon**
4	Lemma 5-awned, these alternating with 6 hyaline lobes	**302 Schmidtia**
3	Rhachilla disarticulating between florets	**303 Cottea**
2	Lemmas with 2(—4) awns	**304 Kaokochloa**

300. Pappophorum Schreb., Gen. Pl. 2: 787 (1791) — P. alopecuroideum Vahl (= P. pappiferum). *Pappophorum sect Polyraphis* Trin. in Mém. Ácad. Sci. Pétersb. sér. 6, 1: 91 (1830) — P. alopecuroideum. *Polyraphis* (Trin.) Lindley, Veg. King.: 115 (1847) nom superfl.

Perennial, with glabrous foliage. Spikelets sometimes with only 1 fertile floret; glumes 1-nerved; lemmas coriaceous, pubescent to villous on keel and margins, with 12—19 scaberulous awns; uppermost florets reduced to a brush-like appendange.

Species 9. Southern USA to Argentina. Grassland and bushland, often on alluvial soils.

301. Enneapogon P. Beauv., Ess. Agrost.: 81 (1812); Burbidge in Proc. Linn. Soc. 153: 52—91 (1941); Renvoize in Kew Bull. 22: 393—401 (1968) — E. desvauxii P. Beauv. *Calotheria* Steud., Syn. Pl. Glum. 1: 199 (1854) in syn sub E. elegans (= E. schimperianus).

Perennial, sometimes annual; leaf-blades usually narrow, often convolute; panicle sometimes spiciform or capitate. Spikelets sometimes with only 1 fertile floret; lemmas chartaceous to coriaceous, smooth or ribbed, villous below middle, with 9 ciliate awns (scaberulous in *E. scaber*); uppermost florets reduced to a brush-like appendage.

Species 28. Tropics and subtropics of the world, especially Australia and Africa. Dry open places in bushland and semi-desert.
A very uniform genus whose species closely resemble one another. A few species (e.g., *E. asperatus*) have cleistogamous inflorescences in the upper leaf-sheaths which are dispersed by disarticulation at the culm nodes, or they have solitary cleistogenes in the basal sheaths.

302. Schmidtia Steud. in Schmidt, Beitr. Fl. Cap. Verd. Ins.: 144 (1852) nom conserv non Moench (1802) nec Tratt. (1816); Launert in Bol. Soc. Brot. sér. 2, 39: 303—319 (1965) — S. pappophoroides Steud. *Antoschmidtia* Boiss., Fl. Or. 5: 559 (1884) nom superfl pro Schmidtia.

Annual or perennial. Spikelets: lemmas subcoriaceous, villous below middle, 6-lobed, the hyaline lobes (these sometimes awn-tipped) alternating with 5 scaberulous awns.

Species 2. Africa and Pakistan. Woodland or bushland on dry sandy soils.

303. Cottea Kunth, Rév. Gram. 1: 84 (1829) — C. pappophoroides Kunth.

Perennial. Spikelets disarticulating between florets; lemmas chartaceous, villous below middle, irregularly lobed, the lobes produced into 7—11 awns.

Species 1. Southern USA to Argentina. Plains and dry hills.
Cleistogenes occur within the lower sheaths.

304. Kaokochloa de Winter in Bothalia 7: 479 (1961) — K. nigrirostris de Winter.

Annual. Spikelets: lemmas coriaceous, villous below middle, usually with 2 narrow awned lobes, one at each margin, the apex between incurved and emarginate, rarely with 1—2 shorter subsidiary lobes.

Species 1. South West Africa. Semi-desert.

30. ORCUTTIEAE

Reeder in Madroño 18: 20 (1965) & Amer. J. Bot. 69: 1082—1095 (1982).

Ligule absent, the sheath and blade scarcely differentiated; leaf-blades viscid, aromatic. Inflorescence a spiciform panicle or single raceme, the spikelets all alike. Spikelets of several to many fertile florets with imperfect florets above, laterally compressed, disarticulating below each floret; glumes present or absent; lemma prominently 13—15-nerved, rounded on back; palea keels glabrous; lodicules 0 or minute.
Genera 3; species 9. California.

Anatomy. Kranz PS type, with unusual mushroom-button microhairs and hooked hairs. Renvoize in Kew Bull. 40: 737—744 (1985).

Chromosomes. The counts apparently represent an aneuploid series based on x = 10.

2n	24	26	28	30	32	40
No of species	2	1	1	1	1	3

The many-nerved glumes and lemmas suggest a relationship with Pappophoreae, but Orcuttieae differs in several features, especially the microhairs (Reeder l.c.). The tribe is not particularly distinctive, but its limited distribution and specialized habitat leave little room for confusion with anything else.

1	Glumes present:	
2	Lemma acuminately 5-lobed	**305 Orcuttia**
2	Lemma erose or denticulate	**306 Tuctoria**
1	Glumes absent	**307 Neostapfia**

305. Orcuttia Vasey in Bull. Torr. Bot. Cl. 13: 219 (1886); Hoover l.c. 68: 149—156 (1941) — O. californica Vasey.

Annual. Inflorescence a single 2-sided raceme, the spikelets sometimes distant but usually ± condensed. Spikelets usually long persistent on the inflorescence, but disarticulating readily when soaked with rain; glumes chartaceous, 5—9-nerved, shorter than lemma, acuminate or irregularly 2—5-toothed; lemma oblong, chartaceous, acuminately 5-lobed; lodicules 0. Embryo without epiblast.

Species 5. California. Vernal pools, lying dormant during drought years and flowering only when inundation adequate (Crampton in Madroño 15: 97—110 (1959).

306. Tuctoria Reeder in Amer. J. Bot. 69: 1090 (1982) — T. fragilis (Swallen) Reeder.

Annual. Inflorescence a dense many-sided raceme. Spikelets like *Orcuttia*, but lemma denticulate to erose, mucronate; lodicules minute, fused to palea.

Species 3. California. Vernal pools.

307. Neostapfia Davy in Erythea 7: 43 (1899) nom nov pro seq. *Stapfia* Davy l.c. 6: 109 (1898) non Chodat (1897) — S. colusana Davy. *Davyella* Hack. in Oest. Bot. Zeit. 49: 134 (1899) nom superfl pro Neostapfia.

Annual. Inflorescence a spiciform panicle, abruptly narrowed and bearing abortive spikelets at the tip. Spikelets: glumes absent; lemma flabellate, membranous, truncate, erose; lodicules minute.

Species 1. California. Vernal pools.

31. ERAGROSTIDEAE

Stapf in Fl. Cap. 7: 316 (1898); Hubbard in Hook. Ic. Pl 34: t 3319 (1936); Phillips in Kew Bull. 37: 133—162 (1982). *Sporoboleae* Stapf in Fl. Cap. 7: 315 (1898). *Jouveae* Pilger, Nat. Pfl.-Fam. ed. 2, 14d: 168 (1956). *Aeluropodeae* Bor in Oest. Bot. Zeit. 112: 184 (1965). *Unioleae* (Clayton) Campbell in J. Arn. Arb. 66: 166 (1985).

Ligule membranous or a line of hairs. Inflorescence a panicle, or of tough unilateral racemes (bilateral with broadside spikelets in *Triodia spicata*; bottle brush in *Harpachne, Viguierella*; embedded spikelets in *Oropetium*), these digitate or scattered along an axis, rarely single, the spikelets alike (except *Sohnsia, Scleropogon, Lycurus, Pereilema, Monanthochloinae*). Spikelets sometimes 1-flowered, typically several—many-flowered with the lower florets fertile and the uppermost ± reduced, usually laterally compressed and sometimes strongly so, commonly disarticulating below each floret but with a wide variety of other abscission modes; glumes mostly persistent (but see *Eragrostis* and allies, *Sporobolus*), usually membranous 0—1-nerved and shorter than lowest lemma, entire (except *Lycurus*, some *Muhlenbergia*); lemmas membranous to coriaceous, 1—3-nerved (some exceptions), entire or 2—3-lobed and then occasionally with small subsidiary teeth between lobes, with or without 1(—3) straight or flexuous terminal awns (*Indopoa* geniculate; *Bewsia* dorsal). Fruit sometimes with free pericarp.

Genera 77; species ± 1000. Tropics and subtropics.

Anatomy. Kranz PS type, usually with short stout microhairs, but these finger-like in 11 genera. Parenchyma sheath separating from bundle in Triodiinae. Renvoize in Kew Bull. 38: 469—478 (1983).

Chromosomes. The basic number is generally 10. Other basic numbers particularly associated with certain genera are: 7 *Blepharidachne*; 8 *Blepharoneuron, Erioneuron, Munroa*; 9 *Acrachne, Eleusine, Eragrostiella, Crypsis, Sporobolus*; 12 *Sporobolus*, a few *Muhlenbergia*.

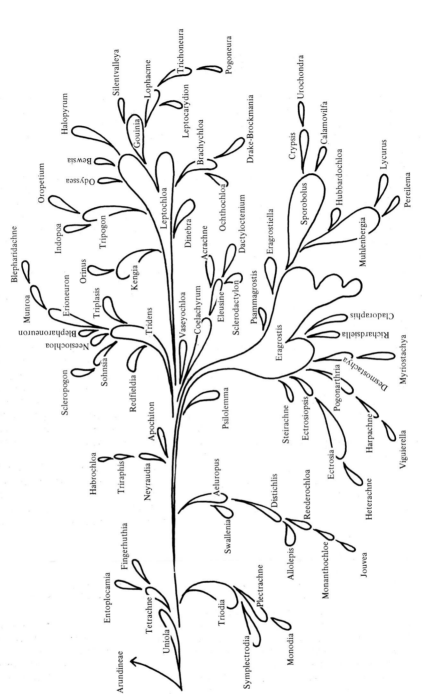

Fig. 15 Diagram of relationships in Eragrostideae.

2n	16	18	20	24	30	32	36	40	42	54	60	80
No of species	11	20	102	18	9	7	33	151	7	6	42	13

The hallmark of Eragostideae is its unspecialized, usually many-flowered, spikelet with (1—)3-nerved lemmas. To the discerning eye there is also a somewhat cartilaginous lemma texture, contrasting with the herbaceous or membranous lemmas prevalent in Poeae and Arundineae. Trends within the tribe (fig 15) include:
1. A transition from panicles to racemes, the latter occasionally deciduous.
2. A transition from many-flowered to 1-flowered spikelets. The reduction is characteristic of Sporobolinae; it occurs in a few genera so closely related to many-flowered neighbours that they cannot reasonably be separated from them; and it crops up occasionally as a local variant among a few species that are normally many-flowered. Some of the 1-flowered genera are difficult to extricate from Cynodonteae, but for the most part they are readily separated from that tribe by the paniculate inflorescence.
3. An extraordinary diversity of spikelet disarticulation. *Eragrostis*, for example, displays most of the possible variations.
4. An unusually large number of xerophytic and ruderal species. Evolution seems to have been particularly active in the direction of physiological adaptations to pioneer and arid habitats.
   Demarcation of the tribe centres upon the treatment of three small groups of genera with typical leaf anatomy but multi-nerved lemmas. The acceptance elsewhere in the tribe of a few anomalous multi-nerved species amongst otherwise orthodox genera weakens the case for excluding these genera altogether, and they are here admitted as subtribes. Similarities between Triodiinae and Uniolinae on the one hand, and the *Spartochloa-Tribolium-Styppeiochloa* group of Arundineae on the other, suggest that these are primitive genera near the point of divergence of the subfamilies. An alternative supposition, based upon the resemblance of *Neyraudia* to *Phragmites*, seems to be a matter of convergence rather than kinship.
   Identification of the tribe rests largely upon its possession of a 3-nerved lemma. It is complicated by the overlap in lemma nervation with Arundineae, and by the intrusion of aberrant 3-nerved species from Pooideae. The latter are sometimes quite difficult to recognize, and leaf sectioning may be required for an unambiguous determination; fortunately they are seldom sympatric with their eragrostoid counterparts.

1　Lemmas 5—13-nerved:
 2　Spikelets bisexual:
  3　Spikelets disarticulating between florets; racemes persistent:
   4　Leaf-blades stiff, pungent or if merely acuminate then distichous:
    5　Plants caespitose with long erect leaf-blades:
     6　Lemma lobes shorter than body of lemma　　**308 Triodia**
     6　Lemma lobes aristulate, longer than body　　**309 Plectrachne**
    5　Plants stoloniferous or rhizomatous, with short distichous leaves:
     7　Glumes shorter than spikelet　　**316 Aeluropus**
     7　Glumes almost as long as spikelet　　**317 Swallenia**
   4　Leaf-blades neither pungent nor distichous:
    8　Ligule membranous:
     9　Lemmas awnless, tuberculate　　*115 Castellia*
     9　Lemmas long awned:

10	Racemes short, stiff and deflexing at maturity	*112 Vulpia*
10	Racemes long and flexuous	**346 Gouinia**
8	Ligule a line of hairs:	
11	Spikelets 1-flowered	*270 Poagrostis*
11	Spikelets several-flowered:	
12	Cleistogamous spikelets concealed within leaf-sheaths	**338 Kengia**
12	Cleistogamous spikelets absent; lemmas awnless; spikelets pubescent (if glabrous see *353 Brachychloa schiemanniana*)	**369 Vaseyochloa**

3 Spikelets not disarticulating between florets:
  13 Spikelets disarticulating above glumes   *387 Lintonia*
  13 Spikelets falling entire (if whole raceme deciduous see *355 Drake-Brockmania*):
    14 Lower florets barren:
      15 Lemmas not spinous:
        16 Racemes many, crowded, overlapping   **312 Uniola**
        16 Racemes few, short, ± their own length apart   **313 Tetrachne**
      15 Lemmas spinous   **314 Entoplocamia**
    14 Lower florets bisexual:
      17 Callus of spikelet obtuse; glumes shortly awned (otherwise see *276 Schismus*)   **315 Fingerhuthia**
      17 Callus of spikelet pungent   **367 Viguierella**

2 Spikelets unisexual:
  18 Female spikelets resembling the ♂, with slender rhachilla:
    19 Glumes present:
      20 Leaf-blades stiff, distichous:
        21 Ligule a ciliate rim   **318 Distichlis**
        21 Ligule membranous   **319 Reederochloa**
      20 Leaf-blades flat, not distichous   **320 Allolepis**
    19 Glumes absent   **321 Monanthochloe**
  18 Female spikelets thorn-like, with thickened rhachilla   **322 Jouvea**

1 Lemmas 1—3-nerved (sometimes with subsidiary nerves in keel of *Eleusine* or lobes of *Astrebla*):
22 Spikelets with 1 fertile floret, sunk in the rhachis of a solitary raceme, edge-ways on, covered by upper glume; lower glume small or suppressed   **342 Oropetium**
22 Not as above:
  23 Spikelets 2- or more-flowered (rarely 1-flowered but then the inflorescence of racemes — *Dinebra, Leptochloa*):
    24 Tip of lemma emarginate to 2—3-lobed, or flanks hairy between lateral nerve and margin, or florets conspicuously bearded from callus:
      25 Leaf-blades rigid, pungent:
        26 Inflorescence open or elongated (if a solitary raceme see *340 Tripogon*):
          27 Spikelets with several fertile florets:
            28 Lemma lobes shorter than body of lemma, this scarious or horny (if membranous see *263 Styppeiochloa*)   **308 Triodia**
            28 Lemma lobes aristulate, longer than body of lemma   **309 Plectrachne**
          27 Spikelets with 1 fertile floret and a deciduous bunch of awns   **310 Symplectrodia**
        26 Inflorescence a short dense ovoid head   **343 Odyssea**

25 Leaf-blades not conspicuously pungent:
29 Grain strongly flattened and concavo-convex, with a free pericarp, mostly rugulose; spikelet disarticulating between florets
368 Coelachyrum
29 Grain seldom strongly flattened and then not with a free pericarp or not disarticulating between florets, mostly smooth:
30 Cleistogamous spikelets concealed within leaf-sheaths of culm:
31 Awn pubescent; palea keels with a dense crest of hairs near tip
329 Triplasis
31 Awn glabrous; palea keels puberulous   **338 Kengia**
30 Cleistogamous spikelets absent; awn, if present, glabrous:
32 Inflorescence a panicle or head, sometimes much reduced:
33 Plants tall, with large plumose panicles
34 Lemma with long ciliate margins   **323 Neyraudia**
34 Lemma glabrous, or villous from the back   *Arundineae* (p 164)
33 Plants shorter:
35 Spikelets with fertile florets below:
36 Lemma 3-awned:
37 Spikelets bisexual   **324 Triraphis**
37 Spikelets unisexual:
38 Awns scarcely exceeding body of lemma   **330 Sohnsia**
38 Awns much longer than body of lemma **331 Scleropogon**
36 Lemma with or without a single awn, rarely the lateral nerves excurrent to a mucro:
39 Palea 2-awned   **326 Apochiton**
39 Palea awnless:
40 Upper florets sterile, long awned   **363 Ectrosia**
40 Upper florets scarcely different from lower:
41 Leaf margins not cartilaginous:
42 Lemmas long awned, or palea keels winged, or floret callus linear, or lowest culm internode persistent:
43 Glumes as long as spikelet; floret callus square
325 Habrochloa
43 Glumes shorter than spikelet, rarely longer but then floret callus linear   *Arundineae* (p 164)
42 Lemmas awnless or with awns shorter than themselves, but not as above:
44 Ligule membranous; lodicules hyaline; embryo up to $\frac{1}{3}$ length of caryopsis; lemmas ± membranous
Go to 43 in Key to Tribes
44 Ligule a line of hairs; rarely membranous (*Tridens, Trichoneura*) but then lodicules fleshy, embryo more than $\frac{1}{3}$ length of caryopsis and lemmas ± cartilaginous:
45 Florets not bearded from callus:
46 Tip of lemma entire; lemma hairs often tubercle-based or spread all over lemma (if glume keels bluntly pectinate see *258 Prionanthium*) **356 Eragrostis**
46 Tip of lemma emarginate to bidentate; lemma hairs confined to pubescent nerves and keel, rarely quite glabrous (if ligule membranous and glumes longer than florets see *350 Trichoneura*) **327 Tridens**

     64   Lateral nerves of lemma conspicuously ciliate or villous:
       65   Ligule membranous; palea keels glabrous **350 Trichoneura**
       65   Ligule a line of hairs; palea keels with a crest of hairs
                                          351 Pogoneura
     64   Lateral nerves of lemma appressed pubescent   **352 Dinebra**
   51 Racemes or secondary branchlets deciduous:
     66   Upper glume 1—5-nerved:
       67   Glumes as long as spikelet, enclosing the florets **352 Dinebra**
       67   Glumes not or scarcely exceeding adjacent lemmas:
          68   Racemes disposed along an axis   **353 Brachychloa**
          68   Racemes digitate   **354 Ochthochloa**
     66   Upper glume conspicuously many-nerved, much longer than
          lower   **355 Drake-Brockmania**
24 Tip of lemma entire, the nerves and flanks glabrous (rarely ciliolate on
    margin itself); florets not conspicuously bearded from callus:
  69 Central axis of inflorescence stout, woody, culm-like, ending in a rigid
      naked point   **357 Cladoraphis**
  69 Central axis of inflorescence slender, rarely stout and then branched to
      the tip:
   70 Inflorescence a panicle:
    71 Upper sterile florets few, smaller but otherwise similar to lower:
     72 Ligule membranous; lodicules hyaline; embryo up to $\frac{1}{3}$ length of
        caryopsis; lemmas ± membranous   *Go to 43 in Key to Tribes*
     72 Ligule a line of hairs; rarely membranous (see *356 Eragrostis* &
        381 Muhlenbergia) but then lodicules fleshy, embryo more than $\frac{1}{3}$
        length of caryopsis and lemmas ± cartilaginous:
      73 Leaf-blades not deciduous; hilum punctiform   **356 Eragrostis**
      73 Leaf-blades falling from sheaths in winter; hilum linear; lowest
        culm internode persistent   *292 Molinia*
    71 Upper sterile florets well developed, longer or noticeably different
      from lower:
     74 Spikelets breaking up between florets; sterile florets resembling the
        lower but longer:
      75 Palea keels wingless   **361 Ectrosiopsis**
      75 Palea keels winged   **362 Steirachne**
     74 Spikelets falling intact above glumes:
      76 Lemma keel wingless; sterile florets usually awned **363 Ectrosia**
      76 Lemma keel winged; sterile florets awnless **364 Heterachne**
  70 Inflorescence of 1 or more racemes:
    77 Raceme single:
     78 Rhachis elongated, bearing numerous spikelets:
      79 Spikelets falling entire:
        80 Glumes longer than lemmas   *154 Pholiurus*
        80 Glumes shorter than lemmas:
          81 Lemmas acute to acuminate   **366 Harpachne**
          81 Lemmas long awned   **367 Viguierella**
      79 Spikelets breaking up at maturity (if awned see *340 Tripogon*):
        82 Spikelets several-flowered   **359 Eragrostiella**
        82 Spikelets strictly 2-flowered   *258 Prionanthium*
     78 Rhachis very short, bearing 1—3 spikelets, the raceme subtended by
        a spatheole   **360 Psammagrostis**

77 Racemes 2 or more:
  83 Inflorescence digitate or ± whorled; fruit with free pericarp (otherwise see *337 Leptochloa*):
    84 Racemes terminating in a fertile spikelet; grain trigonous (if concavo-convex see *368 Coelachyrum*) **370 Eleusine**
    84 Racemes terminating in an abortive spikelet or bare point:
      85 Paleas, or some of them, remaining on rhachilla **371 Acrachne**
      85 Paleas falling with lemmas:
        86 Rhachis terminating in abortive spikelets; leaf-blades terete (if flat see *370 Eleusine*) **372 Sclerodactylon**
        86 Rhachis terminating in a bare point **373 Dactyloctenium**
  83 Inflorescence of racemes disposed singly along a central axis:
    87 Plants dioecious **320 Allolepis**
    87 Plants bisexual:
      88 Spikelets breaking up at maturity:
        89 Leaf-blades pungent **374 Psilolemma**
        89 Leaf-blades not pungent:
          90 Racemes deciduous (if glumes longer than florets see *352 Dinebra*) **365 Pogonarthria**
          90 Racemes persistent **356 Eragrostis**
      88 Spikelets falling entire:
        91 Racemes persistent; glumes acute:
          92 Lowest florets fertile **375 Desmostachya**
          92 Lowest florets sterile **312 Uniola**
        91 Racemes deciduous; glumes awned **376 Myriostachya**
23 Spikelets strictly 1-flowered, or very rarely with rhachilla extension; inflorescence a panicle:
  93 Ligule a line of hairs; pericarp free (except *Hubbardochloa*); lemma usually 1-nerved:
    94 Lemma awnless or with a short awn-point:
      95 Floret not conspicuously bearded from callus:
        96 Spikelets fusiform (or dorsally compressed); glumes and lemmas rounded on back:
          97 Fruit a utricle with free pericarp; leaf-blades linear **377 Sporobolus**
          97 Fruit a caryopsis; delicate plants with broadly linear to ovate leaf-blades *Isachneae* (p 308)
        96 Spikelets strongly laterally compressed; glumes and lemmas keeled; panicle dense, cylindrical to capitate (otherwise see *377 Sporobolus*):
          98 Grain without appendage; annual **378 Crypsis**
          98 Grain beaked; perennial **379 Urochondra**
      95 Floret bearded from callus with hairs ¼ its length or more **380 Calamovilfa**

    94 Lemma with a long awn:
      99 Leaf-blades pungent **311 Monodia**
      99 Leaf-blades not pungent:
        100 Floret callus puberulous **382 Hubbardochloa**
        100 Floret callus long bearded *286 Leptagrostis*
  93 Ligule membranous; fruit a caryopsis; lemma 3-nerved:
    101 Spikelets all alike:
      102 Palea keels densely villous **334 Blepharoneuron**

102   Palea keels not villous   **381 Muhlenbergia**
101   Spikelets of two kinds, fertile and sterile:
103   Spikelets paired, falling together, the lower of each pair smaller and sterile   **383 Lycurus**
103   Spikelets in clusters, the lower spikelets reduced to an involucre of bristles   **384 Pereilema**

a. TRIODIINAE Benth. in J. Linn. Soc. Bot. 19: 30 (1881).

Leaf-blades rigid, conduplicate or convolute and terete when dry, pungent; sheaths often resinous. Inflorescence a panicle or of racemes on a central axis (single raceme in *Triodia spicata*). Spikelets with 1—several fertile florets, ± ovate, disarticulating below each floret; lemmas rounded on back, scarious to horny, 3—9-nerved. Caryopsis ± ellipsoid.

An isolated Australian subtribe without obvious relatives, but some superficial resemblance to *Spartochloa* and *Styppeiochloa* in Arundineae. The leaves are strongly xeromorphic being massively reinforced with sclerenchyma and having their stomata confined to deep grooves. Their chlorenchyma is greatly reduced and occurs as narrow tracts along the stomatal grooves. These tracts are often separated from the bundles, whose parenchyma sheath then becomes partially detached (wholly so in extreme cases such as *T. fitzgeraldii*) to enfold the chlorenchyma (fig 18). Despite these anatomical peculiarities the microhairs unequivocally point to an eragrostoid affinity.

308. Triodia R. Br., Prodr. Fl. Nov. Holl.: 182 (1810); Burbidge in Austr. J. Bot. 1: 121—184 (1953); Jacobs in Proc. Linn. Soc. N.S.W. 96: 175—185 (1971) — T. pungens R. Br. *Triodon* Baumg., Enum. Stirp. 3: 238 (1816) nom superfl pro Triodia.

Tussocky perennial; ligule a line of hairs. Spikelets several-flowered; glumes 1—13-nerved (slightly longer than lemma in *T. irritans*); lemmas sometimes 3-nerved, usually 9-nerved apportioned 3 to each lobe, rarely more, hairy all over or only on margins, rarely glabrous, tridentate to deeply 3-lobed (but *T. irritans*, *T. lanata*, *T. scariosa* often ± emarginate; *T. spicata* acute), the lobes varying from subulate to membranously ovate; palea keels often winged.

Species ± 35. Australia. Arid regions on sandy or stony soils. The genus, popularly known as Spinifex, is an important constituent of arid vegetation, but too harsh to be of much value for grazing.

T. spicata with single raceme and acute lemma is mildly aberrant, but best retained in the genus.

309. Plectrachne Henr. in Viertel. Nat. Ges. Zürich 74: 132 (1929) — P. schinzii Henr.

Like *Triodia*, but glumes longer than adjacent lemmas (scarcely so in *P. Bynoei*) and sometimes as long as spikelet, occasionally awned; lemmas 3-lobed, the lobes aristulate (or rarely the lateral muticous) and longer than body of lemma.

Species 16. Australia. Arid places.

310. Symplectrodia Lazarides in Nuytsia 5: 273 (1985) — S. lanosa Lazarides.

Tussocky perennial; ligule a line of hairs. Spikelets with 1 fertile floret, and a 5-awned bunch of sterile lemmas this readily deciduous; glumes 7-nerved, mostly a little shorter than floret; lemma 3-nerved, pubescent, entire; palea with lower $\frac{1}{3}$ adnate to the stout rhachilla internode.

Species 2. Australia. Sandy soils.

311. Monodia Jacobs in Kew Bull. 40: 659 (1985) — M. stipoides Jacobs.

Tussocky perennial; ligule a line of hairs. Spikelets 1-flowered with brief rhachilla extension; glumes 3—11-nerved, longer than floret; lemma 3-nerved, linear with pungent callus, convolute and covering palea, indistinctly bidentate, with long wavy awn.

Species 1. Western Australia. Stony soils.
The genus imitates *Stipa*.

b. UNIOLINAE Clayton in Kew Bull. 37: 417 (1982).

Leaf-blades flat. Inflorescence a spiciform panicle or of racemes on a central axis. Spikelets with several to many fertile florets (1 in *Fingerhuthia*), ovate, falling entire; glumes shorter than florets; lemmas strongly keeled, chartaceous to coriaceous, (3—)5—11-nerved. Fruit ellipsoid with free pericarp.

A small group, perhaps linking the tribe to *Tribolium* in Arundineae.

312. Uniola L., Sp. Pl.: 71 (1753); Yates in Southw. Nat. 11: 145—189, 372—381 (1966) — U. paniculata L. *Trisiola* Raf., Fl. Ludov.: 144 (1817) & *Nevroctola* Raf., Neogenyton: 4 (1825) nom superfl pro Uniola. *Triunila* Raf. l.c., nom prov pro Uniola. *Leptochloopsis* Yates in Southw. Nat. 11: 382 (1966) — L. virgata (Poir.) Yates.

Perennial; leaves harsh; ligule a line of hairs (obscure in *U. condensata*). Inflorescence of many crowded overlapping racemes (with secondary branchlets in *U. condensata*; not clearly unilateral in *U. paniculata*) on a long central axis. Spikelets falling entire (unusually large in *U. paniculata, U. pittieri*), the lower 1—6 florets barren; glumes acute; lemmas 3—9-nerved, coriaceous, glabrous, subobtuse to acute; palea keels winged.

Species 4. Southern USA to Ecuador. Dunes, salt flats and arid places. *U. paniculata* is a useful sand binder.

Despite its many-nerved lemmas the genus, particularly *U. virgata*, seems closely related to *Desmostachya*. It is somewhat variable but scarcely worth subdividing.

313. Tetrachne Nees, Fl. Afr. Austr.: 375 (1841) — T. dregei Nees.

Perennial. Inflorescence of 5—15 short racemes distant by ± their own length on a central axis. Otherwise like *Uniola*.

Species 1. South Africa and Pakistan. Tropical grassland.
Barely distinct from *Uniola*, but with different distribution and habitat.

314. Entoplocamia Stapf in Fl. Cap. 7: 318 (1898) — E. aristulata (Hack. & Rendle) Stapf.

Annual; ligule a line of hairs. Inflorescence of short often glomerate racemes on a central axis, rarely reduced to a simple raceme. Spikelets falling entire, the lower 2 florets barren; glumes 3—5-nerved, acuminate; lemmas 9—11-nerved, chartaceous above, coriaceous below, ciliate on margins, with a short spinous awn; lodicules 0.

Species 1. South western Africa. Stony slopes and dry river beds.

315. Fingerhuthia Nees in Lehm., Delect. Sem. Horto Hamburg. 1834: 7 (1834) — F. africana Nees. *Lasiotrichos* Lehm. l.c., in syn sub Fingerhuthia.

Perennial; ligule a line of hairs. Inflorescence a spiciform panicle. Spikelets falling entire, of 1 fertile floret with 1—3 smaller ♂ or barren florets above it; glumes shortly awned; lemmas 3-nerved below becoming 5—7-nerved in upper half, firmly membranous, glabrous or pubescent, entire, shortly awned.

Species 1—2. Afghanistan, Arabia, southern Africa. Open places in savanna.
An isolated genus, tentatively associated with *Uniola*. The oddly disjunct distribution resembles that of *Tetrachne*.

c. MONANTHOCHLOINAE Potztal in Willdenowia 5: 472 (1969). *Distichlinae* Parodi, Gram. Bonar. ed. 4: 28 (1946) nom nud. *Aeluropodinae* Jac.-Fél., Gram. Afr. Trop. 1: 94 (1962) sine descr lat.

Leaf-blades short, stiff, flat or rolled, distichous, often pungent (except *Allolepis*). Inflorescence a panicle or of racemes, often reduced to a few spikelets. Spikelets with several to many fertile florets, ± ovate (except *Allolepis, Jouvea, Monanthochloe*), disarticulating below each floret (except *Jouvea*); glumes shorter than lemmas (except *Swallenia*); lemmas rounded on back, chartaceous to coriaceous, 5—13-nerved. Caryopsis ± ellipsoid.

Creeping halophytes with characteristically distichous leaves. Perhaps related to *Psilolemma*, though the similarities are not sufficiently positive to justify separating the latter from Eleusininae. *Odyssea*, another distichously leaved halophyte, is of different affinity within Eleusininae, and apparently unrelated to Monanthochloinae.

316. Aeluropus Trin., Fund. Agrost.: 143 (1822) — A. laevis Trin. (= A. lagopoides). *Chamaedactylis* T. Nees, Gen. Pl. Fl. Germ. 1: 66 (1840) — C. maritima (Schrad.) T. Nees (= A. littoralis). *Aelbroeckia* De Moor, Traité Gram.: 134 (1854) nom superfl pro Chamaedactylis.

Stoloniferous perennial; ligule a very short membrane fringed with hairs. Inflorescence capitate to spiciform, of short densely spiculate racemes appressed to a central axis (sometimes 1 ovoid raceme in *A. lagopoides*). Spikelets: lower glume 1—3-nerved, upper 5—7-nerved; lemmas chartaceous, strongly 9—11-nerved, glabrous or hairy on margins, entire or emarginate, apiculate.

Species 3—4. Mediterranean to northern China; southwards to Ethiopia and Sri Lanka. Saline soils of seashores and deserts.

317. Swallenia Sod. & Deck. in Madroño 17: 88 (1963) nom nov pro seq. *Ectosperma* Swallen in J. Wash. Acad. Sci. 40: 19 (1950) non Vaucher (1803) — E. alexandrae Swallen.

Rhizomatous perennial; ligule a line of hairs. Inflorescence a sparse contracted panicle. Spikelets: glumes almost as long as spikelet, membranous, 7—11-nerved; lemmas chartaceous, 5—7-nerved, villous on margins, mucronate; palea margins villous.

Species 1. California. Sand dunes.

318. Distichlis Raf. in J. Phys. Chim. 89: 104 (1819); Beetle in Rev. Arg. Agron. 22: 86—94 (1955) — D. maritima Raf. (= D. spicata). *Trisiola* Raf., Neogenyton: 4 (1825) non Raf. (1817) — Uniola spicata L.

Rhizomatous perennial; dioecious; ligule a very short membrane fringed with hairs. Inflorescence spicate to ovoid, exserted, of short racemes appressed to a central axis, but occasionally branching into a contracted panicle, or often reduced to a bunch of 2—several spikelets (1 hidden among the leaves in *D. australis*). Female spikelets tardily disarticulating; glumes 3—7-nerved; lemma coriaceous, faintly 7—11-nerved, glabrous, acute; palea margins not enfolding caryopsis, the keels narrowly winged. Male spikelets similar, but of thinner texture.

Species ± 5. Canada to Argentina; Australia. Saline soils of seashores and deserts.

319. Reederochloa Sod. & Deck. in Brittonia 16: 334 (1964) — R. eludens Sod. & Deck.

Stoloniferous perennial; dioecious; ligule membranous. Inflorescence a cluster of 2—4 spikelets, the ♀ sessile among upper leaf-sheaths, the ♂ long exserted. Female spikelets tardily disarticulating; glumes 2—8-nerved; lemma coriaceous, faintly 9—14-nerved, pilose below, acute; palea margins enfolding caryopsis. Male spikelets similar, but smaller thinner and glabrous.

Species 1. Mexico. Alkali flats.

The genus is closely related to *Distichlis* and *Monanthochloe,* all three having microhairs whose lower cell is sunk in the epidermis.

320. Allolepis Sod. & Deck. in Madroño 18: 33 (1965) — A. texana (Vasey) Sod. & Deck.

Perennial with long robust stolons; dioecious; leaf-blades flat, neither distichous nor pungent; ligule membranous with ciliate fringe. Inflorescence of short racemes appressed to an elongated axis. Female spikelets subterete; glumes 3—7-nerved; lemma 3-(occasionally 5-)nerved, glabrous, acute; palea gibbous, coriaceous, the margins overlapping and enfolding caryopsis, the keels narrowly winged. Male spikelets similar but lemmas shorter.

Species 1. Southern USA and Mexico. Open sandy places.

Although lacking the characteristic distichous leaves of its allies, the genus is linked to *Monanthochloe* by its peculiar palea.

321. Monanthochloe Engelm. in Trans. Acad. Sci. St. Louis 1: 436 (1859); Villamil in Kurtziana 5: 369—391 (1969) — M. littoralis Engelm. *Halochloa* Griseb., Symb.: 285 (1879) non Kuetzing (1843) — H. acerosa Griseb. *Solenophyllum* Baillon, Hist. Pl. 12: 235 (1894) in syn sub Monanthochloe.

Stoloniferous perennial; dioecious; leaf-blades subulate; ligule a ciliate rim. Inflorescence a single spikelet embraced and almost concealed by upper leaf-sheaths. Female spikelet subterete, tardily disarticulating; glumes 0; lemma coriaceous, 9-nerved, glabrous, acute; palea coriaceous, the margins overlapping and enfolding caryopsis, the keels with prominent wings which embrace floret above. Male spikelet similar, but smaller and thinner in texture.

Species 2. Southern USA, Mexico, Cuba; Argentina. Seashores in the north; inland salt pans in Argentina.

Linked to *Distichlis* by *D. australis.*

322. Jouvea Fourn. in Bull. Soc. Bot. Belg. 15: 475 (1876); Weatherwax in Bull. Torr. Bot. Cl. 66: 315—325 (1939) — J. straminea Fourn. *Rhachidospermum* Vasey in Bot. Gaz. 15: 110 (1890) — R. mexicanum Vasey (= J. pilosa).

Stoloniferous perennial; dioecious; ligule a line of hairs. Female inflorescence a single spikelet subtended by a prophyll and embraced by an upper leaf-sheath, several of these aggregated into a spiny cluster. Spikelet terete, thorn-like, falling entire, with 2—8 florets embedded in spongy rhachilla; glumes 0; lemma coriaceous, 5—7-nerved, tubular, fused to rhachilla for most of its length, the stigmas protruding from an apical pore; palea small, enclosed by lemma; lodicules 0; caryopsis linear. Male inflorescence an exserted raceme, these borne in axillary fascicles; spikelet many-flowered, producing new florets at tip after lower ones have shed their pollen; lower glume minute or absent, the upper 1-nerved; lemma thinly coriaceous, 3-nerved, acute.

Species 2. Central America. Coastal dunes and mud flats.

The peculiar structure of the ♀ spikelet seems to be a derivation from *Monanthochloe*.

d. ELEUSININAE Dumort., Anal. Fam.: 63 (1829). *Eragrostidinae* Presl, Rel. Haenk. 1: 273 (1830). *Diplachninae* Rouy, Fl. France 14: 159 (1913). *Tripogoninae* Stapf in Fl. Trop. Afr. 9: 22 (1917). *Triraphidinae* Stapf l.c. *Munroinae* Parodi, Gram. Bonar. ed. 4: 28 (1946) nom nud. *Scleropogoninae* Pilger, Nat. Pfl.-Fam. ed. 2, 14d: 167 (1956). *Viguierellinae* A. Camus in Bull. Soc. Bot. Fr. 103: 272 (1956). *Cleistogeninae* Janchen, Cat. Fl. Austr. 1: 786 (1960) nom nud. *Tridentinae* Keng & Keng. f. in Acta Bot. Sin. 9: 67 (1960).

Leaf-blades flat or rolled (stiff and pungent in *Odyssea, Psilolemma*). Inflorescence sometimes a panicle, more often of racemes. Spikelets with 2— many fertile florets (1 in *Blepharidachne, Blepharoneuron, Viguierella,* and occasionally in *Dinebra, Ectrosia, Heterachne, Leptochloa, Lophacme*), orbicular to linear, disarticulating below each floret or otherwise; lemmas keeled or rounded, membranous to cartilaginous, rarely coriaceous, 3-nerved (*Richardsiella* 1; *Vaseyochloa* and species from a few other genera 5—9); palea occasionally persistent. Fruit variable.

The largest and most important subtribe. A study of character correlations in the subtribe (Phillips in Kew Bull. 37: 133—162, 1982) shows that a number of generic groups can be recognized, though these are too indefinite to warrant formal recognition; see the clusters around *Triraphis, Tridens, Leptochloa, Eleusine* & *Eragrostis* in fig 15. In particular this study confirms the apparently tenuous distinction between *Eragrostis* and *Tridens* lemma types, and supports the acceptance of an unusually large number of small genera.

323. Neyraudia Hook.f., Fl. Brit. India 7: 305 (1896); Conert in Bot. Jahrb. 78: 233—245 (1959); Tateoka in Bull. Torr. Bot. Cl. 88: 148 (1961) — N. madagascariensis (Kunth) Hook.f. (= N. arundinacea).

Tall reed-like perennial; ligule a line of hairs. Inflorescence a large plumose panicle. Spikelets with the florets all bisexual or the lowest sterile; glumes sometimes 3-nerved; lemmas keeled, long ciliate on lateral nerves, setaceously bidentate, with a recurved awn. Caryopsis linear, subterete.

Species 2. Old World tropics. Woodland clearings and streamsides.

Neyraudia has slender arundinoid microhairs but its other features, including the embryo, are typically eragrostoid. Its resemblance to *Phragmites* seems due to convergent evolution of the reed habit rather than to taxonomic affinity.

324. Triraphis R. Br., Prodr. Fl. Nov. Holl.: 185 (1810) — T. mollis R. Br.

Annual or perennial; ligule membranous or a line of hairs. Inflorescence an open or contracted, rarely spiciform, panicle. Spikelets: lemmas keeled, villous on lateral nerves, 3-lobed and 3-awned, the central lobe bidentate. Caryopsis linear, trigonous.

Species 7. Africa and Arabia; 1 species in Australia. Savanna, often in stony or sandy places.
An ally of *Neyraudia* with similar slender microhairs.

325. Habrochloa C.E. Hubbard in Hook. Ic. Pl. 37: t 3645 (1967) — H. bullockii C.E. Hubbard.

Annual; ligule a line of hairs. Inflorescence a delicate panicle. Spikelets: glumes as long as spikelet or nearly so; lemmas keeled, ciliate on margins, shortly and bluntly bilobed, with a long flexuous awn. Caryopsis linear.

Species 1. Central Africa. Shady banks.

326. Apochiton C.E. Hubbard in Hook. Ic. Pl. 34: t 3319 (1936) — A. burttii C.E. Hubbard.

Annual; ligule membranous. Inflorescence a panicle. Spikelets: glumes 3-nerved; lemmas keeled, silky pubescent all over lower half, entire, awned; palea 2-awned. Grain ellipsoid, trigonous, concave one face, the pericarp free.

Species 1. Tanzania. Savanna, on seasonally wet soils.
An isolated genus with an unusual 2-awned palea. The paniculate inflorescence suggests a relationship with *Triraphis*, but the microhairs are of the usual eragrostoid type.

327. Tridens Roem. & Schult., Syst. Veg. 2: 34 (1817); Tateoka in Amer. J. Bot. 48: 565—573 (1961) nom nov pro seq. *Tricuspis* P. Beauv., Ess. Agrost.: 77, f 15/10 (1812) non Pers. (1806) — T. caroliniana P. Beauv. (= T. flavus). *Windsoria* Nutt., Gen. N. Amer. Pl. 1: 70 (1818) — W. poiformis Nutt. (= T. flavus). *Gossweilerochloa* Renv. in Kew Bull. 33: 525 (1979) — G. delicatula Renv. *Antonella* Caro in Dominguezia 2: 18 (1981) — A. nicorae (Anton) Caro.

Tufted perennial; ligule a line of hairs (membranous in *T. eragrostoides*). Inflorescence an open, contracted or spiciform panicle, but sometimes the primary branches raceme-like (especially *T. ambiguus*, *T. elongatus*). Spikelets slightly laterally compressed, plump (glumes equalling spikelet in *T. strictus*, the upper 3-nerved in *T. elongatus*); lemmas rounded, nerves and midrib pubescent below (glabrous in *T. albescens*) glabrous above, emarginate to bidentate, rarely subentire, usually mucronate or briefly awned and often the lateral nerves also excurrent to a mucro; palea smooth or ciliolate on keels (ciliate in *T. elongatus,* glandular in *T. nicorae*), glabrous or rarely puberulous between them. Caryopsis dull brown, dorsally compressed, concavo-convex, the embryo not projecting below.

Species 18. Eastern USA to Argentina; 1 species in Angola. Meadows, plains and open woodlands.

Tridens lies at the junction of several divergent lines. It may be confused with the few species of *Coelachyrum* that have an open inflorescence, but their pericarp is free. There is also a resemblance to some Old World species of *Eragrostis* with hairy lemmas, but these do not have an emarginate tip, nor are the hairs in dense lines on nerves and keel.

328. Redfieldia Vasey in Bull. Torr. Bot. Cl. 14: 133 (1887); Reeder in Madroño 23: 434—438 (1976) — R. flexuosa (A. Gray) Vasey.

Rhizomatous perennial; ligule a line of hairs; leaf-blades involute with filiform tip. Inflorescence a delicate panicle. Spikelets cuneate, the callus of each floret bearded; glumes acuminate; lemmas keeled, puberulous on margin at base, acute to acuminate, often mucronate. Caryopsis ellipsoid, flattened.

Species 1. Central USA. Inland sand hills.

The genus is treated here as an offshoot of *Tridens*, but it has an almost equal claim to relationship with *Eragrostis.*

329. Triplasis P. Beauv., Ess. Agrost.: 81 (1812) — T. americana P. Beauv. *Uralepis* Nutt., Gen. N. Amer. Pl. 1: 62 (1818) as "Uralepsis" — U. purpurea (Walt.) Nutt. *Diplocea* Raf. in Amer. J. Sci. 1: 252 (1818) — D. barbata Raf. (= T. purpurea). *Merisachne* Steud., Syn. Pl. Glum. 1: 117 (1854) — M. drummondii Steud. (= T. purpurea).

Annual or perennial; ligule a line of hairs; some of the lower leaf-sheaths slightly inflated and concealing cleistogenes, these dispersed by abscission of the culm at the nodes. Inflorescence a sparse panicle, but sometimes the smaller panicles with simple primary branches. Spikelets linear with long rhachilla internodes; lemmas keeled, margins and midnerve tomentose along their length, bilobed, with a short pubescent awn; palea pubescent on keels with a longer densely ciliate crest near tip, glabrous between them. Caryopsis dull brown, gibbously ellipsoid, the embryo projecting below its base.

Species 2. Eastern USA to Costa Rica. Dry sandy soils.

330. Sohnsia Airy-Shaw in Kew Bull. 18: 272 (1965) nom nov pro seq. *Calamochloa* Fourn. in Bull. Soc. Bot. Fr. 24: 178 (1877) non Calamochloe Reichenb. (1828); Sohns in J. Wash. Acad. Sci. 46: 109—112 (1956) — C. filifolia Fourn. *Eufournia* Reeder in Brittonia 19: 224 (1967) nom nov pro Calamochloa.

Tufted perennial; dioecious; ligule a line of hairs. Inflorescence a panicle in both sexes, the spikelets contracted about primary branches. Female spikelets disarticulating above glumes but only tardily between florets; lemmas subterete, coriaceous, pilose on nerves and midrib, the nerves extended into 3 subulate awns, the central awn arising between 2 hyaline lobes; palea keels narrowly winged. Male spikelets: lemmas slightly laterally compressed, chartaceous, glabrous, with 3 short awn-points.

Species 1. Mexico. Dry hillsides.

331. Scleropogon Phil. in Ann. Univ. Chile 36: 205 (1870); Pilger in Not. Bot. Gart. Berlin 15: 15—22 (1940) — S. brevifolius Phil. *Lesourdia* Fourn. in Bull. Soc. Bot. France 27: 102 (1880) — L. multiflora Fourn. (= S. brevifolius).

Stoloniferous perennial; usually dioecious, but sometimes monoecious or sexes mixed in same panicle; ligule a line of hairs. Female inflorescence a short raceme of 2—8 spikelets condensed into a head; all except uppermost spikelet subtended by a scarious glume-like appendage from tip of rhachis internode; lowermost spikelet usually on a minute branchlet bearing a rudimentary lateral spikelet whose subtending appendage simulates a fourth glume. Female spikelets disarticulating above glumes but not between florets; glumes 2, equalling or exceeding adjacent lemmas, 3-nerved; lemmas terete, tightly rolled around lower half of next lemma above, coriaceous, glabrous, the nerves extended into 3 long slender spreading awns; palea with 2 short awnlets; lodicules 0; upper florets reduced to a bunch of long awns. Male inflorescence a short raceme or much reduced panicle of 2—8 spikelets, without appendages; spikelets oblong, laterally compressed, exserted from glumes; lemmas divergent, glabrous, entire.

Species 1. Southern USA, Mexico, Argentina and Chile. Dry grassy plains.
A complex little genus, related to *Tridens* through *Sohnsia*. Interpretation of the extra spikelet scales is a problem. They fit into a pattern of subtending leaf and prophyll, but this homology is doubtful. It seems better to regard them as new emanations from the internode tip.

332. Neesiochloa Pilger in Feddes Rep. 48: 119 (1940) — N. barbata (Nees) Pilger.

Annual; ligule membranous with ciliate fringe; leaf margins cartilaginous. Inflorescence a very sparse open panicle, most of the long capillary pedicels borne directly upon the central axis, but the lowermost usually bifurcating. Spikelets orbicular; glumes slightly exceeding adjacent lemmas; lemmas oblate, much wider than long, rounded on back, scarious, ciliate on middle third of lateral nerves, broadly truncate and emarginate, shortly awned; palea keels with a central ciliate crest. Caryopsis like *Erioneuron*.

Species 1. NE Brazil. Open disturbed places.
The open inflorescence with long pedicels has the appearance of a panicle, though the extreme paucity of its branching often reduces it, strictly speaking, to a raceme.

333. Erioneuron Nash in Small, Fl. Southeast. U.S.: 143 (1903); Tateoka in Amer. J. Bot. 48: 565—573 (1961) — E. pilosum (Buckley) Nash. *Dasyochloa* Rydberg, Fl. Colorado: 18 (1906); Sanchez in Lilloa 36: 131—138 (1983) — D. pulchella (Kunth) Rydberg.

Tufted perennial (*E. pulchellum* with long stolons bearing fascicles of leaves); ligule a line of hairs; leaf margins cartilaginous. Inflorescence ± condensed into an ovoid or narrowly oblong head, sometimes reduced to only a few spikelets (with very short peduncle and invested by leafy fascicle in *E. pulchellum*). Spikelets plump (glumes almost equalling spikelet in *E. avenaceum, E. pulchellum*); lemmas rounded, margins pilose along their length or with a glabrous gap in the middle, deeply bilobed (emarginate in *E. pilosum*), shortly awned; palea ciliolate to ciliate on keels, villous between them in lower half. Caryopsis translucent, laterally compressed, ovoid, the embryo projecting below its base.

Species 5. Southern USA and Mexico; Argentina. Rocky slopes.
A segregate from *Tridens*, discussed by Tateoka (l.c.).

334. Blepharoneuron Nash in Bull. Torr. Bot. Cl. 25: 88 (1898) — B. tricholepis (Torr.) Nash.

Perennial; ligule membranous; leaf-blades strongly ribbed, involute. Inflorescence a panicle. Spikelets 1-flowered without rhachilla extension; glumes subequal, almost as long as floret; lemma rounded, margins pilose along their length, entire to emarginate, mucronate; palea densely villous on and between keels. Caryopsis ellipsoid, the embryo projecting below its base.

Species 1. Southern USA and Mexico. Dry open places in upland coniferous woodland.
Despite its 1-flowered spikelets *Blepharoneuron* has little in common with *Sporobolus*. It seems in fact to be a relative of *Erioneuron*, sharing the unusual chromosome number of $2n = 16$ with that genus.

335. Munroa Torrey in Rep. Explor. Railroad Pacif. Ocean 4: 158 (1856) as "Monroa", a misspelling of the agrostologist's name; Anton & Hunziker in Bol. Acad. Nac. Cien. Cordoba 52: 229—252 (1978) — M. squarrosa (Nutt.) Torrey. *Hemimunroa* Parodi in Not. Mus. La Plata 2: 4 (1937) — H. andina (Phil.) Parodi.

Annual, with long stolons bearing fascicles of leaves; ligule a line of hairs; leaf margins cartilaginous. Inflorescence of 1—3 spikelets, subsessile within the leaf fascicle, sometimes (especially *M. squarrosa*) the terminal spikelet differing somewhat from the laterals. Spikelets few-flowered, abscissing between the florets, or inflorescence and the two uppermost protective leaf-sheaths shed as a whole; glumes 1—2 (0 in *M. mendocina*); lemmas rounded, often subcoriaceous, with a tuft of hairs halfway up the margin, emarginate to bilobed, mucronate or awned, sometimes the lateral nerves also excurrent; palea glabrous; lodicules sometimes absent; stamens 2—3, or some florets ♀. Caryopsis as in *Erioneuron*.

Species 5. Canada to Mexico; Peru to Argentina. Dry plains.

The genus is evidently related to *Erioneuron pulchellum*, but displays a number of advanced tendencies including spikelet dimorphism, loss of floral parts, and assumption of the role of disseminule by the inflorescence. For an account of these structural modifications, which may show considerable variation even on the same plant, see Anton & Hunziker (l.c.). The distribution is a classical example of a North-South American disjunction.

336. Blepharidachne Hack. in Engl. & Prantl, Nat. Pfl.-Fam. 2, 2: 126 (1887); Hunziker & Anton in Brittonia 31: 446—453 (1979) nom nov pro seq. *Eremochloe* S. Wats. in U.S. Geol. Explor. 40th Par. 5: 382 (1871) non Eremochloa Büse (1854) — E. kingii S. Wats.

Annual or perennial, with short leaves in dense tufts or stoloniferous fascicles; ligule a line of hairs or absent; leaf margins cartilaginous. Inflorescence of few spikelets, shortly peduncled and ± invested by subtending leaves. Spikelets 4-flowered, abscissing above glumes only, the two lowest florets ♂ or barren, the third ♀ or bisexual, the fourth reduced to a 3-awned rudiment; glumes equalling spikelet; lemmas rounded, ciliate on margins (scarcely so in *B. benthamiana*), deeply bilobed, with a ciliate awn and sometimes the lobes also ciliately awned; palea keels ciliate or smooth; lodicules 0; stamens 1—3. Caryopsis similar to *Erioneuron*.

Species 4. USA; Argentina. Deserts, rocky slopes and xerophyllous scrub.

Related to *Munroa*, but with the spikelet reduced to a single fertile floret embraced by 2 sterile florets.

337. Leptochloa P. Beauv., Ess. Agrost.: 71 (1812) — L. virgata (L.) P. Beauv. *Diplachne* P. Beauv. l.c. 80 — D. fascicularis (Lam.) P. Beauv. *Rabdochloa.* P. Beauv. l.c. 84 — R. domingensis (Jacq.) P. Beauv. *Leptostachys* Meyer, Prim. Fl. Esseq.: 73 (1818) nom superfl pro Leptochloa. *Oxydenia* Nutt., Gen. N. Amer. Pl. 1: 76 (1818) — O. attenuata Nutt. (= L. filiformis.). *Diachroa* Nutt. in Trans. Amer. Phil. Soc. ser. 2, 5: 147 (1835) — D. procumbens (Muhl.) Nutt. (= L. fascicularis). *Anoplia* Steud., Syn. Pl. Glum. 1: 210 (1854) in syn sub L. anoplia Nees (= ?). *Disakisperma* Steud. l.c. 287 — D. mexicana Steud. (= L. dubia). *Ipnum* Phil. in An. Univ. Chile 36: 211 (1870) — I. mendocinum Phil. (= L. dubia). *Diacisperma* Kuntze in Post, Lexicon: 169 (1903) nom superfl pro Disakisperma. *Baldomiria* Herter in Rev. Sudamer. Bot. 6: 145 (1940) — B. chloridiformis (Hack.) Herter.

Annual or perennial; ligule membranous, sometimes surmounted by a ciliate fringe (reduced to a line of hairs in *L. choridiformis, L. monticola*). Inflorescence open, of several to many slender racemes on a central axis (subdigitate in *L. chloridiformis, L. digitata*). Spikelets laterally compressed or subterete, the uppermost floret awnless or with a brief awn-point (1-flowered without rhachilla extension in *L. neesii, L. rupestris, L. uniflora*); lower glume shorter than lowest lemma (longer in *L. filiformis & L. uniflora* group); lemmas keeled or rounded, glabrous or appressed hairy on nerves (*L. monticola* villous), obtuse or bidentate rarely acute (*L. gigantea* acuminate with nerves puberulous only at base), sometimes mucronate, rarely with a short awn; stamens 2—3. Caryopsis laterally or dorsally compressed.

Species 40. Throughout the tropics; warm temperate parts of America and Australia. Woodland and savanna, on dry or swampy soils; often as a weed in disturbed places.

A large and somewhat variable genus, whose two sections are tolerably distinct in the Old World, but intergrade in the New (see Phillips in Kew Bull. 37: 142, 1982 on the case for treating as separate genera).

Spikelets laterally compressed, small, 1.5—5(—7) mm long, usually imbricate, on clearly secund racemes (L. caerulescens)   Sect *Leptochloa*
Spikelets subterete, large, 5—15 mm long, usually distant, on indistinctly secund racemes (L. fusca)   Sect *Diplachne*

The 1-flowered *L. uniflora* group fits comfortably here; it has little in common with strictly 1-flowered genera. *L. monticola* is an intermediate species sharing characters with *Gouinia*. *L. dubia* has axillary cleistogenes.

338. Kengia Packer in Bot. Not. 113: 291 (1960) nom nov pro Cleistogenes. *Moliniopsis* Gand., Fl. Eur. 25: 354 (1891) nom nud — K. serotina. *Cleistogenes* Keng in Sinensia 5: 147 (1934) nom inval; Conert in Bot. Jahrb. 78: 208—233 (1959) — C. serotina (L.) Keng.

Perennial; ligule a line of hairs, these sometimes surmounting a very short membrane. Inflorescence of lax racemes on a central axis, or sometimes a sparsely branched panicle (almost a simple raceme in *K. squarrosa*); always associated with axillary cleistogamous spikelets concealed within the upper leaf-sheaths. Spikelets: glumes 1—5(—7)-nerved; lemmas 3—5(—7)-nerved, keeled, pubescent on margins (*K. gatacrei* glabrous), bidenticulate or rarely entire, mucronate to shortly awned; palea keels at most puberulous.

Species ± 10. Southern Europe, Turkey, through southern Russia and Pakistan to China and Japan. Dry open places.

Kengia is apparently related to *Leptochloa*, but its tendency to a paniculate inflorescence and 5—7-nerved lemmas makes it awkward to identify. The name *Cleistogenes* is invalidated by its similarity to the technical term cleistogene, but subject to much controversy on the grounds that this is an English neologism which has never been used in Latin texts.

339. Orinus Hitchc. in J. Wash. Acad. Sci. 23: 136 (1933); Bor in Kew Bull. 6: 453—455 (1951) — O. arenicola Hitchc. (= O. thoroldii).

Rhizomatous perennial; ligule membranous; leaf-blades with setiform slightly pungent tip. Inflorescence of racemes on a central axis. Spikelets: upper glume 3-nerved; lemmas keeled, pilose all over, entire, acute to mucronate; palea keels pilose. Caryopsis cylindrical.

Species 2. Kashmir, Tibet and China. Desert dunes at high altitude, the scaly rhizomes being well adapted to survival in shifting sands.

A specialized genus probably related to *Kengia*.

340. Tripogon Roem. & Schult., Syst. Veg. 2: 34 (1817); Phillips & Launert in Kew Bull. 25: 301—322 (1971) — T. bromoides Roem. & Schult. *Plagiolytrum* Nees in Proc. Linn. Soc. 1: 95 (1841) — P. calycinum Nees (= T. bromoides). *Kralikia* Coss. & Dur. in Bull. Soc. Bot. Fr. 14: 89 (1867) — K. africana Coss & Dur. *Arcangelina* Kuntze, Rev. Gen. Pl. 2: 759 (1891) & *Kralikiella* Batt. & Trab., Fl. Alg. Monocot.: 245 (1895) — nom superfl pro Kralikia.

Slender tufted perennial, usually with filiform leaf-blades (these pungent in *T. pungens*); ligule a narrow membrane fringed with hairs. Inflorescence a single unilateral raceme. Spikelets laterally compressed, broadside to the rhachis, linear to elliptic; both glumes well developed, the upper sometimes 3-nerved (the lowest lemma sterile and glume-like in *T. siamensis, T. wardii*); lemmas lightly keeled or rounded, glabrous, bidentate (sometimes entire in *T. major*), mucronate or awned, the awn straight or rarely flexuous, often the teeth also awned; palea sometimes winged; stamens 1—3. Caryopsis subterete.

Species ± 30. Old World tropics; 1 species in tropical America. Wet flushes on or around rock outcrops, often in upland regions
The genus is quite closely related to *Leptochloa. T. lisboae*, one of the few species with flat leaf-blades, strongly resembles *Eragrostiella*, but the bidentate and mucronate lemma tip shows that the resemblance is merely superficial.

341. Indopoa Bor in Kew Bull. 13: 225 (1958) — I. paupercula (Stapf) Bor.

Like *Tripogon*, but lemma bearing a geniculate awn with twisted column; caryopsis needle-like, occupying a narrow pocket formed along the keel of the lemma.

Species 1. India. On rocks.
A little known genus with extraordinary caryopsis.

342. Oropetium Trin., Fund. Agrost.: 98 (1822); Phillips in Kew Bull. 30: 467. —470 (1975) — O. thomaeum (L.f.) Trin. *Lepturella* Stapf in Mém. Soc. Bot. Fr. 8: 222 (1912) — L. aristata Stapf. *Chaetostichium* C.E. Hubbard in Hook. Ic. Pl. 34: t 3341 (1937) — C. minimum (Hochst.) C.E. Hubbard.

Small tufted perennial, rarely annual; ligule membranous with ciliate margin. Inflorescence a single straight or coiled raceme, the spikelets in two opposite or subopposite (*O. minimum* adjacent) ranks, ± sunk in the rhachis, this tough or fracturing into pieces of 1—4(—8) spikelets. Spikelets 1-flowered (*O. roxburghianum* rarely with an additional ♂ floret) with or without a minute rhachilla extension concealed in callus hairs, dorsally compressed, edgeways to rhachis; lower glume obscure or absent; upper glume exceeding and covering the sunken floret, coriaceous, 1—3-nerved, acute to awned; lemma lightly keeled, hyaline, glabrous to pilose, emarginate to bidentate, mucronate (*O. aristatum* awned). Grain with pericarp reluctantly separable.

Species 6. Africa and India. Bare eroded places, especially the outwash from rocky hills.

A variable genus, whose species form a chain with no gaps large enough to justify partitioning. Though traditionally placed in Cynodonteae, it seems to be a 1-flowered derivative of *Tripogon; T. africanus,* which has 2-flowered spikelets, and *O. roxburghianum* link the two genera together.

343. Odyssea Stapf in Hook. Ic. Pl. 31: t 3100 (1922) — O. paucinervis (Nees) Stapf.

Rhizomatous perennial, with imbricate leaf-sheaths and short stiff pungent distichous flat or rolled blades; ligule a line of hairs. Inflorescence an elliptic to globose head of short crowded racemes. Spikelets slightly laterally compressed; lemmas scarious, rounded, silky villous on nerves, bidenticulate, mucronate. Grain ellipsoid, pericarp free.

Species 2. Ethiopia and Yemen to Transvaal and Namibia. Saline and desert soils.
A xerophytic genus related to *Leptochloa.*

344. Bewsia Goossens in S. Afr. J. Sci. 37: 183 (1941) — B. biflora (Hack.) Goossens.

Perennial; ligule membranous. Inflorescence of racemes on a central axis. Spikelets slightly laterally compressed, 2—4-flowered, disarticulating above glumes but not between florets; lemmas rounded, at least the lowest pubescent on lateral nerves, obtuse or emarginate, shortly awned from ± $\frac{1}{3}$ their length below tip. Caryopsis linear-oblong.

Species 1. Central and southern Africa. Savanna woodland, often on damp soils.
A segregate from *Leptochloa.*

345. Halopyrum Stapf in Hook. Ic. Pl. 25: t 2448 (1896) — H. mucronatum (L.) Stapf.

Perennial with robust stolons; ligule a line of hairs; leaf-blades stiff, convolute, filiform at tip. Inflorescence of short racemes appressed to an elongated axis. Spikelets large (1—3 cm long), the callus of each floret conspicuously bearded; glumes 3—7-nerved; lemmas rounded, coriaceous, asperulous, entire or bidenticulate, mucronate. Caryopsis elliptic, concavo-convex.

Species 1. Shores of Indian ocean from Mozambique to Sri Lanka. Coastal dunes.
A genus of uncertain affinity, perhaps distantly related to *Leptochloa.*

346. Gouinia Benth. in Benth. & Hook., Gen. Pl. 3: 1178 (1883); Swallen in Amer. J. Bot. 22: 31—41 (1935); Tateoka in Bull. Torr. Bot. Cl. 88: 143—152 (1961) — G. polygama Fourn. (= G. virgata). *Pogochloa* S. Moore in Trans. Linn.

Soc. ser. 2, 4: 509 (1895) — P. brasiliensis S. Moore. *Hackelia* Vasey in Beal, Grasses N. Amer. 2: 438 (1896) non Opiz (1838), in syn pro G. polygama.

Perennial; ligule membranous (a line of hairs in *G. barbata*). Inflorescence of racemes on a central axis, the racemes often bare at base and sometimes with a few secondary branchlets (usually so in *G. papillosa*). Spikelets laterally compressed, compact, usually pedicellate, the uppermost floret rudimentary and awned; glumes shorter than lower lemmas, lanceolate, the lower 1—5, the upper (1—)3—7-nerved; lemmas keeled, mostly 3-nerved but sometimes the larger ones 5-nerved (all 5—7-nerved in *G. longiramea*), pilose on margins (*G. paraguayensis* glabrous, but pilose on keel), gradually tapering to an entire or bidentate tip, long-awned (callus bearded in *G. cearensis*); palea glabrous or pubescent on margins (shortly 2-awned in *G. cearensis, G. paraguayensis*). Caryopsis ellipsoid, grooved on one side.

Species 12. Central and South America. Thickets or open places on hill slopes.
A fairly compact genus, closely allied to *Leptochloa*. Although occurring on different continents, genera 346—348 are not easy to separate and must be regarded as doubtfully distinct.

347. Silentvalleya Nair, Sreek., Vaj. & Bargh. in J. Bombay Nat. Hist. Soc. 79: 654 (1982) — S. nairii Nair et al.

Like *Gouinia* but upper glume as long as lemma and 3-nerved, the lower ½ as long and nerveless; lemma 3-nerved, glabrous, entire, awned, its callus bearded.

Species 1. Southern India. Riverside rocks.

348. Lophacme Stapf in Fl. Cap. 7: 316 (1898) — L. digitata Stapf.

Perennial; ligule a line of hairs or an obscure membranous rim. Inflorescence of subdigitate racemes on an axis seldom exceeding their own length. Spikelets cuneate, lax, with 1—3 fertile florets and a bunch of 1—5 sterile florets reduced to little more than their awns; glumes linear, the lower shorter than or equalling lowest lemma; lemmas keeled, thinly pilose, bidentate, long awned.

Species 2. Southern Africa. Seasonally damp places in savanna.
Lophacme is related to *Trichoneura*, the similarity with *Ectrosia* being apparently a matter of parallel evolution. It can be mistaken for *Chloris*, being best distinguished by its membranous lemma texture.

349. Leptocarydion Stapf in Fl. Cap. 7: 316 (1898) — L. vulpiastrum (De Not.) Stapf.

Annual; ligule membranous. Inflorescence a dense elliptic or linear head of numerous long slender crowded racemes. Spikelets: lower glume shorter than lowest lemma; lemmas keeled, conspicuously ciliate on lateral nerves, bidenticulate or entire, long awned; stamens 2. Caryopsis linear, trigonous.

Species 1. Eastern and southern Africa. Dry open places in savanna. Links *Leptochloa* to *Trichoneura*.

350. Trichoneura Anderss. in Kongl. Vet. Akad. Handl. 1853: 148 (1855); Ekman in Ark. Bot. 11, 9: 1—19 (1912) — T. hookeri Anderss. (= T. lindleyana). *Crossotropis* Stapf in Fl. Cap. 7: 317 (1898) — C. grandiglumis (Nees) Rendle.

Annual or perennial; ligule membranous. Inflorescene of stiff spreading or short appressed racemes on a central axis. Spikelets cuneate; glumes narrow, longer than adjacent lemmas and often as long as spikelet, usually tapering to a mucro or awn; lemmas rounded or lightly keeled, conspicuously ciliate on lateral nerves, bidentate, mucronate or shortly awned; palea sometimes capitate pilose between keels. Caryopsis narrow, dorsally flattened, concavo-convex.

Species 7. Tropical Africa and Arabia; Texas; Galapagos Is. Dry sandy or stony soils.
In *T. grandiflora* the whole inflorescence may break off at maturity and function as a tumbleweed.

351. Pogoneura Napper in Kirkia 3: 112 (1963) — P. biflora Napper.

Annual; ligule a line of hairs. Inflorescence of slender racemes on a central axis. Spikelets terete, 2—3-flowered; glumes longer than and enfolding florets; lemmas rounded, villous on lateral nerves, bidentate, shortly awned; palea keels with conspicuous ciliate fringe on upper half. Caryopsis ellipsoid, slightly dorsally flattened.

Species 1. East Africa. Savanna, on clay soils.
An isolated genus, probably related to *Trichoneura*.

352. Dinebra Jacq., Fragm.: 77 (1809); Phillips in Kew Bull. 28: 411—418 (1973) — D. arabica Jacq. (= D. retroflexa).

Annual; ligule membranous. Inflorescence of elongated or cuneate racemes on a central axis, these deciduous or with deciduous secondary branchlets (persistent in *D. perrieri*). Spikelets laterally compressed, cuneate, eventually disarticulating between florets (sometimes 1-flowered with rhachilla extension in *D. retroflexa*); glumes subequal, longer than and enclosing florets, often coriaceous, sometimes 3-nerved, acute to aristate; lemmas keeled, pubescent on nerves or sometimes glabrous in *D. retroflexa*, acute to emarginate, with or without a mucro. Caryopsis elliptic, trigonous in section.

Species 3. Africa to India and Madagascar. Savanna, on seasonally wet clays. *D. polycarpha* links the genus to *Leptochloa*.

353. Brachychloa S.M. Phillips in Kew Bull. 37: 158 (1982) — B. schiemanniana (Schweick.) S.M. Phillips.

Decumbent annual or perennial; ligule a short membrane with ciliate fringe. Inflorescence of racemes on a central axis, these long and deciduous in *B. fragilis*, short persistent and often crowded into a loose head in *B. schiemanniana*. Spikelets disarticulating between florets; glumes subequal, subcoriaceous, not longer than adjacent lemmas, the lower 1—3-nerved, the upper 3—7-nerved; lemmas 3-nerved (*B. fragilis*) or 5—7-nerved (*B. schiemanniana*), lightly keeled, glabrous or pubescent on margins, bidentate, mucronate; palea gibbous. Grain ellipsoid or trigonous, smooth with free pericarp.

Species 2. Mozambique and Natal. Dunes and sandy clearings near coast.

354. Ochthochloa Edgew. in J. As. Soc. Bengal, Nat. Hist. 11: 26 (1842) — O. dactyloides Edgew. (= O. compressa).

Stoloniferous perennial; ligule a short membrane with long ciliate fringe. Inflorescence of (2—)3—5 short secund digitate racemes, these deciduous at maturity. Spikelets strongly laterally compressed, disarticulating above glumes but not between florets; glumes unequal, shorter than adjacent lemmas, membranous, the upper with a thickened 3-nerved keel; lemmas keeled, villous on lower part of margins and keel, entire, acute or with a brief awn-point; palea keels ciliate, not gibbous. Grain ellipsoid, smooth, with free pericarp.

Species 1. Sind, through Arabia, to NE Africa. Semi-desert.
A segregate from *Brachychloa*.

355. Drake-Brockmania Stapf in Kew Bull. 1912: 197 (1912) — D. somalensis Stapf. *Heterocarpha* Stapf & Hubbard l.c. 1929: 263 (1929) — H. haareri Stapf & Hubbard.

Decumbent annual or perennial; ligule membranous. Inflorescence of (2—) 3—10 short compact deciduous racemes on a central axis, this sometimes short and subcapitate. Spikelets strongly laterally compressed, densely imbricate, eventually disarticulating between florets; glumes unequal, chartaceous, the lower 1—3-nerved, the upper conspicuously 6—9-nerved, usually exceeding adjacent lemma and often as long as spikelet, the acuminate tip often reflexed; lemmas (5—7-nerved in *D. somalensis*) keeled, villous on lower part of margins and keel, entire, cuspidate to mucronate; palea keels gibbous, winged or not. Caryopsis ellipsoid.

Species 2. Sudan to Somalia and Tanzania. Damp, often saline, places in savanna.
Linked through *Brachychloa* to *Leptochloa*.

356. Eragrostis Wolf, Gen. Pl. Vocab. Char. Def.: 23 (1776) — E. minor Host. *Erochloe* Raf., Neogenyton: 4 (1825) — Eragrostis spectabilis (Pursh) Steud. *Exagrostis* Steud., Nom. Bot. ed. 2, 1: 622 (1840) nom nud — Eragrostis elongata. *Poa sect Psilantha* K. Koch in Linnaea 21: 405 (1848) — P. collina (Trin.) K. Koch. *Macroblepharus* Philippi in Linnaea 29: 100 (1858) — M. contractus Philippi

(= E. ciliaris). *Vilfagrostis* Doell in Mart., Fl. Bras. 2, 3: 137 (1878) in syn sub Eragrostis. *Triphlebia* Stapf in Fl. Cap. 7: 318 (1898) non Baker (1886) — T. alopecuroides (Hack.) Stapf (= E. tincta). *Stiburus* Stapf l.c.: 696 (1900) nom nov pro Triphlebia. *Acamptoclados* Nash in Small, Fl. Southeast. U.S.: 139 (1903) — A. sessilispicus (Buckley) Nash. *Neeragrostis* Bush in Trans. Acad. Sci. St. Louis 13: 178 (1903); Nicora in Rev. Arg. Agron. 29: 1—11 (1962) — N. weigeltiana (Trin.) Bush (= E. reptans). *Erosion* Lunell in Amer. Midl. Nat. 4: 221 (1915) nom superfl pro Eragrostis. *Thellungia* Stapf in Kew Bull. 1920: 97 (1920) — T. advena Stapf. *Boriskellera* Terekhov, Delect. Sem. Hort. Bot. Kujbyshev: 13 (1938) — B. arundinacea (L.) Terekhov (= E. collina). *Diandrochloa* de Winter in Bothalia 7: 387 (1960) — D. namaquensis (Nees) de Winter (= E. japonica). *Psilantha* (K. Koch) Tzvelev in Bot. Zh. 53: 311 (1968). *Roshevitzia* Tzvelev l.c. — R. diarrhena (Schult.) Tzvelev (= E. japonica).

Annual or perennial, often glandular particularly on leaf-sheaths and inflorescence (*E. reptans* dioecious); ligule a line of hairs (sometimes membranous in sect *Psilantha*); leaf-blades mostly flat, sometimes rolled, rarely pungent. Inflorescence an open, contracted, spiciform or glomerate panicle, very rarely of racemes on a central axis. Spikelets 2—many-flowered (a few lower florets sterile in *E. egregia, E. cenolepis, E. plurigluma*), orbicular to vermiform, variously disarticulating; glumes often deciduous, 1- or rarely 3-nerved (awned in *E. aristiglumis, E. leptophylla, E. variabilis*); lemmas 3-nerved but the laterals sometimes very faint and occasionally suppressed (for example *E. advena, E. airoides, E. habrantha, E. stapfii*), keeled or rounded, membranous to coriaceous, glabrous to asperulous or rarely hairy, entire (3-toothed in *E. dentifera*), obtuse to acuminate, rarely mucronate (short awn-point in *E. dinteri, E. variegata*) or with excurrent lateral nerves; palea keels sometimes winged (conspicuously in *E. invalida*) or ciliate (especially sect *Psilantha*); anthers 2—3. Fruit mostly globose to ellipsoid, usually a caryopsis but sometimes the pericarp free.

Species ± 350. Tropics and subtropics throughout the world. Found in most habitats, but with a predilection for open sites, poor dry soils and weedy places. *E. tef* (Teff) is grown as a staple cereal in Ethiopia (Costanga et al in Econ. Bot. 33: 413—424, 1980); it is probably derived from *E. pilosa. E. curvula* (Weeping Love grass) is cultivated as a pasture species.

A large and variable genus, recognized by its paniculate inflorescence and glabrous entire lemma, but this circumscription needs some qualification. The primary branches of the panicle may be raceme-like if the spikelets are closely clustered about them or the panicle is impoverished (as in *E. flavicans, E. turgida*). In a very few species the primary branches are true racemes; either the usual kind with sub-sessile spikelets (*E. brainii, E. sessiliflora*), or the spikelets on filiform pedicels (*E. canescens, E. hispida*). *E. brainii* has such strongly developed racemes that it is somewhat anomalous here, but scarcely warrants raising to generic rank; the pubescent tips of its rhachilla internodes suggest a link with *Pogonarthria*. Another unusual condition is for the branches to terminate in a sterile bristle (*E.canescens, E. hispida*; sometimes in *E. mollior, E. olivacea*).

The lemmas are hairy in ± 15 Old World species, the hairs often being tubercle-based or spread over the whole surface of the lemma. This invites some risk of confusion with *Tridens*, but that genus has the indumentum confined to a dense pubescence on keel and lateral nerves. Another distinction from *Tridens* is the entire lemma tip, except for *E. dentifera* and a few species (notably *E.*

crassinervis, E. trimucronata) with prominently excurrent lateral nerves; all of these have glabrous lemmas.

The fruit is usually said to be a caryopsis, but in fact there are occasional species throughout the genus whose pericarp may be easily peeled away when moist. Some of these species, notably *E. advena, E. megalosperma* and *E. stapfii*, are very close to *Sporobolus*, and it is evident that the distinction between the two genera is not as great as has been supposed.

There is no modern overall account of the genus, but its taxonomy is evidently closely related to the mode of spikelet disarticulation, which is remarkably diverse. This character is probably subject to some degree of parallel evolution, but the following key provides a tolerable first approximation to natural groups.

Spikelets disarticulating at maturity:
  Disarticulation commencing at tip of spikelet, the rhachilla fragile (E. ciliaris)
    Sect *Psilantha*
  Disarticulation commencing at base of spikelet:
    Paleas retained on rhachilla; rhachilla persistent, or becoming fragile soon
      after lower lemmas start to fall and the upper florets shed singly or in one
      piece (E. cilianensis)   Sect *Eragrostis*
    Paleas falling at same time as lemmas; rhachilla persistent (E. unioloides)
      Sect *Lappula*
Spikelets falling entire (E. superba)   Sect *Platystachya*

The sections probably evolved in the above order. Sects *Psilantha* and *Eragrostis*, the latter containing over half the species in the genus, are world wide; sect *Lappula* principally Old World; and sect *Platystachya* confined to Africa. Evolution seems to have been most active in Africa, where many of the odder members of the genus occur.

E. walteri is anomalous, having non-kranz anatomy though apparently a good member of the genus. It obviously casts doubt upon the conjecture that C_4 metabolism never reverts to C_3, but the implications have yet to be explored (Ellis in S. Afr. J. Bot. 3: 380—386, 1984).

357. Cladoraphis Franch. in Bull Mens. Soc. Linn. Paris 1: 673 (1887) — C. duparquetii Franch. (= C. spinosa).

Perennial; ligule a line of hairs; leaf-blades flat, or rolled and pungent. Inflorescence with a stout woody culm-like central axis ending in a naked pungent tip (not always naked in *C. cyperoides*), and bearing short distant primary laterals with woody rhachis; the laterals secondarily branched and condensed into clusters appressed to the main axis in *C. cyperoides*, but forming simple spreading spine-tipped racemes in *C. spinosa*. Spikelets: glumes eventually deciduous; lemmas rounded, subcoriaceous, glabrous, entire. Grain narrowly oblong with free pericarp.

Species 2. South Africa and Namibia. Sandy desert and coastal dunes.

358. Richardsiella Ellfers & O'Byrne in Kew Bull. 11: 455 (1957) — R. eruciformis Ellfers & O'Byrne.

Annual; ligule a line of hairs. Inflorescence of racemes on a central axis, this with a naked filiform tip; racemes delicately incurved when dry, terminating in a bristle. Spikelets: glumes deciduous, shortly awned, the upper with tubercle-based hairs on keel; lemmas 1-nerved, rounded, margins ciliate; obtuse to obscurely emarginate, mucronate; palea keels pectinate ciliate; stamens 2. Grain ellipsoid, the pericarp free.

Species 1. Zambia. Sandy soils in seasonally damp depressions.
A segregate from *Eragrostis* related to *E. hispida*.

359. Eragrostiella Bor in Indian For. 66: 269 (1940); Lazarides in Contrib. Herb. Austral. 22: 1—7 (1976) — E. leioptera (Stapf) Bor.

Tufted perennial; ligule membranous with ciliate fringe; leaf-blades usually filiform. Inflorescence a single raceme. Spikelets shedding the lemmas leaving persistent rachilla and paleas, but sometimes the upper part shed as a whole; upper glume 1—3-nerved; lemmas keeled, cartilaginous, glabrous, acute to obtuse; palea keels narrowly winged, usually ciliolate. Caryopsis ellipsoid.

Species 5. Eastern Africa to Burma and northern Australia. Dry bushland and grassland on shallow soil.
A homogeneous genus split from *Eragrostis*.

360. Psammagrostis Gardner & Hubbard in Hook. Ic. Pl. 34: t 3361 (1938) — P. wiseana Gardner & Hubbard.

Annual; ligule a line of hairs. Inflorescence axillary, subtended by a spatheole, consisting of a much reduced raceme bearing only 1—3 spikelets, falling entire at maturity together with the short pointed peduncle. Spikelets with clavate rhachilla internodes, not disarticulating; upper glume 3-nerved; lemmas lightly keeled, coriaceous, glabrous, obtuse, mucronate; palea coriaceous, gibbous. Grain oblong, trigonous, reticulately patterned, with free pericarp.

Species 1. W Australia. Sand hills.
An unusual genus without obvious relatives, though the spikelets bear some resemblance to *Eragrostis dielsii*. The peculiar disseminule imitates that of *Thaumastochloa*.

361. Ectrosiopsis (Ohwi) Jansen in Acta Bot. Neerl. 1: 474 (1952) & in Reinwardtia 2: 269 (1953). *Eragrostis sect Ectrosiopsis* Ohwi in Bull. Tokyo Sci. Mus. 18: 1 (1947) — E. subtriflora (Ohwi) Ohwi (= Ectrosiopsis lasioclada).

Perennial, without cleistogamous spikelets; ligule a line of hairs. Inflorescence a contracted panicle. Spikelets linear, moderately loose with glabrous internodes, disarticulating between florets, these becoming a little longer towards tip of spikelet but otherwise not much different; glumes deciduous; lemmas lightly keeled, glabrous, entire, setaceously acuminate to shortly awned; palea wingless; stamens 3. Caryopsis ellipsoid.

Species 1. Australia, New Guinea, Caroline Is. Damp sandy depressions.

Genera 361—367 form a natural group, sharing a number of anatomical and morphological traits, including elongated microhairs and triangular vascular bundles (Decker in Amer. J. Bot. 50: 633, 1963). *Ectrosiopsis* links this group to *Eragrostis*. It has been treated as a primitive member of *Ectrosia,* but morphologically it is even closer to the American *Steirachne.* This is possibly a matter of parallel evolution, but on balance it seems best to accept *Ectrosiopsis* as distinct from both its relatives.

362. Steirachne Ekman in Ark. Bot. 10, 17: 35 (1911) — S. diandra Ekman.

Perennial, with cleistogamous spikelets in leaf axils; ligule a very short ciliate membrane. Inflorescence an open panicle. Spikelets loose, with long rhachilla internodes pubescent at tip; palea keels winged, ciliolate; stamens 2; otherwise like *Ectrosiopsis.* Caryopsis narrowly ellipsoid.

Species 2. Brazil, Guyana and Venezuela. Damp sandy depressions.

363. Ectrosia R. Br., Prodr. Fl. Nov. Holl.: 185 (1810); Hubbard in Hook. Ic. Pl. 34: t 3312 (1936) — E. leporina R. Br.

Annual or perennial; ligule a line of hairs. Inflorescence a panicle, usually contracted, occasionally some of the branches simple and raceme-like. Spikelets slender with long straight rhachilla internodes (zig-zag in *E. anomala*), disarticulating above glumes but not between florets, the lower 1—12 florets bisexual, the upper sterile and progressively transformed into a cluster of long-awned rudiments (not much different from lower and with setaceously acuminate tips in *E. anomala*); glumes deciduous, 1—3-nerved; lemmas lightly keeled, glabrous (hairy and 5—9-nerved in *E. gulliveri*), entire or bidentate, gradually tapering to a recurved acute or awned tip, the awns lengthening towards tip of spikelet; palea wingless (narrowly winged in *E. anomala*), sometimes gibbous; stamens 3. Caryopsis ellipsoid.

Species 11. Northern Australia and Malaysia. Depressions on poor sandy soil.

The genus is readily recognized by the modification of its upper florets into a dispersal device. *E. anomala* is atypical, being halfway to the closely related genus *Heterachne.*

364. Heterachne Benth. in Hook. Ic. Pl. 13: t 1250 (1877); Hubbard l.c. 33: t 3283 (1935) — H. gulliveri Benth.

Annual; ligule a line of hairs. Inflorescence a contracted panicle, this spiciform or condensed about the primary branches. Spikelets oblong to orbicular with zig-zag rhachilla, disarticulating above glumes but not between florets, the lower 1—2 florets bisexual, the upper sterile and forming a fan-like cluster; glumes deciduous, 1—3-nerved; lemmas strongly flattened with winged keels, glabrous (margins obscurely ciliolate in *H. gulliveri*), obtuse; palea prominently gibbous, the keels winged and often ciliate. Caryopsis obliquely ellipsoid.

Species 3. Northern Australia. Damp depressions.

365. Pogonarthria Stapf in Fl. Cap. 7: 316 (1898); Launert in Senck. Biol. 47: 303—307 (1966) — P. falcata (Hack.) Rendle (= P. squarrosa).

Annual or perennial; ligule a line of hairs. Inflorescence of deciduous racemes on a central axis, the spikelets juvenile at first and completing their growth after emergence. Spikelets disarticulating between florets, these decreasing in size upwards; rhachilla internodes (clavate in *P. refracta*) usually tipped with a few short hairs; glumes acute to acuminate; lemmas narrow, divergent, keeled, membranous, glabrous, acuminate to shortly awned. Caryopsis ellipsoid to fusiform.

Species 4. Tropical and South Africa. Open sandy places in savanna or near habitation.
The genus affords a link between *Eragrostis* and *Harpachne*. There is some superficial similarity with *Dinebra*, which has glumes longer than the florets.

366. Harpachne A. Rich., Tent. Fl. Abyss. 2: 431 (1851) — H. schimperi A. Rich.

Perennial; ligule a line of hairs. Inflorescence a single bottle-brush raceme with reflexed spikelets hanging on slender pedicels. Spikelets falling entire together with the pungent or hooked pedicel, the florets gradually increasing in size upwards (not in *H. bogdanii*); lemmas keeled, glabrous except for ciliolate margin, entire, acute to setaceously acuminate; palea gibbous, the keels winged. Caryopsis laterally compressed, obliquely elliptic.

Species 2. North and north east Africa. Open places in savanna.

367. Viguierella A. Camus in Bull. Bimens. Soc. Linn. Lyon 5: 11 (1926) & in Bull. Soc. Bot. Fr. 103: 272—274 (1956) — V. madagascariensis A. Camus.

Annual; ligule a line of hairs. Inflorescence a bottle-brush raceme, the spikelets erect upon a short pedicel, and subtended by a scarious scale ± 1 mm long from tip of each rhachis internode. Spikelets falling entire together with the pungent pedicel, comprising 1 fertile and 1—3 sterile florets, the latter reduced to a bunch of awns; glumes much shorter than lemma, pilose, truncate or asymmetrically bilobed, long-awned, the lower 2-, the upper 3-nerved; fertile lemma 3—5-nerved, keeled, coriaceous, glabrous, entire, long-awned. Caryopsis banana-like.

Species 1. Madagascar. Dry open places.
The subtending bract is an unusual organ. A larger version of it is found in *Scleropogon*.

368. Coelachyrum Hochst. & Nees in Linnaea 16: 221 (1842) — C. brevifolium Hochst. & Nees. *Coeleochloa* Steud., Nom. Bot. ed 2, 1: 394 (1840) nom nud —

C. brevifolium. *Cypholepis* Chiov. in Ann. Ist. Bot. Roma 8: 357 (1908) — C. yemenica (Schweinf.) Chiov. *Coelachyropsis* Bor in Ann. Nat. Mus. Wien 75: 23 (1971) — C. lagopoides (Burm.f.) Bor.

Annual or perennial, usually stoloniferous; ligule membranous, sometimes with a ciliate fringe. Inflorescence rarely a panicle (*C. longiglume*), more often of open or dense racemes, these disposed along an axis or digitate (± capitate in *C. lagopoides*). Spikelets broadly elliptic to ovate; glumes 1—3-nerved; lemma lightly keeled at first but becoming broadly rounded as grain expands, thinly chartaceous (*C. yemenicum* thinly coriaceous), puberulous to villous on flanks and sometimes also on keel (*C. longiglume* asperulous all over; *C. yemenicum* clavate pubescent on back; *C. piercei* sometimes glabrous), obtuse, sometimes mucronate; palea sometimes villous on keels. Grain broadly elliptic to subrotund, strongly flattened, concavo-convex, ± rugulose (*C. yemenicum* smooth), the pericarp free.

Species 8. Africa from Mauritania to Somalia and Tanzania; Arabia and Pakistan; also in South Africa. Dry grassland and semi-desert.

The species vary widely in the form of their inflorescence and lemma indumentum, but are held together by their constant and characteristic grain shape with free pericarp; there seems little to be gained by using the variable characters to create a swarm of small segregate genera. *Coelachyrum* provides a link between *Tridens, Eragrostis* and *Eleusine.*

369. Vaseyochloa Hitchc. in J. Wash. Acad. Sci. 23: 452 (1933) — V. multinervosa (Vasey) Hitchc.

Tufted perennial; ligule a line of hairs. Inflorescence of open racemes on a central axis. Spikelets narrowly ovate, the florets with shortly bearded callus; glumes 3—9-nerved; lemma distinctly 7—9-nerved, rounded, thinly chartaceous, pubescent below, narrowly obtuse; palea splitting longitudinally at maturity, the keels narrowly winged. Grain like *Coelachyrum*, but obscurely striate and with prominent horn-like style bases.

Species 1. Texas. Sandy places.
An anomalous American genus with several-nerved lemmas, but nevertheless clearly related to *Coelachyrum*.

370. Eleusine Gaertn., Fruct. 1: 7 (1788); Phillips in Kew Bull. 27: 251—270 (1972) — E. coracana (L.) Gaertn.

Annual or perennial; ligule membranous, usually with a ciliate fringe; leafblades folded and sheaths strongly keeled. Inflorescence of digitate or subdigitate racemes, the axis shorter than the longest raceme (sometimes longer in *E. multiflora*), the racemes with imbricate spikelets and terminating in a fertile spikelet (a sterile spikelet in *E. semisterilis*). Spikelets disarticulating between florets (persistent in *E. coracana*); upper glume 1—3(—7 in *E. coracana*)-nerved, awnless; lemmas strongly keeled, sometimes the keels thickened and containing 1—3 closely spaced additional nerves, membranous, glabrous, obtuse or acute (sometimes mucronate in *E. multiflora*). Grain ellipsoid to subglobose, trigonous in section, flat or concave on hilar side (sulcate in *E. multiflora*), rugose, with free pericarp.

Species 9. Mostly East & NE tropical Africa, but 1 cosmopolitan weed and 1 species confined to South America. Savanna and upland grassland, often as a weed. *E. coracana* (Finger Millet or Ragi) is widely grown as a cereal in Africa, India and China, especially in upland areas. It is derived from *E. indica*, a diploid cosmopolitan weed (subsp *indica*, 2n = 18) which has a tetraploid race in Africa (subsp *africana*). The morphological characters of the two races overlap so much that they are difficult to separate with any confidence, an uncertainty which leads to their inclusion in a single species. It is convenient to treat the crop as a separate species, but in fact it is a tetraploid which hybridizes readily with subsp *africana*. (Hilu & de Wet in Econ. Bot. 30: 199—208, 1976; de Wet et al in Amer. J. Bot. 71: 550—557, 1984).

Active speciation in East Africa has made this a taxonomically difficult genus. *E. multiflora* links it to *Acrachne* and thence, by further sterilization of the rhachis tip, to *Dactyloctenium*.

371. Acrachne Chiov. in Ann. Ist. Bot. Roma 8: 361 (1907); Lindley, Nat. Syst. ed. 2: 381 (1836) sine descr — A. verticillata (Roxb.) Chiov. (= *A*. racemosa). *Arthrochloa* Lorch in J. Ind. Bot. Soc. 39: 490 (1960) non R. Br. (1823) — A. henrardiana (Bor) Lorch. *Camusia* Lorch in Bull. Res. Counc. Israel 9 D: 155 (1961) — C. perrieri (A. Camus) Lorch. *Normanboria* Butzin in Taxon 27: 301 (1978) nom nov pro Arthrochloa.

Annual; ligule membranous with ciliate fringe. Inflorescence digitate or in whorls along a central axis, the racemes with imbricate spikelets and terminating in an abortive spikelet (sometimes a bare point in *A. perrieri*). Spikelets shedding the lemmas leaving persistent rhachilla and paleas, but sometimes (especially *A. henrardiana*) the upper part shed as a whole; upper glume awned from tip; lemmas strongly keeled, firmly membranous, glabrous, entire or bidentate, tipped with a stout awn-point. Grain ellipsoid, rugose, sulcate on hilar side (smooth and not sulcate in *A. perrieri*), the pericarp free.

Species 3. Old World tropics. Savanna.

372. Sclerodactylon Stapf in Kew Bull. 1911: 318 (1911) — S. juncifolium Stapf (= S. macrostachyum). *Arthrochlaena* Benth. in J. Linn. Soc. Bot. 19: 107 (1881) in syn sub. S. macrostachyum.

Tufted perennial; ligule a line of hairs; leaf-blades stiff, terete, pungent. Inflorescence of paired or digitate racemes, these bearing imbricate spikelets and terminating in an abortive spikelet. Spikelets disarticulating between florets or several florets falling together; upper glume with or without a brief awn-point from just below tip; lemma strongly keeled, coriaceous, glabrous, acute; palea winged. Grain ellipsoid, smooth, the pericarp free.

Species 1. Madagascar, Indian Ocean islands and adjacent east African coast. Coral rocks by seashore.

A grass related to *Dactyloctenium*, but adapted to a specialized habitat. The leaf-blades are rush-like and elliptical in section.

373. Dactyloctenium Willd., Enum. Hort. Berol.: 1029 (1809); Fischer & Schweickerdt in Ann. Natal Mus. 10: 47—77 (1941) — D. aegyptium (L.) Willd.

Annual or perennial; ligule membranous (blades pungent in *D. hackelii, D. robechii*). Inflorescence of paired or digitate racemes, these bearing imbricate spikelets, terminating in a bare pointed rhachis extension, and eventually disarticulating from culm though sometimes very tardily. Spikelets disarticulating above glumes, but not usually between florets; upper glume with an oblique awn from just below tip; lemmas strongly keeled, membranous, glabrous, acute to shortly awned and often recurved at tip. Grain like *Eleusine*.

Species 13. Hinterland of Indian Ocean from Natal to north India; 1 cosmopolitan weed; 1 species confined to Australia. Mostly on dry sandy soils, with some species adapted to dune or saline habitats. *D. aegyptium* is a common weed, now established throughout the world.
A close-knit but taxonomically difficult genus, undergoing active speciation and introgression in east Africa.

374. Psilolemma S.M. Phillips in Kew Bull. 29: 267 (1974) — P. jaegeri (Pilger) S.M. Phillips.

Perennial; ligule a line of hairs; leaf-blades stiff, distichous, pungent. Inflorescence of short racemes bearing (1—)2—3(—5) spikelets and appressed to an elongated axis. Spikelets: lemmas rounded, glabrous, obtuse. Grain ellipsoid, the pericarp free.

Species 1. East Africa. Fringing mud flats and pans on alkaline soil.
A specialized segregate from *Eragrostis*.

375. Desmostachya (Hook.f.) Stapf in Fl. Cap. 7: 316 (1898) non Desmostachys Miers (1852). *Eragrostis sect Desmostachya* Hook.f., Fl. Brit. India 7: 324 (1897) — E. cynosuroides (Retz.) P. Beauv. (= D. bipinnata). *Stapfiola* Kuntze in Post, Lexicon: 532 (1903) nom nov pro Desmostachya.

Perennial; ligule a line of hairs. Inflorescence of numerous racemes on a long central axis, the spikelets densely imbricate. Spikelets sessile, falling entire; glumes acute; lemmas keeled, glabrous, acute. Caryopsis ovoid.

Species 1. Northern Africa, through the Middle East to India and Indo-China. Arid regions with water table near surface.
The genus is evidently closely related to *Eragrostis*. Its name is expressly permitted by the International Code of Botanical Nomenclature, as unlikely to be confused with *Desmostachys*.

376. Myriostachya (Benth.) Hook.f., Fl. Brit. India 7: 327 (1897). *Eragrostis sect Myriostachya* Benth. in J. Linn. Soc. Bot. 19: 117 (1881) — E. wightiana (Steud.) Benth.

Perennial; ligule a line of hairs; leaf-blades broad. Inflorescence of numerous deciduous racemes on a long central axis. Spikelets pedicellate, falling entire together with the pedicel; glumes tapering to a long subulate awn; lemmas keeled, glabrous, acuminate to a subulate tip. Caryopsis oblong.

Species 1. South India to Indo-China. Margins of tidal swamps.

e. SPOROBOLINAE Benth. in J. Linn. Soc. Bot. 19: 30 (1881). *Crypsidinae* Maire & Weiler, Fl. Afr. Nord 2: 89 (1953) sine descr lat. *Lycurinae* Pilger, Nat. Pfl.-Fam. ed. 2, 14d: 167 (1956). *Muhlenbergiinae* Pilger l.c.: 168. *Hubbardochloinae* Auquier in Bull. Jard. Bot. Belg. 50: 246 (1980).

Leaf-blades usually flat, rarely convolute and pungent. Inflorescence a panicle. Spikelet 1-flowered without rhachilla extension (a few rare exceptions), fusiform to lanceolate, disarticulating below floret (falling entire in *Lycurus* and some species of *Crypsis, Pereilema*); lemma rounded on back, membranous to chartaceous, 1—3-nerved; palea often resembling lemma in size and texture. Fruit variable.

The subtribe has a characteristic facies by virtue of its paniculate inflorescence and 1-flowered spikelets. Although favouring secondary habitats, it has not followed the tribal tendency towards a swarm of specialized peripheral segregates, but consists essentially of two very large genera. Nor has it exploited the 1-flowered condition in the manner of Cynodonteae. In fact the single-floret character is not entirely stable, since sporadic 2-flowered spikelets may occur in some species of *Calamovilfa, Muhlenbergia* and *Sporobolus*.

It is clearly linked to *Eragrostis* through *Sporobolus*. The derivation of *Muhlenbergia* is less clear, though there seems little doubt that it is an offshoot of the *Eragrostis—Sporobolus* complex.

377. Sporobolus R.Br., Prodr. Fl. Nov. Holl.: 169 (1810) — S. indicus (L.) R.Br. *Agrosticula* Raddi, Agrost. Bras.: 33 (1823) — A. muralis Raddi (= S. tenuissimus). *Bennetia* Raf. in Bull. Bot. Genève 1: 220 (1830) non Bennettia Gray (1821) — B. juncea (Kunth) Jacks. *Triachyrum* A. Br. in Flora 24: 712 (1841) — T. adoense A. Br. (= S. discosporus). *Spermachiton* Llanos, Frag. Pl. Filip.: 25 (1851); Pilger, Nat. Pfl.-Fam. ed. 1, 14d: 54 (1956) as "Spermatochiton" — S. involutum Llanos (= S. fertilis). *Cryptostachys* Steud., Syn. Pl. Glum. 1: 181 (1854) — C. vaginata Steud. (= S. vaginiflorus). *Diachyrium* Griseb. in Abh. Ges. Wiss. Gött. 19: 257 (1874) — D. arundinaceum Griseb. (= S. rigens). *Bauchea* Fourn., Mex. Pl. 2: 87 (1886) — B. karwinskyi Fourn. (= S. wrightii).

Annual or perennial; ligule a line of hairs. Panicle open or contracted, rarely spiciform, exserted from uppermost sheath (lowest whorl of branches sterile in *S. panicoides*). Spikelets fusiform, often small, rounded on back (laterally compressed and keeled in *S. asper, S. clandestinus, S. neglectus, S. platensis, S. vaginiflorus*), glabrous or very rarely puberulous (with rhachilla extension in

S. subtilis; sporadically 2-flowered in *S. mitchellia*); glumes deciduous (persistent in a few species from temperate N & S America), awnless (*S. molleri, S. myrianthus, S. pectinellus* mucronate), the upper usually longer than lower and resembling lemma; lemma thinly membranous and often shiny, 1-nerved (*S. subtilis, S. clandestinus, S. vaginiflorus* 3-nerved, the two latter chartaceous), entire, awnless (*S. molleri* with subulate tip); palea resembling lemma, depressed between keels, and often splitting lengthways as grain grows; lodicules 2; stamens 2—3 (*S. monandrus* 1). Grain globose to ellipsoid, rounded or truncate, not beaked; pericarp free, commonly swelling when wet and expelling seed to tip of spikelet.

Species ± 160. Tropics and subtropics. Habitats variable, the commonest being open places in savanna on dry or stony soils subject to trampling or grazing; there is also an important group of species which specialize in seasonally flooded heavy clay or saline soils; *S. virginicus* grows in coastal salt flats and mangrove swamps.

The genus may be roughly partitioned according to whether the inflorescence branches are whorled or not, but formal subdivisions seem impractical. In fact the species intergrade to such an extent that their limits are seldom sharply defined, and they sometimes seem to take the form of noda in a continuum of variation; note the contrast with *Eragrostis*, whose species are also closely interrelated but are nevertheless usually disjunct. *S. subtilis* is mildly aberrant; as also are the allies of *S. asper*, whose chartaceous keeled lemmas verge towards *Calamovilfa* but lack its distinctive callus beard.

It is distinguished from *Eragrostis* by its 1-flowered spikelets and 1-nerved lemmas, but the boundary between the genera is blurred by a number of intermediates which have been arbitrarily assigned to *Eragrostis* on account of their 2-flowered spikelets. The mucilaginous pericarp is characteristic, but by no means diagnostic.

S. rigens has solid cylindrical leaf-blades (Böcher in Bot. Not. 125: 344—360, 1972).

378. Crypsis Ait., Hort. Kew. 1: 48 (1789) nom conserv; C.E. Hubbard in Hook. Ic. Pl. 35: t 3457 (1947); Lorch in Bull. Res. Counc. Israel 11D: 91—126 (1962) — C. aculeata (L.) Ait. *Pallasia* Scop., Introd.: 72 (1777) non Pallassia Hout. (1775) — unnamed species (= C. aculeata). *Antitragus* Gaertn., Fruct. 2: 7 (1791) nom superfl pro Crypsis. *Heleochloa* Host ex Roem., Collect.: 233 (1807) — H. alopecuroides (Pill. & Mitt.) Roem. *Pechea* Lapeyr., Suppl. Pl. Pyr.: 8 (1818) in syn sub C. schoenoides (L.) Lam.; Steud., Nom. Bot. ed. 2, 1: 449 (1840) as "Pachea". *Raddia* Mazziari in Ionios Antol. 2: 448 (1834) non Bertol. (1819) — R. aculeata Mazziari. *Ceytosis* Munro in J. Linn. Soc. Bot. 6: 54 (1862) nom nud — Crypsis aculeata. *Torgesia* Bornm. in Mitt. Thür. Bot. Ver. ser. 2, 30: 83 (1913) — T. minuartioides Bornm.

Prostrate or ascending annual; ligule a line of hairs. Panicle spiciform, cylindrical and ± exserted, or ovoid to capitate and then partially enclosed by 1—2 bract-like leaf-sheaths. Spikelets strongly laterally compressed and keeled, sometimes falling entire; glumes narrow, almost equalling floret, acute or with a short awn point; lemma membranous, 1-nerved, acute or with a short awn-point; palea 1—2-nerved; lodicules 0; stamens 2—3. Grain ellipsoid, without beak, the pericarp free and sometimes swelling when wet.

Species 8. Centred on Mediterranean and Middle East, but extending to China and central Africa; naturalized in South Africa and America. Wet, often saline, soils.

Related to *Sporobolus*, especially *S. spicatus*, differing mainly in the laterally compressed spikelets.

379. Urochondra C.E. Hubbard in Hook. Ic. Pl. 35: t 3457 (1947) — U. setulosa (Trin.) C.E. Hubbard.

Caespitose perennial; ligule a line of hairs; leaf-blades rigid, convolute, pungent. Panicle spiciform, cylindrical, exserted from uppermost sheath. Spikelets strongly laterally compressed and keeled; glumes narrow, almost equalling floret, awnless; lemma membranous, 1-nerved, mucronate; palea 2-nerved; lodicules 0; stamens 3. Grain ellipsoid, surmounted by a pallid beak ± $\frac{1}{3}$ its length; pericarp free, swelling when wet.

Species 1. Sudan and Somalia to Sind. Sandy seashores.

Differs from *Crypsis* mainly in the peculiar beak, formed from thickened connate style bases.

380. Calamovilfa (A. Gray) Scribn. in Hack., True Grasses: 113 (1890); Reeder & Ellington in Brittonia 12: 71—77 (1960); Thieret in Castanea 31: 145—152 (1966). *Calamagrostis sect Calamovilfa* A. Gray, Man. Bot.: 582 (1848) — C. brevipilis (Torr.) Beck.

Perennial; ligule a line of hairs. Panicle open or contracted. Spikelets lanceolate, laterally compressed, keeled (sporadic 2-flowered spikelets may occur); glumes membranous, shorter than or equal to floret, awnless; lemma chartaceous, 1-nerved, acute, its callus bearded with hairs ¼ to almost equalling its length; palea depressed between keels. Grain elliptic to linear, the pericarp free.

Species 4. North America. Dry or marshy pine barrens, inland dunes and sandy prairie.

381. Muhlenbergia Schreb., Gen. Pl. ed. 8: 44 (1789); Soderstrom in Contrib. U.S. Nat. Herb. 34: 75—189 (1967) — M. schreberi Gmel. *Dilepyrum* Michaux, Fl. Bor. Am. 1: 40 (1803) — D. minutiflorum Michaux (= M. schreberi). *Podosemum* Desv. in Nouv. Bull. Sci. Soc. Philom. 2: 188 (1810) — P. capillare (Lam.) Desv. *Clomena* P. Beauv., Ess. Agrost.: 28 (1812); Roem. & Schult., Syst. Veg. 2: 18, 383 (1817) as "Cleomena" — C. peruviana P. Beauv. *Tosagris* P. Beauv., Ess. Agrost.: 29 (1812) nom prov — T. agrostoidea P. Beauv. (= M. capillaris). *Trichochloa* DC., Cat. Hort. Monsp.: 151 (1813) nom superfl pro Podosemum. *Anthipsimus* Raf. in J. Phys. Chim. 89: 105 (1819) — A. gonopodes Raf. (= M. schreberi). *Sericrostis* Raf., Neogenyton: 4 (1825); Steud., Nom. Bot. ed. 2, 2: 568 (1841) as "Serigrostis" —Stipa sericea Michaux (= M. capillaris). *Epicampes* Presl, Rel. Haenk. 1: 235 (1830) — E. strictus Presl (= M. robusta). *Dactylogramma* Link, Hort. Berol. 2: 248 (1833) — D. cinnoides Link (= M. glomerata). *Acroxis* Steud., Nom. Bot. ed. 2, 1: 22 (1840) in syn sub Muhlenbergia. *Calycodon* Nutt. in Proc. Acad. Nat. Sci. Philad. 4: 23 (1848) — C. montanum Nutt. *Vaseya* Thurber l.c. 15: 79 (1863) — V. comata Thurber (= M. andina). *Crypsinna* Fourn., Mex. Pl. 2: 90 (1886) — C. macroura (Kunth) Fourn. *Lepyroxis* Fourn. l.c.: 92 in syn sub Polypogon canadensis (= M. mexicana). *Chaboissaea* Fourn. l.c.: 112; Sohns in J. Wash. Acad. Sci. 43: 405—407 (1953) — C. ligulata Fourn. *Bealia* Scribn. in Hack., True Grasses: 104 (1890) — B. mexicana Scribn. (= M. biloba).

Annual or perennial; ligule membranous (rarely briefly so and hair fringed). Panicle open, contracted or spiciform. Spikelets typically lanceolate, lightly laterally compressed, rounded or keeled, often hairy (sporadic 2-flowered spikelets occur in *M. subbiflora* and a few other species; 2—3-flowered spikelets usual in *M. ligulata; M. microsperma, M. appressa* have additional cleistogenes enclosed in and falling with reduced indurated lower sheaths); glumes 0—1(—3)-nerved, characteristically subequal and shorter than lemma (minute in *M. implicata, M. parviglumis, M. schreberi, M. seatonii*) but sometimes exceeding it, usually entire, occasionally awned or tridentate; lemma usually firmer than glumes, 3-nerved (the laterals faint in a few species), entire or bidenticulate (*M. biloba* bilobed), usually with a terminal or subterminal awn. Caryopsis usually fusiform, rarely ellipsoid.

Species ± 160. New World, especially southern USA and Mexico; ± 8 species in southern Asia. Habitat variable, but commonly dry open grassland in subtropical and warm temperate climates.

Soderstrom (l.c.) recognized two subgenera, placing the tall caespitose perennials in subgen *Podosemum*, but basing his distinction mainly upon leaf anatomy. There is no satisfactory overall treatment of the genus or sectional classification available. *M. ligulata* with its 2—3-flowered spikelets is anomalous, but it cannot readily be separated from species such as *M. subbiflora* which are occasionally 2-flowered.

The genus is allied to *Sporobolus*, from which it can usually be distinguished readily enough by the ligule, caryopsis or 3-nerved awned lemma, but it is very variable, and no single character is completely reliable. The basic chromosome number is 10, rarely 12 (for *Sporobolus* x = 9, 10 or 12, but 9 is commonest). The short glumes and long awn distinguish it from most pooid genera, but species lacking these features run some risk of confusion.

382. Hubbardochloa Auquier in Bull. Jard. Bot. Belg. 50: 241 (1980) — H. gracilis Auquier.

Annual; ligule a line of hairs. Panicle open. Spikelets fusiform, rounded; glumes 1-nerved, longer than floret, acute; lemma hyaline, thinner than glumes, 1-nerved, entire, with a long flexuous terminal awn; palea 0; lodicules 0. Caryopsis fusiform.

Species 1. Rwanda, Burundi and Zambia. Stony slopes in savanna.
Apparently a segregate from *Muhlenbergia*, though the latter has not been found in Africa.

383. Lycurus Kunth in Humb. & Bonpl., Nov. Gen. Sp. 1: 141 (1816); Reeder in

Phytologia 57: 283—291 (1985) — L. phleoides Kunth. *Pleopogon* Nutt. in Proc. Acad. Nat. Sci. Philad. 4: 25 (1848) — P. setosum Nutt.

Perennial; ligule membranous. Panicle spiciform, bearing paired spikelets falling intact together, the lower resembling upper but usually smaller and sterile. Spikelets laterally compressed, lightly keeled; glumes subequal, shorter than floret, the lower with 2 (very rarely 1) slender awns, the upper with 1; lemma firmer than glumes, 3-nerved, with a slender terminal awn. Caryopsis fusiform.

Species 3. Southern USA to Argentina. Plains and rocky hills.
Reeder (l.c.) reports that the sex of the paired spikelets is rather variable.

384. Pereilema Presl, Rel. Haenk. 1: 233 (1830) — P. crinitum Presl.

Annual; ligule membranous. Panicle spiciform or contracted about primary branches, bearing persistent (*P. ciliatum* deciduous) clusters of a few fertile spikelets subtended by several sterile, the latter ± reduced to an involucre-like bunch of awns. Spikelets laterally compressed, keeled, shedding the floret; glumes subequal, shorter than floret, emarginate, 1-awned (often reduced to ciliate bristles in *P. ciliatum*); lemma firmer than glumes, 3-nerved, with a slender terminal awn (*P. ciliatum* sometimes mucronate). Caryopsis ellipsoid.

Species 3. Mexico to Brazil. Hillsides and weedy places in savanna.
A relative of *Muhlenbergia*. *P. ciliatum* superficially resembles *Cenchrus*.

32. LEPTUREAE

Holmberg in Bot. Not. 1926: 71 (1926); Hansen & Potztal in Bot. Jahrb. 76: 251—270 (1954). *Lepiureae* Dum., Obs. Gram. Belg.: 83 (1824) nom inval. *Monermeae* C.E. Hubbard in Hutch., Brit. Flow. Pl.: 332 (1948) sine descr lat.
Lepturinae Benth. in J. Linn. Soc. Bot. 19: 31 (1881). *Monerminae* Janchen in Phyton 5: 60 (1953) nom nud.

Ligule membranous with ciliate margin. Inflorescence a single cylindrical bilateral raceme, the spikelets alike, alternate (*L. geminata* opposite), borne edgeways on and embedded in hollows in the fragile rhachis. Spikelets 1-flowered plus rhachilla extension and sometimes a vestigial floret (this fertile in *L. xerophilus*, sporadically so in other species), dorsally compressed, falling entire; lower glume minute or suppressed (but well developed in terminal spikelet); upper glume appressed to rhachis, exceeding and covering the sunken floret, coriaceous, 5—12-nerved, acute to caudately awned (*L. pulchellus* obtuse); lemma 3-nerved, membranous, rounded on back, obtuse to acute. Grain ellipsoid with free pericarp.
Genus 1; species ± 8. Old World tropics.

Anatomy. Kranz PS type with short stout microhairs.

Chromosomes. 2n = 18, 42, 54.

Lepturus has characteristic sunken spikelets and a specialized seashore habitat. Its leaf anatomy is typically chloridoid, but its precise affinity is contentious. Its 1-flowered spikelets point to Cynodonteae, but there is no obvious place for it in that tribe. In fact its nearest relatives are *Oropetium* — an anomalous member of Eragrostideae, and *Lepturopetium* — a poorly known genus tentatively assigned to Cynodonteae. With so much in doubt it seems best to accept Leptureae as a monotypic tribe for the time being. It bears a remarkable superficial resemblance to the pooid genus *Hainardia* (Tateoka in Evolution 13: 418—420, 1959).

1	Upper glume 5—12-nerved:	
2	Lateral nerves of lemma extending almost to tip	**385 Lepturus**
2	Lateral nerves of lemma less than ½ its length	*157 Hainardia*
1	Upper glume 1—3-nerved	*342 Oropetium*

385. Lepturus R. Br., Prodr. Fl. Nov. Holl.: 207 (1810) — L. repens (Forst.) R. Br. *Monerma* P. Beauv., Ess. Agrost.: 116 (1812) & *Leptocercus* Raf. in Amer. Monthly Mag. 4: 190 (1819) & *Lepiurus* Dum., Obs. Gram. Belg.: 90, 140 (1824) — nom superfl pro Lepturus. *Ischnurus* Balf. f. in Proc. Roy. Soc. Edinb. 12: 98 (1883) — I. pulchellus Balf.f.

Perennial, often stoloniferous. Description as for tribe.

Species ± 8. Shores of Indian and western Pacific oceans. Sandy beaches, some species extending to the coastal hinterland.
A uniform genus whose taxonomy is complicated by the variability of *L. repens*, leading to wide differences in the number of species accepted.

33. CYNODONTEAE

Dumort., Obs. Gram. Belg.: 83 (1824). *Chlorideae* Reichenb., Consp. Reg. Veg.: 48 (1828). *Lappagineae* Endl., Fl. Poson.: 100 (1830). *Spartineae* Gren. & Godr., Fl. France 3: 434 (1855). *Zoysieae* Benth. in J. Linn. Soc. Bot. 19: 29 (1881). *Nazieae* Hitchc., Gen. Grasses U.S.: 15 (1920). *Trageae* Hitchc. in Contrib. U.S. Nat. Herb. 24: 559 (1927). *Perotideae* C.E. Hubbard in Bor, Grasses Burma Ceylon India Pak.: 686 (1960). *Pommereulleae* Bor, Grasses Burma Ceylon India Pak.: 686 (1960).

Ligule a short membrane with ciliate margin, but often one or other of the components predominant. Inflorescence of tough unilateral racemes, these single digitate or scattered along an axis, often deciduous (very short and forming a cylindrical false raceme in Zoysiinae), the spikelets alike or the sexes separate. Spikelets with 1 fertile floret (except Pommereullinae, *Tetrapogon, Neostapfiella*), with or without additional ♂ or barren florets, cuneate to subterete, laterally or dorsally compressed, disarticulating above glumes but not between florets, or falling entire; glumes usually persistent on pedicel or falling with spikelet, herbaceous to membranous, 1—3(—5)-nerved (more in *Astrebla, Hilaria, Lepturopetium, Schaffnerella*), shorter than floret or enclosing it, sometimes the lower absent; lemma membranous to coriaceous, (0—)3-nerved (more in *Lintonia, Pommereulla* and lobes of *Astrebla, Chloris humbertiana*), often ciliate on nerves, entire or 2—3(—5)-lobed, with or without 1—3(—5) terminal or subapical awns, these usually straight; callus usually very short and obtuse. Fruit sometimes with free pericarp.

Genera 59; species ± 300. Tropics, extending into the North American prairie.

Anatomy. Kranz PS type with short stout microhairs.

Chromosomes. The basic number is 10, sometimes 9.

2n	18	20	21	22	28	30	36	40	42	56	60	72	80
No of species	16	47	6	5	13	10	18	85	11	7	15	6	7

The tribe is very close to Eragrostideae, with obvious similarities between the *Leptochloa* and *Chloris* groups of genera. It differs principally in the reduction of the fertile florets to one per spikelet, a development which has opened the way to a new range of evolutionary trends including:
— participation of sterile florets in the construction of the disseminule
— retreat of the floret within enclosing glumes
— shedding of the spikelet as a whole
— abbreviation of the raceme, and its conversion to a disseminule.
Lesser features are that the tribe has forsaken panicles, and that it often assumes a characteristic facies with cuneate spikelets and membranous glumes. It has evidently taken a different evolutionary course to Eragrostideae, and its recognition as a separate tribe seems justified. Suggested relationships within Cynodonteae are shown in fig 16.

Though not so strongly weedy and xerophytic as Eragrostideae, it commonly occurs in seral and disclimax communities, for which its generally short or mat forming stature is well suited. Although essentially a tropical tribe, Boutelouinae has successfully extended into the temperate American prairie; and *Spartina* into cool marine habitats (Long et al in Nature 257: 622—624, 1975).

It is usually easy to recognize from its single fertile floret, 3-nerved lemma and racemose inflorescence. Note however that spikelets with 2 female florets (but no fracture between them) may occasionally be found, particularly among species which normally have a well developed male second floret. Pommereullinae are always several-flowered, but seem more closely related to *Chloris* than *Leptochloa*, and are here treated as primitive Cynodonteae.

1   Spikelets containing 2—5 fertile florets:
  2   Body of lemma 5—11-nerved:
    3   Floret cluster rounded at base   **387 Lintonia**
    3   Floret cluster prolonged below into a pungent stipe   **388 Pommereulla**
  2   Body of lemma 3-nerved:
    4   Fertile lemma deeply 3-lobed   **386 Astrebla**
    4   Fertile lemma entire to bidentate:
      5   Lemma flanked by hyaline wings   **389 Tetrapogon**
      5   Lemma not winged   **390 Neostapfiella**
1   Spikelets (or most of them) containing 1 fertile floret:
  6   Fertile lemma entire to bilobed, with or without a single awn, rarely 3-awned and then either racemes subdigitate or lemma deeply cleft into 2 hyaline lobes:
    7   Racemes persistent; spikelets breaking up at maturity:
      8   Lemma exposed; one or both glumes shorter than florets, or if longer then divergent:
        9   Upper glume muticous or awned from near tip:
          10   Leaf-blades linear to filiform with midrib, not clearly distichous; glumes, or at least the lower, shorter than spikelet (except *Austrochloris, Schoenefeldia*):

11 Spikelets 2—several-flowered, or the lemma sinuously awned:
12   Grain trigonous to subterete; lemma laterally compressed:
13   Upper glume 1(—3)-nerved:
14   Lemma awnless or with a straight awn:
15   Raceme single   **404 Harpochloa**
15   Racemes digitate:
16   Callus of fertile floret inconspicuous, at most conical:
17   Upper glume acute to bidenticulate, awnless or rarely with a
                 very short awn; lemma nearly always long awned, usually
                 pallid (if lemma membranous and rhachilla terminating in a
                 tuft of awns see *348 Lophacme*)   **391 Chloris**
17   Upper glume obtuse to bilobed, distinctly awned; lemma
                 awnless or almost so, dark brown   **392 Eustachys**
16   Callus of fertile floret acicular, pungent   **393 Oxychloris**
14   Lemma produced into a long sinuous awn   **413 Schoenefeldia**
13   Upper glume 5—7-nerved   **395 Lepturopetium**
12   Grain and lemma dorsally compressed:
18   Fertile lemma 1-awned:
19   Upper glume 3-nerved   **394 Austrochloris**
19   Upper glume 1-nerved (if spikelet laterally compressed see *389
           Tetrapogon*)   **396 Enteropogon**
18   Fertile lemma with 3 deep lobes or awns:
20   Lemma awned but not lobed   **397 Trichloris**
20   Lemma with hyaline lateral lobes   **398 Afrotrichloris**
11 Spikelets 1-flowered:
21   Raceme single   *141 Libyella*
21   Racemes several:
22   Spikelets dorsally compressed:
23   Lemma thinly membranous   **399 Willkommia**
23   Lemma coriaceous   **400 Polevansia**
22   Spikelets laterally compressed:
24   Racemes digitate:
25   Lemmas nearly always awned; glumes acute to truncate, erose
                                                            408 Daknopholis
25   Lemmas awnless; glumes acute   **409 Cynodon**
24   Racemes scattered along a central axis (if lemma awned see *287
           Dichaetaria*)   **402 Schedonnardus**
10 Leaf-blades narrowly lanceolate, without midrib, distichous; glumes
     subequal, as long as spikelet   **403 Gymnopogon**
9   Upper glume with an oblique dorsal awn:
26   Fertile floret without sterile lemmas below it   **405 Kampochloa**
26   Fertile floret with 2 sterile lemmas below it   **406 Ctenium**
8   Lemma concealed; both glumes exceeding and closed around florets:
27   Spikelets subterete to dorsally compressed:
28   Raceme 1(—2); rhachis semiterete   **407 Microchloa**
28   Racemes several; rhachis flat   **401 Craspedorhachis**
27   Spikelets laterally compressed:
29   Racemes single or digitate:
30   Glumes thinner than lemma in texture   **410 Chrysochloa**
30   Glumes firmer than lemma in texture:
31   Glumes broad, not gaping; spikelets imbricate   **411 Brachyachne**

31 Glumes narrow, soon gaping; spikelets overlapping ½ their length
412 Lepturidium
29 Racemes borne upon an axis and crowded into a spiciform head (if
distant see *337 Leptochloa*) **414 Pogonochloa**
7 Racemes deciduous or spikelets falling entire:
32 Spikelets 2—several-flowered, or at least with a rhachilla extension:
33 Raceme single:
34 Raceme unilateral *116 Psilurus*
34 Raceme like a bottle-brush; lemma awned (if not see *439 Decaryella*)
367 Viguierella

33 Racemes many, scattered along an axis:
35 Glumes awn-like, hirsute **419 Melanocenchris**
35 Glumes not awn-like:
36 Glumes subequal, much exceeding floret, coriaceous, aristate
352 Dinebra

36 Glumes scarcely or not exceeding floret, membranous
418 Bouteloua
32 Spikelets 1-flowered, without rhachilla extension:
37 Racemes of 3 sessile spikelets, 1 ♀ and 2 ♂ or barren (if both laterals
pedicelled see *428 Aegopogon*) **431 Hilaria**
37 Racemes of single or paired spikelets, if more then with a definite
rhachis:
38 Upper glume 3—5-awned **425 Schaffnerella**
38 Upper glume with or without 1 awn:
39 Inflorescence of long unilateral persistent racemes **415 Spartina**
39 Inflorescence cylindrical, or of very short deciduous racemes:
40 Lower glume very small or suppressed:
41 Spikelets 2 or more on short racemelets:
42 Spikelets shed separately from raceme rhachis **432 Catalepis**
42 Spikelets falling in clusters:
43 Upper glume awned, the nerves forming scaberulous ribs
433 Monelytrum
43 Upper glume awnless, the nerves forming spinose ribs
434 Tragus
41 Spikelets borne singly on the central axis **435 Zoysia**
40 Lower glume well developed:
44 Inflorescence not unilateral:
45 Glumes not bristle-like:
46 Racemelets comprising 2—3 spikelets separated by short
rhachis internodes **436 Dignathia**
46 Racemelets comprising 1 spikelet, or a pair of spikelets side by
side:
47 Spikelets awnless:
48 Racemelets pedunculate:
49 Lower glume (one of them if spikelets paired) flat,
recurved, not clasping floret **437 Leptothrium**
49 Lower glume clasping floret, resembling a bird's head
438 Lopholepis

48 Racemelets sessile:
50 Spikelets paired **439 Pseudozoysia**
50 Spikelets single **442 Mosdenia**
47 Spikelets awned:

51   Glumes coriaceous, 5-nerved, subulately awned
                                    440 Decaryella
51   Glumes membranous, 1-nerved; flexuously awned
                                    441 Perotis
  45   Glumes bristle-like   **443 Tetrachaete**
  44   Inflorescence unilateral   **444 Farrago**
6   Fertile lemma 3-awned or with 3 triangular lobes, with or without short additional lobes; inflorescence of solitary or scattered racemes:
  52   Racemes persistent, the spikelets disarticulating above glumes:
    53   Inflorescence of 1—6 distant racemes   **416 Chondrosum**
    53   Inflorescence of numerous closely spaced racemes **417 Neobouteloua**
  52   Racemes deciduous or spikelets falling entire:
    54   Racemes of more than 3 spikelets, sometimes fewer but then not in dimorphic triads:
      55   Inflorescence bisexual; racemes deciduous:
        56   Lower glume narrowly lanceolate to ovate, sometimes with a glabrous setaceous tip (if lemma membranous see *428 Aegopogon bryophilus*)
                                    418 Bouteloua
      56   Lower glume filiform to acicular, hirsute:
        57   Raceme rhachis terminating in a cluster of rudimentary florets
                                    419 Melanocenchris
        57   Raceme rhachis prolonged as a forked bristle   **420 Pentarrhaphis**
    55   Inflorescences unisexual:
      58   Upper glume not indurated; female racemes ± elongated:
        59   Racemes deciduous:
          60   Awns of rudiment scaberulous:
            61   Upper glume 3—5-nerved   **421 Buchlomimus**
            61   Upper glume 1-nerved   **422 Cyclostachya**
          60   Awns of rudiment ciliate   **423 Pringleochloa**
        59   Raceme rhachis persistent, the spikelets deciduous   **424 Opizia**
      58   Upper glume indurated; female racemes much condensed, burr-like
                                    426 Buchloe
    54   Racemes reduced to triads of 1 ♀ and 2 ♂ spikelets:
      62   Inflorescence bisexual:
        63   Central spikelet 3-flowered:
          64   Upper lemma 3-awned   **427 Cathestecum**
          64   Upper lemma 5—9-awned   **428 Griffithsochloa**
        63   Central spikelet 1-flowered   **429 Aegopogon**
      62   Inflorescences unisexual   **430 Soderstromia**

a. POMMEREULLINAE Potztal in Willdenowia 5: 471 (1969). *Astreblinae* Clayton in Kew Bull. 37: 417 (1982).

Inflorescence of single or subdigitate unilateral racemes, these persistent. Spikelets alike, with 2—4 fertile florets, disarticulating above glumes; glumes shorter than or equalling florets; lemma rounded on back, 3-nerved at base but usually branching above, emarginate to 4-lobed, awned. Grain elliptic, dorsally compressed, the pericarp free.

An anomalous group of genera having more than 1 fertile floret per spikelet,

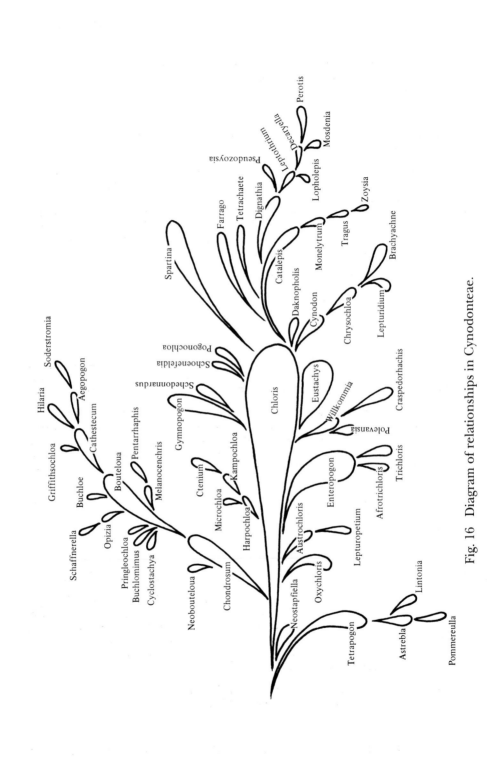

Fig. 16   Diagram of relationships in Cynodonteae.

and unusual branching lemma nervation. The tough rhachilla, as well as the shape and texture of their spikelets, ally them to *Tetrapogon* in Cynodonteae rather than to Eragrostideae.

386. Astrebla F. Muell. in Benth., Fl. Austral. 7: 602 (1878) — A. pectinata (Lindl.) F. Muell.

Perennial. Racemes single or rarely paired. Spikelets plump, laterally compressed to almost ovoid, with 2—4 fertile florets, followed by 0—5 progressively smaller sterile florets; glumes broad, scarious, the upper as long as lemmas and 7—16-nerved, the lower shorter, divergent, acuminate; lemmas coriaceous, silky villous, the body 3-nerved but sometimes with subsidiary nerves in the membranous lateral lobes, deeply 3-lobed, the central (and lateral in *A. squarrosa*) lobe with a stiff often reflexed awn.

Species 4. Australia. Dry grassland. All the species (Mitchell grasses) are of grazing value.
An isolated genus, with no obvious relatives in Eragrostideae, but some resemblance to *Tetrapogon*.

387. Lintonia Stapf in Hook. Ic. Pl. 30: t 2944 (1911) — L. nutans Stapf. *Negria* Chiov. in Ann. Bot. Roma 10: 410 (1912) non F. Muell. (1871) — N. melicoides Chiov. (= L. nutans). *Joannegria* Chiov. l.c. 11: 1 (1913) nom nov pro Negria.

Perennial. Racemes 2—several, digitate or on a short central axis. Spikelets ± ovoid, with 2—4 fertile florets followed by progressively smaller sterile florets; glumes membranous, 1—3-nerved, shorter than lemmas; lemmas membranous, pubescent at least on flanks, with 5—11 indurated nerves the laterals coalescent below, emarginate to bilobed, with a short subapical awn.

Species 2. Eastern Africa. Dry savanna.
An isolated genus whose lemmas, with their curious branching lateral nerves, seem to be derived from the 3-nerved state; in fact they recall the lobe nervation of *Astrebla*.

388. Pommereulla L.f., Nov. Gram. Gen.: 31 (1779) — P. cornucopiae L.f.

Stoloniferous perennial. Raceme single. Spikelets turbinate, with 1—2 empty lemmas followed by 2—3 fertile florets and a terminal rudiment, the floret cluster prolonged below into a pungent stipe; glumes membranous, the upper 3-nerved and as long as spikelet, the lower shorter; lemmas coriaceous, tomentose below, 7—9-nerved, 4-lobed these with mucronate or aristulate tips, the outer lobes much longer than inner, dorsally awned.

Species 1. Southern India and Sri Lanka. Open places.
An isolated genus related to *Astrebla* & *Lintonia*.

b. CHLORIDINAE Presl, Rel. Haenk. 1: 286 (1830). *Spartininae* Maire & Weiler,

Fl. Afr. Nord 2: 211 (1953) sine descr lat. *Cynodontinae* (Dum.) Tzvelev in Bot. Zh. 53: 311 (1968).

Inflorescence of single, digitate or sometimes scattered unilateral racemes, these persistent. Spikelets alike, of 1 fertile floret (except *Tetrapogon, Neostapfiella*) with or without additional sterile florets, disarticulating above glumes (except *Spartina*); glumes shorter than floret or exceeding and enclosing it; lemma keeled or rounded, entire or bilobed, with or without a central awn (3 lobes or awns in *Trichloris, Afrotrichloris,* some *Chloris*). Fruit a caryopsis or the pericarp free.

This is the basic pantropical stock of the tribe, most of it closely related to *Chloris* itself.

389. Tetrapogon Desf., Fl. Atlant. 2: 388 (1799) — T. villosus Desf. *Codonachne* Steud., Nom. Bot. ed. 2, 1: 393 (1840) nom nud — T. tenellus. *Lepidopironia* A. Rich., Tent. Fl. Abyss. 2: 442 (1851) — L. cenchriformis A. Rich. *Cryptochloris* Benth. in Hook. Ic. Pl. 14: t 1376 (1882) — C. spathacea Benth. (= T. cenchriformis).

Tufted annual or perennial. Racemes 1—3, digitate, dense, often hairy. Spikelets laterally compressed, cuneate, with 2—5 fertile florets (occasionally only 1 in *T. ferrugineus, T. villosus*), the rhachilla terminating in a clavate cluster of sterile lemmas; glumes broad, thinly membranous, the upper almost as long as spikelet the lower shorter, divergent, acuminate; lemmas rounded (keeled in *T. tenellus*), coriaceous, ciliate on nerves and keel, the nerves flanked by hyaline wings above, entire to bidentate, with a subapical awn. Grain elliptic, dorsally compressed (laterally compressed and trigonous in *T. tenellus*), the pericarp free.

Species 5. Africa, Middle East and India. In savanna, generally on poor soils.
Despite its several fertile florets *Tetrapogon* is obviously close to *Chloris*, perhaps providing a link between that genus and *Leptochloa* or *Bewsia*.

390. Neostapfiella A. Camus in Bull. Soc. Linn. Lyon 5: 4 (1926) & Not. Syst. 11: 189—192 (1943) — N. perrieri A. Camus.

Annual. Racemes 1—4, digitate. Spikelets laterally compressed, cuneate, with 2 fertile florets, both alike or the upper a little smaller (and occasionally ♂ or barren), the rhachilla not produced; glumes membranous, shorter than spikelet, acute; lemmas keeled, coriaceous, ciliate near margins, the nerves not flanked by wings, bidentate, with a long subapical awn; callus oblong (*N. chloridiantha*) to linear and pungent (*N. perrieri*). Caryopsis lanceolate, trigonous.

Species 3. Madagascar. In savanna.
Very similar to *Chloris*, particularly *C. filiformis* whose second floret is occasionally fertile.

391. Chloris Sw., Prod. Veg. Ind. Occ.: 25 (1788); Anderson in Brigham Young

Univ. Sci. Bull., Biol. Ser. 19(2): 1—133 (1974) — C. cruciata (L.) Sw. *Chlorostis* Raf., Princ. Fond. Somiol.: 26 (1814) nom superfl pro Chloris. *Actinochloris* Steud., Nom. Bot. ed. 2, 1: 352 (1840) & *Apogon* Steud. l.c. non Elliott (1822) & *Geopogon* Steud. l.c. 353 — in syn sub Chloris. *Phacellaria* Steud. l.c. 2: 343 (1841) nom nud non Benth. (1880) — C. submutica. *Agrostomia* Cerv. in Naturaleza 1: 345 (1870) — A. mutica Cerv. (= C. submutica). *Heterolepis* Boiss., Fl. Or. 5: 554 (1884) non Cassini (1820), in syn sub C. meccana (= C. virgata). *Chloris subgen Pterochloris* A. Camus in Bull. Soc. Bot. Fr. 97: 227 (1950) — C. humbertiana A. Camus. *Pterochloris* (A. Camus) A. Camus in Bull. Mus. Hist. Nat. sér. 2, 29: 349 (1957).

Annual or perennial; leaf-blades linear or rarely filiform, with midrib; sheaths not usually strongly compressed and keeled. Racemes digitate (very rarely single), occasionally in 2 or more whorls (digitate and bound together by interlocking hairs in *C. berroi*; densely crowded on an elongated axis in *C. paniculata, C. roxburghiana*), the spikelets pectinate or appressed (dangling at right angles to rhachis in *C. cruciata*). Spikelets laterally compressed, with 1 fertile floret, sometimes a smaller ♂ floret (this occasionally bisexual in a few spikelets of the inflorescence), the rhachilla terminating in 1 or more reduced lemmas; glumes narrow to broad and membranous, 1-nerved, shorter than floret, divergent, acute to acuminate, rarely bidenticulate and mucronate or with a short awn; fertile lemma keeled with a V-shaped section, cartilaginous to coriaceous (*C. robusta* membranous), mostly pallid to tawny rarely brown to black, often decoratively ciliate on margins, not or scarcely winged (except *C. humbertiana* which has a subsidiary nerve in the wing), entire or bilobed (awned lateral lobes in *C. lobata, C. pumilio*), conspicuously awned from tip or just below it (*C. amethystea, C. cucullata, C. flabellata, C. submutica* almost awnless); callus inconspicuous (conical in *C. amethystea*); sterile lemmas variable, but always with a recognizable body (this small in *C. radiata*). Grain ellipsoid and trigonous to lanceolate and subterete, the pericarp free though sometimes reluctantly.

Species ± 55. Tropical and warm temperate regions of both hemispheres. Habitat variable, but mainly in short grassland on the poorer soils and in disturbed places. *C. gayana* (Rhodes grass) is an important tropical forage species.

Several species clusters can be recognized, notably those centred upon *C. barbata, C. ciliata, C. radiata* and *C. verticillata*, but there are too many minor clusters and isolated species for formal subdivisions to be of much practical value. Indeed the genus is unusually rich in mildly aberrant peripheral species, most of which are mentioned in the description above.

392. Eustachys Desv. in Nouv. Bull. Sci. Soc. Philom. 2: 188 (1810) — E. petraea (Sw.) Desv. *Schultesia* Spreng., Pl. Pugill. 2: 17 (1815) nom superfl pro Eustachys. *Langsdorffia* Regel in Ind. Sem. Hort. Petrop.: 26 (1863) non Mart. (1818), in syn sub E. distichophylla. *Chloroides* Regel l.c. 28, in syn sub E. petraea.

Annual or perennial; leaf-blades usually obtuse, the sheaths strongly keeled. Racemes 2—many, digitate, the spikelets pectinate. Spikelets laterally compressed with 1 fertile floret, rarely a smaller ♂ floret, and a rhachilla terminating in a little clavate lemma; glumes membranous, shorter than floret, the upper obtuse to bilobed with a short subapical awn; fertile lemma keeled, cartilaginous to coriaceous, dark brown, acute to emarginate, awnless or with a very short subapical awn-point. Grain ellipsoid, trigonous, the pericarp reluctantly free.

Species 10. Tropics, principally New World. Savanna.

A close-knit group of species possessing a particular combination of characters, but otherwise barely separable from *Chloris*; *C. flabellata* is intermediate between the genera.

393. Oxychloris Lazarides in Nuytsia 5: 283 (1985) — O. scariosa (F. Muell.) Lazarides.

Perennial. Racemes digitate. Spikelets like *Chloris,* but fertile floret with winged lemma and long acicular callus; sterile florets enlarged, papery, 5—7-nerved.

Species 1. Australia. Dry savanna.

394. Austrochloris Lazarides in Austral. J. Bot., Suppl. 5: 33 (1972) — A. dichanthioides (Everist) Lazarides.

Perennial; leaf-blades linear, with midrib. Racemes 2—3, digitate, the rhachis triquetrous. Spikelets dorsally compressed, with 1 fertile floret and a cuneate sterile lemma; glumes narrow, much longer than floret, divergent, the upper deciduous, 3-nerved, acuminate; fertile lemma broadly rounded, subcoriaceous, acute, subapically awned. Grain elliptic, dorsally compressed, lenticular in section, the pericarp free.

Species 1. Australia (Queensland). Savanna.

Although dorsally compressed the lemma is unlike that of *Enteropogon,* and the genus probably has more in common with *Chloris.*

395. Lepturopetium Morat in Adansonia 20: 377 (1981) — L. kuniense Morat.

Perennial. Racemes 1—3, digitate, the spikelets broadside on and partly sunk in shallow hollows in the unilateral rhachis. Spikelets laterally compressed, with 1 fertile floret and a lanceolate sterile lemma; glumes narrow, divergent, the lower 1-nerved and $\frac{1}{2} - \frac{2}{3}$ the length of the floret, the upper 5—7-nerved and exceeding floret, acuminate; fertile lemma weakly keeled, cartilaginous, bidentate, awned. Grain unknown.

Species 1. New Caledonia and Eniwetok. Coastal hinterland.

Although seemingly related to *Austrochloris, Lepturopetium* closely imitates *Lepturus,* leaving some doubt as to its true affinities.

396. Enteropogon Nees in Lindley, Nat. Syst. ed. 2: 448 (1836); Clayton in Kew Bull. 21: 105—110 (1967) — E. melicoides (Rottl.) Nees (= E. monostachyos). *Macrostachya* A. Rich., Tent. Fl. Abyss. 2: 408 (1851) nom nud — E. macrostachyus. *Saugetia* Hitchc. & Chase in Contrib. U.S. Nat. Herb. 18: 378 (1917) — S. fasciculata Hitchc. & Chase.

Annual or perennial. Racemes single or subdigitate (sometimes with short central axis in *E. brandegei, E. chlorideus*). Spikelets dorsally compressed, with 1 fertile floret, sometimes a smaller ♂ floret, the rhachilla terminating in an awned rudiment (awnless in *E. fasciculatus*; cluster of rudiments in *E. longiaristatus, E. prieurii*); glumes subulate to lanceolate, membranous, the upper shorter than or equalling floret, divergent, acute to shortly awned; lemma broadly rounded to almost flat, with prominently raised midnerve, subcoriaceous, often scabrid, bidentate, awned; callus very short to linear. Grain narrowly elliptic, dorsally compressed, concavo-convex in section, the pericarp free.

Species 17. Tropics. Short grass savanna.
Often confused with *Chloris*, but sharply differentiated from that genus by the shape of lemma and grain. *E. chlorideus* has rhizanthogenes on underground rhizomes.

397. Trichloris Benth. in J. Linn. Soc. Bot. 19: 102 (1881) — T. pluriflora Fourn. *Chloridopsis* Hack. in Engl. & Prantl, Nat. Pfl.-Fam. 2, 2: 59 (1887) in syn sub T. blanchardiana (= T. crinita). *Chloropsis* Kuntze, Rev. Gen. Pl. 2: 771 (1891) nom superfl pro Trichloris. *Leptochloris* Kuntze l.c., in syn sub T. crinita.

Perennial. Racemes digitate. Spikelets and grain like *Enteropogon,* except the lemma tip branching into 3 awns.

Species 2. Tropical and subtropical South America. Dry plains and hillsides.
A derivative of *Enteropogon,* unrelated to 3-awned Boutelouinae.

398. Afrotrichloris Chiov. in Ann. Bot. Roma 13: 371 (1915) — A. martinii Chiov.

Perennial. Raceme single. Spikelets with 1 fertile floret and a cluster of sterile lemmas; glumes thinly membranous, 3—5-nerved, shorter than lemmas, divergent, acuminate; fertile lemma broadly rounded, thinly coriaceous below, pilose, cleft to beyond the middle into 2 hyaline acuminate or aristulate lobes, awned from sinus; sterile lemmas like the fertile but smaller. Grain elliptic, dorsally compressed, the pericarp free.

Species 2. Somalia. Dry savanna bushland.
Readily recognized by the elaborately lobed lemmas, and apparently related to *Enteropogon.*

399. Willkommia Hack. in Verh. Bot. Ver. Brand. 30: 145 (1888) non Nyman (1879 nom nud) — W. sarmentosa Hack. *Willbleibia* Herter in Rev. Sudamer. Bot. 10: 132 (1953) — W. texana (Hitchc.) Herter.

Annual or perennial. Racemes several on an elongated axis, bearing inclined spikelets on a flat rhachis. Spikelets dorsally compressed, the single floret with pungent callus (*W. texana* acute) and no rhachilla extension; glumes unequal, the upper deciduous, equalling and embracing spikelet, the lower ± ⅔ its length, both broadly rounded, membranous, obtuse to acute; lemma almost as long as upper glume, broadly rounded, thinly membranous, acute or obtuse, briefly awned (*W. texana* mucronate). Caryopsis ellipsoid.

Species 4. Southern tropical Africa and Texas; introduced to Argentina. Sandy savanna.
Note the unusual disjunct distribution.

400. Polevansia de Winter in Bothalia 9: 130 (1966) — P. rigida de Winter.

Perennial. Like *Willkommia* but callus of floret short, obtuse; lemma subcoriaceous, acute, awnless.

Species 1. Lesotho and South Africa. Old fields and rock outcrops.

401. Craspedorhachis Benth. in Hook. Ic. Pl. 14: t 1377 (1882) — C. africana Benth.

Perennial. Racemes several (rarely 1), digitate or along a central axis, bearing appressed spikelets on a flat rhachis. Spikelets dorsally compressed, the single floret with obscure callus and no rhachilla extension; glumes subequal, the lower keeled, the upper deciduous and broadly rounded, both firmly membranous, enclosing florets, acute; lemma $\frac{1}{3}$ — $\frac{1}{2}$ as long as glumes, hyaline, obtuse. Caryopsis obovoid.

Species 2. Southern tropical Africa. Sandy savanna.
An isolated genus. with similarities to both *Willkommia* and *Microchloa*.

402. Schedonnardus Steud., Syn. Pl. Glum. 1: 146 (1854) — S. texanus Steud. (= S. paniculatus). *Spirochloe* Lunell in Amer. Midl. Nat. 4: 220 (1915) nom superfl pro Schedonnardus; Pilger, Nat. Pfl.-Fam. ed. 2, 14d: 100 (1956) as "Sporichloe".

Perennial. Racemes several, on a central axis, stiff, bearing distant appressed spikelets on a triquetrous rhachis; central axis eventually elongating and coiling into a loose spiral, the inflorescence then shed as a whole. Spikelets laterally compressed, 1-flowered without rhachilla extension, disarticulating above glumes; glumes unequal, the upper as long as spikelet the lower shorter, slightly divergent, tapering to a stiff subulate point; lemma keeled, firmly membranous, acuminate; lodicules 0. Caryopsis fusiform.

Species 1. North America; introduced to Argentina. Prairie.
An isolated genus, perhaps related to *Gymnopogon*. Note the tumbleweed dispersal mode.

403. Gymnopogon P. Beauv., Ess. Agrost.: 41 (1812); Smith in Iowa State J. Sci. 45: 319—385 (1971) — G. racemosus P. Beauv. (= G. ambiguus). *Anthopogon* Nutt., Gen. N. Am. Pl. 1: 81 (1818) & *Alloiatheros* Elliott ex Raf. in Bull. Bot. Genève 1: 221 (1830); Elliott, Sketch Bot. 1: 145 (1821) nom prov — nom superfl pro

Gymnopogon. *Biatherium* Desv., Opusc.: 72 (1831) — B. foliosa (Willd.) Desv. *Sciadonardus* Steud. in Flora 33: 229 (1850) nom nud — G. ambiguus. *Monochaete* Doell in Mart., Fl. Bras. 2, 3: 78 (1878) — M. fastigiata (Nees) Doell. *Doellochloa* Kuntze, Rev. Gen. Pl. 2: 773 (1891) nom superfl pro Monochaete.

Annual or perennial; leaf-blades narrowly lanceolate, stiff, without midrib, acuminate, conspicuously distichous from imbricate keel-less sheaths. Racemes subdigitate or closely spaced on an axis scarcely longer than themselves, long, stiff, spreading or ascending, bearing distant appressed spikelets, sometimes naked at base. Spikelets laterally compressed, with 1 fertile floret, rarely a smaller sterile floret, and a rhachilla extension, this naked or supporting a floret reduced to little more than an awn (2—3 awns in *G. delicatulus*, *G. foliosus*); glumes narrow, 1-nerved, subequal, longer than floret, slightly divergent; fertile lemma lightly keeled, membranous, bidentate, subapically awned (*G. burchellii* awnless); callus usually short (*G. foliosus* linear). Caryopsis narrowly ellipsoid, dorsally compressed or terete.

Species ± 15. Southern USA and South America; 1 species India to Thailand. Open places or light woodland on dry sandy soils.
A homogeneous genus adjacent to *Chloris*, but distinguished by the distichous leaves, long glumes and obsolete terminal floret. The latter may be absent or represented by an awn, but seldom has a recognizable lemma body.

404. Harpochloa Kunth, Rév. Gram. 1: 92 (1829) — H. capensis Kunth (= H. falx).

Perennial. Inflorescence a single raceme bearing pectinate spikelets on a semiterete (crescentic in section) rhachis. Spikelets laterally compressed, with 1—3 ♂ or sterile florets above the fertile; glumes unequal, the upper deciduous as long as spikelet and rounded on back, the lower shorter and keeled, divergent, acute, awnless; lemma keeled, cartilaginous, bidenticulate, awnless. Caryopsis elliptic, trigonous.

Species 2. Central and southern Africa. Open grassland.

405. Kampochloa Clayton in Kew Bull. 21: 103 (1967) — K. brachyphylla Clayton.

Perennial. Raceme single. Spikelets with a dorsally awned ♂ or sterile floret above the fertile, the rhachilla terminating in a bunch of 1—4 long-awned vestigial lemmas; glumes and fertile lemma like *Ctenium*.

Species 1. Angola and Zambia. Rocky places.
Evidently related to *Ctenium*, but with no trace of sterile florets below the fertile.

406. Ctenium Panzer, Id. Rev. Gräser: 36, 59 (1813) nom conserv; Clayton in Kew Bull. 16: 471—476 (1963) — C. carolinianum Panzer (= C. aromaticum).

Campulosus Desv. in Nouv. Bull. Sci. Soc. Philom. 2: 189 (1810) nom rejic — C. gracilior Desv. (= C. aromaticum). *Campuloa* Desv. in J. Bot. Agric. 1813, 2: 69 (1813) nom superfl pro Campulosus. *Monocera* Elliott, Sketch Bot. 1: 176 (1816) —M. aromatica (Walt.) Elliott. *Triatherus* Raf. in Amer. Monthly Mag. 3: 99 (1818) non Triathera Desv. (1810) & *Monathera* Raf. l.c. 4: 190 (1819) & *Aplocera* Raf., Med. Fl. 2: 193 (1830) — nom superfl pro Monocera.

Annual or perennial; leaf-blades often aromatic. Racemes single or digitate, the spikelets borne pectinately on a semiterete (crescentic in section) rhachis. Spikelets laterally compressed, with two awned empty or rarely ♂ lemmas (the lowest vestigial in *C. sesquiflorum*) below the fertile floret, the rhachilla terminating in 1(—3) rudimentary florets (suppressed in *C. sesquiflorum*), these at most shortly awned; glumes narrow, the upper as long as spikelet the lower much shorter, divergent, entire or aristulate at tip, the upper obliquely awned from back; fertile lemma keeled, membranous, entire or bidentate with a terminal or subapical awn. Caryopsis ellipsoid.

Species ± 17. Africa, Madagascar and America. Savanna.
The sterile lemmas below the fertile and the dorsally awned upper glume are unusual features.

407. Microchloa R. Br., Prodr. Fl. Nov. Holl.: 208 (1810); Launert in Senck. Biol. 47: 291—301 (1966) — M. setacea R. Br. (= M. indica). *Micropogon* Pfeiffer, Nom. Bot. 2: 310 (1847) nom superfl pro Microchloa. *Rendlia* Chiov. in Ann. Bot. Roma 13: 53 (1914) — R. obtusifolia Chiov. (= M. altera?).

Annual or perennial. Raceme single (rarely 2), bearing inclined or pectinate spikelets on a semiterete (crescentic in section) rhachis. Spikelets subterete to subcylindrical, 1-flowered without rhachilla extension, or with a second well-developed ♂ floret; glumes subequal, both or only the upper deciduous, the lower keeled the upper rounded, firmly membranous to thinly coriaceous, enclosing florets, acute; lemma shorter than glumes, keeled, thinly membranous, acute to bilobed, sometimes mucronulate. Caryopsis ellipsoid.

Species ± 6. Throughout the tropics. Bare open places in savanna.
The distinctive rhachis shape links the genus to *Harpochloa* and *Ctenium*.

408. Daknopholis Clayton in Kew Bull. 21: 102 (1967) — D. boivinii (A. Camus) Clayton.

Stoloniferous annual. Racemes digitate. Spikelets strongly laterally compressed, 1-flowered plus minute rhachilla extension; glumes membranous, subequal, much shorter than floret, the upper acute to truncate, erose at tip; lemma keeled, cartilaginous, bidentate, awned or rarely awnless. Grain narrowly elliptic, laterally compressed, the pericarp free.

Species 1. East African coast, Madagascar, Indian Ocean islands. Open places near seashore.
An awkward intermediate, resembling both *Chloris* (especially *C. pycnothrix*) and *Cynodon*, but fitting comfortably in neither.

409. Cynodon Rich. in Pers., Syn. Pl. 1: 85 (1805) nom conserv; de Wet & Harlan in Taxon 19: 565—569 (1970) — C. dactylon (L.) Pers. *Capriola* Adans., Fam. Pl. 2: 31, 532 (1763) nom rejic — C. dactylon (L.) Kuntze. *Dactilon* Vill., Hist. Pl. Dauph. 2: 69 (1787) nom rejic; Asch., Fl. Brand. 1: 810 (1864) as "Dactylus" — D. officinale Vill. (= C. dactylon). *Fibichia* Koel., Descr. Gram.: 308 (1802) nom rejic — F. umbellata Koel. (= C. dactylon).

Perennial, mostly rhizomatous or stoloniferous and sward-forming. Racemes digitate, with flat or semiterete rhachis, sometimes in 2 or more closely spaced whorls. Spikelets strongly laterally compressed, 1-flowered, with or without a rhachilla extension (this very rarely bearing a tiny vestigial floret); glumes narrow, herbaceous, very short to as long as floret, divergent, acute; lemma keeled, firmly cartilaginous, entire, awnless. Caryopsis ellipsoid, laterally compressed.

Species ± 8. Old World tropics; 1 species pantropical and extending into warm temperate regions. Inhabited, grazed or weedy places. *C. dactylon* (Dhub, Bermuda or Star Grass) is the commonest tropical lawn grass, and sometimes features as a troublesome weed of arable land; *C. transvaalensis* is also occasionally used for lawns. Some of the taller Star grasses, notably *C. aethiopicus* and *C. plectostachyus*, are important forage species.

A complex genus of morphologically similar and genetically introgressing species at two ploidy levels, 2n = 18, 36 (Harlan, de Wet & Richardson in Amer. J. Bot. 56: 944—950, 1969). It is related to *Chloris*, with which it will hybridize.

410. Chrysochloa Swallen in Proc. Biol. Soc. Wash. 54: 44 (1941) nom nov pro seq. *Bracteola* Swallen in Amer. J. Bot. 20: 118 (1933) nom inval, coincident with technical term — B. lucida Swallen (= C. subaequigluma).

Annual or perennial. Racemes single or digitate, bearing imbricate appressed spikelets on a flat rhachis. Spikelets strongly laterally compressed, 2-flowered, acute; glumes subequal the upper deciduous, keeled, membranous, enclosing florets, acute to acuminate occasionally with a short subterminal awn; fertile lemma ± as long as glumes, keeled, coriaceous, mucronate or with a short subapical awn; upper floret well developed but ♂ or sterile and smaller than fertile. Caryopsis elliptic, trigonous.

Species 4. Tropical Africa. Seasonally waterlogged soils.

411. Brachyachne (Benth.) Stapf in Fl. Trop. Afr. 9: 20 (1917) & in Hook. Ic. Pl. 31: t 3099 (1922). *Cynodon sect Brachyachne* Benth. in Benth. & Hook., Gen. Pl. 3: 1164 (1883) — C. convergens F. Muell.

Annual or perennial. Racemes single or digitate, bearing imbricate appressed spikelets on a flat or triquetrous rhachis. Spikelets strongly laterally compressed, 1-flowered usually with a rhachilla extension (this rarely with a tiny vestigial floret), commonly golden brown and obtuse, not gaping; glumes broad, subequal, deciduous, both keeled (the upper with a narrow flat back in *B. ciliaris*, *B. prostrata*), thinly coriaceous (*B. tenella* membranous), enclosing floret, blunt;

lemma shorter than glumes, membranous, bilobed to acute, rarely with a short mucro. Caryopsis ellipsoid.

Species 9. Tropical Africa; Java to Australia. Rock pools and seasonally wet places.
The flat spikelets point to a derivation from *Cynodon*; but *B. ciliaris* and *B. prostrata* verge towards *Microchloa*, though easily distinguishable by their digitate racemes and flat rhachis.

412. Lepturidium Hitchc. & Ekman, Man. Grasses W. Ind.: 111 (1936) — L. insulare Hitchc. & Ekman.

Perennial. Raceme single, bearing appressed spikelets overlapping ± ½ their length on a triquetrous rhachis. Spikelets laterally compressed, 2-flowered, the upper sterile or represented only by a rhachilla extension, acute, at first closed but soon gaping; glumes narrow, subequal, the lower keeled the upper rounded, thinly coriaceous, enclosing florets, acute; lemma almost as long as glumes, thinly membranous, bidenticulate, mucronulate.

Species 1. Cuba. Salt flats.
A rare genus barely distinct from *Brachyachne*.

413. Schoenefeldia Kunth, Rév. Gram. 1: 86 (1829) — S. gracilis Kunth.

Annual or perennial. Racemes single or digitate. Spikelets laterally compressed, strictly 1-flowered or with a rhachilla extension terminating in a tiny long-awned rudimentary floret; glumes narrow, longer than floret, divergent, acuminate to shortly lawned; lemma keeled, cartilaginous, bidentate, with a long sinuous awn. Grain ellipsoid, laterally compressed, the pericarp free.

Species 2. Africa, Madagascar and India. Open places in savanna, especially hardpans and seasonally flooded flats.
A somewhat isolated genus related to *Chloris*, with delicately braided awns.

414. Pogonochloa C.E. Hubbard in Hook. Ic. Pl. 35: t 3421 (1940) — P. greenwayi C.E. Hubbard.

Perennial. Racemes very short, closely spaced on an elongated axis to form a spiciform head. Spikelets laterally compressed, 2—3-flowered, the second ♂ or sterile, the third reduced to an awn; glumes subequal, keeled, membranous, enclosing florets, shortly awned; lemma much shorter than glumes, membranous, with a long flexuous awn. Caryopsis fusiform.

Species 1. Zambia and Zimbabwe. Stream banks.
An isolated genus, perhaps related to *Schoenefeldia*.

415. Spartina Schreb., Gen. Pl. ed 8: 43 (1789); Mobberley in Iowa J. Sci. 30:

471—574 (1956) — S. cynosuroides (L.) Roth. *Trachynotia* Michaux, Fl. Bor. Am. 1: 63 (1803) & *Limnetis* Rich. in Pers., Syn. Pl. 1: 72 (1805) — nom superfl pro Spartina. *Ponceletia* Thouars, Fl. Trist. Acugn.: 36 (1811) non R. Br. (1810) — P. arundinacea Thouars. *Tristania* Poir., Encycl. Suppl. 4: 526 (1816) nom prov pro Ponceletia. *Psammophila* Schult. in Roem. & Schult., Syst. Veg. 1 Mant. 1: 231 (1822) nom nov pro Ponceletia. *Solenachne* Steud., Syn Pl. Glum. 1: 12 (1854) — S. phalaroides Steud. (= S. ciliata). *Chauvinia* Steud. l.c. 362 non Bory (1829) — C. chilensis Steud. (= S. densiflora).

Perennial. Racemes subdigitate or disposed along an axis, bearing appressed or pectinate spikelets on a triquetrous rhachis. Spikelets strongly laterally compressed, 1-flowered without rhachilla extension, falling entire; glumes unequal, the upper exceeding the floret the lower shorter, firmly membranous, acute to shortly awned; lemma keeled, firmly membranous, acute; lodicules often absent. Grain fusiform, the pericarp reluctantly free.

Species ± 15. Both coasts of the Americas, Atlantic coast of Europe and Africa, especially temperate and subtropical regions. Mainly intertidal mud flats, but some species extend to coastal dunes and inland freshwater swamps; S. *pectinata* ranges from salt marsh in eastern to dry prairie in central USA. Some species, especially S. *anglica,* are of value in stabilizing mud flats, but may also accelerate the silting of harbours.

The genus, whose species show little variation and are often difficult to distinguish, is remarkable for its adaptation to a marine habitat; note the salt-secreting hydathodes in the leaf epidermis (Levering & Thomson in Planta 97: 183—196, 1971).

It also contains a classical example of a species in the making. The American S. *alterniflora* (2n = 62) was introduced to Britain some time prior to 1829, probably in ship's ballast. It encountered the native S. *maritima* (2n = 60) and formed a sterile hybrid, S. × *townsendii* (2n = 62), first collected in 1870. By 1892 a fertile amphidiploid, S. *anglica* (2n = 124), had arisen, and the situation has since become further complicated by the emergence of back-crosses and poly-haploids. The final stage has been suppression of the parental species by competition, and they are now almost extinct in Britain.

Spartina lacks close relatives, but there is no compelling reason to detach it from Chloridinae.

c. **BOUTELOUINAE** Stapf in Fl. Trop. Afr. 9: 22 (1917).

Inflorescence of single or scattered unilateral racemes, these usually deciduous and sometimes condensed into a cluster. Spikelets alike or dimorphic, of 1 fertile floret usually with additional sterile florets, disarticulating above glumes or falling entire; glumes usually narrow, the upper ± as long as floret, the lower shorter; lemma usually ± rounded on back, the tip 3-awned or with 3 pointed lobes, sometimes with shorter additional lobes. Fruit a caryopsis, ± ellipsoid.

A New World offshoot from Chloridinae (note the similarity in facies between *Harpochloa* and *Chondrosum*) with a distinctive trilobed lemma. Digitate inflorescences are noticeably absent, and there are strong trends towards deciduous abbreviated racemes and dicliny. Many of its genera are very narrowly defined, but the alternative is an unreasonably broad circumscription of *Bouteloua.*

416. Chondrosum Desv. in Nouv. Bull. Sci. Soc. Philom. 2: 188 (1810) — C. procumbens (Dur.) Desv. (= C. simplex). *Actinochloa* Roem. & Schult., Syst. Veg. 2: 22, 417 (1817) nom superfl pro Chondrosum. *Antichloa* Steud., Nom. Bot. ed. 2, 1: 108 (1840) in syn sub Actinochloa. *Erucaria* Cerv. in Naturaleza 1: 347 (1870) non Gaertn. (1791) — E. glandulosa Cerv. (= C. hirsutum).

Annual or perennial. Racemes 1—6, disposed singly and about their own length apart along an axis, persistent, ending in a point or a spikelet, the latter often rudimentary, bearing numerous (20—100) densely and pectinately (appressed in *C. eriopodum, C. eriostachyum*) arranged spikelets. Spikelets laterally compressed, with 1—2 sterile florets, the second rudimentary; lemma keeled or sometimes rounded, membranous, usually pubescent, stiffly 3-awned, sometimes the central awn flanked by 2 teeth or short lobes, less often the laterals also flanked by a lobe; palea nerves sometimes excurrent; sterile floret usually subtended by a tuft of hair, the body of its lemma reduced and awns exaggerated, lobes if any obtuse.

Species 14. Canada to Argentina, but centred on south west USA and Mexico. Hill slopes and open plains. The genus contributes several valuable grazing species, such as *C. gracile* (Blue Grama), to the North American grasslands.
Chondrosum bears an outward resemblance to *Ctenium,* and is evidently related to Chloridinae. It is often included in *Bouteloua;* though closely related, and with some overlap of individual characters, the two genera seem distinct enough.

417. Neobouteloua Gould in Bol. Soc. Arg. Bot. 12: 106 (1968) — N. lophostachya (Griseb.) Gould.

Perennial. Racemes numerous, closely spaced on an elongated central axis, persistent, slender, the spikelets appressed to rhachis. Spikelets laterally compressed, with 1 fertile floret and a cluster of 2—4 rudiments; lemma keeled, membranous, 3-awned; rudimentary florets not subtended by a hair tuft, prominently 3-awned.

Species 1. Argentina and Chile. Dry plains and hillsides.
A segregate from *Chondrosum.*

418. Bouteloua Lag. in Varied. Ci. 2, 4: 134 (1805) as 'Botelua', emend Lag., Gen. Sp. Nov.: 5 (1805) nom conserv; Gould in Ann. Miss. Bot. Gard. 66: 348—416 (1979) — B. racemosa Lag. (= B. curtipendula). *Atheropogon* Willd., Sp. Pl. 4: 937 (1806) — A. apludoides Willd. (= B. curtipendula). *Heterosteca* Desv. in Nouv. Bull. Sci. Soc. Philom. 2: 188 (1810) — H. juncifolia Desv. (= B. repens). *Triathera* Desv. l.c. — T. americana (L.) Desv. *Polyodon* Kunth in Humb. & Bonpl., Nov. Gen. Sp. 1: 174 (1816) — P. distichus Kunth. *Triaena* Kunth l.c.: 178 — T. racemosa Kunth (= B. triaena). *Eutriana* Trin., Fund. Agrost.: 161 (1822) — E. curtipendula (Michaux) Trin. *Eutriana sect Aristidium* Endl., Gen. Pl.: 94 (1836) — E. aristoides

(Kunth) Trin. *Eutriana sect Triplathera* Endl. l.c. — E. multiseta Nees (= B. megapotamica). *Pleiodon* Reichenb., Nom. Gen. Pl.: 38 (1841) nom superfl pro Polyodon. *Nestlera* Steud., Nom. Bot. ed. 2, 2: 192 (1841) nom nud non Spreng. (1818) — B. repens. *Aristidium* (Endl.) Lindley, Veg. King.: 116 (1846). *Triplathera* (Endl.) Lindley l.c.

Annual or perennial. Racemes 7—80, disposed singly along an axis, short, deciduous, ending in a straight or forked point, bearing 1—10(—20) appressed spikelets (pectinate in *B. chondrosioides*), sometimes the lowermost spikelets ± reduced (especially *B. media, B. reflexa*). Spikelets subterete, usually with a sterile floret above the fertile (2—3 in *B. megapotamica*) rarely this reduced to a rhachilla extension; lower glume narrowly lanceolate to ovate, membranous, glabrous or rarely pubescent, acute to acuminate sometimes with a glabrous setaceous tip (bidentate and shortly awned in *B. rigidiseta* and allies); lemma thinly coriaceous, glabrous or rarely sparsely pubescent, acute or more often the nerves produced into 3 short awns, sometimes the central awn flanked by 2 teeth; palea nerves sometimes excurrent; sterile floret variable even within a species, not subtended by hairs (except *B. williamsii*), occasionally resembling fertile floret but more often the body reduced and awns exaggerated, lobes if any pointed.

Species 24. Canada to Argentina, but centred on Mexico. Hill slopes and open plains. An important genus of forage grasses, the best known being *B. curtipendula* (Side-oats Grama).

419. Melanocenchris Nees in Proc. Linn. Soc. 1: 94 (1841); Nair & Nayar in Bull. Bot. Surv. India 16: 141—144 (1974) — M. royleana Nees (= M. jacquemontii). *Roylea* Steud., Nom. Bot. ed. 2, 2: 475 (1841) nom nud non Benth (1829) — M. jacquemontii. *Ptiloneilema* Steud., Syn. Pl. Glum. 1: 201 (1854); Hook.f., Fl. Brit. India 7: 284 (1897) as "Ptilonema" — P. plumosum Steud. (= M. abyssinica). *Gracilea* Hook.f., Fl. Brit. India 7: 283 (1897) — G. nutans Hook.f. (= M. monoica).

Annual or perennial. Racemes disposed along an axis, short, cuneate, deciduous, ending in a forked bristle, generally with 1—2 fertile and 2—3 progressively smaller sterile spikelets. Fertile spikelets dorsally compressed, 2-flowered, the upper ♂ or sterile, with rhachilla extension; glumes side by side, hirsute, the lower awn-like (sometimes missing from upper spikelets of a raceme), the upper similar but with a narrowly expanded base; lemma chartaceous, shortly 3-awned (lower lemma of *M. monoica* entire); palea 2-awned.

Species 3. Chad to India and Sri Lanka. Dry plains and hillsides.
Melanocenchris seemingly has no Old World relatives, and must be attached to the otherwise New World Boutelouinae.

420. Pentarrhaphis Kunth in Humb. & Bonpl., Nov. Gen. Sp. 1: 177 (1816) — P. scabra Kunth. *Polyschistis* Presl, Rel. Haenk. 1: 294 (1830) — P. paupercula Presl (= P. scabra). *Strombodurus* Steud., Nom. Bot. ed. 2, 2: 299 (1841) in syn sub P. scabra.

Annual or perennial. Racemes disposed along an axis, short, cuneate, deciduous, ending in a forked bristle, bearing 2 spikelets, one of these aborted and represented by 2 hirsute awn-like glumes (both spikelets well developed in *P. polymorpha*). Spikelets dorsally compressed, 2-flowered, the upper ♂ or sterile; lower glume a hirsute bristle, upper glume acicular to lanceolate; lemma cartilaginous, 3-awned, the central awn flanked by 2 teeth; palea nerves sometimes excurrent.

Species 3. Mexico to Colombia. Dry scrubland.

The species with a bunch of 5 bristles (2 glumes from the aborted spikelet, 1 from the fertile, and a forked rhachis prolongation) at the base of a single spikelet are distinct enough. Unfortunately the commonest species, *P. polymorpha*, has both spikelets well developed and is halfway to *Bouteloua*.

421. Buchlomimus J & C Reeder & Rzedowski in Brittonia 17: 29 (1965) — B. nervatus (Swallen) J & C Reeder & Rzedowski.

Stoloniferous perennial; dioecious; ligule a line of hairs. Female inflorescence of (1—)2—3 straight or curved deciduous pectinate racemes disposed along an axis, exserted from leaf-sheath but lying prostrate on the ground. Female spikelets dorsally compressed, of 1 fertile floret and a cluster of three 3-awned rudiments; glumes narrow, membranous, the lower short, the upper as long as spikelet and prominently 3—5-nerved; lemma cartilaginous, tapering to a shortly 3-awned tip; rudiments with body much reduced, the awns long and glabrous. Male inflorescence like female, but erect and racemes persistent. Male spikelets 1-flowered with or without a rudiment; glumes as long as floret, usually 1-nerved; lemma with 3 awn points.

Species 1. Mexico. Dry slopes.

The spikelets of *Buchlomimus* resemble those of *Cyclostachya*, and its unusual linear microhairs are matched by *Pringleochloa*. These three rare Mexican grasses are evidently closely related, and might almost be included in the same genus. They are more distantly related to *Opizia* and *Buchloe*. The *Chondrosum*-like ♂ inflorescences of all 5 genera are remarkably similar, and seem to have been undisturbed by the evolutionary pressures which have shaped the female plants.

422. Cyclostachya J & C Reeder in Bull. Torr. Bot. Cl. 90: 195 (1963) — C. stolonifera (Scribn.) J & C Reeder.

Stoloniferous perennial; dioecious; ligule membranous, not ciliate. Inflorescence of both sexes a single pectinate raceme, shortly exserted from sheath, curling into a circle and deciduous as a whole at maturity. Female spikelets dorsally compressed, of 1 fertile floret and a cluster of 2—3 three-awned rudiments; glumes narrow, 1-nerved, as long as floret, acuminate-aristate; lemma cartilaginous, tapering to a 3-awned tip; palea nerves excurrent; rudiments with body much reduced, the awns long and glabrous. Male spikelets with 1 ♂ floret and a shortly 3-awned rudiment; lemma with 3 awn-points.

Species 1. Mexico. Dry open places.

The Reeders (l.c.) observe that the exserted ♀ inflorescence and deciduous ♂ inflorescence are imperfect adaptations to dicliny, suggesting that it may be of recent origin in this genus.

423. Pringleochloa Scribn. in Bot. Gaz. 21: 137 (1896) — P. stolonifera Scribn.

Stoloniferous perennial; monoecious or dioecious; ligule a line of hairs. Female inflorescence a head of 3—5 short deciduous racemes, these contiguous upon a short common axis, the whole partially enclosed by upper leaf-sheaths. Female spikelets dorsally compressed, of 1 fertile floret and a cluster of 2—3 many-awned rudiments; glumes as long as floret, pubescent, the lower subulate, the upper 1—3-nerved; lemma cartilaginous, the tip with a large mucronate central lobe and 2 short stiff lateral awns; rudiments represented by a fan-like spread of ciliate awns. Male inflorescence of 3—6 pectinate racemes distant upon a common axis, long exserted. Male spikelets like *Buchlomimus*, but strictly 1-flowered.

Species 1. Mexico. Dry calcareous plains.

424. Opizia Presl, Rel. Haenk. 1: 293 (1830) — O. stolonifera Presl. *Casiostega* Galeotti in Bull. Acad. Brux. 9: 232 (1842) nom nud — O. stolonifera.

Stoloniferous sward-forming perennial; monoecious or dioecious; ligule membranous, not ciliate. Female inflorescence of 1(—2) straight racemes partially enclosed by uppermost leaf-sheath. Female spikelets falling entire, laterally compressed, of 1 fertile floret and a prominently 3-awned rudiment; lower glume minute or suppressed; upper glume narrow, membranous, shorter than floret; lemma keeled, coriaceous, bearing 3 long awns between 4 short hyaline teeth; palea keels broadly winged above, adnate to rhachilla below. Male inflorescence long exserted, of 1—3 pectinate racemes. Male spikelets 1-flowered; lemma entire.

Species 1. Mexico and West Indies, but probably introduced to the latter. Shallow soils on dry hillsides.

425. Schaffnerella Nash, N. Amer. Fl. 17: 141 (1912) nom nov pro seq. *Schaffnera* Benth. in Hook. Ic. Pl. 14: t 1378 (1882) non Schaffneria Moore (1857) — S. gracilis Benth.

Annual; ligule membranous, not ciliate. Raceme single, very short, bearing 1—3 appressed spikelets; 1 to several such racemes, each subtended by a hyaline bract, aggregated into a fascicle partly enclosed by a spathiform leaf-sheath, the fascicles both terminal and lateral on the culm. Spikelets falling entire, laterally compressed, 1-flowered without rhachilla extension; lower glume suppressed; upper glume broad, chartaceous, shorter than floret, 7—9-nerved, bilobed, 3—5-awned; lemma keeled, membranous, bilobed or entire, subapically awned; palea wingless.

Species 1. Mexico. Hillsides.

An isolated genus apparently related to *Opizia*, but with well developed compound inflorescence.

426. Buchloe Engelm. in Trans. Acad. Sci. St. Louis 1: 432 (1859) nom conserv —B. dactyloides (Nutt.) Engelm. *Calanthera* Hook. in Hook. J. Bot. 8: 18 (1856) nom nud — B. dactyloides. *Lasiostega* Benth., Pl. Hartw.: 347 (1857) nom nud —B. dactyloides. *Bulbilis* Raf. ex Kuntze, Rev. Gen. Pl. 2: 763 (1891) nom superfl pro Buchloe.

Stoloniferous sward-forming perennial; monoecious or dioecious. Female inflorescence of usually 2 modified racemes embraced by inflated upper leaf-sheath, the raceme rhachis so shortened that its 3—5 spikelets form a globular burr, this deciduous. Female spikelet dorsally compressed, 1-flowered; lower (inner) glume reduced or suppressed; upper glume strongly indurated, forming an involucre on the outside of the burr, the margins inflexed and enclosing the floret, the tip with 3—5 rigid acuminate lobes; lemma subcoriaceous, shortly trifid. Male inflorescence long exserted, of 1—4 distant pectinate racemes. Male spikelet with 2 ♂ florets; lemma entire.

Species 1. USA and Mexico. Dry plains. *B. dactyloides* (Buffalo grass) is one of the most important grazing species of the Great Plains.

427. Cathestecum Presl, Rel. Haenk. 1: 294 (1830); Swallen in J. Wash. Acad. Sci. 27: 495—501 (1937) — C. prostratum Presl.

Annual or perennial, decumbent or stoloniferous. Racemes cuneate, deciduous, disposed along a central axis, each raceme bearing a triad of dimorphous spikelets, the rhachis sometimes prolonged as a bristle. Central spikelet shortly stipitate, 3-flowered, the lower floret ♀, the others ♂ or barren, with a rhachilla extension (the florets all ♂ in some inflorescences of *C. brevifolium, C. erectum*); lower glume a tiny flabellate scale, the upper well developed; lemmas firmly cartilaginous, 3-awned, the lower 2-lobed but the upper more deeply cleft and usually 4-lobed; palea nerves often excurrent. Lateral spikelets sessile, 2-flowered, both ♂ or barren (the lower ♀ in *C. varia*), with or without a rhachilla extension; lower glume often well developed, otherwise like central spikelet.

Species 5. Southern USA to Guatemala. Dry hills in open scrub.
Triads in *Cathestecum* and its allies follow a general pattern of fertile central and sterile lateral spikelets, but sexuality is subject to a certain amount of sporadic variation.

428. Griffithsochloa Pierce in Bull. Torr. Bot. Cl. 105: 134 (1978) — G. multifida (Griffiths) Pierce.

Perennial, caespitose. Inflorescence like *Cathestecum*. Central spikelet shortly stipitate, 3-flowered, the lower floret ♀, the second ♂, the upper reduced to a bunch of 5—9 awns; glumes well developed, linear; lemmas firmly cartilaginous, the lower 3-lobed, the second deeply cleft into 5—7 awned lobes. Lateral spikelets sessile, 2-flowered, both ♂ or barren, with or without a rhachilla extension; otherwise similar to central spikelet.

Species 1. Mexico. Dry open scrub.

429. Aegopogon Willd., Sp. Pl. 4: 899 (1806); Beetle in Univ. Wyoming Publ. 13: 17—23 (1948) — A. cenchroides Willd. *Hymenothecium* Lag., Gen. Sp. Nov.: 4 (1816) — H. tenellum Lag. *Atherophora* Steud., Nom. Bot. ed. 2, 1: 167 (1840) nom nud — A. tenellus. *Schellingia* Steud. in Flora 33: 231 (1850) — S. tenera Steud. (= A. tenellus).

Annual. Inflorescence like *Cathestecum* but markedly secund. Central spikelet sessile or pedicelled, 1-flowered, fertile, without rhachilla extension; glumes cuneate, shorter than floret, 1-nerved, truncate to bilobed, awned from midnerve and sometimes also from lateral lobes; lemma membranous, 3-awned, with a narrow tooth outside each lateral awn (spikelets awnless in *A. tenellus var abortivus*); palea 2-awned. Lateral spikelets pedicelled, 1-flowered, ♂ or barren (rarely fertile), very variable from almost as large as central to rudimentary (sometimes 1 of them suppressed in *A. bryophilus*).

Species 3. Southern USA to Peru. Dry open places.

430. Soderstromia Morton in Leafl. W. Bot. 10: 327 (1966) nom nov pro seq. *Fourniera* Scribn. in U.S. Dept. Agric. Div. Agrost. Bull. 4: 7 (1897) non Fourn. (1873) — F. mexicana Scribn.

Perennial, stoloniferous; monoecious or dioecious. Female inflorescence exserted, of numerous deciduous racemes on a central axis, each raceme bearing a triad of dimorphous spikelets. Central spikelet of 1 ♀ floret and a 3-awned rudiment; lower glume absent, the upper cuneate, 1-nerved, truncate; lemma stipitate, cartilaginous, the tip with a triangular central lobe and 2 short stiff lateral awns; lateral spikelets each reduced to a cuneate 3—5-nerved glume. Male inflorescence like the ♀. Central spikelet of 2 ♂ florets; lower glume absent, the upper ovate and ½ as long as floret; lower lemma entire, the upper tridentate; lateral spikelets each reduced to a tiny ovate glume.

Species 1. Mexico to Honduras. Short grassland.

431. Hilaria Kunth in Humb. & Bonpl., Nov. Gen. Sp. 1: 116 (1816); Sohns in J. Wash. Acad. Sci. 46: 311—321 (1956) — H. cenchroides Kunth. *Pleuraphis* Torrey in Ann. Lyceum Nat. Hist. New York 1: 148 (1824) — P. jamesii Torrey. *Hexarrhena* Presl, Rel. Haenk. 1: 326 (1830) — H. cenchroides Presl. *Symbasiandra* Steud., Nom. Bot. ed. 2, 1: 767 (1840) in syn sub H. cenchroides. *Schleropelta* Buckley, Prelim. Rep. Geol. Agr. Survey Texas app.: 1 (1866) — S. stolonifera Buckley (= H. belangeri).

Perennial. Inflorescence spike-like, composed of deciduous racemes appressed to a central axis, each raceme bearing a triad of dimorphous spikelets. Central spikelet subsessile, laterally compressed and almost hidden by the laterals, with 1 ♀ or bisexual floret, rarely a second ♂ or empty floret; glumes shorter than floret, narrow, deeply cleft into 2 or more lobes, these often slender and awned, the awns sometimes dorsal; lemma membranous, sometimes tapering upwards into a long neck, 2-lobed awned or not. Lateral spikelets sessile, dorsally compressed, 1—5-flowered, ♂ or empty; glumes almost as long as spikelet, flabellate, chartaceous, or coriaceous and then connate below, 3—7-nerved, strongly asymmetric, the tip acute or variously lobed usually with 1 or more awns; lemmas membranous, bilobed.

Species 9. Southern USA to Guatemala. Dry plains.

The spikelet scales can be confusing due to the extreme asymmetry and variability of the large involucral glumes. Species having these free at the base are often treated as subgenus *Pleuraphis*. The genus is rather isolated but, despite the bilobed lemma, its spikelet triads strongly suggest a link with the *Cathestecum* group of genera.

d. ZOYSIINAE Benth., Fl. Austral. 7: 453 (1878); Clayton & Richardson in Kew Bull. 28: 37—48 (1973).

Inflorescence spiciform, ± cylindrical (except *Farrago*), of numerous deciduous racemelets disposed along a central axis, the racemelets very short and sometimes reduced to a single spikelet. Spikelets alike or the upper reduced, 1-flowered without rhachilla extension, falling entire; glumes often much modified and oddly shaped; lemma usually rounded, membranous to hyaline (except *Tetrachaete*), entire; lodicules often much reduced. Fruit a caryopsis (pericarp reluctantly free in *Catalepis*).

Zoysiinae marks the culmination of several cynodontoid trends. The racemes are deciduous, and so reduced that the inflorescence as a whole imitates a raceme; or becomes a raceme, though this condition can be interpreted as the reduction of each racemelet to a single spikelet on a pedicel-like rhachis. The spikelets are also much modified, being 1-flowered with insignificant lemma and large, often bizarre, protective glumes.

These characters, particularly the unusual bottle-brush inflorescence, impart a certain unity to this assortment of Old World curios. It is distinct from Chloridinae, though *Catalepis* hints at a possible derivation from there, and is excluded from Boutelouinae by the entire lemma. Parallel reductions occur in Boutelouinae, but these are difficult to disentangle from the rest of the subtribe; their existence however undermines the traditional status of Zoysiinae as a full tribe.

432. Catalepis Stapf & Stent in Kew Bull. 1929: 11 (1929) — C. gracilis Stapf & Stent.

Perennial. Inflorescence a spiciform head of numerous short racemes (1—9 spikelets) closely spaced on an elongated axis, the triquetrous raceme rhachis deciduous when or soon after spikelets fall. Spikelets separately deciduous; lower glume reduced to a subulate rudiment; upper glume as long as or longer than floret, laterally compressed, narrow, membranous, acuminate; lemma keeled, acute.

Species 1. South Africa. Stony hillsides and disturbed places.
The clearly racemose inflorescence suggests a link with Chloridinae.

433. Monelytrum Hack. in Verh. Bot. Ver. Brand. 30: 140 (1888); Schweick. in Blumea, Suppl. 3: 71—82 (1946) — M. luederitzianum Hack.

Perennial. Inflorescence a cylindrical false raceme; racemelets shortly pedunculate, of 2—4 fertile and 1—3 awn-like rudimentary spikelets on a short plumose rhachis. Spikelets: lower glume a little hyaline scale; upper glume not much longer than floret, dorsally compressed, subcoriaceous, the nerves forming 5—7 low scaberulous ridges, tapering to a long slightly recurved awn; lemma briefly awned.

Species 1. SW Africa. Stony soils and edge of pans.

434. Tragus Haller, Hist. Stirp. Helv. 2: 203 (1768) nom conserv; Anton in Kew Bull. 36: 55—61 (1981) — T. racemosus (L.) All. *Nazia* Adans, Fam. Fl. 2: 31, 581 (1763) nom rejic — N. racemosa (L.) Kuntze. *Lappago* Schreb., Gen. Pl. ed. 8: 55 (1789) nom superfl pro Tragus. *Echinanthus* Cerv. in Naturaleza 1: 351 (1870) —unnamed species (= T. berteronianus).

Annual or perennial. Inflorescence a cylindrical false raceme; racemelets shortly pedunculate (long in *T. pedunculatus*), of 2—5 spikelets, these contiguous or on a short rhachis, sometimes the upper reduced. Spikelets: lower glume a tiny scale or suppressed; upper glume scarcely exceeding floret, rounded, its 5—7 nerves forming prominent ribs bearing stout hooked prickles, acute to acuminate; lemma acute.

Species 7. Throughout tropics. Weedy places.

435. Zoysia Willd. in Ges. Nat. Freunde Berlin Neue Schr. 3: 440 (1801) nom conserv; Pers., Syn. Pl. 1: 73 (1805) as "Zoydia" — Z. pungens Willd. (= Z. matrella). *Matrella* Pers. l.c. — M. juncea Pers. (= Z. matrella). *Brousemichea* Bal. in J. Bot. Paris 4: 163 (1890) — B. seslerioides Bal. *Osterdamia* Necker ex Kuntze, Rev. Gen. Pl. 2: 781 (1891) nom superfl pro Zoysia.

Mat-forming perennial. Inflorescence a cylindrical raceme (reduced to a single spikelet in Z. *minima*) of deciduous spikelets on persistent pedicels. Spikelets: lower glume 0: upper glume enclosing floret, laterally compressed, rounded on back, coriaceous (Z. *seslerioides* chartaceous), smooth, acute or with a short awn-point; lemma 1—3-nerved, acute to emarginate.

Species ± 10. Tropical and subtropical Asia and Australasia. Coastal sands extending to grazed or trodden places inland. Several species have been widely introduced for lawns in the tropics.
Note the peculiar inflorescence of Z. *minima*, with a single spikelet perched at the tip of the culm.

436. Dignathia Stapf in Hook. Ic. Pl. 30: t 2950 (1911) — D. gracilis Stapf.

Annual or perennial. Inflorescence a cylindrical false raceme; racemelets pedunculate, of 1—2 spikelets and a rudiment separated by the internodes of a short curvaceous rhachis. Spikelets: glumes longer than floret, laterally compressed, thickly indurated, ± gibbous, scaberulous to lanose, the upper larger and caudate to a stiff point or awn; lemma keeled, briefly awned.

Species 5. East Africa to NW India (Cutch). Dry bushland.

437. Leptothrium Kunth, Rév. Gram. 1: 156 (1829) — L. rigidum Kunth. *Latipes* Kunth l.c. 53 — L. senegalensis Kunth.

Perennial. Inflorescence an open false raceme; racemelets of (1—)2 spikelets side by side on the truncate top of a cuneate rhachis. Spikelets: glumes longer than floret, indurated, smooth or muricate-spinulose, the lower modified into a long flat recurved acuminate tail (less so in second spikelet of pair) the upper laterally compressed and enfolding floret (very rarely resembling the lower); lemma 1-nerved, acute.

Species 2. Senegal to Pakistan; Caribbean. Dry bushland.

438. Lopholepis Decaisne in Arch. Mus. Hist. Nat. 1: 147 (1839) nom nov pro seq. *Holboellia* Hook. in Bot. Misc. 2: 144 (1831) non Wall. (1824) — H. ornithocephala Hook.

Annual. Inflorescence a cylindrical false raceme; racemelets of 1 spikelet on a cuneate rhachis. Spikelets: glumes enclosing floret, laterally compressed, thinly coriaceous with prominent ciliate fringe, acute to acuminate, the upper larger and obliquely constricted into a comical resemblance of a bird's head; lemma nerveless, acute.

Species 1. Southern India and Sri Lanka. Disturbed places on dry sandy soil. This is one of the oddest shaped spikelets in the Gramineae.

439. Pseudozoysia Chiov., Pl. Nov. Min. Not. Aeth.: 20 (1928) — P. sessilis Chiov.

Perennial. Inflorescence a cylindrical false raceme embraced below by inflated leaf-sheath; racemelets of 2 sessile contiguous spikelets. Spikelets: glumes longer than floret, thickly indurated, shallowly tuberculate, acute, the lower ovate, the upper subglobose and enclosing floret; lemma obtuse.

Species 1. Somali Republic. Coastal dunes.

440. Decaryella A. Camus in Bull. Soc. Bot. Fr. 78: 177 (1931) — D. madagascariensis A. Camus.

Annual. Inflorescence an open raceme, each spikelet borne upon a long pungent pedicel and falling with it. Spikelets sometimes with 2 fertile florets; glumes subequal, longer than floret, slightly laterally compressed, coriaceous, 5-nerved, smooth, tapering to a stiff awn; lemma 1—3-nerved, obtuse or acute.

Species 1. Madagascar. Dry bushland.

441. Perotis Ait., Hort Kew. 1: 85 (1789) — P. latifolia Ait. (= P. indica). *Xystidium* Trin., Fund. Agrost.: 102 (1822) — X. maritimum Trin. (= P. hordeiformis).

Annual or perennial. Inflorescence a cylindrical raceme, the spikelets borne on a short pedicel and falling with it (*P. patens* sessile). Spikelets: glumes subequal, longer than floret, rounded, membranous, scaberulous, long awned; lemma 1-nerved, acute.

Species ± 10. Old World tropics. Weedy places.

442. Mosdenia Stent in Bothalia 1: 170 (1923) — M. waterbergensis Stent (= M. leptostachys).

Perennial. Like *Perotis* but spikelets sessile and glumes firmly membranous, smooth, awnless.

Species 1. South Africa. Dry bushland.

443. Tetrachaete Chiov. in Ann. Ist. Bot. Roma 8: 28 (1902) — T. elionuroides Chiov.

Annual. Inflorescence a spiciform false raceme embraced by inflated leaf-sheath; racemelets of 2 sessile contiguous spikelets. Spikelets: glumes much longer than floret, bristle-like, involucral, plumose; lemma ovate, strongly keeled, gibbous, coriaceous, 3-nerved, long awned.

Species 1. Ethiopia to Tanzania; Arabia. Dry stony places.
Tetrachaete has no obvious relatives in Zoysiinae. It bears a striking resemblance to *Melanocenchris*, but the lemma shape lends no support to a close relationship.

444. Farrago Clayton in Kew Bull. 21: 125 (1967) — F. racemosa Clayton.

Annual. Inflorescence a unilateral false raceme; racemelets of 1 fertile and 2 vestigial spikelets, the latter each represented by an awn slightly widened at its base, one of them upon a pedicel-like rhachis. Spikelets: glumes much longer than floret, dorsally compressed, membranous, the lower asymmetrical and long awned, the upper symmetrical and shortly awned; lemma a tiny hyaline nerveless truncate scale.

Species 1. Tanzania. Crevices in rock outcrops.
An odd little genus with surprisingly complex racemelets; somewhat aberrant in Zoysiinae, but even more so elsewhere.

VI. SUBFAMILY PANICOIDEAE

A. Br. in Ascherson, Fl. Prov. Brand. 1: 799 (1864). *Andropogonoideae* Rouy, Fl. France 14: 15 (1913).

Herbs, usually with linear leaf-blades. Frequent external characters: panicle, racemes or compound inflorescence, the spikelets single or paired; 2-flowered dorsally compressed spikelets falling entire, the florets dimorphic and rhachilla reduced to a callus; glumes or upper lemma indurated.

Lodicules 2, cuneate, fleshy, truncate; stamens 3, rarely fewer; stigmas 2, rarely 1 (*Neurachne* 3). Caryopsis with large embryo commonly ⅓—½ its length, usually with round or oval hilum; embryo panicoid P-PP.

Chlorenchyma radiate or not; bundle sheaths single or double; microhairs slender or stout; stomatal subsidiary cells triangular or domed; epidermal cells rarely papillate; midrib simple or occasionally complex; fusoid cells present in *Homolepis* & *Streptostachys*. Anatomy mixed, including non-kranz, kranz MS and kranz PS types.

The special feature of the subfamily is its 2-flowered spikelet with the lower floret ♂ or barren; for the most part the spikelets fall entire so that glumes and lower lemma participate in the disseminule. The selection pressures responsible for this distinctive arrangement are unknown, though it is clear that the subfamily has adapted to stable habitats in mesic conditions or in climax grasslands. It is a fascinating group whose genera lend themselves to arrangement in an orderly sequence of increasing morphological complexity.

It comprises two groups of tribes clustered around Paniceae and Andropogoneae, which share the same embryo and dimorphic florets, but differ in the relative induration of glumes and lemmas. Their leaf anatomy is mixed and therefore unhelpful in establishing outgroup relationships, though their cuneate lodicules link them to the other tropical subfamilies. Andropogoneae is related to Arundinelleae, and there is sufficient similarity between primitive members of that tribe and of Arundineae to envisage a common ancestry for the group. The origin of Paniceae is more obscure because there are no obvious precursors. It is tempting to speculate that the fusoid cells of *Homolepis* and the 3 stigmas of *Neurachne* are a bambusoid legacy implying an early divergence from the Arundinoid line, but there is no other evidence to support this proposition.

34. PANICEAE

R. Br. in Flinders, Voy. Terra Austral. 2: 582 (1814); Hsu in J. Fac. Sci. Tokyo 9: 43—150 (1965); Butzin in Willdenowia 6: 179—192 (1970). *Cenchreae* Reichenb., Consp. Reg. Veg.: 47 (1828). *Paspaleae* Reichenb. l.c. 49. *Spinificinae* Dumort., Anal. Fam.: 64 (1829). *Tristegineae* Nees in Hook. & Arn., Bot. Beech. Voy.: 237 (1836) nom nud. *Melinideae* Hitchc., Gen. Grasses U.S.: 18 (1920). *Boivinelleae* A. Camus in Bull. Mus. Hist. Nat. 31: 393 (1925). *Anthephoreae* Potztal in Willdenowia 1: 771 (1957). *Lecomtelleae* Potztal l.c. *Trachideae* Potztal l.c. *Cyphochlaeneae* Bosser in Adansonia 5: 413 (1965). *Arthropogoneae* Butzin in Willdenowia 6: 515 (1972). *Neurachneae* Blake in Contrib. Queensl. Herb. 13: 4 (1972).

Ligule a combination of short membrane and long ciliate fringe but proportions vary (absent in some *Echinochloa*). Inflorescence an open to spiciform panicle or of unilateral racemes (Spinificinae and some *Pennisetum* compound), usually terminal, the spikelets all alike or occasionally some sterile (sexes separate in *Cyphochlaena, Hygrochloa, Lecomtella, Spinifex, Thuarea, Zygochloa*), sometimes paired but then similar (except *Cyphochlaena*), when racemose the lower glume usually turned away from rhachis (abaxial). Spikelets 2-flowered without rhachilla extension (exceptions in *Alloteropsis, Brachiaria, Lasiacis, Panicum*), usually dorsally compressed, falling entire, rarely awned; glumes membranous or herbaceous rarely coriaceous, the upper often as long as spikelet, the lower usually shorter and sometimes rudimentary; lower floret ♂ or barren (except *Dissochondrus*), its lemma usually membranous or herbaceous and as long as spikelet, rarely indurated, with or without a palea; upper floret bisexual, the lemma and palea ± indurated (Arthropogoninae, *Cyphochlaena, Neurachne* hyaline), the radicle emerging through a frangible flap at its base. Linear hilum reported in *Acroceras, Homolepis, Louisiella, Mesosetum, Oplismenopsis, Streptostachys, Tatianyx* and some *Panicum*.

Genera 101; species ± 2000. Tropics.

Anatomy. The tribe contains three different types of leaf anatomy — non-kranz, kranz MS and kranz PS (fig. 17). The anatomy is usually uniform within each genus, but in four genera (*Alloteropsis, Chaetium, Neurachne* and *Panicum*) and one species (*Alloteropsis semialata*) it is mixed.

Chromosomes. The basic number is usually 9; it is 10 in *Axonopus, Hymenachne, Ichnanthus, Paspalum* and a few smaller genera. Intermediate numbers are unusually well represented. In particular 2n = 16 is common in *Mesosetum* and 2n = 34 in *Cenchrus*.

2n	14	18	20	24	27	28	30	32	34
No of species	7	215	92	5	10	8	15	12	24

2n	35	36	40	42	45	48	50	54	60
No of species	5	265	110	9	11	15	6	108	36

2n	68	70	72	80	90	108	120
No of species	6	6	50	15	5	9	4

The hallmark of Paniceae is its indurated upper floret which tightly encloses the caryopsis. The assumption of a protective role by the upper lemma and palea diminishes the importance of the glumes, which are usually thin and the lower often rudimentary. The lower floret is likewise often reduced to an empty lemma, though the degree of reduction seems of little taxonomic significance above species level. Nevertheless glumes and lower lemma participate in the fruit, for the spikelet nearly always falls as a whole though occasionally the upper floret is readily shed from it. In a few genera protection is augmented by induration of the upper glume, lower lemma or, curiously, the keels and flanks of the lower palea, but these are clearly derived from the normal form.

There are two important exceptions to the above rule. The first is Neurachninae, which may well represent a primitive state. The second is Arthropogoninae, whose anatomy indicates derivation though its origins are otherwise conjectural.

The inflorescence is usually paniculate or racemose, but with a high proportion of intermediate states — panicles contracted about primary branches or racemes with secondary branchlets — which make it an awkward taxonomic character; unfortunately it is difficult to avoid in diagnosis since the spikelets are so uniform. A special modification of the inflorescence, which is unusually well developed in the tribe, involves sterilization of the panicle branches and their modification into involucral bristles. Compound panicles make their appearance, but are restricted to a few genera.

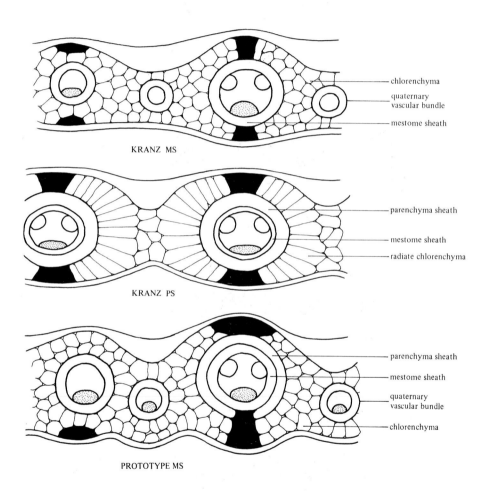

Fig. 17 Leaf anatomy in transverse section: kranz types. From top to bottom the species are — *Odontelytrum abyssinicum, Eleusine coracana* and *Chaetium cubanum.*

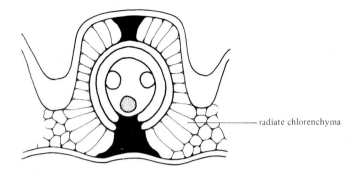

DOUBLE PHOTOSYNTHETIC SHEATH

— radiate chlorenchyma

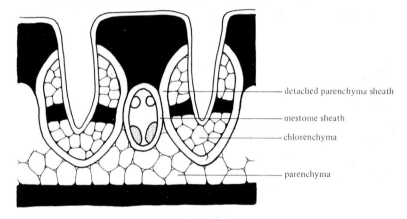

DETACHED PARENCHYMA SHEATH

— detached parenchyma sheath

— mestome sheath

— chlorenchyma

— parenchyma

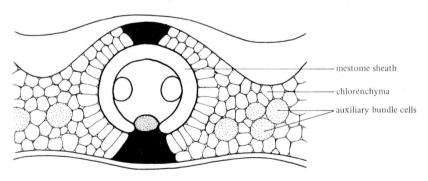

AUXILIARY BUNDLE CELL VARIANT

— mestome sheath

— chlorenchyma

— auxiliary bundle cells

Fig. 18   Leaf anatomy in transverse section: aberrant kranz types. From top to bottom the species are — *Aristida congesta*, *Triodia mitchellii* and *Arundinella nepalensis*.

In a racemose inflorescence much importance is traditionally attached to the orientation of the spikelet — whether the lower glume and lower floret have their backs against the rhachis (adaxial) or turned away from it (abaxial) — but its value has been overrated. It is a satisfactory diagnostic character when the spikelets are borne singly, but ambiguous when they are paired. The lower glume of the sessile spikelet then faces the pedicel whose divergence from the rhachis determines the orientation of the spikelet, though sometimes the top of the raceme bears a few single spikelets from which the orientation may be established. Paired spikelets, one sessile the other pedicelled, are common, inviting comparison with Andropogoneae, but the advantages of this arrangement in Paniceae are unclear since the spikelets are dimorphic only in *Cyphochlaena*. Apomixy is very common, as might perhaps be expected when the flower is so tightly enclosed, and the resultant swarms are often a source of great taxonomic difficulty at species level.

The leaf anatomy is unusually variable, and includes intermediates which throw some light on the probable course of evolution (fig. 17). Thus some C_3 genera, such as *Echinolaena* and *Hylebates,* have radiate chlorenchyma and seem pre-adapted for conversion to kranz PS. Alternatively *Arthropogon* is a C_4 genus with 2 bundle-sheaths and quarternary bundles, possibly representing an intermediate kranz MS form prior to loss of the outer sheath. Some caution should be exercised in regarding the non-kranz genera as primitive in any absolute sense, for the tribe has tended to specialize in mesic tropical habitats, at whose wet and shady extremes selection pressure favouring C_4 metabolism is likely to be relaxed.

It is not easy to find a satisfactory way to partition the tribe owing to the uniformity of its spikelets. The primary taxonomic sequence employed here reflects the evolutionary progression from non-kranz to kranz, and is divided into two parallel lines according to the texture of the upper lemma. Differences in lemma texture are certainly characteristic of the major generic clusters around *Panicum, Digitaria* and *Rhynchelytrum,* but the character is rather plastic and allowance must be made for exceptions. The differences are least clear among some of the non-kranz genera, whose partitioning is therefore somewhat arbitrary. The spikelet shape is a valuable intuitive aid to recognizing genera, though largely ignored here due to difficulty in specifying it precisely. The presence of a linear hilum is sometimes given generic weight; it occurs sporadically in a number of apparently unrelated genera, but its distribution has not been fully explored and its taxonomic significance remains uncertain.

The tribe is pantropical with a very wide adaptability. It has a particular affinity for damp and shady habitats, but has produced successful desert species and has reached into the temperate latitudes of North America. Generic diversity is weak in tropical Asia. The New World is notable for the extraordinary proliferation of species in three large genera — *Panicum, Paspalum* and *Axonopus.*

The tribe is usually easy to recognize, though species with suppressed lower glume and barren lower floret can imitate the 1-flowered spikelets of *Milium* or Olyreae.

1 Inflorescence simple, rarely (*Pennisetum*) borne on axillary branches and aggregated into a loose compound panicle:
2 Spikelets not subtended by bristles, or if so these persistent on branches:
3 Glumes both as long as spikelet, at least the upper indurated; spikelet callus bearded; panicle spiciform:
4 Glumes subulate-acuminate:

5   Glumes similar in texture with prominent nerves   **445 Neurachne**
5   Glumes dissimilar, the lower membranous, the upper coriaceous
                                                    446 Paraneurachne
4 Glumes obtuse, the lower with a hyaline patch at base **447 Thyridolepis**
3 Glumes, or at least the lower, shorter than spikelet or awn-like, rarely as
    long and then not as above:
  6 Upper lemma coriaceous to bony at maturity with inrolled or flat margins,
     sometimes thinner but then margins inrolled:
    7 Inflorescence a single raceme, the spikelets alternately abaxial and
       adaxial in one row on a winged rhachis   **497 Thrasya**
    7 Inflorescence various, but if a 1-rowed raceme then spikelets all facing
       the same way:
     8 Spikelets not subtended by bristles, nor raceme rhachis prolonged
        into a subulate point:
      9 Upper floret laterally compressed:
       10 Upper lemma without a crest; inflorescence of racemes:
        11 Upper lemma membranous to coriaceous:
         12 Upper glume neither gibbous nor armed with hooks
                                     448 Poecilostachys
         12 Upper glume gibbous, armed with hooks at maturity
                                  449 Pseudechinolaena
       11 Upper lemma hyaline; spikelets dimorphic   **450 Cyphochlaena**
      10 Upper lemma with a little green crest at tip; inflorescence a
        panicle:
       13 Upper lemma semirotund   **472 Cyrtococcum**
       13 Upper lemma lanceolate   **475 Microcalamus**
     9 Upper lemma dorsally compressed or gibbously terete:
      14 Upper lemma with decurrent wings or scars at the base:
       15 Spikelets all bisexual:
        16 Inflorescence a panicle or of open racemes:
         17 Glumes rounded; spikelets dorsally compressed:
          18 Upper floret borne upon a decurrently winged or excavated
             stipe   **455 Panicum**
          18 Upper floret borne upon a cylindrical stipe with apical
             auricles   **483 Yakirra**
        17 Glumes keeled; spikelets laterally compressed **452 Ichnanthus**
       16 Inflorescence of pectinate racemes   **453 Echinolaena**
      15 Spikelets mainly ♂   **454 Lecomtella**
    14 Upper lemma without basal wings or scars:
      19 Leaf surface raised into sinuous lamellae   **467 Hydrothauma**
      19 Leaf surface not lamellate:
       20 Spikelets supported on a globular bead (if spikelets gibbously
        plump see *476 Echinochloa callopus*)   **488 Eriochloa**
       20 Spikelets without a bead, though sometimes with a cylindrical
        stipe:
        21 Base of lower glume thickened into a rim projecting down-
         wards   **473 Streptostachys**
        21 Base of lower glume not toroidal:
         22 Inflorescence a panicle, sometimes irregularly contracted
          about primary branches:
          23 Upper glume muticous or acuminate to a slender awn-point:
           24 Upper floret sessile:

25 Upper lemma without a green crest:
26 Spikelets rarely gibbous and then dorsally compressed
in an open panicle:
27 Palea of lower floret unmodified or absent:
28 Rhizanthogenes absent:
29 Upper lemma seldom acuminate and then upper
glume and lower lemma membranous:
30 Upper lemma rarely excavated and then not woolly:
31 Spikelets without hooked hairs:
32 Pedicel tip truncate (if glumes equal and enclosing a lanceolate spikelet see *464 Homolepis*)
455 Panicum
32 Pedicel tip oblique **491 Tatianyx**
31 Spikelets armed with tubercle-based hooked
(*A. maidenii* merely flexuous) hairs
456 Ancistrachne
30 Upper lemma with a shallow excavation and tuft
of wool at the tip **457 Lasiacis**
29 Upper lemma acuminate; upper glume and lower
lemma coriaceous **482 Scutachne**
28 Rhizanthogenes present; upper lemma acuminate
458 Amphicarpum
27 Palea of lower floret developing enlarged keels or
flanks at maturity:
33 Upper glume as long as spikelet:
34 Lower lemma 3-nerved **459 Steinchisma**
34 Lower lemma 4-nerved **460 Plagiantha**
33 Upper glume much shorter than spikelet
461 Otachyrium
26 Spikelets gibbous, panicle usually spiciform
465 Sacciolepis
25 Upper lemma with a green crest **474 Acroceras**
24 Upper floret borne on a brief filiform (if stout see *483
Yakirra nulla*) internode:
35 Panicle branches not deciduous; lower lemma sulcate
492 Whiteochloa
35 Panicle branches deciduous **484 Arthragrostis**
23 Upper glume with a long stiff awn **479 Oryzidium**
22 Inflorescence of ± unilateral racemes, the spikelets usually
single or paired but sometimes in irregular clusters or short
secondary racemelets:
36 Glumes or lemmas awned:
37 Inflorescence of several racemes:
38 Spikelets laterally compressed, in 2 rows; awns often
sticky **451 Oplismenus**
38 Spikelets dorsally compressed:
39 Spikelets estipitate (or some *Echinochloa* with a barrel-
like stipe):
40 Upper lemma awned, crisply chartaceous
481 Alloteropsis
40 Upper lemma awnless, coriaceous

40   Upper lemma awnless, coriaceous
  41 Spikelets paired or clustered, densely packed in 4 rows   **476 Echinochloa**
  41 Spikelets borne singly, in open racemes   **477 Oplismenopsis**
39 Spikelets supported on a linear bearded stipe   **478 Chaetium**
37 Inflorescence of 1 raceme   **499 Mesosetum**
36 Glumes and lemmas awnless or at most mucronate:
42 Spikelets all alike:
  43 Lower glume present (except *Brachiaria breviglumis*):
  44 Upper lemma pubescent all over   **469 Entolasia**
  44 Upper lemma glabrous, or pubescent only at tip:
    45 Glumes equal, shorter than spikelet   **468 Ottochloa**
    45 Glumes unequal, or both as long as spikelet:
    46 Upper glume 11—17-nerved; inflorescence of 1—2 racemes   **498 Thrasyopsis**
    46 Upper glume 3—9-nerved:
     47 Inflorescence of 1 raceme   **499 Mesosetum**
     47 Inflorescence of several racemes:
     48 Spikelets paired or in racemelets:
      49 Tip of upper palea reflexed and slightly protruberant, or tip of upper lemma forming a little green crest:
       50 Tips of upper glume and lower lemma laterally nipped; racemes loose (if dense see *485 Brachiaria*)   **474 Acroceras**
       50 Tips of upper glume and lower lemma not nipped, often acuminate   **476 Echinochloa**
      49 Tip of upper palea not reflexed; upper lemma not crested:
       51 Upper lemma rarely mucronate and then spikelets plump:
        52 Upper glume and lower lemma caudate-acuminate; lower glume short, truncate   **480 Louisiella**
        52 Upper glume and lower lemma seldom acuminate and then lower glume not as above:
         53 Upper palea not gaping after anthesis (if upper floret stipitate see *492 Whiteochloa*):
          54 Spikelets narrowly elliptic, ± acute (but see *P. obtusum*)   **455 Panicum**
          54 Spikelets broadly elliptic, plump, ± obtuse   **485 Brachiaria**
         53 Upper palea gaping after anthesis; upper glume and lower lemma strongly ribbed; lower glume evanescent   **494 Anthaenantiopsis**
       51 Upper lemma mucronate; spikelets plano-convex, cuspidate   **487 Urochloa**
     48 Spikelets single:
     55 Spikelets adaxial:
      56 Upper floret sessile   **485 Brachiaria**

56 Upper floret raised on a sinuous internode; upper glume and lower lemma resembling woven fabric **486 Eccoptocarpha**
55 Spikelets abaxial **487 Urochloa**
43 Lower glume absent, rarely minute (some exceptions in *Paspalum*):
57 Spikelets plano-convex, abaxial:
58 Upper glume present, rarely absent and then upper lemma crustaceous **495 Paspalum**
58 Upper glume absent; upper lemma thinly coriaceous **496 Reimarochloa**
57 Spikelets biconvex:
59 Spikelets not turbinate:
60 Lower lemma deeply sulcate; upper glume 11—12-nerved **498 Thrasyopsis**
60 Lower lemma not sulcate; upper glume 0—9-nerved:
61 Cleistogenes frequent in leaf axils; habit wiry **470 Cleistochloa**
61 Cleistogenes absent:
62 Spikelets single:
63 Spikelets neatly and closely appressed to a strongly unilateral rhachis **500 Axonopus**
63 Spikelets loosely disposed along an indistinctly unilateral filiform rhachis **489 Yvesia**
62 Spikelets paired:
64 Spikelets glabrous **493 Acostia**
64 Spikelets pilose **494 Anthaenantiopsis**
59 Spikelets turbinate:
65 Spikelet callus blunt; upper glume extended downwards into a spur **501 Centrochloa**
65 Spikelet callus long, pungent; upper glume not spurred **502 Spheneria**
42 Spikelets of 2 kinds, the upper ♂ portion of the raceme folding over 1—2 bisexual spikelets **490 Thuarea**
8 Spikelets, at least those terminating a branch, subtended by 1 or more bristles, or the raceme rhachis prolonged into an often obscure point:
66 Inflorescence axis tough:
67 Spikelets all alike:
68 Lower floret unlike the upper, ♂ or barren:
69 Upper glume membranous to herbaceous:
70 Keels of lower palea not thickened:
71 Inflorescence usually a panicle, all or most of the spikelets subtended by bristles **503 Setaria**
71 Inflorescence of racemes, only the terminal spikelet (sometimes also the lowest when paired or clustered) subtended by an inconspicuous bristle or point (if racemes in pockets on a broad main axis see *512 Stenotaphrum*; if lower glume absent see *495 Paspalum*) **504 Paspalidium**
70 Keels of lower palea at first inconspicuous, later indurated and winged:
72 Lower lemma sulcate **505 Holcolemma**
72 Lower lemma not sulcate **506 Ixophorus**

```
      69   Upper glume broad, indurated, auriculate       507 Setariopsis
      68   Lower floret resembling the upper, bisexual  508 Dissochondrus
      67   Spikelets dissimilar, ♀ on lower racemes, ♂ on upper
                                                              511 Hygrochloa
    66   Inflorescence axis fragile                     513 Uranthoecium
6  Upper lemma cartilaginous to chartaceous or rarely hyaline, the
   margins flat and usually hyaline:
  73   Branches of the inflorescence ending in a long bristle
                                                           530 Pseudoraphis
  73   Branches of the inflorescence ending in a spikelet:
    74   Inflorescence axillary, cylindrical              537 Snowdenia
    74   Inflorescence terminal:
      75   Lemma margins wrapped around palea, or palea absent:
        76   Spikelets laterally compressed:
          77   Lower glume absent or minute; upper glume usually emarginate
               to bilobed:
            78   Upper lemma dorsally compressed         514 Tricholaena
            78   Upper lemma laterally compressed:
              79   Upper lemma awned               515 Mildbraediochloa
              79   Upper lemma awnless:
                80   Upper glume 5-nerved, gibbous    516 Rhynchelytrum
                80   Upper glume 7-nerved, straight on the back    517 Melinis
          77   Lower glume well developed; upper glume entire:
            81   Inflorescence of racemes                    Go to 11
            81   Inflorescence a panicle (if spiciform see 465 Sacciolepis):
              82   Lower glume awn-like             528 Arthropogon
              82   Lower glume narrowly oblong, membranous, bilobed
                                                            529 Reynaudia
        76   Spikelets dorsally compressed:
          83   Inflorescence a panicle:
            84   Lower glume shorter than spikelet:
              85   Lower lemma awnless:
                86   Panicle open; leaf-blades filiform (if flat see 524 Digitaria)
                                                            462 Triscenia
                86   Panicle spiciform or contracted:
                  87   Upper glume and lower lemma membranous; upper palea
                       free from lemma towards tip (if enclosed see 455 Panicum)
                                                            463 Hymenachne
                  87   Upper glume and lower lemma smoothly coriaceous
                                                            466 Thyridachne
                85   Lower lemma briefly awned             518 Hylebates
            84   Lower glume as long as spikelet:
              88   Glume nerves not ribbed                464 Homolepis
              88   Glume nerves raised into prominent ridges  520 Homopholis
          83   Inflorescence of racemes:
            89   Spikelets awned:
              90   Racemes several:
                91   Racemes spread along a central axis    519 Acritochaete
                91   Racemes digitate (if upper lemma awned see 524 Digitaria)
                                                            521 Stereochlaena
              90   Raceme single:
                92   Rhachis winged                       522 Baptorhachis
```

92   Rhachis terete   **471 Calyptochloa**

89   Spikelets awnless:

    93   Inflorescence of very short racemes embedded in an enlarged central axis   **512 Stenotaphrum**

    93   Inflorescence not of embedded racemes:

       94   Racemes not deciduous:

          95   Lower glume as long as spikelet   **523 Megaloprotachne**

          95   Lower glume suppressed or up to ¼ length of spikelet:

             96   Upper glume present though sometimes small; upper lemma firm with broad hyaline margins (if clasping only margins of palea and upper glume without clear nerves see *495 Paspalum saccharoides*)   **524 Digitaria**

             96   Upper glume absent; upper lemma membranous with narrow margins   **496 Reimarochloa**

       94   Racemes deciduous, appressed, the inflorescence spiciform   **525 Tarigidia**

  75   Lemma margins gaping, the palea free:

    97   Spikelets dorsally compressed; upper lemma hyaline at the tip   **526 Leptocoryphium**

    97   Spikelets laterally compressed; upper lemma firm to the tip   **527 Anthenantia**

2   Spikelets, singly or in clusters, subtended by 1 or more bristles, bracts or sterile spikelets and deciduous with them:

  98   Upper lemma crustaceous, rugulose, with narrow inrolled margins; inflorescence branches raceme-like:

  99   Bristles in fascicles   **509 Plagiosetum**

  99   Bristle single   **510 Paractaenum**

  98   Upper lemma cartilaginous to thinly coriaceous with flat margins:

    100   Inflorescence spiciform:

      101   Bristles several along a short deciduous branch   **532 Pseudochaetochloa**

      101   Bristles borne singly or in a rosette without evident axis:

        102   Involucre composed of bristles, spines or a herbaceous cupule:

          103   Involucral bristles several to many:

            104   Involucral bristles free throughout, ± filiform   **533 Pennisetum**

            104   Involucral bristles flattened and connate below, often forming a cup   **534 Cenchrus**

          103   Involucral bristle or scale solitary, subtending a single spikelet:

            105   Spikelet invested by a herbaceous lobed cupule   **535 Odontelytrum**

            105   Spikelet subtended by a bristle and supported on a slender stipe (if sessile see *533 Pennisetum*):

              106   Upper glume very short   **536 Paratheria**

              106   Upper glume as long as spikelet   **531 Chamaeraphis**

        102   Involucre composed of sterile spikelets or several glumaceous bracts; bristles absent:

          107   Involucre of shortly pedicelled sterile spikelets   **538 Chaetopoa**

          107   Involucre of sessile scales   **539 Anthephora**

    100   Inflorescence with distant or conjugate raceme-like branches; involucre ± spinous:

      108   Rhachis of primary branches not foliaceous   **540 Streptolophus**

      108   Rhachis of primary branches foliaceous:

a. NEURACHNINAE (S.T. Blake) Clayton & Renvoize, Gen. Gram: 377; Blake in Contrib. Queensl. Herb. 13: 1—51 (1972).

Inflorescence a spiciform or capitate panicle. Spikelets dorsally compressed, the callus bearded; glumes as long as spikelet, ± indurated, the upper broader and densely hairy on margins; upper lemma hyaline to membranous, or coriaceous with membranous tip, the margins narrow and covering only edge of palea. Anatomy: *Thyridolepis* non-kranz; *Paraneurachne* kranz PS; *Neurachne* non-kranz and kranz PS.

A group of closely related genera recognized by their large tough glumes. In *Neurachne* the upper lemma is much thinner than the glumes, but in the other genera it is close to the typical panicoid form affording no good reason for excluding this group from the tribe. The anatomy is mixed, *Neurachne* itself containing both kranz and non-kranz species (Hattersley et al in Bot. J. Linn. Soc. 84: 265—272, 1982).

The affinity of the subtribe is uncertain, though the inclusion of non-kranz anatomy, unspecialized upper lemmas and 3 stigmas suggests an early split from the mainstream of Paniceae.

445. Neurachne R. Br., Prodr. Fl. Nov. Holl.: 196 (1810) — N. alopecuroides R. Br.

Perennial. Spikelets: glumes subulate-acuminate, both subcoriaceous with ribbed nerves; lower lemma similar to glumes but glabrescent and subacute, ♂, embracing upper floret; upper lemma hyaline to membranous, acute; stigmas 3, though often 1 of them rudimentary.

Species 6. Australia. Heath, woodland and scrub.

446. Paraneurachne S.T. Blake in Contrib. Queensl. Herb. 13: 20 (1972) — P. muelleri (Hack.) S.T. Blake.

Perennial. Spikelets: glumes subulate-acuminate, the lower membranous, the upper smoothly coriaceous below and ribbed above; lower lemma gibbous below with strongly indurated nerves, ♂, free from upper floret above; upper lemma coriaceous with rostrate membranous tip; stigmas 2.

Species 1. Australia. Dry grassland.

447. Thyridolepis S.T. Blake in Contrib. Queensl. Herb. 13: 25 (1972) — T. mitchelliana (Nees) S.T. Blake.

Perennial. Spikelets: glumes obtuse, the lower with bristly transverse boss across the centre and depressed hyaline patch below, the upper coriaceous below and ribbed above; lower lemma membranous, barren, tightly clasping upper floret; upper floret like *Paraneurachne*.

Species 3. Australia. Dry grassland and scrub.

b. SETARIINAE Dumort., Obs. Gram. Belg.: 137 (1824). *Paspalinae* Griseb., Fl. Roumel. Bithyn. 2: 468 (1846). *Panicinae* Stapf in Fl. Trop. Afr. 9: 12 (1917). *Boivinellinae* (A. Camus) Pilger, Nat. Pfl.-Fam. ed. 2, 14e: 101 (1940). *Lecomtellinae* Pilger l.c.: 103, nom. nud. *Thuareinae* Ohwi in Acta Phytotax. Geobot. 11: 55 (1942). *Paspalidiinae* Keng, Fl. Illustr. Pl. Prim. Sin.: 718 (1959) sine descr lat. *Brachiariinae* Butzin in Willdenowia 6: 189 (1970). *Microcalaminae* Butzin l.c.: 180 *Otachyriinae* Butzin l.c.: 182. *Uranthoeciinae* Butzin l.c.: 184. *Reimarochloinae* Caro in Dominguezia 4: 41 (1982).

Inflorescence a panicle or of racemes. Spikelets usually dorsally compressed; lower glume variable, the upper glume and lower lemma usually as long as spikelet; lower floret ♂ or barren and then usually without palea (*Dissochondrus* bisexual); upper lemma coriaceous to bony or occasionally thinner, usually with narrow inrolled margins covering only edge of palea but these sometimes flat. Anatomy: non-kranz, kranz PS, kranz MS (see fig. 19).

Setariinae is characterized by its hard upper lemma, though there are exceptions. The lemma surface may be rugose, granular or highly polished; the latter makes the floret difficult to pick up and may be a counter to bird predation.
   The subtribe is dominated by the large, anatomically variable genus *Panicum*, and the host of segregate genera scattered around its periphery. Some of these form fairly well marked clusters, informally listed as:
1   Broad-leaved forest group (*Ichnanthus, Poecilostachys*)
2   Spiciform group (*Sacciolepis*)
3   Aquatic group (*Acroceras, Echinochloa*)
4   PS group (*Brachiaria*)
5   MS group (*Axonopus, Paspalum*)
   A second major group centres on *Setaria*, which is distinguished from *Panicum* by the presence of bristles subtending the spikelets. The diagnostic criterion is easily overlooked when only the terminal spikelet is accompanied by a bristle, and is scarcely apparent when this is reduced to a brief subulate extension of the rhachis. The gradualness of the boundary discourages separation of the *Panicum* and *Setaria* groups in separate subtribes.

448. Poecilostachys Hack. in Sitz. Akad. Wiss. Wien 89: 131 (1884) — P. hildebrandtii Hack. *Chloachne* Stapf in Hook. Ic. Pl. 31: t 3072 (1916) — C. secunda Stapf (= P. oplismenoides).

Trailing perennial; leaf-blades linear to lanceolate. Infloresence of racemes on a central axis, these unilateral but often lax, bearing paired spikelets

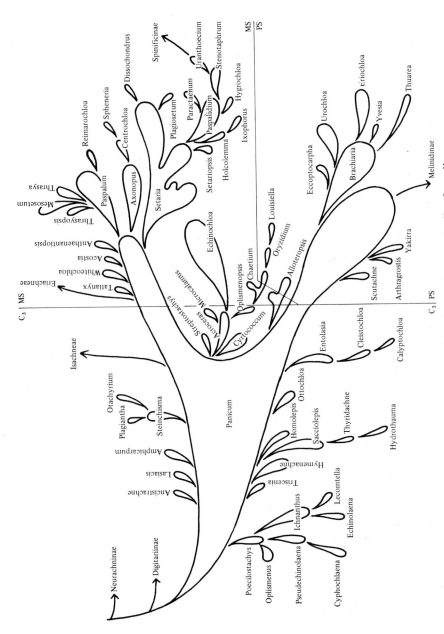

Fig. 19 Diagram of relationships in Paniceae subtribe Setariinae

(sometimes little clusters in *P. oplismenoides*). Spikelets laterally compressed; glumes ⅓—¾ length of spikelet, the lower awned (*P. geminata, P. oplismenoides, P. viguieri* acute to mucronate), the upper acute to mucronate (upper glume and lower lemma of *P. oplismenoides* armed with stiff tubercle-based bristles); upper lemma strongly laterally compressed, membranous to cartilaginous with flat or inrolled margins.

Species ± 20. Madagascar; 1 species tropical Africa. Forest shade.

449. Pseudechinolaena Stapf in Fl. Trop. Afr. 9: 494 (1919); Bosser in Adansonia 15: 121—137 (1975) — P. polystachya (Kunth) Stapf. *Perulifera* A. Camus in Bull. Soc. Bot. France 74: 889 (1928) — P. madagascariensis A. Camus. *Loxostachys* Peter in Feddes Rep., Beih. 40, 1: Anh. 55 (1930) nom superfl pro Pseudechinolaena.

Trailing annual; leaf-blades lanceolate. Inflorescence of slender racemes along a central axis, these lax, bearing paired spikelets but the sessile often reduced. Spikelets laterally compressed; glumes ¾ to as long as spikelet, the lower acute to awned, the upper gibbous, eventually armed with tubercle-based hooks and sometimes with wings, acute or rarely awned; lower lemma chartaceous to subcoriaceous, but membranous on margins and centre of base; upper lemma laterally compressed, cartilaginous to coriaceous with flat or inrolled margins.

Species 6. Madagascar; 1 species pantropical. Forest shade.

The inflorescence is variable in appearance, partly because the hooks only develop after fertilization, and partly because the flowering period is often extended by delayed maturation of the sessile spikelets. Both are adaptations to animal dispersal in a forest environment (Lucas in Isleya 1: 115—139, 1979).

450. Cyphochlaena Hack. in Oest. Bot. Zeitschr. 51: 465 (1901); Bosser in Adansonia 5: 411—413 (1965) — C. madagascariensis Hack. *Boivinella* A. Camus in Bull. Soc. Bot. Fr. 72: 175 (1925) & Bull. Mus. Hist. Nat. 31: 389—393 (1925) —B. sclerioides A. Camus. *Sclerolaena* A. Camus in Bull. Soc. Bot. Fr. 72: 622 (1925) non R. Br. (1810), in syn sub Boivinella comorensis (= C. madagascariensis).

Trailing annual or perennial. Infloresence of unilateral racemes along a central axis, bearing paired spikelets, the one sessile and ♂ or sterile, the other pedicelled and ♀ or bisexual. Female spikelets laterally compressed; lower glume ½—⅔ length of spikelet, usually with a deciduous apical awn; upper glume coriaceous; lower lemma similar but gibbous; upper lemma laterally compressed, hyaline. Male spikelet like ♀ but upper glume and lower lemma membranous; often reduced, sometimes to a single glume

Species 2. Madagascar. Damp places.

The paired dimorphic spikelets have attracted a false comparison with Andropogoneae. In fact the genus is related to *Pseudechinolaena* in which incipient dimorphism can be observed.

451. Oplismenus P. Beauv., Fl. Owar. 2: 14 (Sept 1810) nom conserv; Poir., Encycl. Suppl. 4: 271 (1816) as "Ophismenus"; Hassk., Cat. Hort. Bogor.: 16 (1844) as "Hoplismenus"; Davey & Clayton in Kew Bull. 33: 147—157 (1978); Scholz, Monogr. Oplis. (1981) — O. africanus P. Beauv. (= O. hirtellus). *Orthopogon* R. Br., Prodr. Fl. Nov. Holl.: 194 (Apr 1810) nom rejic — O. compositus (L.) R. Br. *Hekaterosachne* Steud., Syn. Pl. Glum. 1: 118 (1854) — H. elatior Steud. (= O. hirtellus). *Hippagrostis* Kuntze, Rev. Gen. Pl. 2: 776 (1891) nom superfl pro Oplismenus.

Trailing annual or perennial; leaf-blades lanceolate to ovate. Infloresence of unilateral racemes along a central axis, bearing paired spikelets (but the lower often reduced). Spikelets laterally compressed; glumes ½—¾ length of spikelet, the lower or both tipped by a viscid (*O. burmannii* & *O. thwaitesii* scaberulous, the latter short) awn; lower lemma acute to shortly awned; upper lemma dorsally compressed, acute, indistinctly crested.

Species 5. Tropical & subtropical regions. Forest shade.
A genus of very closely related species. The sticky secretion on the awn is an unusual means of fruit dispersal in the grasses.

452. Ichnanthus P. Beauv., Ess. Agrost.: 56 (1812); Stieber in Syst. Bot. 7: 85—115 (1982) — I. panicoides P. Beauv. *Ischnanthus* Roem. & Schult., Syst. Veg. 2: 28 (1817) nom superfl pro Ichnanthus. *Navicularia* Raddi, Agrost. Bras.: 38 (1823) non Fabric. (1759) — N. lanata Raddi (= I. leiocarpus).

Annual or perennial; leaf-blades linear to ovate. Inflorescence a panicle, diffuse or the primary branches simple and raceme-like. Spikelets laterally compressed; glumes keeled, membranous, the lower 3(—5)-nerved (*I. breviscrobs, I. panicoides, I. riedelii* 5—7-nerved) and ½—¾ length of spikelet. (*I. longiglumis, I. riedelii* longer), mostly acute to acuminate; upper lemma with flat or inrolled margins; callus of upper floret semicircular to oblong, expanded laterally into 2 membranous wings adnate to base of lemma, these often represented only by scars.

Species 33. New World tropics, 1 species pantropical. Mainly forest shade, but extending into grassland and disturbed places.
A genus of varying habit from tall canes (*I. bambusiflorus*) to *Olyra*-like forest herbs (*I. panicoides*) and rambling weeds (*I. pallens*), which includes several polymorphic complexes of great taxonomic difficulty. It is divided into Sect *Ichnanthus* with firm wings; and Sect *Foveolatus* with delicate wings which shrink to a mere scar on drying. The function of these appendages is unknown. The appendage scars of *I. breviscrobs, I. camporum, I. grandifolius, I. mayarensis* and *I. procurrens* are small, indistinct and easily overlooked; the laterally compressed spikelets help to distinguish these species from *Panicum*.
Appendages also occur in the unrelated genus *Yakirra* where their form is slightly different, being auricles at the tip of a distinct rhachilla internode.

453. Echinolaena Desv. in J. Bot. Agr. 1: 75 (1813); Spreng., Gen. Pl. ed. 9: 65 (1830) as "Echinochlaena" — E. hirta Desv. (= E. inflexa). *Chasechloa* A. Camus in Bull. Soc. Bot. France 95: 330 (1949) — C. madagascariensis (Baker) A. Camus.

Annual or perennial; leaf-blades linear to lanceolate. Infloresence of 1—several pectinate racemes on a central axis, these bearing paired spikelets (but the sessile often aborted) and ending in a spikelet whose lower glume simulates a rhachis extension. Spikelets: lower glume ½ to exceeding rest of spikelet, membranous to coriaceous, 3—9-nerved, keeled or the nerves forming prominent ribs, armed with tubercle-based bristles, acute to shortly awned; callus of upper floret with narrow wings or scars adnate to base of lemma.

Species 8. South America and Madagascar. Savanna.

A somewhat heterogeneous genus with anomalous distribution. *E. minarum* links it to *Ichnanthus*.

454. Lecomtella A. Camus in Comptes Rend. Acad. Sci. 181: 567 (1925); Stapf in Hook. Ic. Pl. 32: t 3123 (1927) — L. madagascariensis A. Camus.

Perennial. Infloresence a contracted panicle, each main branch with several ♂ spikelets below and a bisexual spikelet at tip. Bisexual spikelet weakly laterally compressed; glumes ½—¾ length of spikelet; lower floret ♂, its lemma as long as spikelet; upper floret ♀, borne upon a short stipe with 2 apical wings, its lemma crustaceous with flat firm margins, tuberculate at tip. Male spikelets similar, but both florets ♂ with membranous lemmas.

Species 1. Madagascar. Forest margins.

455. Panicum L., Sp. Pl.: 55 (1753); Ard., Animad. Spec. Alt.: 14 (1764) as "Paniculum" — P. miliaceum L. *Milium* Adans., Fam. Pl. 2: 34 (1763) non L. (1753) — unnamed species (= P. miliaceum vel aff). *Monachne* P. Beauv., Ess. Agrost.: 49 (1812) — M. racemosa P. Beauv. *Eatonia* Raf. in J. Phys. Chim. 89: 104 (1819) — E. purpurascens Raf. (= P. virgatum). *Talasium* Spreng., Syst. Veg. 4, Cur. Post.: 22 (1827) — T. montevidense Spreng. (= P. racemosum). *Eriolytrum* Kunth, Rév. Gram. 1: 219 (1829) in syn sub P. reptans (= P. racemosum). *Panicum sect Dileucaden* Raf. in Bull. Bot. Genève 1: 220 (1830) — P. dichotomum L. *Panicum sect Phanopyrum* Raf. l.c. — P. gymnocarpon Ell. *Dileucaden* (Raf.) Steud., Nom. Bot. 2: 252 (1841) in syn. *Coleataenia* Griseb. in Abh. Ges. Wiss. Gött. 24: 308 (1879) — C. gynerioides Griseb. (= P. prionites). *Phanopyrum* (Raf.) Nash in Small, Fl. Southeast U.S.: 104, 1327 (1903). *Panicum subgen Dichanthelium* Hitchc. & Chase in Contrib. U.S. Nat. Herb. 15: 142 (1910) — P. dichotomum. *Chasea* Nieuw. in Amer. Midl. Nat. 2: 64 (1911) nom nud — P. clandestinum. *Polyneura* Peter in Feddes Rep. Beih. 40, 1: Anh. 53 (1930) non Kylin (1924) — P. squarrosa Peter (= P. peteri). *Psilochloa* Launert in Mit. Bot. Staats. Münch. 8: 156 (1970) — P. pilgeriana (Schweick.) Launert. *Dichanthelium* (Hitchc. & Chase) Gould in Brittonia 26: 59 (1974); Gould & Clark in Ann. Miss. Bot. Gard. 65: 1088—1132 (1979); Gould in Brittonia 32: 353—364 (1980).

Annual or perennial of varied habit. Inflorescence a panicle (shed entire as a tumbleweed in *P. olyroides*), sometimes condensed about primary branches (eg, *P. auritum, P. infestum, P. laxum, P. rivulare*), rarely spiciform (*P. trinii* & allies) or of racemes. Spikelets dorsally or weakly laterally compressed, usually symmetrical (gibbous in *P. brevifolium* group; tilted obliquely in *P. anceps* and a few others), seldom hairy (*P. cinereum, P. lagostachyum, P. racemosum* & their allies villous to woolly); lower glume mostly shorter than spikelet but sometimes equalling it, truncate to awn-pointed, often with an internode between glumes this sometimes forming a brief stipe at base of spikelet; upper glume as long as spikelet (*P. nudiflorum* and a few others shorter), truncate to awn-pointed (*P. aristellum* shortly awned); lower lemma usually similar to upper glume (*P. infestum* sulcate; *P. chapadense* glandular; *P. quadriglume* with a second sterile lemma); upper floret sessile (supported on a decurrently winged and excavated stipe in *P. cervicatum*, *P. lagostachyum*, *P. trinii*); upper lemma coriaceous to bony, sometimes cartilaginous but palea never free and margins usually inrolled, glabrous or pubescent at tip (woolly tip *P. discrepans*; pubescent all over *P. macranthum*, *P. ramosum*, *P. trichidachne*; turgid basal hairs *P. olyroides*), obtuse to acute or obscurely apiculate (acuminate in *P. auritum*, *P. elephantipes*; slight green crest *P. hubbardii*, *P. peteri*; slight crater *P. comorense*, *P. robynsii*). Hilum round to oval (*P. glutinosum*, *P. macranthum*, *P. pilgerianum* and their allies linear).

Species ± 470. Pantropical, extending to temperate regions of N. America. Desert, savanna, forest and swamp. *P. miliaceum* (Proso millet) is grown as a cereal crop; *P. sonorum* (Sauwi) and *P. sumatrense* (Sama) have also been domesticated, the latter derived from the wild species *P. psilopodium* (de Wet et al in J. Agr. Trop. Bot. Appl. 30: 159—168, 1983). *P. maximum* (Guinea grass) and *P. coloratum* (Buffalo grass) are widely grown for fodder. *P. turgidum* deserves mention as a desert forage species (Williams & Farias in Econ. Bot. 26: 13—20, 1972).

A large genus with fairly uniform spikelets but much variation in the habit, which ranges from woody shrubs (*P. turgidum*) to low cushions (*P. koolauense*). The leaves are likewise variable, from filiform to ovate (*P. latissimum* up to 10 cm wide), and from pungent to scale-like (*P. cupressifolium*).

Partial infrageneric classifications have been given by Stapf in Fl. Trop. Afr. 9 638—650 (1920), Pilger in Nat. Pfl.-Fam. ed. 2, 14e: 8—25 (1940) and Hitchcock in Man. Grasses U.S. ed. 2: 626—706 (1950), but none is wholly satisfactory. The most important variations are summarized in the following approximate key to informal groups:

Upper lemma verruculose; glumes and lower lemma semi-deciduous at about
    the time spikelets disarticulate (P. baumannii)   *Verruculosa*
Upper lemma not verruculose:
  Inflorescence branches bearing clavellate hairs; glumes often lacerate (P. ecklonii)
         Clavelligera
  Inflorescence branches without clavellate hairs:
    Basal leaves differing from those on culm, forming a winter rosette (P.
    dichotomum)   *Dichanthelium*
    Basal and culm leaves similar:
      Leaf-blades rigid, flat or terete, pungent, indistinctly demarcated from sheath
      (P. chnoodes)   *Lorea*
      Leaf-blades not as above:
        Inflorescence of racemes (P. pilosum)   *Stolonifera*
        Inflorescence a panicle (P. miliaceum)   *Panicum*

Non-kranz anatomy occurs in all groups; *Clavelligera* also has PS species, and the large residual *Panicum* group both PS and MS. It is remarkable that a genus which displays so much plasticity in its leaf anatomy should have such uniform spikelets; certainly there is insufficient correlation between the two sets of characters to support dismemberment. Furthermore both types of hilum occur; species with a linear hilum do not form natural units, either among themselves (*P. pilgerianum* is PS, the others non-kranz) or when transferred to other genera, and it seems better to regard *Panicum* as also variable in this feature. The warts on the upper lemma of *Verruculosa* are, in fact, 2-celled microhairs (Scholz in Willdenowia 8: 511—515, 1979).

The genus lies at the heart of a sprawling complex of interrelated neighbours. Some of these are minor satellites, dependent upon a subjective judgement as to whether they warrant recognition at generic level; this judgement has, perhaps, been exercised more critically in the Old World than the New. Others are certainly of generic status, but their circumscription is complicated by the presence of intermediate species linking them to *Panicum*. The following genera contain intermediates which are difficult to separate from Panicum: *Ancistrachne, Cyrtococcum, Eriochloa, Homolepis, Hylebates, Hymenachne, Ichnanthus, Paspalidium, Sacciolepis, Tricholaena, Whiteochloa* and *Yakirra*. Note also the presence of isolated characters more typical of other genera, such as a hairy or cartilaginous upper lemma or an incipient crater or crest at its tip.

Brachiaria is particularly difficult to separate. The essential difference is the contrast between paniculate and racemose inflorescences. However, racemes occur in *Panicum* when the inflorescence is sparse (as in *P. robynsii*), and are often imitated by condensation about the primary branches. True racemes occur in *Stolonifera*; this group certainly belongs in *Panicum*, being linked by intermediates such as *P. laxum* and *P. polygonatum*, and excluded from *Brachiaria* by its non-kranz anatomy. Conversely *Brachiaria* can verge upon a paniculate inflorescence; compare *B. comata* and *P. polygonatum*. In these marginal species there seems to be no unequivocal generic criterion, and separation rests unsatisfactorily upon a subjective assessment of spikelet shape.

There remain a few anomalous species. *P. obtusum* has a racemose inflorescence resembling *Brachiaria*, but its MS leaf anatomy suggests a closer affinity with *Paspalidium reverchonii*. *P. quadriglume* has 2 sterile florets below the fertile (see also *Lasiacis*). *P. trinii* (non-kranz) and *P. cervicatum* (PS) have a distinctive winged stipe below the upper floret, but so little else in common that the character would not appear to be of much taxonomic significance; the dorsally compressed spikelet excludes them from *Ichnanthus*.

456. Ancistrachne S.T. Blake in Univ. Queensland Papers 1, 19: 4 (1941) — A. uncinulata (R. Br.) S.T. Blake.

Perennial with wiry culms. Inflorescence a depauperate panicle, the primary branches often simple and few-flowered but not unilateral. Spikelets obliquely tilted on pedicel; lower glume rudimentary or up to ½ length of spikelet; upper glume and lower lemma prominently nerved, bearing tubercle-based hooked (*A. maidenii* merely flexuous) hairs; upper lemma thinly coriaceous with flat margins, slightly laterally pinched at tip (this puberulous in *A. numaeense*).

Species 4. Australia, Philippines and New Caledonia. Forest.

457. Lasiacis (Griseb.) Hitchc. in Contrib. U.S. Nat. Herb. 15: 16 (1910); Davidse in Ann. Miss. Bqt. Gard. 65: 1133—1254 (1979). *Panicum sect Lasiacis* Griseb., Fl.

Brit. W. Ind.: 551 (1864) — P. divaricatum L. *P. subgen Pseudolasiacis* A. Camus in Bull. Soc. Bot. France 73: 974 (1927) — P. leptolomoides A. Camus. *Pseudolasiacis* (A. Camus) A. Camus in Bull. Soc. Linn. Lyon 14: 72 (1945).

Perennial; culms creeping or scandent, usually woody and cane-like; leaf-blades linear to ovate. Inflorescence a panicle. Spikelets subglobose, tilted obliquely on pedicel; lower glume shorter than spikelet, saccate; upper glume and lower lemma ± as long as spikelet (*L. anomala* with a second sterile lemma), pubescent at tip, blackening at maturity; upper lemma brown, with a shallow excavation and tuft of wool at the tip, the palea tip also excavated.

Species 20. New World tropics; Madagascar. Forest margins, sea level to 2000 m or more.
A rhachilla extension, in the form of a conical boss between the florets, occurs in *L. grisebachii* and *L. ruscifolia*. *L. anomala* goes further by interpolating a second sterile lemma below the fertile, but is otherwise indistinguishable from *L. ruscifolia*. This is presumably an indication of residual genetic mutability in the panicoid spikelet (see also *Panicum quadriglume*), but there is no supporting evidence to suggest that *Lasiacis* itself is particularly primitive; it is certainly fallacious to invoke the superficial similarity with bamboo culms in this context. Note the disjunct geographical distribution, recalling that of *Echinolaena*.
At maturity the glumes and lower lemma turn black and their epidermis becomes packed with oil globules, thus rendering the spikelets attractive to fruit-eating birds, and effecting dispersal by passage of the tough upper floret undigested through the gut (Davidse & Morton in Biotropica 5: 162—167, 1973).

458. Amphicarpum Kunth, Rév. Gram. 1: 28 (1829) — A. purshii Kunth.

Annual or perennial. Inflorescence a panicle contracted about primary branches. Spikelets: lower glume small or absent; upper lemma coriaceous with narrow hyaline margins, acuminate. Rhizanthogenes, larger than aerial spikelets, borne singly at tips of underground rhizomes.

Species 2. South-eastern USA. Sandy pine woods.
Distinguished from *Panicum* mainly by the rhizanthogenes, though the reduced lower glume and acuminate upper lemma are helpful supporting characters.

459. Steinchisma Raf. in Bull. Bot. Genève 1: 220 (1830) — S. hians (Elliot) Nash.

Perennial. Inflorescence a panicle, ± contracted. Spikelets: lower glume short, the upper almost as long as spikelet; lower lemma 3-nerved; lower palea flanks becoming indurated at maturity.

Species 4. Southern USA to Argentina. Damp grassland.
Steinchisma, Plagiantha and *Otachyrium* are difficult to distinguish from *Panicum* until the fruit ripens and the palea develops its characteristic thickening.

460. Plagiantha Renvoize in Kew Bull. 37: 323 (1982) — P. tenella Renvoize.

Annual. Inflorescence a panicle. Spikelets obliquely tilted on pedicel; lower glume short, upper almost as long as spikelet; lower lemma 4-nerved, the 2 inner prominent and forming keels, sulcate and nerveless along midline; lower palea hyaline between keels, the flanks becoming coriaceous.

Species 1. Brazil. Damp places.

461. Otachyrium Nees, Agrost. Bras.: 271 (1829); Sendulsky & Soderstrom in Smiths. Contrib. Bot. 57: 1—24 (1984) — O. junceum Nees (= O. pterigodium).

Annual or perennial. Inflorescence a panicle, open or contracted about primary branches. Spikelets: glumes both short, up to ½ length of spikelet; lower lemma 3-nerved (*O. piligerum, O. succisum* sulcate); lower palea at first unexceptional, but after fertilization the keels arching back to grip edges of upper floret, and the flanks expanding laterally into hyaline wings (*O. piligerum, O. succisum* without wings); upper lemma thinly coriaceous to chartaceous with inrolled margins, pallid to black

Species 7. South America. Marshy places.

462. Triscenia Griseb. in Mem. Amer. Acad. Arts ser. 2, 8: 534 (1863) — T. ovina Griseb.

Perennial; leaf-blades filiform. Inflorescence a panicle with simple, sparse, almost racemose primary branches. Spikelets: lower glume ½ length of spikelet; upper lemma chartaceous with firm flat margins.

Species 1. Cuba. Streamsides.
A little known genus, doubtfully separated from *Panicum* by its thin upper lemma with flat margins.

463. Hymenachne P. Beauv., Ess. Agrost.: 48 (1812) — Agrostis monostachya Poir. (= H. amplexicaulis).

Perennial. Inflorescence a panicle, this or its primary branches spiciform. Spikelets: upper glume as long as spikelet, the lower up to ½ as long; lower lemma acute, acuminate or shortly awned; upper lemma membranous, acute, gripping edges of palea below but free towards tip.

Species 5. Tropics. Swamps.
A segregate from *Panicum*, differing from *P. rivulare* by little more than the free upper palea. There is also a resemblance to *Sacciolepis*, but the culms are filled with aerenchyma whereas those of *Sacciolepis* are hollow (Pohl & Lersten in Brittonia 27: 223—227, 1975).

464. Homolepis Chase in Proc. Biol. Soc. Wash. 24: 146 (1911) — H. aturensis (Kunth) Chase.

Annual or perennial. Inflorescence a panicle. Spikelets lanceolate; both glumes as long as spikelet and enclosing it; lower lemma margins pilose (*H. isocalycia* glabrous); upper lemma cartilaginous with firm flat margins (*H. isocalycia* thinly coriaceous), acute.

Species 3. Mexico to Brazil. Grassland and thicket.
Superficially resembling *Panicum*, but the combination of long glumes, lanceolate spikelet and thin upper lemma never occurs in that genus. The leaf-blade anatomy is peculiar, with complex midrib and fusoid cells.

465. Sacciolepis Nash in Britton, Man. Fl. North. States: 89 (1901); Simon in Kew Bull. 27: 387—406 (1972) — S. gibba (Elliott) Nash (= S. striata). *Rhampholepis* Stapf in Fl. Trop. Afr. 9: 15 (1917) — S. curvata (L.) Chase.

Annual or perennial. Inflorescence a spiciform panicle (*S. curvata, S. striata* open or contracted; *S. ciliocincta, S. cingularis, S. clathrata* with sterile basal spikelets). Spikelets laterally compressed (*S. africana, S. interrupta* dorsally), asymmetrical; glumes prominently ribbed, the lower ¼—¾ length of spikelet, the upper equalling spikelet and gibbous; lower lemma resembling upper glume but less gibbous and sometimes with a transverse row of hairs (*S. fenestrata* with 2 hyaline patches at base); upper lemma dorsally compressed, thinly coriaceous to cartilaginous, with inrolled or flat but never hyaline margins, the floret readily deciduous.

Species 30. Tropics, but mainly Africa. Damp places or shallow water.
Recognized by its spiciform inflorescence. The two species with an open panicle could be mistaken for *Panicum*, but have the gibbous ribbed spikelets characteristic of *Sacciolepis*.

466. Thyridachne C.E. Hubbard in Kew Bull. 4: 363 (1949) — T. tisserantii C.E. Hubbard. *Tisserantiella* Mimeur in Rev. Bot. Appl. 29: 593 (1949) non P. Varde (1941) — T. oubanguiensis Mimeur (= T. tisserantii).

Annual. Inflorescence a very slender spiciform panicle, sometimes imitating a raceme but not unilateral. Spikelets dorsally compressed, falcate in profile; lower glume up to ¼ length of spikelet, hyaline, nerveless; upper glume and lower lemma as long as spikelet, thinly coriaceous, the former gibbous; upper lemma cartilaginous, with firm flat margins.

Species 1. Zaire and Central African Republic. Shallow pools.
Allied to *Sacciolepis*, its inflorescence being derived by reduction from a spiciform panicle.

467. Hydrothauma C.E. Hubbard in Hook. Ic. Pl. 35: t 3458 (1947) — H. manicatum C.E. Hubbard.

Annual; leaf-blades floating, the lower on long false petioles, the upper surface raised into sinuous longitudinal lamellae. Inflorescence a slender spiciform panicle, sometimes reduced to a unilateral raceme with paired spikelets. Spikelets dorsally compressed; lower glume ½ length of spikelet, hyaline, truncate; upper glume and lower lemma as long as spikelet, the former gibbous.

Species 1. Zambia and Zaire. Shallow pools.

An aquatic genus related to *Sacciolepis*. The strange lamellae presumably improve the buoyancy of the leaves by entrapping air bubbles. The culm and false petiole contain air canals.

468. Ottochloa Dandy in J. Bot. 69: 54 (1931) nom nov pro seq; Henrard in Blumea 4: 530—531 (1941). *Hemigymnia* Stapf in Fl. Trop. Afr. 9: 741 (1920) non Griff. (1842) — Panicum nodosum Kunth.

Rambling perennial; leaf-blades lanceolate. Inflorescence of racemes along a central axis, each with slender weakly unilateral rhachis, bearing the spikelets singly in neat appressed secondary racemelets. Spikelets: glumes subequal, ½—⅔ length of spikelet.

Species 4. Old World tropics. Damp shady places.

469. Entolasia Stapf in Fl. Trop. Afr. 9: 739 (1920) — E. olivacea Stapf.

Wiry or rambling perennial; leaf-blades linear to lanceolate. Inflorescence of racemes along a central axis, the spikelets borne singly on the rhachis or in neat appressed secondary racemelets. Spikelets adaxial; lower glume short, triangular, the upper as long as spikelet; upper lemma uniformly pubescent.

Species 5. Tropical Africa and Australia. Marshy places and dry woodland.

470. Cleistochloa C.E. Hubbard in Hook. Ic. Pl. 33: t 3209 (1933) — C. subjuncea C.E. Hubbard. *Dimorphochloa* S.T. Blake in Univ. Queensland Papers 1, 19: 1 (1941) — D. rigida S.T. Blake.

Wiry perennial; leaf-blades eventually disarticulating. Inflorescence a single loose ± bilateral raceme, or of short racemelets on a central axis. Spikelets adaxial; lower glume minute or absent; upper glume and lower lemma membranous, acute to truncate; upper lemma thinly coriaceous, ciliolate on margins, rarely with a few sparse hairs on back. Cleistogenes frequent in leaf axils; like chasmogamous spikelets but upper glume and lower lemma coriaceous.

Species 3. Australia and New Guinea. Dry sandstone ridges.

Cleistogenes appear to be the normal mode of reproduction, supplemented by chasmogamous inflorescences when rainfall is adequate.

471. Calyptochloa C.E. Hubbard in Hook. Ic. Pl. 33: t 3210 (1933) — C. gracillima C.E. Hubbard.

Creeping perennial. Inflorescence a loose untidy raceme of 5—8 spikelets borne singly on a slender rhachis. Spikelets adaxial; lower glume vestigial, the upper as long as spikelet and stiffly pilose on margins and back; upper lemma chartaceous with flat narrow margins, shortly awned. Cleistogenes present in upper axils, the subtending sheaths becoming indurated and dispersed with the spikelets by disarticulation of culm.

Species 1. Australia (Queensland). Woodland shade.
Probably related to *Cleistochloa*, though also with some resemblance to *Alloteropsis*.

472. Cyrtococcum Stapf in Fl. Trop. Afr. 9: 15, 745 (1917) — C. setigerum Stapf (= C. chaetophoron).

Decumbent annual or perennial; leaf-blades linear to narrowly ovate. Inflorescence a panicle. Spikelets laterally compressed, asymmetrical; glumes shorter than spikelet, the upper obtuse; lower lemma obtuse; upper lemma laterally compressed (weakly in *C. multinode*), gibbously semiorbicular with a little greenish crest near the tip.

Species 11. Old World tropics. In shade, sometimes forming ground layer in light woodland.
C. multinode links the genus to *Panicum*.

473. Streptostachys Desv. in Nouv. Bull. Sci. Soc. Philom. 2: 190 (1810); Zuloaga & Soderstrom in Smiths. Contrib. Bot. 59: 42—55 (1985) — S. asperifolia Desv.

Perennial. Inflorescence a panicle, the spikelets in pairs along the stiff primary branches, these with occasional short secondary branches or reduced to racemes. Spikelets narrowly oblong; lower glume almost as long as spikelet, the base toroidally thickened to form a downward projecting rim; lower lemma thinly coriaceous.

Species 1. Trinidad to Brazil. Savanna.
A segregate from *Panicum*, whose stiff inflorescence branches and linear hilum hint at affinity with *Acroceras*. Fusoid cells present.

474. Acroceras Stapf in Fl. Trop. Afr. 9: 621 (1920) — A. oryzoides (Sw.) Stapf (= A. zizanioides). *Commelinidium* Stapf l.c.: 627— C. gabonense Stapf. *Neohusnotia* A. Camus in Bull. Mus. Hist. Nat. 26: 664 (1921) — N. tonkinensis (Bal.) A. Camus.

Sprawling annual or perennial; leaf-blades linear to lanceolate (*A. gabonensis* ovate). Inflorescence generally of loose racemes, but sometimes approaching a panicle due to irregular secondary branching (true panicle in *A. attenuata*). Spikelets paired, dorsally or weakly laterally compressed, glabrous; lower glume ½—¾ length of spikelet; upper glume and lower lemma thickened and laterally compressed at tip as if nipped by pincers (scarcely so in *A. attenuata*); upper lemma dorsally compressed, the tip glabrous (*A. gabonensis* puberulous) with a little green crest; palea usually with reflexed tip slightly protruding from lemma.

Species 19, including 12 Madagascan endemics. Tropics. Damp places, shallow water and forest shade.

The genus can be recognized by the nipped tip of its upper glume and lower lemma. The crested upper lemma is also characteristic, but is imitated by some *Brachiaria*. *A. attenuata* is a marginal species linking the genus to *Cyrtococcum*.

475. Microcalamus Franch. in J. Bot. Paris 3: 282 (1889) — M. barbinodis Franch.

Perennial; leaf-blades lanceolate to ovate. Inflorescence a panicle, often contracted about primary branches. Spikelets laterally compressed; glumes up to $\frac{2}{3}$ length of spikelet; lower lemma a little shorter than spikelet; upper lemma exserted, weakly laterally compressed, lanceolate, acute with a little green crest.

Species 1. Cameroun to Gabon. Forest shade.

The genus is sometimes mistaken for a herbaceous bamboo, but is related to *Acroceras gabonensis*.

476. Echinochloa P. Beauv., Ess. Agrost.: 53 (1812) nom conserv; Gould et al in Amer. Midl. Nat. 87: 36—59 (1972) — E. crusgalli (L.) P. Beauv. *Tema* Adans., Fam. Pl. 2: 496 (1763) nom rejic — unnamed species (= E. crusgalli). *Ornithospermum* Dumoulin in Dur., Fl. Bourg. 1: 495 (1782) nom rejic —unnamed species (= E. crusgalli).

Annual or perennial; ligule often absent. Inflorescence of racemes along a central axis. Spikelets paired or in short secondary racemelets, typically densely packed in 4 (*E. callopus* 2) rows, narrowly elliptic to subrotund, flat on one side gibbous on the other, often hispidulous, sometimes prolonged below into a short cylindrical (*E. callopus* globose) stipe, cuspidate or awned at tip (*E. obtusiflora, E. rotundiflora* obtuse); glumes acute to acuminate, the lower $\frac{1}{3}$ length of spikelet; lower lemma often stiffly awned; upper lemma terminating in a short membranous, laterally compressed, incurved beak (*E. obtusiflora, E. rotundiflora* without beak); upper palea acute, the tip briefly reflexed and slightly protruberant from lemma.

Species 30—40. Tropical and warm temperate regions of the world. In water or damp places, but also as a weed. *E. frumentacea* (Sawa) is a minor grain crop in India, domesticated fairly recently from *E. colona*; *E. utilis* is a similar cereal in China and Japan, but derived from *E. crusgalli* (de Wet et al in Econ. Bot. 37: 283—291, 1983). *E. oryzoides* is a serious weed of rice fields, owing its success to mimicry of the crop; this makes it difficult to eradicate but also narrows its lifestyle to dependence on the crop. It is the antithesis of a general farmland weed such as *E. crusgalli* (Barnyard grass), characterized by broad ecological tolerance and high colonizing ability (Barrett in Econ. Bot. 37: 255—282, 1983).

A difficult genus of numerous intergrading forms, its diversity apparently stemming from self-pollination combined with fluent adaptation to a wide range of aquatic and ruderal habitats. There is much uncertainty as to how this complex should be divided into species, and no reliable key to distinguish them.

The genus can usually be recognized by its hispidulous cuspidate or awned spikelets in 4 rows; in case of doubt the reflexed palea tip seems the best diagnostic character, but it needs careful dissection. The chief anomalies, in an otherwise homogenous genus, are *E. obtusiflora* and *E. rotundiflora* whose obtsue spikelets are easily mistaken for *Brachiaria*; as also the 2-rowed racemes of single spikelets in *E. callopus*. Despite the difficulty in finding clear distinguishing characters, *Echinochloa* and *Brachiaria* have different leaf anatomy and seem not to be closely related.

477. Oplismenopsis Parodi in Not. Mus. La Plata Bot. 2: 2 (1937) — O. najada (Hack. & Arech.) Parodi.

Perennial with spongy culms; leaf-blades lanceolate to narrowly ovate. Inflorescence of loose racemes along a central axis. Spikelets single, adaxial, lanceolate; lower glume $\frac{1}{3}$—$\frac{1}{2}$ length of spikelet, awned; upper glume as long as spikelet, caudate-aristate; lower lemma acuminate to shortly awned; upper lemma tip not laterally compressed.

Species 1. Argentina. Floating in water.
A genus of indeterminate origin in the C_3 group, but superficially similar to *Echinochloa* and apparently giving rise to a line of aquatic grasses.

478. Chaetium Nees, Agrost. Bras.: 269 (1829) — C. festucoides Nees. *Berchtoldia* Presl, Rel. Haenk. 1: 323 (1830) — B. bromoides Presl.

Perennial. Infloresence of loose racemes along a central axis. Spikelets paired, lanceolate, tapering below into a slender bearded stipe; glumes flexuously awned, the upper as long as spikelet, the lower similar (*C. bromoides*) or reduced to an awn; lower lemma acuminate to awned; upper lemma shortly awned (*C. cubanum* awnless).

Species 3. Mexico to West Indies and Brazil. Grassland.
C. bromoides links the genus to *Echinochloa*, the latter being distinguished by its short lower glume and stiff awns. The leaf anatomy is equivocal; although all 3 species are apparently C_4, they each show a mixture of PS and MS characters.

479. Oryzidium Hubbard & Schweick. in Kew Bull. 1936: 326 (1936) — O. barnardii Hubbard & Schweick.

Perennial with spongy culms. Inflorescence a panicle. Spikelets lanceolate; lower glume small, obtuse; upper glume as long as spikelet, stiffly awned; lower lemma acuminate; upper floret separated from the lower by an internode ± 1.5 mm long.

Species 1. Zambia to SW Africa. Floating in water.

480. Louisiella Hubbard & Léonard in Bull. Jard. Bot. Brux. 22: 316 (1952) — L.

fluitans Hubbard & Léonard.

Perennial with spongy culms. Inflorescence of racemes along a short central axis. Spikelets paired or in short appressed racemelets, lanceolate; lower glume short, truncate; upper glume and lower lemma long acuminate; upper lemma with a few hairs at tip.

Species 1. Sudan and Zaire. Floating in water or decumbent in mud.

481. Alloteropsis Presl, Rel. Haenk. 1: 343 (1830); Butzin in Willdenowia 5: 123—143 (1968) — A. distachya Presl (= A. semialata). *Coridochloa* Nees in Edinb. New Phil. J. 15: 381 (1833) — C. cimicina (L.) Chase. *Bluffia* Nees in Lehm., Del. Sem. Hort. Hamb.: 8 (1834) — B. eckloniana Nees (= A. semialata). *Holosetum* Steud., Syn. Pl. Glum. 1: 118 (1854) — H. philippicum Steud. (= A. semialata). *Pterochlaena* Chiov. in Ann. Bot. Roma 13: 47 (1914) — P. catangensis Chiov. (= A. semialata). *Mezochloa* Butzin in Willdenowia 4: 209 (1966) — M. aubertii (Mez) Butzin (= A. paniculata).

Annual or perennial; leaf-blades convolute to lanceolate. Inflorescence of irregular racemes, these digitate or in whorls on a short common axis, each with a slender weakly unilateral rhachis, this sometimes bare at the base. Spikelets paired or clustered, ovate to elliptic; glumes acute to briefly awned, the upper as long as spikelet and ciliate on margins, the lower ½ as long; upper lemma crisply chartaceous with inrolled margins, shortly awned (*A. semialata* often with minute rhachilla extension).

Species 5. Old World tropics. Marshy and weedy places.
A nondescript genus prone to misidentification because the untidy racemes of awned spikelets are not immediately recognizable as panicoid. It is remarkable in containing species possessing non-kranz, PS and MS leaf anatomy. In fact one of the species, *A semialata,* comprises non-kranz and PS races which cannot be distinguished with certainty from their external morphology (Ellis in S. Afr. J. Sci. 70: 169—173, 1974; Gibbs-Russell in Bothalia 14: 205—213, 1983; Frean et al l.c.: 901—913). Probably a segregate from *Panicum,* but its origin is not clear.

482. Scutachne Hitchc. & Chase in Proc. Biol. Soc. Wash. 24: 148 (1911) — S. dura (Griseb.) Hitchc. & Chase.

Perennial. Inflorescence a panicle contracted about primary branches (these simple and almost racemose in *S. amphistemon*). Spikelets: lower glume ½ as long as spikelet, separated from the upper by an internode; upper glume and lower lemma as long as spikelet, coriaceous (*S. amphistemon* thinly so); upper lemma acuminate to a puberulous point.

Species 2. West Indies. Rocky slopes.

483. Yakirra Lazarides & Webster in Brunonia 7: 292 (1984) — Y. pauciflora (R. Br.) Lazarides & Webster.

Annual or short-lived perennial. Inflorescence a panicle this open and terminal, or (*Y. australiensis, Y. foliolosa*) ± contracted and axillary. Spikelets elliptic; lower glume ½ as long as spikelet; upper floret borne on a stout cylindrical internode, this tipped by 2 membranous auricles (none in *Y. nulla*).

Species 6. Burma and Australia. Woodland.

Unlike *Ichnanthus* the auricles are never adnate to the lemma base, and the two genera appear to have developed this character independently. The auricles may serve as elaiosomes attracting dispersal by ants (Berg in Austral. J. Bot. 33: 579—583, 1985). *Y. nulla,* possessing a stout upper internode without auricles, links the genus to *Panicum.*

484. Arthragrostis Lazarides in Nuytsia 5: 285 (1984) — A. deschampsioides (Domin) Lazarides.

Annual. Inflorescence a panicle with deciduous branches. Spikelet: lower glume ½ length of spikelet; upper floret borne on a filiform internode, its lemma ½ length of spikelet and obtuse.

Species 1. Australia (Queensland). Open scrub.

485. Brachiaria (Trin.) Griseb. in Ledeb., Fl. Ross. 4: 469 (1853). *Panicum subtaxon Brachiaria* Trin. in Mém. Acad. Sci. Pétersb. sér. 6, 3: 194 (1834) — P. caucasicum Trin. (= B. eruciformis). *Leucophrys* Rendle, Cat. Afr. Pl. Welw. 2: 193 (1899) — L. mesocoma (L.) Rendle. *Pseudobrachiaria* Launert in Mitt. Bot. Staats. Münch. 8: 158 (1970) — P. deflexa (Schumach.) Launert.

Annual or perennial. Inflorescence of racemes along a central axis, with filiform to ribbon-like rhachis (*B. serpens* capitate; *B. glomerata* glomerate). Spikelets single or paired, rarely in fascicles or secondary racemelets (e.g., *B. comata, B. malacodes*), sessile or pedicelled (especially *B. deflexa*), adaxial, plump, sometimes the lowest internode elongated accrescent to the sheathing base of the lower glume and forming a short cylindrical stipe (e.g., *B. nigropedata*; pungent in *B. pungipes, B. turbinata*); lower glume sometimes equalling spikelet (*B. humidicola* & *B. jubata* & allies, *B. mesocoma*), but mostly shorter (small in *B. eruciformis* & allies; minute in *B. breviglumis*); upper lemma (readily deciduous in *B. eruciformis* & allies; accompanied by rhachilla extension in *B. glomerata, B. tatianae*) obtuse to acute, occasionally mucronate (green crest in *B. paucispicata*).

Species ± 100. Tropics, mainly Old World. Wide habitat range from semi-desert to swamp. A variety of *B. deflexa* is cultivated as a minor cereal in West Africa (Portères in Agron. Trop. 6: 38—42, 1951). Several species are grown for pasture, the more successful being *B. arrecta* (Tanner grass), *B. brizantha* (Palisade grass), *B. decumbens* (Surinam grass) and *B. mutica* (Para grass).

A variable genus for which no satisfactory infrageneric classification is available. Species with a neatly racemose inflorescence present no problem, but the genus is contiguous with a number of other genera and discrimination among intermediate species can be difficult. The principal problems are:

Panicum. The two genera intergrade, diagnosis resting upon a distinction between panicle and raceme that becomes rather arbitrary when there are secondary racemelets or loose racemes with long pedicels. The plumper spikelets of *Brachiaria* provide a helpful, but highly subjective supporting character. The problem can sometimes be resolved by considering nearest relatives; the doubtful *B. deflexa*, for example, is closely related to *B. ramosa*.

Urochloa. The mucronate upper lemma of *B. lata* and *B. reptans* imitates *Urochloa*; the spikelets are paired and their orientation ambiguous, but they are plump with an evident similarity to *B. ramosa*. *B. gilesii*, *B. notochthona* and *B.ophyrodes* are intermediate, resembling *Urochloa* except for the spikelet orientation.

Eriochloa. The stipe of *Brachiaria*, when present, is cylindrical and accompanied by a lower glume; *E. meyeriana* is intermediate.

Acroceras. The upper lemma mucro of *Brachiaria* is sometimes laterally nipped rather than subulate. In *B. paucispicata* this approaches the crested condition of *Acroceras*, but the racemes are denser and the anatomy PS. *Panicum hubbardii* also has a slight crest and dense inflorescence; it has been accommodated in both *Acroceras* and *Brachiaria*, but its MS anatomy is compatible with neither. Note the rhachilla extension of *B. glomerata* and *B. tatianae*, a rare phenomenon in Paniceae.

486. Eccoptocarpha Launert in Senck. Biol. 46: 124 (1965) — E. obconiciventris Launert.

Annual. Inflorescence of racemes along a central axis. Spikelets single, adaxial, obovate; lower glume ¾ length of spikelet; upper glume and lower lemma as long as spikelet, prominently net-veined and resembling woven fabric; upper floret raised upon a slender sinuous internode, this eventually straightening to extrude the floret.

Species 1. Tanzania and Zambia. Savanna.
A peculiar genus, but with obvious similarities to *Brachiaria humidicola* and its allies. The leaf anatomy is equivocal, displaying a mixture of PS and MS characters.

487. Urochloa P. Beauv., Ess. Agrost.: 52 (1812) — U. panicoides P. Beauv.

Annual or perennial. Inflorescence of racemes along an axis (rhachis membranously winged in *U. platyrrhachis*). Spikelets single or paired, abaxial, plano-convex, cuspidate to acuminate; lower glume shorter than spikelet (except *U. paspaloides*); upper glume and lower lemma membranous to firmly chartaceous (*U. sclerochlaena* coriaceous; lemma of *U. platyrrhachis* with hyaline median line); upper lemma obtuse with a long mucro housed within spikelet (*U. platyrrhachis* emucronate; *U. rudis* acuminate).

Species 12. Old World tropics, mainly Africa. Savanna.
The genus is defined by the abaxial orientation of its spikelets, with which is associated a plano-convex shape, cuspidate tip and mucronate upper lemma. When the spikelets are paired their orientation becomes ambiguous and diagnosis then rests upon their facies. Unfortunately orientation and facies are not wholly correlated, some intermediates being noted under *Brachiaria*, and it is a moot point whether generic rank is justified. The number of species is

probably too high, as the characters separating members of the central *U. trichopus* complex have been shown to intergrade.

488. Eriochloa Kunth in Humb. & Bonpl., Nov. Gen. Sp. 1: 94 (1816) — E. distachya Kunth. *Helopus* Trin., Fund Agrost.: 103 (1820) — H. pilosus Trin. (= E. procera). *Oedipachne* Link, Hort. Berol. 1: 51, 273 (1827) nom prov — E. punctata. *Panicum sect Glandiloba* Raf. in Bull. Bot. Genève 1: 220 (1830) — P. molle Michaux (= E. michauxii). *Aglycia* Steud., Nom. Bot. ed. 2, 1: 37 (1840) & l.c.: 66 as "Alycia", nom nud — E. polystachya. *Glandiloba* (Raf.) Steud. l.c.: 687 in syn.

Annual or perennial. Inflorescence of racemes along a central axis (sometimes only 1 raceme in *E. distachya*; a panicle contracted about primary branches in *E. meyeriana*). Spikelets single, paired or clustered, adaxial, elliptic, thinly biconvex, with a little globose bead at the base; lower glume vestigial (*E. meyeriana* small; *E. rovumensis* as long as spikelet); upper glume as long as spikelet, often with an awn-point; upper lemma usually mucronate.

Species 30. Tropics. Damp soil and weedy places.
A uniform genus of indistinctly separated species. It is distinguished by a little bead at the base of each spikelet, but may be confused with *Echinochloa callopus* which has a similar structure. The bead is formed from the lowest rhachilla internode which becomes swollen and fused to the lower glume (Shaw & Smeins in Amer. J. Bot. 66: 907—913, 1979 & in Isleya 2: 15—19, 1983); it is evidently an elaboration of the basal stipe found in some *Brachiaria*. *E. meyeriana* provides a link with *Brachiaria mutica*, and its semi-paniculate inflorescence may lead to confusion with *Panicum*.

489. Yvesia A. Camus in Bull. Soc. Bot. France 73: 687 (1927) — Y. madagascariensis A. Camus.

Annual. Inflorescence delicate, ovate, of subdigitate indistinctly unilateral racemes with filiform rhachis. Spikelets single, borne loosely on short pedicels, adaxial, lanceolate; lower glume absent; upper glume and lower lemma as long as spikelet, pilose, sharply acute; upper lemma mucronate.

Species 1. Madagascar. Rocks and streamsides.
A minor segregate from *Brachiaria*.

490. Thuarea Pers., Syn. Pl. 1: 110 (1805) — T. sarmentosa Pers. (= T. involuta). *Microthuareia* Thouars, Gen. Nova Madag.: 3 (1806) nom superfl pro Thuarea. *Ornithocephalochloa* Kurz in J. Bot. 13: 332 (1875) — O. arenicola Kurz (= T. involuta). *Thouarsia* Kuntze in Post, Lexicon: 558 (1903) nom superfl pro Thuarea.

Creeping perennial. Inflorescence a single deciduous raceme with foliaceous rhachis bearing 1—2 persistent bisexual spikelets below and several deciduous ♂ spikelets above, the ♂ portion of the rhachis folding onto the fertile spikelets after anthesis thus enclosing them in a capsule. Bisexual spikelets adaxial, biconvex; lower glume small or suppressed; upper glume and lower lemma as long as spikelet; upper lemma with flat firm margins. Male spikelets similar, but smaller with thinner scales.

Species 2. Madagascar to Polynesia. Sandy seashores.
Probably related to *Brachiaria*. The inflorescence is borne on a very short culm, and the capsules either become buried in the sand or float away in the sea.

491. Tatianyx Zul. & Sod. in Smiths. Contrib. Bot. 59: 56 (1985) — T. arnacites (Trin.) Zul. & Sod.

Perennial. Inflorescence a panicle. Spikelets borne on a brief callus, this attached obliquely to pedicel tip; lower glume ± ½ as long as spikelet; upper glume and lower lemma villous.

Species 1. Brazil. Savanna.
A minor satellite of *Panicum*.

492. Whiteochloa C.E. Hubbard in Proc. Roy. Soc. Queensland 62: 111 (1952); Lazarides in Brunonia 1: 69—93 (1978) — W. semitonsa (Benth.) C.E. Hubbard.

Annual or perennial. Inflorescence a panicle (primary branches sometimes reduced to racemes bearing paired spikelets in *W. semitonsa*). Spikelets dorsally or slightly laterally compressed; upper glume as long as spikelet and tuberculate-ciliate on the nerves (*W. airoides, W. capillipes* glabrous, laterally nipped at tip), the lower ½ as long; lower lemma membranous to thinly coriaceous, sulcate; upper floret borne on a very short filiform internode (obscure in *W. airoides*), its lemma somewhat gibbous, ± equidimensional in section, acute to acuminate.

Species 5. Australia. Sandy alluvial soils in savanna.
A variable genus, difficult to distinguish from *Panicum* as the characteristic upper rhachilla internode requires careful dissection. The supporting characters are helpful but inconstant.

493. Acostia Swallen in Bol. Soc. Arg. Bot. 12: 109 (1968) — A. gracilis Swallen.

Perennial. Inflorescence of loose racemes along a central axis. Spikelets paired; lower glume tiny or absent; upper glume and lower lemma equalling spikelet.

Species 1. Ecuador. River bank.
Superficially similar to *Digitaria*; distinguished from *Panicum* mainly by the rudimentary lower glume.

494. Anthaenantiopsis Pilger in Not. Bot. Gart. Berlin 11: 237 (1931); Parodi in Not. Mus. La Plata 8: 85—92 (1943) — A. trachystachya (Nees) Pilger.

Perennial. Inflorescence of racemes along an axis. Spikelets paired, plumply biconvex, stiffly pilose; lower glume small or absent; upper glume and lower lemma as long as spikelet, prominently nerved; upper lemma thinly crustaceous, sometimes pubescent at tip, its palea gaping after anthesis.

Species 2. Brazil to Argentina. Savanna.

Easily mistaken for *Brachiaria*, though the different leaf anatomy indicates that the two genera are unrelated.

495. Paspalum L., Syst. Nat. ed. 10: 855 (1759) — P. dimidiatum L. (= P. dissectum). *Digitaria* Fabric., Enum.: 207 (1759) nom rejic non Hall. (1768) — unnamed species (= Paspalum sp). *Sabsab* Adans., Fam. Pl. 2: 31, 599 (1763) nom superfl pro Paspalum. *Cleachne* Roland. ex Rottb. in Acta Lit. Univ. Hafn. 1: 285 (1778) in syn sub Paspalum. *Ceresia* Pers., Syn. Pl. 1: 85 (1805) — C. elegans Pers. (= P. ceresia). *Reimaria* Flügge, Gram. Monogr. Pasp.: 213 (1810) — R. candida (Kunth) Flügge. *Paspalanthium* Desv., Opusc.: 59 (1831) — P. stoloniferum Desv. (= P. racemosum). *Moenchia* Steud., Nom. Bot. ed. 2, 2: 153 (1841) nom nud non Ehrh. (1788) — P. saccharoides. *Anachyris* Nees in Hook. J. Bot. 2: 103 (1850); Steud., Syn. Pl. Glum. 1: 33 (1854) as "Anachyrium" — A. paspaloides Nees (= P. malacophyllum). *Maizilla* Schlecht. in Bot. Zeit. 8: 601, 605 (1850) nom superfl pro Paspalanthium. *Dichromus* Schlecht. l.c. 10: 17 (1852) nom nud — P. pulchellum. *Cerea* Schlecht. l.c. 12: 820 (1854) nom superfl pro Ceresia. *Cymatochloa* Schlecht. l.c. 821 — C. fluitans (Ell.) Schlecht. *Dimorphostachys* Fourn. in Compt. Rend. Acad. Sci. 80: 441 (1875) — D. monostachya Fourn. (= P. pilosum). *Wirtgenia* Doell in Mart. Fl. Bras. 2, 2: 40 (1877) in syn sub P. malacophyllum.

Annual or perennial. Inflorescence of single, digitate or scattered racemes; rhachis flat, sometimes broadly winged and then often with a sterile tip. Spikelets single or paired, abaxial, in 2—4 rows, plano-convex, orbicular to ovate; lower glume suppressed, rarely minute; upper glume and lower lemma as long as spikelet (except sect *Anachyris*); upper lemma usually obtuse, coriaceous to crustaceous, rarely thinner.

Species ± 330. Tropics, predominantly New World. Savanna, forest margins and damp places; *P. distichum* and *P. vaginatum* in coastal and inland salt marshes. A race of the weedy wild species *P. scrobiculatum* has been domesticated as a cereal (Kodo) in India, probably about 3000 years ago (de Wet et al in Econ. Bot. 37: 159—163, 1983). Several species, notably *P. dilatatum* (Dallis grass) and *P. notatum* (Bahia grass), are grown for fodder. *P. conjugatum* (Sour grass) and *P. dilatatum* are sometimes troublesome as weeds.

The genus is best recognized by its plano-convex abaxial spikelets, often with a hemispherical or oblong shape. The lack of a lower glume is also a useful diagnostic feature, but in about 10 species a tiny lower glume is irregularly present. Variation is summarized in the following simplified key (Pilger, Nat. Pfl.-Fam. ed. 2, 14e: 58—67, 1940). Three quarters of the species belong to sect *Diplostachys*.

Rhachis not membranous, foliaceous or winged:
  Spikelets glabrous or weakly hairy:
    Upper glume present:

Upper glume not winged (P. scrobiculatum)   Sect *Diplostachys*
Upper glume winged (P. fimbriatum)   Sect *Pterolepidium*
Upper glume absent; upper lemma often prominently ribbed (P. pulchellum)
                                                             Sect *Anachyris*
Spikelets conspicuously hairy:
  Upper lemma coriaceous:
    Spikelets silky hairy (P. erianthum)   Sect *Erianthum*
    Spikelets with stiff tubercle-based hairs; raceme solitary (P. ekmanianum)
                                                             Sect *Eriolepidium*
  Upper lemma cartilaginous; spikelet bearing silky hairs several times longer
    than itself (P. saccharoides)   Sect *Moenchia*
Rhachis membranous or foliaceous, mostly broad and winged:
  Rhachis foliaceous, green, often deflexed; spikelets glabrous or weakly hairy (P.
    repens)   Sect *Paspalum*
  Rhachis membranous, colourful; upper glume and lower lemma scarious,
    usually ciliate, sometimes winged; upper lemma thinly coriaceous (P. stellatum)
                                                             Sect *Ceresia*

P. amphicarpum bears rhizanthogenes on short subterranean branches.

496. Reimarochloa Hitchc. in Contrib. U.S. Nat. Herb. 12: 198 (1909) — R. acuta (Flügge) Hitchc.

Perennial. Inflorescence of subdigitate racemes. Spikelets borne singly, abaxial, lanceolate, acute to acuminate; both glumes absent; lower lemma as long as spikelet; upper lemma membranous to thinly coriaceous with narrow margins, the palea free from them for nearly ½ its length.

Species 4. Southern USA to Argentina. Damp places.
An odd little genus resembling *Digitaria*, but probably related to *Paspalum vaginatum*.

497. Thrasya Kunth in Humb. & Bonpl., Nov. Gen. Sp. 1: 120 (1816) — T. paspaloides Kunth. *Tylothrasya* Doell in Mart., Fl. Bras. 2: 295 (1877) — T. petrosa (Trin.) Doell.

Perennial. Inflorescence a single raceme with herbaceously winged (*T. reticulata* narrow) rhachis folded around base of spikelets and usually extending beyond uppermost spikelet. Spikelets paired but the pedicel wholly or partly adnate to rhachis, producing an orientation alternately abaxial and adaxial in a single row; lower glume small or absent; upper glume as long as spikelet (*T. scandens* much shorter), membranous, 5—7-nerved; lower lemma thinly coriaceous, 5-nerved, medially sulcate and readily splitting into two halves (*T. achlysophila, T. parvula, T. scandens* chartaceous and weakly sulcate), its palea eventually becoming indurated on flanks; upper lemma often hairy at tip.

Species ± 20. Central and South America. In savanna and by water.
The genus is characterized by its single row of spikelets with their unusual alternating orientation. The latter is a consequence of their paired origin, though this is not apparent in species whose pedicel is wholly adnate to the

rhachis. The split lower lemma is a further aid to identification, but is not always well developed. In fact the genus grades into *Paspalum* through *T. reticulata* and *P. cultratum* (sulcate lower lemma but 2 irregularly oriented rows of spikelets), and the distinction between the two genera is rather arbitrary.

498. Thrasyopsis Parodi in Bol. Soc. Arg. Bot. 1: 293 (1946); Burman in Phyton 23: 101—116 (1983) — T. rawitscheri Parodi (= T. juergensii).

Perennial. Inflorescence of 1—2 racemes, their rhachis with scanty or prominent herbaceous wings. Spikelets paired, in 2 or more rows, biconvex; lower glume small (*T. juergensii*) or ¾ length of spikelet; upper glume as long as spikelet, coriaceous, prominently 11—17-nerved, with an obtuse hooded tip; lower lemma coriaceous, 7—9-nerved, sulcate, its palea indurated on the keels.

Species 2. Brazil. Savanna.
The two species are dissimilar in appearance, but share the unusual many-nerved upper glume. *T. juergensii* links them to *Thrasya*.

499. Mesosetum Steud., Syn. Pl. Glum. 1: 118 (1854); Swallen in Brittonia 2: 363—392 (1937) — M. cayennense Steud. *Panicum sect Bifaria* Hack. in Oest. Bot. Zeitschr. 47: 75 (1897) — P. bifarium Hack. *Bifaria* (Hack.) Kuntze, Rev. Gen. Pl. 3: 359 (1898) non Van Tiegh. (1896). *Peniculus* Swallen in Amer. J. Bot. 19: 581 (1932) — P. angustifolius Swallen (= M. filifolium).

Annual or perennial. Inflorescence a single raceme (rhachis membranously winged in *M. ansatum*). Spikelets single, adaxial; glumes ⅔ to as long as spikelet (lower awned in *M. bifarium* and allies), the upper 3—7-nerved; lower lemma usually hyaline down the centre line; upper lemma acute to mucronate.

Species 30. Mexico to Brazil. Savanna.

500. Axonopus P. Beauv., Ess. Agrost.: 12 (1812); Dedecca in Bragantia 15: 295 (1956); Black in Adv. Front. Pl. Sci. 5: 1—186 (1963) — A. compressus (Sw.) P. Beauv. *Cabrera* Lag., Gen. Sp. Nov.: 5 (1816) — C. chrysoblepharis Lag. *Anastrophus* Schlecht. in Bot. Zeit. 8: 681 (1850) — Paspalum platyculmum Nees (= A. compressus). *Lappagopsis* Steud., Syn. Pl. Glum. 1: 112 (1854) — L. bijuga Steud.

Perennial, rarely annual. Inflorescence of 2—many racemes, mostly subdigitate but sometimes along a central axis. Spikelets borne singly, adaxial, oblong-elliptic, thinly biconvex; lower glume absent; upper glume and lower lemma as long as spikelet.

Species ± 110. Tropical and subtropical America; 1 species in Africa. Savanna, forest clearings and weedy places. *A. compressus* (Carpet grass) has become widely naturalized and is used for lawns in the humid tropics.
Inflorescence and vegetative characters are remarkably uniform and the genus is easy to recognize, but these factors also make it taxonomically difficult,

for the differences between its many species are slight. It can be divided into 3 sections, but 90% of the species belong to sect *Axonopus*.

Rhachis and spikelets glabrous to pubescent (A. compressus)   Sect *Axonopus*
Rhachis or spikelets bearing stiff tubercle-based bristles:
    Bristles white, mainly on spikelets (A. brasiliensis)   Sect *Lappagopsis*
    Bristles golden, mainly on rhachis (A. aureus)   Sect *Cabrera*

501. Centrochloa Swallen in J. Wash. Acad. Sci. 25: 192 (1935) — C. singularis Swallen.

Annual. Inflorescence of subdigitate racemes. Spikelets borne singly, adaxial, turbinate with a short blunt callus, sessile; lower glume absent; upper glume as long as spikelet, extending below the callus as a long tapering spur, transversely bearded below tip; upper lemma tip puberulous.

Species 1. Brazil. Savanna.
The peculiarly shaped spikelets are apparently derived from *Axonopus*.

502. Spheneria Kuhlm. in Comm. Linh. Telegr. Matto Grosso Annexo 5, Bot. 11: 57 (1922) — S. setifolia (Doell) Kuhlm. (= S. kegelii).

Perennial. Inflorescence of few racemes along a short central axis. Spikelets borne singly, abaxial, turbinate with a long pungent callus obliquely articulated to a pedicel; lower glume absent; upper glume as long as spikelet, transversely bearded below tip.

Species 1. Guyana to Brazil. Savanna.
Easily mistaken for *Centrochloa*, whose spur imitates a pungent callus.

503. Setaria P. Beauv., Ess. Agrost.: 51 (1812) nom conserv; Rominger in Illinois Biol. Monogr. 29 (1962) — S. viridis (L.) P. Beauv. *Miliastrum* Fabric., Enum.: 206 (1759) & ed. 2: 372 (1763) nom nud — S. pumila. *Chaetochloa* Scribn. in US Dept. Agric. Div. Agrost. Bull. 4: 38 (1897) nom superfl pro Setaria. *Acrochaete* Peter in Feddes Rep. Beih. 40, 1: Anh. 54 (1930) non Pringsheim (1863) — A. pseudaristata Peter. *Cymbosetaria* Schweick. in Hook. Ic. Pl. 34: t 3320 (1936) — C. sagittifolia (A. Rich.) Schweick. *Camusiella* Bosser in Adansonia sér. 2, 6: 105 (1966) — C. vatkeana (Schum.) Bosser. *Tansaniochloa* Rauschert in Taxon 31: 561 (1982) nom nov pro Acrochaete.

Annual or perennial. Inflorescence a panicle, either spiciform or with spikelets ± contracted about primary branches, these occasionally reduced to racemes, all or most of the spikelets subtended by 1 or more scabrid (*S. orthosticha* and a few others ciliate) bristles which persist on axis. Spikelets ± gibbous; glumes shorter than spikelet, or the upper equalling it, membranous to herbaceous; lower lemma sometimes sulcate (*S. fiherenensis, S. vatkeana* coriaceous on the back with broad membranous margins); upper lemma often rugose.

Species ± 100. Tropics and subtropics. Habitat variable, including grassland, woodland and weedy places. *S. italica* (Foxtail millet) is a major cereal crop in China, and is grown as a minor cereal or for birdseed in Europe and elsewhere. It is derived from *S. viridis*, and was probably domesticated at several independent European and Asian centres ± 7000 years ago. It is suited to semi-arid warm-temperate conditions (de Wet in J. Agric. Trad. Bot. Appl. 26: 53—60, 1979). *S. sphacelata* is grown for pasture; it illustrates the complexity of a successful polymorphic species, being diploid to decaploid and crossing freely between the levels (Hacker in Austral. J. Bot. 16: 539—544 & 551—554, 1968). The shoots of *S. palmifolia* are cultivated as a vegetable in New Guinea; this species is also grown as a hothouse ornamental. *S. verticillata* and *S. viridis* are noxious weeds.

A heterogeneous genus whose traditional subdivisions usefully summarize the major facies, but are of doubtful practical value due to the large number of intermediate species.

Panicle open or contracted:
  Leaf-blades not pleated:
    Upper lemma rounded (S. longiseta)   Sect *Panicatrix*
    Upper lemma keeled (S. sagittifolia)   Sect *Cymbosetaria*
  Leaf-blades pleated (S. palmifolia)   Sect *Ptychophyllum*
Panicle spiciform (S. pumila)   Sect *Setaria*

The most characteristic feature is modification of the tips of the panicle branches into bristles subtending the spikelets (Butzin in Willldenowia 8: 67—79, 1977; Sohns in J. Wash. Acad. Sci. 44: 116—122, 1954). This is associated with contraction of the panicle along two diverging lines which lead, on the one hand to racemose branches, and on the other to a cylindrical spike. *S. verticillata* and a few other species have retrorsely scabrid bristles which cling tenaciously to clothing.

The leaf-blades display a number of peculiarities being often plicate, sometimes falsely petiolate and rarely (*S. appendiculata, S. fiherenensis, S. sagittifolia, S. vatkeana*) sagittate.

Minor segregates pose a problem for their recognition is largely a matter of subjective opinion; *Camusiella* and *Cymbosetaria* seem marginally better retained in *Setaria*, the other satellite genera have been accepted. *S. humbertiana* links the genus to *Paspalidium*.

504. Paspalidium Stapf in Fl. Trop. Afr. 9: 582 (1920) — P. geminatum (Forssk.) Stapf.

Perennial. Inflorescence of short racemes, these overlapping or distant along a central axis and ending in an inconspicuous point or bristle, the spikelets borne singly and often in 2 neat rows, sometimes the lower paired or clustered and then pedicel or branchlet ending in a point, otherwise without subtending bristles (*P. rarum* often reduced to 1 spikelet per raceme). Spikelets abaxial; glumes membranous to herbaceous, the upper as long as spikelet, the lower shorter; lower lemma resembling upper glume, the palea when present permanently hyaline and narrower than upper floret.

Species ± 40. Throughout tropics. Habitat varied; swamp, forest and dry slopes.

Typically the genus has distant racemes with neatly imbricate spikelets, which seem very different from *Setaria*. In fact the gap is bridged by intermediate species with looser racemes so that the diagnostic criterion — most of the spikelets lacking bristles — is rather arbitrary, though seldom difficult to apply.

The rhachis tip is easily overlooked and the genus can then be confused with *Urochloa* or *Panicum*; in fact the intermediate species are sometimes treated as *Panicum sect Paurochaetium*.

505. Holcolemma Stapf & Hubbard in Kew Bull. 1929: 244 (1929); Clayton l.c. 32: 773—774 (1978) — H. canaliculatum (Nees) Stapf & Hubbard.

Annual or perennial. Inflorescence a panicle contracted about the short appressed (*H. dispar* spreading and raceme-like) primary branches, the terminal spikelet of each branch subtended by an inconspicuous bristle (longer in *H. transiens*). Spikelets: glumes shorter than spikelet, membranous (upper glume of *H. dispar* chartaceous, 13-nerved); lower lemma herbaceous, sulcate to lyrate; lower palea at first hyaline, later the flanks thinly coriaceous and inrolled, the keels developing indurated wings which clasp edge of upper floret; upper lemma sometimes much shorter than lower.

Species 4. East Africa, southern India and Sri Lanka; Australia. Weedy or shady places.

Note that the palea keels, which principally distinguish the genus from *Paspalidium*, do not assume their distinctive form until after anthesis.

506. Ixophorus Schlecht. in Linnaea 31: 420 (1861) — I. unisetus (Presl) Schlecht.

Annual. Inflorescence of secund racemes closely spaced along a central axis, the spikelets borne singly and each subtended by a sticky bristle. Spikelets abaxial; glumes herbaceous, the upper almost equalling spikelet, the lower much shorter; lower lemma cartilaginous; lower palea at first hyaline, later circular with expanded coriaceous flanks and winged keels clasping edge of upper floret.

Species 1. Mexico. Weedy places.

507. Setariopsis Scribn. & Millsp. in Publ. Field Mus. Bot. Ser. 1: 288 (1896) — S. latiglumis (Vasey) Scribn. & Millsp.

Annual. Inflorescence a contracted or spiciform panicle, each spikelet subtended by a bristle. Spikelets gibbous; lower glume shorter than spikelet, oblate; upper glume as long as and broader than rest of spikelet with conspicuous nerves, auriculate, indurated at maturity; lower lemma lyrate, becoming indurated, the floret barren with small hyaline palea.

Species 2. Mexico to Colombia. Weedy places.

508. Dissochondrus (Hillebr.) Kuntze, Rev. Gen. Pl. 2: 770 (1891). *Setaria subgen Dissochondrus* Hillebr., Fl. Haw. Isl.: 503 (1888) — S. biflora Hillebr.

Perennial. Inflorescence a spiciform panicle, each spikelet subtended by 1 to several bristles. Spikelets like *Setaria* but both florets similar, bisexual, crustaceous.

Species 1. Hawaii. Shady slopes.
The subtending bristles and MS anatomy clearly indicate that the genus is allied to *Setaria* rather than to Isachneae.

509. Plagiosetum Benth. in Hook. Ic. Pl. 13: 33 (1877) — P. refractum (Muell.) Benth.

Annual. Inflorescence of cuneate deciduous racemes along a central axis, these bearing few spikelets each subtended by several bristles, the rhachis ending in a fan of bristles. Spikelets like *Paspalidium*.

Species 1. Australia. Sandhills.
The deciduous racemes recall *Paractaenum*, but the multiple bristles point to an independent derivation from *Setaria sect Setaria*.

510. Paractaenum P. Beauv., Ess. Agrost.: 47 (1812) — P. novae-hollandiae P. Beauv.

Perennial. Inflorescence of deciduous racemes along a central axis, the spikelets borne singly, 1 or more at the base subtended by a bristle and the rhachis itself ending in a point. Spikelets like *Paspalidium*.

Species 1. Australia. Sandy places and dunes.
A derivative of *Paspalidium* with deciduous racemes.

511. Hygrochloa Lazarides in Brunonia 2: 86 (1979) — H. aquatica Lazarides.

Annual or short-lived perennial. Inflorescence of short racemes appressed along a central axis and ending in an inconspicuous point, the lower racemes ♀, the upper ♂, bearing single spikelets. Female spikelet: glumes membranous, the upper $\frac{2}{3}$ as long as spikelet, the lower shorter; lower lemma membranous, the floret barren; upper lemma thinly coriaceous with flat hyaline margins covering much of palea. Male spikelet similar to ♀, but larger and both florets ♂.

Species 2. Australia (Northern Territory). In or near water.
The genus is very similar to *Paspalidium*, despite the *Digitaria*-like upper lemma. The leaf-blades are densely papillose above, the trapped air presumably assisting flotation.

512. Stenotaphrum Trin., Fund. Agrost.: 175 (1822); Saur in Brittonia 24: 202—222 (1972) — T. glabrum Trin. (= S. dimidiatum). *Ophiurinella* Desv., Opusc.: 75

(1831) — O. micrantha Desv. *Diastemenanthe* Steud., Syn. Pl. Glum. 1: 360 (1854) — D. platystachys Steud. (= *S. secundatum*).

Annual or perennial. Inflorescence of very short racemes bearing few single spikelets and sunk in pockets on one or both sides of a foliaceous or corky axis, variously disarticulating at maturity, the raceme rhachis ending in a point (racemes reduced to 1 spikelet without rhachis extension in *S. clavigerum, S. oostachyum*). Spikelets: glumes membranous, both short or the upper as long as spikelet; lower lemma coriaceous (*S. helferi, S. unilaterale* chartaceous); upper lemma chartaceous (*S. helferi* coriaceous) with flat margins.

Species 7. Tropics and subtropics. Seashores or near the coast, rarely inland. *S. secundatum* (St Augustine grass) is used for lawns.

Derived from *Paspalidium* by a progressive reduction of the racemes and expansion of the central axis, as shown in the sequence: *S. helferi* — racemes occupying shallow pockets in a foliaceous axis, the spikelets individually deciduous; *S. secundatum* — racemes sunk in a corky axis, this disarticulating into segments; *S. clavigerum* — 1-spikelet racemes embedded in a clavate axis, deciduous as a whole. Concommitant with retreat of the upper floret into the axis is the transfer of protective induration from the upper lemma to the lower; but *S. helferi*, the least modified species, has retained a coriaceous upper floret.

The swollen inflorescence axis is presumably an adaptation to dispersal by sea, but it only remains buoyant for about a week.

513. Uranthoecium Stapf in Hook. Ic. Pl. 31: t 3073 (1916) — U. truncatum (Maiden & Betche) Stapf.

Annual. Inflorescence of short racemes appressed to a slender fragile central axis; each raceme comprising 2—4 single spikelets and an inconspicuous pointed rhachis extension, deciduous with adjacent axis internode. Spikelets: glumes firmly chartaceous, truncate, the lower ¼, the upper ½ length of spikelet and gibbous; lower lemma as long as spikelet, membranous along midline with coriaceous flanks, caudate-acuminate; upper lemma coriaceous with flat margins, tapering to a subulate beak.

Species 1. Australia. Grassland on clays.

c. MELINIDINAE (Hitchc.) Pilger, Nat. Pfl.-Fam. ed. 2, 14e: 95 (1940); Butzin in Willdenowia 6: 285—289 (1971). *Tristegininae* Harvey, Gen. S. Afr. Pl. ed. 2: 428 (1869) nom illegit.

Inflorescence a panicle (except *Rhynchelytrum sp*). Spikelets laterally compressed; lower glume small or absent; upper glume as long as spikelet, emarginate to bilobed (except *Tricholaena*); lower floret ♂ or barren, its lemma resembling upper glume; upper lemma cartilaginous, smooth, readily deciduous, the margins firm and flat. Anatomy: kranz PS.

A close-knit group of genera recognized by their panicle, reduced lower glume and cartilaginous upper floret. Presumably derived from the PS branch of *Panicum*.

514. Tricholaena Schult., Syst. Veg. Mant. 2: 8, 163 (1824); Kuntze in Post, Lexicon: 569 (1903) as "Trichochlaena" — T. micrantha Schult. (= T. teneriffae). *Xyochlaena* Stapf in Fl. Trop. Afr. 9: 16 (1917) — X. monachne (Trin,) Stapf. *Eremochlamys* Peter in Feddes Rep. Beih. 40, 1: Anh. 19 (1930) — E. littoralis Peter (= T. monachne).

Annual or perennial. Spikelets: upper glume membranous, indistinctly 5-nerved, subacute, awnless; upper lemma dorsally compressed.

Species 4. Mediterranean and Africa to India. Sandy and stony places. Easily mistaken for *Panicum*.

515. Mildbraediochloa Butzin in Willdenowia 6: 288 (1971) — M. reynaudioides (C.E. Hubbard) Butzin.

Perennial. Spikelets: upper glume membranous, 5-nerved, awned; upper lemma laterally compressed, awned.

Species 1. Annobon Is. Cliffs.

516. Rhynchelytrum Nees in Lindley, Nat. Syst. ed. 2: 446 (1836) as "Rhynchelythrum", corr Nees, Fl. Afr. Austr.: errata (1841) — R. dregeanum Nees (= R. repens). *Monachyron* Parl. in Hook., Niger Fl.: 190 (1849) — M. villosum Parl. (= R. repens).

Annual or perennial. (Inflorescence of racemes along a central axis in *R. tanatrichum*). Spikelets: upper glume gibbous, chartaceous to coriaceous below, thinner and often tapering to a beak above, 5-nerved, awned or awnless (separated from lower by an elongated internode in *R. repens* and a few others); upper lemma laterally compressed.

Species 14. Africa. Savanna and open or disturbed places. *R. repens* (Natal grass) is a common though usually innocuous weed, now distributed throughout the tropics.
A difficult genus of closely related species.

517. Melinis P. Beauv., Ess. Agrost.: 54 (1812) — M. minutiflora P. Beauv. *Suardia* Schrank, Pl. Rar. Horti Monac.: 58 (1820) — S. picta Schrank (= M. minutiflora). *Tristegis* Nees, Hor. Phys. Berol.: 47, 54 (1820) nom superfl pro Suardia.

Annual or perennial. Spikelets: upper glume not gibbous, uniformly membranous to chartaceous (*M. ambigua* thinner at tip), 7-nerved (*M. tenuissima* 5-nerved), awned or awnless; upper lemma laterally compressed.

Species 11. Tropical and South Africa. Savanna woodland, open grassland and disturbed places. *M. minutiflora* (Molasses grass) is cultivated for forage, particularly in South America; its leaves are covered in sticky hairs smelling of linseed oil.
A homogeneous genus of barely distinct species. It is sometimes taken to

include *Rhynchelytrum*, but the two genera differ in spikelet shape. There is some intergradation (notably *M. ambigua*), but the upper glume nervation provides a reasonable diagnostic criterion.

d. DIGITARIINAE Butzin in Willdenowia 6: 509 (1972).

Inflorescence sometimes a panicle, more often of racemes. Spikelets dorsally compressed (except *Anthenantia*); lower glume small or absent (except *Homopholis, Megaloprotachne*); upper glume usually almost as long as spikelet (exceptions in *Digitaria, Stereochlaena*); lower floret usually reduced to an empty membranous lemma as long as spikelet; upper lemma chartaceous to cartilaginous, its flat hyaline margins enfolding and concealing ½ to most of the palea (margins open in *Anthenantia, Leptocoryphium*). Anatomy: *Hylebates, Acritochaete, Homopholis* non-kranz; the rest kranz MS (fig 20).

Definition of the subtribe rests upon its spikelet facies in general and upper lemma in particular, but it is difficult to reduce these to unequivocal diagnostic criteria. Lemma thickness alone is an unreliable criterion and some genera with thin lemmas, but whose spikelet shape allies them to members of Setariinae, have been excluded.

518. Hylebates Chippindall in J. S. Afr. Bot. 11: 127 (1945) — H. cordatus Chippindall.

Annual. Inflorescence a panicle. Spikelets: lower glume small; lower lemma tipped by an awnlet; upper floret acute.

Species 2. Central Africa. Woodland and riverine forest, in shade.
The genus outwardly resembles *Panicum,* and is easily mistaken for it.

519. Acritochaete Pilger in Bot. Jahrb. 32: 53 (1902) — A. volkensii Pilger.

Annual. Inflorescence of several racemes along a central axis. Spikelets single, pedicelled, adaxial; lower glume small, the upper awned; lower lemma sparsely hispid, its awn coiling at the tip and entangling its neighbours; upper floret acuminate to aristulate.

Species 1. Cameroun to Ethiopia and Tanzania. Mountains, in forest shade.

520. Homopholis C.E. Hubbard in Kew Bull. 1934: 126 (1934) — H. belsonii C.E. Hubbard.

Perennial. Inflorescence a panicle with long radiating primary branches bearing 1—3 spikelets near the tip. Spikelets: lower glume as long as spikelet, its nerves raised into prominent thickened ribs, the upper glume and lower lemma similar; upper lemma ½ length of spikelet, briefly rostrate.

Species 1. Australia (Queensland). Woodland shade.

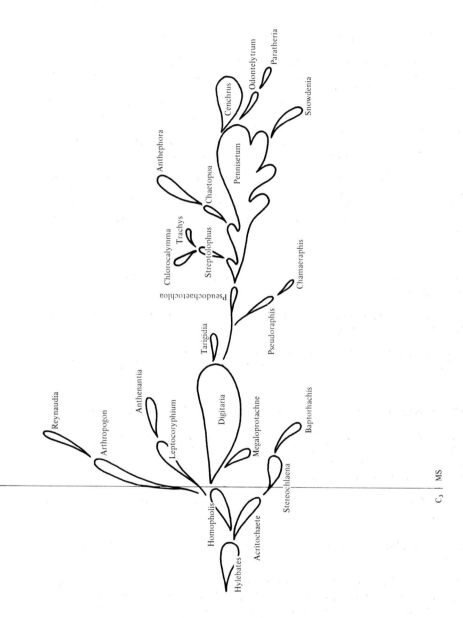

Fig. 20 Diagram of relationships in Paniceae subtribes Arthropogoninae, Digitariinae and Cenchrinae.

The inflorescence resembles that of *Digitaria sect Pennatae*, but is not deciduous.

521. Stereochlaena Hack. in Proc. Rhod. Sci. Ass. 7, 2: 65 (1908); Clayton in Kew Bull. 33: 295—297 (1978) — S. jeffreysii Hack. (= S. cameronii). *Chloridion* Stapf in Hook. Ic. Pl. 28: t 2640 (1900) non Chloridium Link (1824) — C. cameronii Stapf.

Annual or perennial. Inflorescence of paired or digitate racemes with narrow rhachis. Spikelets paired; lower glume tiny or suppressed, the upper from tiny to almost as long as spikelet and sometimes awned; lower lemma scabrid, prominently nerved (coriaceous lateral keels in *S. tridentata*), entire to tridentate, terminating in a straight awn; upper floret acute to acuminate.

Species 5. Tanzania to South Africa. Savanna woodland.

522. Baptorhachis Clayton & Renvoize, Gen. Gram.: 377 — Stereochlaena foliosa Clayton.

Annual. Inflorescence a solitary raceme with broad colourful foliaceous rhachis. Spikelets paired; lower glume suppressed; upper glume and lower lemma as long as spikelet, 3-nerved the laterals thickened and bearing a dense tuft of hair, bilobed with an awn from the sinus; upper floret acute.

Species 1. Mozambique. Stony slopes.
Loosely related to *Stereochlaena tridentata*.

523. Megaloprotachne C.E. Hubbard in Kew Bull. 1929: 320 (1929) — M. albescens C.E. Hubbard.

Annual. Inflorescence of digitate racemes. Spikelets paired; lower glume as long as spikelet, 5-nerved, with obtuse hyaline tip, the upper shorter and 3-nerved; lower floret ♂ with palea; upper floret acuminate.

Species 1. Southern Africa. Savanna, on sand.
Easily mistaken for *Digitaria*.

524. Digitaria Hall., Stirp. Helv. 2: 244 (1768) nom conserv non Fabric. (1759); Henr., Monogr. Digitaria (1950); Veldkamp in Blumea 21: 1—80 (1973) — D. sanguinalis (L.) Scop. *Valota* Adans., Fam. Pl. 2: 495 (1763) nom rejic non Vallota Herb. (1821) — V. insularis (L.) Chase. *Sanguinella* Gleichen in Neu. Reich. Pl. 2: 4, f 8 (1764) — unnamed species (= D. sanguinalis). *Syntherisma* Walt., Fl. Carol.: 76 (1788) — S. praecox Walt. (= D. sanguinalis). *Acicarpa* Raddi, Agrost. Bras.: 31 (1823) non Acicarpha Juss. (1803) — A. sacchariflora Raddi (= D. insularis). *Trichachne* Nees, Agrost. Bras.: 85 (1829) nom nov pro Acicarpa. *Gramerium* Desv., Opusc.: 61 (1831) — G. convolutum Desv. (= D. phaeothrix). *Panicum sect Elytroblepharum* Steud., Syn. Pl. Glum. 1: 37 (1854) — P. eminens Steud. *Elytroblepharum* (Steud.) Schlecht. in Linnaea 26: 533 (1855). *Eriachne* Phil. in An.

Univ. Chile 36: 207 (1870) non R. Br. (1810) — E. rigida Phil. (= D. californica). *Sanguinaria* Bub., Fl. Pyr. 4: 256 (1901) non L. (1753), nom superfl pro Digitaria. *Leptoloma* Chase in Proc. Biol. Soc. Wash. 19: (1906) — L. cognata (Schult.) Chase. *Digitariopsis* C.E. Hubbard in Hook. Ic. Pl. 35: t 3420 (1940) — D. redheadii C.E. Hubbard. *Digitariella* de Winter in Bothalia 7: 467 (1961) — D. remotigluma de Winter.

Annual or perennial. Inflorescence of racemes these digitate or on an elongated central axis, occasionally single or with secondary branchlets (panicle in *D. cognata, D. tomentosa*). Spikelets usually in groups of 2—3, imbricate to effuse the latter often on notably long and unequal pedicels, puberulous to villous typically in stripes between the well-defined nerves, rarely glabrous; lower glume reduced to a little scale up to ¼ length of spikelet or suppressed; upper glume variable, sometimes much reduced; lower lemma usually as long as spikelet, rarely much reduced; upper floret subacute to acuminate, rarely rostrate (*D. aristulata* awned), pallid to black.

Species ± 230. Tropical and warm temperate regions. Habitat variable. *D. exilis* (Acha, Fonio) and *D. iburua* are minor west African cereals tolerant of infertile soils. Forms of *D. eriantha* (notably Pangola grass) are cultivated as pastures. *D. didactyla* (Blue Couch) is used for lawns. *D. sanguinalis* (Crab grass) and *D. ciliaris* are serious weeds. *D. connivens* colonizes sandy beaches.

The genus is extremely variable in inflorescence, relative length of spikelet scales, and spikelet indumentum; the latter may display different combinations of appressed pubescence, glassy bristles and marginal cilia within the same species or even between the two members of a spikelet pair. Despite this the overall facies of the spikelet is surprisingly uniform, and the genus is seldom difficult to recognize.

Henrard (l.c.) constructed an elaborate classification, whose flavour is indicated below by a simplified key to the clearer of his groups. However there is so much intergradation that few of his characters are reliable, and the practicability of recognizing formal infrageneric taxa is open to doubt.

Spikelets sessile, single, nestling in two rows on a winged rhachis (D. pacifica)
　　　　　　　　　　　　　　　　　　　　　　　　　Sect *Solitaria*
Spikelets pedicelled, often in groups:
　Pedicel bearing stiff hairs as long as spikelet (D. diagonalis)　　Sect *Setariopsis*
　Pedicel at most shortly pilose:
　　Racemes stiffly radiating, sparsely spiculate; inflorescence deciduous as a
　　　tumbleweed (D. divaricatissima)　　　　　　　　Sect *Pennatae*
　　Racemes not stiffly radiating:
　　　Upper glume minutely gibbous or spurred below (D. flaccida)
　　　　　　　　　　　　　　　　　　　　　　　　Sect *Flaccidulae*
　　　Upper glume not gibbous:
　　　　Spikelets ternate; hairs verruculose or clavate (D. ternata)　Sect *Ischaemum*
　　　　Spikelets binate:
　　　　　Upper glume longer than lower lemma, separated from lower glume by a
　　　　　　short internode (D. debilis)　　　　　　　Sect *Debiles*
　　　　　Upper glume shorter than lower lemma:
　　　　　　Glumes separated from lower lemma by a very short internode (D.
　　　　　　　insularis)　　　　　　　　　　　　Sect *Trichachne*
　　　　　　Glumes not separated from lower lemma (D. ciliaris)　　Sect *Digitaria*

Variation is greater in the Old World with nearly half the species occurring in Africa, though sect *Trichachne* is predominantly New World.

The paniculate species are sometimes separated as *Leptoloma*, but this treatment is unsatisfactory because *D. cognata* is imperfectly distinct from sect *Pennatae*, whereas *D. tomentosa* is not a tumbleweed and seems more closely related to the *D. junghuhniana* group of sect *Digitaria*.

525. Tarigidia Stent in Kew Bull. 1932: 151 (1932) — T. aequiglumis (Goossens) Stent.

Perennial. Inflorescence spiciform, cylindrical, of numerous short deciduous racemes imbricate along a central axis; racemes oblong, compact, the basal spikelets sometimes vestigial. Spikelets subsessile: glumes ⅔ length of spikelet, the lower 1-nerved linear, the upper 3-nerved lanceolate; upper floret acute.

Species 1. Southern Africa.
Tarigidia combines the characters of *Digitaria* and certain Cenchrinae, forming a link between the two subtribes. Loxton (Bothalia 11: 285—286, 1974) suggests that it is a hybrid between *Digitaria* and *Anthephora*, but there is no positive evidence of this.

526. Leptocoryphium Nees, Agrost. Bras.: 83 (1829) — L. lanatum (Kunth) Nees.

Perennial. Inflorescence a panicle. Spikelets lanceolate, dorsally compressed; lower glume absent, the upper as long as spikelet; upper lemma flat, becoming hyaline towards tip, its hyaline margins gaping and leaving the palea free.

Species 1. Mexico to Argentina. Savanna.
The upper lemma is unusual in not gripping the palea, but otherwise it conforms to Digitariinae.

527. Anthenantia P. Beauv., Ess. Agrost.: 48, 151, expl pl 10 (1812) — A. villosa (P. Beauv.) Michaux. *Aulaxanthus* Elliott, Sketch Bot. 1: 102 (1816) — A. ciliatus Ell. (= A. villosa). *Aulaxia* Nutt., Gen. N. Am. Pl. 1: 47 (1818) nom superfl pro Aulaxanthus.

Like *Leptocoryphium* except: spikelets elliptic, laterally compressed; upper lemma boat-shaped, firm to the tip.

Species 2. Southeastern USA. Pine barrens.
Anthenantia is the etymologically correct version of three alternative spellings given by Beauvois. The genus is barely distinguishable from *Leptocoryphium*.

e. ARTHROPOGONINAE Butzin in Willdenowia 6: 516 (1972); Tateoka in Bot. Mag. Tokyo 76: 286—291 (1963).

Inflorescence a panicle. Spikelets laterally compressed; glumes firmly membranous to coriaceous, awned; lower floret ♂ with palea or reduced to an empty lemma, this resembling upper glume but the awn usually shorter; upper lemma hyaline, the palea absent or very small. Anatomy: kranz MS, but *Arthropogon* the intermediate form with 2 bundle sheaths (fig 17).

Laterally compressed spikelets with tough glumes and hyaline upper floret do not accord with the usual image of Paniceae, and the assignment of these genera has been controversial. In fact a relationship with *Leptocoryphium,* whose upper lemma is partially hyaline, seems likely. The leaf anatomy of *Arthropogon* is unusual, and may represent an intermediate stage in development from non-kranz. The anatomy does not support a link with Melinidinae, despite some superficial similarity in the spikelets.

528. Arthropogon Nees, Agrost. Bras.: 319 (1829); Filguieras in Bradea 3: 303—322 (1982) — A. villosus Nees. *Achlaena* Griseb., Cat. Pl. Cub.: 228 (1866) — A. piptostachya Griseb.

Perennial. Spikelets with bearded callus (*A. piptostachys* stipitate); lower glume linear to awn-like; upper glume as long as spikelet, coriaceous, entire or bidentate (*A. xerachne* deeply bifid), awned; lower lemma awned or awnless.

Species 6. Brazil and West Indies. Savanna.

529. Reynaudia Kunth, Rév. Gram. 1: 195 (1830) — R. filiformis (Schult.) Kunth.

Perennial. Spikelets: glumes firmly membranous, strongly nerved, bilobed, awned, the upper almost equalling spikelet, the lower ½ as long; lower lemma mucronate; stamens 2.

Species 1. Cuba. Savanna.

f. CENCHRINAE Dumort., Obs. Gram. Belg.: 139 (1824). *Pennisetinae* Reichenb., Consp. Reg. Veg.: 51 (1828). *Anthephorinae* Benth. in J. Linn. Soc. Bot. 19: 30 (1881). *Trachidinae* Pilg., Nat. Pfl.-Fam. ed. 2, 14e: 103 (1940) sine descr lat. *Pseudoraphidinae* Keng, Fl. Ill. Pl. Prim. Sin.: 716 (1959) sine descr lat. *Snowdeniinae* Butzin in Willdenowia 6: 516 (1972).

Inflorescence a highly modified panicle (compound in some *Pennisetum*). Spikelets dorsally compressed, borne singly or in clusters, subtended by 1 or more bristles or bracts (except *Snowdenia*) these often forming an involucre, all deciduous together (except *Pseudoraphis*); both glumes shorter than spikelet (except *Chamaeraphis, Pseudoraphis*), the lower often absent; lower floret usually reduced to a membranous lemma ± as long as spikelet, rarely ♂ with palea; upper lemma cartilaginous to thinly coriaceous with flat thin margins covering ½—⅔ of palea, usually lanceolate and acute. Anatomy: kranz MS.

The subtribe is easily recognized by the presence of bristles or scales subtending the spikelet and deciduous with it. The bristles are derived from sterile panicle branches (Sohns in J. Wash. Acad. Sci. 45: 135—143, 1955; Butzin in Willdenowia 8: 67—79, 1977), and display great versatility in forming involucres or burs around the spikelets with varying degrees of adaptation to protection or dispersal. The primitive form is probably a deciduous branch (*Pseudochaetochloa*), whence modification of the bristles to compact involucres has been achieved by three different routes (fig 20):

— Condensation to a rosette of unbranched bristles (*Pennisetum*), thence forming a cup by coalescence (*Cenchrus*) or a single bristle by reduction (*Paratheria*);
— retention of a sterile spikelet at the bristle tip and its transformation to a scale (*Chaetopoa*);
— retention of a forked branch structure in miniature (*Streptolophus*), usually coupled with the development of leafy wings from the principal axis.

A soft upper lemma is characteristic and suggests a derivation from Digitariinae, perhaps *Tarigidia*. It contrasts with the crustaceous upper lemma of the *Setaria* group whose similar, though persistent, sterile bristles can be ascribed to parallel evolution. It also indicates that *Paractaenum* and *Plagiosetum*, possessing a hard upper lemma, should be placed in Setariinae despite their deciduous bristles.

530. Pseudoraphis Griff., Not. Pl. As. 3: 29 (1851) — P. brunoniana (Griff.) Griff.

Perennial. Inflorescence of persistent racemes on a short common axis; raceme rhachis slender, bearing 1—several distant spikelets, with a bristle only at the tip. Spikelets: lower glume very small, the upper as long as spikelet and thinly coriaceous; lower lemma resembling upper glume, acute to acuminate or briefly awned; upper floret ½ as long, the grain eventually much larger and filling spikelet.

Species 6. India to Japan and Australia. Marsh.
Anomalous in Cenchrinae due to its persistent bristles, but no less anomalous if placed elsewhere or if separated from *Chamaeraphis*. The simple inflorescence is apparently primitive, but tangential to the main evolutionary line.

531. Chamaeraphis R. Br., Prodr. Fl. Nov. Holl.: 193 (1810) — C. hordeacea R. Br. *Setosa* Ewart in Ewart & Davies, Fl. N. Terr.: 33 (1917) — S. erecta Ewart & Cookson (= C. hordeacea).

Perennial. Inflorescence densely spiciform, of imbricate racemelets in 2 opposite rows; each racemelet composed of a single spikelet with pungent callus and subtended by a stout bristle. Spikelets like *Pseudoraphis*.

Species 1. Australia. Open sandy places.
The genus is remarkably like *Paratheria*, but this seems to be a matter of parallel evolution rather than kinship for it is apparently derived by reduction from *Pseudoraphis*.

532. Pseudochaetochloa Hitchc. in J. Wash. Acad. Sci. 14: 492 (1924) — P. australiensis Hitchc.

Perennial. Inflorescence subspiciform, of numerous deciduous branchlets spread along a central axis; branchlets bearing 2—5 spikelets interspersed with bristles, often with a few smaller sterile spikelets irregularly disposed at the base. Spikelets: both glumes membranous and shorter than spikelet; upper lemma firmly membranous, scarcely different from lower.

Species 1. Australia. Stony slopes.
A primitive genus whose clusters take the form of branchlets with a clearly defined axis but which is otherwise similar to *Pennisetum*.

533. Pennisetum Rich. in Pers., Syn. Pl. 1: 72 (1805) — P. typhoideum Rich. (= P. glaucum). *Penicillaria* Willd., Enum. Hort. Berol.: 1036 (1809) nom superfl pro Pennisetum. *Gymnotrix* P. Beauv., Ess. Agrost.: 59 (1812) — G. thuarii P. Beauv. (= P. caffrum). *Catatherophora* Steud. in Flora 12: 465 (1829) — C. hordeiformis (L.) Steud. (= P. alopecuroides). *Pentastachya* Steud., Nom. Bot. ed. 2, 2: 299 (1841) nom nud — P. squamulatum. *Sericura* Hassk. in Flora 25 Beibl. 2: 2 (1842) — S. elegans Hassk. (= P. macrostachyum). *Loydia* Delile, Ind. Sem. Hort. Monsp. (1844) non Lloydia Reichenb. (1830) — L. peregrina Delile (= P. petiolaris). *Beckeropsis* Fig. & De Not., Agrost. Aegypt. 2: 49 (1853); Clayton in Hook. Ic. Pl. 37: t 3643 (1967) — B. nubica Fig. & De Not. *Eriochaeta* Fig. & De Not. l.c. 58 — E. secundiflora Fig. & De Not. (= P. pedicellatum). *Macrochaeta* Steud. in Zoll., Syst. Verz. Ind. Archip.: 60 (1854) nom superfl pro Sericura. *Amphochaeta* Anderss. in Vet. Acad. Handl. Stockholm 1853: 156 (1855) — A. exaltata Anderss. (= P. pauperum).

Annual or perennial, prostrate to 3.5 m high; ligule a line of hairs, rarely membranous. Inflorescence spiciform, cylindrical to subglobose, terminal or sometimes axillary and then often aggregated into a leafy compound panicle, bearing rosette-like clusters which may be wholly sessile, prolonged below into a stipe, or borne on peduncle-stumps from the rhachis; each cluster composed of 1—4 spikelets surrounded by an involucre of bristles (supplemented by ♂ spikelets in sect *Heterostachya*), these simple (*P. lanatum* branched), flexuous, filiform (*P. basedowii, P. ramosum* flattened), often plumose, free to the base. Spikelets: glumes and lower lemma variable, absent to almost equalling spikelet; upper lemma obtuse to acute.

Species ± 80. Throughout the tropics. Woodland, savanna and weedy places. *P. glaucum* (Pearl millet) is the most drought tolerant of the tropical cereal crops. It was probably domesticated in West Africa about 2000—3000 BC from the wild ruderal species *P. violaceum*; subsequently there arose a third species, *P. sieberianum*, which mimics the crop and is adapted to live as a weed within it. The three members of this complex interbreed and are sometimes treated as subspecies of a single species (Brunken in Amer. J. Bot. 64: 161—176, 1977; Brunken, de Wet & Harlan in Econ. Bot. 31: 163—174, 1977). *P. purpureum* (Elephant grass) and *P. clandestinum* (Kikuyu grass) are grown for pasture.
Pennisetum is linked to *Pseudochaetochloa* through *P. lanatum*. It is a variable genus foreshadowing many of the trends in Cenchrinae. No satisfactory modern revision is available, but its variability may be appreciated from the following simplified key. Some two thirds of the species are concentrated in sect. *Gymnotrix*.

Involucral bristles branched (P. lanatum)   Sect *Dactylophora*
Involucral bristles simple:

Upper floret persistent, not strongly indurated:
Spikelets of two kinds, a whorl of ♂ spikelets surrounding 1 bisexual spikelet
  (P. squamulatum)   Sect *Heterostachya*
Spikelets all bisexual:
  Involucre plumose, surrounding 1—4 spikelets (P. purpureum)
                                              Sect *Pennisetum*
  Involucre glabrous, surrounding 1 spikelet   Sect *Gymnotrix*
  Inflorescence terminal (P. divisum)   Subsect *Acrostigma*
  Inflorescence axillary, sometimes forming a compound panicle:
    Bristles several to many (P. bambusiforme)   Subsect *Pleurostigma*
    Bristle 1 (P. unisetum)   Subsect *Beckeropsis*
Upper floret deciduous, its lemma hard and shining (P. polystachion)
                                        Sect *Brevivalvula*

Beckeropsis, with its compound panicle and single bristle, is sometimes treated as a separate genus, but it is barely distinct from *P. trisetum* of subsect *Pleurostigma* which has 2—5 bristles. *P. clandestinum* is a peculiar species in which the inflorescence is reduced to a single spikelet cluster hidden within the uppermost leaf-sheath from which the elongated stigmas and filaments protrude. It is linked to the body of sect *Pennisetum* through *P. longistylum*.

The spikelets are sometimes difficult to interpret due to reduction or suppression of the lower scales, and it is usually easier to count backwards from the upper lemma. The genus is not sharply separated from *Cenchrus* and can easily be confused with *C. ciliaris*.

534. Cenchrus L., Sp. Pl.: 1049 (1753); DeLisle in Iowa J. Sci. 37: 259—351 (1963) — C. echinatus L. *Echinaria* Fabric., Enum.: 206 (1759) non Desf. (1749) & *Raram* Adans., Fam. Pl. 2: 35, 597 (1763) — nom superfl pro Cenchrus. *Cenchropsis* Nash in Small, Fl. Southeast. U.S.: 109 (1903) — C. myosuroides (Kunth) Nash. *Nastus* Lunell in Amer. Midl. Nat. 4: 214 (1915) non Juss. (1789) nom superfl pro Cenchrus.

Annual or perennial (leaves pungent in *C. distichophyllus*). Inflorescence spiciform, cylindrical, bearing rosette- or bur-like deciduous clusters, these sessile or with an obconical base; each cluster composed of 1—8 spikelets surrounded by an involucre of 1 or more whorls of bristles, these flexuous or more often spinous and then sometimes retrorsely barbed, ± flattened and united below (at least the inner whorl), the degree of union varying from a small basal disc to a deep cupule. Spikelets: glumes shorter than spikelet, sometimes the lower suppressed; upper floret protogynous, without lodicules.

Species 22. Throughout the tropics. Bushland, open grassland and weedy places. *C. ciliaris* (Buffel grass) is a forage species resistant to drought and hard grazing. *C. echinatus* is an obnoxious weed whose retrorsely barbed spines cling tenaciously to clothing

The genus can usually be recognized by its prickly burs, but it approaches closely to *Pennisetum*, especially *P. basedowii* and *P. ramosum* in which the bristles are somewhat flattened. *C. ciliaris*, in which the connate portion of the involucre amounts only to a little disc ± 1 mm across, lies on the boundary; its inclusion in *Cenchrus* is justified by its intergradation with *C. pennisetiformis*, which has a definite cupule.

535. Odontelytrum Hack. in Oest. Bot. Zeitschr. 48: 86 (1898); Stapf in Hook. Ic. Pl. 31: t 3074 (1916) — O. abyssinicum Hack.

Prostrate perennial. Inflorescence spiciform, bearing deciduous racemelets appressed to the axis; each racemelet composed of a single spikelet, this supported on a blunt oblong stipe and embraced below by a lobed herbaceous involucre, one of the lobes awn-like. Spikelets: lower glume absent or minute, the upper small; upper lemma narrowly obtuse; stigma 1.

Species 1. Yemen and eastern Africa. In running water.
The herbaceous involucre is presumably homologous to the *Cenchrus* cupule.

536. Paratheria Griseb., Cat. Pl. Cub.: 236 (1866) — P. prostrata Griseb.

Prostrate perennial. Inflorescence laxly spiciform, bearing deciduous racemelets appressed to the axis; each racemelet composed of a single spikelet, this supported on a long pungent stipe and subtended by a stout bristle. Spikelets: both glumes very small; lower lemma membranous; upper lemma as long as spikelet.

Species 2. Madagascar; western Africa; West Indies and South America. In and near water.
Cleistogamous spikelets, lacking the bristle, occur at the base of the inflorescence and in upper leaf-sheaths.

537. Snowdenia C.E. Hubbard in Kew Bull. 1929: 30 (1929) & in Hook. Ic. Pl. 37: t 3647 (1967) — S. microcarpha C.E. Hubbard. *Beckera* Fresen. in Mus. Senck. 2: 132 (1837) non Beckeria Bernh. (1800) — B. polystachya Fresen.

Annual or perennial. Inflorescence raceme-like, cylindrical, axillary, bearing pedicellate spikelets singly and without trace of subtending bristles. Spikelets: both glumes very short; lower lemma as long as spikelet, usually awned; upper palea less than ½ length of floret.

Species 4. Northeast tropical Africa. Forest margins.
The genus is very similar to *Pennisetum subsect Beckeropsis,* and was probably derived from it by suppression of the bristle.

538. Chaetopoa C.E. Hubbard in Hook. Ic. Pl. 37: t 3646 (1967) — C. taylori C.E. Hubbard.

Annual; ligule membranous. Inflorescence spiciform, cylindrical, bearing cuneate deciduous clusters, these sessile; each cluster composed of 5—7 shortly pedicelled sterile (rarely ♂) spikelets forming an involucre around 1 sessile bisexual spikelet. Bisexual spikelet: lower glume subulate or suppressed, the upper shorter than spikelet and ± lanceolate; upper lemma acuminate to an awn-point. Sterile spikelets like bisexual, but smaller with both glumes long and awn-like.

Species 2. Tanzania. Soil pockets on rock.

The genus is clearly related to *Pennisetum sect Heterostachya*. The latter seems best left in *Pennisetum* for it has bristles surrounding the ♂ spikelets, linear to ovate glumes and a ligular line of hairs.

539. Anthephora Schreb., Beschr. Gräser 2: 105 (1779); Reeder in Trans. Amer. Microsp. Soc. 79: 211—218 (1960) — A. elegans Schreb. (= A. hermaphrodita). *Hypudaerus* A. Br. in Flora 24: 275 (1841) nom nud — A. pubescens.

Annual or perennial. Inflorescence spiciform, cylindrical, bearing oblong to conical deciduous clusters, these sessile (pungent stipe in *A. pungens*); each cluster composed of 3—11 spikelets surrounded by an involucre of stiffly coriaceous narrowly elliptic several-nerved bracts, these free almost to the base (*A. cristata* connate in lower $\frac{1}{3}$) and obtuse to awned at the tip. Spikelets: lower glume absent, upper subulate from a broad base with its back facing inwards.

Species 12. Africa and Arabia; 1 species tropical America. Savanna.

The involucral bracts are often interpreted as lower glumes, but in Paniceae the general tendency is for lower lemmas, rather than lower glumes, to become indurated. It seems more likely that the bracts are derived from involucral sterile spikelets like those of *Chaetopoa*. *A. cristata*, with its basally connate scales, imitates *Cenchrus*.

540. Streptolophus Hughes in Kew Bull. 1923: 178 (1923) — S. sagittifolius Hughes.

Annual; leaf-blades sagittate, falsely petiolate. Inflorescence of several deciduous cuneate branchlets loosely scattered along a central axis; branchlets stipitate below, divided above into a dwarf branch system with recurved spinous tips, this formed into a basket-like involucre about the several spikelets borne upon it. Spikelets: both glumes small.

Species 1. Angola. In thicket.

541. Chlorocalymma Clayton in Kew Bull. 24: 461 (1970) — C. cryptacanthum Clayton.

Annual. Inflorescence of 2—3 deciduous raceme-like branches distant on a central axis; branches estipitate, ramifying on the underside into flattened partly accrescent recurved spines which form an elongated involucre about the spikelets borne upon them, the whole enveloped by foliaceous wings from the dorsal rhachis of the branch to form an ovoid capsule. Spikelets: lower glume small, upper shorter than spikelet; lower lemma laterally winged.

Species 1. Tanzania. Open bushland.

542. Trachys Pers., Syn. Pl. 1: 85 (1805) — T. mucronata Pers. (= T. muricata). *Trachyozus* Reichenb., Consp. Reg. Veg.: 48 (1828) & *Trachystachys* Dietr., Sp. Pl. 2:

16 (1833) — nom superfl pro Trachys.

Annual. Inflorescence a pair of unilateral raceme-like primary branches, their rhachis foliaceously winged and disarticulating into segments; each segment with a compact cluster of spikelets on the underside, this borne upon dwarf branchlets tipped by recurved spines, the distal spikelets sterile and often smaller. Spikelets: both glumes subulate to linear, shorter than spikelet, coriaceous; lower lemma expanded and rigidly indurated to form a broadly ovate involucral scale.

Species 1. India, Burma, Sri Lanka. Sands, mainly coastal.

g. SPINIFICINAE Ohwi in Acta Phytotax. Geobot. 11: 56 (1942). *Xerochloinae* Butzin in Willdenowia 6: 184 (1970).

Dioecious or bisexual. Inflorescence compound, composed of several to many single racemes or small panicles attended by prophylls and spathate sheaths, and condensed into a compact head or fascicle. Spikelets dorsally compressed; upper lemma firmly membranous to crustaceous, with flat margins covering much of the palea. Anatomy: kranz MS, but atypical in some *Spinifex*.

A group of heterogeneous, but apparently related, genera sharing compact compound inflorescences and adaptation to arid habitats. A resemblance between *Xerochloa imberbis* and *Uranthoecium* suggests a possible origin for the subtribe.

543. Xerochloa R. Br., Prodr. Fl. Nov. Holl.: 196 (1810); Stapf in Bot. Jahrb. 35: 64—68 (1904) — X. imberbis R. Br. *Kerinozoma* Steud., Syn. Pl. Glum. 1: 358 (1854) — K. suraboja Steud. (= X. imberbis).

Perennial or annual. Inflorescence of several single racemes condensed into a fascicle sessile on each of the upper culm nodes; racemes short, deciduous, bearing 2—5 spikelets with abbreviated internodes, the rhachis prolonged in a short subulate point. Spikelets: glumes shorter than spikelet, membranous; lower lemma as long as spikelet, firmly chartaceous, medianly grooved, the floret ♂ with large lemma-like palea; upper lemma fusiform tapering to a falcate beak, cartilaginous with firm margins.

Species 3. Australia. Dry stream beds and clay flats.

544. Zygochloa S.T. Blake in Univ. Queensland Papers 1, 19: 7 (1941) — Z. paradoxa (R. Br.) S.T. Blake.

Perennial shrub; dioecious. Female inflorescence terminal on culm and axillary branches, globose, of several single racemes; raceme reduced to 1 spikelet subtended by 3 expanded papery 'bracts' (see below), all deciduous together; glumes as long as spikelet, chartaceous; lower lemma similar, the floret barren with palea; upper lemma crustaceous, its firm margins flat above inrolled below. Male inflorescence terminal on culms and axillary branches, globose, of

307

several oblong spiciform panicles, the subtending sheaths reduced to cymbiform spatheoles; spikelet resembling ♀ but glumes shorter and both florets ♂.

Species 1. Australia. Desert and hills.
The papery bracts aid wind dispersal. They are similar in appearance but probably of varied homology; from the lowest upwards they are believed to represent a prophyll, spatheole and rhachis extension.

545. Spinifex L., Mant.: 163, 300 (1771) — S. squarrosus L. (= S. littoreus). *Ixalum* Forst. f., Fl. Ins. Austr. Prodr.: 92 (1786) nom nud — S. sericeus.

Perennial; dioecious or sometimes androdioecious (leaf-blades of *S. littoreus* rigid, ferociously pungent). Female (or bisexual) inflorescence terminal, stellately globose, falling entire, composed of numerous single racemes; each raceme bearing a single basal spikelet hidden among subtending spathes, its rhachis prolonged into a long spinous quill; glumes as long as spikelet, chartaceous; lower lemma similar, sometimes with palea and then ♂; upper lemma firmly membranous with hyaline margins. Male inflorescence terminal or incorporating 1—2 upper culm nodes, fasciculate, composed of many single racemes; raceme exserted, bearing several spikelets and ending in a short point; spikelets resembling ♀, but scales coriaceous, glumes shorter and both florets ♂.

Species 4. India to China and Australia. Seashore sand dunes.

35. ISACHNEAE

Benth. in J. Linn. Soc. Bot. 19: 30 (1881); C.E. Hubbard in Hook. Ic. Pl. 35: t 3432 (1943). *Isachninae* Stapf in Fl. Trop. Afr. 9: 13 (1917).

Ligule a line of hairs, occasionally absent. Inflorescence a panicle or of racemes, terminal, the spikelets all alike. Spikelets 2-flowered without rhachilla extension (*Sphaerocaryum* and some *Coelachne* 1-flowered), dorsally compressed, awnless, disarticulating below florets and, sometimes tardily, between them; glumes tardily deciduous (*Coelachne* persistent), membranous, shorter than or equalling spikelet; florets similar or dissimilar, the lower bisexual (♂ in *Limnopoa*, some *Isachne*), the upper ♀ or bisexual; lemmas membranous to coriaceous, obscurely 0—7-nerved, rounded on back, glabrous or puberulous, the margins inrolled and clasping edges of palea. Caryopsis ellipsoid to plano-convex; hilum round or oval (*Limnopoa* linear).
Genera 5; species ± 110. Tropics.

Anatomy. Non-kranz with slender or stout microhairs; polygonal intercostal epidermal cells; mesophyll radially elongated in upper half of transverse section — fig 10 (Potztal in Bot. Jahrb. 75: 551— 569, 1952; Tateoka in Bot. Mag. Tokyo 70: 119—120, 1957).

Chromosomes. Basic number 10.

2n	20	40	60
No of species	9	7	4

Isachneae is characterized by 2 fertile disarticulating florets and by certain anatomical trends, though these features are not always fully expressed and the tribe then approaches very closely to Paniceae. Its status is arguable, but on balance it seems more appropriate to treat it at tribal level than to accept an anomalous group in Paniceae.

Presumably the proto-panicoid spikelet had both florets bisexual, and Isachneae is sometimes regarded as primitive on that account. However, *Isachne* is so similar to *Panicum sect Verruculosa* that a derived status, with reversion to bisexuality of the lower floret, seems more likely. There is little doubt that *Dissochondrus* arose from *Setaria* in this way; nor can Eriachneae, with similar bisexual florets but kranz MS anatomy, be classed as primitive.

The tribe has specialized in aquatic and forest shade environments.

1 Spikelets subtended by bristles   *508 Dissochondrus*
1 Spikelets not subtended by bristles:
  2 Upper lemma indurated:
    3 Inflorescence a panicle   **546 Isachne**
    3 Inflorescence of racemes:
      4 Racemes several   **547 Heteranthoecia**
      4 Raceme single   **548 Limnopoa**
  2 Upper lemma membranous; inflorescence a panicle:
    5 Glumes persistent; spikelets nearly always 2-flowered   **549 Coelachne**
    5 Glumes deciduous; spikelets 1-flowered   **550 Sphaerocaryum**

546. Isachne R. Br., Prodr. Fl. Nov. Holl.: 196 (1810) — I. australis R. Br. (= I. globosa)

Annual or perennial. Inflorescence a panicle. Florets similar or dissimilar, separated by an abbreviated internode, the lower sometimes ♂; glumes subequal, ¾ to as long as spikelet, 5—9-nerved; lower lemma variable — see sectional key; upper lemma orbicular to broadly elliptic, crisply chartaceous to coriaceous, glabrous or pubescent, obtuse.

Species ± 100. Throughout the tropics, but mainly Asia. Marshy and shady places.

A difficult genus of barely separable species. The lower floret provides a basis for division into two sections, though the distinction is bridged by intermediates. Both sections occur throughout the tropics.

Lemmas similar or the lower a little longer, ± hemispherical, coriaceous, fertile
  (I. buettneri)   Sect *Isachne*
Lemmas dissimilar, the lower up to twice as long as upper, elliptic, membranous,
  often ♂ (I. polygonoides)   Sect *Paraisachne*

The genus resembles *Panicum sect Verruculosa*, which has a verrucose upper lemma and 3-nerved lower glume (*P. margaritiferum* 5-nerved), this usually shorter than the upper. The relationship between these taxa is unclear, but sect *Verruculosa* is confined to Africa and seems to have arisen independently from *Panicum*.

547. Heteranthoecia Stapf in Hook. Ic. Pl. 30: t 2927 (1911) — H. isachnoides Stapf (= H. guineensis).

Trailing annual. Inflorescence of short unilateral racemes on a central axis, the raceme rhachis terminating in a point. Florets dissimilar; lemmas thinly coriaceous, puberulous, the lower narrowly ovate and acute, the upper ½ as long elliptic and obtuse.

Species 1. Tropical Africa. Swamps and shallow water.

548. Limnopoa C.E. Hubbard in Hook. Ic. Pl. 35: t 3432 (1943) — L. meeboldii (Fischer) C.E. Hubbard.

Trailing annual. Inflorescence a solitary unilateral raceme, the spikelets paired on its flattened rhachis, alike but one sessile the other pedicelled. Florets dissimilar, the lower ♂; lemmas obtuse, the lower membranous narrowly ovate and glabrous, the upper ⅔ as long cartilaginous elliptic and puberulous.

Species 1. Southern India. Forming mats on the surface of water.

549. Coelachne R. Br., Prodr. Fl. Nov. Holl.: 187 (1810) — C. pulchella R. Br.

Low-growing annual or perennial; leaf-blades linear to lanceolate. Inflorescence an open or contracted panicle. Florets dissimilar, separated by a slender internode (*C. japonica* sometimes 1-flowered); glumes persistent, subequal, ⅓—⅔ length of spikelet, obtuse; lemmas membranous, nerveless or obscurely nerved, glabrous or pubescent, usually obtuse, the upper ⅔ to almost as long as lower; stamens 2—3.

Species 10. Old World tropics. Streamsides and marshy places.
A homogeneous genus of barely separable species.

550. Sphaerocaryum Hook.f., Fl. Brit. India 7: 246 (1896) — S. elegans (Steud.) Hook.f. (= S. malaccense). *Graya* Steud., Syn. Pl. Glum. 1: 119 (1854) non Endl. (1841) — G. elegans Steud. *Sieudelella* Honda in J. Fac. Sci. Tokyo Bot. 3: 258 (1930) nom superfl pro Sphaerocaryum.

Trailing annual; leaf-blades ovate, amplexicaul, with obscure cross-nerves. Inflorescence a panicle. Spikelets 1-flowered; glumes deciduous, obtuse; lemma membranous, 1-nerved, pubescent, obtuse. Fruit a caryopsis.

Species 1. India to China and Indonesia. Damp or swampy places.
The panicle is easily mistaken for *Sporobolus*, but that genus never has ovate leaf-blades.

36. HUBBARDIEAE

C.E. Hubbard in Bor, Grasses India Burma Ceylon Pak.: 685 (1960).

Ligule absent. Inflorescence a scanty axillary panicle, the spikelets all alike.

Spikelets 2-flowered without rhachilla extension, dorsally compressed, awnless, disarticulating above glumes; glumes persistent, membranous, as long as spikelet, 5—7-nerved; florets similar, but the lower empty, the other bisexual; lemmas membranous, 7—9-nerved, rounded on back; paleas absent. Caryopsis fusiform; hilum oval.
Genus 1; species 1. India.

Anatomy. Non-kranz with slender microhairs; intercostal epidermal cells polygonal; leaf very delicate with only 2 layers of mesophyll cells (Clifford in Kew Bull. 21: 169—174, 1967).

Chromosomes. Not known.

The tribe is characterized by the absence of paleas, and is apparently derived from Isachneae.

551. Hubbardia Bor in Kew Bull. 5: 385 (1951) — H. heptaneuron Bor.

Delicate trailing annual. Description as for tribe.

Species 1. Gersoppa Falls, India. In spray of waterfall. Now probably extinct due to damming of river.

37. ERIACHNEAE

(Ohwi) Eck-Borsboom in Blumea 26: 128 (1908). *Eriachninae* Ohwi in Acta Phytotax. Geobot. 11: 183 (1942).

Ligule a line of hairs. Inflorescence a terminal panicle, the spikelets all alike. Spikelets 2-flowered without rhachilla extension, slightly laterally compressed, disarticulating below each floret; glumes persistent, of variable length, membranous to chartaceous, (1—)7—14-nerved, acute to acuminate; florets similar, both fertile, narrowly elliptic, dorsally compressed, the lemma sometimes cartilaginous but mostly coriaceous to crustaceous, (3—)5—9-nerved, hairy, the margins inrolled and clasping palea keels, entire, with or without a straight or curved awn. Caryopsis ellipsoid to linear.
Genera 2; species ± 42. Mainly Australia.

Anatomy. Kranz PS type with slender or stout microhairs (Tateoka in Bull Torr. Bot. Cl. 88: 11—20, 1961).

Chromosomes. No counts available.

An awkward little tribe whose embryo structure and indurated lemmas with inrolled margins clearly ally it to Isachneae and Paniceae, but whose combination of bisexual florets, awned lemmas and kranz anatomy points to a direct link with neither. The awnless species (especially *E. glabrata*) are not unlike *Isachne*, but can be distinguished by the hairy acute lemmas and the harsher leaves adapted to an open savanna habitat.

Glumes equal   **552 Eriachne**
Glumes unequal   **553 Pheidochloa**

552. Eriachne R. Br., Prod. Fl. Nov. Holl.: 183 (1810) — E. squarrosa R. Br. *Achneria* P. Beauv., Ess. Agrost.: 72 (1812) — A. obtusa (R. Br.) P. Beauv. *Massia* Bal. in J. Bot. Paris 4: 165 (1890) — M. triseta (Steud.) Bal.

Annual or perennial; leaves mostly rolled (distichous and pungent in *E. mucronata, E. scleranthoides*). Panicle open, contracted or spiciform. Spikelets (*E. anomala* occasionally 1-flowered): glumes subequal, ½ as long to greatly exceeding lemma; lemma pilose (*E. glabrata* pubescent), sometimes merely acute but usually awned, its callus short and blunt; palea keels usually distant, the nerves often excurrent and sometimes forming long awns (especially *E. triseta*); stamens 3, rarely 2. Caryopsis ± ellipsoid, dorsally compressed.

Species ± 40. Mainly Australia, but extending through SE Asia to Sri Lanka. Open places in savanna.

553. Pheidochloa S.T. Blake in Proc. Roy. Soc. Queensland 56: 20 (1945); Veldkamp in Blumea 19: 60—63 (1971) — P. gracilis S.T. Blake.

Annual. Panicle depauperate, sometimes of only 3—4 spikelets and then raceme-like. Spikelets: glumes unequal, separated by an internode, the lower as long as lemma, the upper twice as long; lemma pubescent, awned, its callus pungent; palea keels close, deeply sulcate between, the tip obtuse; stamens 2. Caryopsis linear, concavo-convex.

Species 2. Australia and New Guinea. Damp sandy heaths.
The spikelets are usually cleistogamous.

38. STEYERMARKOCHLOEAE

Davidse & Ellis in Ann. Miss. Bot. Gard. 71: 994 (1984).

Ligule absent; vegetative culms reduced to a short stack of closely spaced scale-clad basal nodes and bearing a single leaf, this comprising a long cylindrical culm-like sheath and linear blade; flowering culms with aerial nodes bearing bladeless clasping sheaths. Inflorescence a spiciform panicle of unisexual spikelets, ♂ below, ♀ above. Female spikelet 2-flowered plus rhachilla extension bearing a rudiment, terete, falling entire; glumes both shorter than spikelet; lower floret barren without a palea, its lemma herbaceous and shorter than spikelet; upper floret ♀ with herbaceous, 5—13-nerved lemma; upper palea much thickened, well exserted from lemma, falcate, tightly convolute around flower, 5—11-nerved, sulcate along midline; lodicules 0; stigmas 2, terminally exserted. Male spikelets with both florets ♂ (rarely some bisexual); lemmas herbaceous; paleas membranous; stamens 2. Caryopsis fusiform, the hilum linear; embryo unknown.
Genus 1; species 1. Tropical America.

Anatomy. Non-kranz, without microhairs. Sheath and blade traversed by air spaces.

Chromosomes. Not known.

A most peculiar tribe. Its leaf, aerenchyma and spongy (buoyant?) palea seem to be adaptations to a seasonally inundated habitat. Its spikelets are occasionally bisexual in the zone between ♂ and ♀ portions of the panicle, providing evidence for the evolution of monoecy from a gynomonoecious precursor.

Its origins are uncertain. Those features which are not unique tend to be panicoid, with an obvious resemblance to *Hymenachne.* On the other hand a rhachilla extension is very rare among panicoids, and for that reason the tribe has been regarded as arundinoid. Embryo details are required to resolve the problem.

554. Steyermarkochloa Davidse & Ellis in Ann. Miss. Bot. Gard. 71: 995 (1984) —S. unifolia Davidse & Ellis.

Perennial. Description as for tribe.

Species 1. Colombia. Streamsides in savanna.

39. ARUNDINELLEAE

Stapf, Fl. Cap. 7: 314 (1898); Hubbard in Kew Bull. 1936: 317—322 (1936); Jac.-Fél. in Rev. Bot. Appl. 30: 418—424 (1950); Conert in Bot. Jahrb. 77: 226—354 (1957); Phipps in Kirkia 4: 87—124 (1964), 5: 235—258 (1966) & Blumea 15: 477—517 (1967); Clayton in Kew Bull. 21: 199—124 (1967) & 26: 111—123 (1971); Phipps in Canad. J. Bot. 50: 1309—1336 (1972). *Garnotieae* Tateoka in J. Jap. Bot. 32: 277 (1957).

Arundinellinae Honda in J. Fac. Sci. Tokyo Bot. 3: 228 (1930). *Garnotiinae* Pilger, Nat. Pfl.-Fam. ed. 2, 14d: 167 (1956). *Trichopteryginae* Jac.-Fél., Gram. Afr. Trop. 1: 92 (1962) sine descr lat.

Ligule usually a line of hairs, sometimes membranous. Inflorescence a panicle, the spikelets all alike, usually immature at emergence and completing their growth on the panicle, often in triads, these sometimes with connate pedicels; peduncle (rarely pedicel) sometimes developing a fragile hook-like flexure at maturity, the triads then falling entire though subsequently shedding the upper floret. Spikelets 2-flowered without rhachilla extension (except *Garnotia*), lanceolate, slightly laterally compressed, shedding one or both florets; glumes persistent, the upper as long as spikelet the lower usually shorter, membranous to coriaceous, often brown or beset with tubercle-based hairs, rarely awned; lower floret ♂ or barren (except *Chandrasekharania*), its lemma resembling upper glume, often persistent, 3—9-nerved, usually accompanied by a narrow palea; upper floret bisexual, subterete; lemma thinly coriaceous, often decorated with hair tufts, bidentate or bilobed, awned from sinus; awn geniculate with flat or terete spiral column and often deciduous (some exceptions in *Arundinella, Chandrasekharania, Garnotia*); hilum often linear. Genera 12; species ± 175. Tropics, mainly Old World.

Anatomy. Non-kranz in *Chandrasekharania* and *Jansenella*; kranz MS type in the rest of the tribe. The smallest vascular strands of *Garnotia* and some *Arundinella* are peculiar in that they lack phloem or xylem, being reduced to a little cluster of "auxiliary bundle cells", whose position relative to the chlorenchyma shows them to be functionally equivalent to bundle sheath cells (Renvoize in Kew Bull. 37: 489—495 & 497—500, 1982 & l.c. 40: 470, 1985). Anatomical variation within the *Loudetia—Tristachya* group of genera has been studied by Li & Phipps (Canad. J. Bot. 51: 657—680, 1973), who found that it was not very strongly correlated with spikelet characters.

Chromosomes. The basic number is 10 or 12, occasionally 9 (Phipps & Mahon in Canad. J. Bot. 48: 1419—1423, 1970).

2n	18	20	24	34	36	40	48	60	80
No of species	3	24	15	3	3	7	11	4	3

The most remarkable feature of the tribe is a tendency for its spikelets to cluster in triads; in more advanced forms the pedicels are connate, so that the triad mimics a single spikelet, and the peduncle may kink into a fragile hook from which the triad abscisses before the florets start to shed. Another peculiarity is the emergence of the panicle long before the spikelets are mature, and juvenile specimens with undeveloped awns often puzzle the unwary. The callus at the base of the upper floret is of taxonomic significance; it is readily seen if a mature floret is gently pulled out of the spikelet.

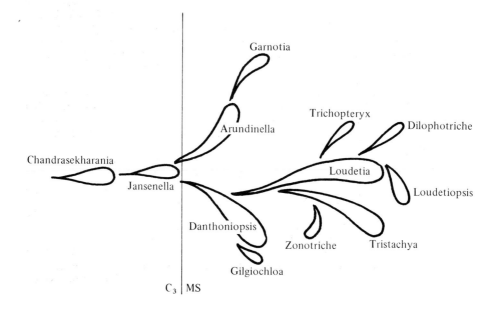

Fig. 21   Diagram of relationships in Arundinelleae.

The tribe suffers from an over-abundance of potentially significant generic characters, occuring in a bewildering number of different combinations. The reduction of the consequent reticulate pattern of relationships to a practical taxonomy inevitably leaves much scope for subjective interpretation in the matter of character weighting and the level at which generic rank should be pitched. The history of these treatments may be pursued among the references cited above. Perhaps the most important point is a gradual appreciation that triadism has developed along several parallel lines rather than in a single sequence, but detailed relationships (fig 21) remain controversial.

The tribe includes two primitive non-kranz genera, which suggest an origin among primitive Arundineae (there is a plausible alternative link with *Thysanolaena*, but this is probably false). Thereafter evolution has branched to *Arundinella* and *Garnotia* on the one hand, and to the loudetioid genera on the other. There is a noticeable tendency for the tribe to specialize in shallow soils and rocky places

Apart from the anomalous genera *Chandrasekharania* and *Garnotia*, the tribe is not difficult to recognize by its spikelets with deciduous dimorphic florets and geniculate awns. The prevalence of colourful lanceolate spikelets beset with tubercle-based hairs is a useful aid to recognition.

1   Spikelets 1-flowered, falling entire   **558 Garnotia**
1   Spikelets 2-flowered, usually breaking up:
  2   Both florets bisexual   **555 Chandrasekharania**
  2   Lower floret ♂ or barren:
    3   Ligule shortly membranous; hilum round; stamens 3:
      4   Upper lemma hairy   **556 Jansenella**
      4   Upper lemma scaberulous   **557 Arundinella**
    3   Ligule a line of hairs; hilum linear; upper lemma hairy or quite smooth:
      5   Lower lemma 5—9-nerved; stamens 3 (otherwise see *Loudetia togoensis*):
        6   Callus of upper floret square to oblong, obtuse or rarely 2-toothed:
          7   Spikelets with free pedicels; palea of upper floret winged (otherwise see *Loudetiopsis*):
            8   Palea of lower floret membranous   **559 Danthoniopsis**
            8   Palea of lower floret woody   **560 Gilgiochloa**
          7   Spikelets in triads with connate pedicels   **562 Zonotriche**
        6   Callus of upper floret conical, pungent   **561 Tristachya**
      5   Lower lemma 3-nerved:
        9   Lobes of upper lemma awned, with a tuft of hairs below each lobe:
          10   Callus of upper floret very short, obtuse to truncate
              563 Trichopteryx
          10   Callus of upper floret oblong to linear, truncate to acute
              564 Dilophotriche
        9   Lobes of upper lemma awnless (if with hair tufts see *Danthoniopsis*):
          11   Spikelets paired or single, rarely in loose groups of three with long pedicels   **565 Loudetia**
          11   Spikelets in close triads (if callus pungent see *Tristachya avenacea*)
              566 Loudetiopsis

555. Chandrasekharania Nair in Proc. Ind. Acad. Sci. 91: 79 (1982) — C. keralensis Nair.

315

Annual; ligule an obscure membrane. Panicle capitate. Spikelets brown, both florets fertile; glumes shortly awned; lemmas firmly membranous, 5-nerved, smooth, bidentate, with a short straight awn; callus short; palea wingless. Hilum round.

Species 1. Southern India.
An anomalous 2-flowered genus somewhat resembling *Zenkeria*; but its papery brown spikelets, and leaf anatomy almost identical to *Jansenella*, suggest it may be better regarded as the most primitive member of Arundinelleae.

556. Jansenella Bor in Kew Bull. 10: 96 (1955) — J. griffithiana (C. Muell.) Bor.

Annual; ligule shortly membranous. Panicle spiciform, the spikelets mostly paired. Spikelets purplish; lower lemma 5-nerved, awned; upper lemma with 2 hair tufts, bilobed, the lobes aristulate; callus short, truncate; palea wingless, papillose between keels.

Species 1. India. Moist places in hill country.
A primitive C_3 genus intermediate between *Arundinella* and *Danthoniopsis*.

557. Arundinella Raddi, Agrost. Bras.: 36 (1823); Keng in Nat. Centr. Univ. Sci. Rep. Biol. 2 (3): 1—68 (1936); Bor in Kew Bull. 10: 377—414 (1955); Phipps in Canad. J. Bot. 45: 1047—1057 (1967) — A. brasiliensis Raddi (= A. hispida). *Goldbachia* Trin. in Spreng., Neue Ent. 2: 81 (1820) nom rejic non DC. (1821) — G. mikani Spreng. (= A. hispida). *Acratherum* Link, Hort. Berol. 1: 230 (1827) — A. miliaceum Link (= Arundinella nepalensis). *Calamochloe* Reichenb., Consp. Reg. Veg.: 52 (1828) nom nov pro Goldbachia. *Thysanachne* Presl, Symb. Bot. 1: 11 (1829) — T. scoparia Presl (= A. hispida). *Brandtia* Kunth, Rév. Gram. 2: 511 (1831) — B. holcoides Kunth. *Riedelia* Kunth, Enum. Pl. 1: 515 (1833) in syn sub Goldbachia.

Annual or perennial; ligule a very short membrane. Panicle open or contracted (rarely spiciform), often with simple raceme-like primary branches, the spikelets usually paired. Spikelets purplish; lower lemma 3—5-nerved; upper lemma scaberulous, entire or bidenticulate, sometimes the awn straight or missing, occasionally the lateral teeth also awned; callus short, rounded; palea wingless, rarely papillose between keels, sometimes the margins auriculate below.

Species ± 50. Tropics and subtropics but mainly in Asia. Commonly on rocky slopes.
A homogeneous genus, somewhat isolated from the rest of the tribe.

558. Garnotia Brongn. in Duperr., Voy. Coq. Bot. Phan. 132, f 21 (1832); Gould in Kew Bull. 27: 515—562 (1972) — G. stricta Brongn. *Miquelia* Arn. & Nees in Nova Acta Acad. Leop.-Carol. Nat. Cur. 19, Suppl. 1: 177 (1843) non Meisner (1838) — M. courtallensis Arn. & Nees. *Berghausia* Endl., Gen. Pl. Suppl. 3: 57 (1843) nom nov pro Miquelia.

Mostly perennial and often caespitose, some annual; ligule a short membrane fringed with hairs. Panicle open or contracted. Spikelets 1-flowered, falling entire; glumes as long as spikelet; lemma cartilaginous, 3-nerved, entire or bidentate, with geniculate or straight awn, sometimes awnless; palea auriculate at base. Hilum round.

Species 29. Tropical Asia, Polynesia and Queensland. Light woodland and moist rocky slopes.

The genus is homogeneous, but much given to minor morphological variation between populations, so that over 75 species have been described. Gould (l.c.) has reduced these to 29, but even so they are mostly endemic or locally distributed, only 3 being relatively widespread.

At first sight *Garnotia* has no place in Arundinelleae, but it shares with *Arundinella* its auriculate palea and unusual auxiliary bundles. Indeed *Arundinella* is more closely related to *Garnotia* than to the rest of the tribe, and there is no case for maintaining a tribal distinction between the two genera.

559. Danthoniopsis Stapf in Hook. Ic. Pl. 31: t 3075 (1916) — D. gossweileri Stapf (= D. viridis). *Loudetia sect Pleioneura* C.E. Hubbard in Kew Bull. 1936: 321 (1936) — L. ramosa (Stapf) C.E. Hubbard. *Rattraya* Phipps in Kirkia 4: 100 (1964) — R. petiolata Phipps. *Jacquesfelixia* Phipps l.c. 115 — J. dinteri (Pilger) Phipps. *Gazachloa* Phipps l.c. 116 — G. chimanimaniensis Phipps. *Petrina* Phipps l.c. 117 — P. pruinosa (C.E. Hubbard) Phipps. *Xerodanthia* Phipps l.c. 5: 230 (1966) — X. barbata (Nees) Phipps. *Pleioneura* (C.E. Hubbard) Phipps in Bol. Soc. Brot. ser. 2, 46: 418 (1972) non Rechinger (1951).

Perennial, rarely annual (with false petiole in *D. petiolata*). Panicle open or contracted, bearing spikelets in groups of 2—3. Spikelets purplish, the glumes nearly always glabrous; lower lemma 5—9-nerved (*D. parva, D. pruinosa* 3-nerved); upper lemma usually with 2—8 transversely arranged tufts or lines of hair, sometimes glabrous, bilobed (lobes aristulate in *D. chimanimaniensis*); callus square to oblong, obtuse (narrowly oblong and 2-toothed in *D. barbata*); palea keels winged, the wings clasped by inrolled margins of lemma and often terminating in a clavate swelling or auricle, sometimes papillose between keels.

Species ± 20. Mainly central and south Africa; also Guinée, Sierra Leone, and Sudan to Pakistan. Rocky fire-free places in savanna woodland or desert fringe.

A variable, but reasonably compact, genus with characteristically winged upper palea, and a short blunt callus. It is linked to *Loudetia* by *D. pruinosa* and *D. ramosa*.

560. Gilgiochloa Pilger in Bot. Jahrb. 51: 415 (1914) — G. indurata Pilger.

Annual. Panicle spiciform, the pedicels ± accrescent to the axis. Spikelets purplish; lower glume awned; lower lemma 5—7-nerved, its palea becoming thickened and hardened like a chip of wood; upper lemma with hair tufts on margins and at base of awn, bilobed, the lobes aristulate; callus oblong, truncate; palea keels winged, the wings clasped by the lemma margins and terminating in a clavate swelling.

Species 1. Central Africa. Open places in thicket and woodland.
A segregate from *Danthoniopsis* with an extraordinary thickened palea.

561. Tristachya Nees, Agrost. Bras.: 458 (1829) — T. leiostachya Nees.
Monopogon Presl, Rel. Haenk. 1: 324 (1830) — M. avenaceus Presl. *Loudetia* A. Br.
in Flora 24: 713 (1841) nom superfl pro Tristachya. *Tristachya sect Apochaete* C.E.
Hubbard in Kew Bull. 1936: 322 (1936) — T. hispida (L.f.) K. Schum. (= T.
leucothrix). *Tristachya sect Dolichochaete* C.E. Hubbard l.c. — T. rehmannii Hack.
Apochaete (C.E. Hubbard) Phipps in Kirkia 4: 105 (1964). *Muantijamvella* Phipps
l.c. 106 — M. huillensis (Rendle) Phipps. *Veseyochloa* Phipps l.c. — V.
viridearistata Phipps. *Dolichochaete* (C.E. Hubbard) Phipps l.c. 109. *Isalus* Phipps
l.c. 5: 146 (1965) — I. humbertii (A. Camus) Phipps.

Perennial, rarely annual. Panicle open or contracted (raceme of triads in *T.
thollonii*), the spikelets sometimes in groups of 2—3 on long unequal pedicels,
but usually in triads, these mostly with connate pedicels (and a fragile hooked
peduncle in *T. viridearistata*). Spikelets brown, often large; lower lemma 5—7-
nerved (*T. avenacea* 3-nerved); upper lemma usually pubescent, rarely with 2—8
hair tufts, bilobed, the lobes aristulate or not; callus conical, pungent (*T.
huillensis* narrowly obtuse to acute); palea keels thickened but not winged.

Species ± 22. Central and south Africa; Madagascar; central and south
America. Savanna woodland and flood plains.
A variable genus defined by the pungent callus and divisible into four
sections:

Pedicels distinct, often unequal and then the spikelets sometimes paired
                                                        Sect *Tristachya*
Pedicels connate:
  Upper lemma lobes acute to acuminate   Sect *Apochaete*
  Upper lemma lobes aristulate:
  Upper floret terete, the lemma pubescent, with or without 2—8 hair tufts
                                                        Sect *Dolichochaete*
  Upper floret turbinate, the lemma with vertical lines of hairs Sect *Veseyochloa*

It seems unnecessarily divisive to treat these sections as separate genera. The
primitive species of sect *Tristachya* point to a relationship with *Loudetia*.

562. Zonotriche (C.E. Hubbard) Phipps in Kirkia 4: 113 (1964). *Tristachya sect
Zonotriche* C.E. Hubbard in Kew Bull. 1936: 322 (1936) — T. decora Stapf.
Tristachya sect Piptostachya C.E. Hubbard l.c. — T. inamoena K. Schum.
Piptostachya (C.E. Hubbard) Phipps in Kirkia 4: 108 (1964). *Mitwabochloa* Phipps
in Bol. Soc. Brot. ser. 2, 41: 199 (1967) — M. brunnea Phipps.

Perennial. Panicle bearing spikelets in triads with connate pedicels, the
peduncle developing a fragile hook at maturity. Spikelets brown; lower lemma
5-nerved; upper lemma with or without a row of 6—8 hair tufts, bilobed, the
lobes aristulate or not; callus short, broadly rounded; palea keels with or without
narrow wings, but these not clasped by lemma.

Species 3. Central Africa. Savanna woodland.
Apparently a derivative of *Tristachya*, but with a blunt danthoniopsoid callus.

563. Trichopteryx Nees in Lindley, Nat. Syst. ed. 2: 449 (1836) as "Trichopteria", corr Nees in Fl. Afr. Austr.: 339 (1841) — T. dregeana Nees.

Annual or perennial, mostly trailing with wiry culms. Panicle open or contracted, the spikelets single or paired. Spikelets brown; lower lemma 3-nerved; upper lemma with marginal hair tufts, bilobed, the lobes aristulate; callus short, rounded or truncate; palea keels wingless; stamens 2.

Species 5. Western, central and southern Africa; Madagascar. Wet flushes on rocky slopes.
A very uniform genus; somewhat isolated, but possibly a distant relative of *Loudetia*.

564. Dilophotriche (C.E. Hubbard) Jac.-Fél. in J. Agr. Trop. Bot. Appl. 7: 407 (1960). *Tristachya sect Dilophotriche* C.E. Hubbard in Kew Bull. 1936: 322 (1936) —T. tristachyoides (Trin.) C.E. Hubbard.

Annual or perennial. Panicle bearing spikelets in triads with short subequal pedicels, or (*D. occidentalis*) with long slender pedicels developing a fragile hook at maturity. Spikelets purplish; lower lemma 3-nerved; upper lemma with 2 hair tufts and aristulate lateral lobes; callus oblong to linear, truncate or acute; palea keels wingless; stamens 3.

Species 3. Senegal to Ivory Coast. Damp pockets on rock outcrops.
A small genus loosely related to *Trichopteryx* and *Loudetiopsis*.

565. Loudetia Steud., Syn. Pl. Glum. 1: 238 (1854) nom conserv non A. Br. (1841) — L. elegans A. Br. (= L. simplex).

Perennial, rarely annual. Panicle open, contracted or spiciform, bearing single or paired spikelets (loose triplets with long pedicels in *L. togoensis*). Spikelets brown; lower lemma 3-nerved (5-nerved and lacking a palea in *L. togoensis*); upper lemma glabrescent to pilose, bidentate; callus oblong to linear, truncate, 2-toothed or obliquely pungent; palea keels thickened, wingless; stamens 2, rarely 3 (anther tips penicillate in *L. togoensis*).

Species 26. Tropical and south Africa; Madagascar; South America. Savanna woodland, often on poor shallow soils. Grain of the Sudanese *L. esculenta* is eaten, but the plant is not deliberately cultivated.
A reasonably uniform genus, apart from *L. togoensis*; though aberrant, the latter is best accommodated here.

566. Loudetiopsis Conert in Bot. Jahrb. 77: 277 (1957) — L. ambiens (K. Schum.) Conert. *Tristachya sect Diandrostachya* C.E. Hubbard in Kew Bull. 1936: 322 (1936)

— T. chrysothrix Nees. *Diandrostachya* (C.E. Hubbard) Jac.-Fél. in J. Agr. Trop. Bot. Appl. 7: 408 (1960).

Perennial, rarely annual. Panicle bearing spikelets in dense triads with short pedicels, the peduncle often developing a fragile hook. Spikelets brown; lower lemma 3-nerved *(L. baldwinii, L. falcipes, L. trigemina* 5—7-nerved); upper lemma glabrescent to pubescent, bidentate; callus square to oblong, truncate or 2-toothed; palea keels thickened or not, wingless; stamens 2 (3 in *L. baldwinii, L. falcipes, L. trigemina).*

Species 11. West tropical Africa; South America. Occasionally in swamps, more often savanna woodland or shallow pockets on bare rocks.

Some of the species are barely separable from *Loudetia*; others are uncomfortably variable, but seem more closely related to each other than to anything else.

40. ANDROPOGONEAE

Dumort., Obs. Gram. Belg.: 84 (1824); Hack. in DC., Monogr. Phan. 6 (1889); Clayton in Kew Bull. 27: 457—474 (1972) & 28: 49—57 (1973). *Sacchareae* Dumort., l.c. 83. *Maydeae* Dumort., l.c. 84, nom inval. *Zeeae* Reichenb., Consp. Reg. Veg.: 55 (1828). *Ophiureae* Dumort., Anal. Fam.: 64 (1829). *Rottboellieae* Kunth, Rév. Gram. 1: 150 (1829). *Imperateae* Gren. & Godr., Fl. France 3: 471 (1855). *Coiceae* Nakai, Ord. Fam. etc: App. 223 (1943). *Euchlaeneae* Nakai l.c. *Tripsaceae* Nakai l.c.

Ligule usually scarious to membranous. Inflorescence composed of fragile (very rarely tough) racemes, these sometimes in a large panicle, but usually single, paired or digitate, terminating the culm or axillary and numerous, in the latter case each true inflorescence subtended by a modified leaf-sheath (spatheole) and often aggregated into a leafy compound panicle. Racemes bearing the spikelets in pairs (rarely singly or in threes, but usually terminating in a triad), nearly always with one sessile and the other pedicelled, these sometimes alike but usually dissimilar, the sessile being bisexual and the pedicelled ♂ or barren (very rarely the sexes reversed); occasionally with 1 or more of the lowermost pairs in the raceme (homogamous pairs) alike, infertile and persisting for some time after the other spikelets have fallen. Sessile spikelet 2-flowered without rhachilla extension, usually dorsally compressed, falling entire at maturity with adjacent pedicel and internode (unless the latter tough), the pedicelled spikelet usually falling separately; glumes enclosing the florets and ± hardened, the lower facing outward and very variable in shape and ornamentation, the upper usually boat-shaped and fitting between internode and pedicel; lower floret ♂ or barren (very rarely suppressed), the lemma membranous or hyaline and awnless (except *Polliniopsis*), the palea usually suppressed when floret barren; upper floret bisexual, its lemma membranous or hyaline, with or without a geniculate awn with spirally twisted column, its palea short or absent. Pedicelled spikelet sometimes similar to sessile, but commonly ♂ or barren, awnless, and smaller or even vestigial (though occasionally large and colourful); rarely the pedicel absent or fused to internode.

Genera 85; species ± 960. Throughout the tropics, particularly the savanna zone, extending into warm temperate regions.

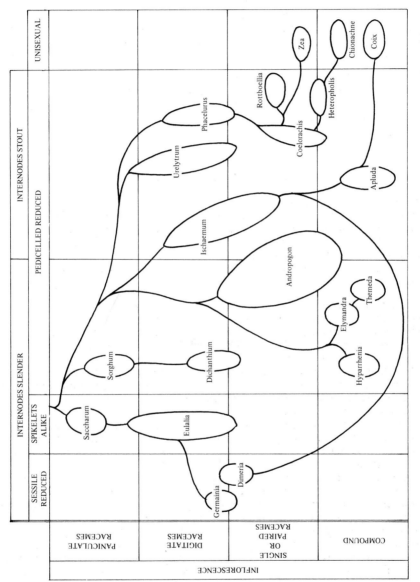

Fig. 22　Evolution of Andropogoneae. Schematic diagram showing selected genera on two axes of increasing morphological complexity.

Anatomy. Shows little variation, being universally of the kranz MS type (Renvoize in Kew Bull. 37: 315—321, 1982).

Chromosomes. The usual basic number is 5; a basic number of 9 occurs sporadically throughout the tribe, becoming quite common in Rottboelliinae. The counts of 2n = 38 were all obtained from *Miscanthus.* Unusually low counts of 2n = 6 & 8 occur in *Iseilema.*

2n	10	18	20	30	36	38	40	50	54	60	72	120
No of species	11	23	155	25	28	8	101	12	6	58	7	8

The most characteristic feature of the tribe is the possession of fragile racemes bearing paired spikelets. In a few of the simpler genera both spikelets of the pair are alike and functionally independent, but it is more usual for the pedicelled spikelet to lose its sexuality and differ in shape. There is then a tendency for the whole raceme-segment (internode, sessile spikelet, pedicel and pedicelled spikelet) to function as a single unit of remarkable variability, all parts of which may participate in the investment of the fertile spikelet. The sex of the pedicelled spikelet has long been regarded as taxonomically important, but it is not infallible and allowance must be made for occasional anomalous species. Sterilization of both spikelets in a segment leads to yet another spikelet shape, that of the homogamous pair; these occur at the base of the raceme, and are sometimes modified to form a kind of involucre.

Loss of sexual function in the florets, typically leaving only one ovary in each spikelet pair, may make it quite difficult to identify the spikelet scales correctly, for their paleas are usually small and often altogether absent. It is thus common to find that the sessile spikelet contains only two scales between the glumes: a lower lemma, which is often 2-keeled like a palea; and an upper lemma, which may be no more than the flattened base of a large awn (but see discussion under *Microstegium*). Even these scales may be missing in the pedicelled and homogamous spikelets. Traditional classifications often employ the tip of the upper lemma, whether entire or bilobed, as a primary character, but it is not well correlated with other trends, and is here regarded as of secondary importance.

Large terminal panicles occur in some of the more primitive genera, but throughout the tribe there is a strong tendency to reduction of the inflorescence, ultimately to a single short raceme. This is coupled with a tendency to multiply the number of inflorescences by repeated axillary branching, and to enclose them within the subtending sheaths; the latter are at first leaf-like, but become progressively more bladeless and inflated with successive degrees of branching, the most distal of them being termed spatheoles. These themes culminate in the compound panicle, where the whole elaborate structure of axillary branches and greatly modified leaves is crowded towards the top of the culm, so that it imitates a panicle; note the analogous inflorescence morphology of Bambuseae. Racemes may be exserted terminally from the spatheole by elongation of the common peduncle or, if paired, they may burst forth laterally by deflexion of the stalks (raceme-bases) supporting the individual racemes. These bases, and the accrescent pair of homogamous spikelets, are homologous to a raceme-segment with twin internodes, such as may occasionally be seen in abnormal branched racemes. Usually one of the bases, conventionally termed the lower, is very short; the other may equal or exceed it.

By ingeniously exploiting the possibilities for morphological variation inherent in the raceme-segment and compound panicle, the tribe has evolved some of the most complex structures found in the Gramineae. A suggested phylogeny, based on advancement along raceme-segment and inflorescence axes, is shown in fig 22. The upshot of the modifications is often to place additional protective envelopes around the flower and fruit, variously derived from the pedicel, pedicelled spikelet, internode, homogamous spikelets and subtending leaf-sheath. This tendency may perhaps be related to the tribe's success in open savanna habitats, whose climate is characterized by strongly contrasting seasons of high rainfall and drought, and where bush fires are an annual event. Generic diversity is prolific in the Old World, slight in the New.

There is little difficulty in defining or recognizing the tribe, except for a few genera, placed at the beginning of the key, which have completely lost their pedicels and pedicelled spikelets. In some other genera the pedicel is so reduced or modified that it is easily overlooked. The complete suppression of the lower floret may also be misleading; it occurs occasionally in the first three subtribes, and the 2-flowered nature of the spikelet must then be inferred from the orientation of the upper lemma.

The most likely derivation of the tribe is via Arundinelleae, which shares the dimorphic florets and geniculate awn.

1 Spikelets not paired, unaccompanied by a vestige:
  2 Inflorescence a panicle: **588 Cleistachne**
  2 Inflorescence of single or digitate racemes:
    3 Raceme rhachis tough   **605 Dimeria**
    3 Raceme rhachis fragile:
      4 Spikelet awnless; callus strongly oblique (otherwise see *640 Ophiuros*)
                  641 Oxyrhachis
      4 Spikelet awned:
        5 Awn arising from bidentate tip of lemma   **602 Pogonachne**
        5 Awn arising from low down on back of lemma   **610 Arthraxon**
1 Spikelets paired, but sometimes one of them vestigial:
  6 Spikelets, or at least one of each pair, bisexual:
    7 Rhachis internodes and pedicels slender, sometimes thickened upwards but then the upper lemma awned or the callus rufously bearded:
      8 Pedicelled spikelet similar to the sessile, both fertile (occasionally the pedicelled ♂ in *578 Microstegium*)
        9 Inflorescence a panicle, with elongated central axis:
          10 Lower glume chartaceous, convex, the nerves raised
                  567 Spodiopogon
          10 Lower glume membranous to coriaceous, the nerves flat (rarely raised but then the lower glume membranous):
            11 Raceme rhachis fragile; one spikelet of the pair sessile:
              12 Panicle ample, with long loose racemes, these mostly white hairy
                    568 Saccharum
              12 Panicle narrow, with short appressed racemes, these rufous or tawny
                    569 Eriochrysis
            11 Raceme rhachis tough; both spikelets pedicelled:
              13 Panicle loose; glumes cartilaginous to coriaceous   **570 Miscanthus**
              13 Panicle contracted or spiciform; glumes membranous
                  571 Imperata
        9 Inflorescence of single or subdigitate racemes:
          14 Inflorescences axillary:
            15 Spikelets laterally compressed   **576 Pogonatherum**

15   Spikelets dorsally compressed; nerves of lower glume raised (if raceme glabrous see *609 Schizachyrium kwiluense*)   **577 Eulaliopsis**
14   Inflorescence terminal:
16   Spikelets in groups of 3, two sessile and one pedicelled
574 Polytrias
16   Spikelets paired:
17   Lower glume convex to flat, rarely slightly concave; erect grasses with narrow leaf-blades; spikelets conspicuously hairy:
18   Raceme rhachis tough; both spikelets of the pair pedicelled; callus obtuse   **570 Miscanthus**
18   Raceme rhachis fragile, rarely tough but then the upper glume awned or callus pungent:
19   Lower glume as long as the upper, ± villous, seldom truncate:
20   Callus short, obtuse; spikelets dorsally compressed **572 Eulalia**
20   Callus long, acute; spikelets terete (if rhachis tough see *582 Trachypogon*)   **573 Homozeugos**
19   Lower glume of fertile spikelet shorter than upper, laterally compressed, with a transverse row of hair tufts, truncate (if dorsally compressed and villous see *580 Apocopis*)
575 Lophopogon
17   Lower glume concave to grooved along median line; rambling grasses with broad leaf-blades; spikelets seldom copiously hairy:
21   Lemma of lower floret awnless   **578 Microstegium**
21   Lemma of both florets awned   **579 Polliniopsis**
8   Pedicelled spikelet differing from the sessile in shape and sex (or some similar the rest represented by barren pedicels in *Sorghastrum*):
22   Sessile spikelet ♂ or barren, the pedicelled fertile:
23   Raceme fragile; sessile spikelet rudimentary   **602 Pogonachne**
23   Raceme tough:
24   Lower spikelet of the pair sessile, dorsally compressed, imbricate
581 Germainia
24   Lower spikelet of the pair shortly pedicelled, subterete, not imbricate   **582 Trachypogon**
22   Sessile spikelet fertile, the pedicelled ♂, barren or suppressed (rarely fertile in anomalous species of *Ischaemum, Rhytachne, Coelorachis*):
25   Inflorescence a panicle with elongated central axis; raceme internodes never with a translucent median line:
26   Lower glume of sessile spikelet dorsally compressed:
27   Pedicels all bearing an awnless spikelet:
28   Lower glume of sessile spikelet flat on the back, 2-keeled for most of its length (if raceme internodes hairy see *568 Saccharum*)
583 Hemisorghum
28   Lower glume of sessile spikelet broadly convex, keeled only at tip:
29   Glumes of sessile spikelet coriaceous; panicle usually loose, of short racemes   **584 Sorghum**
29   Glumes of sessile spikelet firmly cartilaginous; panicle dense, of moderately long racemes   **585 Pseudosorghum**
27   Pedicels sterile, rarely some of them bearing an awned spikelet (if panicle branches simple and callus pungent see *Sorghum angustum*):
30   Upper glume of sessile spikelet broadly convex
586 Sorghastrum

        30   Upper glume of sessile spikelet laterally compressed and keeled
                                                        587 Asthenochloa
  26   Lower glume of sessile spikelet laterally compressed:
    31   Raceme composed of several to many spikelet pairs; awns slender
            or inconspicuous   **589 Vetiveria**
    31   Raceme reduced to a triad; awns usually prominent
                                                        590 Chrysopogon
25   Inflorescence of single or subdigitate racemes, sometimes with an
        elongated central axis but then raceme internodes with a translucent
        median line:
  32   Sessile spikelet fused to cruciform homogamous pairs and awned
                                                        623 Iseilema
  32   Sessile spikelet separately deciduous (rarely attached to homogamous
          pairs but then awnless):
    33   Pedicels and internodes with a translucent median line:
      34   Inflorescence a panicle; racemes of 1—5(—8) sessile spikelets
                                                        594 Capillipedium
      34   Inflorescence of single or subdigitate racemes, rarely paniculate
              and then racemes bearing more than 8 sessile spikelets:
        35   Racemes without homogamous pairs   **595 Bothriochloa**
        35   Racemes with homogamous pairs   **596 Euclasta**
    33   Pedicels and internodes without a translucent median line:
      36   Lower floret of sessile spikelet ♂, with a palea:
        37   Pedicel barren:
          38   Sessile spikelet truncate, not rugose   **580 Apocopis**
          38   Sessile spikelet acute, rugose   **598 Thelepogon**
        37   Pedicel bearing a spikelet:
          39   Ligule membranous:
            40   Sessile spikelet dorsally compressed; racemes usually 2 or
                    more   **597 Ischaemum**
            40   Sessile spikelet laterally compressed; racemes single, spathate:
              41   Raceme reduced to a triad   **599 Apluda**
              41   Raceme containing several sessile spikelets:
                42   Lower glume of sessile spikelet not grooved
                                                        600 Kerriochloa
                42   Lower glume of sessile spikelet grooved   **601 Triplopogon**
          39   Ligule a line of hairs:
            43   Glumes inconspicuously winged, the upper awned
                                                        603 Sehima
            43   Glumes prominently winged, muticous   **604 Andropterum**
      36   Lower floret of sessile spikelet barren and reduced to a lemma:
        44   Upper lemma of sessile spikelet awned from low down on
                back   **610 Arthraxon**
        44   Upper lemma awned from tip, or sinus of bilobed tip, rarely
                awnless:
          45   Lower glume of sessile spikelet 2-keeled (merely sharply
                  inflexed in some spp of *Schizachyrium*); callus ± inserted in
                  hollowed internode tip:
            46   Callus of sessile spikelet obtuse, usually very short:
              47   Racemes digitate or paired, rarely single and then the
                      lower glume nerveless along the midline; lower glume of
                      sessile spikelet concave or grooved between the keels,
                      these lateral or dorsal (rarely slightly convex):

48 Lower glume of sessile spikelet with a broad membranous wing; upper glume trilobed; raceme-bases terete   **607 Bhidea**

48 Lower glume of sessile spikelet with or without a narrow wing (sometimes broader but then racemes deflexed):

    49 Racemes not deflexed (except *A. pumilus, A. pusillus*), borne upon unequal terete racemes-bases; leaves not aromatic   **606 Andropogon**

    49 Racemes usually deflexed at maturity and borne upon subequal flattened raceme-bases, seldom exceeding the spatheole in length; leaves nearly always aromatic; compound panicle dense, profusely branched   **608 Cymbopogon**

47 Racemes single; lower glume of sessile spikelet ± convex, the keels lateral to frontal, with intercarinal nerves   **609 Schizachyrium**

46 Callus of sessile spikelet acute to pungent   **611 Diheteropogon**

45 Lower glume of sessile spikelet convexly rounded without keels, sometimes with a median groove but then the callus applied obliquely to the internode with its tip free (or raceme reduced to a single spikelet); internodes and pedicels linear:

    50 Upper lemma bidentate, awned:

      51 Callus of pedicelled spikelet obscure or absent, sometimes oblong to broadly conical but then the sessile spikelet grooved:

        52 Lower glume of sessile spikelet rounded on back; racemes paired (sometimes single in *Hyparrhenia mobukensis* & *Parahyparrhenia*, otherwise see *591 Dichanthium*,):

          53 Upper raceme-base up to 9 mm long, but usually much shorter; lower glume of sessile spikelet not herbaceous at tip   **612 Hyparrhenia**

          53 Upper raceme-base 15—25 mm long; lower glume of sessile spikelet herbaceous at tip   **613 Exotheca**

        52 Lower glume of sessile spikelet with a median groove:

          54 Raceme-base produced at the tip into a long scarious appendage   **614 Hyperthelia**

          54 Raceme-base without distinct appendage   **615 Parahyparrhenia**

      51 Callus of pedicelled spikelet distinct, narrowly oblong to linear, sometimes the spikelet itself missing or vestigial:

        55 Racemes paired (except *E. gossweileri*), with 1—10 homogamous pairs at the base of the lower or both   **616 Elymandra**

        55 Racemes single, without homogamous pairs:

          56 Spatheoles linear to narrowly lanceolate: racemes loose, the internodes visible   **617 Anadelphia**

          56 Spatheoles cymbiform; racemes dense, the internodes ± concealed   **618 Monocymbium**

    50 Upper lemma entire (if awnless and racemes paired see *612 Hyparrhenia*, subdigitate see *610 Arthraxon*):

      57 Raceme with 2 large homogamous pairs at the base, forming an involucre   **622 Themeda**

      57 Raceme with or without homogamous pairs, if present not forming an involucre:

        58 Sessile spikelet dorsally compressed, the callus obtuse:

59 Inflorescence terminal, sometimes axillary but then subtending sheath not inflated:
  60 Spikelets wingless **591 Dichanthium**
  60 Spikelets broadly winged **592 Pseudodichanthium**
59 Inflorescence spathate:
  61 Racemes digitate, enclosed by a large membranous spathe **593 Spathia**
  61 Racemes single, the spatheoles in bunches **619 Pseudanthistiria**
58 Sessile spikelet subterete, the callus pungent:
  62 Lower glume of sessile spikelet medianly grooved **620 Agenium**
  62 Lower glume of sessile spikelet not grooved **621 Heteropogon**
7 Rhachis internodes and pedicels stout, thickening upwards; upper lemma awnless:
63 Pedicels free from internodes:
  64 Callus of sessile spikelet obtuse to acute, with oblique articulation scar (if racemes reduced to a triad see *599 Apluda;* if spikelet with median groove see *578 Microstegium*):
    65 Sessile spikelet lower floret ♂, with palea; its lower glume without hair tufts or oil streaks:
      66 Pedicelled spikelet nearly always awned; callus pubescent, the hairs mostly concealed **624 Urelytrum**
      66 Pedicelled spikelet awnless (except *L. strigosa*); callus bearded, displaying a ring of hairs at each node **625 Loxodera**
    65 Sessile spikelet lower floret reduced to a lemma; its lower glume with hair tufts or oil streaks (otherwise see *609 Schizachyrium salzmannii*) **626 Elionurus**
  64 Callus of sessile spikelet truncate, with transverse articulation often reinforced by a central peg (if raceme internodes flat on back see *597 Ischaemum*):
    67 Internode and pedicel columnar to inflated:
      68 Raceme silky villous **630 Lasiurus**
      68 Raceme glabrous to pubescent:
        69 Pedicelled spikelet with a distinct callus **627 Phacelurus**
        69 Pedicelled spikelet without a callus:
          70 Lower glume of sessile spikelet produced into a long flattened tail **628 Vossia**
          70 Lower glume of sessile spikelet without a herbaceous tail:
            71 Racemes several to many **627 Phacelurus**
            71 Raceme single:
              72 Sessile spikelet smooth or variously roughened:
                73 Ligule a fringe of hairs; inflorescence axillary; lower floret ♂ **634 Chasmopodium**
              73 Ligule membranous:
                74 Lower floret ♂ (except *R. gracilis*) with large palea; usually the raceme terminal, and lower glume wingless (if with full-sized pedicelled spikelet and chartaceous glumes see *627 Phacelurus speciosus*) **631 Rhytachne**
                74 Lower floret barren, with or without a small palea; usually the racemes axillary, and lower glume winged **632 Coelorachis**

a. SACCHARINAE Griseb., Fl. Rumel. Bithyn. 2: 472 (1844). *Erianthinae* Griseb.
in Nachr. Ges. Wiss. Gött. 3: 89 (1868).

Inflorescence terminal (except *Eulaliopsis, Pogonatherum*) of solitary, digitate
or paniculate racemes with tough or fragile rhachis, and usually slender

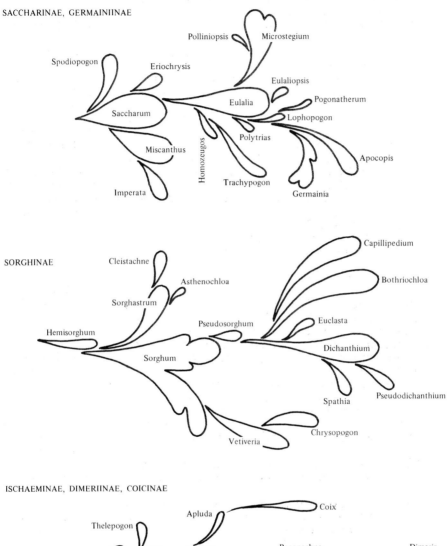

SACCHARINAE, GERMAINIINAE

Polliniopsis Microstegium

Spodiopogon Eriochrysis

Eulaliopsis

Eulalia Pogonatherum

Saccharum Lophopogon

Polytrias

Homozeugos

Miscanthus

Apocopis

Imperata Trachypogon Germainia

SORGHINAE Cleistachne

Capillipedium

Asthenochloa Bothriochloa

Sorghastrum

Pseudosorghum Euclasta

Hemisorghum Dichanthium

Sorghum

Spathia Pseudodichanthium

Vetiveria Chrysopogon

ISCHAEMINAE, DIMERIINAE, COICINAE

Apluda Coix

Thelepogon

Pogonachne Dimeria

Ischaemum

Kerriochloa

Sehima Triplopogon

Andropterum

Fig. 23   Diagram of relationships in Andropogoneae (see also fig. 24).

internodes. Spikelets paired (except *Polytrias*), alike, one sessile the other pedicelled but both pedicelled if rhachis tough, usually dorsally compressed, often plumose, the callus rounded with cupuliform or truncate articulation (except *Homozeugos, Lophopogon*); lower glume mostly thin, convex, or flat on the back and 2-keeled (concave or grooved in *Microstegium, Polliniopsis*); lower floret mostly represented by a barren lemma, occasionally ♂, rarely represented by a palea or absent; upper lemma lanceolate to oblong or sometimes cordate, entire or bilobed, with or without an awn, this usually glabrous.

This is regarded as the most primitive subtribe, since both spikelets of the pair retain their fertility and the rhachis internodes are unspecialized. It may be divided into two groups of genera (fig 23).

The first group has a paniculate inflorescence, which is thought to represent the primitive condition. It tends to have thin glumes and weak awns, which are sometimes also said to be primitive, but they are associated with plumose spikelets and spreading callus hairs, and are more likely to be adaptations to wind dispersal. The rhachis may be fragile or tough, the latter correlated for some reason with both spikelets of the pair being pedicelled. The tough rhachis is quite widely dispersed in the subtribe, and its value for generic delimitation has often been overrated. The derived chromosome number of *Miscanthus* suggests that the tough rhachis may also be a secondary condition. It may, in fact, be a further adaptation to wind dispersal, leaving the spikelets unencumbered by the weight of internode and pedicel.

The second group has a digitate inflorescence, and comprises a number of divergent lines radiating from *Eulalia*. Adaptations to wind dispersal are much in evidence, though abandoned by the shade-loving *Microstegium*. Uncommon characters associated with this group are truncate glumes and cordate lemmas. It is also notable for the variability of its lower floret, some species showing several degrees of reduction in the same inflorescence.

567. Spodiopogon Trin., Fund. Agrost.: 192 (1822) — S. sibiricus Trin. *Eccoilopus* Steud., Syn. Pl. Glum. 1: 123 (1854) — E. andropogonoides Steud. (= S. cotulifer).

Perennial, rarely annual, sometimes with falsely petiolate leaf-blades. Inflorescence an open or contracted panicle, its primary branches typically flexuous and bearing 1 or more racemes with fragile or tough rhachis; internodes linear (*S. rhizophorus* clavate). Spikelets puberulous to villous usually with white hairs, the callus glabrous to shortly bearded (involucral beard in *S. pogonanthus*); lower glume chartaceous, pallid, convex, with prominent nerves raised into ridges; upper lemma bifid for $\frac{1}{3}$—$\frac{3}{4}$ its length, awned.

Species 9. Subtropical Asia from Turkey and India to Japan and Thailand, but *S. sibiricus* extending northwards to Irkutsk. Grassy hillsides.

A homogeneous genus, characterized by the texture and nervation of the lower glume; there is insufficient reason to separate *Eccoilopus* solely on account of its tough rhachis. It is related to *Saccharum*, being linked by the intermediate species *Saccharum beccarii,* whose spikelets resemble *Saccharum* in shape, texture and callus hairs, but have raised nerves.

568. Saccharum L., Sp. Pl.: 54 (1753) — S. officinarum L. *Erianthus* Michaux, Fl.

Bor. Am. 1: 54 (1803); Mukherjee in Lloydia 21: 157—188 (1958) — E. saccharoides Michaux (= S. giganteum). *Saccharifera* Stokes, Bot. Mat. Med. 1: 131 (1812) nom superfl pro Saccharum. *Ripidium* Trin., Fund. Agrost.: 169 (1822) non Bernhardi (1800) — R. ravennae (L.) Trin. *Andropogon subgen Lasiorhachis* Hack. in DC., Monogr. Phan. 6: 471 (1889) — A. hildebrandtii Hack. *Lasiorhachis* (Hack.) Stapf in Hook. Ic. Pl. 32: t 3124 (1927). *Narenga* Bor in Indian For. 66: 267 (1940) — N. porphyrocoma (Hance) Bor (= S. narenga).

Tufted or rhizomatous perennial, often tall. Inflorescence a panicle, often large and plumose, bearing numerous racemes on its branches; rhachis fragile; internodes slender, rarely slightly clavate. Sessile spikelet typically small, with a copious, often involucral, white (rarely rufous) beard from the callus (*S. baldwinii, S. hildebrandtii, S. williamsii* beardless); lower glume cartilaginous to coriaceous, flat to broadly convex, ± 2-keeled but otherwise nerves indistinct (except *S. beccarii, S. velutinum*); upper lemma sometimes almost suppressed, entire or bidentate (up to ⅓ its length), with or without a short awn; stamens 2—3. Pedicelled spikelet similar to sessile, but sometimes more rounded on back (often ± reduced in *S. hildebrandtii* and allies).

Species 35—40. Throughout tropics and subtropics. Mostly riversides and valley bottoms, but some species on open hillsides. Sugar cane is cultivated throughout the tropics. It is usually known as *S. officinarum*, but two segregates, *S. barberi* and *S. sinense*, are often also accorded specific rank. It seems to have originated in New Guinea, and comprises a complex aggregate of hybrids based principally on *S. robustum* and *S. spontaneum* (Stevenson, Genetics and breeding of sugar cane, 1965). Another segregate, *S. edule*, has an arbortive inflorescence which is cooked and eaten as a vegetable from New Guinea to Fiji.

Saccharum is commonly split into several genera, but the characters relied on are more appropriate to infra-generic categories. In particular the traditional division into awned (*Erianthus*) and awnless species seems wholly artificial, and *Narenga*, with its coriaceous glumes, seems no more than the extreme expression of a trend found elsewhere in the genus. *Lasiorhachis* is a problem, for its pedicelled spikelets vary from fertile to rudimentary within the same panicle. It lies between *Saccharum* (especially *S. sikkimense*) and *Hemisorghum*, but is insufficiently distinct to stand on its own.

Grassl (in 9th Congr. Int. Soc. Sugar Cane Tech., 1956) has suggested that the 2-keeled lowermost spikelet scale is a prophyll, and the next two scales are the true glumes. However, when extended beyond *Saccharum*, for example to *Ischaemum* where the lower floret is male, his theory is clearly shown to be untenable.

Saccharum will hybridize with its neighbours, and it is clear that genera 567—572 form a close-knit group. It will also hybridize with *Sorghum* (Gupta et al. in Amer. J. Bot. 65: 936—942, 1978). Hybrids with *Zea* remain unproven; those with *Bambusa* are definitely false, the reports being based on apomictic reproduction in the *Saccharum* parent (Nair & Ratnambal in Vistas Pl. Sci. 3: 1—62, 1978).

569. Eriochrysis P. Beauv., Ess. Agrost.: 8, f 4/11 (1812) — E. cayennensis P. Beauv. *Plazerium* Kunth, Enum. Pl. 1: 474 (1833) in syn sub Eriochrysis. *Saccharum subgen Leptosaccharum* Hack. in DC., Monogr. Phan. 6: 127 (1889) — S. filiforme

Hack. (= E. holcoides). *Leptosaccharum* (Hack.) A. Camus in Bull. Soc. Bot. Fr. 70: 737 (1923); Stapf in Hook. Ic. Pl. 32: t 3125 (1927) where it is mistakenly compared with Leptocoryphium.

Tufted perennial. Inflorescence narrow, rufous or tawny, with several racemes ± appressed along a central axis; racemes short, dense, fragile, bearing pairs of almost similar spikelets; internodes short, sometimes clavate. Sessile spikelet bisexual, bearded with ± rufous hairs from the callus; lower glume chartaceous to coriaceous, broadly convex, the nerves generally indistinct; upper lemma entire, awnless. Pedicelled spikelet ♀, a little smaller than the sessile.

Species 7. Africa and tropical America; 1 species in India. Moist or swampy soils.

A homogeneous group of species allied to *Saccharum,* but distinguished by the compact rufous racemes and slightly dimorphic spikelets.

570. Miscanthus Anderss. in Oefvers. Kon. Vet.-Akad. Forh. 12: 165 (1856); Lee in J. Jap. Bot. 39: 196—204, 257—265, 289—298 (1964) — M. capensis (Nees) Anderss. (= M. ecklonii). *Imperata subgen Triarrhena* Maxim., Prim. Fl. Amur.: 331 (1859) — I. sacchariflora Maxim. *Saccharum subgen Sclerostachya* Hack. in DC., Monogr. Phan. 6: 121 (1889) — S. fuscum Roxb. *Xiphagrostis* Cov. in Contrib. U.S. Nat. Herb. 9: 400 (1905) nom nud — M. floridulus. *Miscanthidium* Stapf in Fl. Trop. Afr. 9: 89 (1917) —M. teretifolium (Stapf) Stapf. *Sclerostachya* (Hack.) A. Camus in Lecomte, Fl. Gén. Indo-Chine 7: 243 (1922). *Triarrhena* (Maxim.) Nakai in J. Jap. Bot. 25: 7 (1950), as "Tiarrhena".

Tufted or rhizomatous perennial, often tall. Inflorescence subdigitate or paniculate, often large and plumose, of numerous racemes (only 1—5 in *M. oligostachyus*) with tough rhachis; internodes slender. Spikelets small, with a spreading often involucral beard from the callus (except *M. fuscus*); lower glume cartilaginous to coriaceous, broadly convex (as in the pedicelled spikelets of *Saccharum*) or sometimes weakly 2-keeled, without raised nerves; upper lemma entire or bidentate (up to $\frac{1}{3}$ its length), the awn small or rarely absent; stamens 2—3.

Species ± 20. Mainly SE Asia, but extending westward to Africa. Open places, such as hillsides and marshes. Several of the larger species with handsome inflorescences, notably *M. sinensis,* are grown as ornamentals.

The inflorescence is subdigitate in most Asian species, but has an elongated axis in the African. The latter are sometimes placed in a separate genus, *Miscanthidium,* but the distinction is blurred by intermediates such as *M. floridulus.* There is even less justification for separating *Sclerostachya,* which has much in common with *M. ecklonii.* An interesting oddity is the suppression of the leaf lamina in *M. teretifolius,* resulting in a quill-like blade formed from the midrib.

The genus has the unusual basic chromosome number of 19, possibly originating as an amphidiploid between species with x = 9 and x = 10 (Adati & Shiotani in Bull. Fac. Agric. Mie Univ. 25: 1—24, 1962).

Miscanthus is closely related to *Saccharum,* with which it hybridizes. The distinction afforded by the tough raceme rhachis is undoubtedly somewhat artificial, and is justified mainly by its practical convenience.

571. Imperata Cyr., Pl. Rar. Neap. 2: 26 (1792) — I. arundinacea Cyr. (= I. cylindrica). *Syllepis* Fourn., Mex. Pl. 2: 52 (1886) — S. ruprechtii Fourn. (= I. brasiliensis).

Rhizomatous perennial. Inflorescence a silky spiciform (loosely contracted in *I. conferta*) panicle, whose branches bear numerous very short racemes with tough rhachis. Spikelets very small, ± terete, enveloped in long silky white hairs from callus and glumes; glumes membranous; upper lemma entire, awnless; lodicules 0; stamens 1—2.

Species 8. Throughout the tropics, extending to warm temperate regions. Open spaces subject to cultivation and disturbance. *I. cylindrica* is an aggressively rhizomatous weed.
A homogeneous group of species allied to *Miscanthus,* but distinguished by the contracted panicle and deficient floral parts.

572. Eulalia Kunth, Rév. Gram. 1: 160 (1829) — E. aurea (Bory) Kunth. *Pseudopogonatherum* A. Camus in Ann. Soc. Linn. Lyon. n.s. 68: 202 (1921) — P. irritans (R. Br.) A Camus. *Puliculum* Haines, Bot. Bihar Orissa: 1018 (1924) — P. articulata (Trin.) Haines (= E. contorta).

Tufted perennial with erect culms and linear leaf-blades, rarely annual. Inflorescence of 1-many digitate racemes (short axis in *E. fastigiata)* with fragile rhachis (often tough in *E. contorta, E. irritans),* conspicuously hairy. Spikelet with short obtuse callus (longer in *E. irritans, E. monostachya),* this not long bearded; lower glume cartilaginous to subcoriaceous, ± flat and usually nerveless on back, 2-keeled or the sides becoming rounded in the lower half, acute to obtuse or truncate, rarely biaristulate; upper glume as long as the lower, sometimes awned; upper lemma linear to oblong or sometimes cordate, bifid ($^1/_3$—$^2/_3$ its length) or shortly bidentate, the awn glabrous or rarely hairy (awnless in *E. manipurensis).*

Species ± 30. Old World tropics. Open grassy places.
The genus is variable, but without clear subdivisions. The possession of a tough rhachis has sometimes been made the basis of a distinct genus (*Pseudopogonatherum*), but the two species concerned also have varieties with a fragile rhachis which are inseparable from *Eulalia.*
It is related to *Saccharum,* differing mainly in the digitate racemes and tendency for the wind-dispersed spikelets to rely upon hairs from glumes and internode rather than from the callus; the latter character helps to place the otherwise intermediate *E. fastigiata.* Indeed the genus stands at the junction of several divergent lines, the truncate glumes of *E. ridleyi* suggesting a link with *Polytrias* and *Lophopogon,* and the large callus of *E. monostachya* foreshadowing *Homozeugos.*

573. Homozeugos Stapf in Hook. Ic. Pl. 31: t 3033 (1915); Clayton in Garcia Orta, Bot. 1: 11—12 (1973) — H. fragile Stapf.

Tufted perennial; leaf-sheaths often auriculate. Inflorescence of 1—several digitate racemes, these villous with fragile rhachis. Spikelet terete, with sharply conical to pungent callus attached obliquely to the internode; lower glume coriaceous, convex, with evenly spaced nerves, obtuse; upper lemma linear, bidentate, with a hairy awn.

Species 5. Tanzania to Angola. Savanna.

A homogeneous genus of barely separable species. It is evidently a segregate from *Eulalia* with long callus and terete spikelets.

574. Polytrias Hack. in Engl. & Prantl, Nat. Pfl.-Fam. 2, 2: 24 (1887) — P. praemorsa (Steud.) Hack.(= P. amaura). *Aethonopogon* Kuntze, Rev. Gen. Pl. 2: 788 (1891) in syn sub Polytrias.

Creeping perennial. Inflorescence a single raceme, this with fragile rhachis and bearing the spikelets in threes, 2 sessile and 1 pedicelled. Spikelet long pilose; lower glume cartilaginous, flat on the back with 2 nerves between the sharply inflexed sides, truncate; upper glume longer than lower, truncate; upper lemma cordate, bidentate, awned.

Species 1. SE Asia. Waste land and roadsides. Sometimes employed as a lawn grass in the humid tropics.

Very closely related to some species of *Eulalia,* being distinguished mainly by its unusual spikelet arrangement.

575. Lophopogon Hack. in Engl. & Prantl, Nat. Pfl.-Fam. 2, 2: 26 (1887) & in DC., Monogr. Phan. 6: 253 (1889); Bor in Hook. Ic. Pl. 37: t 3648 (1967) — L. tridentatus (Roxb.) Hack.

Tufted annual or perennial. Inflorescence of 2 short racemes closely appressed to form an ovate head; raceme with fragile rhachis, bearing imbricate pairs of similar spikelets on short obliquely tipped internodes (but 3—5 of the lowermost sessile spikelets larger, ♂, dorsally compressed and awnless). Fertile spikelets ± laterally compressed; lower glume subcoriaceous, convex, distinctly nerved, with a transverse row of hair tufts across the middle, truncate; upper glume longer than lower, awned; upper lemma linear, bilobed, awned; lodicules 0; stamens 2.

Species 2. India. Open places.

A small genus whose truncate glumes indicate a relationship with *Polytrias*. It introduces a suite of characters — sterile basal spikelets, oblique pedicel tip, exserted upper glume and reduced floral parts — which are developed further in subtribe Germainiinae.

576. Pogonatherum P. Beauv., Ess. Agrost.: 56 (1812) — P. saccharoideum P. Beauv. (= P. paniceum). *Homoplitis* Trin., Fund. Agrost.: 166 (1822) nom superfl pro Pogonatherum. *Pogonopsis* Presl, Rel. Haenk. 1: 333 (1830) — P. tenera Presl (= P. crinitum).

Delicate trailing perennial. Inflorescence axillary, comprising a single raceme with fragile rhachis borne on a flexuous peduncle. Spikelet laterally compressed, the callus obtuse with an involucral beard; lower glume cartilaginous, strongly convex, obtuse; upper glume slenderly awned; upper lemma oblong, bifid ($\frac{1}{3}$—$\frac{1}{2}$ its length), with a long slender awn; stamens 1—2.

Species 3. Tropical Asia. Favours damp rocks and steep banks. *P. paniceum* is sometimes grown as an ornamental.

A homogeneous genus, whose species are barely separable. It occupies a rather isolated position, but bears some resemblance to *Lophopogon.*

577. Eulaliopsis Honda in Bot. Mag. Tokyo 38: 56 (Mar. 1924) — E. angustifolia (Trin.) Honda (= E. binata). *Pollinidium* Haines, Bot. Bihar Orissa: 1020 (Apr. 1924) — P. angustifolium (Trin.) Haines (= E. binata).

Tufted perennial. Inflorescence axillary, of 2—4 digitate racemes with fragile rhachis, conspicuously hairy. Spikelet with involucral hairs from the callus; lower glume chartaceous, pallid, convex, with raised nerves, 2—3-toothed; upper glume with or without a short awn; upper lemma entire or minutely bidentate, shortly awned.

Species 2. Afghanistan to China and the Philippines. Dry hillsides.

A rather isolated genus, whose ridged lower glume recalls *Spodiopogon;* but similar glumes occur in some species of *Apocopis,* and it seems that *Eulaliopsis* might be better regarded as another derivative of *Eulalia.*

578. Microstegium Nees in Lindley, Nat. Syst. ed. 2: 447 (1836); Bor in Kew Bull. 7: 209—223 (1952) — M. willdenowianum Nees (= M. vimineum). *Ephebopogon* Steud., Nom. Bot. ed. 2, 1: 556 (1840) nom nud — M. vagans. *Leptatherum* Nees in Proc. Linn. Soc. 1: 92 (1841) — L. royleanum Nees (= M. nudum). *Psilopogon* Hochst. in Flora 29: 117 (1846) — P. capensis Hochst. (= M. nudum). *Nemastachys* Steud., Syn. Pl. Glum. 1: 357 (1854) — N. taitensis Steud. (= M. glabratum). *Ischnochloa* Hook.f. in Hook. Ic. Pl. 25: t 2466 (1896) — I. falconeri Hook.f. *Coelarthron* Hook. f., Fl. Brit. India 7: 163 (1896) — C. brandisii Hook. f. (= M. eucnemis).

Creeping or rambling annual or perennial with broadly linear to lanceolate leaf-blades, these narrowed at the base and often with a short false petiole. Inflorescence of 1—many subdigitate racemes; raceme with fragile rhachis (*M. japonicum, M. falconeri* tough), slender, sparsely hairy (*M. stapfii, M. dispar* villous), rarely (*M. stapfii*) with homogamous pairs at the base; internodes filiform to clavate or inflated. Sessile spikelet: lower glume herbaceous to cartilaginous, the back with a deep groove or broadly concave median channel, the margins sharply inflexed and usually keeled; upper glume often shortly awned; lower floret well developed, reduced to a palea or absent; upper lemma linear to cordate, bidentate or sometimes bifid, rarely entire, awned (except *M. vimineum, M. rufispicum*), usually accompanied by a small palea; stamens 3, rarely 2 (*M. nudum, M. japonicum*). Pedicelled spikelet resembling sessile but less concave, occasionally slightly smaller and ♂.

Species ± 15. Tropical Asia; also Africa but probably introduced there. Shady places.

A variable genus, recognised by the characteristic, though sometimes rather obscure, median concavity of the lower glume.

The lower floret of Andropogoneae is often reduced to a single scale whose homology can only be established by its orientation, or by seeking rudiments of the missing parts. Such evidence is not always easy to find, but when available it indicates that the surviving scale is the lower lemma. This is taken to be the normal reduction mode, and single scales of indeterminate homology are conventionally referred to as lemmas. However certain species of *Microstegium,* such as *M. vagans,* sometimes have a reduced lower floret containing rudimentary stamens, whose positioning shows that the lower lemma is missing and that the surviving scale is a full-sized lower palea, the upper palea being present as a little scale. This alternative reduction mode is apparently confined to *Microstegium.*

Tiny cordate lemmas occur in only a few genera, and their presence in *Microstegium* strongly suggests kinship with *Eulalia; M. stapfii* bears a marked resemblance to the latter.

579. Polliniopsis Hayata, Ic. Pl. Formosa 7: 76, f 45 (1918) — P. somai Hayata.

Creeping, with lanceolate leaf-blades. Inflorescence of paired racemes with tough rhachis. Spikelet: lower glume shallowly concave; upper glume awned; both lemmas linear, bidentate, awned; palea absent.

Species 1. Formosa.
A rare genus related to *Microstegium japonicum.*

b. GERMAINIINAE Clayton in Kew Bull. 27: 465 (1972). *Apocopidinae* Keng in Sinensia 10: 278 (1939) sine descr lat.

Inflorescence terminal, of solitary or digitate racemes with tough or fragile rhachis and slender internodes. Spikelets paired, dissimilar. Sessile spikelet ♂ or barren and persistent (bisexual and deciduous in *Apocopis*), sometimes enlarged or involucral at base of raceme; lower glume obtuse, truncate or retuse; florets ♂, reduced to a lemma or suppressed. Pedicelled spikelet fertile (sometimes suppressed at base of raceme or throughout), subterete, the callus obtuse to pungent; lower glume coriaceous, obtuse; lower floret reduced to a lemma or suppressed; upper lemma linear, entire or bidentate, with a hairy awn.

In the strictest sense Germainiinae is probably paraphyletic since *Germainia* and *Trachypogon* have different nearest relatives among extant genera, though both are derived from the same genetic potential latent in *Eulalia*. The point is debatable, but there is certainly some didactic advantage in separating these highly modified derivatives of *Eulalia* from the relatively homogeneous Saccharinae (Fig 23).

Apocopis conforms to the general trend of modification in Andropogoneae by reducing its pedicelled spikelets. But *Trachypogon* and *Germainia* have adopted the opposite course, reducing the sessile spikelet and transforming it into a shield behind which the fertile pedicelled spikelet shelters until maturity.

This would seem to be a less effective arrangement, affording no scope for the protective devices of the raceme, which may include modified internodes and pedicels, to be retained by the disseminule. Note that spikelet sexuality can be a treacherous character in this subtribe, for specimens with both spikelets fertile occur in certain species of *Apocopis* and *Trachypogon*.

580. Apocopis Nees in Proc. Linn. Soc. 1: 93 (1841); Bor in Kew Bull. 7: 101—116 (1952) — A. royleanus Nees (= A. paleaceus). *Amblyachyrum* Steud., Syn. Pl. Glum. 1: 413 (1854) — A. mangalorense Steud.

Annual or perennial. Inflorescence of 1—3 digitate racemes; raceme with fragile rhachis, bearing imbricate spikelets, sometimes with a few of the lowermost spikelets enlarged, barren and awnless. Sessile spikelet bisexual, deciduous, dorsally compressed, with obtuse callus; lower glume chartaceous to coriaceous, convex, with evenly spaced nerves, these sometimes raised into ridges, truncate; upper glume longer than lower, truncate; lower floret ♂; upper lemma linear, entire or notched at the tip, with puberulous awn (*A. collinus, A. paleaceus* awnless); lodicules 0; stamens 2. Pedicelled spikelet usually reduced to a little barren pedicel adnate at its base to margin of lower glume of sessile spikelet, rarely with some or most of the spikelets well developed.

Species ± 15. Tropical Asia. Dry shallow soils in open places, often on slopes or pans.

The curious little pedicels are characteristic of *Apocopis,* but its circumscription is complicated by species in which the pedicelled spikelets are often, but not always, well developed. In *A. anomalus* they are ♂ and almost as large as the sessile, thus verging upon *Eulalia*. In *A. wrightii* (and rarely in *A. collinus)* they are ♀, small and subterete, so that the species might be placed in *Germainia* were it not for the fertile sessile spikelet. The derivation of the genus is clearly indicated by the suite of characters which it shares with *Lophopogon*.

581. Germainia Bal. & Poitr. in Bull. Soc. Hist. Nat. Toulouse 7: 344 (1873); Chaianan in Thai For. Bull. 6: 29—47 (1972) — G. capitata Bal. & Poitr. *Balansochloa* Kuntze in Post, Lexicon: 58 (1903) nom superfl pro Germainia. *Sclerandrium* Stapf & Hubbard in Hook Ic. Pl. 33: t 3262 (1935) — S. truncatiglume (F. Muell.) Stapf & Hubbard. *Chumsriella* Bor in Dansk. Bot. Ark. 23: 467 (1968) —C. thailandica Bor.

Tufted perennial, sometimes annual. Inflorescence of 1—2(—6) digitate racemes; raceme with tough rhachis, the large imbricate sessile spikelets shielding smaller pedicelled spikelets, but the latter sometimes suppressed at base of raceme; internodes short, or negligible and then inflorescence capitate being wholly enclosed by an involucre of sessile spikelets. Sessile spikelet ♂ or barren, dorsally compressed, larger than the pedicelled; lower glume coriaceous (*G. pilosa, G. tenax, G. thailandica* chartaceous), broadly convex, truncate or denticulate or retuse; upper glume longer than the lower (scarcely so in *G. thailandica*), truncate; upper lemma, if present, muticous or rarely weakly awned. Pedicelled spikelet fertile, subterete, the callus pungent (*G. tenax, G. thailandica* obtuse) and obliquely attached to pedicel; lower floret sometimes suppressed; upper lemma entire, with pubescent awn; lodicules 0; stamens 2.

Species 9. SE Asia and northern Australia. Savanna.

The genus comprises a complex of inter-related species, broadly divisible into three facies:-

1. *Germainia* proper; inflorescence capitate, with 1—7 pedicelled spikelets enclosed by an involucre of 2—10 greatly enlarged sessile spikelets. However, the racemes of *G. capitata* and *G. lanipes* are sometimes ± elongated, and verge towards *Sclerandrium*.

2. *Sclerandrium*; inflorescence of several elongated racemes, without sterile pairs at the base, the sessile spikelets coriaceous. *G. truncatiglumis* is distinct enough, but *G. grandiflora* intergrades with the previous group.

3. *Chumsriella*; inflorescence a lax raceme, without sterile pairs, the sessile spikelets chartaceous. The glume texture is distinctive, but *G. tenax* links the group to *Sclerandrium*, and *G. pilosa* to *Germainia*.

In short there are more intermediate than typical species, thus effectively undermining attempts to formalize the facies into discrete genera.

The derivation of the genus is clear from the similarity between *G. truncatiglumis* and *Apocopis wrightii*; there is also some resemblance between *G. tenax* and *Lophopogon*.

582. Trachypogon Nees, Agrost. Bras.: 341 (1829) — T. montufari (Kunth) Nees.
Homopogon Stapf in Mém. Soc. Bot. Fr. 8: 103 (1908) — H. chevalieri Stapf.

Tufted annual or perennial. Inflorescence of 1—several digitate racemes; raceme with tough rhachis bearing pairs of pedicelled spikelets, elongated, the internodes clearly visible. Subsessile spikelet ♂ or barren and awnless (sometimes fertile and awned in *T. chevalieri*), otherwise resembling the pedicelled. Pedicelled spikelet bisexual, subterete, the callus pungent and obliquely attached to pedicel; upper lemma entire, with pubescent to villous awn; lodicules 2; stamens 3.

Species ± 3. Africa and tropical America. Savanna.

Trachypogon has a similar raceme structure to *Germainia*, but this has apparently been achieved by a slightly different route for it resembles *Homozeugos* rather than *Lophopogon*.

c. SORGHINAE Bluff, Nees & Schauer, Comp. Fl. Germ. ed. 2, 1: 46 (1836).
Bothriochloinae Keng in Sinensia 10: 282 (1939) sine descr lat.

Inflorescence terminal or rarely axillary, of single or digitate or paniculate racemes, the latter often in whorls; racemes with fragile rhachis and slender internodes, sometimes reduced to triads or single spikelets, occasionally with homogamous pairs. Spikelets paired, dissimilar, seldom plumose. Sessile spikelet bisexual, usually dorsally compressed, the callus usually obtuse with cupuliform or truncate articulation but the latter sometimes oblique (always so when callus pungent); lower glume usually firm, ± convex on the back and abruptly rounded on the flanks (except *Hemisorghum*); lower floret reduced to a barren lemma; upper lemma linear to oblong, entire or bidentate, usually with a glabrous awn. Pedicelled spikelet ♂ or barren, sometimes much reduced, rarely with a small callus.

Saccharinae and Sorghinae both have primitive paniculate or digitate inflorescences, and their common origin is suggested by the close relationship between *Saccharum* and *Sorghum*. Sorghinae differs mainly in the lost fertility of its pedicelled spikelets. The sessile spikelets are of a simple type, employing a toughened convex lower glume, and showing little specialization for wind dispersal. The raceme of Andropogoneae usually terminates in 2 pedicelled spikelets, one of them presumably homologous to a rhachis extension, and a recurrent theme in Sorghinae is the abbreviation of the raceme to a triad of 1 sessile and 2 pedicelled spikelets. Unusual features are the pitted glumes and partly hyaline rhachis internodes found in a few genera.

The two main groups of genera, centred upon *Sorghum* and *Dichanthium* respectively, share a similar spikelet structure and are linked by *Pseudosorghum* (fig 23). There is some parallelism between the *Dichanthium* group and certain Anthistiriinae, but no convincing evidence for a direct relationship.

583. Hemisorghum C.E. Hubbard in Bor, Grasses Burma Ceylon India Pak.: 686 (1960) — H. mekongense (A. Camus) C.E. Hubbard.

Tufted perennial. Inflorescence a panicle, its primary branches subdivided, bearing long loose racemes with glabrous or scabrid internodes. Sessile spikelet callus obtuse; lower glume thinly coriaceous, flat on the back, 2-keeled for most of its length, the margins becoming sharply inflexed towards the base; upper lemma awnless, or bidentate and awned; lodicules glabrous. Pedicelled spikelet well developed or much reduced.

Species 2. Tropical Asia. Hillsides and riverbanks.

A small genus whose 2-keeled glumes form a link between *Sorghum* and *Saccharum* (especially *S. hildebrandtii*).

584. Sorghum Moench, Meth.: 207 (1794) nom conserv; Hubbard in Hook. Ic. Pl. 34: t 3364 (1938); Garber in Univ. California Publ. Bot. 23: 283—361 (1950); Snowden in J. Linn. Soc. Bot. 55: 191—260 (1955); Celarier in Cytologia 23: 395—418 (1959); Ivanyukovich & Doronina in Trudy Prikl. Bot. Genet. Selek. 69: 18—27 (1980) — S. bicolor (L.) Moench. *Blumenbachia* Koel., Descr. Gram.: 28 (1802) nom rejic non Schrad. (1825) — B. halepensis (L.) Koel. *Sarga* Ewart & White in Proc. Roy. Soc. Victoria n.s. 23: 296 (1911) — S. stipoidea Ewart & White.

Annual or perennial, tufted or sometimes rhizomatous, mostly robust. Inflorescence a large panicle, its primary branches simple or subdivided, bearing short dense racemes (triads in *S. intrans*) with hairy internodes. Sessile spikelet callus obtuse or pungent; lower glume coriaceous (cartilaginous in *S. burmahicum*), convex, rounded on the flanks but becoming 2-keeled and winged near the tip, usually hairy; upper lemma awnless, or bidentate and awned; lodicules ciliate (glabrous in *S. macrospermum*). Pedicelled spikelet well developed or reduced to a glume (suppressed in *S. angustum*).

Species ± 20. Tropics and subtropics of the Old World; 1 endemic species in Mexico. Forest margins and savanna, often with a preference for ruderal habitats and alluvial plains. Sorghum (*S. bicolor*) is an important tropical cereal, derived from *S. arundinaceum*. It was probably first domesticated in the Sudan zone over 3000 years ago, spreading thence throughout tropical Africa, and eventually into east Asia. Snowden (The cultivated races of Sorghum, 1936) divided it into 28 species, but these are now treated as cultivars grouped into 5 basic races (de Wet in Amer. J. Bot. 65: 477—484, 1978). There are special cultivars which yield syrup from the stem, or coarse brush bristles from the panicle branches. Several species are grown for forage including Johnson grass (*S. halepense*), Sudan grass (*S.* x *drummondii* = *S. arundinaceum* x *S. bicolor*) and *S.* x *almum* (= *S. bicolor* x *S. halepense*). *S. halepense* can also be a troublesome weed.

The taxa of agricultural importance are closely related to *S. arundinaceum*, forming a complex whose many variants have attracted a deluge of specific names. These are gradually being reduced as cytogenetic understanding of the group improves (de Wet, Harlan & Price in Amer. J. Bot. 57: 704-707, 1970). Variation outside this group is best indicated by the following key to subgenera (from Garber l.c.):

Nodes glabrous or pubescent; panicle branches subdivided (except Chaetosorghum); awns seldom prominent:
  Pedicelled spikelet containing lemmas; Old World (S. arundinaceum)
                                                 Subgen **Sorghum**
  Pedicelled spikelet without lemma; Australia
    Glumes of pedicelled spikelet equal in length (S. macrospermum)
                                     Subgen **Chaetosorghum**
    Glumes of pedicelled spikelet unequal (S. laxiflorum)
                                     Subgen **Heterosorghum**
Nodes bearded; panicle branches simple, awns prominent:
  Callus obtuse; Old World (S. versicolor)   Subgen **Parasorghum**
  Callus pointed; Australia (S. plumosum)   Subgen **Stiposorghum**

Subgenera *Parasorghum* & *Stiposorghum* (x = 5) are thought to be somewhat distant from the rest of the genus (x = 10). Subgen *Sorghum* is perhaps related to *Saccharum*, with which it will hybridize.

The pedicels lack spikelets in *S. angustum*, but this species has the bearded nodes, simple panicle branches and hairy lodicules typical of subgen *Stiposorghum*. It seems that reduction has occurred independently, and that the species is not closely related to *Sorghastrum*.

585. Pseudosorghum A. Camus in Bull. Mus. Hist. Nat. Paris 26: 662 (1920) — P. fasciculare (Roxb.) A. Camus.

Decumbent annual. Inflorescence a small dense panicle (sometimes the central axis short, rarely subdigitate), with subdivided but very short primary branches, bearing moderately long narrow racemes; internodes ciliate, without translucent line. Sessile spikelet callus obtuse; lower glume firmly cartilaginous, rounded on the flanks, glabrous; upper lemma bilobed, awned; lodicules glabrous. Pedicelled spikelet well developed.

Species 2. Tropical Asia. Damp or shady places.

The characters separating *Sorghum* and *Pseudosorghum* are rather weak, except that the latter superficially resembles *Bothriochloa bladhii*. Its status as a link between these genera deserves cytogenetic investigation, but meanwhile it seems best to accept it as distinct.

586. Sorghastrum Nash in Britton, Man. Fl. North. States: 71 (1901) — S. avenaceum (Michaux) Nash (= S. nutans). *Poranthera* Raf. in Bull. Bot. Genève 1: 221 (1830) non Rudge (1811) — P. nutans (L.) Jacks. *Dipogon* Steud., Nom. Bot. ed. 2, 1: 518 (1840) nom nud — S. stipoides.

Annual or perennial. Inflorescence a panicle, the subdivided primary branches bearing short racemes, these sometimes reduced to triads. Sessile spikelet callus obtuse or pungent (with involucral beard in *S. pogonostachyum*); lower glume coriaceous, convex, keeled only at tip; upper glume broadly convex; upper lemma bidentate, awned; lodicules glabrous. Pedicelled spikelet reduced to a barren pedicel (but often present and resembling sessile on some pedicels of *S. fuscescens, S. pogonostachyum*).

Species ± 16. Africa and tropical America. Savanna and woodland margins.

A relative of *Sorghum* with characteristic barren pedicels. The generic circumscription is stretched by *S. fuscescens* & *S. pogonostachyum* in which many of the pedicels bear fertile awned spikelets (they also occur very rarely in *S. stipoides* and some other species), but whose spikelets are otherwise so typical of *Sorghastrum* that they would be misplaced in *Saccharum*. Nevertheless they clearly indicate a strong link with that genus.

587. Asthenochloa Büse in Miq., Pl. Jungh.: 367 (1854) — A. tenera Büse. *Garnotiella* Stapf in Hook. Ic. Pl. 25: t 2494 (1896) — G. philippinensis Stapf (= A. tenera).

Decumbent annual. Inflorescence a panicle with subdivided primary branches, bearing racemes reduced to triads. Sessile spikelet small (2 mm), its callus obtuse; lower glume firmly cartilaginous, broadly convex, rounded on the flanks; upper glume laterally compressed, keeled; lower floret suppressed; upper lemma bilobed, awned; lodicules 0; stamens 2. Pedicelled spikelet reduced to a tiny barren pedicel concealed in the callus beard.

Species 1. SE Asia. Damp places.

A segregate from *Sorghastrum,* distinguished by its keeled upper glume and reduced floral parts.

588. Cleistachne Benth. in Hook. Ic. Pl. 14: t 1379 (1882) — C. sorghoides Benth.

Coarse annual. Inflorescence a panicle, its primary branches bearing racemes at regular intervals along their length, each raceme reduced to a single sessile spikelet (whose apparent pedicel is homologous to the raceme peduncle). Sessile spikelet callus obtuse; lower glume coriaceous; upper lemma bidentate, awned; lodicules ciliate. Pedicelled spikelet and pedicel completely suppressed.

Species 1. Tropical Africa and India. Old farmland.

The genus can be baffling due to the extreme reduction of its racemes, but the spikelets unmistakably ally it to *Sorghum*.

589. Vetiveria Bory in Lem.-Lisanc. in Bull. Sci. Soc. Philom. 1822: 43 (1822) —V. odoratissima Bory (= V. zizanioides). *Lenormandia* Steud. in Flora 33: 229 (1850) non Sonder (1845), nom nud pro seq. *Mandelorna* Steud., Syn. Pl. Glum. 1: 359 (1854) — M. insignis Steud. (= V. nigritana).

Tufted perennial; ligule a line of hairs. Inflorescence a panicle, its primary branches whorled, simple, each bearing a raceme; raceme typically long and slender, comprising (2—)3—10 spikelet pairs. Sessile spikelet laterally compressed, its callus obtuse to pungent, often large and conical; lower glume chartaceous to coriaceous, spinulose; upper glume shortly awned; upper lemma bidentate (*V. pauciflora* entire), with a slender or inconspicuous awn (*V. zizanioides* awnless). Pedicelled spikelet well developed.

Species 10. Old World tropics. Flood plains and stream banks. *V. zizanioides* is cultivated for the aromatic oil obtainable from its roots, which is used in perfumery.
Vetiveria is related to *Sorghum subgen Parasorghum. V. pauciflora*, with only 2—3 spikelet pairs per raceme, links it to *Chrysopogon*.

590. Chrysopogon Trin., Fund. Agrost.: 187 (1822) nom conserv — C. gryllus (L.) Trin. *Rhaphis* Lour., Fl. Cochin.: 552 (1790) nom rejic — R. trivialis Lour. (= C. aciculatus). *Pollinia* Spreng., Pl. Pugill. 2: 10 (1815) nom rejic — P. gryllus (L.) Spreng. *Centrophorum* Trin., Fund. Agrost.: 106 (1822) — C. chinense Trin. (= C. aciculatus). *Trianthium* Desv., Opusc.: 69 (1831) in syn sub Rhaphis. *Chalcoelytrum* Lunell in Amer. Midl. Nat. 4: 212 (1915) nom superfl pro Chrysopogon.

Perennial, mostly tufted (*C. pauciflorus* annual); ligule a short membrane or a line of hairs. Inflorescence like *Vetiveria*: raceme reduced to a triad, but rarely some racemes with 2 sessile spikelets (usually so in *C. sylvaticus*). Sessile spikelet laterally compressed, its callus elongated, acute to pungent; lower glume cartilaginous to coriaceous, often spinulose; upper glume usually awned; upper lemma entire or bidentate, its awn glabrous to pubescent and usually prominent (*C. setifolius* awnless). Pedicelled spikelet well developed (but often rudimentary in *C. sylvaticus*).

Species 26. Tropical and warm temperate regions of the Old World, principally in Asia and Australia; 1 species in Florida and West Indies. Open, often disturbed, habitats from subdesert to rain forest. *C. aciculatus* is often used for lawns in the humid tropics.
Chrysopogon intergrades with *Vetiveria* via *C. sylvaticus*, and the separation of these genera is somewhat arbitrary, particularly in Australia. It is marginally justified by the convenience of treating the compact cluster of species with triads as a single entity.

591. Dichanthium Willemet in Usteri, Ann. Bot. 18: 11 (1796); de Wet & Harlan in Bol. Soc. Arg. Bot. 12: 206—227 (1968) — D. nodosum Willemet (= D. annulatum). *Lepeocercis* Trin., Fund. Agrost.: 203 (1822) — L. serrata (Retz.) Trin. (= D. caricosum). *Diplasanthum* Desv., Opusc.: 66 (1831) — D. lanosum Desv. (= D. caricosum). *Eremopogon* Stapf in Fl. Trop. Afr. 9: 182 (1917) — E. foveolatus (Del.) Stapf.

Annual or perennial; leaves sometimes aromatic. Inflorescence terminal or sometimes also axillary, of single or subdigitate racemes, these sometimes conspicuously pedunculate, usually with 1 or more homogamous pairs; internodes and pedicels solid, truncate to oblique at the tip. Sessile spikelets often imbricate, with obtuse callus; lower glume chartaceous to cartilaginous, broadly convex to slightly concave, sometimes pitted, acute to broadly obtuse; upper lemma entire (*D. foveolatum, D. mucronulatum* sometimes bidentate), with a glabrous awn (*D. mucronulatum* hairy); stamens (2—)3. Pedicelled spikelet much like the sessile, rarely herbaceous, occasionally with a short oblong callus.

Species ± 20. Old World tropics. Open places from subdesert to marshland, particularly when subject to disturbance.
Dichanthium may be recognized by its homogamous pairs and obtuse sessile spikelets, but some species lack these features and approach closely to *Bothriochloa*, from which they are rather arbitrarily separated by the solid pedicels.

592. Pseudodichanthium Bor in Indian For. 66: 271 (1940) & in Hook. Ic. Pl. 36: t 3598 (1962) — P. serrafalcoides (Cooke & Stapf) Bor.

Annual. Inflorescence terminal and axillary, of a single raceme with imbricate spikelets and 2—3 homogamous pairs; internodes and pedicels solid, with crateriform tip. Sessile spikelet callus obtuse; lower glume cartilaginous, broadly convex, the margins expanded into wings; upper lemma entire, awned. Pedicelled spikelet larger than sessile, membranous, winged.

Species 1. India. In partial shade.
The culm is unusual, since the nodal swelling occurs at the base of the internode; most grasses have it at the node itself or at the base of the sheath. The genus is presumably related to *Dichanthium*, but is isolated by the broadly winged lower glume.

593. Spathia Ewart in Ewart & Davies, Fl. North. Territ.: 26 (1917) — S. neurosa Ewart & Archer.

Annual. Inflorescence terminal and axillary, of digitate racemes enclosed in a large membranous spathe; raceme with 1 homogamous pair; internodes and pedicels solid, oblique at the tip. Sessile spikelet callus obtuse; lower glume coriaceous, convex, acute; upper lemma entire, awned. Pedicelled spikelet well developed, with a short oblong callus.

Species 1. Australia. Grassy plains.
The genus is distinguished by its spathe. It has plump *Sorghum*-like spikelets, but the internode tip and pedicelled spikelet callus suggest a derivation from *Dichanthium*.

594. Capillipedium Stapf in Fl. Trop. Afr. 9: 169 (1917) — C. parviflorum (R. Br.) Stapf. *Filipedium* Raiz. & Jain in J. Bombay Nat. Hist. Soc. 49: 682 (1951) — F. planipedicellatum (Bor) Raiz. & Jain.

Annual or perennial, mostly rambling; leaves sometimes aromatic. Inflorescence a delicate panicle, with subdivided branches bearing short racemes of 1—5(—8) sessile spikelets and no homogamous pairs; internodes and pedicels hyaline and translucent between thickened margins (greatly expanded in *C. planipedicellatum*). Sessile spikelet callus obtuse; lower glume cartilaginous, broadly convex to slightly concave, acute to obtuse; upper lemma entire, with a glabrous or puberulous awn (*C. planipedicellatum* awnless). Pedicelled spikelet usually well developed.

Species ± 14. Eastern Africa, tropical Asia and Australia. Open grassy places.
A homogeneous genus related to *Bothriochloa*, but with paniculate inflorescence and short racemes often reduced to triads. *B. bladhii* lies midway between the two genera.

595. Bothriochloa Kuntze, Rev. Gen. Pl. 2: 762 (1891) — B. anamitica Kuntze (= B. bladhii). *Andropogon subgen Gymnandropogon* Nees, Fl. Afr. Austr.: 103 (1841) — A. radicans Lehm. *Gymnandropogon* (Nees) Duthie in Atkinson, Gaz. NW Prov. & Oude 10: 638 (1882). *Amphilophis* Nash in Britton, Man. Fl. North. States: 71 (1901) — A. torreyanus (Steud.) Nash (= B. saccharoides).

Perennial; leaves sometimes aromatic. Inflorescence digitate or subdigitate, sometimes paniculate with simple or rarely subdivided branches and then the racemes with more than 8 sessile spikelets, without homogamous pairs; internodes and pedicels hyaline and translucent between thickened margins. Sessile spikelet callus obtuse; lower glume mostly cartilaginous, broadly convex to slightly concave, sometimes with 1—3 circular pits, acute; upper lemma entire (*B. biloba, B. erianthoides* bilobed), with a glabrous awn (*B. exaristata* awnless); stamens (1—)3. Pedicelled spikelet much like the sessile, or smaller.

Species ± 35. Throughout the tropics. Open grassy places.
The essential oils of *Bothriochloa*, and their taxonomic implications, have been studied by de Wet & Scott in Bot. Gaz. 126: 209—214 (1965). Heslop-Harrison (Phytomorph. 11: 378—383, 1961) believes that the glume pits play a part in cleistogamous flowering by obstructing the emergence of the anthers.
The boundaries between *Bothriochloa, Capillipedium* and *Dichanthium* are somewhat blurred, largely due to a complex pattern of hybridization created by rapacious introgression from *B. bladhii* (de Wet & Harlan in Evolution 24: 270—277, 1970). In recognition of its capacity for genetic mixing De Wet & Harlan have called *B. bladhii* a compilospecies (Amer. J. Bot. 53: 94—98, 1966), and have advocated uniting the three genera (Taxon 19: 339—340, 1970). However, apart from this one promiscuous species and its immediate neighbours, the genera are acceptably distinct both morphologically and genetically.

596. Euclasta Franch. in Bull. Soc. Hist. Nat. Autun 8: 335 (1895) — E. glumacea Franch. (= E. condylotricha). *Indochloa* Bor in Kew Bull. 9: 75 (1954) — I. clarkei (Hack.) Bor.

Rambling annual. Inflorescence terminal and axillary, of delicate solitary or subdigitate racemes, these pedunculate with 1—3 large herbaceous homogamous pairs at the base; internodes and pedicels with a translucent median line. Sessile spikelet callus obtuse; lower glume chartaceous to cartilaginous, ± flat, narrowly obtuse; upper lemma entire, with a glabrous or pubescent awn. Pedicelled spikelet large, herbaceous.

Species 2. India, tropical Africa and tropical America. In partial shade or among taller grasses.

Euclasta has *Bothriochloa*-like pedicels, but the resemblance between *E. clarkei* and *Dichanthium oliganthum* suggests an even closer affinity with *Dichanthium*. There is also a remarkable, but apparently superficial, similarity between *E. condylotricha* and *Agenium villosum*.

d. ISCHAEMINAE Presl, Rel. Haenk. 1: 328 (1830). *Apludinae* Hook.f., Fl. Brit. India 7: 4 (1897).

Inflorescence of single, paired or digitate racemes, these usually terminal, sometimes axillary, rarely spathate; racemes with fragile rhachis and linear to obovoid internodes, without homogamous pairs. Spikelets paired, dissimilar. Sessile spikelet bisexual (except *Pogonachne*), dorsally or laterally compressed, the callus blunt and fitting a truncate or shallowly hollowed internode tip; lower glume chartaceous to crustaceous, convex or concave, 2-keeled or rounded on the flanks, with or without a median groove; lower floret ♂, with palea; upper lemma oblong, bidentate or bifid, nearly always with a glabrous awn. Pedicelled spikelet variable.

Reduction of the inflorescence to 1 or 2 racemes is firmly established, but the subtribe retains a number of primitive features, notably the male lower floret and occasional bisexuality of the pedicelled spikelet, which suggest a derivation from *Eulalia*. On the other hand the appearance of strongly 2-keeled glumes, thickened internodes which may assume a protective function, and spatheoles places it at the branching point of several divergent lines where these trends are developed further (figs 22 & 23).

597. Ischaemum L., Sp. Pl.: 1049 (1753) — I. muticum L. *Schoenanthus* Adans., Fam. Pl. 2: 38, 602 (1763) nom superfl pro Ischaemum. *Colladoa* Cav., Ic. Pl. 5: 37 (1799) — C. distachia Cav. (= I. rugosum). *Meoschium* P. Beauv., Ess. Agrost.: 111 (1812) — M. aristatum (L.) P. Beauv. *Ischaemopogon* Griseb., Fl. Br. W. Ind.: 560 (1864) — I. latifolius (Spreng.) Griseb. *Ischaemum subgen Digastrium* Hack. in DC., Monogr. Phan. 6: 250 (1889) — I. fragile R. Br. *Digastrium* (Hack.) A. Camus in Bull. Mus. Hist. Nat. Paris 27: 372 (1921). *Argopogon* Mimeur in Rev. Bot. Appl. 31: 211 (1951) — A. vuilletii Mimeur (= I. fasciculatum).

Perennial, sometimes annual, often decumbent; leaves mostly with sheath auricles, sometimes sagittate or falsely petiolate. Inflorescence terminal and axillary, of paired (occasionally single or digitate) racemes, these generally 1-sided and interlocked back to back thus simulating a single spike, mostly exserted but sometimes embraced by a spatheole; internodes and pedicels stoutly linear to obovoid, usually exposed on the back of the raceme as a U- or V-shaped segment, occasionally the pedicel very short and the spikelets almost side by side. Sessile spikelet dorsally compressed; lower glume chartaceous to coriaceous, convex (*I. afrum* concave), 2-keeled or rounded on flanks, often rugose, sometimes winged, entire or bilobed; upper glume with or without an awn; upper lemma awnless in *I. muticum* and a few other spp. Pedicelled spikelet as large as the sessile (much reduced in *I. decumbens, I. fragile, I. roseo-tomentosum;* with elongated callus in *I. latifolium*), dorsally or laterally compressed, often asymmetrical, occasionally bisexual with the upper lemma weakly awned.

Species ± 65. Throughout the tropics, but mainly in Asia. Mostly damp or shady places. *I. rugosum* is a weed of rice fields.

There is no adequate treatment of the genus available, but variation within it is indicated by the following key (modified from Pilger, Nat. Pfl.-Fam. 14e: 125, 1940).

Sessile spikelet rounded in the lower half; pedicelled spikelet laterally
    compressed:
  Racemes digitate (I. fasciculatum)   Sect *Fasciculata*
  Racemes 1—2 (I. indicum)   Sect *Ischaemum*
Sessile spikelet 2-keeled throughout; pedicelled spikelet dorsally compressed:
  Internodes and pedicels rounded on the back (I. afrum)   Sect *Coelischaemum*
  Internodes and pedicels flat on the back:
    Lower glume of sessile spikelet rugose or at least knobbly on the flanks,
      coriaceous; upper glume awnless (I. rugosum)   Sect *Aristata*
    Lower glume of sessile spikelet not rugose, chartaceous; upper glume awned
      (I. aureum)   Sect *Aurea*

The sections probably evolved in the order shown above, sect *Fasciculata* being closely related to *Eulalia*. The genus is often quite difficult to distinguish from *Andropogon,* but the shape of the rhachis segment exposed on the back of the raceme is usually characteristic (except sect *Coelischaemum*).

598. Thelepogon Roem. & Schult., Syst. Veg. 2: 46 (1817) — T. elegans Roem. & Schult. *Rhiniachne* Steud., Syn. Pl. Glum. 1: 360 (1854) in syn sub Jardinea abyssinica (= T. elegans).

Coarse annual. Inflorescence terminal, of digitate racemes with clavate internodes. Sessile spikelet dorsally compressed: lower glume crustaceous, broadly convex, rounded on the flanks, rugose, wingless, entire; upper glume rugose, wingless. Pedicelled spikelet absent, represented by a flattened linear pedicel.

Species 1. Mainly tropical Africa, extending eastwards to Indonesia. Weedy places.

Distinguished from *Ischaemum* mainly by the barren pedicel.

599. Apluda L., Sp. Pl.: 82 (1753) — A. mutica L. *Calamina* P. Beauv., Ess. Agrost.: 128 (1812) nom superfl pro Apluda.

Rambling perennial; leaf-blades often falsely petiolate. Inflorescence a single raceme embraced by a boat-shaped spatheole, these numerous and crowded into a compound panicle; raceme comprising 1 sessile and 2 pedicelled spikelets, the pedicels flat and broad forming, together with its lower glume, a triangular box around the sessile spikelet. Sessile spikelet laterally compressed, with a large bulbous callus; lower glume coriaceous, convex, without keels or wings, bidentate; upper glume awnless; upper lemma sometimes awnless. Pedicelled spikelets awnless, unequal, the one ♂ or bisexual and as large as the sessile, the other much reduced and sterile.

Species 1. Tropical Asia. Among thickets and forest margins.
A relative of *Ischaemum* with highly modified pedicels.

600. Kerriochloa C.E. Hubbard in Hook. Ic. Pl. 35: t 3494 (1951) — K. siamensis C.E. Hubbard.

Perennial. Inflorescence terminal and sometimes also axillary, of single racemes partly enclosed in a spatheole; internodes cuneate. Sessile spikelet laterally compressed; lower glume thinly coriaceous, convex, wingless, acute; upper glume awned. Pedicelled spikelet lanceolate, much reduced.

Species 1. Thailand and Indo-China. Open places.
Related to *Ischaemum,* particularly *I. decumbens.*

601. Triplopogon Bor in Kew Bull. 9: 52 (1954) — T. spathiflorus (Hook.f.) Bor (= T. ramosissimus).

Annual. Inflorescence of single racemes subtended by spatheoles and forming a scanty compound panicle; internodes linear. Sessile spikelet laterally compressed; lower glume coriaceous, strongly convex, with a longitudinal median groove and rounded flanks, wingless, bidentate; upper glume awnless; grain laterally compressed. Pedicelled spikelet longer than sessile, slender, subterete.

Species 1. India. Forest margins.
Apparently related to *Kerriochloa,* but also with some similarity to *Sehima sulcatum.*

602. Pogonachne Bor in Kew Bull. 4: 176 (1949) — P. racemosa Bor.

Annual. Inflorescence of single racemes subtended by spatheoles and forming a scanty compound panicle; raceme with linear internodes, these tardily disarticulating after spikelets have fallen. Sessile spikelet rudimentary or completely suppressed. Pedicelled spikelet bisexual, strongly laterally compressed; lower glume coriaceous, narrowly convex, without keels or wings, entire; upper glume awnless.

Species 1. India
The nearest relative of this odd genus seems to be *Kerriochloa.* It is quite unrelated to Germainiinae, the only other group with sex-reversed spikelets.

603. Sehima Forssk., Fl. Aegypt.-Arab.: 178 (1775) — S. ischaemoides Forssk. *Hologamium* Nees in Edinb. New Phil. J. 18: 185 (1835) — H. nervosum (Rottler) Nees.

Annual or perennial; ligule a line of hairs. Inflorescence a single terminal raceme; internodes stoutly linear to subclavate. Sessile spikelet slightly dorsally compressed to ± square in section, fitting between internode and pedicel; lower glume coriaceous, concave or with a median groove (*S. galpinii* convex), laterally 2-keeled or lyrate with the keels becoming dorsal towards the base, scarcely winged, bidentate; upper glume awned; upper lemma awn glabrous or pubescent along the coils; grain dorsally compressed. Pedicelled spikelet large, lanceolate, strongly dorsally compressed, distinctly nerved.

Species 5. Old World tropics. Dry bushland.
Although variable in certain key characters, the genus is remarkably uniform in general facies, the shape and nervation of the pedicelled spikelet being particularly characteristic. It can be regarded as a segregate from *Ischaemum*.

604. Andropterum Stapf in Fl. Trop. Afr. 9: 38 (1913) — A. variegatum Stapf (= A. stolzii).

Rambling perennial; ligule a line of hairs. Inflorescence terminal and axillary, of single racemes with clavate internodes. Sessile spikelet laterally compressed, squeezed between internode and pedicel; lower glume cartilaginous, 2-keeled, the keels dorsal, almost contiguous and separated by a narrow groove, wingless, entire; upper glume winged towards top of keel. Pedicelled spikelet larger than sessile, laterally compressed, its lower glume with a broad asymmetrical wing.

Species 1. Central Africa. Forest margins.
The lower glume of the sessile spikelet and the ligule indicate a relationship with *Sehima*.

e. DIMERIINAE Hack. in Engl. & Prantl, Nat. Pfl.-Fam. 2, 2: 22 (1887).

Inflorescence terminal, of single or digitate racemes with tough rhachis. Spikelets single, shortly pedicelled, strongly laterally compressed; glumes subcoriaceous, usually keeled, often winged; lower floret reduced to a barren lemma; upper lemma oblong, bilobed, with a glabrous awn.

An apparently anomalous subtribe, whose spikelets are borne singly with no trace of pairing, though their structure is unmistakably andropogonoid. The few species with distant spikelets on terete pedicels, such as *D. leptorhachis,* are revealing for they are not unlike *Pogonachne*. It seems reasonable therefore to regard Dimeriinae as derived from Ischaeminae by suppression of the sessile spikelet.

605. Dimeria R. Br., Prodr. Fl. Nov. Holl.: 204 (1810); Bor in Kew Bull. 7: 553—592 (1953) — D. acinaciformis R. Br. *Haplachne* Presl, Rel. Haenk. 1: 234

(1830) — H. pilosissima Presl (= D. chloridiformis). *Didactylon* Zoll. & Mor. in Mor., Syst. Verz. Zoll. Pfl.: 99 (1846) — D. simplex Zoll. & Mor. (= D. ornithopoda). *Psilostachys* Steud., Syn. Pl. Glum. 1: 413 (1854) non Turcz. (1843) — P. hohenackeri Steud. *Pterygostachyum* Steud. l.c. — P. lehmannii Steud. *Woodrowia* Stapf in Hook. Ic. Pl. 25: t 2447 (1896) — W. diandra Stapf (= D. stapfiana).

Annual or perennial, often straggling or delicate. Raceme rhachis triquetrous or flattened, the spikelets usually imbricate but sometimes distant, on squatly clavate or rarely terete pedicels. Spikelets with truncate callus (*D. avenacea* oblique) and awned upper lemma (*D. lehmannii, D. glabra* awnless); stamens 2.

Species 35—40. SE Asia from India and China to Indonesia and Australia; 3 species in Madagascar. Glades and open places in or near forest.

A homogeneous genus with many, perhaps too many, narrowly defined species. *D. woodrowii* is unusual, for its spikelets are not deciduous; at maturity the pair of racemes coil inwards to form a ball, and the inflorescence is shed as a whole.

f. ANDROPOGONINAE Presl, Rel. Haenk. 1: 331 (1830). *Arthraxoninae* Benth. in J. Linn. Soc. 19: 67 (1881).

Inflorescence of single, paired or sometimes digitate racemes, these terminal, or axillary and aggregated into a compound panicle; racemes with fragile rhachis and filiform to ovoid internodes, the homogamous pairs inconspicuous or lacking (except *Diheteropogon*). Spikelets paired, dissimilar. Sessile spikelet bisexual, dorsally compressed or squeezed between internode and pedicel, the callus blunt (except *Diheteropogon*) and ± inserted in the cupuliform or crateriform internode tip; lower glume mostly firm, 2-keeled or at least sharply inflexed (except *Arthraxon*), often depressed or grooved between the keels, sometimes winged; lower floret reduced to a barren lemma; upper lemma narrowly oblong, nearly always bilobed with a glabrous awn (but see *Arthraxon, Diheteropogon*). Pedicelled spikelet very variable, without a distinct callus (except *Bhidea*).

The subtribe is closely related to Ischaeminae, and is often difficult to distinguish from it. It is characterized by 2-keeled glumes and a callus inserted into the hollowed internode tip, but it must be admitted that these are relative terms, open to some degree of subjective interpretation.

606. Andropogon L., Sp. Pl.: 1045 (1753); Clayton in Hook. Ic. Pl. 37: t 3644 (1967) — A. distachyos L. *Anatherum* P. Beauv., Ess. Agrost.: 128 (1812) — A. bicorne (L.) P. Beauv. *Diectomis* Kunth in Mém. Mus. Hist. Nat. Paris 2: 69 (1815) nom conserv non P. Beauv. (1812) — D. fastigiata (Sw.) P. Beauv. *Dimeiostemon* Raf., Neogenyton: 4 (1825) — D. vaginatus (Ell.) Jacks. (= A. virginicus). *Hypogynium* Nees, Agrost. Bras.: 364 (1829) — H. spathiflorum Nees (= A. virgatus). *Arthrostachys* Desv., Opusc.: 74, f 6/2 (1831) — A. gracilis Desv. (aff sect Piestium?). *Eupogon* Desv. l.c. 67, in syn sub A. juncifolius (= A. gracilis). *Heterochloa* Desv. l.c. 66 — H. alopecurus Desv. *Andropogon subgen Athrolophis* Trin. in Mém. Acad. Sci. Pétersb. sér. 6, 2: 268 (1832) nom superfl pro subgen

Andropogon. *Homoeatherum* Nees in Lindley, Nat. Syst. ed. 2: 448 (1836) — H. chinense Nees. *Eriopodium* Hochst. in Flora 29: 115 (1846) in syn sub A. eucomus Nees. *Euklastaxon* Steud., Syn. Pl. Glum. 1: 412 (1854) — E. tenuifolius Steud. (= A. leucostachyus). *Athrolophis* (Trin.) Chiov. in Bull. Soc. Bot. Ital. 1917: 57 (1917) as "Arthrolophis", nom superfl. *Leptopogon* Roberty, Monogr. Androp.: 193 (1960) non Borzi (1907) — L. carinatus (Nees) Roberty.

Annual or perennial, often robust; leaves never aromatic. Inflorescence typically of paired racemes but these sometimes digitate or rarely single, terminal or axillary, the latter often crowded into a compound panicle; raceme-bases terete, not deflexed (flattened and divergent in *A. pumilus*; terete deflexed and bearing 1—2 homogamous pairs in *A. pusillus*); internodes filiform to obovoid, sometimes plumose, the tip not usually fimbriate. Sessile spikelet dorsally or laterally compressed; lower glume membranous to coriaceous, flat to concave or grooved (rarely slightly convex in sect *Andropogon*; pitted in *A. lacunosus, A. pusillus*), 2-keeled, the keels lateral or dorsal and sometimes narrowly winged; upper glume occasionally awned; upper lemma bilobed with glabrous or puberulous awn, sometimes entire and awnless; stamens sometimes 1. Pedicelled spikelet varying from large and colourful to suppressed, not concave (except *A. burmanicus*).

Species ± 100. Tropics. One of the dominant savanna genera, but some species of sect *Andropogon* have adapted to tropical highlands. *A. gayanus* is an important pasture species.

The genus shows a progression from digitate to single racemes, and from terminal to compound inflorescences, but the main source of variation is the shape of the sessile spikelet lower glume, and sectional classification is based on this (Clayton l.c.):

Rhachis internodes filiform to linear; lower glume ± lanceolate:
  Lower glume thinly coriaceous with 3—9 intercarinal nerves, its keels lateral and often winged; racemes usually terminal; tropics & Mediterranean (A. distachyos)   Sect *Andropogon*
  Lower glume membranous, without intercarinal nerves, its keels lateral to dorsal and wingless; racemes in a compound panicle, delicate and often plumose; sometimes the sessile spikelet awnless or the pedicelled spikelet suppressed; mainly America, also Africa (A. leucostachyus) Sect *Leptopogon*
Rhachis internodes clavate to obovoid; inflorescence mostly a compound panicle; lower glume coriaceous:
  Lower glume linear, squeezed between internode and pedicel, the back deeply concave with dorsal keels almost meeting over the depression; 2—4(—6) closely spaced nerves in each keel, but none between; tropics, mainly Africa (A. schirensis)   Sect *Piestium*
  Lower glume lanceolate, the back flat with a median groove and lateral keels; intercarinal nerves 6—10; Africa, mainly western (A. gayanus)
        Sect *Notosolen*

Sect *Andropogon* has the least modified spikelets and inflorescence, and is thereby regarded as the most primitive. It intergrades with sect *Leptopogon* (the largest section with 55 narrowly circumscribed species), whose spikelets are small, thin-textured and often plumose, showing an evident trend towards wind dispersal. Sects *Piestium* and *Notosolen* are more distinct; they are characterized by tough glumes with exaggerated keels (dorsal and lateral respectively), enlarged protective internodes and pedicels, and the elaboration of compound panicles. However none of the sections is sufficiently clear-cut to recommend elevation to generic rank.

Bowden (J. Linn. Soc. 59: 77—80, 1964 & 64: 77—80, 1971) comments on the occurrence of a membranous rim, called an external ligule, on the abaxial side of the leaf-sheath of *A. gayanus*; the same species also has false petioles and leaf nectaries.

The raceme-bases help to distinguish *Andropogon* from its neighbours, for they are terete and often fairly long, even peduncle-like in *A. polyptichos*. Exceptions are *A. pumilus*, with *Cymbopogon*-like raceme-bases, but spikelets typical of sect *Piestium*; and *A. pusillus* with *Hyparrhenia*-like bases, but whose spikelets closely resemble *A. lacunosus*, itself clearly assignable to sect *Andropogon*. Species with single racemes are unusual, and liable to be confused with *Schizachyrium*. They differ from the latter in possessing a ± concave lower glume nerveless along the midline, such as can be matched among sects *Andropogon*, *Leptopogon* and *Piestium*.

607. **Bhidea** Bor in Kew Bull. 3: 445 (1949) — B. burnsiana Bor.

Annual. Inflorescence terminal and axillary, of paired racemes embraced by a spatheole; raceme-bases terete; internodes linear with truncate tip. Sessile spikelet dorsally compressed; lower glume flat, laterally 2-keeled, without intercarinal nerves, the keels with large asymmetrical membranous wings; upper glume trilobed, the central lobe produced into a long tail; upper lemma bilobed, awned. Pedicelled spikelet large, with a small square callus, the lower glume asymmetrically winged.

Species 2. India. Open places on dry soils
The genus is a peripheral segregate from *Andropogon* sect *Andropogon*, barely deserving separate recognition.

608. **Cymbopogon** Spreng., Pl. Pugill. 2: 14 (1815); Bor in J. Bombay Nat. Hist. Soc. 51: 890—916 (1953) & 52: 149—183 (1954); Soenarko in Reinwardtia 9: 225—375 (1977) — C. schoenanthus (L.) Spreng. *Cymbanthelia* Anderss. in Nova Acta Soc. Sci. Uppsala ser. 3, 2: 254 (1856) nom nud — Cymbopogon tortilis. *Gymnanthelia* Schweinf., Beitr. Fl. Aeth.: 299 (1867) nom nud — C. commutatus.

Perennial, rarely annual, often tall; leaves aromatic (except *C. gidarba, C. microtheca*). Inflorescence of short paired racemes ± enclosed in a spatheole, these crowded into a compound panicle which is often large and complex; raceme-bases short, flattened, deflexed (except ser *Proceri*), the lower bearing a homogamous pair, internodes linear (*C. gidarba, C. microtheca* clavate), sometimes the pedicel of the homogamous pair swollen and ± fused to the internode. Sessile spikelet dorsally compressed; lower glume ± chartaceous, often streaked with oil glands, concave, 2-keeled, the keels usually lateral and often winged near the apex, with or without intercarinal nerves; upper lemma bilobed with a short glabrous awn, occasionally awnless (awned and entire in *C. densiflorus*). Pedicelled spikelet well developed, never concave on the back.

Species ± 40. Old World tropics and subtropics; introduced to tropical

America. Savanna. *C. citratus, C. flexuosus, C. martinii, C. nardus* and *C. winterianus* are cultivated for the essential oils which can be distilled from their leaves and used as an inexpensive perfume (Guenther, The essential oils, vol 4, 1950). *C. citratus* is also appreciated as a medicinal and culinary herb throughout the tropics.

A fairly homogeneous genus of narrowly circumscribed species, which are often difficult to distinguish. The range of variation is indicated by the following key to series (Soenarko l.c.):

Raceme-bases ± cylindrical, not usually deflexed; lower glume concave, wingless;
    Australia (C. bombycinus)   Ser *Proceri*
Raceme-bases flattened, deflexed:
  Pedicelled spikelets pungent; Australia (C. refractus)   Ser *Refracti*
  Pedicelled spikelets acute to acuminate:
    Sessile spikelet flat or concave on back:
      Lower glume of sessile spikelet flat, ± winged; Africa, India (C. nardus)
         Ser *Citrati*
      Lower glume of sessile spikelet concave, wingless; Old World (C. schoenanthus)   Ser *Cymbopogon*
    Sessile spikelet with a V-shaped median groove in the lower half of the back; Old World (C. martinii)   Ser *Rusae*

The raceme segments of *C. refractus* show an unusual adaptation to dispersal, having developed slender recurved pungently tipped pedicelled spikelets which catch the fur of passing animals.

The concave 2-keeled sessile spikelet of *Cymbopogon* clearly indicates an affinity with *Andropogon*, from which it differs mainly in its elaborate compound panicle with deflexed raceme-bases; the straight bases of ser *Proceri* are taken to be a primitive character. Another distinguishing feature is the aromatic flavour when a leaf is chewed. Only two species lack this; both have clavate internodes reminiscent of *Andropogon*, but their raceme-bases are typically *Cymbopogon*-like. Though obviously peripheral to the genus, they are insufficiently distinct to justify removal from it.

609. Schizachyrium Nees, Agrost. Bras.: 331 (1829) — S. brevifolium (Sw.) Büse. *Schizopogon* Spreng., Gen. Pl. ed. 9, 1: 55 (1830) — unnamed species (= S. brevifolium?). *Pithecurus* Kunth, Rév. Gram. 2: 571 (1832) in syn sub S. myosurus. *Ystia* Compère in Bull. Jard. Bot. Brux. 33: 400 (1963) — Y. stagnina Compère (= S. kwiluense).

Annual or perennial, often tall but sometimes delicate. Inflorescence of single slender racemes, these axillary and arranged in a compound panicle, rarely terminal; internodes filiform to clavate, sometimes plumose, the tip usually with fimbriate rim. Sessile spikelet lanceolate to linear, dorsally compressed or squeezed between internode and pedicel; lower glume chartaceous to coriaceous, convex (*S. impressum, S. muelleri, S. sulcatum* concave), 2-keeled or at least with sharp inflexions, the keels lateral to frontal, with several intercarinal nerves though these sometimes faint, wingless; upper glume rarely awned; upper lemma bilobed, or bifid almost to the base (*S. pulchellum, S. scintillans* entire), with a glabrous awn, this usually short and sometimes inconspicuous (*S. kwiluense, S. salzmannii* awnless). Pedicelled spikelet commonly smaller than sessile (bisexual in *S. kwiluense*).

Species ± 60. Throughout the tropics. Savanna; *S. pulchellum* on sandy beaches.

The genus is very closely related to *Andropogon* sect *Leptopogon*, being distinguished by its single racemes. The intercarinal nerves and fimbriate internode tip serve to separate it from the few species of *Andropogon* which also have single racemes. *S. kwiluense* has an anomalous bisexual pedicelled spikelet, but otherwise resembles *Schizachyrium*, particularly *S. mukuluense.*

610. Arthraxon P. Beauv., Ess. Agrost.: 111, f 11/6 (1812); van Welzen in Blumea 27: 255—300 (1981) — A. ciliaris P. Beauv. (= A. hispidus). *Pleuroplitis* Trin., Fund. Agrost.: 174 (1822) — P. langsdorfii Trin. (= A. hispidus). *Lucaea* Kunth, Rév. Gram. 2: 489 (1831) — L. gracilis Kunth (= A. hispidus). *Batratherum* Nees in Edinb. New Phil. J. 18: 180 (1835) — B. echinatum Nees. *Lasiolytrum* Steud. in Flora 29: 18 (1846) — L. hispidum (Thunb.) Steud. *Alectoridia* A. Rich., Tent. Fl. Abyss. 2: 447 (1851) — A. quartiniana A. Rich. (= A. micans)

Annual or perennial, slender, often trailing; leaf-blades lanceolate. Inflorescence of subdigitate, rarely single, slender racemes, these terminal and axillary but not spathate; internodes linear. Sessile spikelet dorsally or laterally compressed; lower glume membranous to coriaceous, convex, with or without lateral keels, often spinulose; upper lemma entire, awned from low down on back (*A. submuticus* awnless); stamens 2—3. Pedicelled spikelet well developed, reduced to a pedicel or subulate point, or completely suppressed.

Species ± 10. Old World tropics, but mainly in India. Rocky slopes, shady glades and old farmland.

A homogeneous genus with a basic chromosome number of 9, and several unusual features which make it difficult to place in the system. The most plausible comparison is with *Schizachyrium*, in which the awn is also sometimes basal though from a bifid lemma, a comparison supported by the 2-keeled lower glumes of some *Arthraxon* species.

611. Diheteropogon (Hack.) Stapf in Hook. Ic. Pl. 31: t 3093 (1922); Clayton in Kew Bull. 20: 73—76 (1966). *Andropogon sect Diheteropogon* Hack. in DC., Monogr. Phan. 6: 647 (1889) — A. grandiflorus Hack.

Annual or perennial. Inflorescence of paired (very rarely single) racemes, these terminal or gathered into a scanty compound panicle; raceme-bases terete, not deflexed, bearing 1—many homogamous pairs; internodes linear. Sessile spikelet subterete, its callus pungent and deeply inserted into the hollow internode tip; lower glume coriaceous, hollowed or deeply grooved, 2-keeled, the keels dorsal ± rounded and each 2—7-nerved; upper lemma bilobed, with puberulous to hirsute awn. Pedicelled spikelet much larger than the sessile.

Species 5. Tropical and South Africa. Savanna.

A small homogeneous genus which links *Andropogon* sect *Piestium* (particularly *A. ivorensis*) to *Parahyparrhenia*. Indeed its separation from *Andropogon* is barely justified.

g. ANTHISTIRIINAE Presl, Rel. Haenk. 1: 347 (1830).

Inflorescence of single or paired racemes, these usually axillary and aggregated into a compound panicle; racemes with fragile rhachis and slender internodes, often with the lower pairs homogamous. Spikelets paired, dissimilar. Sessile spikelet bisexual, mostly subterete, the callus (usually pointed) applied obliquely to top of internode with its tip free; lower glume usually coriaceous, rounded on back and sides; lower floret reduced to a barren lemma; upper lemma mostly stipitiform, entire or bilobed with a glabrous or hairy, often large, awn. Pedicelled spikelet sometimes with an elongated callus.

Compound panicles, often of considerable complexity or augmented by involucral homogamous pairs, are the rule. The major trends are a reduction in the number of racemes from two to one, and a shortening of the raceme itself. A minor trend, particularly associated with this subtribe, is the development of a long stipe-like callus at the base of the pedicelled spikelet. Apart from *Iseilema* the disseminule remains simple, being represented by a tough sessile spikelet, but it often has a large awn. This seems rather inefficient as a dispersal agent, but its hygroscopic twisting effectively drives the seed into cracks or beneath crumbs on the soil surface.

The subtribe is distinguished from Andropogoninae by a pointed callus applied obliquely to the internode tip, rather than blunt and sunk into it. Similarities with *Diheteropogon* and *Cymbopogon* suggest that its ancestry lies somewhere in the common ground between them (fig 24).

612. Hyparrhenia Fourn., Mex. Pl. 2: 51 (1886); Clayton in Kew Bull. Addit. Ser. 2 (1969) — H. foliosa (Kunth) Fourn. (= H. bracteata). *Dybowskia* Stapf in Fl. Trop. Afr. 9: 382 (1919) — D. seretii (De Wild.) Stapf (= H. dybowskii).

Annual or perennial, usually caespitose with tall culms, rarely trailing; leaf-blades never aromatic. Inflorescence a pair of racemes (sometimes single in *H. mobukensis*), embraced or enclosed by a spatheole, this linear to ovate and often colourful, crowded into a large compound panicle; raceme short, with up to 2 homogamous pairs, these sometimes involucral; raceme-bases terete or flattened, often deflexed at maturity. Sessile spikelet dorsally compressed or subterete, the callus obtuse to pungent; lower glume without median groove or herbaceous tip; upper glume awnless; upper lemma bidentate, bearing a stout hairy awn (*H. exarmata, H. mutica* awnless; *H. mobukensis* glabrous). Pedicelled spikelet usually a little longer than the sessile, without a callus.

Species 55. Mainly Africa, a few species extending to other tropical regions, one to the Mediterranean. Almost confined to savanna, and often dominant there. Widely used for thatching in Africa; *H. rufa* has been introduced to many tropical countries as a forage grass.

The genus is noteworthy for its elaborate compound panicles, an important element of which is the raceme-base. This may be adapted to deflex at maturity, or to supplement the spatheole by supporting an inner protective cover of long bristles or involucral homogamous spikelets; in *H. filipendula* the upper base is exceptionally long, placing the racemes almost end-to-end. Sectional classification is based on the various forms of these bases (Clayton l.c.).

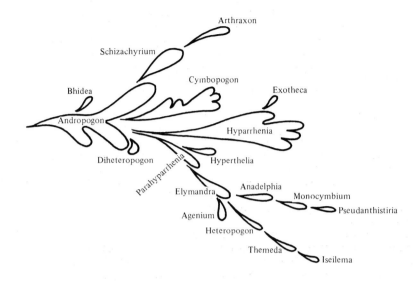

ROTTBOELLIINAE, TRIPSACINAE, CHIONACHNINAE

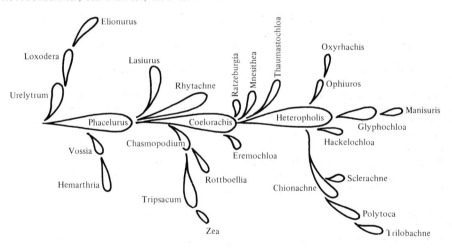

Fig. 24   Diagram of relationships in Andropogoneae (continued from fig. 23).

Callus of sessile spikelet broadly rounded; spikelets glabrous; raceme-bases
    unequal (H. glabriuscula, H. mobukensis)   Sect *Strongylopodia*
Callus of sessile spikelet acute to pungent, rarely obtuse but then not as above:
    Upper raceme-base terete, usually much longer than the lower, glabrous to
        softly hirtellous; spatheoles generally narrow (H. filipendula, H. hirta, H.
        rufa)   Sect *Polydistachyophorum*
    Upper raceme-base flattened, scarcely exceeding the lower:
        Homogamous pairs at base of lower raceme only; raceme-bases bearded with
            long bristles:
            Raceme-base without appendage; spatheoles generally inflated (H. cymbaria)
                 Sect *Pogonopodia*
            Raceme-base extended into a short scarious appendage (H. bracteata)
                 Sect *Hyparrhenia*
        Homogamous pairs at base of both racemes, often forming an involucre:
            Homogamous spikelets pectinate ciliate on the margin (H. arrhenobasis)
                 Sect *Arrhenopogonia*
            Homogamous spikelets scabrid on the margin (H. diplandra)
                 Sect *Apogonia*

The genus is notorious for introgression among its species, many of which are
difficult to distinguish. The sections also intergrade, and there is no case for
raising any of them to generic rank. They are arranged above in a logical
sequence of morphological advancement, but there is evidence, mainly from
geographical distribution, that except for sect *Strongylopodia* they actually
evolved in almost the reverse of this order (Clayton l.c.). *H. glabriuscula,* rated as
one of the most primitive species, bears a close superficial resemblance to
Cymbopogon and provides a link between these two genera.

613. Exotheca Anderss. in Nova Acta Soc. Sci. Uppsala ser. 3, 2: 253 (1856);
Clayton in Kew Bull. 20: 447 (1966) — E. abyssinica (A. Rich.) Anderss.

Perennial. Inflorescence a pair of racemes subtended by a narrow spatheole,
these grouped into a scanty compound panicle; racemes short, each with 2
involucral homogamous pairs at the base; raceme-bases unequal, the upper
terete, very long, the racemes thereby arranged head to tail. Lower glume of
sessile spikelet with herbaceous tip. Otherwise like *Hyparrhenia.*

Species 1. East Africa and Viet Nam. Upland grassland.
The end-to-end arrangement of the raceme-pair imitates a single raceme,
perhaps thereby avoiding mutual interference. This and the basal involucre are
encountered in *Hyparrhenia,* though not in combination. It is clearly a
peripheral segregate from that genus, the differences being just sufficient to
justify separation. The distribution is odd, but a number of African grasses are
known to have disjunct records in Indo-China perhaps as a result of coastal
trading going back to antiquity.

614. Hyperthelia Clayton in Kew Bull. 20: 438 (1966) — H. dissoluta (Steud.)
Clayton.

Annual or perennial, tall. Inflorescence a pair of racemes embraced or subtended by a linear to lanceolate spatheole, these crowded into a large compound panicle; racemes short, containing (1—)2(—10) sessile spikelets per pair, with 1 pair of homogamous spikelets at the base of the lower; raceme-bases terete, sometimes deflexed, the tip very oblique and produced into a scarious appendage, this 3—20 mm long, flat or rolled into a funnel about the base of the raceme. Sessile spikelet terete, the callus pungent; lower glume with median groove and herbaceous or membranous tip; upper glume with or without a short awn; upper lemma bidentate, bearing a stout hairy awn. Pedicelled spikelet about as long as the sessile, narrowed at the base to a short conical callus.

Species 6. *H. dissoluta* throughout Africa and introduced to tropical America, the remaining species localized in southern Sudan and Central African Republic. Savanna. Wild stands of *H. edulis* are harvested for grain.

The genus resembles *Hyparrhenia*, but this may be misleading for it has more features in common with *Parahyparrhenia*. *H. colobantha* shows an unusual variant of the raceme-reduction theme, for its upper raceme is abortive, being reduced to a single ♂ spikelet.

615. Parahyparrhenia A. Camus in Bull. Mus. Hist. Nat. Paris sér. 2, 22: 404 (1950); Clayton in Kew Bull. 20: 434 (1966) — P. jaegeriana A. Camus (= P. annua).

Annual or perennial. Inflorescence a single or pair of racemes, terminal and also axillary but scarcely forming a compound panicle; raceme fairly long, the homogamous spikelets inconspicuous; raceme-bases terete, not deflexed, without appendages. Sessile spikelet subterete, the callus acute to pungent; lower glume often awned; upper lemma bidentate, bearing a stout ± hairy awn. Pedicelled spikelet ± as long as the sessile, with or without a small oblong callus.

Species 5. Senegal to Sudan, also in India and Thailand. Open savanna grassland, or shallow pools on ironstone outcrops.

A small genus which links *Diheteropogon* to *Elymandra; P. tridentata* approaches closely to the latter.

616. Elymandra Stapf in Fl. Trop. Afr. 9: 407 (1919); Clayton in Kew Bull. 20: 287—293 (1966) — E. androphila (Stapf) Stapf. *Pleiadelphia* Stapf in Hook. Ic. Pl. 30: t 3121 (1927) — P. gossweileri Stapf.

Annual or perennial with tall culms. Inflorescence a pair of racemes (single in *E. gossweileri*), long-exserted from narrow spatheoles and gathered into a compound panicle; racemes slender, with 1—10 homogamous pairs at the base of the lower or both, the homogamous spikelets narrowly lanceolate and olive or brownish green; raceme-bases filiform, unequal, not deflexed (except *E. archaelymandra*). Sessile spikelet subterete, at length dark brown, the callus pungent; lower glume not grooved; upper glume obliquely awned (*E. androphila* awnless); upper lemma bilobed, bearing a stout ± hairy awn. Pedicelled spikelet about as long as the sessile, with narrow linear callus.

Species 6. Tropical Africa, 1 species also in Brazil. Savanna woodland.

The species vary somewhat, but all have a distinctive facies imparted by the olive-green homogamous spikelets and dark sessile spikelets. In general, species with the most homogamous pairs tend to have the fewest fertile spikelets, sometimes only 1 per raceme; *E. archaelymandra* has 2 homogamous pairs separated by an internode at the base of each raceme, thus approaching the involucral condition. The pedicelled spikelet callus suggests a relationship with *Parahyparrhenia.*

617. Anadelphia Hack. in Bot. Jahrb. 6: 240 (1885); Clayton in Kew Bull. 20: 275—285 (1966) — A. virgata Hack. (= A. leptocoma). *Diectomis* P. Beauv., Ess. Agrost.: 132, f 23/5 (1812) nom rejic non Kunth (1815) — D. fasciculata P. Beauv. (= A. leptocoma). *Andropogon sect Pobeguinea* Stapf in J. Bot. Paris 19: 100 (1905) —A. afzeliana Rendle. *Monium* Stapf in Fl. Trop. Afr. 9: 399 (1919) — M. macrochaetum Stapf. *Pobeguinea* (Stapf) Jac.-Fél. in Rev. Bot. Appl. 30: 172 (1950).

Annual or perennial. Inflorescence a single raceme, exserted from or enclosed by a narrow spatheole, gathered into a scanty or copious panicle; raceme loose, with few spikelets (sometimes only 1) and long internodes visible between them, without homogamous pairs. Sessile spikelet slightly dorsally compressed to subterete, the callus usually pungent; lower glume not grooved (except A. *scyphofera*); upper glume usually awned; upper lemma bilobed, with glabrous to pubescent awn. Pedicelled spikelet as long as the sessile, linear-lanceolate, acuminate, nearly always glabrous, with narrowly oblong to linear callus, sometimes the spikelet absent and its pedicel much reduced.

Species 14. Senegal to Zambia, but mainly the Fouta Djallon plateau of Guinée. Savanna, often on shallow soils.
The racemes seldom contain many spikelets, and in some species (A. *trichaeta*) may be reduced to a single fertile spikelet with two vestigial pedicels hidden among its callus beard. A. *scyphofera* is odd in having a funnel-like cup at the tip of the peduncle and a medianly grooved sessile spikelet, but is otherwise similar to other members of the genus. The genus is clearly related to *Elymandra.*

618. Monocymbium Stapf in Fl. Trop. Afr. 9: 386 (1919); Hubbard in Kew Bull. 4: 374—375 (1949); Jacques-Félix in Rev. Bot. Appl. 30: 175—177 (1950) — M. ceresiiforme (Nees) Stapf.

Perennial. Inflorescence a solitary raceme, enclosed by a boat-shaped reddish spatheole, and grouped into a loose compound panicle; raceme dense, the spikelets ± concealing the short internodes, without homogamous pairs. Sessile spikelet dorsally compressed, the callus obtuse; lower glume not grooved; upper glume awned; upper lemma bilobed, with glabrous awn. Pedicelled spikelet broadly lanceolate, subacute, hairy or merely spinulose ciliate on the margins, with linear callus.

Species 3. Tropical Africa. Savanna, often on shallow hillside soils.
Monocymbium, with its conspicuous spatheoles, looks very different from *Anadelphia,* but in fact the differences between them are rather slight. On the other hand there are no intermediate species, and the separation of the two genera is marginally justifiable.

619. Pseudanthistiria (Hack.) Hook.f., Fl Brit. India 7: 219 (1896). *Andropogon sect Pseudanthistiria* Hack. in DC., Monogr. Phan. 6: 400 (1889) — A. heteroclitus (Roxb.) Nees.

Trailing annual. Inflorescence a solitary raceme subtended by a spatheole, these in little bunches on flexuous peduncles, several such bunches forming a compound panicle; raceme comprising 2 sessile spikelets with pedicelled attendants, without homogamous pairs. Sessile spikelet dorsally compressed, the callus obtuse; lower glume not grooved; upper glume awnless; lower lemma absent; upper lemma entire, with glabrous awn. Pedicelled spikelet larger than sessile, with narrowly oblong to linear callus.

Species 4. India to Thailand. Open hillsides and disturbed places.
A small homogeneous genus related to *Monocymbium*.

620. Agenium Nees in Lindley, Nat. Syst. ed. 2: 447 (1836); Pilger in Feddes Rep. 43: 80—82 (1938) — A. nutans Nees (= A. villosum).

Perennial. Inflorescence of single or subdigitate racemes, terminal and axillary, without obvious spatheoles; racemes with several conspicuous homogamous pairs at the base; raceme-bases (when digitate) filiform and flexuous. Sessile spikelet subterete, the callus pungent; lower glume with a median groove; upper glume awnless; upper lemma entire, bearing a stout puberulous awn. Pedicelled spikelet larger than sessile, with a short oblong callus, the pedicel with a pigmented median line on one side.

Species 4. Brazil to Argentina. Dry open savanna.
The grooved glume and entire upper lemma place the genus somewhere between *Parahyparrhenia* and *Heteropogon*. The uncanny resemblance between *A. villosum* and *Euclasta condylotricha* seems more superficial than real.

621. Heteropogon Pers., Syn. Pl. 2: 533 (1807) — H. glaber Pers. (= H. contortus). *Spirotheros* Raf. in Bull. Bot. Genève 1: 221 (1830) — Andropogon melanocarpus Ell.

Annual or tufted perennial. Inflorescence a single raceme, terminal and axillary, sometimes loosely aggregated into a compound panicle; raceme linear, with homogamous spikelets for the lower $\frac{1}{4}$—$\frac{2}{3}$ of its length. Sessile spikelet subterete, the callus long and pungent; lower glume not grooved; upper lemma entire, with stout pubescent awn. Pedicelled spikelet larger than sessile, with slender pedicel-like callus, the true pedicel reduced to a little stump.

Species 6. Throughout the tropics and subtropics. Dry open places, often on poor soils.
The homogamous spikelets and well developed pedicelled spikelet callus suggest a loose relationship with *Elymandra*. *H. contortus* has a needle-sharp sessile spikelet callus which readily penetrates clothing and is a ferociously efficient dispersal mechanism.

622. Themeda Forssk., Fl. Aegypt.-Arab.: 178 (1775) — T. triandra Forssk. *Anthistiria* L.f., Nov. Gram. Gen: 35 (1780) & Suppl. Pl.: 13 (1781) — A. ciliata L.f. (= T. quadrivalvis). *Perobachne* Presl, Rel. Haenk. 1: 348 (1830) — P. secunda Presl (= T. arundinacea). *Androscepia* Brongn. in Duperr., Voy. Coq. Bot. Phan.: 77 (1831) — A. gigantea (Cav.) Brongn. *Aristaria* Jungh. in Tijd. Nat. Gesch. 7: 296 (1840) — A. barbata Jungh. (= T. arguens). *Heterelytron* Jungh. l.c. 294 — H. scabrum Jungh. (= T. villosa).

Annual or perennial, tufted. Inflorescence a single raceme embraced by a colourful spatheole, these solitary or more often densely packed in fan-shaped bunches on a flexuous peduncle, gathered into a compound panicle; raceme very short with 2 large involucral homogamous pairs at the base, and 1—2(—4) sessile spikelets with their pedicelled attendants. Sessile spikelet subterete or dorsally compressed, usually deciduous but rarely the raceme shed as a whole; callus mostly pungent, sometimes obtuse; lower glume not grooved (obscurely so in *T. tremula*); upper lemma entire, with pubescent awn (*T. anathera, T. gigantea* and sometimes *T. villosa* awnless). Pedicelled spikelet mostly larger than sessile, with slender pedicel-like callus (this narrowly oblong in *T. anathera, T. gigantea, T. hookeri*), the true pedicel usually much reduced.

Species 18. Tropics and subtropics of the Old World, but mainly in Asia. Open savanna. *T. triandra* (Rooigras) is an important grazing species in South Africa. *T. villosa*, a huge Asiatic species, is sometimes cultivated as an ornamental.

The genus is clearly related to *Heteropogon*, though the nature of the inflorescence is not always easy to perceive as the racemes are much modified and often compacted into dense clusters. The sessile spikelet is normally shed at maturity in the usual way, but in *T. anathera* and *T. gigantea* the whole raceme is deciduous with the sessile spikelets still attached. These species cannot be confused with *Iseilema* for, apart for the awnless sessile spikelets, the homogamous pairs are separated by a short internode.

623. Iseilema Anderss. in Nova Acta Soc. Sci. Upsal. ser. 3, 2: 250 (1856); Hubbard in Hook. Ic. Pl. 33: t 3286 (1935) — I. prostratum (L.) Anderss.

Annual or perennial, often wiry. Inflorescence a single raceme embraced by a boat-shaped spatheole, these solitary or in tightly packed clusters, gathered into a narrow compound panicle; raceme very short, with 2 involucral homogamous pairs at the base, 1 sessile spikelet (very rarely 2) usually borne upon a short internode, and 2 pedicelled spikelets; homogamous spikelets often indurated, all ± pedicelled, arising from the same point in a cruciform arrangement. Sessile spikelet dorsally flattened, lanceolate, coriaceous below and herbaceous above, not deciduous but shed with the whole raceme; callus none, the spikelet base being fused to the rhachis internode; upper lemma entire or bilobed, with glabrous awn. Pedicelled spikelet usually smaller than sessile and sometimes much reduced, deciduous or not, without a callus, borne upon a filiform pedicel.

Species ± 20. India to Australia. Mostly in open grassland. Includes a number of excellent grazing species known as Flinders grass.

Modification of the raceme is extreme, the sessile and homogamous spikelets being fused at their base into a single unit which falls as a whole. *I. macratherum* takes this a step further, for the raceme remains tightly wrapped in its spatheole, falling with it at maturity; while in *I. vaginiflorum* the spatheole becomes strongly indurated before it is shed. There is an obvious similarity with *Themeda*, but no sign of the latter's characteristic pedicelled spikelet callus. It is significiant, therefore, that in neither *T. anathera* nor *T. gigantea*, the species which most resemble *Iseilema*, is the callus well developed.

Iseilema contains a long polyploid series of chromosome numbers, including the unusual diploid counts of 6 and 8; these are probably not primitive, but derived from a basic number of 5 (Rao in Nature 255: 220—221, 1975).

h. ROTTBOELLIINAE Presl, Rel. Haenk. 1: 329 (1830). *Ratzeburgiinae* Hook.f., Fl. Brit. India 7: 4 (1897).

Inflorescence of single or sometimes digitate racemes, these terminal, axillary or spathate; racemes fragile, though sometimes tardily so and rarely tough, the internodes variously thickened or swollen, without homogamous pairs. Spikelets paired, rarely in triplets, usually dissimilar. Sessile spikelet bisexual, dorsally compressed, the callus sometimes obtuse with oblique scar, more often transversely truncate and then commonly reinforced by a central peg; lower glume herbaceous to crustaceous, convex, often sculptured, mostly 2-keeled; lower floret ♂ or barren; upper lemma narrowly ovate, entire, awnless; lodicules truncate, or (especially in *Phacelurus*) retuse or toothed from one corner. Pedicelled spikelet variable, the pedicel sometimes fused to the internode.

Urelytrum and its allies have the thickened internodes and awnless upper lemma characteristic of Rottboelliinae, but some of their other features, particularly the callus, are reminiscent of Ischaeminae and Andropogoninae. They are an intermediate group, almost deserving recognition as a separate subtribe. Apart from these genera, *Phacelurus*, with its digitate racemes and unspecialized internodes, is the least modified member of the subtribe, and points to a derivation from Ischaeminae.

Coelorachis introduces cylindrical racemes with characteristic ball and socket joints, and from it radiate the more specialized members of the subtribe. In these the internode and pedicel combine, and sometimes actually fuse, so as to protect the fertile spikelet within a hard cylindrical box closed by the indurated lower glume. It has been suggested that the ball-joint functions as an eleiosome attractive to ants.

The *Urelytrum* and *Phacelurus* groups have the usual basic chromosome number of 10, but 9 (occasionally 7) is more typical of the genera radiating from *Coelorachis*.

In general, weakly developed and imperfectly separated species clusters are rather common in the subtribe, leaving a good deal of room for subjective interpretation in the choice of generic treatment (fig 24).

624. Urelytrum Hack. in Engl. & Prantl, Nat. Pfl.-Fam. 2, 2: 25 (1887) — U. agropyroides (Hack.) Hack.

Tufted perennial, sometimes annual. Inflorescence terminal, of single or subdigitate (whorled on a long axis in *U. giganteum*) racemes, these cylindrical or slightly flattened, very fragile; internodes clavate, the tip crateriform with lobed scarious rim. Sessile spikelet with short broadly obtuse callus, this inserted (longer and scarcely inserted in *U. henrardii*) and pubescent, the hairs mostly concealed within the node; lower glume coriaceous to crustaceous, the nerves raised only towards the tip, keeled or rounded and often knobbly on the flanks, entire; lower floret ♂, with palea. Pedicelled spikelet well developed or much reduced, its lower glume drawn out into a long curved awn (*U. giganteum, U. henrardii* sometimes awnless); pedicel free, resembling internode.

Species 7. Tropical Africa. Savanna.

The genus can nearly always be recognized by its distinctively awned pedicelled spikelet. Note the remarkable superficial similarity between *U. henrardii* and *Schizachyrium salzmannii*.

625. Loxodera Launert in Bol. Soc. Brot. 37: 80 (1963) — L. rigidiuscula Launert (= L. bovonei). *Plagiarthron* Duv. in Bull. Soc. Bot. Belg. 90: 187 (1958) nom nud. *Lepargochloa* Launert in Bol. Soc. Brot. 37: 82 (1963) — L. rhytachnoides Launert.

Tufted perennial. Inflorescence a single terminal raceme, this stout, flattened, tardily disarticulating; internodes columnar to clavate, the tip crateriform with lobed scarious rim. Sessile spikelet with short broadly obtuse callus, this shallowly inserted and bearded, the hairs forming a ring around each node; lower glume coriaceous, commonly with nerves raised into longitudinal ridges, the flanks keeled or rounded and sometimes knobbly, entire; lower floret ♂, with palea. Pedicelled spikelet well developed or much reduced, awnless (*L. strigosa* shortly awned); pedicel free, resembling internode.

Species 5. Tropical Africa. Damp drainage hollows in savanna.

A homogeneous genus linked to *Urelytrum* by *L. strigosa*.

626. Elionurus Kunth ex Willd, Sp. Pl. 4: 941 (1806) as "Elyonurus", a spelling miscopied from Kunth's manuscript; emend Kunth in Humb. & Bonpl., Nov. Gen. Sp. 1: 192 (1815); Renvoize in Kew Bull. 32: 665—675 (1978) — E. tripsacoides Willd. *Callichloea* Steud., Nom. Bot. ed. 2, 1: 257 (1840) nom nud; Kuntze in Post, Lexicon: 91 (1903) as "Calochloa" — E. elegans. *Habrurus* Hochst. in Flora 39: 90 (1856) nom nud — E. royleanus.

Tufted perennial, occasionally annual; leaves sometimes aromatic; ligule membranous, but very short and densely ciliate. Inflorescence a single raceme, these terminal, or axillary and spathate, flexuous, flattened, usually white hairy; internodes columnar to subclavate, the tip strongly oblique, not hollowed or rimmed (but with a scarious lobe in *E. elegans* group). Sessile spikelet with large cuneate callus attached obliquely to internode; lower glume subcoriaceous, smooth, laterally 2-keeled, the keels prominently ciliate and bordered by a brown oil streak (with pectinate hair tufts and no oil streak in *E. elegans* group), cuspidate to a bilobed or rarely entire tip; lower floret barren, without palea. Pedicelled spikelet well developed, muticous or aristulate; pedicel free, resembling internode.

Species 15. Tropical Africa (extending to Sind) and tropical America: 1 species in Australia. In savanna, often on dry soils. Some species yield an essential oil, but this is not commercially exploited.

A fairly homogeneous genus in which *E. elegans, E. hirtifolius* and *E. royleanus,* with their tendency to a short callus and lobed internode tip, afford a link with *Loxodera.*

627. Phacelurus Griseb., Fl. Rumel. Bithyn. 2: 423 (1846); Clayton in Kew Bull. 33: 175—179 (1978) — P. digitatus (Sibth. & Sm.) Griseb. *Jardinea* Steud., Syn. Pl. Glum. 1: 360 (1854) — J. gabonensis Steud. *Thyrsia* Stapf in Fl. Trop. Afr. 9: 48 (1917) — T. inflata Stapf (= P. huillensis). *Pseudovossia* A. Camus in Bull. Mus. Hist. Nat. Paris 26: 665 (1920) — P. cambogiensis (Bal.) A. Camus. *Pseudophacelurus* A. Camus l.c. 27: 370 (1921) — P. speciosus (Steud.) A. Camus.

Perennial. Inflorescence terminal, usually of ± flattened digitate racemes, these rarely single or paniculate, often tardily disarticulating; internodes columnar to inflated. Sessile spikelet callus truncate, flat or with central peg; lower glume membranous to coriaceous (concave in *P. latifolius*), smooth (muricate in *P. franksae, P. gabonensis*), the keels winged or not; lower floret ♂, or barren and then with or without palea. Pedicelled spikelet usually resembling sessile but rarely bisexual, occasionally vestigial, with an elongated callus in *P. cambogiensis, P. digitata;* pedicel free, resembling internode.

Species 9. Old World tropics, extending northwards to the Mediterranean. Woodland and damp places in grassland.

A variable genus whose species are broadly similar in spikelet structure, but differ considerably in detail. Unfortunately, characters derived from these details are poorly correlated with one another, so that attempts at subdivision have had to rely almost entirely upon the subjective weighting of single characters. On balance it seems better to treat these species as a single diffuse cluster, than as a swarm of perhaps 5 weakly differentiated small genera.

In practice there is not much difficulty in distinguishing it from *Ischaemum,* but it is sometimes quite hard to find unequivocal diagnostic characters, and the two genera are clearly related.

628. Vossia Wall. & Griff. in J. As. Soc. Bengal Nat. Hist. 5: 572 (1836) nom conserv non Adanson (1763) — V. procera Wall. & Griff. (= V. cuspidata).

Perennial. Inflorescence terminal, of digitate (rarely single) racemes, these flattened, tardily disarticulating; internodes clavate, hollowed at tip. Sessile spikelet callus truncate with irregular central convexity; lower glume coriaceous, narrowly winged above and drawn out into a long flattened tail; lower floret ♂, with palea. Pedicelled spikelet similar to the sessile; pedicel free.

Species 1. Tropical Africa and India. In or close to water, often floating.
A segregate from *Phacelurus.*

629. Hemarthria R. Br., Prodr. Fl. Nov. Holl.: 207 (1810) — H. compressa (L.f.)

R. Br. *Lodicularia* P. Beauv., Ess. Agrost.: 108 (1812) — L. fasciculata (Lam.) P. Beauv. (= H. altissima).

Perennial, mostly rambling. Inflorescence axillary, a single flattened dorsiventral raceme with tough rhachis; internodes clavate, usually obliquely articulated. Sessile spikelet callus obtuse to cuneate, rarely truncate; lower glume rigidly herbaceous, smooth, indistinctly winged above, obtuse to caudate (*H. debilis* biaristate); upper glume sometimes awned; lower floret barren, without palea. Pedicelled spikelet resembling sessile, but base truncate and lacking callus; pedicel fused to internode.

Species 12. Old World tropics and subtropics; possibly also native in America. In or near water.
Despite the evidence of the fused pedicel and basic chromosome number of 9, *Hemarthria* seems more closely related to *Phacelurus* than to *Heteropholis*.

630. Lasiurus Boiss., Diagn. Pl. Nov. Or. sér. 2, 4: 145 (1859); Cope in Kew Bull. 35: 451—452 (1980) — L. hirsutus (Vahl) Boiss. (= L. scindicus).

Perennial, the culms somewhat woody below; ligule a fringe of hairs. Inflorescence terminal, a single silky villous raceme, bearing spikelets in pairs, or in triplets of 2 sessile and 1 pedicelled; internodes stoutly clavate. Sessile spikelet callus truncate with central peg; lower glume subcoriaceous, with a short flattened bidentate or entire tail; lower floret ♂, with palea. Pedicelled spikelet well developed, without a tail; pedicel free, resembling internode.

Species 1. Mali to NE India. Subdesert. A useful fodder grass in arid conditions.
An isolated xeromorphic genus, loosely related to *Coelorachis*.

631. Rhytachne Desv. in Hamilt., Prodr. Fl. Ind. Occ.: 11 (1825); K. Schum. in Engler, Pfl. Ostafr. C: 96 (1895) as "Rhytidachne"; Clayton in Kew Bull. 32: 767—771 (1978) — R. rottboellioides Desv. *Lepturopsis* Steud., Syn. Pl. Glum. 1: 357 (1854) — L. triaristata Steud.

Perennial or rarely annual, mostly small plants with narrow or filiform leaf-blades; ligule membranous. Inflorescence terminal (*R. furtiva* axillary), a single cylindrical raceme bearing paired spikelets; internodes clavate, semicylindrical, as long as or longer than spikelets. Sessile spikelet callus truncate with central peg; lower glume chartaceous to crustaceous, smooth, rugose or longitudinally ribbed, 2-keeled or rounded on flanks, wingless (*R. furtiva, R. latifolia, R. perfecta* obscurely winged), rarely awned; upper glume sometimes awned; lower floret ♂ (*R. gracilis* barren), with large palea. Pedicelled spikelet rudimentary or represented by an awn (well developed in *R. glabra*, bisexual in *R. perfecta*); pedicel free, foliaceous (semi-cylindrical in *R. perfecta*).

Species 12. Tropical Africa and America. Moist or seasonally flooded grassland.
Apparently derived from *Phacelurus* via *P. gabonensis*.

632. Coelorachis Brongn. in Duperr., Voy. Coq. Bot. Phan.: 64, f 14 (1831); Clayton in Kew Bull. 24: 309—314 (1970) — figure of C. glandulosa (Trin.) Ridley. *Rottboellia sect Apogonia* Nutt., Gen. N. Amer. Pl. 1: 83 (1818) — R. rugosa Nutt. *Apogonia* (Nutt.) Fourn., Mex. Pl. 2: 63 (1886). *Cycloteria* Stapf in Ind. Lond. 5: 459 (1931) nom nud — C. selloana.

Perennial (*C. clarkei* annual), often robust with broad leaf-blades; ligule membranous. Inflorescence axillary and often spathate (*C. capensis, C. cylindrica, C. selloana* terminal), a single cylindrical or flattened dorsiventral raceme, the spikelets paired or occasionally in triplets of 2 sessile and 1 pedicelled; internodes clavate to pyriform, mostly shorter than spikelets, these often imbricate. Sessile spikelet callus truncate with central peg; lower glume chartaceous to crustaceous, smooth, areolate or cancellate (*C. rugosa, C. tuberculosa* rugose), 2-keeled (*C. khasiana* rounded), the keels winged towards tip (except *C. cancellata*); upper glume awnless; lower floret barren, with or without a small palea. Pedicelled spikelet well developed or vestigial (subsessile and bisexual in *C. parodiana*); pedicel free (but lower part fused to internode in *C. khasiana*), clavate or foliaceous, sometimes auriculate at tip.

Species ± 21. Throughout the tropics. Grassland and open woodland, often favouring damp soils.

A rather variable genus very closely related to *Rhytachne*; no single diagnostic character is wholly reliable, and a few of the species are difficult to assign. Nevertheless the differential characters amount to a considerable difference in facies, and it seems worthwhile to maintain two genera.

The spikelets are sometimes borne in triplets, a character often regarded as diagnostic for the genus *Mnesithea*. However, both pairs and triplets occur in *C. helferi, C. impressa, C. mollicoma* & *C. striata*, often mixed in the same panicle or even the same raceme. Evidently the character is rather plastic, and is an unsound criterion for generic delimitation.

633. Eremochloa Büse in Miq., Pl. Jungh.: 357 (1854); Bor in Kew Bull. 7: 309—316 (1952) — E. horneri Miq. (= E. ciliaris). *Ischaemum sect Pectinaria* Benth. in J. Linn. Soc. Bot. 19: 71 (1881) — I. pectinatum Trin. (= E. muricata). *Pectinaria* (Benth.) Hack. in Engl. & Prantl, Nat. Pfl.-Fam. 2, 2: 26 (1887) non Haworth (1819).

Perennial. Inflorescence terminal (*E. petelotii* axillary), a single strongly flattened tardily disarticulating raceme bearing imbricate spikelets; internodes clavate. Sessile spikelet callus truncate, sometimes with a low central boss; lower glume chartaceous to coriaceous, the keels pectinately spinose (very shortly so in *E. ophiuroides*), sometimes winged at tip; lower floret ♂, with palea. Pedicelled spikelet absent or represented by a bristle; pedicel free, narrowly foliaceous.

Species 9. India to China and Australia. Short grassland. *E. ophiuroides* (Centipede grass) is sometimes used for tropical lawns.

A homogeneous genus related to *Coelorachis*, particularly *C. glandulosa*.

634. Chasmopodium Stapf in Fl. Trop. Afr. 9: 76 (1917) — C. caudatum (Hack.) Stapf.

Annual or perennial, robust with broad leaf-blades; ligule a fringe of hairs. Inflorescence axillary, a single subcylindrical dorsiventral raceme with paired spikelets; internodes squatly clavate, shorter than spikelets. Sessile spikelet callus truncate, with large central knob; lower glume oblong-ovate, crustaceous, smooth, pallid, narrowly winged on keels above; lower floret ♂, with palea; embryo ⅘ as long as caryopsis. Pedicelled spikelet well developed; pedicel free, stout.

Species 2. West Africa from Guinée to Zaire. Savanna.
It has the unusual basic chromosome number of 8 (Dujardin in Bull. Jard. Bot. Nat. Belg. 48: 373—381, 1978), indicating a greater separation from *Rottboellia*, in which x = 10, than the spikelets alone might suggest.

635. Rottboellia L.f., Nov. Gram. Gen: 23 (1779) & Suppl. Pl.: 114 (1781) nom conserv non Scop. (1777) — R. exaltata L.f. (= R. cochinchinensis). *Stegosia* Lour., Fl. Cochin.: 51 (1790) — S. cochinchinensis Lour. *Robynsiochloa* Jac.-Fél. in J. Agric. Trop. 7: 406 (1960) — R. purpurascens (Robyns) Jac.-Fél.

Annual; ligule membranous. Inflorescence axillary, a single flattened or cylindrical raceme; internodes flattened, or semi-cylindrical with sunken spikelets. Sessile spikelet like *Chasmopodium*. Pedicelled spikelet as long as or shorter than sessile, herbaceous; pedicel fused partly or wholly to internode.

Species 4. Old World tropics; introduced to Caribbean. Habitat variable; swamps, disturbed places or dry soils in woodland. *R. cochinchinensis* has developed, within the last decade or so, into a serious tropical weed.

636. Heteropholis C.E. Hubbard in Hook. Ic. Pl. 36: t 3548 (1956); Koning et al in Gard. Bull. Sing. 36: 137—162 (1983) — H. sulcata (Stapf) C.E. Hubbard.

Annual or perennial. Inflorescence axillary, a single cylindrical or slightly flattened dorsiventral raceme; internodes clavate. Sessile spikelet callus transversely truncate with central boss or peg; lower glume oblong, crustaceous, smooth, cancellate or areolar, slightly winged at tip, awnless; lower floret barren, with or without palea. Pedicelled spikelet as large as sessile (reduced in *H. benoistii*); pedicel fused to internode.

Species 5. Africa to Indo-China, the Philippines and Australia. Wooded grassland.
The genus may be likened to *Coelorachis* with fused pedicels. The embryo of *H. sulcata* is unusually large, some ⅘ the length of the caryopsis.

637. Hackelochloa Kuntze, Rev. Gen. Pl. 2: 776 (1891), the description derived from Manisuris sensu Hack. in DC., Monogr. Phan. 6: 314 (1889) — H. granularis (L.) Kuntze. *Rytilix* Hitchc. in U.S. Dept. Agric. Bull. 772: 278 (1920) nom superfl pro Hackelochloa.

Coarse annual. Inflorescence axillary, a single flattened dorsiventral raceme, these aggregated into a compound panicle; internodes oblong. Sessile spikelet callus obliquely truncate with central boss; lower glume hemispherical, crustaceous, rugose to cancellate, wingless; lower floret barren, without palea; embryo as long as caryopsis. Pedicelled spikelet narrowly ovate, herbaceous, smooth, narrowly winged; pedicel fused to internode.

Species 2. Throughout the tropics. Weedy places.
Apart from its unique spikelet shape, the genus differs little from *Heteropholis*.

638. Glyphochloa Clayton in Kew Bull. 35: 814 (1981); Jain in Bull. Bot. Surv. India 12: 6—17 (1970) — G. forficulata (Fischer) Clayton.

Annual. Inflorescence terminal or axillary, a single flattened dorsiventral raceme; internodes oblong, clavate or turbinate, abscissing between segments in usual way. Sessile spikelet callus truncate or oblique with central knob; lower glume ovate to oblong, crustaceous, smooth or more often elaborately sculptured with ridges or spines, with broad membranous wings above, 1—2-awned (sometimes awnless in *G. acuminata*); lower floret barren, with or without palea. Pedicelled spikelet as large as sessile, asymmetrically winged, usually awned; pedicel fused to internode, the spikelet firmly attached to its tip.

Species 8. India. On rocks.
A variant of *Heteropholis* with ornamental spikelets. There is also some resemblance to *Coelorachis clarkei*.

639. Manisuris L., Mant. 2: 164, 300 (1771) — M. myurus L. *Peltophorus* Desv. in Nouv. Bull. Sci. Soc. Philom. 2: 188 (1810) nom superfl pro Manisuris.

Perennial. Inflorescence axillary, a single flattened dorsiventral raceme; internodes stoutly clavate, the abscission line extending beneath pedicelled spikelet belonging to segment below. Sessile spikelet callus truncate with central boss; lower glume oblong, crustaceous, transversely grooved, this interrupting membranous wings on keels, awnless; lower floret barren, without palea. Pedicelled spikelet as long as sessile, longitudinally striate, asymmetrically winged, awnless; pedicel fused to internode of its own segment, base of spikelet to callus of segment above, the spikelet thus forming part of that segment and falling with it.

Species 1. India. Dry places.
An extraordinary derivative of *Glyphochloa* in which the sessile and pedicelled spikelets of each pair are seemingly set side by side, but are actually derived from different segments.

640. Ophiuros Gaertn., Fruct. 3: 3 (1805) — O. corymbosa (L.f.) Gaertn. (= O. exaltatus).

Annual or perennial. Inflorescence of single cylindrical racemes aggregated into a compound panicle, the spikelets borne alternately on opposite sides of the rhachis; internodes semicylindrical with sunken spikelets. Sessile spikelet callus transversely or slightly obliquely truncate with central peg; lower glume oblong, crustaceous, smooth, areolate or cancellate, with or without narrow wings at tip; lower floret ♂, with palea. Pedicelled spikelet absent; pedicel fused to internode, sometimes barely distinguishable from it.

Species 4. NE tropical Africa to southern China and Australia. Damp places in savanna.

A homogeneous genus, whose lower glume sculpturing suggests a relationship with *Heteropholis*.

641. Oxyrhachis Pilger in Not. Bot. Gart. Berlin 11: 655 (1932) — O. mildbraediana Pilger (= O. gracillima).

Perennial. Inflorescence terminal, a single cylindrical raceme, the spikelets borne alternately on opposite sides of the rhachis; internodes semicylindrical with sunken spikelets. Sessile spikelet callus obtuse, strongly oblique; lower glume lanceolate, coriaceous, smooth, rounded on flanks, wingless; lower floret barren, without palea. Pedicelled spikelet and its pedicel completely suppressed (or perhaps the pedicel present but fused to and indistinguishable from internode).

Species 1. Africa and Madagascar. Upland bogs.
An isolated genus, possibly related to *Ophiuros*.

642. Mnesithea Kunth, Rév. Gram. 1: 153 (1829) — M. laevis (Retz.) Kunth. *Diperium* Desv., Opusc.: 76 (1831) — D. cylindricum Desv. (= M. laevis). *Thyridostachyum* Nees in Lindl., Nat. Syst. ed. 2: 379 (1836) nom superfl pro Mnesithea.

Perennial with narrow leaf-blades. Inflorescence terminal and axillary, a single cylindrical raceme, bearing triplets of 2 subopposite sessile spikelets sunk in the rhachis and separated by a slender pedicel (but upper part or whole of depauperate racemes with 1 sessile spikelet and pedicel fused to internode along its length); internodes squatly clavate. Sessile spikelet callus truncate with central peg; lower glume crustaceous, smooth, wingless; lower floret barren, without palea. Pedicelled spikelet absent; pedicel free except for its tip which is fused to top of internode.

Species 1. Afghanistan to Thailand and Indonesia. Damp grassland.
The raceme segment, with paired sessile spikelets and a strap-like pedicel attached only at the tip, is unusual but not wholly diagnostic. Paired sessile spikelets occur sporadically in the racemes of neighbouring genera, and depauperate racemes of *Mnesithea* differ from *Heteropholis* only in the absence of a pedicelled spikelet. Hence acceptance of the genus is contentious. The problem is that although genera 631—644 are not well separated, they form an uncomfortably heterogeneous conglomerate if united.

643. Ratzeburgia Kunth, Rév. Gram. 2: 487 (1831) — R. pulcherrima Kunth.

Aikinia Wall., Pl. As. Rar. 3: 46 (1832) non R. Br. (1832) in syn sub Ratzeburgia.

Perennial. Inflorescence terminal, a single flattened raceme, bearing triplets of 2 opposite sessile spikelets appressed back to back, their edges bordered by a square frame formed from internode and pedicel, these linear. Sessile spikelet callus truncate with central boss; lower glume crustaceous, cancellate, truncately winged at tip; lower floret barren, without palea. Pedicelled spikelet vestigial, pedicel free.

Species 1. Burma. Short grassland.
An elegant variant of the *Mnesithea* theme, in which the highly modified internode and pedicel form a narrow frame protecting the edges of the spikelets.

644. Thaumastochloa C.E. Hubbard in Hook. Ic. Pl. 34: t 3313 (1936); Koning et al in Gard. Bull. Sing. 36: 137—162 (1983) — T. pubescens (Benth.) C.E. Hubbard.

Annual; ligule a short membrane or a line of hairs. Inflorescence axillary and usually compound, a single cylindrical dorsiventral raceme bearing 1—8 spikelets, the raceme fragile but the lowest or only spikelet falling with the peduncle, this becoming stiff, curved, pointed at the base and retrorsely asperulous; internodes semicylindrical to urceolate with sunken spikelets, the terminal internode conical. Sessile spikelet callus transversely or somewhat obliquely truncate with central peg or boss; lower glume oblong, crustaceous, smooth or rugose, wingless; lower floret barren, without palea. Pedicelled spikelet absent; pedicel fused to internode.

Species 7. Australia and New Guinea. Eucalyptus woodland.
A specialized genus with a modified deciduous peduncle which assists in dispersal. In *T. pubescens* only the lowest spikelet remains attached to the peduncle, the rest of the raceme shattering in the normal way; but in more modified species, such as *T. rariflora,* the raceme consists of a single spikelet more or less integral with the peduncle. The genus is probably derived from *Heteropholis.*

i. TRIPSACINAE Dumort., Anal. Fam.: 64 (1829). *Maydinae* Harvey, Gen. S. Afr. Pl. ed. 2: 428 (1868) nom inval. *Zeinae* Tzvel. in Bot. Zh. 53: 312 (1968).

Similar to Rottboelliinae, but the spikelets unisexual, with the sexes borne in separate parts of the same inflorescence or in different inflorescences.

The subtribe is barely distinct from Rottboelliinae. Although advanced in many respects, it retains a remarkable degree of plasticity in the pairing and sex of its spikelets.

645. Tripsacum L., Syst. Nat. ed. 10: 1261 (1759); de Wet, Gray & Harlan in Phytologia 33: 203—215 (1976); de Wet & Harlan in Walden, Breeding and

Genetics of Maize: 129—140 (1978) — T. dactyloides (L.) L. *Digitaria* Adans., Fam. Pl. 2: 38, 550 (1763) non Haller (1768), nom superfl pro Tripsacum. *Dactylodes* Kuntze, Rev. Gen. Pl. 2: 772 (1891) nom superfl pro Tripsacum.

Perennial, often broad-leaved and robust, usually rhizomatous. Inflorescence terminal and axillary, of digitate (occasionaly single or with a short central axis) racemes, each raceme ♀ with fragile swollen internodes below, ♂ with tough narrow internodes in distal half. Female spikelets single without trace of pairing, sessile, deeply sunk in internode, the callus transversely truncate with central ridge or peg; lower glume crustaceous, smooth, slightly winged at tip; lower floret barren, without palea. Male spikelets paired, both sessile or one raised on a free pedicel; glumes chartaceous; both florets ♂.

Species 13. Southern USA to Paraguay, but mainly Central America. Mostly in open woodlands and damp places. Several species are cultivated for forage, especially *T. andersonii* (Guatemala grass), which has been introduced to many tropical countries.

Tripsacum is a difficult genus of closely related species. It is clearly derived from some *Chasmopodium*-like offshoot of *Coelorachis*. It has a different basic chromosome number (x = 9) but will hybridize with *Zea* (x = 10); some of these are counterfeit hybrids, possessing *Zea* chromosomes only in the endosperm (de Wet et al in Amer. J. Bot. 71: 245—251, 1984).

646. Zea L., Sp. Pl.: 974 (1753); Mangelsdorff, Corn its Origin Evolution and Improvement (1974); Galinat in Sprague, Corn and Corn Improvement (1977); Wilkes, The Origin of Corn (1977); Doebley & Iltis in Amer. J. Bot. 67: 982—993 (1980) — Z. mays L. *Mays* Miller, Gard. Dict. ed. 4: (1754) & *Mayzea* Raf., Med. Fl. 2: 241 (1830) — nom superfl pro Zea. *Euchlaena* Schrad., Ind. Sem. Hort. Gött. 1832: 3 (1832) — E. mexicana Schrad. *Reana* Brignoli in Ann. Sci. Nat. Bot. sér. 3, 12: 365 (1849) — R. giovanninii Brignoli (= Z. mexicana). *Thalysia* Kuntze, Rev. Gen. Pl. : 794 (1891) nom superfl pro Zea.

Annual or rarely perennial, broad-leaved, robust. Female inflorescence axillary, a single raceme wrapped in 1 or more spathes, exceptionally tipped by a short ♂ raceme; internodes fragile, swollen, bearing a single sessile spikelet without trace of pairing, distichous (in *Z. mays* the internodes much condensed and fused into a polystichous woody cob with paired spikelets at each node, both sessile). Spikelets deeply sunk and almost enclosed by internode, the callus obliquely truncate, flat (shallowly inserted on surface of cob in *Z. mays,* with short chaffy glumes exposing grain); lower glume crustaceous, smooth, obscurely winged at tip; lower floret barren; style single, very long, silky, pendulous from inflorescence tip. Male inflorescence terminal, of digitate or paniculate racemes; internodes tough, narrow, bearing paired spikelets, one of them on a slender free pedicel; glumes chartaceous; both florets ♂.

Species 4. Central America. Field margins. *Z. mays* (Maize, Corn, Mealies) is a staple cereal of tropical regions; it is also extensively grown as a forage crop, and is an important source of oil, syrup and alcohol. It is not known in the wild, but was apparently domesticated in Central America some 7000 years ago from a species resembling *Z. mexicana* (Teosinte). The gall produced by infection of the cob by *Ustilago maydis* is eaten as a vegetable.

Z. *mays* is so different morphologically from the other three species, that the latter are commonly placed in a separate genus. However the differences, though extreme to the eye, are found to be under relatively simple genetic control, and are such as would be expected between species subject to disruptive selection, meaning that selection pressure on the wild species has been towards efficient dispersal, but on maize it has been in the opposite direction. Indeed some of the differences are sufficiently plastic to respond to changes in photoperiod (Heslop-Harrison in Proc. Linn. Soc. 172: 108—123, 1961). The genus as a whole is clearly related to *Tripsacum*.

j. CHIONACHNINAE Clayton in Kew Bull. 35: 813 (1981); Henrard in Med. Rijks Herb. Leiden 67: 1—17 (1931).

Inflorescence of single axillary racemes, these often gathered into a compound panicle; racemes bearing paired spikelets, with fragile ♀ segments below, and fragile or tardily disarticulating ♂ segments above, the ♀ internodes terete, clavate or columnar, narrower than spikelet, cupuliform at tip (sometimes the terminal and larger lateral inflorescences digitate, and then all ♀ or with a few ♂ spikelets at tip). Female pair dissimilar. Sessile spikelet ♀, dorsally compressed, the callus truncate with central knob; lower glume bony, convex, rounded on flanks, enclosing the spikelet (and often also the internode), usually winged above; lower floret barren; upper lemma oblong, entire, awnless; caryopsis oblong to triangular, its base emarginate with punctiform hilum (except *Trilobachne*). Pedicelled spikelet ♂ or barren, arising laterally near top of internode with its pedicel fused to the latter, sometimes suppressed. Male pair (occasionally triplet) similar, the pedicel free or fused with internode; glumes chartaceous; both florets usually ♂.

A close-knit subtribe, the genera separated by relatively slight differences. The sessile spikelet callus clearly indicates a derivation from Rottboelliinae. The slender composite internode-pedicel is distinctive, but *Chionachne javanica*, which has an unusually wide internode, provides a link with *Heteropholis*.

647. Chionachne R. Br. in Benn., Pl. Jav. Rar.: 15 (1838) — C. barbata (Roxb.) Benth. (= C. koenigii).

Perennial, rarely annual. Inflorescence axillary and usually gathered into a compound panicle, of a single raceme comprising (1—) several ♀ segments and few to many exserted ♂ segments. Female segment: sessile spikelet lower glume not or scarcely constricted (only a little wider than internode in *C. javanica*), winged above (except *C. koenigii*), obtuse, emarginate, bifid or irregularly trilobed; pedicelled spikelet suppressed or vestigial (well developed and ♂ in *C. javanica, C. macrophylla*). Male segment with broadly linear internode and fused pedicel.

Species 7. India, SE Asia, Australia and Polynesia. Forest margins and stream sides.

648. Sclerachne R. Br. in Benn., Pl. Jav. Rar.: 15 (1838) — S. punctata R. Br.

Annual. Inflorescence axillary, a single raceme comprising 1—3 ♀ segments and 1—2 short ♂ segments, the latter almost enfolded by the topmost ♀ spikelet. Female segment: sessile spikelet lower glume with two conspicuous transverse constrictions, winged, emarginate; pedicelled spikelet small or vestigial, barren. Male segment with very short internodes and fused pedicels.

Species 1. Thailand, Indo-China and Indonesia. Forest margins.

649. Polytoca R. Br. in Benn., Pl. Jav. Rar.: 20 (1838) — P. bracteata R. Br. (= P. digitata). *Cyathorhachis* Steud., Syn. Pl. Glum. 1: 403 (1854) — C. wallichiana Steud.

Annual or perennial. Terminal and larger lateral inflorescences digitate; axillary inflorescences of a single raceme having several ♀ segments and a slender ♂ portion. Female segment: sessile spikelet lower glume winged above, obtuse or emarginate; caryopsis with punctiform hilum; pedicelled spikelet well developed, barren. Male segment with slender internode and free or fused pedicel (lower glume awned in *P. wallichiana*).

Species 2. India and SE Asia. Forest margins.

650. Trilobachne Henr. in Med. Rijks Herb. Leiden 67: 4 (1931) — T. cookei (Stapf) Henr.

Broad-leaved annual. Like *Polytoca* but lower glume of female spikelet symmetrically trilobed above, and hilum linear.

Species 1. India. Forest margins.

k. COICINAE Reichenb., Consp. Reg. Veg.: 51 (1828).

Inflorescence axillary, compound, comprising 2 racemes separated by a prophyll, the one sessile and ♀, the other pedunculate and ♂, subtended by a globose or elongated bony utricle derived from a modified leaf-sheath. Female raceme enclosed within utricle, comprising 1 sessile spikelet & 2 pedicels; sessile spikelet ♀, with membranous glumes and lower floret reduced to a lemma; pedicels free, stout, with or without vestigial spikelets. Male raceme projecting from mouth of utricle, the spikelets in pairs or triplets and pedicels free; lower glume chartaceous, laterally winged; both florets usually ♂.

An extraordinary modification in which protection of the disseminule is provided by a hard flask-like spatheole. The presence of a prophyll between ♂ and ♀ racemes indicates that this is a compound structure derived from the union of two separate inflorescences (Jacques-Félix in J. Agr. Trop. 8: 44—56, 1961). The large-free pedicels of the ♀ raceme are quite alien to Tripsacinae or Chionachninae, but hint at a link with *Apluda*.

651. Coix L., Sp. Pl.: 972 (1753); Mimeur in Rev. Bot. Appl. 31: 197—211 (1951) — C. lacryma-jobi L. *Lachrymaria* Fabric., Enum.: 208 (1759) & *Lachryma-jobi* Ort., Tab. Bot.: 30 (1773) & *Lithagrostis* Gaertn., Fruct. 1: 7 (1788) & *Lacryma* Medik, Philos. Bot. 1: 177 (1789) & *Sphaerium* Kuntze, Rev. Gen. Pl. 2: 793 (1891) — nom superfl pro Coix.

Annual or perennial. Species differ mainly in vegetative parts and shape of utricle.

Species ± 5. Tropical Asia. Forest margins and swamps. *C. lacryma-jobi* (Job's Tears) has been introduced throughout the tropics where the utricles, which vary from globose to fusiform, and from white to blue-grey or brown, are used as ornamental beads; Mimeur l.c. gives a varietal classification. It is also employed as a fodder crop, and the utricles are sometimes ground up for flour (Vallayes in Bull. Agric. Congo Belge 39: 247—304, 1948; Jain & Banerjee in Econ. Bot. 28: 38-42, 1974).

HYBRID GENERA

x **Aegilosecale** Ciferri & Giacom., Nom. Fl. Ital. 1: 80 (1950): Aegilops x Secale.

x *Aegilotrichum* A. Camus in Bull. Mus. Hist. Nat. 33: 538 (1927) perperam formatum: = x Aegilotriticum.

x *Aegilotricum* Tschermak in Ber. Deutsch. Bot. Ges. 44: 113 (1926) perp form: = x Aegilotriticum.

x **Aegilotriticum** P. Fourn., Quatre Fl. France: 89 (1935): Aegilops x Triticum.

x **Agrocalamagrostis** Aschers. & Graebn., Syn. Mitteleur. Fl. 2: 223 (1899): Agrostis x Calamagrostis.

x **Agroelymus** A. Camus in Bull. Mus. Hist. Nat. 33: 538 (1927): Agropyron x Elymus.

x **Agrohordeum** A. Camus in Bull. Mus. Hist. Nat. 33: 537 (1927): Agropyron x Hordeum.

x **Agropogon** P. Fourn., Quatre Fl. France: 49 (1934): Agrostis x Polypogon.

x *Agropyrohordeum* A. Camus in Riviera Scientif. 21: 45 (1934): = x Agrohordeum.

x **Agrositanion** Bowden in Canad. J. Bot. 45: 720 (1967): Agropyron x Sitanion.

x *Agrotrigia* Tzvelev in Nov. Sist. Vysh. Rast. 9: 63 (1972): Agropyron x Elytrigia = x Agroelymus.

x **Agrotrisecale** Ciferri & Giacom., Nom. Fl. Ital.: 48 (1950): Agropyron x Secale x Triticum.

x **Agrotriticum** Ciferri & Giacom., Nom. Fl. Ital.: 48 (1950): Agropyron x Triticum.

x **Ammocalamagrostis** P. Fourn. in Monde Pl. 35: 28 (1934): Ammophila x Calamagrostis.

x **Arctodupontia** Tzvelev in Nov. Sist. Vysh. Rast. 10: 91 (1973): Arctophila x Dupontia.

x **Bromofestuca** Prodan. in Bul. Grad. Bot. Univ. Cluj 16: 93 (1936): Bromus x Festuca.

x *Calammophila* Brand in Koch, Syn. Deutsch. Schweiz. Fl. ed. 3, 3: 2715 (1907) nom prov: = x Ammocalamagrostis.

x *Calamophila* O. Schwartz in Mitt. Thüring. Bot. Ges. 1: 88 (1949): = x Ammocalamagrostis.

x **Cynochloris** Clifford & Everist in Proc. Roy. Soc. Queensland 75: 46 (1964): Chloris x Cynodon.

x *Danthosieglingia* Domin in Preslia 13/15: 39 (1935): Danthonia x Sieglingia = Danthonia.

x **Elyhordeum** Zizan & Petrowa in Züchter 25: 164 (1955): Elymus x Hordeum.

x **Elyleymus** Baum in Canad. J. Bot. 57: 947 (1979): Elymus x Leymus.

x *Elymopyrum* Cugnac in Bull. Soc. Hist. Nat. Ardennes 1938: 14 (1938): = x Agroelymus.

x *Elymordeum* Lepage in Nat. Canad. 84: 97 (1957): = x Elyhordeum.

x **Elymostachys** Tzvelev in Nov. Sist. Vysh. Rast. 9: 58 (1972): Elymus x Psathyrostachys.

x *Elymotrigia* Hylander, Nord. Karlväxtfl. 1: 371 (1953) & in Bot. Not. 1953: 358 (1953): Elymus x Elytrigia = Elymus.

x **Elymotriticum** P. Fourn, Quatre Fl. France: 88 (1935): Elymus x Triticum.

x **Elysitanion** Bowden in Canad. J. Bot. 45: 721 (1967): Elymus x Sitanion.

x *Elytrordeum* Hylander, Nord. Karlväxtfl. 1: 369 (1953) & in Bot. Not. 1953: 358 (1953): Elytrigia x Hordeum = x Elyhordeum.

x *Euchlaezea* Bor, Grasses Burma Ceylon India Pak.: 267 (1960): Euchlaena x Zea = Zea.

x **Festulolium** Aschers. & Graebn., Syn. Mitteleur. Fl. 2: 768 (1902): Festuca x Lolium.

x **Festulpia** Stace & Cotton in Watsonia 10: 136 (1974): Festuca x Vulpia.

x *Haynaldoticum* Ciferri & Giacom., Nom. Fl. Ital.: 50 (1950) perp form: Dasypyrum x Triticum.

x *Hibanobambusa* Maruyama & Okamura in Acta Phytotax. Geobot. 30: 151 (1979) perp form: Sasa x Semiarundinaria.

x **Hordale** Ciferri & Giacom., Nom. Fl. Ital.: 180 (1950): Hordeum x Secale.

x *Hordelymus* Bakhtjeev & Darevskaja in Bot. Zh. 35: 191 (1950) non (Jessen) Harz (1885): = x Elyhordeum.

x *Hordeopyrum* Simonet in Compt. Rend. Hebd. Séances Acad. Sci. 201: 1212 (1935): = Agrohordeum.

x *Horderoegneria* Tzvelev, Arkt. Fl. SSSR 2: 241 (1964): Hordeum x Roegneria = x Elyhordeum.

x **Leymopyron** Tzvelev, Fl. Sev.-Vost. Eur. Ch. SSSR 1: 121 (1974): Agropyron x Leymus.

x **Leymostachys** Tzvelev in Nov. Sist. Vysh. Rast. 10: 58 (1973): Leymus x Psathyrostachys.

x *Leymotrigia* Tzvelev, Arkt. Fl. SSSR 2: 250 (1964): Elytrigia x Leymus = x Elyleymus.

x *Maltea* B. Boiv. in Nat. Canad. 94: 526 (1967) perp form: = x Pucciphippsia.

x **Oryticum** Wang & Tang in Acta Phytotax. Sin. 20: 179 (1982): Oryza x Triticum.

x *Polypogonagrostis* Maire & Weiler, Fl. Afr. Nord 2: 151 (1953) perp form: = x Agropogon.

x **Pucciphippsia** Tzvelev in Nov. Sist. Vysh. Rast. 8: 76 (1971): Phippsia x Puccinellia.

Rouxia Husn., Gram. Fr. Belg.: 76 (1899) — R. hordeoides Husn.: = x Elyhordeum.

x *Secalotricum* Kostoff in Rev. Bot. Appl. 16: 251 (1936) perp form: = x Triticosecale.

x **Sitordeum** Bowden in Canad. J. Bot. 45: 722 (1967): Hordeum x Sitanion.

x **Stiporyzopsis** Johnson & Rogler in Amer. J. Bot. 30: 55 (1943): Oryzopsis x Stipa.

x *Terrelymus* Baum in Canad. J. Bot. 57: 947 (1979) perp form: Elymus x Terrellia = Elymus.

x **Trisetokoeleria** Tzvelev, Zlaki SSSR: 279 (1976): Koeleria x Trisetum.

x *Triticale* Muntzing in Züchter 8: 188 (1936): = x Triticosecale.

x **Triticosecale** Wittmack in Sitzungsber. Ges. Naturf. Freunde Berlin 1899: 59 (1899): Secale x Triticum. This hybrid is now widely grown as a crop and should, perhaps, be accorded generic status (Gupta & Baum in Taxon 35: 144—149, 1986).

x *Trititrigia* Tzvelev in Nov. Sist. Vysh. Rast. 10: 59 (1973): Elytrigia x Triticum = x Elymotriticum.

x **Tritordeum** Aschers. & Graebn., Syn. Mitteleur. Fl. 2: 748 (1902): Hordeum x Triticum.

NAMES OF UNCERTAIN APPLICATION

Acophorum Steud., Nom. Bot. ed. 2, 1: 20 (1840) nom nud — A. coerulescens Gaudich. No other information.

Corethrum Vahl in Skr. Naturh. Selsk. 6: 85 (1810) — C. bromoides Vahl. Description suggests either Boissiera or Enneapogon, but the type from Syria has been lost.

Cymbachne Retz., Obs. Bot. 6: 36 (1791) — C. ciliata Retz. Probably based on a damaged specimen of Dimeria, but the holotype is missing at Lund.

Cyrenea Allamand in Nova Acta Leop.-Carol. Nat. Cur. 4: 94 (1770) — no species named. Apparently a grass from Surinam, but otherwise unidentifiable.

Diplachyrium Nees in Flora 11: 301 (1828) — D. rarum Nees. The type is a superfluous name for Polypogon simplex Spreng., itself based on Sieber 94, an unidentified specimen from Australia.

Flexularia Raf. in J. Phys. Chim. 89: 105 (1819) — F. compressa Raf. Probably a species of Muhlenbergia, but the type is lost.

Gramen W. Young, Cat. Arbres Arbustes Pl. Herb. Am.: 36 (1783) nom nud non Séguier (1754). The work is virtually a nurseryman's catalogue, extolling the virtues of 4 unidentifiable American forage grasses.

Kampmannia Steud., Syn. Pl. Glum. 1: 34 (1854) — K. zeylandica Steud. Perhaps a species of Cortaderia, but the type from New Zealand is lost.

Lachnochloa Steud., Syn Pl. Glum. 1: 5 (1854) — L. pilosa Steud. A grass from Senegambia assigned to Oryzeae. Description unidentifiable and type lost.

Leptopyrum Raf. in Med. Repos. New York 5: 351 (1808) nom nud. An American genus supposedly akin to Avena.

Meringurus Murbeck in Acta Univ. Lund 36 Afd. 2, 1: 27 (1900) — M. africanus Murbeck. A Tunisian grass ascribed to Hainardieae. Type missing at Lund.

Reimbolea Debeaux in Rev. Bot. Bull. Mens. 8: 266 (1890) — R. spicata Debeaux. Based on Reimbole 1418 from Sicily, and distributed by Gandoger as Iter Italicum Siculumque. Probably a form of Echinaria capitata, but no type found at Lyon or Paris.

Runcina Allamand in Nova Acta Leop.-Carol. Nat. Cur. 4: 94 (1770) — no species named. From Surinam; description fits Cenchrus.

Trichodiclida Cerv. in Naturaleza 1: 346 (1870) — T. linearis Cerv., T. prolifera Cerv. Possibly synonymous with Erioneuron, but no types located at Madrid.

VALIDATION OF NEW NAMES

Subtribe **Neurachninae** (S.T. Blake) Clayton & Renvoize, subtribus nov.
Tribe *Neurachneae* S.T. Blake in Contrib. Queensl. Herb. 13: 3 (1972). Typus:
Neurachne R. Br.

Baptorhachis Clayton & Renvoize, gen. nov. a *Stereochlaena* Hack. racemo
singulari rhachidi foliacea pictaque et apice lemmatis inferioris bilobato
distinguenda. Typus: *Stereochlaena foliacea* Clayton.

INDEX

to genera and names of higher rank

Printed in the United Kingdom for Her Majesty's Stationery Office
Dd289398 12/89 C4 G3390 10170